THE WORLD'S ELITE FORCES

PAGE ONE *Two Special Boat Squadron personnel with a Klepper canoe.*

THIS PAGE *An Israeli Mirage jet fighter-bomber flies over a Centurion tank on the Golan Heights, 1973.*

THE WORLD'S ELITE FORCES

BRUCE QUARRIE

HAMLYN

CONTENTS

Author's note

Among the many people who have helped in the writing of this book, I would like particularly to put on record David Rosser-Owen, Martin Windrow and John Frost. Will Fowler was also of great help, as was Terry Gander, and for all their unstinting generosity I give great thanks. In addition, I would like to pay tribute to Sue Forster's painstaking editing work. Alan Smith of the John Topham Picture Agency, Bill Rouse of *Soldier* magazine, Christopher F. Foss and Terry Fincher also deserve a vote of thanks. However, this book is dedicated to Samantha Yvonne Quarrie for her timely arrival. . .

Bruce Quarrie, Wellingborough, Northants

First published in 1985 by Octopus Books Ltd

This edition published in 1994 by
The Hamlyn Publishing Group
an imprint of Reed International Books Ltd
Michelin House, 81 Fulham Road
London SW3 6RB
and Auckland, Melbourne, Singapore and Toronto

Reprinted 1995 (three times)

ISBN 0 600 58613 8

A CIP catalogue record for this book is available from the British Library

Printed and bound in Great Britain
by Cox & Wyman Ltd, Reading, Berkshire

CHAPTER ONE

REGARDLESS OF RISK

THE ROLE OF ELITE FORCES

'Regardless of risk, he charged up the hill and, although mortally wounded, succeeded in eliminating the enemy machine-gun nest so that the other men in his section could advance to take their objective.' How bald it sounds, and yet how many citations for the Victoria Cross and other awards for extreme valour read in just this way. Many perfectly ordinary men, faced with a situation which they know will quite probably lead to their own death, find the inner reserves to act with extraordinary courage if the circumstances demand it. The stranger diving into a roaring river torrent to rescue a drowning child, or hurling himself into a blazing building to save the life of an unconscious neighbour, is no less courageous than the soldier who defends his wounded comrade until his ammunition runs out; but there is a difference. Soldiers who have volunteered for their career (rather than being conscripted) know that their choice is one of kill or be killed, and come to an acceptance of the possibility of their death which is foreign to the average civilian. Nowhere is this more true than in the ranks of the élite military forces of the world, volunteers from the word 'go', who undertake even more intensive and rigorous training which will lead them in time of war or emergency into the front line wherever the action is hottest.

Since World War 2, the term 'élite', as applied to military formations, has come to acquire at least three separate connotations. The traditional and historical meaning goes back to the Praetorian Guard of the Caesars, to the Saxon huscarls at Hastings, to Cromwell's Ironsides, Napoleon's Old Guard or the men who died at Camerone, defending the Alamo or marching to the relief of Khartoum. Today, this tradition is maintained by such formations as the British Brigade of Guards.

Since World War 1, though, and even more so since World War 2, a different type of élite soldier has emerged. In the early days he would have been a member of an *ad hoc* battle group, a small unit of volunteers, often using imaginatively improvised weapons, which would be deployed as a 'hit-and-run' assault force during trench raids on the Western Front. By the time of World War 2, more formally structured units were beginning to emerge on both sides. German, British and American paratroops in particular earned a deserved reputation for daring, for toughness and for the use of unconventional methods in the attacks on Eben Emael in Belgium in 1940, Crete in 1941, Normandy and Arnhem in 1944, and elsewhere. The US Marine Corps and Rangers, the British Royal Marine commandos and other Allied units received much media attention, as did such élite German units as the Afrika Korps.

Alongside these relatively large formations, however, there was a parallel development of small, intensely self-disciplined, highly motivated and ruthlessly trained units, whose function was as often covert as it was overt. The Long Range Desert Group and similar semi-official formations led to the birth of today's Special Air Service Regiment and Special Boat Squadron, for example, while, in America, men who trained as both parachutists and underwater swimmers became the nucleus of todays SEAL (Sea-Air-Land) Teams and, in Germany, Otto Skorzeny's brilliantly successful airborne SS commandos showed the way for the type of role this new élite would adopt in the post-war world.

After 1945, however, the face of war changed dramatically – not just because of nuclear weapons. The 'cauldron' was no longer confined to Europe. There had been bloody uprisings in China, India, Africa and elsewhere throughout the 19th century, but now, in the wake of a five-year conflict which had weakened the major powers, the emergent countries of the so-called Third World discovered nationalism and self-determination, and a rapid balkanization of colonial territories ensued. British, Belgian, Dutch and French authorities in the Far and Middle Easts found themselves faced with growing demands for independence which created a seemingly never-ending succession of guerrilla wars and terrorist attacks in Indo-China, Malaya, India, Indonesia, Palestine, Kenya, the Congo, Rhodesia and many other countries.

Developing skills

Regular troops, as the British learned in North America in the 18th century, have an almost impossible task when fighting an elusive foe who can, chameleon-like, fade into the natural background, and who avoids at all costs any form of traditional set-piece battle. Ambushes and traps, the torture and mutilation of prisoners, the quick hit-and-run raid, the use of hostages and international blackmail, hijackings and the slaughter of civilians who might be in the way or just in the wrong place at the wrong time – all of these became part and parcel of a new form of total warfare which the conventional armed forces of the world are largely unable to cope with.

There have been a few exceptions. The British Army won the only true victory over an indigenous terrorist force in Malaya; it is still trying in Northern Ireland, and the scope of the problem is illustrated when one appreciates that troops not only have to undergo several weeks of special training before a tour of duty in Ulster, but also have to undertake a similar retraining course *afterwards*, before they are fit to go back into the 'real' front line in Germany. Many other nations have experienced similar difficulties. The French, and then the Americans, both tried, and lost, in Indo-China/Vietnam. Using similar tactics, but against a largely disorganized opposition, the Jews succeeded in wresting and holding the new state of Israel from their enemies against frightful odds – simultaneously creating a major new trouble spot for the world to watch.

Alongside the emergence of new nations and new power struggles came the international terrorist, the political or religious fanatic who does not care one iota who is killed, how many are killed, or even if he (or she) is killed, as long as a political objective is achieved. Assassination is, of course, nothing new. Organizations such as the Palestinian *El Fatah*, the Japanese Red Army, the German Baader-Meinhof gang and the Provisional Wing of the Irish Republican Army operate, however, on a different level and, in that sense, *are* new. The fact that they so often strike seemingly at random, and at 'soft' targets – not necessarily within the boundaries of the country at whose government their demands are aimed – makes them particularly difficult to deal with on a purely military footing.

The 'brush wars' of the 1950s and '60s had already accelerated the creation of special counter-insurgency forces in many civilized countries, and it is mainly with these that this book deals. In Borneo, Malaya, Aden and elsewhere, the British Special Air Service Regiment established for itself a formidable reputation, and other countries were not slow in imitating it. Commonwealth countries were the first to develop special units on the SAS model, and American commanders were so impressed with the Australian SAS in Vietnam that they set up special training camps with Australian instructors for their own élite troops, such as the men of the Airborne, Marine and Ranger battalions. West Germany, shocked by the Olympic Games massacre at Munich, formed its own special anti-terrorist commando, *Gremzschutzgruppe* (GSG) 9. France cultivated the élite paras of the French Foreign Legion. And, after the Israelis showed the way at Entebbe, these units proved themselves at Mogadishu and Kolwezi.

There are many dramatic and exciting tales of adventure concerning the élite forces of the world, some of which have been selected for inclusion in this volume. They include pitched battles, such as Goose Green, as well as rescue operations, such as Princes Gate and Operation 'Eagle Claw', and their locations cross the world from the jungles of Vietnam, via the deserts of the Middle East, to the bleak inhospitable terrain of the Falkland Islands. The intention of this book is to show through example what defines an 'élite' force, as well as including as much information as is available on organization and weapons.

It is almost impossible to glean reliable information from the other side of the 'Iron Curtain'. That East German commandos regularly exercise in NATO uniforms and with NATO equipment on the island of Hiddensee in the Baltic is no secret, nor is the presence of Soviet airborne troops in Afghanistan. But the main Soviet attempt over the last three decades has been in encouraging and supporting – economically, militarily and politically – the independent terrorist movements which are, for their own motives, trying to destroy the fabric of Western society. Well trained, and just as capable of entering battle 'regardless of risk', these organizations also have a separate section in this book.

The future

The last five years have seen an increased awareness of the need for extremely tough and well-trained quick-reaction forces in both British and American military circles, and new ready-alert brigades, as well as command structures, are currently being implemented. To what extent other countries will follow suit remains to be seen, but one particularly encouraging sign has been the hardening of attitudes towards terrorism in recent years, with the result that few governments today will accede to blackmail, and potential hijackers know that they will not be allowed to escape alive. However, although the protection of the innocent from terrorist blackmail is an important role for today's special forces, their recent and continuing reorganization must also be seen in the context of their role in time of global war, and the ominous implication for Europe in particular is that strategic planners in the Pentagon and elsewhere may have finally decided that it is not worth fighting a nuclear war over that continent. Even while we pray that such a theory is never put to the test, let us also give thanks for the fact that the men of the American, British and other élite forces stand prepared to lay down their lives, causing as much damage as possible to the enemy in order to buy the world time to reach sanity.

CHAPTER TWO

GREAT BRITAIN

THE PARACHUTE REGIMENT • THE SPECIAL AIR SERVICE REGIMENT • THE ROYAL MARINE COMMANDOS • THE SPECIAL BOAT SQUADRON AND RAIDING SQUADRONS

The British Army has for centuries combined the best military qualities of professionalism and individual enterprise, and nowhere can these be seen more clearly than in Great Britain's spearhead units. None of these formations existed prior to World War 2, but all of them proved themselves in action in the Western Desert, the Greek islands, France, Norway, and on mainland Italy, and later in the numerous campaigns around the world in which the British Army has been involved since 1945. The nation's soldiers have taken part, it will surprise many people to learn, in more than 50 campaigns of one type or another since the end of World War 2: in Greece from 1945 to '47; in India, Palestine and Aden; in Northern Ireland, of course, but also in the former Gold Coast and British Honduras; in Eritrea and Somaliland; in Malaya and Singapore; in Korea, Kenya, Cyprus, Suez and Hong Kong; in Belize, Togoland, Muscat and Oman, Jordan and Lebanon; in Jamaica, the Bahamas, British Guiana and Kuwait; in Zanzibar, Swaziland, Uganda, Tanganyika, Mauritius and the Seychelles; in Libya, Anguilla, Dhofar and Rhodesia; and finally, of course, in the Falkland Islands.

During the post-World War 2 withdrawal from Empire, when Britain was granting independence to so many of its former colonies, one campaign stands out as unique in the annals of war. While the French, and later the Americans and Australians, were involved in the long drawn-out and ultimately hopeless war of attrition in Indo-China, Laos and Vietnam, the British Army fought and won a successful campaign against communist-inspired guerrilla forces in Malaya. The Special Air Service and Special Boat Squadron played an especially vital role here during the years 1948 to 1960. Operating in the jungle, living off the land like the guerrillas for weeks at a

WEAPONS OF THE BRITISH ÉLITE FORCES

Designation	Type	Calibre	Magazine	Rate of fire	Range	Remarks
L9A1	Browning automatic pistol	9 mm	13 rounds	Single-shot	40 m	
XL47E1	Walther automatic pistol	7.65 mm	8 rounds	Single-shot	40 m	Modern equivalent of the wartime Walther PP
L2A3	Sterling sub-machine-gun	9 mm	34 rounds	550 rpm cyclic	200 m	
L34A1	Sterling Patchett silenced sub-machine-gun	9 mm	34 rounds	515 rpm cyclic	150 m	
MP5	Heckler and Koch sub-machine-gun	9 mm	15 or 30 rounds	800 rpm	200 m	Used by SAS and SBS
L1A1	Self-loading rifle	7.62 mm	20 or 30 rounds	40 rpm	600 m +	The widely used Belgian FN FAL
L42A1	Sniper rifle	7.62 mm	10 rounds	Single-shot	1000 m+	
M16A1	Armalite assault rifle	5.56 mm	20 or 30 rounds	700–950 rpm cyclic	400 m	
XL70E3	Individual weapon	5.56 mm	20 or 30 rounds	700–850 rpm cyclic	400 m	Just entering service
XL73E2	Light support weapon	5.56 mm	20 or 30 rounds	700–850 rpm cyclic	1000 m	LMG version of Individual Weapon
L4A4	Light machine-gun	7.62 mm	30 rounds	500–575 rpm cyclic	800 m	The faithful Bren gun

time, they used the same tactics that the terrorists were using against them. It was a hit-and-run campaign of hide and seek, with the destruction of the enemy's will to fight being just as important as the destruction of his arms caches and the killing of his soldiers. Similarly, the SAS and SBS waged a parallel 'hearts and minds' campaign among the civil population to deny the guerrillas their traditional refuge of hiding among the innocent. As a result, when the Army left Malaya after 12 years, it was able to hand over the government to a democratically established nation.

With the end of the Empire, the British Army's role has in more recent years been increasingly concentrated in Europe, with its commitment to the North Atlantic Treaty Organization (NATO). As discussed in the following pages, the SAS and SBS have a particularly crucial part to play here, since the behind-the-lines sabotage of Soviet and Warsaw Pact tactical nuclear weapons – particularly the mobile, multi-warhead type, such as the SS-20 – will be essential in the early hours and days of a major conflict. Similarly, it must be assumed that the newly formed 5th Airborne Brigade, the

Designation	Type	Calibre	Magazine	Rate of fire	Range	Remarks
L7A2	Machine-gun	7.62 mm	100-round belt	750–1000 rpm cyclic	1800 m	The widely used 'Gimpy'
L32A1	Automatic shotgun	12 bore (20 mm)	5 rounds	Single-shot	50 m	
M79	Grenade launcher	40 mm	Single-shot	6–10 rpm	150 m	
L9A1	Mortar	51 mm	Single-shot	8 rpm	750 m	
L16A1	Mortar	81 mm	Single-shot	15 rpm	5800 m	
L1A1	Anti-tank missile	66 mm	Single-shot	Not applicable	300 m	Modern equivalent of the old 'bazooka'
LAW80	Anti-tank missile	94 mm	Single-shot	Not available	500 m	Just entering service to replace the L1A1
L14A1 Carl Gustav	Anti-tank missile	84 mm	Single-shot	4–6 rpm	500 m	
Milan	Anti-tank missile	90 mm	Single-shot	3–4 rpm	2000 m	Became known as the 'bunker-buster' in the Falklands
TOW	Anti-tank missile	152 mm	Single-shot	Not available	3750 m	
Blowpipe	Anti-aircraft missile	76.2 mm	Single-shot	Not available	3000 m +	
Stinger	Anti-aircraft missile	70 mm	Single-shot	Not available	Not available	Used by SAS in the Falklands

spearhead of Britain's quick-reaction forces, will perform an equally vital function in neutralizing Soviet front-line airfields, while the Royal Marine commandos will be first into the fray in Norway if a Soviet offensive ever develops on NATO's northern flank.

All four of these units, which are considered 'élite' in the context of this book, have recently proved their capabilities yet again during the recapture of the Falkland Islands; but it must not be forgotten that they also have a peacetime role. This can take the form of the rescue of hostages from terrorists, as happened at Princes Gate in London in 1980; or it can take the form of aid to a country which appeals for help after being devastated by earthquake or flood. Wherever trouble occurs, whether it be a military threat or a natural disaster, a terrorist hijacking or a full-scale war, the officers and men of the Parachute Regiment, the Special Air Service, the Royal Marines and the Special Boat Squadron stand ready and alert for action. Without a shadow of doubt, there are no finer trained troops in the world.

THE PARACHUTE REGIMENT

'Hallo Two, this is Twenty-Three,' came the voice of Private 'Beast' Kirkwood over the Clansman radio.

'Send, over,' came the reply.

'Twenty-Three, for God's sake beam me up, Scotty!' was the heartfelt message.

B Company of the 2nd Battalion the Parachute Regiment (2 Para) was in a very exposed position on the hillside overlooking the ruins of Boca House, on the west side of the narrow isthmus joining the two main land masses of East Falkland. The company was on the right flank of 2 Para's attack on Argentine positions around the settlements of Darwin and Goose Green, and was coming under extremely heavy fire from enemy 105 mm howitzers as well as mortars. Retreat to the reverse side of the slope, out of direct Argentine observation, was the only prudent course, and the company retired from its precarious position.

It was the middle of the afternoon of 28 May 1982, and the Paras had been in action since 06.35. It was essential that the Argentine positions around Darwin and Goose Green be eliminated as quickly as possible, for they posed a distinct threat both to the beach-head at San Carlos and to the flank of the main troop movement eastwards across the island towards Port Stanley. When the SAS had originally reconnoitred the Argentine positions, and laid down their diversionary attack to keep the enemy's head down while the Marines and Paras landed at San Carlos on 21 May, the Argentine garrison had numbered a single battalion of about 500 men. Unknown to 2 Para's commander, Lieutenant-Colonel Herbert ('H') Jones, however, in the intervening period the Argentines had transferred a further two battalions of the 12th Infantry Regiment from Mount Kent to Goose Green, so that, when his battalion attacked, the enemy outnumbered the Paras by nearly three to one. To put the Paras' achievement in its correct context, it is normally recommended that an assault against prepared enemy positions should take place with a ratio of three attackers to one defender – the reverse of the situation 2 Para encountered.

The Regiment goes to war

The 2nd Battalion, the Parachute Regiment, was to see the heaviest fighting of all during the campaign to recapture the Falkland Islands, and they had watched with chagrin as 3 Para had sailed aboard the *Canberra* on 10 April. Five days later, however, they felt better as they embarked aboard the chartered ferry *Norland* and began the same sort of intensive training which was being carried out on the other troopships of the Task Force. Their landing at San Carlos had not been auspicious, though. Climbing into the landing craft (nicknamed 'rubbish skips' by the Paras) was difficult and dangerous, heavily laden as the men were, and one man slipped and broke his pelvis in the gap between the ferry and the landing craft. A

Lance-Corporal with the battalion summed it up. 'We got into this landing craft. Well, you'd think it would be easy, wouldn't you? But we were carrying these bergens [rucksacks] which weighed about 100 lb each. It would take two blokes to help you stand up. There were these Blowpipes as well, and the Blowpipes weigh about 50 lb, and we've got them on our shoulders. Unbelievable!'

However, the men of 2 Para had the honour of setting foot ashore first at San Carlos, although they were not pleased at finding that, while the Marines of 40 Commando on their flank had a shallow, shelving stretch of beach, their own was much steeper and meant they had to wade ashore waist-deep in the icy water. Fortunately, there was no resistance. The Lance-Corporal said, 'It was utter bloody chaos. In the dark, everyone looks the same in a helmet from behind, and there was no way to distinguish between anybody, and everybody was coming up to you and saying, "Do you know where so-and-so is?" Basically, if there had been anybody there it would have been the biggest fiasco ever. All you needed there was a hundred blokes, a couple of sustained-fire machine-guns, or even light machine-guns, a rocket launcher, wait until the boats are almost on the beach and just shoot the rockets straight into the men aboard them. They would have killed us all for sure.'

As they moved up the beach, everyone expected an Argentine air attack, but all they encountered was a group of tired and unshaven SBS men who directed them. The battalion's first task was to secure Sussex Mountain, overlooking San Carlos water.

'When we crossed the river,' the Lance-Corporal continued, 'there was an SBS bloke there helping you up, and I can remember someone asking him, "How long will it take?" It was only 13 km (8 miles) to the actual top of the mountain and the bloke said it would take about maybe five to six hours. We all thought "rubbish", but he was right, almost to the minute.'

When they reached the summit, the Paras began to dig in on the reverse side of the slope in anticipation of an enemy counter-attack (which never materialized) from the Argentines in Darwin. Then the anticipated air attacks began. The Lance-Corporal continued, 'All of a sudden there was this whistling and we all looked round and we could see nothing. Then there was an aircraft. My first thought was for my camera – I wanted to take a photograph. Never mind shooting the damned thing down!'

The aircraft was an Argentine Pucara ground-attack machine, which fired some rockets at both *Argonaut* and *Canberra* and was rapidly engaged by machine-guns and Blowpipe missiles from everywhere in sight. It was soon shot down, having done no damage to the ships. However, this was only a foretaste of what was to come in 'bomb alley'. By the end of the first day of the landings at San Carlos, HMS *Ardent* had been sunk after no fewer than 17 determined attacks by Skyhawks, Mirages, Pucaras and Aermacchis, while *Argonaut* was seriously damaged, and *Antrim*, *Brilliant* and *Broadsword* had all suffered hits, fortunately from bombs which failed to explode. In return, the Argentine air force had lost 16 aircraft. Two days later, HMS *Antelope* was destroyed in the spectacular explosion which made newspaper front pages around the world, and on the 25th *Coventry* also was sunk. But the Argentines had made the fatal mistake of waiting until the troops were ashore before attacking, and all the courage of their pilots could not prevent the counter-invasion succeeding.

By nightfall on the day of their invasion, both Para battalions as well as the Marines were well dug-in, supplies were flowing ashore, the Blues and Royals of the Household Cavalry with their Scorpion and Scimitar light tanks were in position, as were most of the artillery and Rapier anti-aircraft missile batteries. For 2 Para, though, it was the beginning of a very uncomfortable night since, although they were 900 m (3000 feet) above sea level on Sussex Mountain, the bottoms of their trenches were awash with water. Warmth and dryness were luxuries which all the troops on the Falklands, regardless of nationality, soon learned to do without.

Within a few days, despite the repeated air attacks on the ships in San Carlos water, sufficient supplies had been brought ashore, and it was time for the Paras to move on: 3 Para alongside 45 Commando on the long 'tab' ('tabbing' being the Paras' equivalent of the Marines' 'yomping', or forced-marching) to Port Stanley; and 2 Para towards their destiny at Goose Green.

Colonel 'H' Jones' battalion was organized along regular Army lines, but with subtle differences. Because it had been earmarked for duty in Belize at the time the Argentines invaded the Falklands, its men were equipped for the jungle fighting role. Although the terrain and climate on East Falkland could hardly have been more different from the tropical forest of Central America, what this meant was that they were not only issued with twice the normal number of 7.62 mm General Purpose Machine-Guns ('Gimpys') but also with a number of M16 Armalite rifles and M79 40 mm grenade launchers (of the type used so effectively by the Royal Marines' M&AW Cadre in the battle for Top Malo house described on page 41). This weight of firepower was to stand them in good stead. In addition, Colonel Jones had established an experimental, and very successful, dual command structure, with two tactical headquarters; this was to prove invaluable in keeping up the momentum of the Paras' attack on Goose Green when Colonel Jones was killed. Other than this, the battalion comprised the normal headquarters company (split into two), a support company with the mortars and Milan anti-tank missiles, and four rifle companies (A to D). C Company had been designated a special Patrol Company and operated in front of the battalion, confirming SAS reports that the isthmus was held in strength, particularly on Darwin Hill which overlooks the settlement from the south.

At 06.35 on 28 May the battalion moved out, with B Company on the right flank, D Company in the centre and A Company on the left. An Argentine platoon in a farmhouse was rapidly evicted by A Company, who were astounded to discover that the civilians inside had survived their attack. With this position secure (albeit under heavy artillery fire by this time), B Company moved up on the right in a pincer movement, enfilading Darwin from the west, while D Company pressed forward to consolidate the centre, eliminating some Argentine positions which A Company had bypassed, and taking several prisoners. It was during the next phase that Colonel Jones was killed. He was an officer who believed in leading from the front rather than directing matters from the rear, in the finest tradition of the Army, and his tactical headquarters was right forward with A Company when it began an assault up Darwin Hill. Colonel Jones led his own men forward at the same time on A Company's right. Murderous Argentine machine-gun fire forced A Company to fall back with two officers killed, and at this moment a burst of fire from another machine-gun raked Colonel Jones, killing him instantly.

'Sunray is down'

The code message informing him that 'Sunray' ('H' Jones) was 'down' – whether killed or incapacitated was not known at the time – was received by Major Chris Keeble, the second in command, over the radio at a time when 2 Para's main headquarters was itself being barraged by heavy artillery and mortar fire. The situation was perilous, with B Company pinned down on the slope above Boca House and D Company still reorganizing after its mopping-up operations. Following 'H' Jones' example, Keeble moved up to the front and ordered A Company into the assault on Darwin Hill again. Perhaps the death of the commanding officer whom the tough Paras idolized provided the necessary spur, because this time there was no stopping them. While 81 mm mortar rounds and Milan missiles rained into the Argentine positions from the Support Company which Keeble had also brought forward, A Company charged up the hill under cover of smoke grenades, blasting away with every automatic weapon the men possessed. The Argentines crumbled. With 18 of their number dead and another 39 wounded, they surrendered. *Now* Keeble could bring up D Company to outflank the Boca House position which had pinned down B Company. Rockets, grenades and machine-gun fire poured into the Argentine defences from two directions, and the surviving soldiers quickly surrendered.

Lance-Corporal Kevin Lukowiak summed up the Paras' attitude in such a situation: 'Your main instinct in a firefight is, "He's trying to get me, I'm going to get him before he does". A great Army expression is, "You don't kill things, you destroy them". So if you go in to take out a bunker, you waste the bunker before you get to it, then you give it some grenades. And then you blast it with your rifle.'

The Argentine troops on the Falklands, by and large, did not wait for the Paras to do this, but retreated or surrendered first. However, this does not mean that they did not fight with determination and vigour at the beginning of an engagement, as any soldier who was there will testify.

With both Darwin Hill and Boca House secured, Keeble could continue the Paras' advance on the main Argentine forces at Goose Green. Again, an enveloping manoeuvre was planned, with B Company pressing right around the western coast of the isthmus to come back round upon Goose Green unexpectedly from the south, while D Company performed a less extensive sweep so as to come in from the west, and C Company, the Patrol Company, moved through A Company's position on Darwin Hill to attack from the north. The Support Company was also brought forward on to Darwin Hill to lend its firepower to the action.

Both C and D Companies soon encountered problems. Even at this early stage in the land battle, the Paras recognized the Argentine disposition to surrender when threatened by determined aggression and so, despite the fact that they came under murderous fire from artillery pieces, mortars and even anti-aircraft guns as they descended Darwin Hill towards Goose Green and its airstrip, few were surprised when, as they reached the Argentine trenches, a white flag was waved. What happened next is confused. One British journalist is reported as having said that a British machine-gun opened fire, to which an Argentine gun responded. Lieutenant Jim Barry of D Company, who had walked forward to accept the Argentine surrender, was killed together with two NCOs. Private Baz Graham of 11 Platoon, D Company, remembers things differently. 'We were going up the hill and the flag went up. The officer [Barry] called the Sergeant, and they got half-way up the hill. Bang! They let rip into them. Killed them. One guy was hit in the knee and one of the Argies came forward and shot him in the head. He moved forward out of his position and shot him.'

Anyone who has ever been on a battlefield will realize that mistakes occur and that things are not always what they seem; moreover, no two witnesses ever give the same account of events. The effect on C and D Companies, regardless, was electrifying. They went in with everything blazing. The schoolhouse behind the trenches which the Argentines had been occupying was blasted with so many grenades and perforated with such concentrated automatic fire that it was afterwards impossible to determine how many defenders it had held. (The Argentine soldiers did not wear identifying metal 'dog-tags', so no accurate body count of their casualties was ever possible during the campaign.)

At this stage in the evening of 28 May the air forces of both sides came into action. D Company was attacked by four aircraft, two Mirages and two Pucaras, the latter carrying dreaded napalm containers. This was, however, the only occasion during the whole campaign that these loathsome weapons were used, and there were no casualties among the Paras. In retaliation, three Royal Air Force Harriers struck hard at the Argentine defences with cluster bombs and cannon fire. As darkness fell, helicopters could be seen bringing up further Argentine reinforcements.

During the night, a Para patrol entered Darwin settlement itself, and the information gleaned from the local inhabitants changed Major Keeble's ideas about the following day's action. In order to save the lives of his own troops during what was certain to prove hard street-fighting, he had decided to lay on a concentrated artillery barrage and had ordered up more 105 mm guns, mortars and ammunition. However, the patrol discovered that the Argentines held over a hundred British civilians hostage in the community centre in Goose Green. Whatever form an attack took, innocent lives would be lost. Keeble radioed for permission from Brigadier Julian Thompson to ask the Argentine commander to surrender, or at least to release the civilians (who had, it transpired, been incarcerated since 1 May). Thompson agreed, and preliminary negotiations took place over the radio between two British farm managers, one in San Carlos and one in Goose Green. In the morning, two Argentine senior NCOs emerged under a white flag and Chris Keeble, together with two other officers – one a Spanish-speaking SBS officer, Captain Rod Bell – plus a radio operator and two journalists, accompanied them back to the airstrip, where the Argentine commander, Air Vice-Commodore Wilson Pedrozo, agreed to surrender. Then came the surprise. Instead of the 300-odd men expected as a result of the earlier faulty intelligence reports (allowing for those already killed or captured), Argentine troops emerged in their droves from the buildings in and around Goose Green, most of them very happy with the bloodless end to the battle. The Paras had gone in and won at odds of one to three!

The making of the Parachute Regiment

Britain was a late starter in the development of airborne troops, and it was not until late in June 1940, after the dramatic successes of German paratroops and glider-borne forces during the invasion of Belgium and the Netherlands, that Prime Minister Winston Churchill issued an instruction to begin the formation of an airborne corps of at least 5000 men. Thus was the 1st Airborne Division born, and it proved so successful in Tunisia (where British paras – the 'red devils' – met German *Fallschirmjäger* – the 'green devils' – for the first time), and later during the invasions of Sicily and Italy, that in May 1943 the creation of a second division, the 6th Airborne, was authorized. (It should be noted that many military formations, particularly those originated during wartime, are deliberately numbered out of sequence in order to mislead the enemy.) The 6th Airborne spearheaded the British assault on Normandy in the early hours of D-Day, 6 June 1944, while the 1st Division was enjoying a well-earned rest after its labours in the Mediterranean theatre of operations. However, it was the 1st Airborne which won undying glory at Arnhem that autumn.

After World War 2, there was a rapid run-down of all the armed services, and the airborne forces were reduced from 17 to only 3 parachute battalions, the 4th/6th, the 5th (Scottish) and the 7th. Together with supporting artillery and cavalry (light armoured) formations, they became 16 Para Brigade, with headquarters at Aldershot. A quarter of a century later, in 1977, further defence cuts caused the disbandment of the supporting units and, at the time of the Falklands crisis, the Parachute Regiment consisted essentially of just three battalions: 1, 2 and 3 Para.

In the wake of the Falklands' operation, however, considerable rethinking has gone into the Para role. Over recent years it had become fashionable to regard the airborne capability as outmoded, and to treat the Paras merely as especially tough infantrymen. What analysis of the battles for the Falklands shows, on the other hand, is that in almost every case, with the exception of the final assault on Port Stanley, *had* a parachute drop capability existed, Argentine positions could have been captured more quickly and with fewer casualties. It is equally true to say that, without the loss of so many troop-carrying Chinook helicopters aboard *Atlantic Conveyor*, the course of the campaign would have been different. In both cases, the answer is speed and mobility – the prime attributes of the airborne trooper, who can get quickly to where he is, hopefully, least expected, or at any rate before the enemy can prepare adequate defences.

What the Falklands also showed was that Britain had, in the Parachute Regiment, the nucleus of a 'quick-reaction' force second to none – small, maybe, but in the British Army quality has usually counted for more than quantity. 'Small is beautiful' has more than one meaning. The British Army,

Soldiers of the Parachute Regiment bundle their 'chutes together while a second wave descends in the background.

even allowing for the well-trained members of the Territorial Army, is only half the size of those of France or West Germany and a mere fifth the size of that of America. The closest comparison one can draw is that the British troops in the Falklands proved once more the point Wellington made in the Peninsular War against France: a small, trained, motivated and professional force will defeat a far larger conscript army of reluctant soldiers. The only truly professional force the Argentines possessed was their air force, and they frittered it away. Fortunately, official government thinking has finally reached the same conclusion, with the result that, while these words are written, the old British 5th Infantry Brigade is being reconstituted as the new 5th Airborne Brigade. As during the 1970s, its task remains essentially that of principal reserve for commander-in-chief of United Kingdom Land Forces (UKLF). This means that it is principally entrusted, in time of global war, with the internal defence of the United Kingdom. However, the brigade now includes two battalions of the Parachute Regiment together with an armoured reconnaissance regiment whose Scorpions and Scimitars can be transported by air, together with a helicopter support squadron, an air defence troop equipped with Blowpipe surface-to-air missiles, plus signals, ordnance and engineering units. This gives the new brigade far greater flexibility as well as mobility and, despite its small size, shows that the government is not willing to be 'caught napping' by another Falklands-type encounter. Had the 5th Airborne Brigade existed in 1982, it could have been in Stanley before the main Argentine forces arrived. Considering the havoc that the tiny parties of Royal Marines managed to cause, what would the Argentines have accomplished against such an airborne force? And so, today, 5th Airborne, proudly wearing the same maroon beret which meant so much in 1944, stands ready for an almost immediate departure for any one of the world's trouble spots in which British interests or the lives of British civilians may be threatened.

Parachute training

It is common knowledge that the training course for a modern paratrooper is both intense and gruelling. Basic training takes seven weeks and, while principally designed to toughen up recruits physically, it also involves learning weapons use, fieldcraft and rudimentary first aid. The course culminates in a realistic exercise in the Welsh mountains, after which the recruits' performance is examined by a selection committee. Some men are weeded out at this stage as being unsuitable material for the Parachute Regiment (although many of them would be perfectly at home in a regular infantry regiment); others are recommended for further training and a 'second chance'; and the best recruits, after a weekend's leave, begin the second stage of their course. The first three weeks of this involves advanced weapons handling with automatic rifles, machine-guns, sub-machine-guns, anti-tank missiles and grenades, but the physical toughening-up process does not stop either. At the end of this period there is a further selection committee to decide which recruits are suitable to go on for parachute training and which must, regretfully, be passed over.

Unbelievably, the next training stage is even more demanding than the preceding two, but by this time the recruits are in peak physical condition and the knowledge that they are on the 'final lap' promotes confidence. The initial stages involve crossing obstacle courses some 9 m (30 ft) above the ground, taking part in a boxing match designed to test aggression, completing a 16 km (10 mile) forced march in full kit in under two hours, a 12 km (7½ mile) 'stretcher race' carrying a simulated casualty, a 'log race' carrying a simulated box of ammunition, a cross-country steeplechase, and three circuits of the assault course. After the successful completion of all these, the recruit is finally permitted to wear the coveted red beret, but he still has to earn his parachutist's wings.

Following four weeks' advanced training in fieldcraft and tactics in Wales, designed to make them think and act as part of a military team rather than as individuals, the recruits finally proceed to the RAF Station of Brize Norton in Somerset. Here, they are first taught the correct way in which to fall, then proceed to dummy exits from a mock-up of a Hercules transport aircraft, and controlled drops from the hangar roof on rigging lines whose rate of descent is controlled by gears to approximate the 30 km/h (20 mph) speed of an actual parachute drop. Once he has mastered the art of falling correctly and safely, a recruit goes outside to the tower, where he makes further controlled drops of longer duration and learns how to deal with tangled rigging lines and similar problems. Then comes the balloon jump, and it is at this stage that some recruits balk.

However, refusal to jump is the cardinal sin in the Parachute Regiment and any recruits who simply cannot face it are gently and sympathetically made to leave the Regiment. For most of them, though, that first jump from the balloon, in a silence only broken by the wind, is an exhilarating experience, although the seconds before the parachute is pulled open by its static line (fixed to the balloon platform) seem far longer than they really are. Then the recruit is floating gently to earth. He has only a few seconds in which to appreciate the sensation, because the ground is rushing up and it's feet together and hit and roll. I've made it! An incredulous grin. 'Feeling nine feet tall and covered with hair', a recruit at this stage regards the final qualifying seven jumps from a Hercules, three of them with full equipment and one of them at night, with relative equanimity. And, at the end, there are those coveted wings to add to the maroon beret.

Paras in action

The Parachute Regiment has seen extensive service around the world since the end of World War 2. 3 Para was instrumental in seizing Gamil Airport outside Port Said during the Anglo-French occupation of the Suez Canal Zone in 1956, and both 2 and 3 Para saw action in Aden, as well as Borneo, during the late 1950s and mid-1960s. Since 1969, a battalion of Paras has usually been stationed in Northern Ireland, and they have established a reputation for ruthless aggression which makes them unpopular with IRA sympathizers. Until the recent formation of 5th Airborne Brigade, however, their role within NATO in time of major conflict in Europe would largely have been restricted to that of ordinary infantry, since RAF Support Command had only sufficient Hercules transports to air-lift one battalion into action. That situation is now being remedied, and at least two battalions, together with their light armoured vehicles and support weapons, will be available for proper airborne operations in time of war.

The most significant campaign the Paras have fought since 1945, though, was undoubtedly in the Falklands. We have already seen how 2 Para fared at Goose Green following the amphibious landing at San Carlos; while they were making headlines, 3 Para was on the march.

After trudging ashore on 21 May, many of the men soaking wet because a landing craft had struck an unsuspected offshore sandbar, 3 Para entered San Carlos settlement itself to be greeted with joy and hot cups of tea by the locals. The men then established dug-in positions overlooking the settlement and began sending out patrols to clear Fanning Head of remaining Argentine troops. On 27 May, as 2 Para was preparing to move on Darwin and Goose Green, 3 Para was tightening its boots for the long cross-country 'tab' in the company of 45 Commando, via Douglas and Teal Inlet to Estancia and Mount Kent. Led by their CO, Lieutenant-Colonel Hew Pike, the Paras completed the march to Estancia House, an isolated building on the north-west slopes of Mount Kent, in only four days. The house was packed with local civilians who had left Stanley to avoid military action and who were astonished to be awoken during the night of 31 May by a flare bursting overhead and the shouted order, 'Open up! It's the British Army.'

The Paras rapidly dug in, putting up tents over their foxholes and constructing dug-outs using spare timber and sheets of corrugated iron in order to obtain some shelter from the bitter cold. Defensive machine-gun positions were established using piles of cut peat in place of sandbags, and patrols were sent out. A number of Argentine stragglers (a kinder word than deserters) were brought in, weaponless, and, as dawn broke, the Paras were able to look out over Port Stanley and their next objective, Mount Longdon. However, due both to the acute helicopter shortage and to poor flying conditions, it was another three days before Brigadier Thompson was able to get an artillery battery forward to support them.

The formidable and craggy slopes of Mount Longdon were to prove an extremely tough nut to crack, for not only were they defended by the whole of the Argentine 7th Infantry Regiment, supported by marines and snipers from the *Buzo Tactico* equipped with night sights, but also the mountain approaches had been heavily mined. Because of the minefields, there was just one possible approach for the Paras, and it was on a narrow frontage which permitted the deployment of only one company at a time. Naval gunfire support would be provided by HMS *Avenger*, but Mount Longdon was a veritable fortress, and Colonel Pike knew that he was going to need all the support he could muster.

To begin with the operation went well. A and B Companies moved out to the north and south in a pincer movement at 21.00 on 11 June, while C Company took the centre. Guides were provided by the men of D (Patrol) Company who had reconnoitred the approach routes and minefields over the preceding days. It was a brilliant moonlit night and the men made the best use of whatever cover was available to avoid detection through the Argentine night scopes. However, any element of surprise was lost when a Corporal in B Company trod on an anti-personnel mine only about 630 m (700 yd) from the first Argentine trenches. The Argentine mortars, machine-guns and artillery pieces opened up immediately, but two Para platoons raced up the slope, covered by a third platoon which had found good cover in some rocks. Hurling grenades in all directions, they took the first objective without loss but unfortunately missed one Argentine bunker, whose occupants opened fire on their rear. Several Paras had died or been wounded before the bunker fell silent.

Advancing from this position, B Company came under severe fire from Argentine positions further up the slope. The Paras used 66 and 84 mm rockets to eliminate the troublesome heavy-calibre machine-guns, but the Argentines seemed to be everywhere and, the moment one position was knocked out, fire opened up from a different quarter. Two Privates ran forward to take out a 0.50 calibre machine-gun nest with hand grenades – something which is easy to say but which in practice demands the kind of courage and determination which defy description. It was while attempting to deal with another such heavy machine-gun that Sergeant Ian McKay won his posthumous Victoria Cross. McKay was the Sergeant of 4 Platoon, commanded by Lieutenant Bickerdike. As his platoon came under sustained fire from a 0.50 calibre heavy machine-gun, two lighter 7.62 mm machine-guns and a 105 mm recoilless gun, both Lieutenant Bickerdike and his signaller were wounded, the former in the leg and the latter in the mouth. McKay took charge and decided that the heavy machine-gun was the main problem. Gathering a four-man section of 4 Platoon around him, he led the way up the slope towards the well dug-in Argentine position, which was further protected by numerous riflemen in well-sited trenches. The four riflemen with McKay were all hit and fell, but the Sergeant continued alone. As he leapt over the parapet, he was hit by a sniper and was killed instantly. However, in falling he blocked the machine-gun's fire and 5 and 6 Platoons were able to take advantage of the momentary lull to retire.

As the men regrouped and casualties were brought to the rear, a rain of fire fell on the Argentine positions from the Royal Artillery's 105 mm guns and 81 mm mortars. Then B Company moved forward again. 4 and 5 Platoons were merged into one and started forward along the ridge they had so recently evacuated. As they neared the Argentine position, they came under heavy fire from point-blank range and fired a 66 mm rocket at the

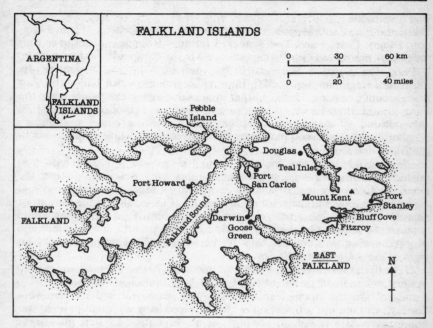

FALKLAND ISLANDS

enemy gunners. Charging forward with their rifles blazing, they discovered several dead Argentine soldiers – but by this time the rest of the company was in trouble, having come under fire from two flanks as they advanced. Once again they were forced to retire, and Colonel Pike decided that their casualties had been so heavy that he would have to pull the survivors back and replace them with A Company.

A Company had its own problems, having come round the northern flank of the mountain to find itself on open ground with little cover, and also under heavy fire. Colonel Pike brought the men back and redirected them up through B Company's position. This time the Paras moved forward painfully on their stomachs, firing as they crawled and launching a barrage of grenades and 66 mm rockets to add to the artillery shells which were still pounding the Argentine strongpoint. As they reached the crest, the artillery fire was called off, but some Argentine soldiers could now be seen fleeing. Fixing bayonets, the Paras grimly began clearing the trenches with brutal efficiency. More and more Argentines began to withdraw, harassed by artillery fire, and, after a battle lasting ten hours – the most costly in the whole campaign – Mount Longdon was finally secured by 3 Para. Twenty-three men had been killed and twice that number wounded, but the Argentine casualties were at least double; once more, due to the lack of dog-tags, it was impossible to make an exact count.

The final battle

While the Paras and Marines consolidated their positions on Mount Long-don, Mount Harriet and Two Sisters, 5 Infantry Brigade moved up so that the Scots Guards and Gurkhas could take Mount Tumbledown. Meanwhile, 2 Para was assigned Wireless Ridge, defended by the Argentine 1st Parachute Regiment and the 7th Infantry Regiment, which had withdrawn from Mount Longdon. Unlike earlier attacks during the campaign, when the Paras and Marines had tried to close with the enemy positions by stealth, it was decided to make this a 'noisy' assault, with a heavy preliminary bombardment, and accompanied by the Scorpion and Scimitar light tanks of the Blues and Royals.

During 13 June the battalion marched around 3 Para's hard-won positions on Mount Longdon in order to approach Wireless Ridge from the north. D Company was to anchor its attack on Mount Longdon, with B Company to its left in the centre position and A Company on the far left, or eastern flank. All the artillery and mortars of both Para battalions would support the attack. C Company would follow behind the main assault and proceed eastwards along the bank of the Murrell River to outflank the far right of the Argentine positions.

The battalion moved up to its start line at 22.30 that evening and moved out just before 01.00 on the 14th, after the Argentines had been subjected to a full half hour's intense artillery fire. The Paras watched the 'firework display' with intense satisfaction as they trudged forward, and the night was not without its element of farce for, as an Argentine 155 mm gun began shelling the advancing Paras, two men dived for cover, only to find themselves at the bottom of an abandoned Argentine latrine! As A and B Companies advanced, they were accompanied by two Scorpion light tanks with 76 mm guns and two Scimitars with quick-firing 30 mm Rarden cannon. The Blues and Royals, commanded by Lieutenant Robin Innes-Ker, were anxious to show what they could do, because so far in the campaign they had not been engaged in a proper battle. They soon proved their usefulness, however. As soon as an Argentine bunker was identified, they would open fire with their main armament and then pursue any Argentine soldiers who tried to escape with their co-axial machine-guns. As one observer commented, 'The Paras loved it!' But it was not all to be so easy.

As A and B Companies advanced in the centre, the supporting artillery fire was switched to the front of D Company on the right flank. Unfortunately, the gunners got the range wrong to begin with, and the Paras cursed as their artillery fire landed among their own ranks. Soon, however, the night was lit up by shell bursts from both directions, the sparkle of flares and the red arcs of tracer. An Argentine attempt at a counter-attack was soon beaten off, pursued by mortar fire. 2 Para's determination had never been grimmer. Even the cooks and clerks came along to help out, acting as stretcher bearers and carrying ammunition. By the early hours of the morning, Wireless Ridge was virtually in the Paras' hands, and they could look down at the old Marines' barracks which Argentine troops had stormed on the first day of the invasion. Argentine artillery in Stanley was still active, but following a second attempt at a counter-attack by men of the 1st Parachute Regiment which was broken up by artillery fire, the heart seemed to go out of the resistance. More than a hundred Argentines had been killed in the attack; 2 Para had lost just three men.

As the daylight grew stronger on the morning of 14 June, the enemy's position was revealed as hopeless. The Argentines were completely surrounded by eager troops on all the high ground around Stanley, and their men were demoralized. Brigadier Thompson flew in to Wireless Ridge by helicopter to observe the situation for himself, and gave his approval for 2 Para to continue down the hill, past the Marines' barracks, into Stanley itself. After having been first ashore at San Carlos, and following Goose Green and Fitzroy, it seemed only just that 2 Para should be first into the islands' capital. Jauntily, the men strolled, sauntered or ran down the slopes, many of them yelling at the tops of their voices. Most of the Argentine troops just stood and watched them, making no attempt to stop the Paras as they started climbing over the Panhard armoured cars and removing souvenirs. At last the guns were silent.

THE SPECIAL AIR SERVICE REGIMENT

At 04.15 on 15 May 1982, Griff Evans, a sheep farmer in the small community on Pebble Island, and his wife Gladys, were awoken by the sound of explosions. Peering through their farmhouse windows, they saw the whole night sky brilliantly illuminated by exploding flares, ammunition and oil drums from the nearby airstrip which the invading Argentine forces had been building as an alternative to Stanley airfield. As Griff and his wife made a cup of coffee and tried to reassure each other, they were unaware of the fact that the darkness outside concealed a troop of men from the Special Air Service Regiment who had been detailed to protect the settlement in case of an Argentine counter-attack. A second troop, led by Captain John Hamilton (who was later to be killed in circumstances of great personal valour), was busy placing charges of plastic explosive in the 11 aircraft on the strip – Pucara ground-attack aircraft, Puma helicopters and a Shorts' Skyvan utility aircraft.

Apart from Port Stanley airfield itself, Pebble Island, lying on the north coast of West Falkland, is the only place in the rocky and mountainous island group where there is a sufficiently long stretch of level ground to accommodate large aircraft. Both the Argentines and the British Task Force commander, Rear Admiral 'Sandy' Woodward, appreciated the strategic value of Pebble Island, and the airstrip had been reconnoitred during the night of 13 May by an eight-man SAS patrol. Landed on Keppel Island the previous night, they had carried their lightweight Klepper canoes down to a sheltered cove from which they were able to observe their objective. As darkness fell, they paddled across Keppel Sound and landed on the south-west shore of Pebble Island. Moving stealthily through the darkness, they established a hidden observation post on First Mount Hill, 290 m (960 ft) high, overlooking the Argentine airstrip with its accompanying radar post and fuel dump. They radioed their observations to the Task Force flagship, *Hermes*, and marked out a landing zone for the Sea King helicopters which would bring in Captain Hamilton and the men of D Squadron, 22 Special Air Service Regiment, plus a Naval Gunfire Support Forward Observer, Captain Chris Brown of 29 Commando Regiment, Royal Artillery. Offshore lay the 'County' Class destroyer *Glamorgan*, whose 4.5-inch guns would soon be brought into play.

The Sea Kings landed after dark on the night of 14 May, and John Hamilton and his men disembarked. They were heavily laden down with machine-guns, 2-inch mortars, bombs, grenades, and plastic explosive charges and detonators, and a strenuous cross-country march lay ahead of them. Eventually, they reached the site that the earlier patrol had selected as a mortar position, and thankfully dropped their loads. Splitting into three groups now – one with the mortars as a support section, one to cover the civilian settlement, and one to sabotage the Argentine aircraft – they were ready to tackle the Argentine air force personnel guarding the airstrip.

As the SAS men settled into position, Chris Brown started relaying target information to *Glamorgan* and the shells began to arrive.

For a soldier, naval gunfire support is terrifying. The ship or ships are lying well offshore, outside the range of normal infantry weapons. With an observer on the ground, as in the case of Chris Brown, the accuracy is point-blank. *Glamorgan*'s 20 kg (46 lb) shells appeared to come from nowhere and were unstoppable. Blast after blast scoured the Argentine positions, carefully timed at one-minute intervals. Nowhere was safe. Ammunition and fuel began exploding, awakening Griff and Gladys Evans and sending the 200 men of the Argentine garrison scurrying to hide from the fury in their dug-outs. Into the confusion slipped the dark shadows of John Hamilton's troopers, festooned with plastic explosive charges, wire and detonators. Working their way, without spoken orders since each man knew exactly his job, from aircraft to aircraft, they placed their charges and detonated them. When daybreak dawned, the Argentine officers surveyed 11 heaps of scrap metal where 11 vital aircraft had been the preceding day. The SAS, meanwhile, had slipped back to their landing ground, picking up the mortars *en route*, and had been flown back to *Hermes*.

'Who Dares Wins'

The Special Air Service Regiment ('Ess-Ay-Ess' to most people, but 'Sass' within the Army) had led a largely secret life from the time of its official post-war establishment in 1950 until that never-to-be-forgotten day in 1980 when the black-garbed figures of SAS men were photographed on the balcony of the Iranian Embassy in London by the eagerly awaiting press and television cameras of the world. 'Sass' is a military organization which has always shunned the glare of publicity, but the rescue of hostages from a group of fanatics in the centre of one of the world's principal cities focused the limelight on them long before the Falkland Islands' confrontation. Suddenly, their motto was on everyone's lips, and at least one fortunate book publisher made a small fortune through having a manuscript on the regiment's history already in production! From the obscurity of the campaigns in Malaya, Aden and elsewhere around the world in which they had won their spurs, suddenly the men of the SAS were exposed to the public gaze.

This exposure has not been welcomed by the Army: the role of 'Sass' is clandestine. The regiment's exact strength and order of battle are not discussed in public, nor will a list of the officers and men in its ranks be found in any published gazetteer. It is officially forbidden to take a photograph of a member of the regiment unless he is sufficiently camouflaged as to be unrecognizable, and even then the practice is frowned upon. The reasons are obvious and understandable. In time of global war, the regiment's duties include the kind of behind-the-lines reconnaissance and sabotage which it accomplished with such panache in the Falklands. In time of 'peace', the regiment is responsible for intelligence gathering and the setting of ambushes against the Irish Republican Army in Ulster, while all of its troopers are specially trained in anti-terrorist duties – specifically, the safe rescue of hostages in a hijack situation. Officers and NCOs of the SAS act as advisers to most of the free world's special forces, and, from America to Australia and back, the crack troops of all the western and aligned nations are organized and trained on the SAS model.

The men who join 'Sass' are an élite even before their special training. For the most part, the regiment recruits from the Brigade of Guards or the Parachute Regiment, although the officers and men of other regiments are entitled to volunteer (Captain John Hamilton, for instance, came from The Green Howards). The SAS is the only remaining regiment in the British Army which does not recruit directly from the general public, and its standards are so high that by no means all of those who apply, even after the gruelling physical and aptitude tests and training needed for their parent regiment, are accepted.

Volunteers, after passing preliminary interviews, have to undertake the SAS's even more rigorous four-week selection course. This not only embraces the 'ordinary' skills of the Para or Commando units, such as rock-climbing, parachuting, skiing, canoeing, swimming and prolonged forced marching in full kit, but a wide variety of psychological tests to ascertain a recruit's ability to respond intelligently and quickly under the most difficult circumstances imaginable. Sensory deprivation tests, in which recruits are spun in a chair similar to those used to train astronauts, but in complete darkness and wearing earplugs, are just one of the many trials a volunteer must endure. At the end of the test, he has to be able to aim and fire at a target which suddenly springs up. In other, Houdini-style tests to judge nerve and susceptibility to panic, recruits are released into darkened swimming pools, laden down with chains, and must release the combination locks on these chains before they can surface to breathe. There *are* casualties during SAS selection and training, and once in a while they hit the headlines, but the effect is to ensure that a man is not admitted to the regiment unless the selection officers are as certain as they can be that he is not only at a peak of physical fitness, but also alert, intelligent and self-motivated.

Once a soldier has passed this initial selection process, which is deliberately made extremely tough in order to weed out as many unsuitable candidates as possible before the more expensive phases of advanced training begin, he enters a two-year training programme. As described by Tony Geraghty in his fine book on the history of the SAS, *Who Dares Wins* (Arms and Armour Press), this training is divided into six phases. The first is a continuation of the basic toughening-up process, which even Paras find strenuous. Route marches of ever-increasing length, with heavier and heavier loads, together with instruction in map-reading and navigation, are accompanied by continuous psychological testing and training in basic security, such as memorizing information instead of writing it down. Phase 2, which lasts three weeks, involves the men being taken to somewhere in the Welsh mountains, or a similar piece of inhospitable terrain, and being given the task of finding their way to a particular rendezvous within a time limit. During this phase a candidate gets very little sleep – another test of stamina and determination – being awoken at 04.00 every morning and having to attend a briefing for the following day's activities at 22.30. Phase 2 ends with a march of 65 km (40 miles) over mountainous terrain, which has to be accomplished within 20 hours.

Candidates who have survived the course to this point now enter Phase 3, which involves both a three-week combat survival course on Exmoor, during which they learn to live off the land, improvise shelter and avoid detection – all vital elements in the training of a soldier who will be expected to operate behind enemy lines in time of war. Phase 3 also includes highly realistic exercises during which candidates are interrogated by experts in just the same way that they would be if captured by an enemy. Having a hood placed over one's head in a bleak cell and not being allowed to sleep because of blaring loudspeakers, or being forced to squat for hours on end in ice-cold water, are just two of the basic techniques. Others include being blindfolded and having to listen to the apparent sounds of a colleague being beaten up, as well as other even more unnerving experiences such as being manacled, blindfolded, to a railway track. The few candidates who survive Phase 3 are judged worthy of entering the SAS and are thereafter entitled to wear the regiment's beige beret and winged-dagger badge.

During Phase 4 the new SAS men can opt for one of four specialist training courses (although many men go on to complete them all, in due course). Each of the SAS's four Sabre squadrons is specially trained for particular duties: one is high-altitude free-fall parachuting; the second, which the SAS shares with the SBS (Special Boat Squadron), is marine operations, including canoeing, landing on a hostile shore at night either from a dinghy or by swimming from a submarine, and sub-aqua work; the third, where training is shared with the Royal Marines' Mountain & Arctic Warfare Cadres, is in their skills; and the fourth, harking back to Long Range Desert Group days, is cross-country mobility, particularly in desert terrain. Once an SAS man has completed his specialist training, Phase 5 begins, which is the all-important counter-terrorist course. Many details of this are necessarily secret, but the use of explosives, stun grenades and the setting (and detecting) of booby traps; planning how to break into a house, airliner or train and kill terrorists while minimizing risk to their hostages; and the use of non-regulation firearms from many countries, all form part of this course.

Finally, the SAS trooper will be allocated to one of the four Sabre Squadrons to begin his work in earnest. Because the regiment may be called upon at any time to go anywhere in the world, and because its men have to act intelligently in the face of a wide variety of possible situations, their training is as broad as possible and never really ends. Numbers of SAS officers and NCOs, for example, learn to fly with the Army Air Corps. Britain's AAC pilots are the most highly trained in the world and, although an SAS trooper escapes their basic training, he still has to do the preliminary ten-week course which covers aerial map reading, aerial observation post duties, the direction of artillery fire, flight servicing, and other essential skills. Within the AAC, a soldier has to spend a minimum of two years acting as an aircrewman/observer before he can apply for pilot training, but for the SAS this is reduced to four weeks. A five-week pre-flying course is followed by a minimum of 60 hours on fixed-wing trainers – Chipmunks and Beagles – before the trainee goes to the civilian Basic Helicopter Flight for a further 60 hours on Bell 47 helicopters. Another week is spent learning aero-medical and ditching procedures before the recruit finally passes to the Advanced Rotary Wing Squadron at the Army Air Corps headquarters at Middle Wallop. A further 115 hours' in-flight instruction on the fast and versatile little Aérospatiale Gazelle follows before the soldier finally gains his wings as a fully qualified helicopter pilot; even more experience is required if he wishes to qualify on the Lynx, Puma or Chinook.

Many SAS officers, because of their behind-the-lines infiltration and intelligence-gathering role in time of war, also spend some time learning intelligence skills with 'I' Corps (the 'MI6' of popular fiction) at its Ashford headquarters. Their studies here include not only photography and photo reduction (to make microdots), but also specialized signals training, surveillance techniques, the use of codes and ciphers, and even lock-picking. Finally, because an understanding of the language in an overseas operation is always an asset, many officers learn German, Russian, Chinese and other languages at the Army School of Languages at Beaconsfield. Within the SAS, indeed more than in any other branch of the Army, learning is something which never ceases, as the highly motivated officers and men in the regiment would chafe at the restrictions of normal Army life.

In Northern Ireland

As a result of this highly specialized training, 'Sass' is much in demand in the constant fight against terrorist outrages in Northern Ireland, and between 120 and 160 members of the regiment are normally stationed in the province. Just as when on duty elsewhere, whether with the British Army of the Rhine, in Hong Kong, Cyprus or Belize, the soldiers of the SAS rarely wear their famous winged-dagger badge or beige beret, but rather the insignia of the regiment to which they are temporarily attached, or something fairly innocuous such as Royal Army Ordnance Corps or Royal Corps of Transport badges. Frequently, only the commanding officer and intelligence officer of a regiment will know the identities of any SAS men in their ranks.

The Army's task in Northern Ireland is neither an easy nor a pleasant one, but it is vital if the province is not to erupt into total civil war. Even before the present troubles began in 1969, the British government maintained a peacetime garrison in Northern Ireland in support of the Royal Ulster Constabulary. As the bombings and shootings increased in frequency and intensity, the Royal Ulster Constabulary was disbanded under political pressure and a new Army regiment was formed to replace it – the Ulster Defence Regiment which, although currently the strongest regiment in the British Army with more than 7000 men and nearly 1000 women in its ranks, is also a part-time regiment, being organized along Territorial Army lines from civilian volunteers. The SAS work closely with the UDR and other Army regiments which are stationed in the province as peace-keeping forces, but particularly closely with the UDR because its members, being local to the area and with friends and relatives all over the province, have their ears more closely to the ground than any mainlander could hope to have, and are vital in securing intelligence.

The SAS's role in Northern Ireland is largely concerned with intelligence gathering and implementing direct action as a result of information gathered. This can involve the setting up of ambushes, especially along the Border, the pursuit of terrorists after an attack, the rescue of Protestant hostages from the IRA, and the tracking down and capturing of hidden arms caches. In this work the SAS liaises closely with the Marines of Commachio Group and the Special Boat Squadron, as well as with the Customs and Excise and the coastguards, and they have become very successful in intercepting smugglers attempting to bring arms and ammunition into Northern Ireland.

As a result of its 15 years of experience in the province, the SAS, and the Army in general, have become highly experienced in dealing with terrorists and terrorist methods, and this has led to SAS officers being in great demand in many other countries, both inside and outside Europe, as instructors for indigenous commando and anti-terrorist units. Of course, the Special Air Service Regiment has a long tradition in this role. In 1940 Winston Churchill called for the establishment of special commando-style units capable of hitting back at objectives inside Nazi-occupied Europe, and in November of that year 11 Special Air Service Battalion was formed from No 2 Commando. Three months later the battalion made its first attack, destroying an aqueduct in Italy, and from then until the end of the war was constantly in action, one of its main tasks being to help equip and train resistance groups in France and Italy. At the same time, in North Africa, an unconventional officer, Colonel David Stirling, was organizing hit-and-run forces for operations behind Rommel's lines, and for many years the bearded men of the Long Range Desert Group, with their jeeps and trucks festooned with machine-guns, became the epitome of the Special Air Service Regiment in the popular imagination. That image has long since disappeared, but the regiment's success at Pebble Island was foreshadowed 40 years earlier in the Long Range Desert Group's destruction of German aircraft and fuel and ammunition dumps in the desert.

By 1942 the SAS had been expanded to the strength of a regiment with the addition of French and Greek battalions. Two years later it was the size of a brigade and comprised one British regiment, one Commonwealth regiment formed from Australian, New Zealand, South African, Rhodesian and Canadian volunteers, two French regiments and a Belgian squadron. At the end of World War 2, the brigade was disbanded, but in 1947 a territorial SAS regiment was raised in London as 21 SAS (which still exists) and, as a result of its success in Malaya during 1948 and '49, in 1950 a regular Army regiment was formed, 22 SAS, which remains to this day.

During the 1950s and '60s, 22 SAS played a vital part, not just in the continuing war in Malaya which finally ended in 1960 (the first time in history a terrorist force operating on its own territory – like the IRA in Ulster – has been so totally defeated), but also in Korea, in Kenya against the Mau-Mau, in Cyprus and Aden, at Suez in 1956, in Muscat and Oman, Jordan, Kuwait, Belize and many of the world's other trouble spots where the SAS's experience and techniques have been welcomed by the governments or rulers of several countries. With the exception of Malaya, Cyprus and Oman, SAS operations received little publicity and the regiment remained largely an unknown quantity to the general public until 1980 and the Princes Gate siege.

Princes Gate

On Monday, 5 May 1980, concealed television cameras, whose presence was not even suspected by the SAS, revealed to an enthralled audience a spectacle which would have done credit to a thriller film. On the balcony, and in the street outside the white, colonnaded façade of the Iranian Embassy in Princes Gate, London, suddenly materialized the sinister figures of a number of armed men carrying automatic weapons and tear-gas grenade launchers. Since the previous Wednesday, 24 men and women, mostly Iranian Embassy staff but including three Britons, had been held hostage by six masked gunmen who were demanding the release of 91 political prisoners held under the Ayatollah Khomeini's administration. Many people sympathized with their aims, especially since American Embassy staff in Tehran were, at the time, being held prisoner by that same evil regime. But when the gunmen began shooting their hostages, there was only one answer – send in the SAS.

Up until this point, at 19.00 on a warm, early summer's day, the normal siege tactics practised by the Special Branch of the Metropolitan Police had seemed to be working well: establish contact with the terrorists, discover their aims, and do everything possible to take the tension out of the situation. Little was known about the gunmen inside, except that they had come from Iraq and were believed to be Arabs from Khuzestan, the southern region of Iran which contains the main oil installations, and yet whose people appeared to be benefiting least from the new government's policies. It gradually emerged that there were five or six men, all with their features concealed by Arab head-dress; five were to die.

In the beginning, the police allowed the terrorists free access to the outside world, laying on telephone and telex links so that they could communicate their demands not only to Tehran but also to the rest of the globe. In response, the terrorists released one of the hostages, BBC reporter Chris Cramer, who was suffering from acute stomach-ache. Later, these facilities were cut off to build up the psychological pressure on the gunmen. Similarly, food and cigarettes which to begin with had been provided on demand were discontinued, and the terrorists were told that they would have to make do with what they had. The reasons were simple: it quickly became clear that the terrorists' demand for the release of unnamed hostages in Iran was something which the Ayatollah's government would not countenance, and, in any case, the British government had no influence with the Iranian authorities. The inescapable conclusion was that the gunmen were purely seeking publicity for their cause rather than tangible results. This changed the whole complexion of the affair, because normal police tactics would not work unless there was a negotiable objective. Thus, although it is quite likely that the SAS had been called in as observers and advisers even before the third day of the siege, there is no doubt that they were involved by this time. However, the 'hard' decision was not going to be taken unless, or until, the terrorists began carrying out their threat to shoot the hostages.

So the seemingly endless, and ultimately pointless, talks dragged on through the weekend. There were 18 men and 6 women held hostage inside the embassy, in different rooms; the men at the front and the women at the rear. Planning for the eventuality for which they had been trained, the SAS Troop of 18 men decided that any assault would have to be made from front and rear simultaneously. Climbing over the rooftops from an adjoining block of flats, the SAS made their preparations, securely attaching ropes to the chimneys at the rear of the embassy down which two sections of four men each would abseil into action once given the word. Around the embassy, other members of the troop mingled anonymously with the police and onlookers.

Inside, a curious rapport was growing up between captors and captured and, when the terrorists were informed on Saturday that their message would be broadcast in full by the BBC, they allowed two hostages to go free – a pregnant woman and a Pakistani journalist. Gunmen and hostages celebrated together as the police sent in a meal for them all; it was the first since Thursday. On the Sunday morning the hostages were even allowed a

Black-garbed men of the Special Air Service Regiment on the front balcony of the Iranian Embassy in Princes Gate.

bath. However, what the terrorists took to be the sounds of preparation for
an attack – the noise of pneumatic drills – soured the increasing *détente* inside
the embassy. The gunmen became more tense and moved the male hostages
to a lower room in the front of the building. They had reason to worry. Two
demands – one for a meeting with Arab ambassadors from other countries in
London, and a second for a safe-conduct by coach to an aircraft at Heathrow
– which the terrorist leader 'Oan' had made by telephone the previous day,
remained unanswered.

By Monday, therefore, the tension was becoming unbearable and
something had to snap. It did. The Iranian assistant press attaché, Abbas
Lavasani, had been pleading with the gunmen since Friday that they kill him
and let the other hostages go. He had been particularly incensed when the
terrorists scrawled 'Death to the Ayatollah' on the wall of the room in which
the male hostages were held. Late on Monday afternoon, Lavasani asked to
go to the toilet, and somehow got hold of the terrorists' radio-telephone. He
began calling the police and 'Oan' cut him down with three shots. The leader
of the gunmen then picked up the telephone to inform the waiting world that
he had just executed one of the hostages and that he would not speak again
until he heard news about the requested meeting with the Arab ambassadors.

A personal message from the Commissioner of Police, Sir David
McNee, brought the senior Iman of the London Central Mosque to the
scene. He pleaded over the radio-telephone for patience, but the leader of
the terrorists shouted, 'Why should we wait any longer?' The sound of
further shots was heard and the line went dead. When, a few minutes later, a
body was pushed out of the front door of the embassy, it was believed, quite
naturally, that a second hostage had been shot. In fact, the firing was a bluff,
but nobody outside the building could have been expected to know that. It
was time to send in the SAS.

The two sections with the trickiest task crossed the roof from an
adjacent skylight at 19.20 and clipped their abseiling clamps to the ropes
which were already affixed to the embassy chimneys. Each pair of troopers
was equipped with a specially tailored frame charge – a rectangular frame
designed to fit the embassy windows exactly and blow them in. Timing is of
the essence in any military operation, but most especially in a situation
where innocent lives are at stake. Hearts stopped as the first pair of men
began abseiling down to the ground-floor terrace, and one trooper's flailing
boot smashed an upper storey window. Inside the embassy, one of the
gunmen asked a hostage what was happening, and received the reply, 'Don't
worry. They wouldn't try anything in daylight.'

As the first pair of troopers reached the terrace, the second two abseiled
down to the first-floor balcony. Then came a hitch – literally. One of the
third pair of troopers managed to get entangled in his rope and was dangling
helplessly outside the second-storey room where the female hostages were
held. The men on the floors below could not now use their frame charges

without risking serious injury to him, so they kicked in the windows and hurled stun grenades (known as 'flash-bangs' in the trade) into the rooms. These grenades are encased in stout cardboard but produce such a concussion shock-wave that, in an enclosed space, they literally paralyse their victims for what can be vital fractions of a second.

As the second pair of troopers swung into the first-floor room, 'Oan', the terrorist leader, ran to the landing and raised his automatic pistol. Only prompt intervention from an unlikely source saved the life of the leading SAS trooper. Police Constable Trevor Lock, a 41-year-old member of the Diplomatic Protection Group, had been on duty at the embassy when it was seized, and had been held hostage ever since. He and a BBC sound engineer, Simeon Harris, had been talking to 'Oan' as the SAS troopers broke in. Now he hurled himself on the terrorist leader and grappled with him until the SAS man shot the Arab. Harris fled towards the front of the building where, little did he know it, the third SAS section had now placed a frame charge and were about to enter. He threw open the curtains and was confronted by what he thought was a frogman on the balcony. In fact, it was an SAS trooper wearing a black balaclava helmet, urgently gesturing for Harris to take cover. Moments later the frame charge exploded and four more SAS troopers entered the embassy through clouds of smoke.

On the second floor, above Harris, the 15 male hostages were listening with horror to the sounds of shooting and explosions. When the attack began, they were guarded by only one man, but now two more ran in and began shooting. Samad-Zadeh, another press attaché, was killed and two other men were wounded. At this point, as if realizing what they had done, the terrorists started throwing down their guns, but it was not to save them. The SAS shot them anyway, in two cases by holding pistols to their heads. Within minutes, only one of the terrorists was still alive – the man who had been guarding the women in a back room.

By this time the embassy was ablaze, and it was only with difficulty that the third SAS section managed to rescue the stranded trooper at the back, who was still dangling from his rope. The wounded were quickly loaded on to stretchers and bustled out to waiting ambulances, while the hostages were hurried out of the building into a waiting coach. As firemen outside tried to control the blaze, guarded by some Special Branch officers with tear-gas dischargers (not least from the howling crowd of Khomeini supporters who had gathered outside the embassy), the SAS teams inside hastily combed the building for any further survivors.

Despite a certain amount of vilification which they received from some sections of the Press for killing at least two of the terrorists while they were apparently trying to surrender, the SAS men rightly received a verdict of 'justifiable homicide' at the inquest, which ended the following February. The coroner, Dr Paul Knapman, said, 'I think it is important to consider the implications to this country if a verdict of unlawful killing were to be recorded, if soldiers were sent in to do a specific job.'

The SAS had been called upon and had done its job. Only one hostage died directly as a result of the assault, but who knows how many others might have perished if 'Oan' had carried out his threat, delivered earlier that evening, to shoot another hostage every half hour if his demands were not met.

Two years later, a different enemy was holding a different community of civilians prisoner, and once again the SAS was to play a vital role in the rescue mission.

To the South Atlantic

When it became obvious, in March 1982, that the Argentines seriously intended invading the Falkland Islands, it was inevitable that the SAS should be one of the first units involved, and it was appropriate that an SAS man should have been the first to run up the Union Jack again on South Georgia. However, victory was preceded by near disaster.

After the Argentine forces, under the command of Lieutenant-Commander Alfredo Astiz, had taken control of South Georgia (see page 46), their garrisons were established at the former whaling stations of Leith and Grytviken. Within days some 60 men of the Mountain and Boat Troops, D Squadron, 22 SAS, together with 2 SBS, were joined on Ascension Island by M Company of 42 Commando. On 10 April they embarked on HMS *Antrim*, accompanied by the Royal Fleet Auxiliary *Tidespring*, for a rendezvous two days later with the ice patrol and research vessel *Endurance*. On board *Endurance*, British Antarctic Survey scientists briefed the SAS and SBS on the conditions they could expect to meet on South Georgia, which were hostile to say the least.

The final attack plan was for the Mountain Troop of D Squadron, 22 SAS, to be landed by helicopter on the Fortuna Glacier, thence to make their way overland to Leith, while the SBS and Boat Troop would land in Gemini inflatable assault boats in Hound Bay and proceed to Grytviken. M Company of 42 Commando would be held in reserve as the main force for the principal attack on Grytviken. The scientists had warned that weather conditions on the glacier could be extreme in the Antarctic autumn, but nobody expected the hell which lay ahead.

At dawn on 21 April a Wessex helicopter took off from HMS *Antrim* in order to reconnoitre the glacier. High winds and driving rain were observed, but these did not deter the SAS. The chopper returned to the ship to pick up the advance party of four men but, by the time it returned to the island, low cloud in addition to the wind and rain made a landing impossible. A few hours later the cloud lifted and a second attempt was made, despite violent changes in wind direction caused by the glacier, and heavy gusts of sleet and snow which obscured visibility. This time the Wessex succeeded in landing, and was rapidly followed by two others which disgorged the remaining 11 men of the Mountain Troop. The helicopters then hurriedly set off back to the ship, flying low to avoid radar detection from the Argentine garrison.

Even midwinter conditions in Norway had not prepared the 15 SAS men for the night which followed, however. The barometer fell by over 50 millibars to 960 mb – a decrease in atmospheric pressure which in itself causes the temperature to drop – while at the same time the wind speed picked up to Force 10 (storm) on the Beaufort scale, carrying snow and ice spicules in gusts of up to 130 km/h (80 mph) across the glacier. Since the effective temperature drops by one degree centigrade for every mile per hour of wind strength once the ambient air temperature falls below zero (the so-called 'wind chill factor'), the SAS patrol had to spend the night in over 55°C (68°F) of frost. Moreover, the blizzard blew away their tents.

By 11.00 on the following morning John Hamilton was forced to radio the ship with the news that, not only had the SAS patrol been unable to move off the glacier, but also that, unless they were picked up within hours, they would perish from frostbite and exposure. The same three Wessex helicopters which had landed the party the previous day took off immediately, but were unable to land because the wind was gusting so violently, from a full gale one moment to virtual calm the next. After three attempts, the helicopters had to return to *Antrim* to refuel. Then they set off again. This time luck appeared to be on their side. They spotted the smoke flare ignited by the desperate men on the glacier and, taking advantage of a momentary lull in the wind, succeeded in landing. However, as the SAS men emplaned, the wind rose again and the driven snow created a total 'white-out'. One Wessex lifted off regardless but, blown sideways by the ferocious wind, tilted. A rotor touched the ice and the helicopter crashed on to its side. Miraculously, no one was seriously hurt. The other two helicopters landed alongside and the troops from the first piled into them while the pilots dumped fuel to accommodate the additional load.

They took off into a roaring white hell, visibility being effectively nil, and flew on radar and compass alone back down the glacier until tragedy struck again. Cresting a ridge, the leading Wessex lurched under a sudden and unexpected gust of wind and struck the ground, rolling on to its side. Its radio was damaged and the pilot of the third helicopter, Lieutenant-Commander Ian Stanley, could not make contact to ascertain the extent of the damage. Undaunted, he flew his overloaded Wessex back to *Antrim* where his passengers were helped out, wrapped in blankets and hustled to sick bay for a hot drink and medical attention. Ian Stanley had not finished yet, however. After refuelling and packing his helicopter with spare blankets, he took off some 30 minutes later to return to the crash site. Miraculously, once again, there had been no serious casualties, and the 17 SAS and Fleet Air Arm personnel piled hastily into Stanley's Wessex. Just over half an hour later they, too, were safely aboard *Antrim*.

The attempt to land SAS and SBS men by Gemini boats fared little better than the Fortuna Glacier venture. Five Geminis were launched, each carrying three men. The engine of one failed almost immediately, and it disappeared helplessly into the blizzard. Somehow, however, it stayed upright and its crew was later rescued by helicopter. A second boat was swept away and just succeeded in landing on the last toehold of South Georgia before being lost forever in the wild, dark wastes of the South Atlantic. The remaining three boats landed safely, but needle-sharp splinters of blown ice from the glacier rapidly punctured the tough rubber hulls, and their crews had to be evacuated by helicopter.

The landings could not have gone worse for the SAS and SBS, and from this point onwards matters could only improve. However, theirs were not to be the only British landings on the island. Knowing of the presence of British warships off South Georgia, the Argentine commander, Astiz, had requested reinforcements, and a party of 40 marines had been dispatched aboard the ex-US Navy Guppy Class submarine *Santa Fe*. Even as John Hamilton's men were being ferried back to Fortuna Glacier during a lull in the blizzard the day after they had been evacuated, the Argentine submarine was detected. *Antrim* went on full alert and, on 25 April, her crew's vigilance was rewarded, for the *Santa Fe* was spotted on radar by one of her Wessex helicopters. Amazingly, the submarine was running on the surface, having dropped her marines at Grytviken, and she was promptly depth-charged by the hovering helicopter. Damaged on her port side and apparently unable to dive, she turned back towards the whaling station, harassed by machine-gun fire from the helicopter and anti-tank missiles from *Endurance*'s Wasp helicopters, which arrived to join the fray. Leaking oil and listing badly, the damaged submarine made a sorry sight as she limped back to Grytviken. The effect on the morale of the Argentine troops on South Georgia was understandable, and Major Cedric Delves, commanding D Company, 22 SAS, was determined to take advantage of it. Thus it was that Major Guy Sheridan assembled his *ad hoc* assault group and landed by helicopter, while *Antrim* and *Plymouth* poured down an intense naval gunfire barrage – not *on* the Argentine positions but 725 m (800 yd) beyond them (at this point, the cruiser *Belgrano* had not been sunk and it was the British government's policy to try to preserve as many lives as possible).

However, after their earlier epic on the glacier, John Hamilton was determined that the SAS should be in at the kill. Even while Guy Sheridan was establishing his positions, Hamilton was leading his men through an Argentine minefield on the outskirts of Grytviken. Walking into the centre of the settlement, he had the Argentine flag hauled down and the Union Jack raised in its place. The thoroughly demoralized Argentine troops began waving white flags and all resistance, or even thought of resistance, ended. Hamilton, who was later to be described by an Argentine Colonel who witnessed his death as 'the most courageous man I have ever seen', had well and truly vindicated the SAS motto.

Ashore on the Falklands

Even before the Marines and Paras landed at San Carlos on 21 May, SAS and SBS patrols, usually of four men apiece, had been landed by boat or helicopter to scour the land, reporting on Argentine positions and troop movements. Following the success of John Hamilton's Pebble Island raid on 15 May, numerous diversionary attacks were made in order to delude General Menendez into thinking that these were going to be the style for the British campaign, and to distract Argentine attention from San Carlos. Similarly, while the San Carlos landings were actually taking place, three SAS Troops engaged the Argentine garrison (at odds of roughly one to ten!) in Darwin to prevent a counter-attack across the Sussex Mountains. The 40-plus SAS troopers were armed with the heavy mixture of machine-guns, rocket launchers and mortars which characterized so many of the Falklands' operations, and kept up such a barrage of fire that, in the darkness, the 500 men in Darwin imagined they were faced by at least a battalion. In this instance, however, it was not the SAS's intent to capture the objective, merely to keep its inhabitants' heads low so that 3 Commando Brigade and the two battalions of the Parachute Regiment could get ashore safely. A full assault on Darwin and Goose Green would have to wait a few days – fatal days, as it turned out for, when 2 Para went in during the night of 27 May, they found the Argentine garrison reinforced to three times its original strength.

Ironically, one of the reasons for the strong resistance the Paras encountered was SAS activity further east, on the slopes of Mount Kent – the highest point overlooking Port Stanley. Here, the SAS Troops (each consisting of 15 troopers and NCOs plus 1 officer, a pattern which is now being adopted throughout the Army) had already established a strong presence in front of, and often among, the well dug-in positions of the Argentine 12th Infantry Regiment. This was a conscript regiment, full of raw troops who did not know enough to avoid presenting silhouettes against the rocks of the mountain slopes, and who were sufficiently ignorant to allow their cooking fires, torches and cigarettes to burn unshielded at night. As a result, men began disappearing, or were found with broken necks as the result of an apparent fall, while the Argentines' sleep was further disturbed by constant alerts and strange noises. This stealthy attrition made morale-sapping inroads into the Argentines' confidence, and many of them must have greeted with relief the news that they were to be ferried by helicopter to Goose Green. Under some circumstances, the prospect of a pitched battle can seem healthier than another night in a dark bunker with an unseen enemy stalking outside.

By the end of May, Mount Kent was effectively in the SAS's hands, but they were insufficiently strong on the ground to have held out against more determined Argentine opposition or counter-attack. 45 Commando were on their way, footslogging across the bleak terrain together with 3 Para, but the SAS needed urgent reinforcements. On 31 May, an attempt to fly in 42 Commando by helicopter was aborted due to the weather, but another attempt the following night was successful. Cedric Delves and John Hamilton were looking out for them, but were distracted by movement in the darkness. An Argentine patrol was approaching the helicopters' landing zone. Once again the SAS troopers went into action, and the deceptively slow-moving streaks of red machine-gun tracer lit the mountainside as the first Sea King arrived, containing 42 Commando's CO, Nick Vaux, and the Special Air Service Regiment's own CO, Lieutenant-Colonel Mike Rose. The Argentine patrol was wiped out and the Marines occupied Mount Kent.

The SAS continued to play an important role in the capture of the other hills around Port Stanley, operating ahead of the main British lines to scout enemy positions and call in artillery fire or naval support, and Mike Rose was involved in the final surrender talks with General Menendez, under the pseudonym 'Colonel Reid'. Before these took place, however, tragedy was to befall the regiment. John Hamilton, having survived the ordeal on Fortuna Glacier, having run up the Union Jack in Grytviken, having assisted in the diversionary attack on Darwin and having survived the Argentine artillery fire on Mount Kent, was on West Falkland – where he had first gone ashore for the Pebble Island raid – observing troop movements in Port Howard. With him was a signaller. Somehow they were detected and Argentine troops moved forward to try to surround them. Both sides opened fire and Hamilton was hit in the back. Knowing he could not escape, he ordered his signaller to 'get the hell out' while he covered his escape. As the signaller crawled away to safety, Hamilton drew himself up and, firing on the run, charged straight at the Argentines. He was hit again, and got up. And again. And again. The fifth time he was hit he did not get up. Among the many awards for gallantry awarded to the soldiers, sailors and airmen involved in the Falklands campaign, Gavin John Hamilton's Military Cross must be one of the most deserved.

Thus ended the SAS's war in the South Atlantic, but not elsewhere, because they still have a vital role to play in Northern Ireland and a potentially even more crucial role to play alongside the newly formed 5th Airborne Brigade which, in 1985, spearheads Britain's quick-reaction force. While there is the possibility of major global confrontation, while there are still terrorists, while there are still 'small' wars like that in the Lebanon, there will still be a place for the SAS and honest citizens can rest more safely in their homes for the presence of these fearless men.

THE ROYAL MARINE COMMANDOS

The twenty-sixth of May 1982 is a date which Sergeant Derek Wilson will not soon forget. As a member of the Royal Marines' crack Mountain and Arctic Warfare Cadre, he had been one of the first ashore during the re-invasion of the Falklands, and had spent the previous 12 days in deep-probing reconnaissance patrols. On this particular day, which dawned dull and snowing but which later cleared and brightened, observers had spotted an unknown number of Argentine soldiers in the isolated Top Malo House, in the middle of the valley to the south of Teal Inlet. As it turned out, there were in fact 16 Argentine soldiers present, all members of 602 Marine Commando Company.

Captain Rod Boswell, commanding the M&AW Cadre on the spot, tried to call up a Harrier strike but no aircraft were available at the time so he decided to launch an assault on foot with the 19 men at his disposal. Shortly after first light, the Marines embarked in a Sea King helicopter which flew them at virtually zero height, hugging the contours of the ground, and dropped them into a partially frozen bog about 1.5 km (1 mile) from the house. The landing was unobserved because the Argentines had posted no sentries during the bitterly cold night. They were shortly to pay a heavy price for this oversight.

Deploying into two parties on either side of the house, a fire section of six men on the left and an assault group of 13 on the right flank, the Marines moved quickly into position, still unobserved. Sergeant Wilson, armed with an American-made M79 40 mm grenade launcher, was with the latter group. As Captain Boswell fired a green flare, the fire section opened up with four L1A1 66 mm rocket launchers (the modern equivalent of the World War 2 'bazooka') which had no trouble in penetrating the walls of the house. Further 66 mm rounds followed, supported by a barrage of 40 mm grenades from the M79s and a withering fusillade of automatic fire from a mixture of SLR and Armalite rifles plus one L42 sniper rifle.

As the Argentines came tumbling out of the house, firing back with vigour, the fire section continued shooting while the assault group charged in on the flank. Within seconds there were two casualties – Sergeant Chris Stone was hit in the chest by a 7.62 mm armour-piercing round which fortunately missed his lung, while another bullet shattered Terry Doyle's upper arm, an injury which still gives him a great deal of pain today. However, realizing they were outnumbered and outgunned, the Argentine soldiers began throwing down their weapons and raising their hands, and the British Marines moved in to encircle, blindfold and search them. The Argentine commander had been killed along with two of his men, and seven others were wounded. Ironically, one of the captured Argentine officers turned out to be married to an English girl, and had been on training courses in Great Britain. This brought caustic comments from the Marines, who told him that if that was the case he should have learned enough to know to post a sentry!

Short and sharp though it was, the attack on Top Malo House well illustrates the calibre of the men in the M&AW Cadre.

Commando organization

The illustrious history of the Royal Marines goes back to 1664, when the first soldiers to be specially trained to fight at sea were formed into the Duke of York's Regiment (later the Lord High Admiral's Regiment), and they have given sterling service to the nation ever since. The first Commandos were trained during World War 2 for amphibious assault operations, but today's organization really dates back to 1956, when the value of helicopters in both the assault and the casualty evacuation roles became apparent during the Anglo-French attempt to seize the Suez Canal. The aircraft carriers *Albion* and *Bulwark* were converted to helicopter-carrying Commando vessels and soon showed their value. In 1961, fearing invasion by Iraq, the Ruler of Kuwait made an urgent plea to the British government for assistance. HMS *Bulwark*, by chance, was in the Gulf of Oman at the time and was able to arrive off the coast of Kuwait within hours. Men of 42 Commando were disembarked in Whirlwind helicopters and the Iraqis backed down.

Since World War 2, all Royal Marines with the exception of the Band Service have been trained as commandos and, indeed, their training today is the toughest and most rigorous in the world, for they are not only expected to be landed by sea, whether from assault boats or helicopters, but may also have to qualify as parachutists.

Commando forces are organized and equipped very much along Army lines but maintain many naval customs and traditions. Their Commandant is a Lieutenant-General, whose office is in Whitehall, but the main Royal

Mountain and arctic warfare training in the bleak Norwegian winter; the helicopter is a Wessex.

Marine establishments are all found in the west of England. Headquarters, Commando Forces, are at Mount Wise, Plymouth, and the Training, Reserve and Special Forces are administered from Eastney, near Portsmouth. Most training is actually carried out at Lympstone, near Exeter, but amphibious assault work is taught at Poole, in Dorset, and airborne training is given at Royal Naval Air Station Yeovilton.

Royal Marines operational units are controlled by Headquarters, 3 Commando Brigade, and comprise Nos 40, 42 and 45 Commando Groups, each equivalent to an Army battalion, and having some 650 men apiece. In addition, there is an air squadron, a signal squadron, an air defence troop, a raiding squadron and a logistics regiment, while three Army units provide additional support. These are 29 Commando Regiment, Royal Artillery; 59 Independent Commando Squadron, Royal Engineers; and a Territorial Army unit, 131 Independent Commando Squadron, RE.

In time of war, it is expected that the main role of the Commando Forces would be on NATO's northern flank, in Norway, and to this end British Commandos train and exercise regularly with two companies of the Royal Netherlands Marine Corps, who would come under British command: these are No 1 Amphibious Combat Group and Whiskey Company, both based at Doorn. The combined force trains for three months of every year, from January to March, in the atrocious weather conditions prevailing in northern Norway, with temperatures often falling as low as $-46°C$ ($-51°F$). For this they are remarkably well equipped, normal disruptive pattern material (DPM) combat clothing being enhanced by the addition of string vests, 'long johns', quilted under-jackets and -trousers, thick parkas and special boots with thermal insoles. (Lack of availability of these for the majority of the troops in the Falklands caused considerable problems due to the continuously damp and cold conditions, and the old World War 1 medical condition known as 'trench foot' became quite prevalent.) Rucksacks, originally designed for the SAS and weighing only 1 kg (2 lb 3 oz), hold everything needed for at least three days in the field under these extreme conditions, including the special arctic, waterproof and down-filled sleeping bag, which is barely heavier than the general service issue. Arctic tents are also provided and, in Norway, Commandos can alternatively sleep in the powered, tracked trailers attached to Volvo Bv202E over-snow tractors, which can each accommodate eight men. In the Falklands, more widespread use was made of the waterproof poncho, which has press studs along its reinforced edges and can be clipped to service sleeping bags to provide a miniature weatherproof tent.

Comacchio Group

Operating independently of 3 Commando Brigade, this company-sized unit is specially trained in the anti-terrorist role, and has a unique task in the protection of Britain's offshore oil rigs against attack or capture. Formed in May 1980 and based in Arbroath, Scotland, the unit was named after a battle fought near Ferrara, in Italy, in 1945. Its techniques and tactics are of necessity secret, but Comacchio Group's personnel are trained in underwater swimming and canoeing in addition to their normal Commando tasks.

All Royal Marines recruits undergo a basic 26-week training course at Lympstone, extended to a full year for officers, who are expected to be able to do everything their men can do, but better and faster. Only at the completion of basic training is a recruit entitled to wear the green beret.

To begin with, training is much the same as in any army today – physical exercise with long cross-country marches and runs to build up muscles and stamina, weapons instruction, and both classroom and field training in tactics and communications. By halfway through the course, the recruits are ready for more advanced instruction, and spend more and more time in practising getting into and out of helicopters and landing craft, and in learning rock-climbing and mountaineering techniques. All this is rounded off with a four-day series of tests involving cross-country runs and hikes, traversing various assault courses, and demonstrating proficiency in weapons use and in swimming.

When basic training is finished, the Royal Marine Commando continues to learn such skills as skiing, diving with both aqualung and oxygen re-breathing equipment (which avoids any tell-tale trail of bubbles to the surface) and parachuting. Those who successfully complete all aspects of this advanced training become qualified swimmer/canoeists and are eligible to volunteer for the Special Boat Squadron or Comacchio Group.

This training was to stand the Royal Marines in good stead in the Falkland Islands.

April Fool's Day recall

Lieutenant Henk de Jaeger was on leave and enjoying his own wedding reception in New York when he received a telegram recalling him to his post as Intelligence Officer with 42 Commando at Bickleigh Barracks, Plymouth. Along with many others in the British armed forces, he was making the best of the Easter break and, when he received the telegram, his first thought, like that of so many others, must have been, 'Come on! April Fool's was yesterday'. What his new wife thought is not on record. . .

The decision to recall all troops on leave and put the Royal Marines on standby alert had been taken by the Cabinet during the evening of 1 April 1982 and Brigadier Julian Thompson, of 3 Commando Brigade, received his orders from Major-General Jeremy Moore at 03.15 on the 2nd, five hours before the Argentines landed. Within minutes RM Poole was on standby, and the following day British railway stations were flooded with posters and announcements recalling troops on leave. Several officers were in Denmark for a NATO planning conference and a couple of dozen others were also abroad on holiday. Admiral Sir Henry Leach, First Sea Lord at the time, had assured Prime Minister Margaret Thatcher that the Task Force would sail five days later.

In a remote outpost in the South Atlantic, however, two groups of Royal Marines were to see action even more rapidly. On East Falkland itself, Major Mike Norman assumed command of Naval Party 8901, relieving Major Gary Noott, at 09.00 on 1 April. Under his command were 80 men, including 12 sailors from the ice patrol vessel *Endurance*. At 15.15, Norman and Noott were summoned by the Governor of the Falkland Islands, Rex Hunt, who showed them a telex from Whitehall advising that an Argentine invasion was imminent. Despite the obvious impossibility of withstanding an invasion attempt, Mike Norman began issuing orders for his troops' dispositions immediately, concentrating on likely landing areas around Port Stanley airfield and to the east of the town itself. The Marines were lightly armed, possessing only two of the 84 mm Carl Gustav anti-tank missile launchers and a few of the lighter 66 mm L1A1 'bazookas'.

Spearheading the Argentine invasion were 150 men of their own special forces, the *Buzo Tactico*, supported by a further 1000 marines and other élite troops. Unfortunately for Mike Norman, the *Buzo Tactico* landed in their helicopters to the *west* of the town and at 06.15 on 2 April were observed attacking the Marines' barracks with automatic weapons and grenades, obviously hoping to catch them still asleep. Mike Norman hastily recalled his troops to Government House, where they managed to beat off the first attack. However, by this time the support troops were beginning to pour ashore, and American-built LVTP-7 Amtrack armoured personnel carriers, which had been landed at Yorke Point, were heading towards Port Stanley. Two were stopped by direct hits fired by Lieutenant Bill Trollope's No 2 Section using one of the Carl Gustavs and an L1A1 but, as the remaining 16 vehicles started deploying and firing their machine-guns, Trollope ordered a prompt retreat to Government House.

The Amtracks were the Marines' biggest problem, because they could stand off outside the British troops' range and blast Government House to pieces. After telephoning various people in Port Stanley to ascertain the outside situation, Governor Hunt reluctantly agreed to see the commander of the Argentine forces present, Admiral Busser. When Busser declined Rex Hunt's invitation to leave the island, and told him that he now had 2800 men ashore and a back-up force of another 2000 on the ships lying off the coast, the Governor instructed the Marines to lay down their arms. It was 09.15 on Day One of the invasion.

South Georgia scrap

South Georgia is even more bleak and inhospitable than the Falklands. Lying 1300 km (800 miles) to their south-west, it is a windswept, mountainous speck in the middle of a vast ocean, and would probably never have been settled were it not for the fact that it was the ideal location for a whaling base. By the mid-1960s, however, the base was no longer viable, and large numbers of abandoned and rusting ships and other debris cluttered the shore. Ninety per cent of the world's population had never even heard of

South Georgia before March 1982, when an Argentine scrap-metal dealer with the unlikely name of Constantio Davidoff arrived with a group of workmen, ostensibly to begin a salvage operation. What caused the British government to protest was his running up of the Argentine flag and, after a week of futile arguing with the junta in Buenos Aires, the ice patrol vessel *Endurance* was ordered to proceed from Port Stanley to South Georgia to evict the scrap merchants. On board were the ship's normal complement of two dozen Royal Marines, plus nine men from Mike Norman's NP8901, all 'armed to the teeth' according to a journalist on board *Endurance*. They were landed at Grytviken under the command of Lieutenant Keith Mills, and prepared defensive positions at the site of the British Antarctic Survey installation on King Edward Point, which was considered the most likely location for a landing from the two Argentine warships known to be heading into the area.

Early in the morning of 3 April, the Argentine ice patrol vessel *Bahia Paradiso*, accompanied by the corvette *Guerrico*, entered the bay. Keith Mills informed the ships, by radio, that South Georgia was occupied by British troops and that any attempt to land would be resisted. Having conveyed this message, he strolled down to the harbour jetty, expecting one of the Argentine vessels to lower a boat containing a negotiator. Instead, an Argentine Puma helicopter landed on the shore behind him and began to disgorge troops, who first pointed their guns at him and then began to open fire. As other helicopters landed, Mills sprinted to cover while his own small force gave covering fire, disabling both a Puma and one of the smaller Gazelle helicopters.

The *Guerrico* now opened fire with its 40 mm guns, the whole episode giving further emphasis to the junta's lie that they did not want to take British servicemen's lives, and Mills' troops retaliated spiritedly, holing the corvette below its waterline with an anti-tank missile and disabling one of its guns. The ferocity of this response forced the ship to withdraw out of range, but Mills and his men were now encircled by the Argentine marines from the helicopter and discretion became the better part of valour. Mills had, in any case, been instructed to put up only a 'token defence'. By this time he had not only made the Argentines' eyes water, but had also given them bloody noses: and they were soon to learn that this was but a foretaste of what the Royal Marines could dish out!

While the main strength of 42 Commando, hastily recalled from leave back in Britain, was preparing to embark aboard the equally hastily converted passenger liner *Canberra*, the 110 men of M Company, under the command of Major Guy Sheridan, were detached to be flown south to join 60–70 SAS and SBS men on Ascension Island: their objective – to recapture the other island Lieutenant Keith Mills had surrendered so reluctantly. As the first piece of British territory to have seen the Argentine flag hoisted, it was only appropriate that South Georgia should also be the first to see it torn down.

South Georgia recaptured

Lieutenant-Colonel Alfredo Astiz had an appalling record on human rights. The presence of such men under the rule of the savagely right-wing junta during the 1970s was hardly surprising. Known as the 'blond angel', he was wanted for questioning by both the French and Swedish governments concerning the disappearance of young women, including two nuns. Yet this was the man appointed by the junta to command the Argentine garrison on South Georgia. He was soon to meet more than his match.

Landing on Ascension Island, the Marines linked up with the Mountain and Boat Troops of 'D' Squadron, 22 SAS, and 2 SBS, and were embarked aboard the old 'County' Class destroyer, HMS *Antrim*, and the Royal Fleet Auxiliary *Tidespring*. As recounted on page 36, several men of the SAS and SBS trans-shipped to HMS *Endurance* when the ships rendezvoused on 12 April, and the epic saga of Fortuna Glacier ensued. However, the Marines were to be in at the kill when Guy Sheridan formed a scratch force of all the available troops aboard *Antrim* – 75 Commandos, SAS and SBS, including headquarters and administrative personnel – to take advantage of the morale-sapping disablement of the Argentine submarine *Santa Fe*.

Landing in Wessex helicopters, during the afternoon of 25 April, Sheridan's mixed force moved in on the Argentine positions, which had been extended beyond those occupied only a few days earlier by Keith Mills' valiant garrison on King Edward Point. Naval gunfire from HMSs *Antrim* and *Plymouth*, even though aimed deliberately to avoid the Argentine positions, clinched the day and Astiz' troops surrendered. Raised by the SAS, the Union Jack flew over South Georgia on 26 April, barely a month after a belligerent scrap merchant had taken it down.

Astiz, after signing the surrender document aboard HMS *Plymouth*, was later returned to Argentina as a prisoner of war and has since been put on trial by the new Argentinian government.

Aboard the 'Great White Whale'

With the exception of Sheridan's small force, the bulk of 42 Commando, together with 40 Commando, a company of 45 Commando, and 3 Para, embarked aboard the Cunard passenger liner *Canberra* which, with her white paint scheme, was quickly re-christened 'the Great White Whale' by the troops of the Task Force. The remainder of 45 Commando shipped aboard the Royal Fleet Auxiliary *Stromness* and the carrier *Hermes*. On all three ships, a rigorous training programme designed to bring the Marines to a peak of physical and mental preparedness was instituted immediately. Aboard *Canberra*, the troops exercised around the Promenade Deck, six circuits of which constituted approximately 1.5 km (1 mile), while lectures – on the geography of the Falkland Islands, on the known capabilities of the Argentine troops, on their weapons and probable dispositions, and on the Marines' own anticipated tasks – were given daily.

Weapons drill was also intensive, particularly in the use of the Marines'

Milan anti-tank missiles. Manufactured under licence by British Aerospace, Milan is a French-designed, second-generation wire-guided missile which is capable of destroying all known main battle tanks at up to 2000 m (2200 yd) range. The Falklands would see its first use in anger by British troops, and it was to prove particularly effective in destroying Argentine bunkers. Each Commando Support Company includes an anti-tank Troop of 48 Marines equipped with 14 Milan launchers.

Training did not stop when *Canberra* reached Ascension Island on 20 April. The Army and RAF personnel already on the island had constructed several firing ranges, and the Marines practised intensively for the two weeks they were there, being dropped by helicopter at Wideawake airfield and then marching – or, more often, running – several miles in full kit to the ranges. When you consider that a man carrying his personal equipment, including rifle and ammunition, plus a Milan missile or launcher, or one of the various other support weapons, was laden down by 54 kg (120 lb), the necessity for the intensive physical training becomes obvious.

Suddenly the training was over. On 1 May huge delta-winged Avro Vulcan bombers attacked Port Stanley airfield, the intention being to damage the runway sufficiently to prohibit Argentine air movements. They were followed by Royal Navy Sea Harriers from the two British carriers, *Hermes* and *Invincible*. The following day the Argentine cruiser *Belgrano* was torpedoed and sunk by the submarine *Conqueror*. To the Marines, as to the rest of the world, came the shocked realization that a real state of war existed in the South Atlantic. Two days later the British destroyer *Sheffield* was hit and mortally damaged by an AM39 Exocet missile launched by an Argentine Super Etendard naval strike aircraft.

While plans for reinforcing the Task Force were hurriedly being implemented back in Britain, including the commissioning of the liner *QE2* as a troopship for 5 Infantry Brigade and the Ghurkas, the men of 3 Commando Brigade and 2 and 3 Para embarked at Ascension on the amphibious assault ships *Fearless* and *Intrepid*. On 10 May, following Task Force commander Rear Admiral 'Sandy' Woodward's decision that the main attack would go in at San Carlos, the Royal Marines' commander, Brigadier Julian Thompson, briefed his own unit commanders.

The San Carlos decision had not been an easy one. Many officers favoured a frontal assault on Port Stanley using landing craft supported by troop-carrying helicopters, but this was abandoned because of uncertainty as to whether the harbour had been mined by the Argentines. There was even a plan for an Entebbe-style raid by the SAS to eliminate the Argentine headquarters in Stanley. Eventually, however, San Carlos was chosen for two reasons. One of the officers with the Task Force, Major Ewen Southby-Tailyour, was a keen amateur yachtsman who had spent most of his leisure time sailing round the coast of the Falkland Islands when he had commanded Naval Party 8901 there four years previously. He reported to Rear Admiral Woodward that San Carlos, 100 km (65 miles) from Port

Stanley, was both sheltered and dominated by high ground, giving good positions for observation posts. SAS teams and men of the Royal Marines M&AW Cadre, who had been landed secretly by helicopter on the islands to reconnoitre, not only confirmed Southby-Tailyour's report, but also discovered that there were no Argentine troops in the immediate vicinity, although there were strong Argentine garrisons within 20 km (13 miles), at Darwin and Goose Green.

On 18 May the assault ships rendezvoused with *Hermes*, which had been reinforced by a dozen Harriers from the ill-fated container ship *Atlantic Conveyor* and by a further four RAF GR Mark 3s which had made the long flight all the way from Britain, via Ascension Island. The Task Force steamed steadily towards East Falkland, and during the night of 20 May entered Falkland Sound. It was a crisp, clear night after the evening's mist, and the sea was calm.

D-Day at San Carlos

After a delay of about an hour, caused partially by a casualty in 2 Para who missed his footing while climbing into his landing craft and smashed his pelvis, and partially by a pump failure aboard *Fearless* which prevented her well deck from being flooded, it was 04.00 on 1 May when the troops began swarming ashore. (The normal landing procedure is to fill the well deck with water, as in dry dock. Since this proved impossible, the captain of *Fearless* simply ordered the forward ramp to be lowered, allowing the sea to flood in.) The first wave comprised 40 Commando, 2 Para and 4 Troop of the Blues and Royals – Household Cavalry equipped with Scorpion and Scimitar light tanks which have an armament of a 75 mm gun and a 30 mm quick-firing cannon, respectively. As expected, there was no opposition to the main landing, although the SAS encountered more trouble than they anticipated from a small Argentine garrison on Fanning Head (overlooking San Carlos water) whose presence had been detected only hours before.

While HMS *Plymouth* bombarded Argentine positions at Goose Green, and other diversionary attacks were taking place elsewhere in the islands, the men of 40 Commando, flanked on their right by 2 Para, waded ashore from their landing craft across the gravel beach and headed up the hillside to begin digging in. The only sign of life so far was a group of Special Boat Squadron Marines who stood leisurely watching the landing craft move in and who gave directions for moving off the beach. However, this was just the lull before the storm.

As the men ashore pushed inland and consolidated their positions, the landing craft returned to the ships to bring in the second wave – 45 Commando on the right of 2 Para in Ajax Bay and 3 Para on the left of 40 Commando on Fanning Head. Meanwhile, helicopters had been busily ferrying in the 105 mm light guns of 29 Commando Regiment, Royal Artillery, and the Blowpipe and Rapier anti-aircraft missiles of the Air Defence Troop, 3 Commando Brigade HQ, and 'T' Battery, 12 Air Defence

Regiment, Royal Artillery. They were none too soon. The first attack by a solitary Argentine Pucara ground-attack aircraft, which was shot down after unsuccessfully firing rockets at *Canberra* and HMS *Broadsword*, was followed half an hour later by a strike delivered by a pair of Mirage supersonic fighters.

Few of the troops ashore recognized the air raid warning for what it was. 'The first air raid was quite frightening,' said one Marine afterwards. 'It became apparent after a while that they were after the boats. As they flew over, everyone opened up on them with everything from Gimpys [General Purpose Machine Guns] to pistols and SLRs [rifles]. Of course, in the excitement, we didn't realize we were firing towards the ships and they were firing back towards us. It really was quite something to see.'

Another man commented, 'We hadn't been told that that was a signal to notify that an air attack was coming in, and we all stood around looking at each other. This 'plane suddenly rolled over the top [of the hill] and everyone just dived for cover. I think he [the pilot] must have been as surprised as we were!'

As the air attacks intensified, the troops became accustomed to them and would let fly with the nearest weapon to hand. The American Stinger anti-aircraft missiles used by some of the SAS proved particularly valuable during the early part of the campaign, as the long voyage and salt air had affected the guidance systems of the normally very effective Rapier missiles. Of the first ten Rapiers fired at attacking aircraft, only three scored hits, but thereafter the 'kill' rate soared and Rapiers accounted for at least 14 Argentine aircraft during the course of the campaign, plus six 'probables'.

What is really surprising is that the Argentines delayed so long before sending in their first air strikes. One of their Canberra high-altitude reconnaissance aircraft had observed the Task Force manoeuvring in Falkland Sound during the evening of 20 May, and it would have been logical for them to have launched an attack at dawn, while the vulnerable landing craft were still coming ashore and before the ground-based anti-aircraft systems were established. Despite the success of their later efforts, and the unquestioned courage and skill of their pilots, by allowing the British Task Force to establish itself ashore the Argentines had effectively lost the campaign.

Casualties mounted over the next few days. HMS *Ardent* was sunk on 21 May, *Antelope* on the 23rd, *Coventry* on the 25th, together with *Atlantic Conveyor*, while other ships were damaged, including *Broadsword* and *Glasgow*. Ashore, the three Commando and two Para battalions dug into the peaty soil and waited. They had established their beach-head and could do nothing but wait for reinforcements before beginning the long slog to Stanley. Brigadier Thompson had intended to leapfrog his units across East Falkland using the heavy-lift Chinook helicopters which were on their way aboard *Atlantic Conveyor*. Their loss caused a complete change in strategy and, on 26/7 May, while 2 Para headed towards their epic battle at Goose

Royal Marine Commandos dig in on the steep slopes overlooking San Carlos Water in anticipation of a counter-attack.

Green, 42 and 45 Commandos and 3 Para prepared for the long cross-country march to the other side of the island and the final goal, Port Stanley. 40 Commando remained at San Carlos to secure the bridgehead against counter-attack.

The long march
A backpacking holiday in one of the moorland and mountain beauty spots of the world is one thing; a forced march carrying some 50 kg (100 lb+) of gear across similar terrain, treacherous rock outcroppings alternating with bogs, streams and ravines, in the cold of the late South Atlantic autumn, is a different matter entirely.

The brunt of the three-day march was borne by 45 Commando and 3 Para who had to 'yomp' (the Marines' name for a forced march) around the northern side of the island, via Douglas and Teal. 42 Commando were luckier, and were in fact the first troops – with the exception of the SAS – to get within sight of Port Stanley. The SAS, as recounted on page 39, had established an observation post on Mount Kent, overlooking Stanley, some days earlier, and by 27 May the mountain was effectively in their hands. Brigadier Thompson's problem was how to reinforce them quickly with the helicopters – already stretched to their limit – at his disposal. After two days' planning it was resolved to fly in one Commando company first, to secure the position, and to fly in the rest of 42 Commando in batches.

The first attempt, on the night of 31 May, failed because a blizzard forced the helicopters to return to San Carlos shortly after taking off. On the following night, however, K Company, commanded by Lieutenant-Colonel Nick Vaux and accompanied by Lieutenant-Colonel Mike Rose of the SAS, took off in their Sea King helicopters which flew virtually 'on the deck' (at or below 6 m [20 ft]) towards their objective. As the evening darkened, passive night sights (light intensifiers) were used by the helicopter pilots to enable them to see where they were going without giving their position away to the enemy. However, when they arrived at their landing zone some 3 km (2 miles) behind the ridge of the mountain, the Marines were surprised to see the flashes and lines of red tracer ammunition of what was obviously a fierce firefight taking place a few hundred metres away. The SAS had intercepted an Argentine patrol, which they eliminated.

K Company swept up the ridge and started digging in. A couple of hours later, an RAF Chinook helicopter brought in a 105 mm light gun, and the Sea Kings began ferrying the rest of 42 Commando. With Port Stanley in sight, they settled in to endure the cold, the wet and the occasional Argentine artillery barrage. Meanwhile, 45 Commando had started their heroic 'yomp' around the other side of the island, an exploit which was to make newspaper headlines and add this new and expressive word to the English language. Charles Lawrence, a distinguished journalist with the *Sunday Telegraph*, marched with them. He found it 'punishingly hard', partly due to the terrain with its coarse tussocks of grass and soft mud, but largely to the enormous weight of equipment everyone had to carry.

After an early morning brew of tea, the men of 45 Commando tightened their bootlaces and marched down to Ajax Bay, where landing craft ferried them to the opposite side of the water. Then they began walking, their leather boots soon becoming soaked through, the weight of their equipment appearing to treble. Breathing hard through open mouths they pressed on, accompanied by Volvo Bv202 over-snow vehicles carrying the heavy equipment. Within a few miles, casualties from turned ankles and sprained muscles began to occur. The advance started to straggle as the men tired, and Colour Sergeant Bill Eades, never lost for words, bellowed out in a parade-ground voice that he didn't know about the assault on Stanley, it 'looks to me more bloody like the retreat from Moscow!'

Just before dark, the commanding officer of 45 Commando, Lieutenant-Colonel Andrew Whitehead, called a brief halt for a meal. Gratefully, the Marines broke out their portable stoves and ration packs, but just at that moment an air raid alert came through and all lights had to be extinguished; the next six hours' march in the freezing night therefore took place on largely empty stomachs. When they reached Newhouse, a deserted sheep farm, most men collapsed into their sleeping bags wherever they were, without bothering about tents. Then it rained. The irrepressible Sergeant Eades commented, 'You've got to laugh, or you would bloody well cry'.

Next day it was still raining, but the Marines reached the comparative comfort of the village of Douglas, where the local inhabitants, who had been locked in the Community Hall by the Argentines, rapidly made them welcome and set peat fires burning. After a good meal and a proper night's rest, 45 Commando was off again, 'yomping' to the next objective, Teal Inlet. For this stage of the march, having seen the difficulties encountered on the first two days, Colonel Whitehead lightened the men's packs, piling as much of the heavier support equipment as possible on to the Volvos. Although the weather had turned colder, with heavy snow, the second stage of the march was easier for the Marines since the cold had hardened the boggy ground. By the time they arrived at Teal, however, the Marines were beginning to run out of supplies, and Colonel Whitehead called a halt while he tried to organize a helicopter airlift for the remaining miles to Mount Kent. However, the weather thwarted this and, after a day's delay, 45 Commando was back on the move. The going was again steady and the men were in good spirits when they made camp on the night of 3 June.

On 4 June, the Marines were awakened before dawn and ordered forward without even the benefit of a hot brew because of the risk from showing any lights. They were allowed a breakfast stop two hours later, though, and reached the camp that K Company had established on Mount Kent in the afternoon, in the middle of a blizzard. There, too, began to make themselves as comfortable as possible in the appalling conditions.

By the end of the first week in June, the Argentines in Port Stanley were surrounded. 42 and 45 Commandos were well dug in, with 3 Para on their flank and 2 Para in reserve, in a line from Bluff Cove Peak to Mount Kent. Meanwhile, the anxiously awaited reinforcements from the second wave of the Task Force had arrived at San Carlos. These comprised 5 Infantry Brigade, 1 Battalion 7th (Duke of Edinburgh's Own) Gurkha Rifles, 2 Battalion Scots Guards and 1 Battalion Welsh Guards. The Argentine positions in and around Stanley were mercilessly bombarded both from the sea with naval gunfire and from the air by RAF Harriers, while the Fleet Air Arm's Sea Harriers provided cover against enemy air attacks.

A constant series of patrols was undertaken at night to scout out and harass the enemy. Typical was the patrol sent out in the early hours of the morning of 10 June. Lieutenant David Stewart of X-Ray Company, 45 Commando, had briefed his men during the previous afternoon, and by midnight they were ready. Heavily armed, with two machine-guns per section plus 66 mm rocket launchers and 2-inch mortars, the Troop moved off stealthily into the moonlit night towards a ridge some 4 km (2½ miles) away where Argentine movement had been observed. Keeping well spaced out because of the good visibility, they moved across the rocky ground using the numerous shell holes for cover, and by 04.00 were set to cross the final stretch of open ground in front of the enemy positions.

Using a shallow stream for cover, they moved up the slope and deployed into position among the rocks in front of the Argentine trenches. With the help of a light-intensifying night scope, they could see sentries moving about. Suddenly, an Argentine machine-gun opened fire and the Marines launched a couple of flares from their 2-inch mortars, firing back with their own machine-guns and rifles. Within seconds three Argentine soldiers and two Marines were dead. Other figures could be seen running on the hill to the left, and four more Argentine soldiers fell to the accuracy of the Marines' fire.

By this time, the Argentine troops further up the slope were wide awake, and a hail of fire forced the Marines to crouch in the shelter of the rocks. The situation was becoming decidedly unhealthy and Lieutenant Stewart decided to retire, with the objective of killing and harassing the enemy well and truly accomplished. However, a machine-gun to the Marines' right was pouring fire over their getaway route, and Stewart sent his veteran Sergeant, Jolly, with a couple of other men to take it out. After a difficult approach with little cover, there was a short burst of fire and the Argentine machine-gun fell silent. Leapfrogging by sections, the Troop retreated to the stream, by which time the Argentine fire was falling short and there were no further casualties. Stewart reported the success of the raid to his company commander, Captain Ian Gardiner, and the weary Marines trekked back to Bluff Cove Peak and a welcome breakfast.

Such raids were invaluable in lowering Argentine morale prior to the main assault, in which the Royal Marines would play a crucial role. As a preliminary to taking Port Stanley itself, the British had first to seize a line of rugged hills in which the Argentines were dug in in strength. 45 Commando was tasked with the capture of Two Sisters and 42 Commando with that of Mount Harriet, while 40 Commando was to remain in reserve with the Welsh Guards, who had been so badly mauled on 8 June when the landing ships *Sir Galahad* and *Sir Tristram* had been bombed at Fitzroy. 3 Para was to assault Mount Longdon. Once these positions had been taken, the plan was that the remainder of the force – 5 Infantry Brigade, the Gurkhas, the Guards and 2 Para – would consolidate, and the Marines would then have the honour of the final assault on Stanley itself; an assault which never took place, as it turned out, because of the Argentine surrender.

Captain Ian Gardiner's X-Ray Company spearheaded the attack on Two Sisters. After assembling at their start-line, the Murrell Bridge at the bottom of Mount Kent, on the day after the raid described above, the Marines began moving forward in the cold, menacing darkness. Argentine fire was intense, with 105 mm guns and 0.50 calibre machine-guns pounding the Marines on the exposed hillside. 45 Commando's CO, Lieutenant-Colonel Andrew Whitehead, realized that a single company could not hope to secure Two Sisters, and brought up the battalion's two other companies. Stealthily, while X-Ray Company continued to draw the brunt of the enemy fire, the Marines crept and crawled up the flanking sides of the ridge, with its distinctive twin peaks. Milan anti-tank launchers were brought into play, hammering at the Argentine bunkers, but the defenders held on grimly. Not all the Argentine troops were under-age conscripts, by any means. Sergeant-Major George Meachin, a career veteran with 21 years' experience, was in the attack on Two Sisters. 'We came under lots of effective fire from 0.50 calibre machine-guns. . . At the same time, mortars were coming down all over us, but the main threat was from those machine-gunners who could see us in the open because of the moonlight. There were three machine-guns and we brought down constant and effective salvoes of our own artillery fire on to them directly, 15 rounds at a time. There would be a pause, and they'd come back at us again. So we had to do it a second time, all over their positions. There'd be a pause, then "boom, boom, boom," they'd come back at us again. Conscripts don't do this, babies don't do this, men who are badly led and of low morale don't do this. They were good steadfast troops. I rate them. Not all of them, but some of them.'

Despite the stubborn resistance, suddenly the Commandos were inside the Argentine positions and the cold, frightened, but still defiant defenders began throwing down their arms. Two Sisters was secure and the weary Marines began wrapping themselves in captured Argentine sleeping bags and ponchos to snatch some sleep in the drifting snow.

For the attack on Mount Harriet, 42 Commando's Lieutenant-Colonel Nick Vaux decided a frontal assault would be suicidal. Accordingly, he led K Company on a dangerously exposed march around the south of the hill, through an Argentine minefield which an earlier patrol had scouted and in which two Marines lost their legs as a result of detonating anti-personnel mines. Once through the minefield, K Company made a 180° turn to come up on the Argentine positions from the rear, while L Company engaged the Argentines' attention from the front and J Company remained in reserve to secure the position.

The battle for Mount Harriet was hard and furious. While the Marines pounded the Argentine bunkers with 66 mm and 84 mm anti-tank missiles, grenades and machine-gun fire, the Argentines responded vigorously with their lethal 0.50 calibre machine-guns, 7.62 mm assault rifles and a mixture of 7.62 mm and 0.45 calibre sub-machine-guns. The noise was horrific, the crunch of explosions and the hammer of automatic weapons blending with the screams of the wounded and the hoarsely shouted orders of officers and NCOs. But by first light Mount Harriet had fallen. K Company collected nearly 70 prisoners and had suffered no fatal casualties, although two officers and five Marines were wounded. When J Company moved up on the bitterly cold morning of 12 June, the total catch was 300 petrified prisoners, many of whom believed they would be shot out of hand.

While the Marines were assaulting Two Sisters and Mount Harriet, 3 Para were completing a similar assault on Mount Longdon and the stage was set for the penultimate act: the taking of Wireless Ridge by 2 Para and of Mount Tumbledown by 5 Infantry Brigade. This was followed by the

Gurkhas' attack on Mount William and the Welsh Guards' assault on Sapper Hill. On 14 June, the Argentines had been forced right back into Port Stanley itself and had no further room to manoeuvre. The Argentine troops in Stanley were mesmerized as the hills in front of them suddenly seemed to come alive with 'thousands' of English troops running down the slopes towards them, yelling and screaming like madmen. They knocked the guns out of the Argentine conscripts' hands, and Marines and Paras both exchanged their steel helmets for their proud green and maroon berets.

Major-General Jeremy Moore ordered the troops to halt at the racecourse as the Argentine commander, General Menendez, had sent a message to say that he was prepared to discuss surrender. Back in England, at 22.12 on 14 June, a jubilant Prime Minister Margaret Thatcher rose to her feet in the House of Commons. 'After successful attacks last night, General Moore decided to press forward. The Argentines retreated. Our forces reached the outskirts of Port Stanley. Large numbers of Argentine soldiers threw down their weapons. They are reported to be flying white flags over Port Stanley.'

To the sounds of cheers from the members of all political parties, Mrs Thatcher concluded: 'Our troops have been ordered not to fire except in self defence. Talks are now in progress between General Menendez and our Deputy Commander, Brigadier Waters, about the surrender of the Argentine forces on East and West Falkland.'

The war was over.

THE SPECIAL BOAT SQUADRON AND RAIDING SQUADRONS

Like the Special Air Service Regiment, the Special Boat Squadron and the three Royal Marine Raiding Squadrons owe their origins to the need during World War 2 for men able to land on an enemy coastline and penetrate inshore on clandestine reconnaissance and sabotage missions, to attempt the capture of high-ranking enemy officers and to perform similar tasks. Again like the SAS, the Special Boat Squadron began its life as an almost unofficial unit, and by the time its existence became officially recognized, on 14 April 1942, it had already seen considerable action, notably in the abortive raid on the North African coast to kill Rommel, in November 1941. The raid failed because Rommel was in Rome at the time and many of the commandos were killed, including their leader, Lieutenant-Colonel Geoffrey Keyes.

As constituted in April 1942, the SBS consisted of just 47 officers and men, commanded by Major R. J. Courtney. Its members were drawn from both the Army and the Royal Marines, and for the remainder of the war they played a sterling role in harassing the Germans and Italians by lightning raids in North Africa, the Aegean and the Adriatic. They trained in the techniques of canoe-handling, landing from submarines, cliff-scaling, mine-laying, underwater sabotage and other necessary skills, in the north of

Scotland, practising landings on the Isle of Arran and elsewhere. The SBS was also active on D-Day and afterwards, demolishing underwater obstacles on the Normandy beaches to clear paths for the waves of landing craft; but its most famous exploit was in December 1942, when five canoes were launched into the estuary of the Gironde river in France and the SBS blew up a number of German ships. This episode formed the basis for the popular film, *The Cockleshell Heroes*.

Throughout the war, the SBS operated closely alongside the SAS and there was a constant interchange of personnel which continues today, even though the SAS is an Army unit, while the SBS is part of the Royal Marines and therefore under Admiralty command. Later, in the 1950s and '60s, the SBS took part in counter-terrorist operations with the SAS in Borneo, Malaya and Indonesia and, as we shall see, 2 SBS played a very active role in the Falkland Islands.

SBS today

Even more so than the SAS, the SBS has always kept a very low profile and neither its strength nor many details of its organization and equipment are discussed in public. Today's recruits for the SBS come primarily from the Royal Marines. Having completed the already rigorous commando training, volunteers take a further 12-month course alongside the SAS, including psychological indoctrination against interrogation, parachute training at Brize Norton, and ski training with the Mountain and Arctic Warfare Cadre in Norway.

For obvious reasons, special attention is paid to teaching the volunteers all aspects of seamanship and diving, and they become well versed in both underwater sabotage and in the protection of British installations, such as oil rigs, against terrorist attack. An obvious role for the SBS would be the rescue of hostages in the event of a ship being hijacked. In these tasks the squadron shares responsibility with Comacchio Group (see page 43), but it also operates alongside the three Royal Marines Raiding Squadrons.

The men for these units are selected from commando volunteers who have shown special talent in boat handling, and train at Poole, in Dorset. Their special skill is in the use of small boats – both inflatables, such as the Gemini, and small glass-fibre launches known as Rigid Raiders. In time of war, the role of the Raiding Squadrons is to ferry commandos or members of the SAS and SBS ashore, usually secretly and by night.

The Falklands campaign

In the Falklands, however, they came 'into the open', operating an invaluable ship-to-shore shuttle service for the Task Force in San Carlos water, even in the middle of Argentine air attacks. However, that the men of these squadrons are not just glorified 'taxi drivers' was clearly shown right at the end of the Falklands campaign, when No 1 Squadron put in a diversionary raid on Port Stanley as 2 Para were taking Wireless Ridge.

Four Rigid Raiders, packed with men from 2 SBS and 22 SAS, sneaked into Port William, the estuary of the Murrell river, during the night of 13-14 June. Unfortunately, they were spotted by the crew of the Argentine survey ship *Bahia Paradiso*, and searchlights flashed across the dark water. Although all hope of taking the Argentines by surprise had now been lost, the four craft, led by Sergeant Plym Buckley, accelerated in to the beach where they were met by a hail of gunfire. A landing was obviously out of the question and the four boats, leaking from several bullet holes, retreated into the cover of the night, dropping their occupants on an unoccupied stretch of the coast. The men stayed low throughout the night, watching the intense firefight taking place on Wireless Ridge, and later witnessed 2 Para's jubilant entry into Stanley.

The SBS, though, had been active in the South Atlantic from the very beginning. As we have seen (page 37), the attempt to land on South Georgia by Gemini inflatables met with near disaster, but SBS patrols were later landed successfully on both East and West Falkland and, indeed, the first people the commandos and paras encountered when they landed at San Carlos were a group of tired and bearded SBS men who had been on the islands for several days, reconnoitring Argentine dispositions. As with the SAS, in time of conflict the men of the SBS and Royal Marine Raiding Squadrons will usually be found first in and last out.

Dressed in SCUBA gear, men of the Special Boat Squadron rehearse a clandestine landing on a hostile shore.

CHAPTER THREE

UNITED STATES

SPECIAL FORCES OPERATIONAL DETACHMENT DELTA • THE 'GREEN BERETS' • THE RANGERS • THE AIRBORNE DIVISIONS • THE MARINE CORPS • THE UNDERWATER DEMOLITION AND SEA-AIR-LAND TEAMS

Firing his Colt Commando in short bursts to preserve ammunition, Sergeant Fred Zabitosky helped keep his own men's morale up and the Vietcong attackers' heads down as he waited for the retrieval helicopters to arrive. The weapon, a cut-down version of the famous Armalite assault rifle, was not always popular with American Special Forces personnel because – particularly at night – its vivid muzzle flash was much too noticeable for comfort. In the daytime this was less of a disadvantage, and Zabitosky and the mixed force of nine Green Berets and South Vietnamese irregulars with him used their weapons with deadly effect, as wave after wave of Vietcong troops broke against their perimeter.

Zabitosky's tiny command was one of the Special Operations Group reconnaissance teams which were used in Vietnam by the Central Intelligence Agency to confirm reports of Vietcong troop movements and assembly points. On 19 February 1968 his 'A' Team had been dropped by helicopter in the dense jungle and tall elephant grass of the junction between the borders of Vietnam, Laos and Cambodia, west of the Special Forces training camp at Dak To. As usual, Zabitosky's team had landed from one of a group of helicopters, each of which came in to hover briefly above a different clearing in the jungle. This decoy manoeuvre meant that, although any Vietcong troops in the vicinity would be aware that an enemy patrol had been dropped, they would not know at which of the landing zones. Unfortunately, on this particular day, Zabitosky's team had landed practically on top of a battalion of Vietcong and had come under heavy fire moments after the transport helicopter's departure.

Retreating towards a clearing where helicopters could come down to rescue his tiny force, Zabitosky tied a couple of white phosphorus smoke flares to a Claymore anti-personnel mine, which he hurled into the leading ranks of the attacking Vietcong. The two heavily armed Skyraider ground-attack aircraft circling overhead were called in and dropped napalm on the white smoke, wiping out the first wave of the attack. As his men pulled further back, Zabitosky repeated the trick, and on their second run the Skyraiders disrupted the Vietcong with high-explosive bombs.

Reaching the landing zone, Zabitosky went from man to man of his team, encouraging them to stay calm and pick their targets, while the Skyraiders – whose ability to carry enormous loads of bombs, napalm containers and rockets had become legendary – continued to blast and strafe the Vietcong. Eventually, three helicopters returned to the landing zone where Zabitosky's team was still, miraculously, intact. Keeping four men with him, the Sergeant ordered the remaining five into the first helicopter, which took off for safety. The second machine spiralled in and the rest of the force eagerly leaped aboard. As it ascended, a Vietcong guerrilla, armed with a grenade discharger attachment on his AK47 assault rifle, fired a grenade at the escaping helicopter.

When Zabitosky regained consciousness, he was lying on the ground with broken ribs and injured spine a few metres away from the crashed helicopter, having somehow been thrown clear. Although the helicopter was burning fiercely, the injured man managed to pull out the dazed pilot and then returned for the unconscious co-pilot. As Zabitosky was pulling him out, the helicopter's fuel tanks exploded, hurling blazing liquid and debris in all directions. Zabitosky rolled in the grass to extinguish his own and the co-pilot's burning clothing, then picked the still-unconscious man up in a fireman's lift and ran towards another helicopter which, seeing the fate which had befallen its companion, had returned to pick up any survivors. Although the co-pilot later died of his injuries, Zabitosky was awarded a well-earned Medal of Honor.

The reconnaissance mission might have been a failure in one sense, but Zabitosky's team and the two Skyraiders succeeded in killing well over 100 Vietcong, and the incident – one of out of hundreds of similar engagements which took place during the Vietnam War – clearly demonstrates the courage and cool thinking of the men in the various élite formations of the US Army, Navy and Marine Corps.

Evolution
The United States seems to have produced more specialist units and formations from its armed forces than any other country. It has been suggested that this is a result of the size of the American armed forces, rivalries between the services, and competition between their supporters in Congress. But it may also derive from using the division (or its equivalent) as the basic administrative unit, and recruiting for it from all over the country. The British use a much smaller unit – the regiment – which has strong local ties and a long history and tradition. Since many of the tasks done by US élite forces are carried out in the British and Commonwealth armed forces, for example, by normal units, there has been some interest in

the US in using the British regimental system, and both the Rangers and 'Delta Force' come close to this.

The Japanese naval air attack on Pearl Harbor on 7 December 1941, which brought the USA into World War 2, resulted in the real development of airborne formations, with the 82nd and 101st Divisions as parachute units. This war was also the birthplace of many of the other élite units which survive today with, for example, the Canadian-American Special Service Force later spawning the US Army Special Forces. After the Korean War (June 1950–July 1953) most of these were wound down, but saw a revival in the late 1950s. British and French experiences in the many guerrilla wars they were fighting at the time had some influence on this.

American involvement in Vietnam produced an upsurge in the élite forces, and gave rise to much of the present-day confusion of units, with each service having élite and specialist forces. Since Vietnam, there has been an attempt to rationalize organization and to eliminate overlaps, and, on 1 January 1984, the Pentagon set up the Joint Special Operations Agency to make the management and response of these forces more unified and efficient. This agency replaces the Joint Special Operations Command, which conducted the Grenada operation in October 1983.

Today, the United States élite forces are as follows. The US Navy has its Underwater Demolition Teams (UDTs) and Sea-Air-Land (SEAL) teams. The US Marine Corps is an élite force all of its own, and includes an Air Wing which flies helicopters and broadly similar combat jets to those of the US Navy, but which is also acquiring the V/STOL (Vertical/Short Take Off and Landing) AV-8B version of the Harrier that performed so well in the 1982 Falklands campaign. The US Army has the greatest number of élite and specialist units, such as the 82nd and 101st Airborne Divisions (currently only the 82nd has a parachute role – the 101st being an air-mobile unit); the 1st Cavalry Division ('Air Cavalry') which used helicopters in Vietnam but is now possibly being superseded by the 101st Airborne; the 75th Infantry Regiment (the Rangers); the US Army Special Forces (the 'Green Berets'); and the 1st Special Forces Operational Detachment Delta (known as 'Delta Force' or just 'Delta', for short).

In most of the operations that the USA has mounted since the Korean War – especially in Vietnam, but also afterwards – in which élite forces have been used, elements of many of these have been working together. For example, the Grenada operation in 1983 involved the Marines, Rangers, SEALs and Airborne; and Operation 'Eagle Claw' in 1980 used US Army Special Forces, Delta, Rangers, USMC, USAF Aerospace Rescue and Recovery Service (ARRS) and 1st Special Operations Wing (SOW). With so much combined activity, it is expected that the joint planning, training and understanding which ought to come about through the presence of the new Joint Special Operations Agency should hone performance to a finer edge.

The need for such an agency is clearly demonstrated in the following pages, where so much duplication of effort and sheer logistic complication

Soldiers of the 1st Air Cavalry Division disembark from helicopters near Dak To in November 1967.

muddies the waters of what should have been clear-cut operational requirements. Instead of one team of men with a close rapport and a single objective, the task forces described have suffered from being muddled together, relying on different chains of command and mission priorities. It is for these reasons that the success rate of American special forces, despite the courage of the individual soldiers concerned, has been lower than that of the British or Israelis, for example. Confused objectives, political considerations – especially in Vietnam – and inter-Service rivalries have also served to inhibit the potential of the US special forces.

Because the disparate units of the American élite forces have been obliged to work together on combined operations, in a way which does not happen in other, smaller, armies, it seems logical, therefore, to consider their origins, organization and status first, before going into details of some of their operations, in order that the reader can understand more fully the difficulties under which they have laboured.

Delta Force

Delta was the brainchild of Colonel Charles Beckwith, and eventually came into being on 19 November 1977. Its official name is Special Forces Operational Detachment Delta, presumably after the other Operational Detachments ('A', 'B', and 'C' Teams) into which the Special Forces are divided. The prime role of Delta is to deal with terrorist incidents affecting the USA and its interests, as a result of studies conducted after the Olympic Games massacre in Munich in August 1972 and the Mogadishu rescue of October 1977. The inspiration for Colonel Beckwith's force was the British 22nd Special Air Service Regiment with which he served in 1962-3, being one of the few US Special Forces' exchangees to gain selection. He developed a great love for the regiment and, on his return to the US Army, tried for a number of years to persuade it to form a unit with the same organization, purpose and functions as the British regiment.

Once his dream had been made reality, Colonel Beckwith proceeded to organize Delta into squadrons (initially there was only 'A' Squadron, but this was split in 1979 to form 'B' Squadron as well) which are subdivided into troops of 16 men. The basic group, or 'chalk', is the 4-man patrol, but the troops can operate in groups of 2, 4, 8 or 16 men. Selection and training in Colonel Beckwith's time closely followed the SAS pattern, and had a strong element of weeding out 'cowboys' and an accent on intelligence and self-reliance. Very high standards of marksmanship are required: snipers must score 100 per cent hits at 600 m (650 yd) and 90 per cent at 1000 m (1100 yd). Special Forces personnel volunteering for Delta are often surprised at the degree of competence demanded by SAS criteria.

Little more is known about Delta, as befits a 'child' of the SAS, and Colonel Beckwith has now retired from the US Army. His brainchild survives, unaffected by the failure of Operation 'Eagle Claw', and will presumably come into the limelight again when some other terrorist activity threatens the lives of US citizens.

The 'Green Berets'

The US Army Special Forces (the 'Green Berets') became well-known to the world during the Vietnam War. They trace their origin – like the British Special Air Service Regiment, with which they have some affinity – back to World War 2, when the Canadian-American 1st Special Service Force was formed on the authority of General George C. Marshall. This force was made up of three regiments of two battalions each, and fought in North Africa, Italy, southern France and the Aleutian Islands. Their tasks included raids and covert strikes, and their members were trained in demolition work, parachuting, amphibious assault, rock-climbing and skiing.

After World War 2, the force was disbanded, but, on 20 June 1952, the concept was revived with the formation of the 10th Special Forces Group at Fort Bragg, North Carolina. On 25 September 1953, the 77th Special Forces Group was born and, on 24 June 1957, the 1st Special Forces Group was activated in Okinawa. In the same year, 1 SFG sent a team to Nha Trang in South Vietnam to train a small group of men from the Army of the Republic of Vietnam (ARVN). Four years later, on 21 September 1961, the 5th SFG was formed at Fort Bragg: it later moved to Vietnam and became responsible for the activities of all personnel from the Special Forces Groups serving in the country. In that same year, President Kennedy authorized the wearing of the now-famous green beret, and ordered the deployment of the first Special Forces personnel to Vietnam in November 1961.

Although the original concept of the 1950s was that of fighting a guerrilla war against conventional troops, this was modified in the light of the new conditions encountered in Vietnam. The Special Forces' expertise fitted them well for a counter-insurgency role, and the tactic of 'setting a thief to catch a thief' was being proved successful at the same time by the British in Malaya, Kenya, Aden and Cyprus. Circumstances and policies were slightly different in Vietnam, however, and the US Army Special Forces acquired the role of helping and instructing the Vietnamese Montagnard tribes to defend themselves against the Vietcong, and later to take a more active part. This was the Civilian Irregular Defense Group (CIDG) programme, and the Special Forces gained considerable expertise in organizing such 'armies', although their value in the field varied enormously and was often unpredictable.

With the end of the Vietnam War, the 'Green Berets' lost some favour in US Army circles, but it was soon realized that such a force was an essential element of a modern army. While retaining their ability to organize counter-insurgency armies for low-intensity warfare, the Special Forces have now rediscovered their intelligence-gathering and covert operations role, bringing them back in line with the SAS.

The basic Special Forces sub-unit is the Operational Detachment or 'A' Team of 12 men, and there are 12 such teams to a company. The companies themselves are formed into battalions and the battalions into groups, of which there are at present seven, with two more battalions and a group headquarters currently being raised. Of the seven groups, two are Army reserve and two are National Guard formations. The other three are regulars. All Special Forces groups now come under command of the 1st Special Operations Command of the Army, which is part of the Joint Special Operations Agency.

All members of the Special Forces are volunteers, who must be parachute-qualified or willing to become so. A rigorous training programme, lasting between 44 and 62 weeks, weeds out unsuitable candidates, after which the accepted recruits undergo a further period of training. All Special Forces soldiers must have at least two particular trades, such as demolitions, intelligence, special weapons or communications, and often they must become proficient in foreign languages. Each group has a coloured shield-shaped patch which is worn on the beret, and on this is set the officers' badges of rank or, for enlisted men, the SF cap badge.

The Rangers

The US Army's Ranger battalions are, in effect, its Light Infantry: their training, equipment, role and history make them what the British Army's Light Division ought to be. In general war, the Rangers' missions include deep reconnaissance into enemy-held territory, strategic raids, ambush patrols, and in low-intensity warfare their tasks are geared to counter-guerrilla and counter-terrorist operations.

At present, there are two Ranger battalions in the US Army with a third on its way. Known generally as the 1st and 2nd (and, presumably, 3rd) Ranger Battalions after their World War 2 predecessors, they are in fact the 1st and 2nd Battalions of the 75th Infantry Regiment (1/75 and 2/75, with 3/75 to follow). The 1st Battalion has its depot at Hunter Army Airfield, Georgia, and the 2nd Battalion is based at Fort Lewis in Washington State. The 3rd Battalion will be based at Fort Benning, Georgia, along with the Ranger Regimental Headquarters and the Ranger School.

First formed during World War 2, the Rangers were disbanded after Korea, but re-activated as a long-range reconnaissance force in Vietnam. In 1969 they were re-formed as the present two battalions of the 75th Infantry Regiment, whose basic combat unit is the squad of 11 men. Officially, the current Ranger mission is 'to conduct special military operations in support of the policies and objectives of the USA'. Typical missions would include operations against targets deep behind enemy lines and in conjunction with conventional forces; rescues; safeguarding US lives, property or invest-ments; protecting US citizens abroad during emergencies; and air-mobile or airborne anti-armour operations in support of larger units. To act effectively, the battalions must be ready to deploy anywhere in the world; manoeuvre with speed and surprise in all types of terrain and climatic conditions by day or night; and to use air, land, water and parachute infiltration to carry out raids, ambushes and attacks against key targets in enemy territory. In addition, the Ranger battalion performs all the other traditional Light Infantry tasks.

Becoming a Ranger is a lengthy business, and the wastage rate is high: less than 50 per cent of the candidates win that black beret. All Rangers are volunteers from a parent Army unit, and do a two-year tour with the 75th Infantry Regiment. This may be extended by six months, on the Com-manding Officer's recommendation. After this time, the Rangers go back to their units, taking their newly acquired skills and their coveted black berets with them.

Candidates need first to have a high-school graduation diploma, a high General Aptitude score, and to be able to gain a 'Secret' security clearance. As most volunteers are infantrymen, they go through basic and advanced training at Fort Benning. After completing the Advanced Individual Training Course, the recruits go on to airborne school, also at Fort Benning. On passing out from this, they begin the four-week Ranger Indoctrination Program, which is designed to perfect their individual battle skills and acquaint them with Ranger standard operating procedures (SOPs).

After about one year in a Ranger battalion, and having proved his leadership qualities, a Ranger is sent to Ranger School. On graduating from this course, he is eligible for certain specialist schools such as Special Forces SCUBA (diving), SF Medical, Sniper, Demolitions, free-fall parachuting, and so on. As the Ranger qualification is a 'trade' available to all Army units, many soldiers complete Ranger School, even if they do not subsequently join a Ranger battalion.

The two battalions have an arduous training schedule. Exercises are conducted all over the USA and abroad in order to find as many different climates and environments as possible, and the training year is divided into two gruelling 5½-month periods with just two fortnight block leaves in between.

The Airborne Divisions

'Airborne!' is the traditional chant and greeting of the members of the United States Army's parachute formations but, today, only one of the two World War 2 US Airborne divisions is 'in role': the other has been turned into an air assault formation, specializing in helicopter operations using the Sikorsky UH-60A Black Hawk. The 82nd Airborne Division (the 'All American' – hence the Double-A formation sign) is currently the US Army's only full-time parachute unit. The other famous Division – the 101st (the 'Screaming Eagles' from the eagle's head divisional sign) – is now a 17,900-man strong air assault formation, but it still keeps 'Airborne' on its sign. Both are part of XVIII Airborne Corps, based at Fort Bragg, North Carolina.

The 82nd Airborne Division is made up of a divisional headquarters, a divisional support command, and three Airborne brigades. Each brigade consists of three parachute battalions with the usual headquarters and support arms. The present 'rig' is the MC1-1B steerable parachute, which gives almost the same manoeuvrability as a hang glider.

Entry into the Airborne forces can be either by direct application or by volunteering from another unit. All candidates must pass a tough selection procedure, followed by a rigorous training and parachute course, after which they get their 'wings' and can wear the maroon beret.

The primary task of any airborne unit is to arrive by air, take control of the ground, and hold it until relieved by main force units. The 82nd Airborne Division is at present the mainstay of the US Rapid Deployment Joint Task Force and as such takes part in the annual 'Bright Star' Exercises in Egypt. One parachute battalion is kept on an 18-hour standby, with one of its companies on 2-hour standby. One of the brigades – the Ready Brigade, which, like the standby battalion, rotates around the division – is on 24-hour notice. The airlift capability for the Division is provided by the Lockheed C-141 Starlifters and C-130 Hercules of the USAF. The 82nd Airborne Division is equipped with three days' combat rations of food, ammunition, POL (petrol, oil and lubricants), spares, water, and clothing; after that period, air resupply is necessary.

United States Marine Corps
The largest élite force in the world is the USMC, with some 194,000 personnel of both sexes; making it larger than the total armed forces of many countries. It is organized into three regular and one reserve divisions, each incorporating a Marine Air Wing. The US Marine Corps has a unique all-arms air-land capability with a particular emphasis on amphibious operations, although it has often fought in conventional battles alongside the Army and the two other air forces.

The general role of the USMC has been put into three broad categories: amphibious capabilities for use with USN fleet operations, land operations which are necessary for successful maritime campaigns, and providing security detachments for US Naval bases and principal warships. The Corps may also, of course, carry out any other duties given it by the President.

The Marine division is larger than its Army counterpart with a strength of 18,000 men and some women (of which the Corps has approximately 4000). Each division is made up of a headquarters and three Marine brigades or regiments, plus supporting artillery, tanks and ancillary formations. A Marine battle group, known as an Amphibious Unit, comprises between 1600 and 2500 men. Number 22 MAU was the USMC contingent in the Grenada operation.

Recruits to the USMC enlist directly into the Corps, going to one of two training depots either at San Diego in California or at Parris Island in South Carolina. There they undergo the 11-week 'Boot Camp', which is analogous to the Royal Marines' Beret Course, passing out at the end as 'leathernecks'. Officer selection is rigorous, and potential officers must endure a tough selection process and training course at Quantico, Virginia, before being commissioned. The USMC does not have its own officers' academy; some officers are accepted from the Naval Academy at Annapolis, but most come from either the Naval Regimental Officers Training College, the Officers Candidate School, or the Platoon Leaders' Class run by the USMC. The Boot Camp and the Quantico course instil in the Marines the Corps' traditional doctrine of aggressive offensive action, which has been the hallmark of their combat engagements.

Underwater Demolition and Sea-Air-Land Teams
The Underwater Demolition Teams and the Sea-Air-Land Teams are the US Navy's principal élite forces. The UDTs were formed during World War 2, mainly to destroy water obstacles laid in the approaches to landing beaches. However, they also perform beach reconnaissance missions, and beach marking. Other activities which they are trained for include the destruction of certain targets near coasts, such as key bridges and crossings over which an enemy would have to move reinforcements to the beach

Two US Marines check out an abandoned Vietnamese village after fierce fighting in the Quang Tri province.

defenders. In general, UDTs and SEALs have a range of tasks equivalent to those of the British Royal Marines' Special Boat Squadrons and the Boat Troops of SAS Squadrons.

SEAL team personnel are recruited from volunteers from the UDTs, and they receive special training to fit them for their role. The UDT members are themselves volunteers from other parts of the Navy. After the selection process, UDT volunteers go through an intensive and physically demanding 24-week course. The first four weeks consist of physical preparation: endurance and speed runs, PT, swimming, and marches. Recruits then embark upon several weeks of classroom work, physical and tactical exercises, open-sea swims, reconnaissance exercises and demolition training. This period is then followed by a week's E-and-E (escape and evasion), survival training and land navigation exercises. Finally, the volunteers go through a three-week parachute course and then to underwater swimming school.

SEAL volunteers go even further: they take foreign language courses and qualifications, study low-intensity warfare, and complete a HALO (high altitude/low-opening) free-fall parachute course. The SEAL teams' role requires them to work in hostile waters with little friendly support, or on land where they may have 'contacts' with the enemy. They may be taken into action by submarine – coming out either while it is still submerged or when it is on the surface – to swim or paddle ashore in inflatable boats. They could also parachute towards their objective: their HALO training would allow them to jump from the aircraft some distance from the target and 'track' towards it. They might also come ashore by the US equivalents of Geminis, Rigid Raiders or canoes.

Both UDTs and SEALs wear standard naval uniform with specialist trade insignia. On exercise or operations, they wear the appropriate gear. SEALs often wear leaf-pattern combat kit, and sometimes also the face-veil *shimag* around the head that has been popularized by the SAS. Jungle hats and camouflaged berets are alternative headgear.

Control over the UDTs and the SEALs and the USN Reserve special forces is under the Naval Special Warfare Groups (NAVSPECWARGRUs) of which there are two. Number 1 (NAVSPECWARGRU 1) commands SEAL Team 1, UDTs 11 and 12, Special Boat Squadron 1 and Swimmer Delivery Vehicle (SDV) Team 1. Its base is the Naval Amphibious Base, Coronado, San Diego, in California, but it also administers Naval Special Warfare Unit 1 at Subic Bay in the Philippines. NAVSPECWARGRU 2 has its depot at Little Creek, Norfolk, Virginia, and has under command SEAL Team 2, UDTs 21 and 22, and a similar spread of units to NAVSPECWAR-GRU 1.

UDTs consist of 15 officers and 111 ratings ('enlisted men'), while SEAL teams consist of 27 officers and 156 ratings. A SEAL team is divided into five self-contained platoons, each of which is able to operate independently.

There is no doubt that the scope of the United States' élite forces, as detailed above, is mindboggling. The number of men – and women – involved, the range of training, and the multiplicity of equipment and skills, might make these formations seem unwieldy and difficult to coordinate in the field. All three of the actions described in the remainder of this chapter were combined operations and in some part may serve to illustrate the advantages, or disadvantages, of having so many independent units on call in times of emergency.

THE MAYAGUEZ RESCUE

The sun had not long risen when the two helicopters reached their destination – the island of Koh Tang. As the Marines looked out from the first helicopter, all that met their gaze was a peaceful, tropical paradise of warm blue seas lapping a deserted beach. Their hopes high, the men dropped to the ground and spread out along the shore. Suddenly, all hell broke loose – the Khmer Rouge had organized a welcoming party.

No one could have expected this complex operation to run like clockwork, given the number of unknown factors, but at least it achieved its objective: the recovery of the SS *Mayaguez* and the rescue of its crew. The *Mayaguez* rescue was, perhaps, the last major US military operation in the south-east Asian conflict.

Following the hurried evacuation of the US embassy in Saigon at the end of April 1975, American air power was concentrated in Thailand and on ships in the Gulf of Thailand. During the first week of May two merchant vessels bound for Thailand were intercepted by Cambodian gunboats: a Korean ship was shot at, but escaped, and, on 7 May, a Panamanian-registered vessel was seized and held for 35 hours, then released. Then, on 12 May, the American-registered freighter SS *Mayaguez* was stopped and held by Cambodian naval gunboats in the Gulf, some 10 km (6½ miles) off Poulo Wai. Before the Cambodians took control, the radio operator had managed to send a message asking for help, which was picked up and relayed to Washington.

At 06.15, three hours after the seizure, the officer of the watch at the State Department's Intelligence and Research Bureau woke up the Secretary of State, Henry A. Kissinger. Dr Kissinger passed the news on to the President, Gerald R. Ford, 1½ hours later. After this briefing, the President called a meeting of the National Security Council for noon. One of the problems of rescue attempts in Vietnam was the delay involved in mounting them: by the time the Council sat down in Washington, the *Mayaguez* had already been in Cambodian hands for 5¾ hours.

The Master of the *Mayaguez*, Captain Charles T. Miller, managed to stall the Cambodians from moving his ship to Sihanoukville (Kompang Som) on the mainland. So, the vessel was still riding at anchor off Poulo Wai, when a US Navy Lockheed P-3C Orion patrol aircraft spotted it just after dawn on 13 May. Later that morning, the headquarters of Pacific Air Force ordered the USAF Aerospace Rescue and Recovery Service units in Thailand to prepare a rescue force for the 39 crewmen being held by the Cambodians. On orders from President Ford, the US Navy Commander-in-Chief Pacific Fleet instructed fighter-bombers and gunships to prevent the ship or its crew from being taken to the mainland. They were to fire warning shots across the bow and, if that failed, they were to strafe the after-deck and stern in an attempt to disable the freighter. If the Cambodians tried to tow the vessel, they would be warned and the tug sunk, if necessary.

The aircrews received these orders late in the afternoon of 13 May. That night, AC-130 Spectre gunships of the USAF special operations units circled over the vessel. A Cambodian gunboat fired at the aircraft, the Spectres attacked and forced the boat aground. During the evening of 13 May, the Joint Chiefs of Staff in Washington ordered eight HH-53 helicopters (callsigns 'JG' – 'Jolly Green') from 3rd Aerospace Rescue and Recovery Squadron, and eight CH-53s (callsigns 'K' – 'Knife') from 21st Special Operations Squadron to the Royal Thai Air Force Base at U-Tapao on the Gulf. They were to carry 75 security policemen from Nakhon Phanom as a possible rescue force. Sadly, a tragic accident happened during the move. One of the 'Knife' helicopters crashed into wooded country 60 km (37 miles) west of Nakhon Phanom, killing all on board: five crewmen and 18 policemen.

At 08.17 the next day, two 'JG' helicopters took off from U-Tapao to look for survivors of a Cambodian gunboat, earlier sunk by strafing from A-7 Corsair IIs. None was found, and the aircraft returned to U-Tapao. The same flight of A-7s which had sunk the gunboat spotted soon after a wooden fishing boat full of people heading for the mainland. Suspecting that the *Mayaguez* crew was on board, they fired warning shots and dropped tear gas all around it. But the gas actually prevented the crewmen and the Thai fishermen from overpowering their Cambodian captors. They were taken to Sihanoukville and later transferred to Kaoh Rong Samloem – a nearby island. Corsairs, Phantoms and Hercules aircraft resumed watch over the *Mayaguez*. In the mid-morning, Corsairs sank a patrol boat towing a barge east of Koh Tang island and, during that night, a Hercules sank another patrol boat as it approached the ship.

Washington was meanwhile trying diplomatic approaches in an attempt to secure the release of the crew. At the same time it was putting rescue plans in motion – just in case! On 14 May, two companies of Marines were flown from Okinawa to U-Tapao, bringing the total number of available USMC personnel to somewhere around 600. American ships were also steaming as fast as they could to the scene. The nearest vessel was the frigate USS *Harold E. Holt*, which was by chance in the area, and the fleet carrier USS *Coral Sea* and the destroyer USS *Henry B. Wilson* were hurrying down from the north-east.

By nightfall on 14 May, nobody knew for certain where the crew of the *Mayaguez* was. Military preparations continued in Thailand and, when it became clear that diplomatic efforts were getting nowhere, President Ford ordered the Joint Chiefs of Staff to take appropriate measures to reclaim the ship and secure the release of the crew: the military in south-east Asia had been given the 'green light'!

The plan was for 60 Marines to be flown out to the *Holt* in three helicopters. These men would board the SS *Mayaguez* and capture the ship. Intelligence estimates indicated that the crew was being held on Koh Tang, guarded by a handful of Cambodian civilians and Khmer Rouge terrorists, but this information proved to be wrong. Up to 600 Marines were to be flown out to the island in helicopters, with an Army interpreter in the first aircraft to tell the Khmer Rouge that the Marines had landed, and that their only hope of safety was to hand over the *Mayaguez* crew unharmed. Eight helicopters would transport an initial wave of Marines for a landing at first light on the two northern beaches of Koh Tang (called West Beach and East Beach) to establish a beach-head. A second wave would then be flown in, and a third was to be held in reserve.

In the early morning of 15 May, eight helicopters (five 'Knife' CH-53s and three 'Jolly Green' HH-53s) flew towards the two beaches carrying the first two waves of Marines. At 06.45 two CH-53s, 'Knife 21' and '22', flew in to West Beach. No resistance was met until most of the Marines off the first chopper – 'Knife 21' – had fanned out across the beach. Then the Khmer

WEAPONS OF THE AMERICAN ÉLITE FORCES

Designation	Type	Calibre	Magazine	Rate of fire	Range	Remarks
L9A1	Browning automatic pistol	9 mm	13 rounds	Single-shot	40 m	Most widely used hand gun in world
M3	Browning sub-machine-gun	0.45 in	30 rounds	450 rpm cyclic	100 m	The faithful old 'grease gun'
M16A1	Armalite assault rifle	5.56 mm	20 or 30 rounds	700–950 rpm cyclic	400 m	
M16A2	Armalite assault rifle	5.56 mm	20 or 30 rounds	600–940 rpm cyclic	400 m	With 3-round burst capability
CAR15	Colt Commando carbine	5.56 mm	20 or 30 rounds	700–800 rpm cyclic	200 m	Carbine version of Armalite
M10	Ingram sub-machine-gun	9 mm or 0.45 in	32 rounds (9 mm), 30 rounds (0.45)	1090 rpm, 1145 rpm	100 m+	Has replaced the unsuccessful Stoner
M11	Ingram sub-machine-gun	9 mm short or 0.38 in	16 or 32 rounds	1200 rpm	100 m	
M60	Machine-gun	7.62 mm	100-round belt	550 rpm	1000 m	Dual-purpose light/heavy machine-gun
M224	Mortar	60 mm	Single-shot	18 rpm	Not available	New section light mortar
L16A1	Mortar	81 mm	Single-shot	15 rpm	5650 m	The standard British mortar

Rouge opened fire at close range with rifles, missiles and mortars, knocking out one of 'Knife 21's' engines as it took off. The helicopter skipped over the waves until it was about a kilometre out, then settled into the water.

'Knife 22' stood by until 'Jolly Green 41' and 'Knife 32' arrived, then headed in to the beach to unload its Marines. 'Knife 32', fully laden, had to dump fuel before its para rescue man could fish the crew of 'Knife 21' out of the water. He managed to save the pilot, co-pilot and one of the crewmen, but tragically the other, Sergeant Elwood E. Rumbaugh, was lost. Showing great bravery, the Sergeant had saved the co-pilot's life by diving down to help him out of the wreckage, but had then disappeared and was presumed drowned. 'Knife 32' managed to land its Marines on the beach, and then returned to U-Tapao with the injured and survivors of 'Knife 21'.

Approaching the beach through a hail of fire all the way, 'Knife 22' took many hits, one of which damaged a fuel line causing a major leak. It was unable to land, and so it struggled back towards Thailand escorted by two 'Jolly Greens'. Just as the disabled helicopter reached the Thai coast, it ran out of fuel and had to make a forced landing on the beach.

Designation	Type	Calibre	Magazine	Rate of fire	Range	Remarks
M79	Grenade launcher	40 mm	Single-shot	6–10 rpm	150 m	
M249	FN Minimi light machine-gun	5.56 mm	30 rounds (box) or 100- or 200-round belts	750–1000 rpm cyclic	600 m	Extremely versatile
G3	Heckler and Koch assault rifle	7.62 mm	20 rounds	500–600 rpm cyclic	400 m	West German design
MP5	Heckler and Koch sub-machine-gun	9 mm	15 or 30 rounds	800 rpm cyclic	200 m	Used by British and Germans
Cobra	Anti-tank missile	100 mm	Single-shot	Not applicable	2000 m	Second-generation weapon
M47 Dragon	Medium anti-tank armour weapon	Not available	Single-shot	Not available	1000 m+	Third-generation weapon
TOW BGM71A	Anti-tank missile	152 mm	Single-shot	Not available	3750 m	
Stinger	Anti-aircraft missile	70 mm	Single-shot	Not applicable	1500 m+	One-shot 'disposable' weapon, also used by British SAS
Redeye	Anti-aircraft missile	70 mm	Single-shot	Not available	Not available	

The East Beach landing was experiencing the same sort of problems. As 'Knife 23' and '31' headed in, they received a hostile welcome from small-arms, heavy machine-guns, rockets and mortars just as they were about to touch down. 'Knife 23' was hit in the rotor system, and was forced to make a controlled crash landing in the surf, its tail boom snapping as it struck. The pilot ordered everyone to abandon the helicopter, and the 20 Marines, together with the air force crew, charged ashore to fight on the beach. 'Knife 31' was also badly damaged and, as it was being ditched in the shallows, it burst into flames. Eight people died in the wreckage. Of the 18 survivors, 4 more were killed and 1 other died later of wounds when they were fired on by the Khmer Rouge as they tried to swim out to sea. The 14 survivors were picked up by a launch from a USN destroyer.

An hour after the attack began, there were 14 Americans dead or missing, 3 helicopters had been shot down and 2 more severely damaged, and there were 54 Marines and USAF personnel pinned down on the two beaches. It was not the happiest of situations.

During these actions, the USS *Holt* came alongside the *Mayaguez* and put the Marine boarding party on to the ship. It found that the vessel had been abandoned, so the *Holt* put a line aboard and towed the *Mayaguez* away from Poulo Wai. Thus, an hour and a half after the main assault at least the ship had been recovered.

Elsewhere, but soon afterwards, the missing crew was rescued. It seems that, together with the crew of the Thai fishing boat, the sailors had managed to escape from their guards at Kaoh Rong Samloem, and had put to sea in the boat. The destroyer *Wilson* was sighted, and the *Mayaguez* crewmen stripped off their underwear to make white flags. The *Wilson* was at battle stations before anyone saw the underwear flying from the fishing boat's mast, but, within an hour, the *Mayaguez* crew was safely in American care.

Attention now centred on extricating the embattled Marines from Koh Tang. With the *Mayaguez's* crew safe, it was now possible to use A-7s, F-4s and AC-130 Spectre gunships to give fire support on the island: previously these had been held back for fear of hitting the captured crew. But while the *Mayaguez* men were approaching the *Wilson*, more Marines had been landed on Koh Tang. 'Jolly Green 42' and '43' approached on their first run in, and 'Jolly Green 41' headed in, after refuelling, to West Beach. They were all driven off by heavy fire, so 'Jolly Green 43' flew down the coast a little way and landed its 29 Marines 800 m (875 yd) south of the main body. It took them many hours to fight their way back to link up. 'Jolly Green 42' managed to land its Marines on West Beach after another try, but put them down on a small patch of sand about 900 m (1000 yd) from the other group. The helicopter sustained heavy damage, and had to be escorted back to U-Tapao by 'Jolly Green 43'. The third helicopter tried again, but was driven back and had to refuel once more. At about 08.00, 'Jolly Green 13' was seriously damaged while trying to pick up the 20 Marines and 5 USAF crew of 'Knife 23' on East Beach, and was left with no option but to return to Thailand.

'Jolly Green 41' did not give up easily: it approached West Beach four times in an attempt to land its troops, but was driven back each time. Finally, it called in a Spectre to shoot at enemy positions with 20 mm, 40 mm and 105 mm rounds. With this support, 'Jolly 41' flew in to the beach to drop off its Marines, with its crewmen furiously shooting up the jungle fringe with their miniguns. Nevertheless the aircraft came under mortar fire as it unloaded; one round passed through the rotor disc and exploded near the chopper, causing serious damage. 'Jolly 41' had to retire to Thailand, after refuelling, with five Marines still on board.

'Cricket', the airborne command post, marshalled the five remaining helicopters to fly in reinforcements. 'Knife 51', 'Knife 52' and 'Jolly Green 43' flew in the first wave, with 'Jolly Green 11' and '12' forming the second wave. 'Knife 51' landed 19 Marines and took out 5 wounded at West Beach, while 'Jolly Green 43' put another 28 Marines ashore, refuelled, and then circled in case it was needed for aircrew recovery. As 'Knife 52' approached the landing zone, it was hit several times in the fuel tank, so the pilot was forced to abort the landing and return to Thailand. The second-wave helicopters managed to put all their Marines ashore, however. 'Jolly Green 12' took on casualties and flew them to the mainland, while 'Jolly Green 11' refuelled from the Hercules tanker and returned to Koh Tang to join 'Jolly Green 43' in orbit. A-7s, F-4s, and OV-10A Broncos strafed, bombed and dropped tear gas on the enemy positions, but the gas was ineffective due to adverse winds.

By midday, there were 222 Americans on the island: 197 on West Beach and 25 on East Beach. The West Beach force managed to fight its way towards East Beach across the 'neck', but could get no further than a clearing about half-way across. At 14.30 another pick-up was attempted after the air attacks. 'Jolly Green 43' again came under heavy fire on its approach, sustaining damage to fuel lines and one disabled engine, but gamely carried on. It landed and took on a full load of Marines, and then precariously skipped over the waves escorted by 'Jolly Green 11' to make a forced landing on the *Coral Sea* 100 km (60 miles) away. 'Jolly Green 11' returned yet again to Koh Tang.

'Cricket' and the airborne forward air controllers directed more tactical strikes against the Khmer Rouge positions before the evacuation was resumed. By this time, only three helicopters were operational, and two others were being hurriedly repaired: 'Jolly Green 44', previously out of commission at Nakhon Phanom, and 'Jolly Green 43' on board USS *Coral Sea*. By 16.00, 'Jolly Green 44' was thankfully back in service and rushing to U-Tapao. It arrived at Koh Tang at 17.30, just as 'Jolly Green 43' was returning from *Coral Sea*, and the two helicopters joined up with 'Jolly Green 11', 'Jolly Green 12' and 'Knife 51'. Before the five went back into action, a Hercules dropped a 6800 kg (15,000 lb) bomb on the centre of Koh Tang island, devastating an area the size of an American football pitch and killing everyone inside a 45 m (50 yd) radius of the explosion.

While the enemy was still reeling, 'Jolly Green 11' headed in to East Beach, supported by minigun fire from 'Jolly Green 12', 'Knife 51' and two machine-guns, mounted in a longboat, from the *Wilson*. It was feared that the 25 men would not survive the night, and rescue was essential. 'Jolly Green 11' came under heavy fire from the Khmer Rouge as soon as it neared the beach. The helicopter hovered at the water's edge, while the party on the beach raced for the chopper in pairs, firing blindly into the jungle as they dived inside the aircraft. The flight mechanic manning the rear ramp minigun, Sergeant Harry W. Cash, was giving covering fire for the Marines and USAF men coming in off the beach. As the last pair scampered aboard, he yelled into his headset for the aircraft to take off, but there was no response: one of the first men aboard had ripped out the intercom system in his hurry. Black-clad figures were pouring out of the undergrowth, and Sergeant Cash swung his minigun to cut them down. One of the figures attempted to throw a grenade, but was killed before he could manage it.

Nevertheless, the grenade rolled inexorably towards the chopper and exploded. The pilot had had enough of this unfriendly treatment, and decided to go, whether or not everyone was on board – fortunately, they were. 'Jolly Green 11' flew the relieved Marines back to the *Coral Sea*.

As darkness approached, there were 202 Marines still to be evacuated off West Beach. 'Knife 51' headed in under intense small-arms fire to pick up 41 of them, 'Jolly 43' took off 54 more, and both choppers flew them to the *Coral Sea*. 'Jolly Green 44' then loaded up with 34 Marines. The pilot decided that he could save the 20-minute round trip to the aircraft carrier by landing the Marines on the *Holt*, as the situation on the beach was becoming increasingly desperate. With one of the crewmen hanging out of the door and giving him directions, the brave pilot managed to get one wheel on the corner of the *Holt's* helicopter pad with barely any clearance for the rotor blades. The Marines got out as fast as they could, and 'Jolly Green 44' hurtled back to the beach.

The remaining 73 men had withdrawn into a 45 m (50 yd) perimeter only a short sprint from the landing zone. OV-10A Broncos and A-7 Corsair IIs strafed the nearby jungle, but still the Khmer Rouge pressed their fierce attacks. At 19.25, the Marine commander on the beach radioed that it looked as though his position would be overrun within 15 minutes. As a Spectre shot up the tree-line beyond them, the Marines assembled a strobe light to guide the incoming helicopters. 'Jolly Green 44' followed the light to the beach and picked up 40 Marines, but due to engine power loss it was forced to fly out to the *Coral Sea*; there was no way that it could repeat the aerobatics at the *Holt*. 'Knife 51' spotted the strobe light and made its way to pick up the remaining Marines, while an OV-10A orbited above the spot, occasionally turning on its landing lights to draw fire away from the rescue chopper. 'Knife 51' touched down on the landing zone, and 27 of the Marines clambered to safety. The para rescue man had to run up the beach to grab the remaining two, who were still courageously giving covering fire. With all 29 on board, 'Knife 51' took off, and America's military involvement in south-east Asia was at an end.

During the action on Koh Tang, around 230 men were landed on the island and then taken out. It had proved a costly operation, both in lives and equipment: 15 men were killed, 49 wounded and 3 were missing; of the 15 helicopters which took part, 4 were destroyed and 9 damaged. But the SS *Mayaguez* and its crew were safe. The operation was a success.

OPERATION 'EAGLE CLAW'

Orange flames from a burning petrol tanker cast shadows darker than the night across the primitive desert road as the pilot of the Sea Stallion helicopter peered anxiously through the sand-pitted windscreen. He was already running nearly a hour behind schedule because of the dust storms and mechanical failures which had plagued the eight choppers ever since they had lifted off from the flight deck of the nuclear-powered carrier *Nimitz* at 19.30. Even as the pilot settled in to land, using the blazing vehicle as a beacon, it was obvious that more than just the weather and the vagaries of sophisticated machinery were conspiring to thwart Operation 'Eagle Claw' – the attempted rescue of American hostages who were being held in Tehran by the fanatical followers of the Ayatollah Khomeini.

On 4 November 1979, a group of Iranian 'students' rushed into the American embassy compound in Tehran and took the 53 occupants hostage; three more Americans were held in the Foreign Ministry. America was outraged. Any prospect of a diplomatic solution was complicated by the nature of the Iranian regime, which appeared to have only a notional control over the captors, and negotiations for the hostages' release proved inconclusive. As time passed, President Carter became increasingly worried for the hostages' safety.

From soon after their capture, one of the options kept under constant review was the possibility of a rescue, and contingency plans were worked out. When the decision was eventually taken to try to bring out the hostages by military means, the plan centred around using Delta Force under Colonel Charles Beckwith, with support from Rangers, Green Berets, the USMC Air Wing, and Special Operations Squadrons of the USAF.

The rescue plan was complicated, to say the least. At its core were eight RH-53D Sea Stallion helicopters. It was agreed from the beginning that an absolute minimum of six Sea Stallions was essential during the later phases of the operation, so, theoretically, there would be two helicopters in reserve.

The mission was to be in three phases, plus some preliminary moves. Delta personnel under Colonel Beckwith were to fly to Masirah airfield (the former RAF base used by the hijackers in the Mogadishu affair) in Oman, via Germany and Egypt, by Lockheed C-141 Starlifter of USAF Military Airlift Command. At Masirah they were to trans-ship to three MC-130E Hercules flown by USAF Special Operations Squadron personnel, which would take them at very low level (to avoid radar detection) across the Gulf of Oman and southern Iran to a remote spot in the Dasht-e Kavir salt desert, some distance north of the town of Yazd and west of the Kuh-e Sorkh mountain. This key site was code-named 'Desert One', and was located some 490 km (306 miles) south-east of Tehran.

The eight RH-53D Sea Stallions were scheduled to arrive at 'Desert One' some 30 minutes after the main party. These helicopters were minesweeping versions of the HH-53 'Super Jolly Green Giant', and had been chosen because of their payload, range and shipboard capability. It was also felt that minesweeping helicopters would attract less notice from prying Arab eyes than troop-carrying versions. These eight aircraft had been deployed to the British airfield at Diego Garcia, in the Indian Ocean, some weeks earlier, and had been picked up by the USS *Nimitz*, which was at the centre of a Carrier Task Force operating in the Indian Ocean and the Gulf of Oman. The Sea Stallions were to be flown by USMC crews from the *Nimitz* at very low level to 'Desert One', where they would refuel from three EC-130E Hercules flown in from Masirah.

Overall command of the operation was in the hands of Major-General James Vaught, the Commander Joint Task Force, who was located at Wadi Kena airfield in Egypt. The commander of 'Desert One' was Air Force Colonel James Kyle – a last minute change of plan – while Colonel Beckwith assumed command of the rescue forces on the ground. Vaught had a satellite link back to Washington, so that he could talk to the Chairman of the Joint Chiefs of Staff, General David Jones, and to the President. Colonel Beckwith had a similar 'satcom' link to General Vaught.

As 'Desert One' lay near a road (albeit little used), a road watch team was included in the main party flown to the spot. Four Department of Defense agents were also to be positioned in Tehran before the operation to organize, or act as, guides. They were to arrange for six Mercedes-Benz trucks: one agent would take the 12-man driving team of 6 drivers and 6 assistants-cum-interpreters to collect the trucks. The agents would first guide the assault group from a forward rendezvous nearer to Tehran to hides, where they would lie up during the day.

The main party at 'Desert One' was to consist of the 12-man driving team, made up of volunteers; the 12-man road watch team, comprising some Delta men and some Rangers from the 75th Infantry Regiment; the Foreign Ministry assault team, made up of a 12-man Green Beret 'A' Team plus one other man; and the main assault group for the embassy. This group consisted of Delta personnel in three 'elements': 'Red' Element (40 men) was to secure the western end of the embassy compound; 'Blue' Element (also 40 men) the eastern sector of the embassy; while 'White' Element (13 men) was to secure Roosevelt Avenue during the rescue action, and then cover the withdrawal.

Phase One of the rescue was the occupation of 'Desert One'. Phase Two consisted of two concurrent actions: the embassy rescue and the Foreign Ministry rescue. Phase Three was the airlift. The first phase called for the six Hercules aircraft (three MC-130Es as troop carriers, and three EC-130E command and control variants to ferry in fuel for the helicopters) to land at 'Desert One' and wait there for the RH-53D Sea Stallions, which were due to arrive about 30 minutes later. The road watch team would deploy to intercept and detain any passers-by. The refuelled helicopters would load the assault teams plus the driving team and fly north-west towards Tehran to a forward landing zone, where the agents would be waiting. The men would be dropped off, and the Sea Stallions would go on to a helicopter hide some 24 km (15 miles) to the north. The agents would guide men to their lying-up point, and, at sundown, one agent would take the driving team to collect the trucks.

At 20.30, the assault teams would board the Mercedes trucks and begin the drive to Tehran. The rescue itself was timed to start between 23.00 and 24.00. At the embassy, the Elements were to take care of the guards and release the hostages. If possible, they were also to clear a landing zone in the compound by removing the poles which the 'students' had erected, so that the helicopters could come in. If this was not possible, the group with the hostages was to go to a nearby football stadium, where the helicopters would collect them. Simultaneously with this action, the 'Green Berets' were to attack the Foreign Ministry and take the three hostages to a nearby park for helicopter pick-up.

While the actions at the US embassy and the Foreign Ministry were taking place, a company of Rangers was to capture Manzarieh airfield, some 55 km (35 miles) south of Tehran. Several C-141s would then fly in to Manzarieh, with General Vaught on board one of them. The Sea Stallions would fly everyone from Tehran to the recently captured airfield, where they would board the Starlifters, and be flown out. The Rangers would leave last and the helicopters would be destroyed at the airfield.

It was a fiendishly complex plan, but the actual execution of Operation 'Eagle Claw' began quite promisingly. The preliminary moves worked, and the first MC-130E duly landed at 'Desert One' carrying Colonels Beckwith and Kyle, 'Blue' Element of the embassy assault group, and the road watch team. This team immediately took up its positions, and then the problems began. As the road watch team scanned the darkening desert landscape, they observed with horror the headlights of an approaching bus. Stepping into the middle of the dusty desert track, they flagged down the vehicle and put the 45 frightened passengers under guard. A few minutes later, however, two more vehicles drove up from the south. The first was a petrol tanker which was hit by an anti-tank missile and burst into flames; the driver ran off to board the second vehicle, which drove off at high speed.

A dramatic scene thus greeted the remaining C-130s as they turned up to deliver their troops. The third MC-130E and the three EC-130Es remained at 'Desert One' while the first two troop carriers returned to Masirah. The men at 'Desert One' could do nothing but wait for the helicopters to arrive before any changes of plan could be carried out.

The eight Sea Stallions had taken off from USS *Nimitz* at 19.30 local time, as scheduled, but complications soon reared their ugly heads. At about 21.45, Number 6 had to land with an impending 'catastrophic blade failure'; the crew destroyed any sensitive documents, and were picked up by helicopter Number 8. About an hour later, the leading RH-53Ds flew into a dust storm. The gritty particles blinded the pilots of the helicopters, who had to rely on instruments alone, and who breathed sighs of relief as the dust finally cleared and the stars re-emerged. Their relief was short-lived, however, since shortly afterwards they met a second, and worse, storm. The commander of the helicopter force, Major Seiffert, had lost his inertial navigation system earlier and was flying blind. Followed by Number 2 helicopter, he flew back out of the first dust storm and radioed General Vaught, who informed him that the weather over 'Desert One' was clear. The two aircraft took off after about 20 minutes and headed for 'Desert

One' once again. At about the same time, Number 5 had a major electrical failure and lost the use of its instruments. It was forced to return to the *Nimitz*, leaving just six helicopters to carry on with the mission. The operation proper had not yet begun, and already the Americans were down to the bare minimum of helicopters.

The first helicopter to clear the dust storms was Number 3, which used the burning petrol tanker as a beacon to land at 'Desert One', about 50 minutes late. The other five helicopters came in from different directions over the following half-hour. They immediately started to refuel, and the assault group began to board their respective aircraft. By this time, the operation was running 90 minutes behind schedule. Then came the final blow: it was discovered that Number 2 helicopter, which had had a hydraulic failure during the flight, could not be repaired with the facilities available and should therefore be counted out.

The rescue force now had less than the minimum number of helicopters for the operation. Nevertheless, Colonel Kyle radioed General Vaught in Egypt and explained the situation. The General suggested that they might try to carry on with the five aircraft they had, but the decision was eventually taken to call off the operation. It is still not known whether this decision came from Washington, as has often been suggested, or was made at 'Desert One', by the men on the spot. Anyway, there seemed no major problem in 'aborting' the mission.

There was a minor hindrance, however. Helicopter Number 4 needed to top up with fuel for the long flight back to the *Nimitz*, as it had been on the ground longest with its engine running. Only one of the EC-130Es had enough fuel left for it and, to clear a space for refuelling, Number 3 took off and banked to the left, but was unable to keep hovering because of its weight – around 19,500 kg (42,000 lb) – and the height above sea level – some 1500 m (5000 ft). At 02.40 it slid back towards the ground, and crashed into the C-130 tanker. Both aircraft exploded, throwing debris in all directions, and ammunition began to detonate. It was a tragic end to an ill-fated mission. Five USAF personnel in the C-130 and three Marines in the Sea Stallion were killed. Amazingly the 64 Delta men in the Hercules managed to escape from the blazing wreckage, rescuing the Hercules' loadmaster in the process. The decision was then taken to abandon the remaining helicopters and return to Masirah in the three remaining C-130s.

Later, the Iranians staged a tasteless propaganda jamboree. The world was treated to the gruesome sight of Ayatollah Khalkhali gloating over the remains of a dead American serviceman. Khalkhali himself was later killed in a bomb explosion in Tehran. As for the hostages, Algerian intermediaries eventually managed to negotiate their release from Khomeini's Iran.

Although the rescue attempt failed, it was not the fault of the forces on the ground. Some of America's allies have raised questions about the operation, the Israelis saying that, in any helicopter operation of that kind, there should be a 100 per cent reserve of aircraft: double the number necessary should have been tasked to 'Desert One' – that is, 16 RH-53D Sea Stallions. Also, the British 22nd Special Air Service Regiment, who had two observers present at some of the planning for the rescue, was unhappy about parts of the plan.

Nevertheless, the very fact that America tried meant something to the luckless captives. It was also a declaration that America will always try to rescue any of its people held unjustly, if diplomacy fails. There is no doubt that Operation 'Eagle Claw' could have succeeded, like the Koh Tang raid or the Grenada rescue.

GRENADA

As the 12 Rangers floated down through the Grenadan sky towards Point Salines airfield, they watched helplessly as the aircraft from which they had just jumped flew off into the distance, carrying with it their comrades from the 1st Battalion, forced to abandon the remainder of the drop by the fierce anti-aircraft fire from below. The 12 said silent prayers as they drifted downwards, easy prey for the enemy below. By some miracle, they all touched down in one piece, but the Rangers' troubles were not over by a long chalk. They were surrounded by hostile forces, with no knowledge of when reinforcements would reach them, and with the clear realization that, until the airfield had been secured, their jeeps and equipment would have to stay put – far above in the clear blue sky!

This incident was, happily, just a hiccup in the relatively smooth rescue by US forces – with a small eastern Caribbean contingent – of some 600 American medical students from the small island state of Grenada: the biggest, and most successful, combined arms operation mounted by the Americans since the Koh Tang SS *Mayaguez* rescue of May 1975. It was the first major campaign under the direction of the Joint Special Operations Command, and is interesting because it involved elements of nearly all the US élite forces.

Political developments on Grenada, a member of the British Commonwealth, had been causing concern to many people, not least the USA and neighbouring eastern Caribbean countries. Finally, on 19 October 1983, martial law was imposed, with an announcement that 'all citizens are asked to remain at home . . . anyone who violates this curfew will be shot on sight'. The same day, the airport, shops, and news media were closed down, and several government officials – including the Prime Minister, Maurice Bishop – were arrested. These people were then shot by troops of General Austin's New People's Revolutionary Army, an act which prompted the Governor, Sir Paul Scoon, to ask for help from neighbouring Caribbean states and America. Britain was unable to assist materially, although HMS *Antrim* and the Royal Fleet Auxiliary *Pearleaf* joined the US Navy Task Force, which sailed for Grenada from the Colombian port of Cartagena, where they had been paying a goodwill visit. A force of some 300 men, from

While smoke rises from burning buildings in the background, men of the 82nd Airborne Division wait at Point Salines.

Jamaica, Barbados, Dominica, St Kitts-Nevis, Antigua/Barbuda and St Vincent, joined the US force. Although small in number, this contingent was politically very important. American worries about the expansion of Cuban and Warsaw Pact influence in the Caribbean were exacerbated by the prospect of US citizens being held hostage, as had happened in Iran earlier.

Joint Special Operations Command contingency plans were put into operation on the directive of the President, Ronald Reagan, and various units were put on ready-alert. The 1st and 2nd Ranger Battalions (1/75 and 2/75 Infantry Regiment) were on standby from about 23 October, and were deployed to their staging base at Savannah, Georgia, on 24 October. The 23rd Air Force was similarly alerted for transport and fire support duties.

A week before the invasion of Grenada took place, a US Navy Task Force of nine vessels was steaming to the Lebanon to relieve the American forces there. While still in the western Atlantic, it was diverted – probably immediately following the arrival of news of Mr Bishop's murder and Sir Paul Scoon's request in Washington DC on or about 20 or 21 October – to rendezvous with another Task Force of six vessels off Grenada.

The nine-vessel force was commanded by Rear Admiral Joseph Metcalf III, flying his flag in USS *Guam*, a special amphibious assault ship equipped as a helicopter landing platform for CH-46 Sea Knight and CH-53 Sea Stallion aircraft, and refitted in 1971 as a sea control ship. He also had with him the USS *Saipan*, a general-purpose amphibious assault ship specially designed and equipped to mount and support a Marine amphibious landing. Among the USMC personnel with the Task Force was the 22nd Marine

Amphibious Unit (22 MAU), commanded by Lieutenant-Colonel Ray Smith, some 400 men strong, and trained and equipped to secure a beach-head against strong opposition. Among their equipment were M-60 Patton main battle tanks and LVTP-7 Amtracks (armed with 0.50-calibre machine-guns). The largest vessel in the group was USS *Independence*, a multi-purpose aircraft carrier equipped with Vought A-7 Corsair II and Grumman A-6 Intruder attack aircraft, as well as Grumman F-14 Tomcats.

A build-up of supplies and equipment at Barbados' Grantley Adams International Airport began. The airport was also used as a staging point for the invasion of Grenada, and several support aircraft were based there, particularly the AC-130 Spectre gunships of the 16th Special Operations Squadron of 1st Special Operations Wing (23rd Air Force).

Facing the US forces were 784 Cubans (of whom 44 were women and 636 were construction workers), all of whom had been given weapon training in Cuba and were competent shots. Colonel Pedro Tortoló Comas had arrived from Cuba on the day preceding the invasion, and was on hand to control the Cubans at Point Salines Airfield. There were certainly some 43 military personnel among the Cubans: one of them, Captain Sergio Grandales Nolasco – a 49-year-old transport and armoured vehicle expert – was killed in the subsequent fighting.

In addition to the Cubans, there was the 1000-strong Grenadan Regular Army under General Hudson Austin, and an indeterminate number of militia personnel. Vast stocks of ammunition and weapons were later found, as Austin had intended to increase the size of the Grenadan Army to some 10,000. Soviet-made armoured personnel carriers were also in evidence and the US Rangers later destroyed two such BTR-70s (armed with 14.5 mm machine-guns) at Point Salines airfield. As most of the Cubans were concentrated at Point Salines, much of the resistance met by the US forces was put up by the Grenadan regulars, militia, and other local troops.

The plan was for the invasion to begin with a covert operation, in which a USN SEAL team would secure the Governor-General's residence and ensure his safety. Point Salines was to be taken during the hours of darkness by the two battalions of the 75th Infantry Regiment in two waves: an initial parachute drop from MC-130s of the 23rd Air Force, followed by the rest of the regiment and the heavy equipment, which would be landed on the runway. AC-130 Spectre gunships were to give airborne fire support. As the Rangers were dropping in on Point Salines, 22 MAU was to be taken by helicopter to Pearls Airport on the western coast of the island, and launch a vertical assault. Once the airfields were secure, the Rangers were to take the True Blue campus of the St George's University Medical School. Some 5000 men of the 82nd Airborne would then be flown in to Point Salines.

The Marines would take the militia barracks at Sauters, and would then be moved round to Grand Mal Bay, north of St George's, while 82nd Airborne would secure the Grand Anse campus of the Medical School, to the south of the capital. The Americans would then have St George's encircled, and could contemplate moving forward to occupy the town.

In the early hours of Tuesday morning, 25 October, the USN SEALs' detachment came ashore on the west coast of the island, just north of St George's, and quickly moved surreptitiously across the kilometre or so that separated them from Government House, in the north-east part of the town. They had secured the house and made certain that Sir Paul Scoon was safe, when the furore caused by the Rangers' action at Point Salines alerted the defenders, and the SEALs found themselves pinned down at Government House by Grenadan fire. They were kept there until 07.45 the next day, when the Governor-General was evacuated by helicopter to the tactical headquarters of 22 MAU at Queen's Park stadium, and thence to the USS *Guam* for discussions with the Task Force Commander, Admiral Metcalf.

The Marines of 22 MAU were taken by helicopter to Pearls Airport at 05.00 local time on Tuesday, 25 October. They had a brief firefight with the Grenadan regulars operating some Soviet-made anti-aircraft guns, who were eventually overcome, but not before one of the helicopters had been hit.

The contingents from the 1st and 2nd Ranger Battalions of the 75th Infantry Regiment left the staging airfield at Barbados, in the early hours of Tuesday morning, in MC-130E aircraft of 8 Special Operations Squadron (23rd Air Force). The plan was to attack Point Salines airfield in two waves. The 1st Battalion (with a 12-man team of 317 Tactical Airlift Wing to supervise the drop) would jump from 300 m (1000 ft) at 05.30 local time. Once the runway was secured, the 2nd Battalion would be landed with the heavy equipment. The men of the 2nd Battalion would drive off the aircraft in their gun-jeeps and occupy the hills surrounding the airfield.

As the first 'stick' of 12 men went out over the dropping zone, the aircraft came under heavy anti-aircraft fire and the drop plans were aborted. This left the 12 Rangers floating down on their parachutes. The C-130s went round to come in at a lower altitude and put the Rangers out at only 150 m (500 ft) – below the AA gunfire. This new situation was radioed to Lieutenant-Colonel Hagler (CO of 2/75th Infantry Regiment). The first 12 Rangers were by this time on the ground and fighting hard. The runway was obstructed by bulldozers and other obstacles, so that the aircraft could not land. Colonel Hagler decided that the 2nd Battalion would re-rig for a low-level jump and recover their jeeps once they had won the airfield.

The 1st Battalion men jumped at 150 m (500 ft) to rejoin their embattled comrades on the ground. Meanwhile, the aircraft carrying the 2nd Battalion was circling above the airfield at high altitude, while the jeeps were hurriedly unloaded of their equipment. Organized chaos reigned way above the ground as rucksacks crammed with ammunition, mortar rounds, Claymore mines, light anti-armour weapons, water and food were repacked for a combat jump. Parachutes (no reserve – 150 m is too low to do anything about a malfunction of the main parachute, other than pray) were put on, with all the problems of water wings, weapons storage, straps, helmets and so on, in the cramped conditions of the Hercules.

Safely on the ground, soldiers of the 82nd Airborne Division prepare to move out in the direction of Grand Anse.

As the Rangers dropped over the runway, there was a possibility that they would under- or over-jump at either end, or even drift to the ocean side of the field, and land in the water. With their 50 kg (110 lb) packs, this would be extremely hazardous. In fact, one Ranger did hit the water but, keeping his head, he allowed himself to sink to the bottom, where he released his gear. Calmly picking up his rifle and pack, he swam to the beach and waded ashore, none the worse for his experience!

AC-130H Spectre aircraft had been called in to deal with the searchlights and the anti-aircraft artillery. The Rangers took on two BTR-70 armoured personnel carriers, which were equipped with 14.5 mm machine-guns. Using 90 mm recoilless rifles, the Rangers managed to immobilize them, and then called up the Spectres to finish them off.

Ranger snipers killed several Cubans and, in another firefight, a Ranger medical orderly, Pfc Underdonk, killed a couple of Cubans and wounded some others. He then administered combat first aid to his victims, and was subsequently recommended for the Silver Star.

By 07.00 the Rangers were in complete control of the airfield. The Cuban military personnel who had been captured were separated from the other combatants. However, Colonel Tortoló and a few others managed to escape and spent some time looking for refuge in St George's, eventually taking sanctuary in the Soviet embassy. The runway was speedily cleared, and at 07.15 the first C-130 landed, and several Sikorsky UH-60A Black Hawk helicopters were brought in. A rapid build-up of men and equipment from the 82nd Airborne Division began. Eventually, a total of some 5000 personnel from the 82nd was on the island.

The next objective was to bring out the medical students from the True Blue campus, which was at the eastern end of the Point Salines runway. At the time of the landing, there were only a few dozen students on the campus, and the majority of those who had not left the island on one of the charter flights the day before were being accommodated in a dormitory block, a couple of kilometres north-east on the St George's road. In an air assault from Black Hawks, 2nd Battalion Rangers came down behind resisting forces and gave covering fire, while the students were emplaned and evacuated, and were then taken out themselves. The operation had begun at 08.30 and was over within 26 minutes.

During the day, AC-130H Spectres and Vought A-7 Corsair II aircraft from USS *Independence*, flown by US Navy and USMC Air Wing pilots, attacked targets and keypoints on the island. Some Spectre strikes were within only a few metres of US troops! One Ranger fire team was engaged in a firefight at night with a superior force across the road from their position. Their officer called in direct to a Spectre for an air strike and gave the coordinates. When told that the enemy was too close, he replied, 'either you shoot them or else they will shoot us!' The Spectre aircraft fired its Gatling guns into the jungle right next to the fire team's position, killing the enemy.

The Navy and Marine A-7s attacked the barracks at Calvigny, on the east side of the island, and certain targets in and around St George's. Just before midday, they attacked Fort Rupert, overlooking the entrance to St George's harbour, destroying the anti-aircraft guns there and scattering their crews with rockets. Butler House, the Prime Minister's office, was hit a number of times and set on fire. As the continuing air strikes drove the fire brigade away, the building was allowed to burn itself out. There was one tragic case of a mistaken target: Fort Matthew (a mental hospital) was attacked in error, instead of the nearby Fort Frederick, and demolished. At least 30 patients were killed, and many inmates wandered dazedly around St George's until rounded up and handed over to the General Hospital.

Whenever an aircraft flew overhead, the Grenadans would fire at it with any weapon to hand. In the middle of Tuesday afternoon, for example, an American helicopter was shot down on the Tanteen field on the other side of the harbour entrance from Fort Rupert, and the pilot was killed. That day, aircraft also attacked the Sauteurs Militia Base at the northern tip of the island, and 22 MAU later captured the base.

The paratroops of 82nd Airborne moved north from Point Salines to close in on the Grand Anse campus of the university in order to free the students staying there. Just before last light on Wednesday, 26 October, men of 82nd Airborne took the campus in an action preceded by attacks from helicopter gunships and Spectres. The 82nd men guarded the students while resistance at Radio Free Grenada was overcome, then loaded the students on to helicopters bound for Point Salines.

In the early hours of the same morning, 26 October, the Marines had been flown around the island to land at Grand Mal Bay, north of St George's, at 04.00. Their disembarkation point was only a few hundred metres north of the city limits, and Colonel Smith, in charge of 22 MAU, established his tactical headquarters at Queen's Park Stadium. Heavy equipment, including M60 Patton main battle tanks, was brought ashore, and three of these tanks were stationed on the St George's road. At 07.45, 22 MAU received the Governor-General and took over his security from the USN SEALs. The aerial bombardment and the numbers of troops surrounding the capital seemed to convince the resisters within St George's to give up, and the city was secured with little more trouble.

That afternoon, 22 MAU Marines climbed up Morne Jaloux ridge to capture Fort Frederick and the Richmond Hill Prison. At about the same time, 60 Rangers of the 2/75th Infantry Regiment were taken around to the east of the island in a trio of Sikorsky UH-60A Black Hawk helicopters to mop up at Calvigny Barracks.

As the Black Hawks finished the 8 km (5 mile) flight they came under fire from a heavy-calibre machine-gun. The first helicopter had just landed and the Rangers were getting out; the pilot of the second helicopter was killed by the gunfire; his chopper crashed into the first one, and Rangers were spilled out of the wreckage. One man was hit by the spinning rotor blades and died instantly. The opposition's fire was concentrated on the landing zone, and the last Black Hawk made a bad touchdown.

The uninjured Rangers attacked the defenders and provided covering fire for the wounded. Sergeant Stephen Trujillo, who had Special Forces medical training, stayed to treat the injured. Using the SF's advanced paramedical techniques, he treated Lieutenant William Eskridge, who was bleeding heavily from a leg wound, and, although the officer eventually lost a leg, Sergeant Trujillo had saved his life. Trujillo was awarded the Silver Star for his actions in aiding the injured. Eventually the defenders were subdued and rounded up, and the Calvigny Barracks were secure.

Although there was much criticism of the American action in Grenada, the Grenadans themselves were mostly delighted to have been saved from a deteriorating situation. The invasion also gave a boost to flagging American morale following recent events in the Middle East. On the Sunday before the invasion was launched, at 02.27, Washington had received news of the bombing of the US Marines' headquarters in Beirut, with many dead and injured. The Grenadan operation restored confidence after the failure of Operation 'Eagle Claw', and seemed to show that the freeing of the crew of the SS *Mayaguez* was not just a flash in the pan. It was also an operation in which nearly all the US élite forces from the Army, Navy, Marines and Air Force were involved, under the control of the Joint Special Operations Command, and they cooperated well together. This success seems to have been the spark which led to the formation of the Joint Special Operations Agency at the Pentagon on 1 January 1984.

CHAPTER FOUR

THE COMMONWEALTH & SOUTH AFRICA

THE AUSTRALIAN SPECIAL AIR SERVICE REGIMENT • THE CANADIAN MOBILE COMMAND • THE RHODESIAN SPECIAL AIR SERVICE, SELOUS SCOUTS AND GREY'S SCOUTS • SOUTH AFRICAN SPECIAL SERVICES • THE NEW ZEALAND SPECIAL AIR SERVICE

Although it may be old-fashioned to talk about the British Commonwealth, it seemed appropriate to group together the special forces of those countries which have always maintained a special relationship with the 'old country', no matter how far politics and politicians may have strained this relationship in recent years.

In the international sphere, Australia and New Zealand have been far more active than the other three countries considered, their Special Air Service troops being modelled on British lines and being largely British trained following joint experiences in Korea and Malaya. Both countries also contributed forces to the futile war in Vietnam, adding to the knowledge and expertise which their SAS veterans have been able to share with others. Canada has retreated into isolationism under the American umbrella ever since Korea, and her special forces have none of the Australian, British or New Zealand experience of counter-insurgency warfare, apart from the brief affray with Québécois separatists in 1970. Rhodesia, now Zimbabwe, in contrast, has the greatest experience in this type of campaigning, while South Africa is readying itself – while pretending not to – for the inevitable conflict to come.

The Australian Special Air Service Regiment

By the time the Australians began pulling out of their involvement in Vietnam in 1970, the 3rd Special Air Service Squadron had killed more than 500 Vietcong guerrillas for the loss of only one man. Introduced into Vietnam as part of the Australian Task Force reinforcement in 1966, for nearly five years this special jungle-trained unit helped first to secure and then to protect, the whole of the Phuoc Tuy province east of Saigon. In fact, they were so successful that General Westmoreland, overall commander of the Allied forces in Vietnam, requested the assistance of the Australian SAS in setting up special training camps for American soldiers with the aim of providing each American brigade or division with at least one long-range patrol company versed in these effective Australian tactics. What makes this surprising is that fact that the Australian Special Air Service Regiment had only recently been formed, following Australian observation of the triumphs of British SAS and SBS units, alongside whom they fought in Malaya and Indonesia.

Since Gallipoli in 1915, the Australian Army has always had a reputation for toughness and endurance in adversity which is second to none. During World War 2, particularly in the Western Desert and in Italy, the Germans had come to respect the Australian infantryman above all others for his doggedness and tenacity, and these same qualities were ably demonstrated in Korea.

In Malaya, the Australians contributed 3000 men in support of the 50,000 British, Gurkha and Malayan regulars who were fighting the communists. (It is ironic that these same communist guerrillas had originally been armed and trained by the British during World War 2 to fight against the Japanese invaders.) In Malaya, the three reinforced battalions of The Australian Regiment learned a great deal from the tactics of the British special forces. In particular, they learned a lesson which neither the French nor the Americans in Vietnam ever seemed to understand: that in a campaign of this type it is necessary not merely to defeat a guerrilla army in the field, but that in some ways it is even more important to win over the

A Centurion tank and M113 armoured personnel carrier of the Australian Regiment during operations in Vietnam.

hearts and minds of the local civilian populace so that they will refuse to hide or support the terrorists.

This knowledge proved vital in Indonesia when President Soekarno tried to 'liberate' the Dutch East Indies and what had been British North Borneo. Indonesian troops would frequently disguise themselves as innocent farmers or fishermen in their attempts to infiltrate behind the Australian and British lines, and the Allies' persistence in feeding, clothing and educating the local population, in providing them with medical centres, schools, roads and bridges, meant that the inhabitants of the threatened provinces would usually deny the Indonesians shelter at the least, and give them away to Australian or British patrols at the best. Even had Soekarno not been overthrown by a Muslim junta which called off the campaign, it is likely that Allied tactics would, in any case, have provided the same ultimate end to the conflict as in Malaya.

The Australians entered Vietnam reluctantly, and to begin with provided just 30 advisers to help train the Army of the Republic of Vietnam (ARVN) but, by the time they withdrew, the strength of the Australian contingent had grown to over 8000 infantrymen, aircrew and warship crewmen. The original 30 advisers gradually increased in number to 100, and their training activities were stepped up to a point where Australian officers and NCOs would lead South Vietnamese offensive patrols in search-and-destroy operations against the Vietcong.

Four Victoria Crosses

Warrant Officer K. A. Wheatley was just one of four members of the Australian Army Training Team to win the Victoria Cross in Vietnam. Like the rest of the soldiers in the team, which included several other SAS men, Wheatley had been selected from the toughest and most experienced veterans of Korea, Malaya and Indonesia, and was a professional soldier through and through. On 13 November 1965 he was part of a company-sized patrol of Vietnamese Civil Irregulars commanded by Captain F. Fazekas, another Australian adviser. Wheatley was in the right-hand platoon, together with Warrant Officer Swanton, as the patrol marched from the Tra Bong Special Forces camp down the Tra Bong valley. They had not gone far, and were walking across open rice paddies, when Wheatley's platoon came under heavy fire from concealed Vietcong positions. He sent a radio message to Captain Fazekas, whose own platoon in the centre of the company was still forcing its way through the jungle towards the rice fields.

The heavily outnumbered Australians and Vietnamese Irregulars continued to fire back at the unseen enemy in the jungle on the other side of the paddy fields, but then Warrant Officer Swanton was hit and the Irregulars fled. Left on his own, apart from the dying Swanton and one Vietnamese soldier, Dinh Do, Wheatley asked Fazekas to call an air strike on the Vietcong positions; then, abandoning the radio, he picked up Swanton's inert body and began to struggle back towards the safety of the jungle from which the platoon had emerged. Dinh Do urged him to leave Swanton but Wheatley refused, so the Vietnamese Private took to his heels. By this time the Vietcong had emerged from the jungle on the other side of the clearing and were running to encircle Wheatley. Laying Swanton's body on the ground, he primed two hand grenades and stood over his friend, calmly awaiting the enemy. Moments later, Captain Fazekas heard the sound of two explosions. In staying with his dying comrade, Wheatley had deliberately sacrificed himself, and the citation to his Victoria Cross stated: 'His acts of heroism, determination and unflinching courage in the face of the enemy will always stand as examples of the true meaning of valour'.

The Australians' use of small patrols in Vietnam, living off the land for up to a fortnight at a time, paid dividends when compared with the more conventional American tactics. Dropped by helicopter deep behind Vietcong lines, the men of the 3rd Special Air Service Squadron, in particular, created havoc. Although good soldiers when they controlled the situation, the Vietcong were basically lazy, and their discipline became slack when they felt themselves safe from observation. SAS patrols often caught them unawares in their base camps, where they carelessly lit cooking fires and became drunk and rowdy on rice wine and native beer. Sentries were rarely posted, and the Australians were often able to creep silently through the dark jungle to encircle an encampment without being observed. Then they would open up with their Bren guns to send the Vietcong into a state of pandemonium. In the face of such an attack, most of the guerrillas would attempt to flee into the jungle, where many were caught by the patiently waiting SAS men standing motionless behind rubber trees. Then, when the guerrillas had either all been killed or had fled, the SAS could move in to destroy the camp, being careful to watch out for booby traps and the cunningly concealed pits which the Vietcong had dug, their bottoms lined with sharpened stakes smeared with human excrement to cause wounds to fester and septicaemia to set in.

It was a lonely, dangerous and demanding war – both mentally and physically – for the SAS patrols, particularly during the monsoon season, when it was impossible to keep anything dry, when the humidity sapped strength and willpower, and when skin diseases and leeches were prevalent. However, the SAS had a demoralizing effect on the enemy, who were frequently astonished to see a squadron of Phantom or Skyhawk fighter-bombers materializing out of nowhere to blast with rockets and napalm a concealed encampment which the Vietcong troops had thought hidden and inviolate.

The SAS patrols also brought back much vital information on Vietcong dispositions and strengths to assist in the planning of major American offensives, many of which failed even then because, by the time the Americans, with their large numbers of men and noisy tanks and other vehicles, reached their objective, the Vietcong could easily have slipped away into the jungle.

WEAPONS OF THE COMMONWEALTH ÉLITE FORCES

Designation	Type	Calibre	Magazine	Rate of fire	Range	Remarks
L9A1	Browning automatic pistol	9 mm	13 rounds	Single-shot	40 m	
L1A1	Self-loading rifle	7.62 mm	20 or 30 rounds	40 rpm	600 m	The Belgian FN FAL
Parker Hale	Sniper rifle	7.62 mm	Single-shot	Single-shot	1000 m+	Australia only
F1	Sub-machine-gun	9 mm	34 rounds	640 rpm cyclic	100 m	
M3	Browning sub-machine-gun	0.45 in	30 rounds	450 rpm cyclic	100 m	
Uzi	Sub-machine-gun	9 mm	25 or 32 rounds	600 rpm cyclic	100 m	Israeli-made; Australia and South Africa
BXP	Sub-machine-gun	9 mm	22 or 32 rounds	800 rpm cyclic	100 m	South Africa
Galil RAM	Assault rifle	5.56 mm	35 or 50 rounds	650 rpm cyclic	400 m	South Africa only
M16A1	Armalite assault rifle	5.56 mm	20 or 30 rounds	700–950 rpm cyclic	400 m	
L2A3	Sterling sub-machine-gun	9 mm	34 rounds	550 rpm cyclic	200 m	Particularly favoured in Canada
L4A4	Light machine-gun	7.62 mm	30 rounds	500–875 rpm cyclic	800 m	New Zealand and Zimbabwe

The Australian SAS today

Organized and trained in exactly the same way as is the British SAS, in four squadrons, the Australian Special Air Service Regiment is an élite unit which, with Aussie nonchalance, does not regard itself as an élite. Its men are all volunteers from other regiments in the Australian Army, particularly from The Australian Regiment which, although composed of one-third national-service conscripts, maintained the nation's reputation for producing tough soldiers in many operations in Vietnam.

Amphibious and jungle operations obviously form a much greater part of the Australian SAS's training than they do for its British counterparts, because in time of global war it would be committed to ANZUS, the mutual defence pact between Australia, New Zealand and the United States, and the theatre of operations would be the islands of Australasia and the mainland of Malaysia, Indo-China, Korea and China. The men are well experienced and equipped for this role, but they also have other duties in the counter-terrorist task. The Philippines, Japan and Korea are also members of ANZUS, and Australian SAS advisers are on call to all three countries to help cope with hijackings and other terrorist threats.

Designation	Type	Calibre	Magazine	Rate of fire	Range	Remarks
M1919A4	Machine-gun	7.62 mm	250-round belt	400–500 rpm cyclic	1000 m	Canada only
FN MAG	Machine-gun	7.62 mm	100-round belt	600–1000 rpm cyclic	1200 m	New Zealand, Zimbabwe
M60	Machine-gun	7.62 mm	100-round belt	550 rpm cyclic	1000 m	Australia
M2HB	Machine-gun	0.5 in	50-round belt	450–600 rpm cyclic	1500 m	South Africa
2 in mortar	Light mortar	2 in	Single-shot	15 rpm	800 m	New Zealand, Zimbabwe
L16A1	Mortar	81 mm	Single-shot	15 rpm	5800 m	
ENTAC	Anti-tank missile	60 mm	Single-shot	Not applicable	500 m	Australia only; obsolescent
L1A1	Anti-tank missile	66 mm	Single-shot	Not applicable	300 m	Canada only
Carl Gustav	Anti-tank missile	84 mm	Single-shot	4–6 rpm	1100 m	Canada only
Redeye	Anti-aircraft missile	70 mm	Single-shot	Not available	Not available	Australia only
Blowpipe	Anti-aircraft missile	76.2 mm	Single-shot	Not available	3000 m +	Canada only

(Most Commonwealth nations use much the same weapons, but where an entry is applicable only to one country this is indicated in the remarks column.)

In fact, the main role of the whole Australian Army today can largely be seen as one of counter-insurgency. Since 1972, when its strength was reduced from 32,000 men in three divisions, each of five battle groups plus a support group, to the present single division of six infantry battalions, one armoured and two mechanized infantry regiments, four artillery regiments, two signals regiments and other supporting services, the Australian Army has only a minor role to play in a global context.

The Army is organized along British lines, and volunteers, who train at Duntroon or Portsea, Victoria, serve for an initial period of six years. However, as in World Wars 1 and 2, one can be assured that Australian recruiting stations would be full if any major international emergency arose.

The Canadian Mobile Command

Canadian armed forces have not seen action since Korea, when a brigade was committed to help staunch the communist offensive and, particularly since the country opted for unilateral nuclear disarmament, there has been a steady run-down of Canadian military power until, today, the entire Army consists of only 18,000 regulars and 15,000 reservists. This force is extremely stretched, both physically and financially, and is devoted solely to internal defence, with the exception of the 3000 men of the Mechanized Brigade Group Europe based at Baden-Söllingen in Germany. Canada is also committed to the United Nations peace-keeping role, and one air-mobile battalion of the Airborne Regiment, based at Edmonton, Alberta, is on permanent 12-hour standby.

Mobile Command comprises three brigade groups, of which one is airborne, each consisting of two or three infantry battalions plus light armoured and artillery regiments, and support services.

As with all the Canadian forces, the Airborne Regiment is composed of both English- and French-speaking soldiers, and consists of the *1er Commando Aéroporté*, the 2nd Airborne Commando, and the 1st Airborne Battery of 105 mm air-portable guns. Each of the Commandos is of approximately battalion size (600–700 men) and would be taken into action by transport and attack helicopters.

Canadian troops are extremely well trained in mountain and arctic warfare techniques as well as mountain search and rescue operations, and they have acted on several occasions as peace-keeping forces under United Nations auspices in Egypt, the Congo, Kashmir, Cyprus and Lebanon, wearing the UN's blue beret.

The Rhodesian Special Air Service, Selous Scouts and Grey's Scouts

From the time that Ian Smith made his unilateral declaration of independence (UDI) in 1965 and took Rhodesia out of the British Commonwealth, until the creation of the modern state of Zimbabwe in 1979–80, the country suffered from one of the worst internal struggles in history. Black nationalism had been particularly prevalent in southern Africa ever since 1959, when Northern Rhodesia was granted independence as Zambia, and from 1960 black insurgents mounted an escalating campaign of terror against Rhodesian whites which eventually resulted in the country being carved up into a string of armed fortresses. In the early days, the terrorist attacks and incidents were relatively mild, ranging from communist-incited riots in African townships to petrol-bomb attacks on government offices. Although there were also several murders, of both blacks and whites, the Rhodesian police succeeded in containing the incidents until 1965 and UDI.

By this time, the Russian- and Chinese-trained African nationalist guerrillas, armed with Eastern Bloc weapons, were becoming more organized, and Ian Smith's declaration lit the fuse to a powder keg of violence. Terrorists slipped across Rhodesia's borders by night and infiltrated into the black townships on sabotage and murder missions, but their attempts at achieving really spectacular successes, such as blowing up the Kariba power lines or the oil pipeline from Mozambique, were foiled, largely due to the efforts of the Rhodesian Special Air Service Regiment.

Comprising three squadrons, each of 60 white men, and organized and trained along British lines, the Rhodesian SAS played much the same role as does the British SAS in Northern Ireland, particularly in information-gathering, surveillance and the laying of ambushes. In these duties, the SAS was ably helped by the élite Selous Scouts, a mixed force of more than 1000 blacks and whites, and by the smaller force of horsemen in Grey's Scouts. Like so many other military formations in southern Africa, the origins of these two units date back to the Zulu and Boer Wars, and the Selous Scouts in particular were adept at tracking and 'hot pursuit' tactics, chasing and running down terrorists even across the borders into neighbouring African countries. While the Rhodesian SAS was recruited exclusively from white Rhodesian Army units – the élite Rhodesian Light Infantry, for example – the Selous Scouts employed a mixture of blacks and whites from all walks of life, including numerous mercenaries from Europe and North America. They were commanded by Lieutenant-Colonel Ron Reid-Daly who had fought earlier with the British SAS in Malaya. Grey's Scouts never amounted to more than a quarter the strength of the Selous Scouts, some 250–300 men, but they were all first-class horsemen and were mainly employed on border patrol work, riding up and down the barbed wire fences protecting Rhodesia's borders and looking for signs of terrorist intruders.

As the terrorist campaign mounted in intensity, the need for men trained in counter-insurgency work increased, and the Rhodesian Army eventually became the most skilled in the world in this field, with the possible exception of the British Army in Northern Ireland. South Africa sent military assistance in 1968, and for a few months it seemed as though the terrorists had been beaten back outside Rhodesia's borders (a lull which happened to coincide with Ian Smith's referendum on UDI, and which may have contributed to its result). In 1970, however, the intrusions resumed, many whites being killed during an attack on Chisuma police camp, although an attempt to sabotage the main railway line from Salisbury to South Africa was foiled.

By 1973, the terrorists were stepping up their campaign even further, and were now organized in commandos of up to 100 men armed with modern Soviet automatic weapons, rocket launchers, mortars and grenades. Their favourite tactics were hit-and-run assaults on isolated farmhouses and rural police stations, after which they would disappear back into the bush. The Selous Scouts, on permanent alert, could usually be at the scene of an incident within half an hour and, using helicopters as well as skilled native trackers, proved very successful at bringing such groups to ground. Even so, there were casualties.

A typical hit-and-run incident

Robin 'Brown' was a relative newcomer to the Scouts and was out on his first bush training exercise when the terrorists struck. The patrol, under the command of a veteran Sergeant-Major, had been dropped by truck deep in the bush and the men had been marching for seven hours. There had already been one mock attack from two Bren guns which suddenly opened fire, sending the recruits sprawling to the ground before they realized that the Sergeant-Major was still standing, and the men had practised their own marksmanship on targets concealed in the scrub which suddenly sprang up when activated by the Sergeant. By 17.00 the six trainees in the patrol were hot, tired, footsore, thirsty, and barely aware of their surroundings as they stumbled along under the Sergeant's baleful eye. As they sank gratefully to the ground for a brief rest, the men did not realize that they were under observation from a nearby kopje by two blacks, both armed with Kalashnikov AK-47 assault rifles, who had been attracted by the earlier firing. The terrorists could not resist a sitting target and opened fire from a distance of less than 50 m (55 yd). To begin with, Robin did not react, thinking that it was another exercise like the one which had scared him in the morning. Then he noticed that the Sergeant-Major had crumpled to the ground, a red stain spreading across his thin bush shirt. Another man screamed, tried to run, was hit, stumbled, was hit again, and also fell. Robin and the remaining four Scouts fell prone and began firing their 7.62 mm FN rifles at the rocky outcrop. Being untrained, the men soon exhausted the four magazines of ammunition each carried, and would have been easy targets for the terrorists had the two blacks not already slipped away. Too late, a Gazelle helicopter, which had been sent to pick up the patrol, arrived

A Grey's Scout checks his weapons before moving off on patrol.

on the scene. However, it raced off after the terrorists and succeeded in catching and mowing one down with the pintle-mounted machine-gun in the open helicopter door.

In 1975, South Africa withdrew military support from Rhodesia, and the terrorist attacks intensified still further. Black nationalist sympathizers also began infiltrating Rhodesia from Mozambique and Botswana for the first time, and the Smith government set up four regional military commands to try to contain the situation – 'Tangent' on the Botswana front, 'Repulse' with responsibility for the Port Victoria area and the vital rail link to South Africa, 'Thrasher' in the eastern highlands, and 'Hurricane' at Bindura in the north. However, despite these efforts, the rapidly combining groups of freedom fighters were becoming so strong that the border areas of Rhodesia began to resemble World War 1 battlefields, with fortified blockhouses and farms protected by barbed wire fences, minefields, searchlights, electronic warning devices and machine-guns, while civilians wishing to travel more than a few miles did so in convoys under the protection of heavily armed armoured cars and personnel carriers.

The regime could not last, nor did it, despite all the efforts of the élite forces (among which one should really include the paramilitary Police Anti-Terrorist Units, or PATU, formed from volunteers in the British South Africa Police, which operated for weeks at a time in the border areas on intelligence-gathering and infiltration missions), and ultimately the Smith regime had to fall, to be replaced by a black democracy which is still finding its feet.

South African Special Services

Little is said in public about the crack quick-reaction and counter-insurgency forces of South Africa, which today has one of the largest armies in the Western world, comprising some 18,000 regulars and 60,000 national servicemen, plus 130,000 members of the Citizen Force and 110,000 men in the Commandos. (The latter, although today basically a 'home guard', maintain their original Boer names and traditions. There are ten Commandos in all, most bearing famous names such as Wynberg or Tugela, and their role is much the same as that of the UDR in Northern Ireland.)

Because of the country's schizophrenic politics, all white males are subject to conscription, but all blacks and Indians in the armed forces have to be volunteers. Moreover, the units themselves are segregated by the controversial policy of apartheid, blacks and Indians serving in the separately administered Cape Corps. Needless to say, there are not many volunteers for the latter.

The mainstay of South Africa's counter-insurgency forces, many of whose members have direct experience of fighting against terrorists in Rhodesia, are the 1st Parachute Battalion and Tank Squadron, and 1st Special Service Brigade, which are based at Bloemfontein and fall under the Orange Free State Command, plus the Parachute Commando based at

Kroonstat. Since the Sharpeville crisis in 1960, which made the Republican National Party realize for the first time the very real threat from black African nationalism, the South African special forces have been fighting a rearguard action against the inevitable.

Although the government has always claimed to have a vital role to play in the defence of the West by providing a second Gibraltar between the Atlantic and Indian Oceans, thereby keeping open the sea lanes from Europe to Australia and New Zealand, the argument rings hollow when one considers that over two-thirds of South Africa's army is dedicated to preserving internal order rather than to any possible external obligations. Moreover, since 1963 South Africa has been subject to a United Nations arms embargo (made mandatory in 1977 but still flouted by France and other countries). This has restricted progress in the Army's acquisition of modern battlefield weapons, although, since it was established in 1969, the Armaments Development and Production Corporation of South Africa (ARMSCOR) has made great strides in the design and development of armoured vehicles intended for counter-insurgency operations and manufactures under licence many small-arms of European origin.

The New Zealand Special Air Service

Although isolated geographically, New Zealand's tiny standing army of 5500 regulars (supported by 6000 territorials and 1500 reservists) is one of the best-trained, most experienced and most capable of rapid deployment in the world. Like the Australians, New Zealand troops have long been known for their fighting quality, a reputation which was upheld during World War 2 at the battles of El Alamein and Monte Cassino, to name just two of the most significant. Since World War 2, the New Zealand Army has taken an active part in the counter-insurgency campaigns in Malaya, fought bravely in Korea, and even contributed a token force of 550 men to the support of the Australians in Vietnam. Here, the two squadrons of the NZ Special Air Service Battalion proved as adept as their Australian counterparts in dealing with the enemy on his own terms – and small wonder, for New Zealand does not maintain a military academy of her own, so all her officers are trained either at Sandhurst or at Duntroon.

New Zealand abolished conscription in 1973 and since then has severely curtailed her military commitments, although she has maintained a battalion-strength garrison in Singapore under the terms of the 1971 Five Power Defence Arrangement which has been abandoned by both Australia and Britain, and continues to adhere to other defence agreements with Indonesia, New Guinea, Fiji and Tonga. Other than this, New Zealand is still a signatory of SEATO, the South-East Asia Treaty Organization, and contributes troops to United Nations' peace-keeping missions, but is otherwise primarily concerned with the defence of her own long and rugged coastline from infiltration or attack, and with protecting the sealanes which are so vital to her economy.

CHAPTER FIVE

WESTERN EUROPE

FRANCE: THE 2ND PARACHUTE REGIMENT OF THE FOREIGN LEGION • HOLLAND: THE ROYAL NETHERLANDS MARINE COMMANDOS • WEST GERMANY: GSG 9

As the forces of international terrorism flexed their muscles during the 1970s, the governments of France, Holland and West Germany began training military and paramilitary units to counteract this new menace. The Olympic Games murders in Munich in 1972 shocked the world, while the Israelis' success at Entebbe gave inspiration.

The French Foreign Legion has, of course, always been one of the toughest of all fighting forces, and the establishment of parachute units which trained alongside the fledgling British airborne forces during World War 2 produced a new élite within an élite. From Indo-China to Algeria, the men of the *2ᵉ Régiment Etranger Parachutiste* acquired a reputation for courage and skill in adversity second to none, and their training and experience proved invaluable in May 1978, when they parachuted into the little mining town of Kolwezi, in Zaïre, to rescue technicians and their families from a bloodthirsty group of Katangese rebels.

Earlier, in 1975, Dutch Marines had rescued hostages from a train which had been hijacked by South Moluccan extremists, while in 1977 the élite West German commandos of GSG 9 had successfully emulated the Israeli action at Entebbe, freeing the passengers of a hijacked Boeing 737 from Red Army fanatics who were demanding the release of prisoners in a German jail.

What all three countries – as well as Britain – have clearly demonstrated is a determination, which must be maintained, not to give in to terrorism in any way, shape or form. If terrorists know that their demands will not be met, and that the best they can hope for is their own deaths, then they will have to pause for thought.

THE FRENCH FOREIGN LEGION

At about 15.15 on 19 May 1978, in a sweltering bungalow where he had been hiding with his family for the past six days, an Italian mineworker named Rafaello Rubeis thought he heard the sound of heavy aircraft engines. He crept to the window and peered at the western sky, taking care not to show himself to the wandering gunmen who had subjected this little mining town of Kolwezi, in Zaïre's Shaba Province, to a reign of terror ever since they had burst from the bush at dawn on the 13th. The whistling roar in the sky grew louder and, as Rafaello peered at the strip of sky visible at the top of his window, the silhouette of a C-130 Hercules transport aircraft floated slowly into view, only about 200 m (600 ft) above the shanty roofs of the native Old Town. The transport's doors were open, and a long line of green parachutes was blossoming across the sky behind the aircraft. Rafaello snatched up a camera and took a hasty photograph: he wanted to remember this moment, when his life had been handed back to him after he had despaired of ever leaving the town alive.

The gift came by courtesy of the legionnaires of the *2ᵉ Régiment Etranger Parachutiste* (REP) – France's 2nd Foreign Parachute Regiment: one of the crack 'fast-reaction' units of the French Army, and one of the most formidable fighting regiments in the world.

The Legion takes to the air

The French Foreign Legion, swollen by a flood of recruits from a ravaged Europe in the years immediately after World War 2, played a major part in France's war against the Communist Viet Minh in Indo-China between 1946 and 1954. As the conflict grew in intensity, and guerrilla attacks flared all over France's colonies in Vietnam, the 150,000-man Expeditionary Force of French, Arab, and Foreign Legion troops was spread dangerously thin. Most of them were tied down in small garrisons, scattered up and down the network of roads and towns, which inadequately controlled a vast, wild land of jungle, mountain and swamp. In such wars the advantage always lies with the elusive guerrilla bands, who can pick their time and place to fight, and melt away into the bush before the security forces can bring their superior firepower to the threatened sector along the few, easily ambushed roads.

In this kind of fighting mobility is everything; and France, desperately short of troops capable of forming a mobile reserve to take the war into enemy-held country, soon began to pin her hopes on the possibility of 'vertical envelopment' – the paratrooper's unique ability to drop right into a battle without first slogging through swamps, scrambling up mountain ridges or fighting his way along mined and ambushed roads. Although always short of transport aircraft to drop and re-supply the paratroopers, the French command began to build up a precious reserve of airborne troops, to use both as a 'fire brigade' for stamping out sudden Viet Minh initiatives, and as a weapon of sudden attack when enemy refuges in the mountain jungles were identified. In April 1948, the 3rd Foreign Infantry Regiment of the Legion, rich in wartime veterans including a number of former German paras, formed an experimental 'integral parachute company'. Operating with a battalion of French paras, the company proved itself a success. Shortly afterwards, a parachute school was established near the Legion's Algerian headquarters at Sidi-bel-Abbès, and in November 1948 the 1st Foreign Parachute Battalion – *1er Bataillon Etranger Parachutiste* (BEP) – arrived in the Far East. It was soon followed by the 2e BEP. The para company of the *3e Régiment Etranger d'Infanterie* (REI) was absorbed by the 1er BEP, and a third battalion was formed and retained in Algeria, acting as a pool for training the replacements for the two units in Vietnam.

For the next five years, both of the Legion para units were heavily committed to the increasingly savage war in Vietnam. Thanks to Chinese support, the Viet Minh's General Giap was able to build up his forces from scattered guerrilla bands into large and well-equipped units able to face the French in pitched battle. The fighting grew in scope and intensity. Given their special capability and role, it was inevitable that the paras would often be dropped in an attempt to save already disastrous situations: their casualties were commensurately high. Jumping over appallingly rough drop zones in thick forest or on to the tops of precipitous cliffs, against an enemy of unknown but usually far greater strength, with little hope of serious support unless they could fight their way through to a major road, the paras fought like tigers – but paid a heavy price.

In September and October 1950 the French suffered a disastrous defeat on the Cao Bang ridge, which runs along the northern edge of Tonkin immediately south of the Chinese border. The French garrisons were pulled out, and began a retreat along the single road through the jungled cliffs. They were ambushed by the Viet Minh in massive strength – as were their would-be rescuers, pushing up Route Coloniale 4 to meet them. Both columns were virtually annihilated; among several battalions wiped out were the 1er BEP, and Giap captured enough weapons to equip a division.

With the Communist Chinese border now open to them, the Viet Minh enjoyed safe refuge, training camps, and a steady flow of weapons. Soon Giap had a force of some half-a-dozen conventional divisions of about 10,000 men each, with modern small-arms, plentiful machine-guns, mortars, and heavy artillery support. The war moved towards its climax. Some of Giap's early attempts to fight pitched battles were premature, and he suffered costly reverses at the hands of paras, legionnaires, tanks, artillery and French air power; but he learned from his mistakes.

Encouraged by their success at Na San, a fortified camp reinforced, supplied and supported entirely from the air, the French command planted a much more ambitious 'airhead' in the valley of Dien Bien Phu in late 1953. Far behind Viet lines, and surrounded by hills, 11,000 French Union infantry, paras, artillery and tank men in inadequate entrenchments were soon surrounded by 50,000 Viet Minh, backed up by some 200 well-camouflaged artillery pieces and strong anti-aircraft batteries. The trap closed on 13 March 1954, with a shattering artillery barrage. For two months the French garrison clung on, in one of the epic defences of modern warfare. Among the original garrison were the legionnaires of the 1er BEP, and their sister battalion was parachuted into the shrinking perimeter to reinforce them during the battle. By the end of the siege, in early May, the few survivors of the 1er and 2e BEP were fighting in a small, composite battalion. They resisted like heroes, but the cause was hopeless. On 8 May 1954 Dien Bien Phu fell; three months later France had signed a cease-fire, and was pulling out of her Asian colonies.

The agony of Algeria

The mauled survivors returned to the Legion's adopted homeland of Algeria in time to be pitch-forked straight into another bloody guerrilla war. Retitled the 1st and 2nd Foreign Parachute Regiments (*Régiment Etranger Parachutiste*), and brought up to strength with new recruits and transfers from other units, the two green-beret regiments saw almost continuous active operations between 1955 and 1961. They became famous as two of the most effective units of the French mobile reserve – but the 1er REP also became tainted with a reputation for brutal interrogation of suspects, which clung to the whole 10th Parachute Division, after its ruthless crushing of the Algerian liberation ALN terrorist network in Algiers city in 1957.

Parachute drops played no major part in the Algerian War. The airborne units would be inserted into the harsh mountains of the interior, by helicopter or simply by truck, after an ALN unit had been spotted. Then they would take off after the enemy on foot, setting a killing pace despite the scorching heat of summer or the freezing snows of winter, while the French command used air reconnaissance and radio to weave a net around the guerrillas. The Legion paras usually ran their quarry to earth: by the end of the war in 1962 the 2e REP had recorded 4000 enemy killed, for a loss of 598 legionnaires. This impressive combat record made all the more inevitable and tragic the traumatic episode which accompanied the end of the war.

Humiliated in 1940, and defeated despite heroic sacrifices in Vietnam, the French Army had been determined not to lose again in Algeria. And they had not: Algeria was a military victory. The ALN never achieved the formation of large, conventional units in the Viet Minh tradition. The soldiers they trained in camps in Morocco and Tunisia never managed to penetrate the effective French frontier defences in any numbers. The guerrillas were limited, by 1960, to the same furtive raids and dispersed hide-outs in the mountains that had characterized the outbreak of rebellion in 1954. Nevertheless, President de Gaulle knew that France had to go with the tide of history. The time for colonies was past, and the military successes, won with such effort, merely gave him strong bargaining counters in the negotiations over Algerian independence. The pride of the army, the future of the large white settler community, and the lives of the Algerians

WEAPONS OF THE PRINCIPAL EUROPEAN ÉLITE FORCES

Designation	Type	Calibre	Magazine	Rate of fire	Range	Remarks
Automatic pistol	Browning	9 mm	13 rounds	Single-shot	40 m	
Automatic pistol	Walther PP	7.65 mm	8 rounds	Single-shot	40 m	
M3	Browning sub-machine-gun	0.45 in	30 rounds	450 rpm cyclic	100 m	Holland only
Uzi	Sub-machine-gun	9 mm	25 or 32 rounds	600 rpm cyclic	100 m	West Germany and Holland
FAMAS	Individual weapon	5.56 mm	25 rounds	950 rpm cyclic	400 m	France only
MP5	Heckler and Koch sub-machine-gun	9 mm	15 or 30 rounds	800 rpm cyclic	200 m	
G3	Heckler and Koch assault rifle	7.62 mm	20 rounds	500–600 rpm cyclic	400 m	
FR-F1	Sniper rifle	7.5 mm	10 rounds	Single-shot	1000 m+	France only
FN FAL	Self-loading rifle	7.62 mm	20 or 30 rounds	40 rpm	600 m+	
FN MAG	Machine-gun	7.62 mm	250-round belt	600–1000 rpm cyclic	1200 m	
MG3	Machine-gun	7.62 mm	50- or 100-round belt	700–1300 rpm cyclic	1000 m+	Modern equivalent of the wartime MG42 'Spandau'
AA-52	Light machine-gun	7.5 mm	250-round belt	800 rpm cyclic	1000 m	France only
L7A2	Machine-gun	7.62 mm	100-round belt	750–1000 rpm cyclic	1800 m	
L16A1	Mortar	81 mm	Single-shot	15 rpm	5800 m	British-made
Soltan	Mortar	120 mm	Single-shot	10 rpm	6500 m	Israeli-made; France and West Germany
Cobra	Anti-tank missile	100 mm	Single-shot	Not available	Not available	
SS-11	Anti-tank missile	164 mm	Single-shot	Single-shot	3000 m	French-made
Milan	Anti-tank missile	90 mm	Single-shot	3–4 rpm	2000 m	
LRAC-89	Anti-tank missile	89 mm	Single-shot	Not available	400 m	France only
Carl Gustav	Anti-tank missile	120 mm	Single-shot	4–6 rpm	500 m	
TOW	Anti-tank missile	152 mm	Single-shot	Not available	3750 m	

who had stayed loyal to the mother country, must all be sacrificed to extricate France from a position she could not maintain in the long term.

When it became clear, in 1960, that France was going to abandon her colony, the men of the Foreign Legion were faced with an agonizing choice. The corps had been raised in 1831 specifically to fight in Algeria, and had played a major role in the colony's history ever since. Without Algeria where would they go? What would be the justification for their existence? Cheated of what they felt to be their just rewards, some of the finest units in the French army collapsed in mutiny. The 1st Foreign Parachute Regiment, wiped out twice in four years in the service of the Republic, now spearheaded the coup led by four generals in April 1961. It was an almost bloodless episode. The remainder of the army, and the nation, remained loyal to de Gaulle, and on 30 April the 1er REP was disbanded for the last time. A number of former members of this and other Legion units went underground to pursue, in the ranks of the Secret Army Organization, what quickly became a futile career as gangsters.

The Legion reborn

The early 1960s were years of low morale throughout the Legion. Some critics called for its disbandment: they claimed that in the post-colonial world there was no need or place for 'foreign mercenaries' of uncertain loyalty. Gradually, however, a more far-sighted attitude prevailed. France still had colonies, which needed rather more hard-bitten garrisons than conscript national servicemen could provide. She still had a network of defence agreements with former possessions in troubled parts of Africa. The Legion, reduced in size, was posted to new bases in France, Corsica, French Guiana, the Horn of Africa and Polynesia. It was at Camp Raffali, at Calvi in Corsica, that the 2e REP worked tirelessly to fit itself for its new role. France still needed units of full-time professional, long-service soldiers who would accept the toughest training and conditions in preparation for rapid intervention in overseas emergencies. The 2e REP was determined to become trusted and respected once more, as the finest 'fast-reaction' unit in the army.

The regiment transformed itself from a tough but basically conventional parachute infantry unit into an extraordinarily flexible air-commando regiment. Apart from its conventional mission – for which it recruited more selectively, and trained more mercilessly, than any other unit in the army – the 2e REP equipped itself with a wide range of special skills: mountain and arctic warfare, amphibious and 'scuba' operations, night fighting, demolition and sniping, and deep penetration and intelligence-gathering. Using the network of Legion garrisons scattered from South America to the Persian Gulf, the 2e REP honed its techniques in environments ranging from snow-clad peaks to steaming jungle and arid desert. As part of France's 11th Parachute Division, the regiment was given several opportunities to show off its new skills under combat conditions.

In the stricken city of Algiers, a Moslem civilian submits to a search by two grim French soldiers.

In the 1960s and '70s the 2ᵉ REP, in detachments and in full strength, served in the harsh deserts of Chad in support of the government of this ex-colony against various rebel elements. Companies rotated regularly through Djibouti, supporting the permanent garrison provided by the Legion's 13th Half-Brigade in this strategic corner of Africa. In 1982, the unit was sent into Beirut as part of the multi-national force supervising the withdrawal of the PLO guerrillas. But the most famous operation of the past few years was undoubtedly the rescue of the European community trapped in the rebel-held mining town of Kolwezi, Zaïre, in May 1978.

Operation 'Leopard'
There were about 2300 Belgian, French, Italian, Portuguese and other white technicians and their families living in the New Town of Kolwezi in May 1978. During the previous year, an attempt to invade Shaba Province from camps in Angola had been made by the Katangese rebels of the Congolese National Liberation Front – FNLC – who were armed and trained by Cuban instructors. It had been repelled by General Mobutu's Zaïrean army, stiffened by Moroccan and French advisers. Now the FNLC were back, and this time they drove the small garrison out of the town without difficulty.

They seemed to have no strategic plan for advancing further towards the provincial capital, Lubumbashi, and they made no very serious attempts to fortify the town against counter-attack. Their precise strength is unknown, but there were between 1500 and 4000 men armed with modern Soviet and Belgian small-arms, machine-guns, mortars and rocket launchers, and supported by a few captured Zaïrean army AML armoured cars. The FNLC seemed content to settle down to a leisurely, medieval sack of the town. They smashed in the doors of shops and houses, helping themselves to what they wanted. At first under some kind of discipline, they later degenerated into drunken savages. The European quarter was searched repeatedly, though in a random fashion. The first unfortunates to fall prey to the FNLC's impromptu 'courts' and firing parties were those whom they decided were 'Moroccan and French mercenaries': anyone who had an Arab appearance, or a French passport. Later, the violence became an end in itself. Men, women and children, black and white alike, were tortured, raped, murdered and mutilated. The stench of death and the sound of swarming flies haunted the wrecked, empty streets. For days on end, terrified families hid in their barricaded bungalows, helpless to intervene as their neighbours suffered.

The situation in Kolwezi was known: a radio operator at the Gécamines offices had stayed on the air long enough to inform his head office at Kinshasa, the national capital. The Zaïrean Army was obviously incapable of mounting a serious operation. The Belgian government – the logical choice for a rescue mission, since they had intervened before in their former colony to rescue hostages, and since the largest group of whites at Kolwezi were Belgians – was indecisive. It was willing to supply transport, and an escort to bring out refugees – but not to fight. At last, after four days, an appeal from President Mobutu reached Paris, through the offices of the French ambassador and military advisors in Kinshasa. The appeal was accepted, and, early on the morning of 17 May, a warning order reached Lieutenant-Colonel Erulin of the 2ᵉ REP at Calvi. His regiment was placed on six hours' notice of immediate movement.

The sheer speed of the operation was dazzling. There was no time to construct the perfect plan; there was reason to fear that hints of a rescue operation were already reaching the FNLC 'Tigers' over transistor radios, and that they might begin a wholesale massacre (this fear was well founded). The legionnaires would have a rich opportunity to show their skill in obeying the Foreign Legion's unofficial motto: '*Démerdez-vous!*' ('Make do!').

By 20.00 on the night of the 17th, Erulin had somehow managed to gather together the personnel and sub-units of his regiment, which had been dispersed in the normal routine of exercises and courses. All through the night they frantically prepared to fly out; and at 01.30 on the 18th the movement order arrived. By 08.00 that morning, the bulk of the regiment was assembled at Corsica's Solenzara airfield.

During the day, the first echelon – 650 men of the four rifle companies, regimental tactical headquarters, and reconnaissance and mortar platoons – would fly the 6000 km (3750 miles) to Kinshasa in five French DC-8 airliners: an eight-hour flight. The second echelon, with the unit vehicles, had to wait to be flown direct to Lubumbashi on USAF C-141 and C-5 transports. By 23.30 on that stifling night, Erulin and the first of his men were on the ground at Kinshasa, facing their second sleepless night as they struggled to improvise a battalion combat drop with inadequate and unfamiliar facilities in a few hasty hours. The rest of the paras arrived during the night, joining the grim, purposeful chaos on the overcrowded airfield. Kit was hastily off-loaded and repacked, weapons were checked, ammunition was issued, and a minimal briefing was handed round on duplicated slips of paper.

To hot, exhausted, jet-lagged NCOs like Sergent-Chef Paul Fanshawe of the 3rd Company, the preparations heralded a paratrooper's nightmare. A six-year veteran of the US Army and Marine Corps, and eight years a legionnaire, Fanshawe was grimly amused as each new surprise was revealed. Jumping out of an aircraft under tactical conditions is a complex and dangerous business, and familiarity with the aircraft and the equipment is essential. Fanshawe's paras were to be crammed into a C-130 Hercules – a fine machine, but completely strange to all but the few Americans in the ranks. It transpired that only four serviceable C-130s and one C-160 were available; so 80 men had to ride in an aircraft built for 66. To save time, space and weight, the 2e REP had left their own parachutes in Corsica, and were issued at Kinshasa with American T-10 rigs – again, fine pieces of equipment, but incompatible with the jump-bags in which the legionnaires carried their gear on the drop. They would have to hitch rucksacks to their leg-straps as best they could, and tie the rest of their weapons and kit to the harness with cord, tape and fervent prayers. Squad light-machine-gunners could not use the quick-release valises to dangle the 9 kg (20 lb) guns below them before hitting the ground. As Fanshawe watched Legionnaire Misse struggle to strap the AA-52 and 2000 rounds of belted ammo across his chest, he reflected, 'The poor bastard's in for a real experience!'

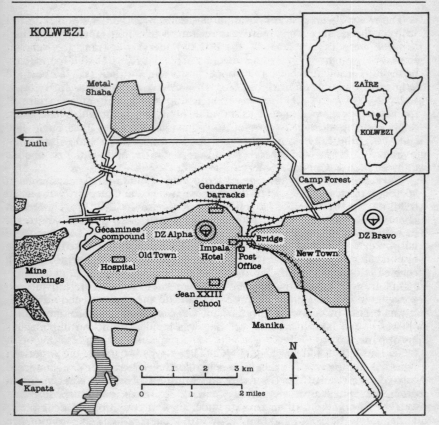

KOLWEZI

Metal-Shaba

Luilu

Camp Forest

Gendarmerie barracks

Gécamines compound

DZ Alpha

Bridge

DZ Bravo

Mine workings

Old Town

Impala Hotel

Post Office

New Town

Hospital

Jean XXIII School

Manika

N

0   1   2   3 km

0   1   2 miles

Kapata

ZAÏRE

KOLWEZI

    The paras would carry minimal kit on the drop: two water canteens, two ration packs, a poncho, a sweater, and ammunition. Even this last was in short supply. Most of the legionnaires would jump over an unprepared and 'hot' drop zone armed with – incredibly – just 40 rounds each for their FSA-49/56 self-loading rifles, or about 200 rounds for the MAT-49 sub-machine-gun, plus perhaps four hand grenades. Their mission briefing told them little more than that they were to get on the ground, deal with any opposition as best they could, rescue civilians wherever they found them, and hold on till further orders. . . They could expect no re-supply for three days. Fanshawe's platoon was less than amused to be told that there would be no medical back-up in the first wave: each man was on his own, with the contents of his small personal first aid pouch.

    The emplaning process the following morning nearly drove Fanshawe crazy with frustration. Zaïrean and French jumpmasters got in each other's

way; awkwardly loaded, red-eyed paras shuffled aboard the strange aircraft
with no idea of the correct loading procedure; and 'sticks' (sections of paras)
became muddled. At last, at about 11.30 on 19 May, the five aircraft
lumbered into the sky. They carried, crowded in their bellies in intense
discomfort, Lieutenant-Colonel Erulin and just 405 of his 1st, 2nd and 3rd
Companies, and a reduced HQ. After four hours of hot, miserable flight,
Sergent-Chef Fanshawe was shouting and shoving his muddled sticks of
paras into some sort of order as they shuffled towards the door. The green
light came on and, to a welcome of machine-gun fire, the 2e REP tumbled
awkwardly into thin air in the regiment's first full combat drop since Dien
Bien Phu. It was just a day and a half since the unit had received its
movement order thousands of miles away in Corsica.

'DZ Alpha' was an expanse of scrub, huge termite-hills and patches of
tall grass at the eastern end of the Old Town. The 1st Company was tasked
with moving south to the Jean XXIII School; the 2nd with marching west
through the town towards the hospital (where it was thought civilians might
be held hostage) and the Gécamines compound (from whose motor pool the
paras hoped to acquire transport). The 3rd Company was to take the Impala
Hotel and Post Office, and set up a blocking position on the bridge leading
across the railway towards the New Town.

Not surprisingly, the drop was badly scattered: ten paras were so
thoroughly lost that they did not rejoin their comrades until the next day.
Sergent-Chef Fanshawe hit the ground a kilometre off course, only 100 m
(110 yd) from his objective – the railway overpass. Quickly releasing his
harness, he dashed for the bridge. He could see many parachutes hung up in
the tall bush, but, thanks to the 90 sq m (108 sq yd) area of the big American
canopies, there turned out to be surprisingly few injuries – even Misse and
his AA-52, who hit the ground particularly hard, was only shaken. Even
more surprising was the lack of organized opposition. Apart from those first
bursts of firing, the drop zone was almost eerily quiet.

It was later discovered that the FNLC had indeed got wind of the
forthcoming rescue, and many of them had fled for the Angolan border.
Plenty remained, however, scattered all over the Old and New Towns in
hidden positions, waiting to fight it out. The companies assembled as fast as
possible, heading off towards their objectives without waiting for stragglers,
as they were terribly aware of the need for speed if a massacre of hostages
was to be prevented.

Just south of the railway overpass to the New Town, Fanshawe managed
to assemble all but six of his 2nd Platoon, and established a blocking
position. He was agonizingly short of support weapons, and faced the
possibility of a major attack with only two light machine-guns, nine rifle
grenades, and one LRAC anti-tank launcher with just two rounds. He had
not been in position long when three captured AML armoured cars charged
out of the New Town on to the approach to the overpass. At the last minute,
the leading AML was knocked out cleanly, only 50 m (55 yd) from the 2nd

Platoon positions, with one of the precious rockets. After firing several rounds of 90 mm and 60 mm shells from their cannon, the other two armoured cars retreated in a hail of small-arms fire. The bridge was not attacked again before nightfall, but heavy firing could be heard all around.

The 1st and 2nd Companies were advancing through a maze of alleys, shanties and patches of scrub in a hectic, confused running fight. They came under constant harassing fire, and dealt with each position as they met it, fast and hard; but they could build up no picture of the overall situation against such a dispersed enemy. As they pushed on they saw dreadful sights in the streets and the wrecked buildings. The 'Tigers' had been as brutal in their treatment of the native inhabitants as of the whites. The first of the Europeans were now showing themselves, often running dazedly into the middle of firefights in their confused delight at seeing white soldiers. Erulin's HQ team tried to keep a tally of them by radio, and assembled several hundred of them in the Jean XXIII School when it was secured that evening.

Shortly before nightfall, the transport aircraft reappeared overhead with the second wave of the 2ᵉ REP. Erulin 'waved them off' to Lubumbashi, however, with orders to return at first light. His three companies had secured all the main objectives for the day, and he did not want disoriented troopers falling all over the drop zone in the dark, and shooting at each other in their confusion.

The temperature fell quickly. Huddled in their ponchos in hastily dug rifle pits, the paras sat out the night of 19/20 May – their third without sleep – wherever darkness found them. Swallowing dexedrine tablets from their first aid pouches, they tried to keep alert. There was heavy gunfire all over Kolwezi throughout the night, as prowling units of the FNLC ran into Legion positions without warning. At about 22.00 one group made another attempt on Fanshawe's bridge-block, led – rather strangely – by an FNLC Major in a Volkswagen 'Beetle'! After a brisk exchange of automatic and rifle fire, and some rocket-propelled grenades from the FNLC, the attack was beaten off. (The VW was shot to pieces by the two AA-52s, enabling Fanshawe to examine the Major's papers.) Later, Fanshawe heard that a larger enemy unit and an AML armoured car had been prowling his area, but they did not attack.

At first light on the 20th the second wave dropped: the mortars, reconnaissance platoon and remaining HQ element on 'DZ Alpha', and the 4th Company on 'DZ Bravo', east of the New Town. In not much more than an hour they had combed right through the New Town, silencing all resistance and releasing the European inhabitants from their long ordeal. Meanwhile, the 1st Company finally cleaned up the southern area of the Old Town, and the 2nd mopped up the western area. The reconnaissance platoon moved north, clearing Camp Forrest and the old Gendarmerie barracks, and part of the 3rd Company pushed south into the labyrinth of the Manika housing estate. The HQ was established at the Impala Hotel.

From here, Erulin was able to begin organizing the evacuation of the Europeans from the airstrip some way outside the town, where Belgian troops and various medical teams had now landed.

Some of the clashes on the 20th had been heavy. Sergent-Chef Daniel of the 4th Company was killed during the clearing of the Metal-Shaba estate that afternoon, and other paras were wounded. The 4th was quickly supported by the 2nd, the mortars and the reconnaissance platoon, and some 80 rebels were killed. Here, as all over Kolwezi, large numbers of weapons and explosives were found, including two recoilless rifles, heavy bazooka-type cannon. Many legionnaires, short of ammunition for their FSA-49/56 rifles, helped themselves to FN/FALs, Russian AK-47 assault rifles, and American M-16 Armalites from the rebel booty.

The night of the 20th was disturbed only by sporadic sniping, and some paras at last managed to have a few hours' sleep. Ambush positions secured all routes into the cleared area, and the men lying awake on guard had plenty to think about. Hideous sights encountered in the New Town had filled them all with a grim rage. In a single charnel-house room in block P2, no less than 38 men, women and children had been found heaped in a pile. Nevertheless, a large number of Europeans had been saved, some after miraculous escapes. The Pansalfin family had emerged from a tiny hiding place in the cavity between their house's double walls. One woman had been found in the hospital, with her limbs riddled with bullets, having lain for nearly 12 hours, holding her dead baby, under the bodies of her neighbours.

The operation was by no means over. For another week, using requisitioned civilian lorries, and their own jeeps and trucks which arrived after driving from Lubumbashi on the 21st, the 2ᵉ REP spread out on wide-ranging patrols, covering more than a 300 km (190 mile) radius. On the 21st there was fighting during the clearing of Kapata to the south-west, and casualties were taken during a fierce clash near Luilu, where several searches were carried out during the period 24–28 May. On that day most of the regiment finally pulled out and drove to Lubumbashi, some of them having received no rations since the first drop.

By 4 June the 2ᵉ REP was back in Corsica. They had saved more than 2000 lives; killed more than 250 rebels, and captured 163; and accounted for two armoured cars, four recoilless cannon, 15 mortars, 21 rocket launchers, 10 machine-guns, 38 sub-machine-guns, and 216 rifles. They had lost 5 legionnaires, and 25 had been wounded.

The 2ᵉ REP today
The Legion, in these days of high unemployment, can turn away all but the best would-be recruits. And of those who survive the extremely punishing basic training, and who apply for transfer to the élite parachute regiment, an even more testing ordeal awaits. There is fierce competition to serve in the 2ᵉ REP, the most famous of the Legion's nine regiments, and the paras can afford to be highly selective.

Today, the regiment has about 1300 officers and men divided into six companies: Command and Services; Reconnaissance and Support; and four numbered rifle companies. Each company is trained to fight as a conventional parachute infantry company within the battalion combat mission. In addition, each has a particular specialist role for which it is highly trained, and maintains a cadre of experts. There is considerable cross-training between these specialities. The 1st Company concentrates on anti-tank, night-fighting and urban fighting techniques. The 2nd specializes in mountain and arctic warfare, and general obstacle-crossing. The 3rd is the amphibious warfare company, and the 4th specializes in sniping, demolition and sabotage.

The Command and Services Company provides HQ, signals, repair, medical, and other general facilities. The Recce and Support Company – 237 men, with 77 vehicles – has a reconnaissance platoon, two platoons of Milan anti-tank missiles with eight launchers each, a platoon of 20 mm electrically operated anti-aircraft cannon, a mortar platoon with eight 81 mm and four 120 mm tubes, and the 'pathfinder' platoon. The last named is intensively trained in a wide range of skills: high-altitude jumps with steerable 'ram-air' canopies which allow a long horizontal approach to a target; concealment and intelligence-gathering behind enemy lines; and such special tasks as hostage rescue.

The recruit who gains the coveted grenade-and-dragon badge of the 2ᵉ REP has a better chance than any other legionnaire of seeing action during his five-year enlistment. He is certain of travelling widely, and of carrying out exercises under tactical conditions in jungle, mountains and desert, often with foreign armies. He will earn at least a third more than his earth-bound comrades. And he will have the satisfaction, ever afterwards, of having proved himself in the company of some of the most skilled and dangerous soldiers on earth.

THE ROYAL NETHERLANDS MARINE COMMANDOS

Holland very nearly had a 'first', which would have gone down in history alongside the Entebbe and Mogadishu rescues, when South Moluccan extremists hijacked an express train at Beilen, near Assen, on the main line from Groningen to Zwolle, on Tuesday, 2 December 1975. The South Moluccan cause is one which few people in the outside world had heard of prior to this date, and goes back to the granting of Indonesian independence in 1950. The Moluccan inhabitants of the region, who had fought fiercely for the Dutch against the Japanese invaders during World War 2, had also resisted the independence movement, and feared reprisals under the new regime. As a result, some 15,000 of them emigrated to Holland after being given a guarantee that the Dutch government would negotiate, on their behalf, with the new Indonesian rulers for the establishment of a separate, and independent republic of South Molucca. Many of these *émigrés* were given temporary accommodation in former Nazi concentration camps, which cannot have inspired confidence, and, by 1975, a quarter of a century after the Dutch government had first made its promise to them, the younger members of the community had run out of patience.

From 1970 onwards, South Moluccan extremists had been causing the Dutch government concern through such activities as raids with petrol bombs on the Indonesian embassy in the Hague, but, in 1975, members of

Front-page headlines as the South Moluccan hijackers open fire on their hostages.

the youth movement within the Moluccan government-in-exile decided upon even more drastic measures. Six men boarded the express train at Groningen at 09.33 on 2 December, with a sub-machine-gun and automatic pistols wrapped up as a Christmas parcel. They stopped the train at Beilen, shooting the 30-year-old driver, Hans Braam, and herded the passengers into one carriage. Another man who tried to escape was also shot.

Dutch marines, a 25-strong squad trained in counter-terrorist techniques alongside the SAS, were flown in by helicopter to assess the situation and take advantage of any opportunity which arose, but the wide train windows offered the terrorists an excellent view of events outside, while they themselves were concealed from the marines by the crush of 80 passengers.

The flat countryside provided little cover for the marines, although there was one waterlogged ditch which would have given an approach up to 45 m (50 yd) from the train, but the terrorists appeared alert and a frontal approach was ruled out. Instead, the bright-yellow train, standing in the middle of the bleak farmland, was eventually surrounded by an 'overkill' force of some 1000 Dutch policemen, soldiers and marines, including 60 highly skilled snipers.

Over the next 13 days the Moluccans continued to reiterate their demands for the Dutch government to give them a fair hearing on international radio and television, and released a large number of hostages in small groups as a goodwill gesture in return for the food and warm clothing with which they were supplied. During this period, older and saner members of the Moluccan government-in-exile continued to try to act as mediators, even though they had been fired upon at their first attempt. For once, psychological tactics worked. The increasingly cold weather, coupled with the Dutch government's refusal to cooperate in any way with the terrorists' demands and the constant threat of the marines and snipers only metres away from the marooned train, finally broke the hijackers' will, and they released the remaining 25 hostages, surrendering themselves to police custody, on Sunday, 14 December.

Holland and NATO

The Netherlands, having been overrun by the Nazis in 1940, is one of the most active member nations of NATO, since it has no wish to repeat such an experience under the Russian jackboot. Despite the small size of the country, and the extreme anti-militaristic and anti-authoritarian attitude of Dutch youth which made the country such a haven for American deserters and draft-evaders during the Vietnam conflict, its army is one of the best trained, equipped and motivated in Europe, with no fewer than three divisions committed to the northern flank of NATO (ie, Norway). The Dutch Army consists nominally of 28,500 men, of whom 60 per cent are regulars and the balance conscripts called up for the mandatory 12 months' service. Dutch marines – *Korps Commandetroepen* – are as fit and well trained as the British commandos (despite their beards and long hair), and share in joint mountain and arctic warfare exercises in Norway every spring. Armed with a mixture of American, British, German and Israeli equipment, they are a formidable fighting force.

Norway

Although a founder-member of NATO, Norway has an even smaller army than that of Holland, with only some 2500–3000 regulars. The balance of the 20,000-strong force comprises conscripts between the ages of 20 and 45, who serve for a year before becoming part of the reserve. However, the reserve is 120,000-strong and, like the Dutch, the Norwegian people remember the Nazis too well to welcome being overrun by the Soviet Union. As a result they have a very firm defence policy and welcome the British, Dutch and others who come to practise mountain and arctic warfare techniques in Norway, but they have no élite troops of their own committed to offensive operations.

WEST GERMANY'S GSG 9

The atmosphere was euphoric on the modern, brightly lit concourse of Frankfurt Airport on the afternoon of Tuesday, 18 October 1977. Sipping a drink in the cocktail lounge above the departure area, while waiting for my own flight to Heathrow to be called, I watched with other outward-bound passengers as the Lufthansa Boeing 737 taxied slowly up to the terminal, surrounded by a bevy of official cars and airport vehicles. Landing steps were brought up to the exit hatches, and moments later people began to emerge. One little boy was carried down the steps by an airline official. All around me, people were smiling, laughing and talking animatedly. It certainly made a great contrast to the previous days of tension.

Five days earlier, on Thursday, 13 October, the Boeing 737 had lifted off from the holiday resort of Palma, Majorca, with 86 passengers and a crew of 5, headed for Frankfurt. Unknown to anyone at the time, two men and two women aboard the aircraft were carrying small-arms and plastic explosive. Shortly after take-off, the terrorists broke into the flight deck and threatened the pilot, Captain Jürgen Schumann, and co-pilot Jürgen Vietor, with a Colt revolver and a 9 mm automatic pistol. The two men were ordered to fly the Boeing to Rome, while the hijackers made their demands to the West German government for the release of 11 members of the notorious Baader-Meinhof gang, including Andreas Baader himself, from the top-security Stammheim prison. The hijackers, later identified as members of the notorious Red Army faction, which has activists in practically every country in the world, also demanded a ransom of £9 million.

Aftermath of Munich
The West German government's attitude towards terrorists had hardened considerably since the murder of Israeli athletes by Palestinian gunmen in Munich in 1972, and it had established a special commando unit of 60 men, under the command of Ulrich Wegener, to deal with any similar outrages. Known as Gremzschutzgruppe 9, it was drawn from volunteers in the German police, army and frontier guards, and was trained in counter-hijacking and other tactics by advisors from both Britain's Special Air Service Regiment and the Israeli secret service. However, Chancellor Helmut Schmidt's government was in political difficulties, and to begin with it seemed likely that Germany would take the 'soft' rather than the 'hard' option by acceding to the hijackers' demands. In particular, left-wing movements in West Germany were incensed at the government's proposals to limit the rights of lawyers defending terrorists and to reintroduce the death penalty, so that many observers thought that Chancellor Schmidt would follow the same course as he had in 1975, when five members of the Baader-Meinhof gang had been released from prison following the kidnapping of Berlin's Mayor-elect, Peter Lorenz.

However, Schmidt was well aware what that had led to: the released terrorists took over the German Embassy in Stockholm in April 1976, capturing 12 hostages and demanding the release of all convicted Baader-Meinhof personnel in German jails. When Chancellor Schmidt refused to give in, the terrorists exploded a bomb inside the embassy, which caught fire. Armed Swedish police stormed the building, killing two of the terrorists and capturing the others, but not before the West German military attaché, Andreas von Mirbach, had been killed.

As the hijacked Boeing refuelled at Rome, Chancellor Schmidt was in urgent consultation not only with his own cabinet but also with other Western European government leaders, including Prime Minister James Callaghan in Britain and President Giscard d'Estaing in France. It had been known for some time that one of the headquarters of international terrorism was in Algiers, where members of the Japanese Red Army had hijacked a Japan Airlines aircraft at the beginning of October 1977 and had blackmailed the Tokyo government into freeing terrorist prisoners in Japanese prisons. Chancellor Schmidt was therefore calling for united pressure on Algeria's dictator, Colonel Boumédienne, in order to persuade him to deny a home to the terrorists.

Meanwhile, the hijacked Lufthansa jet was eastward-bound across the Mediterranean towards its next refuelling stop in Cyprus. From there it flew to Bahrain where it remained overnight, surrounded by police and military vehicles carefully concealed from the hijackers' vision. As the pressure mounted, newspapers around the world were questioning whether anyone had the right to gamble with 86 lives, and left-wing groups began agitating for the Bonn government to give in to the terrorists' demands. Behind the scenes, however, GSG 9 was preparing its equipment – Heckler and Koch sub-machine-guns, 9 mm automatic pistols and plastic explosive – in case it became necessary to blow open the doors of the airliner. A seating plan of the Boeing 737 was obtained from Lufthansa, and various methods of assaulting the aircraft were discussed. Two British SAS officers from Hereford flew out to West Germany to give the benefit of their own expertise and to issue the German commandos with a quantity of their special concussion grenades, which shock and immobilize without killing. However, no final plans could be laid until it was known where the airliner would finally come to rest.

On to Dubai

From Bahrain it flew on Friday to Dubai, where the Defence Minister of the United Arab Emirates, Sheik Mohamed bin Raschid, installed himself in the control tower to handle negotiations. He was joined by the West German ambassador, Dr Hans Neumann, and for hours they tried to talk the terrorists into surrender, promising safe conduct if they would only give up their impossible demands. Periodically during the day, one or other of the hijackers would come to the forward door of the aircraft to throw out rubbish or collect food, while the white-shirted leader, Harda Mahmoud, a Palestinian, could frequently be seen in the aircraft's cockpit by the troops, armed with light machine-guns, who ringed the Boeing.

At 14.15 Mahmoud called the control tower and shouted, 'We gave the German government 60 hours of ultimatum to release our prisoners. Nothing has happened. There is no response. We hold the German government responsible for what happens to the passengers. We hold Helmut Schmidt responsible. Our deadline is 12 GMT [1 hour 20 minutes later]. It will not be a second more.'

The German ambassador tried to placate the terrorists by telling them that a Minister of State was on his way from Bonn, but this only enraged Mahmoud even more. 'There is no more time. We are going to our second destination. We are not going to wait a second after our deadline.'

Sheik Mohamed asked Mahmoud what the hijackers' next destination was to be and was told Masirah, a former RAF base on an island off the coast of Oman. Meanwhile, the aircraft's captain, Jürgen Schumann, had been talking to the air traffic controller in the tower at Dubai and had managed to pass over information on the number of hijackers and how they were armed by means of code phrases inserted into the technical conversation about the aircraft's status. Now he asked, 'Headings for Masirah, please', and at 15.19 – 41 minutes before the expiry of the terrorists' deadline – the fully refuelled Boeing took off into the heat haze. However, instead of proceeding to Masirah, it turned west towards Sallala, the provincial capital of Dhofar in Oman, and circled for a while before being refused permission to land. Thwarted, the hijackers directed Captain Schumann to fly on to South Yemen (formerly Aden), where the aircraft landed again at 18.15 local time. The landing was not a good one and the aircraft touched down very violently, damaging its undercarriage. It is possible that Captain Schumann did this deliberately, in an attempt to 'ground' the plane, but this will never be known for certain.

Now the drama began to move into its final phase. Captain Schumann was allowed to leave the aircraft to inspect the undercarriage, and made a run for freedom. He actually reached the control tower, where he had obviously hoped to give Yemeni officials further information about the disposition of the terrorists and, in particular, to tell them how the plastic explosives had been placed. Mahmoud screamed over the radio, saying that he would blow the aircraft up immediately if the pilot was not returned.

Back aboard the aircraft, Captain Schumann was ordered to take off again. To begin with he objected, saying that the undercarriage was unsafe, but Mahmoud insisted. Then, as the plane rose into the sky, Mahmoud told co-pilot Jürgen Vietor to take the controls and Captain Schumann was man-handled back into the passenger cabin. He was forced to his knees in the aisle while the terrorist leader screamed at him to admit his guilt. A moment later he was shot in the back of the head in front of the shocked and terrified passengers, who included seven children.

The end of the road

The aircraft flew on towards its next destination, Mogadishu, in Somalia. On the ground, nobody knew what had happened in the aircraft, but the West German commando team was already on a Boeing 707, having flown from Frankfurt to Crete while the hijacked 737 was at Dubai. They had wanted to storm the aircraft there, but were thwarted by Sheik Mohamed's insistence that Dubai troops should participate in the assault. This would have proved fatal, for they were completely untrained in the tactics and techniques needed for carrying out such an operation with minimal risk to the hostages.

As the Boeing landed at Mogadishu, the terrorists opened one of its doors and Captain Schumann's body was thrown callously on to the runway. Chancellor Schmidt, and the GSG 9 commandos, knew that time was running out. If the terrorists were prepared to kill one hostage, they were obviously prepared to kill more. Thus, as the hijacked aircraft rested on the runway at Mogadishu in the short tropical dusk, the commandos' 707 began winging its way eastwards from Crete. Inside the aircraft, the commandos checked their weapons and applied black grease-paint to their faces, while Chancellor Schmidt conferred over the hot line with President Barre of Somalia. The Somali government was fully in agreement with the rescue attempt and made no objection as the commando 707 landed in the darkness at Mogadishu, its engines throttled back to reduce noise and all its lights extinguished.

The commandos jumped from the plane and, following their carefully rehearsed schedule, approached the hijacked Boeing from the rear, where there was least chance of their being spotted by the terrorists in the cockpit. Moving silently with rubber-soled boots, grenades primed and their sub-machine-gun safety catches off, the commandos assembled underneath the aircraft beside the emergency release points which would jettison the aircraft's doors, even if they had been locked from the inside. Two men beside each door held light aluminium scaling ladders ready.

At a pre-arranged moment, all the doors were blown, the ladders were slapped into place and the first commandos stormed into the plane. It all happened so quickly that the passengers barely had time to react. One woman said later: 'I didn't hear a thing. Then somebody fell on top of us, covering us with his body – and all we heard was "Heads down, don't be scared".'

Another man said, 'We really did not know what was going on. Suddenly there were explosions [as the commandos threw their grenades] and men came pouring into the plane shouting "Hinlegen! Hinlegen!" ["Lie down!"] as the shooting began.'

It was all over in a matter of seconds. Blood from the hijackers' bullet-riddled bodies seeped into the airliner's carpet as the commandos gently led the relieved passengers to the waiting ladders. First out of the aircraft was one of the three air hostesses, who had received a minor wound in the leg during the shooting. None of the other passengers was hurt, but they were all suffering from the tension and deprivations of the past few days, and another Boeing carrying a special team of doctors and nurses was already *en route* to Mogadishu to care for them. Chancellor Schmidt's brave gamble had paid off.

In a bizarre postscript to the Mogadishu rescue, the three leaders of the Baader-Meinhof gang – Andreas Baader, his mistress, Gudrun Ensslin, and Jan Carl Raspe – committed suicide. The two men shot themselves, which caused the West German police to tighten security in Stammheim prison, and Ensslin hanged herself from the barred window of her cell. A fourth terrorist, Irmgard Moller, tried to stab herself to death with a breadknife but later recovered in hospital to face the charge of bombing the American embassy in Heidelberg, five years earlier.

For Ulrich Wegener and his commandos there was the sense of satisfaction in a job well done, and for other terrorists around the world there was a clear warning that the élite GSG 9 – successors to Otto Skorzeny's famous wartime SS commandos who had rescued Mussolini from his mountain-top prison at Gran Sasso in Italy – is fit and ready to tackle any similar situation in the future.

Training and recruitment

Although recruited from a variety of different sources, GSG 9 is basically a product of the *Bundesgrenzschutz* (BGS, or Federal Border Guard), which was formed in 1950. Equipped with armoured cars and personnel carriers, it is a paramilitary force whose principal role is that of safeguarding a 30 km (19 mile) border against intrusion from the east, and it is well trained in surveillance and detection techniques. The whole BGS comprises some 20,000 men organized in five commands, each of which controls *Gruppen* (Groups) of regimental size organized in two or three battalions.

When the Federal Republic of Germany became a member of NATO, a large number of BGS personnel transferred to form the nucleus of today's 9th *Luftlandedivision* (air-landing division), based in Bruchsal, and the 8th *Gebirgsdivision* (mountain division), based in Garmisch-Partenkirchen; subsequent volunteers for GSG 9 are thus well-versed in either (or both) airborne or mountain and arctic warfare techniques where the training parallels that of British and Dutch paras and commandos. GSG 9 volunteers also undergo specialist indoctrination and courses in military technology at Darmstadt, languages and psychological warfare at Euskirchen, and intelligence at Bad Ems. Their training thus follows the British SAS pattern which inspired it.

CHAPTER SIX

ISRAEL

TANK, AIRBORNE AND MOUNTAIN FORCES

Born in war, the state of Israel has fought a major war once every decade since it came into existence, and has been continuously involved in counter-insurgency operations against the Palestinian guerrillas who also claim the country as their own. This has meant that every member of the population, male and female, has had to serve as a soldier, with the result that the Israeli Army, *Zahal*, has become the most finely honed and efficient fighting machine in the world.

Israel is surrounded by potential enemies, with the exception of Egypt – which finally recognized the country's existence under the inspired leadership of the late President Anwar Sadat – and, since 1983, Lebanon. Nor are Israel's enemies insignificant: Saudi Arabia, Iraq, Syria, Jordan and Libya all possess excellent armies with modern equipment and vastly outnumber *Zahal*. The reason Israel has not been crushed so far is mainly the superior quality of the men and women who are prepared to lay down their lives to preserve a dream which finally came true in 1948, after centuries of Jewish wandering and persecution, although rivalries between the Arab states opposed to them, and super-power intervention, have also played a part.

However, before examining Israel's achievements in conventional warfare in more detail, there is one accomplishment which, in the eyes of many people, exemplifies the spirit, determination, military expertise and imagination of *Zahal*.

The most daring raid of all

It was one minute past midnight, local time, at Entebbe Airport, a 50-minute drive from Kampala, the capital of Uganda. Inside the new airport control tower, traffic controllers Badrew Muhindi, Tobias Rwengeme and Lawrence Mawenda were feeling increasingly confused. Only moments earlier an African Airways Boeing 707 *en route* from

Nairobi, Kenya, had mysteriously disappeared from the operators' radar screens. Now, suddenly, they were being called up by Israeli Flight 166, which was only three minutes from touchdown. The flight was not unexpected, merely unannounced and far earlier than anyone had predicted. However, as they peered through the green-tinted glass of the control tower windows, the three men were astonished to see not one, but *two* Lockheed C-130 Hercules transports, both in military camouflage, drop on to the main runway of the airport. Moreover, the telephones seemed to be out of order and the controllers could obtain no advice from Kampala.

Out of their sight, behind a rise in the ground, Ugandan soldiers were equally surprised to see a third Hercules touch down. Rapidly reversing propeller pitch to slow down, the huge aircraft taxied towards the old control tower where 104 men, women and children had been incarcerated for the past few days. As the aircraft came to a halt, its rear loading ramp dropped and a Land Rover emerged, closely followed by a black Mercedes-Benz 220 with curtains drawn around the passenger compartment, and a second Land Rover. Although this was totally unexpected, the Ugandan soldiers were used to the unpredictable behaviour of their President, Idi Amin, and in recent days had become accustomed to his visits to the old control tower.

Once off the aircraft's ramp, the small convoy drove at a smart pace towards the front of the control tower and old terminal building, watched by men armed with machine-guns on the roof as well as by two startled Germans, Wilfred Boese and Gabrielle Tiedemann. As the soldiers on the brightly lit tarmac snapped to attention, thinking that their President had returned unannounced from the Organization for African Unity conference in Mauritius, Boese darted back into the building.

The cars slowed as they approached the terminal, and suddenly one of the watching soldiers shouted in alarm. The men in the leading Land Rover were not armed with the usual Russian-designed Kalashnikov AK-47 assault rifles, but with stubby Israeli Uzi sub-machine-guns. At the Ugandan's shout, the windows of all three vehicles suddenly spurted flame, the stutter of the Uzis blending with the harder 'crack' of Galil assault rifles wielded by the concealed Israeli commandos in the rear seats of the Mercedes. The Ugandan soldier who had raised the alarm was the first to fall.

The Entebbe raid was on!

The hijack

One week previously, in the early hours of 27 June 1976, sleepy passengers had begun boarding the scheduled flight from Kuwait which was due to arrive in Athens at 07.00. No one took any notice of the 28-year-old German lawyer and his girlfriend who had first-class tickets through to Paris, while even less attention was paid to a pair of anonymous young Arabs travelling in tourist class. Within hours, however, their names were to be on everyone's lips around the world.

At Athens, the attractive German couple and the two Arabs went straight through to the transfer lounge without having to go through any form of security check. The German lawyer, Wilfed Boese, excused himself to his girlfriend and entered the men's toilets. He was joined by one of the Arabs, who was carrying two tins of dates. Inside the toilet, the tins were rapidly opened and the Arab handed Boese two Czech 7.65 mm automatic pistols and a pair of hand grenades; then the two men separated. The girl donned a blonde wig and the four sauntered to join the queue of people waiting to board Air France Flight 139 for Paris; the girl carried two grenades and a pistol in her handbag while her companion had the other pistol in his pocket. Her name was Gabrielle Tiedemann, and both she and Boese were members of the dreaded Baader-Meinhof gang.

In the cockpit of the Air France Airbus, Captain Michel Barcos completed his routine pre-flight checks and the aircraft taxied out to the runway. In the cabin, an air hostess was serving drinks to the first-class passengers. The Airbus lifted off into the cloudless sky and banked on to its course across the Aegean towards Paris. As it did so, the elegant but hard-faced German girl rose to her feet. To the horror of the air hostess and the other first-class passengers, Tiedemann raised a grenade aloft in each hand. 'Sit down!' she commanded. 'Everyone must sit down.' Her companion stood up, holding the automatic pistol, and walked forward to the flight deck. Back in the tourist section of the Airbus, the two Arabs, one wearing a bright-red shirt, the other a yellow one, had also arisen, and there were shrieks of fear from several passengers as they spotted the guns in the Arabs' hands.

From the flight deck, Boese spoke over the cabin intercom, while the two Arabs – who throughout the operation were only referred to by the code numbers 39 and 55 – began tying what appeared to be innocent boxes of chocolates to two of the aircraft's emergency exit doors. The boxes, Boese informed the stunned passengers, contained plastic explosive. As the aircraft was flying at over 10,000 m (30,000 ft), their detonation would produce explosive decompression which would cause the airliner to disintegrate in mid air. However, Boese said that all the passengers would be safe if they did as they were told by his colleagues. They were being taken to a safe destination, he continued, where they would be held hostage against the release of Palestine Liberation Organization 'freedom fighters' in Israel, and Baader-Meinhof gangsters in West Germany.

After the Airbus had crossed the Mediterranean, Boese ordered Captain Barcos to contact the control tower at Benghazi, in Libya, where arrangements had already been made for the airliner to land and refuel before departing for its final, and as yet undisclosed, destination. Then the aircraft took off again on the longest leg of its flight, across the barren Bayuda Desert where Lord Wolseley's Camel Corps had battled so valiantly a century before in their attempt to rescue General Charles Gordon, besieged in Khartoum. Eventually the aircraft crossed the border between

Sudan and Uganda and began descending towards Lake Victoria and Kampala's main airport at Entebbe. The Airbus landed in the still, pre-dawn air on Monday, 28 June, but few of the passengers realized where they were until Boese announced over the intercom that they had landed in Uganda. There were smiles and the occasional hand-clap among the 257 passengers as the aircraft doors were opened to let out the stale air, and a Ugandan truck delivered hundreds of cartons of cool, soft drinks. Many of the hostages had fallen under the spell of the eloquent and persuasive German lawyer, and had begun to believe that their ordeal might really be over. The next five days were to show how ill-founded these hopes were.

After several hours' acute discomfort in the cramped confines of the aircraft, the passengers were told that it was time to disembark. Blinking in the hot African sunlight, they emerged unsteadily to face a cordon of armed Ugandan soldiers, and the full horror of the situation came home to them. The troops' automatic rifles were directed not at the hijackers, but at the passengers!

The hostages were herded between two lines of soldiers towards the old control tower and terminal complex. Although the buildings were falling into disrepair, the rooms and toilets inside had been freshly cleaned, and the hostages' spirits lifted again as airport personnel began to bring round more cold drinks together with hot food. However, the staple Ugandan diet of rice, bananas and badly cooked meat would soon pall, and the toilets were

WEAPONS OF THE ISRAELI ÉLITE FORCES

Designation	Type	Calibre	Magazine	Rate of fire	Range	Remarks
Uzi	Sub-machine-gun	9 mm	25 or 32 rounds	600 rpm cyclic	100 m	
Galil ARM	Assault rifle	5.56 mm	35 or 50 rounds	650 rpm cyclic	400 m	
Galil SAR	Assault carbine	5.56 mm	35 rounds	750 rpm cyclic	300–400 m	Paras and tank crews
FN FAL	Self-loading rifle	7.62 mm	20 or 30 rounds	40 rpm	600 m +	
FN MAG	Machine-gun	7.62 mm	100-round belt	600–1000 rpm cyclic	1200 m	
M65	Mortar	120 mm	Single-shot	10 rpm	6500 m	
Cobra	Anti-tank missile	100 mm	Single-shot	Not applicable	2000 m	
SS11	Anti-tank missile	164 mm	Single-shot	Not applicable	3000 m	
LAW	Light Armour Weapon	94 mm	Single-shot	Not applicable	500 m	
TOW	Anti-tank missile	152 mm	Single-shot	Not applicable	3750 m	
Redeye	Anti-aircraft missile	70 mm	Single-shot	Not available	Not available	

soon to become blocked. Sickness and diarrhoea would be added to the hostages' misery. To begin with, though, their situation did not seem too frightening, and many people applauded when Idi Amin, the paranoid Ugandan dictator and former British Army NCO, paid his first visit to them. Amin, wearing, of all things, Israeli paratrooper's wings on his camouflage uniform, made a long speech in which he defended the right of the Palestinian people to their homeland. However, he said, 'You must not worry. I will take care of you like a father. I will see that you are released.' He was to say much the same on every visit.

On Tuesday, 29 June, the Jews among the hostages were terrified when Boese entered the main hall of the terminal building and announced that he had an answer to the overcrowding, which was becoming more and more of a problem. The wooden slats which had barred entry to the adjoining lounge were torn away by Palestinian guerrillas – their numbers now swollen to ten with new arrivals – and Boese began reading names from a list. It rapidly became apparent that all the names were Jewish: the terrorists were segregating their prisoners. A few of the older Israelis remembered the Holocaust – some had actually survived the Nazi concentration camps – and it seemed to them that history was repeating itself.

The terrorist leader did not appear to understand the Jews' consternation. Confronted with the problem, he frowned and assured the hostages that there was nothing sinister in his actions. 'It is simply,' he said, 'that we have to put about a hundred of you in the other room and, as there are about that many Jews, it is better that you be together.' However, several of the hostages later reported that Boese looked worried at the situation, almost as if he resented any implication that his group might be capable of behaving like the SS. Whether this had anything to do with subsequent events is impossible to decide; certainly the discussion was resumed later in the week. Whatever the case, on the following day, Wednesday, 30 June, the hijackers released 47 of their prisoners, while Ugandan soldiers brought blankets for the remainder since, although the days were hot, the nights were very cold. However, no one missed the fact that none of those released was Jewish.

On Thursday, the Israeli cabinet submitted – as far as the outside world was concerned – to the hijackers' demands. The terrorists held in Israeli jails whose release Boese was demanding would be set free as soon as the hijackers could give satisfactory assurances about the safety of the hostages. Boese reacted swiftly and within hours had released a further 101 hostages, who were flown back to Paris.

The remaining 104 prisoners, with the exception of the Air France Airbus crew, who bravely refused to leave, were all Jews. If it had not been clear before, it was now obvious that Boese's target was Israel.

On the Friday morning, Idi Amin paid his third visit to Entebbe, this time accompanied by both his wife and young son. They were on their way to Mauritius for the conference of the Organization for African Unity. He repeated his earlier words of reassurance.

He then appealed to the remaining hostages to help him, urging them all to sign a letter, which would be read over the radio, begging the Israeli government to capitulate completely. As he departed for Mauritius, the prisoners began arguing hotly amongst themselves, some being in favour of writing such a letter and others being totally opposed. Eventually a form of agreement was reached and a letter drafted; a letter which carefully concealed in its syntax a plea to the Israeli government to act positively rather than negatively. Unknown to those who penned the letter, the Israeli government *was* acting positively.

Operation 'Thunderbolt'

On Monday, 28 June 1976, the Knesset, Israel's parliament, was in emergency session. Prime Minister Yitzhak Rabin and opposition leader Menachem Begin had spent the previous day at Ben Gurion airport, tracing the course of the hijacked Airbus as it proceeded first to Libya and then on to Uganda. While the politicians talked, Israel's military leaders began planning. Defence Minister Shimon Peres, Chief-of-Staff General Mordecai Gur, his second in command, Major-General Yekuti Adam, and air force commander, General Beni Peled, discussed the information which was so far available to them. By any standards, the prospects for a successful military solution to the problem looked gloomy. The hijacked Airbus was 2000 miles away in a country whose dictator was openly hostile to Israel. As well as the Palestinian and Baader-Meinhof terrorists themselves, numerous regular Ugandan troops were guarding the hostages. There were two squadrons of Russian-built MiG-17s and -19s at Entebbe, and the air routes to Uganda from Israel all passed over Arab countries. In contrast to a rescue attempt on an airliner grounded in a friendly or neutral country, therefore, any military operation would have to be aimed at seizing the entire airport and neutralizing the jet fighters as well as rescuing the hostages themselves.

At 17.30, Peres and Gur went to Jerusalem to meet with the crisis cabinet summoned by Prime Minister Rabin. At this stage, barely 30 hours after the hijack, they had to confess that they could not see a viable military option. The cabinet therefore decided against making any immediate decision on the hijackers' demands. While the government would continue to negotiate with the terrorists in the hope of bringing a bloodless end to the crisis, the military was instructed to carry on pursuing ideas for a feasible rescue operation.

Several plans were considered and discarded over the next hours, including a parachute assault and the possibility of dispatching an airliner, ostensibly carrying the prisoners from Israeli jails whose release the terrorists were demanding, but in fact packed with commandos. None of the ideas were viable because they would all alert the hijackers and so their chances of success seemed remote. Speed, secrecy and surprise were the essentials. The Israelis had to get a strong force on to the ground undetected. They then had to free the hostages from wherever they were being held prisoner; they had to neutralize the hijackers and the Ugandan troops at Entebbe; they had to destroy the MiGs; and they had to be clear of the airfield in less than an hour, or strong Ugandan reinforcements from Kampala would be on top of them. It seemed an impossible task, but Peres and Gur appointed various sub-committees to work out plans for each phase of the operation – the undetected approach, the rescue of the hostages in the middle of a firefight to secure the airfield, and the escape. The large number of hostages – 257 – was in itself a problem, because it meant that at least three aircraft would have to be used in the operation. But gradually ideas began to gel, and ultimately a number of separate but concurrent operations emerged as the best possible answer.

While the military planners continued to polish the basic concepts for the rescue operation, the Knesset was meeting again and, on Thursday, 1 July, it finally agreed to discuss with the hijackers the release of some of the prisoners in Israeli jails. The hijackers responded by releasing a second batch of hostages, who were questioned closely by Israeli secret service agents in order to ascertain from them as many details as possible relating to the condition of the remaining hostages, where they were being kept, and the disposition of their guards.

Although there was natural concern in Israel about the fact that all the remaining hostages, with the exception of the Air France crew, were Jews, the fact that there were now only just over 100 of them in Entebbe made the military option much more feasible. The plan had several parts. First, three Lockheed C-130 transports would be used for the main assault. They would fly from Israel's southernmost air base, Sharm el-Sheik, at an extremely low level to avoid radar detection from Egypt, Libya, Saudi Arabia and the Sudan, at the same time flying in very close wingtip-to-wingtip formation so that, if they were spotted, they would register on a radar screen only as a single aircraft. This way, if they were detected, they could claim that they were a special flight laid on to ferry the terrorist prisoners to Entebbe. Meanwhile, 10,000 m (30,000 ft) above them, a specially equipped Boeing 707 aerial command post would fly in close company with a scheduled airline flight from Tel Aviv to Nairobi, in Kenya. Reaching the vicinity of Kampala, the scheduled aircraft – which in fact was being hastily refitted as a mobile hospital – would bank over Lake Victoria towards Nairobi, while the aerial command post would accelerate to its maximum speed of nearly 300 knots and enter the blind zone of the Entebbe radar: this was a cone which, at 10,000 m (30,000 ft) was 25 km (16 miles) in diameter; since the Boeing's turn radius was only 8 km (5 miles), the command post could circle undetected in this zone for as long as needed to complete the operation.

Further activity was taking place on the ground. Israeli agents had been filtering into Uganda from Kenya during the middle of the week, their prime task being to gain access to the airfield in the guise of airport workers and airline crew, and to sabotage all the telephone lines out of the airport in order to make it more difficult for the Ugandans to summon help from outside. Meanwhile, in Israel itself, the crack troops who were going to carry out the main assault were rehearsing.

The man chosen to lead the operation on the ground was an exceptional soldier with a remarkable record. Although only aged 39, Dan Shomron was already a brigadier. He had joined the paras in 1955, taking part in the 1956 Suez operation and the later Six-Day War, and had afterwards specialized in counter-terrorist raids against Palestinian camps in the Jordan valley. During the Yom Kippur war he commanded a tank brigade, and he was highly regarded as an intelligent and incisive officer.

The term 'hand-picked volunteer' is something of a contradiction in terms, but that is exactly what the force which Shomron assembled at Sharm el-Sheik consisted of. Israel is an egalitarian state, and its predominantly civilian army does not encourage élitism. Nevertheless, many units in the Israeli Defence Forces had made themselves into an élite through sheer performance, drive, determination and skill rather than through any special training. And within the armed forces there were few men who would not have wanted to be part of such a rescue operation, despite the fact that casualty estimates for the strike force ran as high as 40 per cent. In other words, it was anticipated that, of the 200 soldiers taking part in the operation, at least 30 would be killed and another 50 seriously wounded.

So, they assembled at Sharm el-Sheik, 200 bronzed, highly fit young men from the paras, the armoured forces and the Golani mountain troops. First, Brigadier Shomron briefed them on the situation and the obstacles to be overcome, then the men turned the airfield into a full-size replica of Entebbe, marking out the positions of the key buildings, the parked MiGs and other features. The three Hercules aircraft they would be using were taxied into the positions they would occupy on Entebbe airfield and the troops embarked, together with their vehicles. Other soldiers acted the part of the hostages. Again and again the men ran through the exercise: the disembarkation from the aircraft, the dash to the old terminal building, taking out the control towers, sabotaging the MiGs – all these phases were rehearsed extensively. Other Israelis played the part of Ugandan soldiers and terrorists, and a grim mock battle using blank ammunition ensued. Officers watched it all with stop-watches in hand. Instructors pointed to casualties, who had to lie down and be carried back to the aircraft. Eventually the timing improved and, by late on the afternoon of Friday, 2 July, Brigadier Shomron knew that his men could be out of their aircraft and fully deployed within 45 seconds of the loading ramps dropping.

A key figure in the attack was Lieutenant-Colonel Yonatan ('Yoni') Netanyahu, who was leading the strike force in the Hercules with the trickiest task of all – storming the old terminal building without, hopefully, causing any casualties among the hostages. Netanyahu, aged 30, had been born in New York, but his parents had emigrated to the new state of Israel in 1948. He had led a distinguished life in the army, being wounded during the storming of the Golan Heights during the Six-Day War and later defending the same position against Syrian attacks in the Yom Kippur War. Now he was drilling his commandos mercilessly, and, by 16.00 on the Friday afternoon, he was able to report that his men were as ready as possible.

While the assault force was training on the ground, the pilots who would fly the three Hercules were also rehearsing, flying at low level while vigilant Israeli radar operators on the ground tried to spot them, and practising pin-point navigation exercises over the empty wastes of the Sinai Desert. They flew wingtip-to-wingtip in complete radio silence until the pilots also pronounced themselves ready. As darkness fell, Generals Gur and Peled were confident that everything that could be done to make the mission a success had been done. The Chief-of-Staff and air force commander flew back to Jerusalem to report on the day's exercises to the crisis cabinet. Their description of how they intended to carry out the operation brought a burst of applause from the assembled politicians, who had become increasingly concerned at the hijackers' refusal to allow a United Nations force to supervise the exchange of prisoners, even though the West German government had finally capitulated, under protest, and had said that it was prepared to release the Baader-Meinhof prisoners in German jails. Prime Minister Rabin sat quietly for a timeless moment, then looked up at his assembled colleagues. 'I am in favour,' he announced. The news was received with acclaim at Sharm el-Sheik.

The rescue

On that crucial Sabbath morning, 3 July, Brigadier Shomron carried out a final briefing of all his unit commanders in the presence of Generals Gur and Peled. All the men understood the critical importance of timing, and here the Boeing aerial command post, flying in the radar blind spot above Entebbe, became a vital link in the chain. It could receive line-of-sight transmissions from the small portable radios carried by the troops on the ground and coordinate their activities, as well as being able to monitor radio traffic from Kampala and warn the strike force of any Ugandan troop movements towards the airfield.

After a final dress rehearsal, Brigadier Shomron ordered his men to rest. 'We go at 16.00 hours,' he said. It was a difficult decision to take, for the Israeli meteorological service had reported a severe storm developing, which would be at its worst while the Hercules were flying towards Uganda. It was a further complication to add to the already difficult task of precision flying at low level at night, but it had become apparent that the hijackers' patience was running out and that a delay of even 24 hours could prove fatal.

There was a party in Tel Aviv that night in aid of the United Jewish Appeal, and many of the hundred or so guests remarked on the absence of Generals Gur and Peled. Little did they know that the three Hercules were at that moment thundering 60 m (200 ft) above the Red Sea, while the scheduled Boeing Flight LY167 to Nairobi, closely accompanied by the aerial command post, was sailing 10,000 m (30,000 ft) above them.

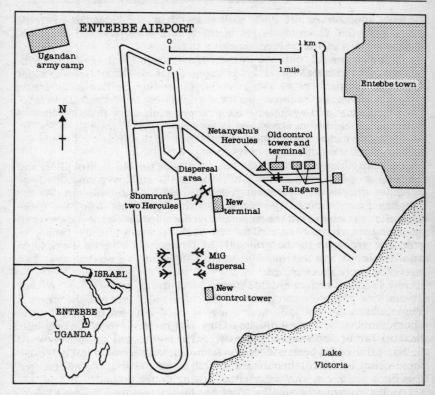

In the old terminal building at Entebbe, conditions had become unbearable during that long, hot Sabbath. With inadequate water and toilet facilities, the hostages were existing in unadulterated squalor. Many were by now seriously ill, weak and feverish, and constantly haunted by the prowling figure of Gabrielle Tiedemann, who seemed to relish their plight. By contrast, Wilfrid Boese was clearly disturbed at their condition and spent most of his time outside the building. Finally, he requested help for the hostages and two Ugandan Army doctors arrived. To their credit, they were appalled by conditions inside the terminal, and immediately set about organizing soldiers to clean out the toilets and supply fresh water, while they themselves moved among the Jews, administering drugs to alleviate the suffering.

As they settled down to sleep that night, none of the hostages could have realized that help was at hand, and that Israeli secret agents were already in action on the airfield, laying plastic explosive charges to demolish all the telephone and telex links with the outside world. When the Hercules suddenly appeared on the flight path at midnight, the Ugandan air-traffic controllers tried frantically to get in touch with Kampala, and could not understand why all the 'phones appeared to be dead.

Although severely buffeted by the storm through which they had flown, the three Hercules had succeeded in keeping station and in avoiding radar detection, assisted by a fortuitous strike among Sudanese air-traffic controllers. Now, as the three gigantic aircraft swept majestically in to land, the commandos inside gripped their weapons even more tightly. Many of them had suffered from airsickness during the rough journey, and for the last hour they had been sitting in total darkness so that their eyes would not have to adjust when the cargo ramps dropped.

As Yoni Netanyahu's aircraft drew up outside the old control tower and the ramp dropped, he shouted 'Go!'. The two Land Rovers and the black Mercedes wheeled down the ramp and headed for the buildings. As the Ugandan guard shouted the alarm and fire broke out from the three vehicles, the remainder of the commandos concealed inside the dark maw of the Hercules charged out. Ugandan soldiers were already falling in grotesque heaps on to the brilliantly lit tarmac as Gabrielle Tiedemann raised her pistol. She had time for just one shot before she was cut down by a burst of sub-machine-gun fire.

Boese, who had re-entered the control tower to pick up his own sub-machine-gun as the unannounced Hercules landed, ran into the terminal lounge where the hostages were lying, startled into wakefulness by the sudden shooting. He raised his gun to fire. Ilan Hartuv, one of the prisoners who had earlier discomfited Boese by comparing his actions with those of the Nazis, raised his head and looked calmly into the terrorist leader's eyes. Boese visibly hesitated, then turned and ran out of the door. As he emerged from the building he, too, was smashed, dying, to the ground.

As the commandos, led by Yoni Netanyahu, reached the building, a loud hailer was already calling to the hostages 'Tishkavu! Tishkavu!' ('Lie down!'). As Yoni pounded down the corridor towards the stairs leading to the roof and control tower, a burst of firing sounded from the terrace. He flattened himself against a wall while the two men with him detached hand grenades from their harness webbing and primed them. Bursting through the door at the top of the stairs, the trio was met by a hail of fire and ducked back hastily, throwing two grenades into the room. The three Palestinian terrorists inside screamed in fear, but were caught in the blast of shrapnel as the grenades exploded. The Israeli commandos swept the room with sub-machine-gun fire in case any of the terrorists had escaped, but they were all dead. A signaller radioed to the circling command post overhead: 'We are in the terminal. Yoni is going for the roof.'

The roof was soon cleared of terrified Ugandan soldiers, and Yoni and his men descended. He was moving towards the Land Rovers when a Ugandan soldier fired a burst in his direction, and Yoni Netanyahu fell dead with a bullet in his back.

Inside the terminal lounge there was consternation and panic. Most people obeyed the commandos' injunction to lie down, parents shielding their children's bodies with their own, wives clinging to husbands. As soldiers appeared at the terminal windows, one young student leapt to his feet in terror. The commandos were spraying the room with automatic fire at waist to chest height and he fell instantly. An old lady also forced her way to her feet, despite the efforts of those around her to pull her down, and she too fell. Another man was mortally wounded and one woman was hit in the leg by a ricochet. It was a scene of utmost terror and confusion, but gradually order emerged from the chaos. The disbelieving hostages could still hear a fierce firefight going on outside, but the dazed realization that a rescue operation was actually in progress was beginning to sink in.

The firing continued for about a quarter of an hour, then gradually died away as those Ugandan troops who had not been killed, fled. Now Israeli soldiers entered the lounge, moving among the hostages, urging them to their feet and outside to the waiting Land Rovers. Many of the people were so weak that they had to be helped or carried and several of them were in their nightwear. Other commandos encircled the buildings and the dispersal area in a ring of steel, watchful eyes scanning the darkness outside the brilliance of the terminal lights. On the roof of the buildings, snipers with Galil rifles fitted with night sights sought further targets. More Israelis scoured the buildings to ensure that nobody had been left behind.

The people filed into the waiting Hercules, which had been refuelled by a special squad while the fighting was still going on, and, Allison engines roaring, it lifted into the night sky.

Across the airfield at the new terminal and dispersal area, Brigadier Dan Shomron's two Hercules had landed at the same time as Yoni Netanyahu's, and their cargo ramps were being lowered even as the aircraft taxied to a standstill. Jeeps, a command car and an armoured personnel carrier mounting a heavy machine-gun accelerated out, splitting to left and right to encircle the new terminal. Within the 45 seconds achieved during the dress rehearsal, commandos were racing through the building, shooting at anything which moved. However, they could not gain access to the roof, which was held by a strong force of Ugandans armed with light machine-guns whose fire was sweeping the open ground. Dan Shomron ordered the armoured personnel carrier to lay down a withering hail of covering fire to keep the Ugandans' heads down while other commandos stormed the stairs. One Israeli was killed but others hurled hand grenades into the tower and on to the roof, and the Ugandan resistance suddenly ceased.

Meanwhile, another squad was racing towards the parked MiGs, which were heavily guarded. A brief firefight took place before a hand grenade exploded the fuel tanks of one of the fighters, which blew up dramatically, showering the area with debris and burning fuel, and setting light to other aircraft.

Strangely, the Israelis who had been detached to join the waiting secret agents on the approaches to the Ugandan army camp on the airfield perimeter, found themselves without a job to do. The paranoid dictator, Amin, fearing treachery while he was away in Mauritius, had stripped the troops of their weapons, which were locked in the armoury. The incarcerated Ugandan soldiers, 2000 strong, spent the hour of the raid getting drunk!

With the terminal secured and the MiGs a blazing pile of wreckage, the Israeli commandos scoured the area in order to divert any possible counter-attack by Ugandan troops who might have regrouped, while tanker trucks pumped fuel into the thirsty tanks of the two Hercules. It seemed that time was running out. The circling command post overhead had reported troop movements from the direction of Kampala. Then, with a sigh of relief, Brigadier Shomron watched as the third Hercules with its still disbelieving cargo of passengers lifted off from the old runway. The tanker trucks were quickly disconnected, whistles urgently sounded the recall, and the commandos ran for the ramps of the waiting aircraft. The aerial command post proudly radioed the message 'Mission successful' back to the Israeli government, and an astonished world awoke the following morning to the story of one of the most daring and remarkable feats of arms in history. It was a superb achievement.

THE WAR OF INDEPENDENCE

During World War 2, Jews living in the British Protectorate of Palestine suffered divided loyalties because, although they wanted to expel the British military government from 'their' country, they were obviously anti-Nazi. As a result, while many Jews served alongside the Allies in the Jewish Brigade, others began preparing for the hiatus which was bound to follow the end of the war in Europe, and formed the *Haganah*, a terrorist organization dedicated to the expulsion of the British Army. Their activities reached a peak just after the war with the bombing of the King David hotel in Jerusalem, but tension was maintained during 1947, since Britain had agreed to grant independence to Egypt in 1949 and began moving military forces from Egypt into Palestine. In this confused situation, the opposing Jewish and Arab groups, both determined to win control of the country after the British finally withdrew, were in constant armed conflict, and atrocities were committed by both sides, including the Jewish massacre of 250 men, women and children in one village and the Arab slaughter of 77 Jewish doctors and nurses in retaliation. The increasing violence and obvious Jewish determination to gain control of Palestine after the British withdrawal, caused hundreds of thousands of Arabs to flee from the affected areas, and by May 1948 it was estimated that the Arab population of Palestine had dropped from 700,000 to a mere 170,000. Herein lay the genesis of the Palestinian problem.

The War of Independence proper lasted from March 1948 to January 1949, with two truces during that period, and resulted in a military defeat for the Arab Legion by the indigenous Palestinian Jews, whose ranks were swollen by refugees from the Holocaust in Europe. Thus, although Israel had declared its independence on 14 May 1948, and *Zahal* had been formally created 12 days later, the country effectively came into existence at the beginning of 1949.

Israeli armour and paras in action

'Shamir and Zebra. This is Tirah. Sunrays to the mike. Over!'

'Tirah, this is Shamir. Sunray speaking. Over.'

'Tirah, this is Zebra. Sunray speaking. Over.'

'Shamir and Zebra. This is Tirah. Move now and good luck. Over.'

The time was 08.15 on 5 June 1967. General Israel Tal, alias Tirah, had just given the order to advance to his two subordinates, Colonels Shmuel and Raphoul. The Israeli 'blitzkrieg' was about to break upon unsuspecting Egyptian heads, and its armoured spearhead was General Tal's division in the north. Tal, the founder of modern Israeli tank forces, was then 43 years old. He had fought with the Jewish Brigade in North Africa during World War 2 and had risen rapidly through *Zahal's* ranks after independence, becoming General Officer Commanding Armoured Corps (GOCAC) in 1964. His formation was now charged with the task of creating an initial Israeli breakthrough, its objective the strategically important rail centre of El Arish with its accompanying airfield. At his disposal were three brigades equipped with approximately 150 to 300 Centurion and Patton tanks, facing the Egyptian 7th Infantry Division reinforced by an artillery brigade and accompanied by an estimated 100 tanks, holding strong defensive positions protected by deep minefields.

Tal's force was the strongest of the three Israeli spearheads in 1967, the others being the divisions under Generals Abraham Yoffe and Arik Sharon (the founder of the Israeli parachute force, known popularly as 'The Guys'), which were operating in the centre and south respectively on a front stretching from Rafa to Kuntilla. Its component forces were 'S' armoured brigade, under Colonel Shmuel, 'Z' parachute brigade under Colonel Raphoul, and 'M' reserve brigade under Colonel Men.

Ever since the conclusion of the 1956 Sinai campaign – when the Israelis had cooperated with British and French forces in seizing the Suez Canal, which had been nationalized by Gamal Nasser – border intrusions and terrorist raids on Israeli *kibbutzim* (communal farms) had been mounting. Under United Nations censure, the British and French forces had been obliged to withdraw from Egypt with great loss of national prestige, while Israel was also forced to withdraw from the territory which *Zahal* had captured in the Sinai. This meant abandoning the airfield at Sharm el-Sheik but, in return, passage of Israeli shipping through the Straits of Tiran was guaranteed by a UN peace-keeping force. As the border incidents continued

Israeli tank commanders suffered heavy casualties in exchange for better visibility and therefore faster reactions.

to increase, in November 1966 Israel launched a massive reprisal raid against *El Fatah* camps in Jordan, and in April 1967 her air force bombed Syrian artillery batteries which had been bombarding *kibbutzim* workers. President Gamal Nasser, who had signed a secret defence agreement with Syria, now demanded the withdrawal of the UN peace-keeping force from the Canal Zone, and closed the Straits of Tiran to Israeli shipping. In May, King Hussein of Jordan flew to Cairo and also signed a defence agreement with Nasser, while Iraq agreed to provide military support in the event of a war between Jordan and Israel. The noose was tightening around the neck of Israel and, in utmost secrecy, a lightning campaign was planned.

The remarkable efficiency of Israel's 'citizen army' was to be proved time and again over the next few days, but in many ways its most dramatic expression came in the speed of the call-up. Brigade commanders summoned battalion commanders, who telephoned or raced around to see company commanders, who organized their Sergeants to notify their men – and women. Shopkeepers, accountants, typists, journalists, schoolteachers, mechanics, salesmen – they all responded to the call and went home to change into their uniforms. After presenting themselves at their respective assembly points, they were issued with arms and ammunition and proceeded to wait. Gradually the tension mounted.

The battle commences

The Israeli cabinet finally took the decision to attack during the long night of 3/4 June 1967, and the time of waiting was over. The preliminary air strike went in at 07.45 on 5 June, and half an hour later the tanks and armoured personnel carriers began to roll.

The Sinai Desert is a harsh and barren wasteland, broken only by the occasional clump of scrub grass, scoured clean by a constant burning wind and inhabited solely, under normal circumstances, by the odd nomadic bedouin. Like all desert landscapes, it appears virtually flat to the uneducated eye, but the successful tank commander is the one who can spot the shallow depressions and low ridges which will enable him to enter into a hull-down position with just his turret showing to the enemy, and who can recognize from afar the deceptively smooth areas of soft sand which will hinder his vehicle's advance. Israeli tank commanders, like their earlier counterparts in the Afrika Korps and 8th Army (and unlike Arab tank commanders, who go into action with all their hatches battened down), have the slow-moving, distant gaze of men accustomed to 'the blue'.

On 5 June, the normally uninhabited Sinai was crowded. By this time the Egyptians had concentrated no fewer than seven divisions in the arena: 4th Armoured, 2nd, 3rd, 6th and 7th Infantry, 20th PLA (Palestine Liberation Army), and a special armoured battle group of divisional strength without a number. Against this might the Israelis had but three divisions – one armoured (Tal's), one mechanized (Sharon's) and one reserve (Yoffe's). Numerically, the Egyptians had a three-to-one superiority in men and tanks over the Israelis. As with the British paras at Goose Green, this did not deter the Israeli troops.

For the armoured attack in the north or Mediterranean flank, General Tal split his force into two: Colonel Shmuel's 'S' Brigade was to attack northwards, capturing Khan Yunis and Rafa, while Colonel Raphoul's 'Z' Parachute Brigade was to outflank the southern edge of the Egyptian 7th Infantry Division. 'S' Brigade would then head for Sheik Zuweid, while 'Z' Brigade swung north to take out the Egyptian artillery.

'In war,' General Tal once said, 'nothing ever goes according to plan, but there is one thing you must stick to: the major designation of the plan.' How right he was to be proved. 'S' Brigade struck north on the 6.5 km (4 mile) route to Khan Yunis and immediately ran into trouble from the PLA Brigade, which included a 25-pounder artillery battalion and a combined tank and anti-tank gun battalion. Egyptian artillery fire began falling, and the advance was slowed by anti-tank ditches and minefields while, when they reached the town itself, the tank crews became confused in the narrow streets. S/14 Battalion was entrapped and had to summon the help of S/10 which was to have bypassed the town to the south. The two battalions met at the railway station, by which time the PLA defenders were beating a hasty retreat, and together they pushed on towards Rafa. However, six tanks had already been incapacitated and no fewer than 35 tank commanders killed or wounded, largely through machine-gun fire as a result of going into action with their heads and shoulders exposed in their tanks' turrets. Four more tanks were damaged by mines *en route* to Rafa.

S/10 entered the town, meeting minimal opposition, but again S/14 ran into trouble against a heavily defended strongpoint with cunningly dug-in and camouflaged anti-tank guns. The Egyptian gunners put up a stubborn resistance and once again S/10 had to come to S/14's assistance, racing down on the Egyptian position from the rear. The gunners began fleeing, with the exception of one brave man, who attempted to knock out the nearest tank with an old American bazooka.

In the meantime, Tal's southern pincer, comprising 'Z' Parachute Brigade with 'M' Brigade in reserve, had also encountered stiff resistance, including an Egyptian battalion of Joseph Stalin III heavy tanks, which forced Raphoul's tanks to fight, so leaving the paras in their armoured half-tracks dangerously exposed. Fierce hand-to-hand fighting took place during the afternoon, but eventually the paras won through and, by late afternoon on the first day of the war, General Tal's northern force had reached El Arish, while the Egyptian positions south of the Rafa junction were in Raphoul's hands. However, there was an unpleasant surprise in store for, although they did not know it at the time, the Israelis had completely missed the southernmost of the Egyptian brigades. The first inkling of this came when helicopters, brought in to evacuate Israeli wounded, came under intense fire from the ground. The paras launched an immediate attack, and fighting for this position continued until well after dark.

Further south still, General Yoffe's mechanized division had had a much easier day. Advancing through an area of deep sand dunes which the Egyptians had thought impassable, his troops covered close on 96 km (60 miles), reaching the vicinity of Bir Lahfan at around 18.00 without a single casualty. Here, however, the Israelis encountered Egyptian reinforcements being sent north towards El Arish. Fighting continued through the night of 5/6 June, during which several Egyptian tanks were destroyed, and in the morning an Israeli air raid sent the remainder packing, hotly pursued by a group of Yoffe's own tanks.

On the Israeli left, or southern flank, General Sharon had split his force into two, one advancing parallel to Yoffe's towards Abu Agheila in the centre, the other even further south towards Kuntilla. Abu Agheila was a vital communications centre which had to be captured before the Israeli advance could continue any further, and naturally it was heavily defended by the incumbent Egyptian 2nd Infantry Division reinforced with 80 to 90 tanks and 6 artillery regiments. General Sharon's plan of attack involved a complex interleaving of all arms: artillery to pin the enemy frontally, followed by four assault columns alternating armour and infantry, with Israeli paras lastly being dropped by helicopter on the Egyptian artillery positions in their rear.

By 15.00 on 5 June, Sharon's forces were in position about 8 km (5 miles) from the Abu Agheila defences. The northernmost of the four assault columns ran into Egyptian tanks which forced Sharon's men to retire, but by dint of renewed effort they pushed through, and, by later in the afternoon, they had reached the Abu Agheila–El Arish road. After dark they pushed further forward, ready to strike southwards in support of the other assault columns. Similarly, the southernmost of the four columns had reached the Kusseima–Abu Agheila road so that, by nightfall, all the Egyptians' lines of communication had been cut. At dusk, helicopters landed a battalion of paras behind the enemy lines while their attention was diverted by the approach of the two central Israeli columns and an intense artillery barrage. Shortly before 23.00 the final attack took place – tanks from the front and north, mechanized infantry from the south and the paras

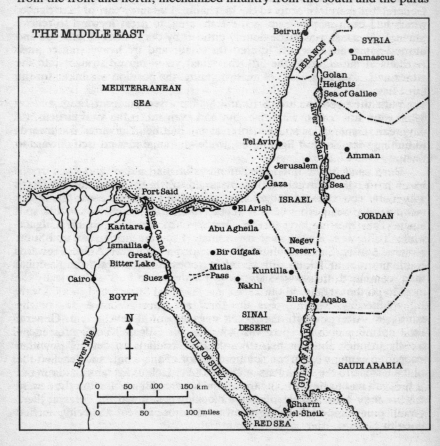

THE MIDDLE EAST

from the rear. Flares and tracer lit the desert sky as the Israelis pressed in on the Egyptian positions with fixed bayonets. There was fierce hand-to-hand fighting in the trenches, but within five hours most of the Egyptian positions were in Israeli hands. As dawn broke, the tanks – which had been largely useless in the dark – moved forward to complete the rout and, by 06.00 on 6 June, Sharon was able to order a further advance towards Kusseima.

Returning to Tal's forces in the north, S/14 had again run into trouble in the Jiradi area. While part of the battalion broke through the strong defences, it soon found itself cut off and another fierce battle took place during which the battalion commander, Major Elad, was killed. The remainder of the battalion broke through in the wake of S/14, but also found itself cut off as the Egyptians regrouped behind, and the reserve 'M' Brigade was unable to help because Colonel Men's tanks were practically out of fuel. General Tal therefore ordered the mechanized infantry part of 'S' Brigade, which had been mopping up in the Rafa area, to press forward to relieve Shmuel. This task was made doubly difficult by the dozens of wrecked and burned-out vehicles which littered the road, and by heavy traffic jams. Arriving at midnight on the 5th, the infantrymen moved straight into the attack and, after four hours of heavy fighting, the position was taken for the third time.

With their rear secure, S/10 and S/14 pressed on from Jiradi and by 04.00 were not only in El Arish, but had even taken the vital airfield. At daybreak, General Tal split his force again, half being diverted southwards to link up with Yoffe at Bir Lahfan, while the remainder pressed onward to Qantara and the Suez Canal.

Deep sand dunes aided the defenders at Bir Lahfan, and Tal's troops had a hard fight of it before they managed to win through and join forces with Yoffe's columns around midday on the 6th. From here, they planned to move jointly westward as far as Jebel Libni, after which they would split again, Tal's men striking further west towards Ismailia, via Bir Gifgafa, while Yoffe went south, heading ultimately for the Mitla Pass and Suez. Simultaneously, Sharon would first strike down from Abu Agheila towards Nakhl in order to link up with his other troops pressing west from Kuntilla; then, combined, they would also head for the Mitla Pass, strategically the most important feature in the Sinai.

Wednesday, 7 June, was the third and most decisive day of the campaign. After a short, sharp tank engagement at Jebel Libni, General Tal's northern division sped west towards Bir Gifgafa. Yoffe pressed on rapidly through Bir Hassneh towards Bir Thamada to cut off Egyptian troops retreating west in the southern sector of the front, and reached the vital entrance to the Mitla Pass at about 18.00. Half of his tanks had run out of fuel and had to be towed by those which were still mobile, but they could still fire their guns. Tal established a blocking position at Bir Gifgafa; there would be no escape for the Egyptian tanks whose retreat was being hurried along by Sharon – they would have to fight.

After a pause during the Wednesday night in order to allow his troops – most of whom had been constantly on the move since early Monday morning – to sleep, Sharon continued his long southward trek towards Nakhl. *En route* he came across an amazing sight: an entire brigade of Joseph Stalin III tanks abandoned in the middle of the desert. Their Egyptian commander had heard of the Israeli successes and, deciding that discretion was the better part of valour, had fled with his men in the brigade's half-tracks!

At Nakhl, Sharon laid a trap for the Egyptian forces still retreating from Kuntilla. Leaving the bulk of his tanks deployed on the southern outskirts of the town, he took the remainder in a long loop to the north-east. The Egyptians ran into the blocking force at Nakhl and were then taken in the rear by the rest of Sharon's force. It was slaughter.

At Bir Gifgafa, Tal's similar blocking force of two battalions had a more difficult task against an Egyptian armoured brigade, whose assault was actually accompanied by ground-attack aircraft – one of the few occasions during the war when the Egyptian MiGs saw action, since most of them had been destroyed on the ground during the preliminary Israeli air strike on the Monday morning. The situation at Bir Gifgafa became critical during the Wednesday night, when a new force of Russian-built T-54 main battle tanks blundered unwittingly into the Israeli positions. The Israelis had only the light, French-built, AMX-13 tanks on the spot, and these were no match for the heavier, better-armed and better-armoured T-54s. After a couple of hours, during which the Israelis tried to use their superior speed and mobility to counteract the Egyptians' advantages, Tal withdrew his battalions until heavier armour could be brought forward to reinforce them. The arrival of a company of Centurions redressed the balance, allowing the Israelis to re-occupy their original positions, and Tal then sent a further armoured brigade southwards to come round and attack the Egyptians from the rear. Outnumbered, and having already lost several tanks, the Egyptian brigade was soon overwhelmed.

Yoffe's force at the Mitla Pass, a solitary brigade under Colonel Iska, also found itself in difficulties as thousands of Egyptian troops tried to pour through the 23 km (15 mile) gap towards Suez and, by 22.00 on Wednesday night, he was surrounded and in grave danger of being overrun, despite the courage with which his paras were fighting. A second brigade was ordered to make a night march to relieve Colonel Iska. Advancing through the darkness, it suddenly found itself, like a comedy scene in a bad film, moving alongside a large column of Egyptian tanks headed in the same direction. The Egyptians took the Israeli tanks for friends in the darkness, but the Israelis, knowing that there were none of their own troops in the vicinity, began shooting up the thoroughly confused Egyptians with rare abandon!

Leaving their disorganized foe behind trying to work out what had happened, the fresh brigade pressed on and came as a godsend to Iska's men, who had been fighting continuously now for 72 hours and who were running very short of ammunition. Relieving them in the middle of a pitched battle was not easy, but was finally accomplished on Thursday morning, the fourth day of the war. Unable to break through the stubborn Israelis, and unable to retreat because of General Sharon's approach, several Egyptian tanks actually tried to climb the steep walls of the pass, where they became 'stuck like flies', in General Yoffe's words.

During the Thursday afternoon, Yoffe's new brigade battled its way to the western end of the Mitla Pass, where it encountered strongly defended Egyptian positions blocking any further advance towards the Suez Canal. Yoffe ordered a daring night attack, his tanks charging forward with headlights blazing, and the petrified Egyptians abandoned their positions and fled. By 02.00 on Friday, 9 June, Yoffe's forces had reached the canal. One armoured brigade was sent north towards Ismailia, but ran into heavy opposition from Egyptian tanks occupying hull-down positions behind the crests of dunes. The Israelis countered by splitting their force, two companies moving through the dunes while the remainder advanced along the road to draw the Egyptians' fire and make them reveal their positions. By this method the relatively small Israeli force succeeded in destroying some 70 Egyptian tanks for the loss of only 10 of their own.

While this was happening, on Thursday night Nasser asked for a cease-fire. In one of the fastest and most decisive military operations of all time, Israeli forces had succeeded in breaking the hitherto proud Egyptian Army, in capturing over 700 tanks and 5000 officers (Egyptian other ranks, after being given food, water and medical attention, were allowed to swim home across the canal, where a large number of them were inadvertently machine-gunned by their own troops on the western bank).

The battle for Jerusalem

It must be remembered that, at the beginning of the June 1967 campaign, which has ever afterwards been known as the Six-Day War, Jerusalem was still, like Berlin, a divided city: half Jewish and half Arab. As soon as King Hussein of Jordan received news of the Israeli advance into the Sinai, Jordanian forces in Jerusalem and on the West Bank of the River Jordan began opening fire and moved forward to occupy Mount Scopus, which was taken by midday on 5 June, followed by Government House in the early afternoon. Israeli tanks and paratroopers began moving forward and, by 16.00, had retaken the latter strongpoint. The heavily defended Police School was another story. Occupied by about 200 fanatical members of the Arab Legion, it took 500 Israeli paras several hours to capture, and did not finally succumb until 04.00 on Tuesday, after the courageous defenders had lost more than half their men.

By 10.00, most of the fighting in the former demilitarized zone was over, and the Israelis turned their attention to the Old City. This proved a more difficult task, since neither side wished to use heavy weapons which could damage the many historic and religious sites, and in the ensuing firefight the Israelis were at a disadvantage, having to move through the open while the

Arabs were well dug-in. To the north-east of the city, however, Mount Scopus finally fell to the Israelis after the collapse of the defence in the Police School.

On Wednesday morning, the Israelis attacked once more, the regiment on Mount Scopus advancing uphill to Augusta Victoria, while infantry attacked the Old City again. This time heavy weapons *were* employed, although great care was taken to avoid the Holy Places, and, by 10.00, the Temple Mount and Wailing Wall were Israeli territory.

With Jerusalem firmly in Israeli hands, *Zahal* was ready to complete operations on the West Bank. There had been only minor activity here on the 5th, when Israeli forces moved down from the north in the direction of Jenin. On the 6th, a further attack in the north from Sandala had reached Jenin and Qabatiya, a third force had advanced eastwards from Kalkilya, and a fourth had reached Ramallah, just north of Jerusalem, and had taken it in a night attack. In the north, around Jenin, the Jordanians had a strong force of M-47 Patton tanks, but they were left in a difficult situation because the Israeli air force made repeated attacks on their supply columns. In the end, nearly half the tanks had to be abandoned for want of supplies.

Now, on the Wednesday, the road seemed clear for the projected Israeli pincer movement – General Elazar's forces moving down from the north, and Colonel Uri Ben-Ali's moving east and north from Ramallah. Ben-Ali pressed on to Jericho, which fell without need of trumpets, while south of Jerusalem Colonel Amitai broke through the Jordanian positions and advanced on Bethlehem and Hebron. By dusk on 7 June, therefore, this phase of operations was complete. Jerusalem, the West Bank, and the Sinai as far west as the Suez Canal were all in Israeli hands. Next came the turn of the Syrians, who had remained ominously quiet so far.

Assault on the Golan Heights

The Golan Heights were the key to the Syrian positions. High, bleak and rugged, they were defended by complex fortifications some 16 km (10 miles) in depth, with dug-in tank, artillery and rocket launcher batteries. For two solid days the Israeli air force plastered these defences with everything in their arsenal, but the Syrian fortifications were deep and strong. However, the Arabs' morale began cracking under the merciless bombardment, with a new air raid every ten minutes. They were still strongly in evidence on the Friday morning, though, as Israeli bulldozers began advancing up the slopes to clear a path for the following tanks and armoured personnel carriers. The Israeli engineers suffered heavy casualties from well dug-in Syrian tanks, which eventually had to be destroyed by infantry with hand grenades.

Two more attacks further south, in the Gonen and Ashmura vicinities, were also successful, and by nightfall the Israelis had two footholds on the Heights. On the following morning both forces struck towards Qnaitra through the difficult, rocky terrain, reaching it by 13.00 and capturing it after an hour's fighting. Meanwhile, in the south, a further attack by infantry and tanks up the Yarmouk Valley succeeded in pinning down the Syrians while a paratroop force was dropped by helicopter in their rear. By the Saturday evening, therefore, the Heights were firmly in Israeli hands, and both sides accepted the cease-fire for which the United Nations Security Council had been calling since Friday morning.

The Six-Day War left Israel in a stronger position than at any time since her temporary occupation of the Sinai in 1956–7. She had possession of the crucial Golan Heights; Jerusalem was a united city once more; the West Bank had been cleared of hostile troops; and Israeli soldiers sat on the banks of the Suez Canal. Sharm el-Sheik had fallen, with its vital airfield defending access to the Red Sea, and, for the first time, Israel had territory to trade in exchange for time if ever counter-attacked.

For the next few years, an uneasy peace settled over the Middle East, a peace interrupted only by Israeli engineers building fortified defence posts along the east bank of the Suez Canal, while desultory Egyptian artillery barrages bombarded them, and during which the strong Syrian defences on the Golan Heights were turned to the Israelis' advantage. Known as the 'War of Attrition', this period lasted until 1970, when President Nasser died. His successor, Anwar Sadat, was determined to restore Egyptian prestige and redress the humiliating military defeat of 1967. After first expelling all the Soviet advisers in Egypt, Sadat shortly afterwards relented, and a new flood of Soviet arms and equipment began to enter the country. By April 1973 a new war seemed imminent. A partial mobilization of Israeli forces took place the following month in response to a strong build-up of Egyptian forces on the west bank of the Suez Canal, but nothing happened and *Zahal* reverted to its normal alert status. However, the mobilization had cost several million Israeli pounds and would be remembered when a similar situation arose later in October of the same year.

This time, the Arab leaders were determined that the 'boot' should be on the other foot, and were planning to take Israel by surprise. There were secret talks between Egypt, Syria and Jordan, and further discussions with the Gulf States – particularly Saudi Arabia – aimed at producing an oil embargo to prevent super-power intervention.

THE YOM KIPPUR WAR

Despite the vast strides in training, morale and equipment which had been made in the Egyptian Army since 1967, its task in 1973 was not an easy one, thanks to the high ramparts on the Israeli side of the Suez Canal which made a tank crossing impossible. The initial assault thus had to be made by infantry, equipped with scaling ladders and sufficient supplies and ammunition to hold their own for at least 24 hours. Breaches were to be blown in the Israeli ramparts not by explosives, but by high-pressure water hoses, no fewer than 80 special units being created and trained for this specific task. After consolidating their bridgeheads, Egyptian forces were supposed to head for the Mitla and other passes into the Sinai, but in fact this second phase never materialized, due to the speed of the Israeli response.

The Egyptian assault was planned for 6 October for both military and psychological reasons. It was not only a moonlit night, but also the tide in the canal was just right for crossing. Moreover, October is the Muslim fast month of *Ramadan*, during which *Zahal* was unlikely to expect an attack, and the 6th itself is the Jewish feast day of *Yom Kippur*, when defences were confidently expected to be at a low ebb. Secrecy was total. Right up until the last moment, Egyptian soldiers thought that they were merely going on yet another exercise. Indeed, they were not informed until the morning of the attack that this time it was 'for real', and only 5 out of 18 officers of Colonel and Lieutenant-Colonel rank were let in on the plan before the day itself.

To a large extent, the Israeli Defence Force (IDF) had been lulled into a sense of complacency, partly as a result of its success in the Six-Day War, and partly because of the non-event of the alert earlier in the year. Besides, it was a national holiday and the reserves were on stand-down when the attack materialized. The Egyptians had 3 armies mobilized along the canal, consisting of 4 infantry divisions, 3 mechanized divisions, 2 armoured divisions and 2 independent armoured brigades, and 16 artillery brigades. Against this, Israel had five under-strength 'divisions'. However, the Suez Canal constituted only half the picture. Five Syrian divisions, two of which were armoured, were also in place and ready to go on the eastern front, while Israeli defences on the Golan Heights were slim.

At dawn on 6 October, General Eli Zeira, the Director of *Mossad* – the Israeli secret service – received a telephone call from an agent which confirmed that an attack was imminent. He immediately notified Defence Minister Moshe Dayan and General Elazar, who contacted General Beni Peled, commander of the air force, as well as General Tal, and an urgent meeting was held at 05.50. Unfortunately, Israeli intelligence had got the time of the attack wrong – 18.00 instead of 14.00. The traditional times for an attack are dawn and dusk, whichever puts the sun in the defender's eyes, and 18.00 would have been ideal for an Egyptian attack. However, this would have acted in the Israelis' favour on the Syrian front, so the two Arab allies had selected the completely unlikely hour of 14.00 as a compromise.

While the Israeli high command uncharacteristically dithered, calling up only part of the reserves and refusing suggestions for a pre-emptive air strike, the Arabs completed their preparations and, at 13.45, a Syrian artillery bombardment erupted upon Mount Hermon. Helicopter-borne commandos followed and rapidly overran the Israeli positions as the massed tank and infantry formations began rolling forward. Unfortunately for the Syrians, their sheer weight of numbers ensured that the comparatively small force of Israeli tanks and guns could hardly miss, and the leading wave of Syrian troops fell in droves. However, numerical superiority did begin to tell, and in the south the Israeli 137th Armoured Brigade was cut to pieces and overrun. In the north, however, the crack 7th Armoured Brigade held on manfully, despite being completely surrounded on several occasions. The arrival of a fresh armoured brigade helped to stabilize the situation for the Israelis on Sunday, 7 October, although their forces on the Golan Heights were still heavily outnumbered. By midnight on that day, though, the Syrians had advanced as far as the Israelis were going to let them. Their casualties were often in the ratio of five or even ten to one and, in one notable engagement, three Israeli Centurion tanks succeeded in destroying or immobilizing no fewer than 35 Russian-built T-55s.

Throughout Monday the beleaguered 7th Brigade continued to fight against overwhelming odds. The Syrians' new Soviet T-62 tanks were fitted with what were then sophisticated night vision 'scopes, which gave them an enormous advantage over the ageing Israeli tanks, and by Tuesday morning the 7th had very few serviceable vehicles left. The Syrians then unleashed a massive bombardment with artillery, rockets and ground-attack aircraft, under cover of which the T-62s, supported by infantry, began to inch forward. The Israelis retired a few hundred metres and prepared for the onslaught. As the Syrians breasted the skyline, the remaining 15 Centurions and Pattons opened fire and then, incredibly, counter-attacked. The astonished Syrians fell back momentarily, as a Great Dane will when menaced by a Jack Russell, but within minutes the Israeli force had been depleted to only seven tanks, and they were running out of ammunition. As in a film, the 'cavalry' arrived in the nick of time in the form of a scratch force of another 13 tanks, and the demoralized Syrians, who had expected a walkover, began to retire.

By the Wednesday, the delayed Israeli mobilization of the reserves was really taking effect, however, and, despite still being outnumbered, the forces on the Golan Heights turned on the offensive. Although their tank crews continued to put up a stiff fight, the Syrian infantry did not give them the support they deserved and, by midday on 10 October, all Syrian forces had been pushed back behind their original start lines. The road was clear for an Israeli invasion of Syria itself.

D-Day on the Suez Canal

Meanwhile, in Egypt, the Yom Kippur War had begun with an intensive air strike by some 240 aircraft against Israeli anti-aircraft missile batteries, radar stations and strongpoints, accompanied by a massive artillery barrage from some 2000 muzzles against the tiny force of just 436 Israeli soldiers guarding the strongpoints, strung at 11 km (7 mile) intervals along the 175 km (110 mile) canal line. This bombardment was followed by an assault by 8000 Egyptian infantry, who carefully selected landing sites in the gaps between the Israeli blockhouses. They were followed by special assault teams whose assignment was to eliminate the blockhouses while Egyptian Army engineers began construction of ten bridges across the canal.

The task of the Israeli commander in charge of the armoured brigades east of the canal was not an enviable one. General Abraham Mandler was aware that the Egyptians were attacking, but he did not know where to concentrate his forces for a counter-thrust. Should he try to destroy the bridges which the enemy was building, or should he attempt to join up with surviving forces in the blockhouse line? It was a situation at which many top-rate commanders would have balked but, unfortunately, General Mandler made the mistake of deciding to commit his tanks in small groups in order to find out exactly what was happening. They were met enthusiastically by Egyptians soldiers armed with new Soviet wire-guided anti-tank missiles, and were destroyed piecemeal. By nightfall, Mandler had lost nearly two-thirds of his original force of 280 tanks.

At 09.00 on Sunday the 7th, the first Egyptian armoured units began swarming across the newly built bridges over the canal. The plight of the surviving defenders in the Israeli strongpoints was desperate, but Mandler had been ordered to let them fend for themselves and to concentrate his remaining armour against the Egyptian tanks. There are many tales of heroism from this period of the war, but one of the most outstanding must be that of the southernmost Israeli garrison at Port Tewfik, where 42 defenders held out for an entire week against a whole Egyptian army, defying all attempts to enter their position and finally surrendering only when all their medical supplies and ammunition were exhausted.

At 11.40 on Sunday, Dayan himself arrived to review the situation in the Sinai, and he took the immediate decision to withdraw from the canal zone to the high ground east of it. The next few days witnessed a battle of containment as the Egyptians fought to break out into the Sinai, and the Israelis doggedly held them back. Egyptian tactics during this phase of the war can only be described as suicidal. They would prepare for an attack under cover of darkness, sending their infantry forward to within 1800 m (2000 yd) of the Israeli defences. At dawn, a short but intense artillery barrage would announce the assault, and then the infantry, supported by tanks, would move forward. Only one such attack, on Tuesday the 9th, achieved partial success, before being thrown back by an armoured Israeli counter-thrust. By Wednesday (at which time the Israelis were pushing off the Golan Heights), the Egyptians had run out of steam, and it was the Israelis' turn to attack.

Counter-attack

The basic plan was for a two-division assault across the canal at the junction of the Egyptian 2nd and 3rd Armies, for which a special prefabricated bridge had been prepared. This was a dangerous scheme, because the bulk of the Egyptian armoured reserves were on the west bank of the canal, but, as we have seen elsewhere, 'who dares, wins'.

Coincidentally, the Egyptians were also summoning their strength for another attempt at breaking out and, unknown to each other, both sides chose 14 October as the day of attack. The Egyptians attacked first in four columns, one in the north from Qantara, one from Ismailia, one towards the

Mitla Pass, and one in the south along the Gulf of Suez. However, the Israelis were fully prepared and had learned the danger of the Egyptian anti-tank wire-guided missiles. Keeping to the high ground, they used the highly accurate 105 mm guns on their Centurion and Patton tanks to knock out the Egyptian missile operators, moving rapidly from one position to another in order to spoil the Egyptians' aim.

The Israelis revised their basic plan, to take advantage of the situation. Instead of crossing the canal opposite Ismailia, as originally envisaged, the attack would now take place further south at Deversoir, just north of the Great Bitter Lake. The offensive began to roll late in the afternoon of the 15th, three armoured columns supported by paras and a rolling artillery bombardment moving rapidly towards the canal, while a diversionary attack pinned down the Egyptians in front of Ismailia. Heavy resistance was encountered in the Chinese Farm area, but Israeli 'watch and dodge' tactics, in which one tank moved while a second spotted for anti-tank missiles, were largely successful in minimizing casualties from these missiles.

The Israelis were handed one present on a plate, when the brigade commanded by Colonel Amnon suddenly found that it had broken through in the junction between the Egyptian 2nd and 3rd Armies, and was actually behind the lines. Pandemonium broke out among the Egyptians. Soldiers and tanks raced hither and thither in total confusion, while Amnon's tanks coolly blasted away at ammunition dumps, fuel depots, radar and missile sites, tanks and trucks. By the early morning of the 16th, the brigade entrusted to secure a foothold across the canal was on the west bank, the infantry crossing on rafts which were then sent back for the tanks. Israeli reinforcements, who were bringing pontoons in order to build bridges, pushed forward through the gap in the Egyptian lines created by Colonel Amnon's brigade, but were unable to reach the bank of the canal before dawn, and it would have been suicidal to try to build bridges in daylight.

Inevitably, the Egyptians counter-attacked on the 17th, but their attempt to throw the Israelis back from the canal failed, with the loss of 86 T-62 tanks against a mere 4 Israeli tanks destroyed. Thus, during the night of 18/19 October, Israeli engineers assembled the pontoon bridge in position and their tanks pressed across, splitting into two columns heading northwards and southwards along the west bank. By the evening of the 18th, the southern force had secured the strategically important Geneifa Hills and, on the following day, they seized Fayid airport.

However, Soviet Premier Kosygin telephoned President Sadat on the evening of the 20th and persuaded him to agree to a cease-fire, while American envoy Henry Kissinger convinced the Israelis.

Towards Damascus

Back in the east, on 11 October, Israeli forces had begun a major counter-attack in the northern sector of the Golan Heights, but the terrain and the multiplicity of Syrian anti-tank missiles held them up, and they could only make slow progress. Further south, another Israeli division launched an attack straight down the Damascus road, but it too ran into stiff opposition, and an entire armoured brigade was surrounded and virtually annihilated before being relieved by horrified paras the following morning. However, the Syrians were virtually at the end of their strength, and the Egyptian attack on the 14th has often been interpreted as an attempt to take Israeli pressure off them while reinforcements, in the form of an Iraqi armoured division, could be brought forward. However, this fared no better than the Syrian armoured formations had. The build-up was spotted by the Israeli commander on the southern flank, General Laner, and he prepared a classic trap: a three-sided killing-ground into which the oblivious Iraqi tanks obligingly trundled. Battle was joined at a distance of only 50 m (55 yd) and, hit in both flanks, the Iraqi forces reeled back in disorder, losing 80 tanks. Israeli casualties were zero.

The next attack came from Jordanian Centurion tanks every bit as good as the Israelis' own. They moved forward with determination but did not receive coordinated support from their Syrian and Iraqi allies, and were unable to make any headway against the Israeli bridgehead. A final attack by Iraqi forces against the northern flank of the bridgehead resulted in a seven-hour battle, again often at point-blank range, until an Israeli assault on the Iraqis' flank finally won the day. Meanwhile, Mount Hebron had been taken by the Golani Brigade, which advanced frontally, while Israeli paras were dropped by helicopter behind the Syrian lines. On 22 October, the Syrian government agreed to the cease-fire and the war was over.

THE LEBANON

Denied of their bases in Jordan after King Hussein expelled them just prior to the Yom Kippur War, the Palestine Liberation Organization guerrillas established their headquarters in Beirut. Following the Arab defeat in that campaign, the PLO intensified its raids across the border as well as other terrorist activities, which came to a head with the shooting of the Israeli ambassador in London in June 1982. The Israelis retaliated with an air strike on the PLO arms depot in Beirut's sports stadium, and the PLO escalated the conflict by means of an artillery bombardment of Israeli border settlements. Prime Minister Begin's patience finally snapped, and Israeli tanks were ordered into Lebanon, where the situation was already confused because of the internecine war which had been going on for some years between Lebanese Christians and Muslims. To begin with, the Israeli attack was purely defensive, being aimed at clearing a 40 km (25 mile) strip of southern Lebanon in order to push the PLO artillery back out of range of the northern settlements in Israel. However, the war soon escalated into more than this for, while Israeli sympathies largely lay with the Christian faction in Lebanon, Syria supported the Muslim cause and had maintained a strong military presence in the country ever since 1976.

Sunday, 6 June 1982. The war in the Falkland Islands was drawing to a close, but Colonel Eli Geva's thoughts were elsewhere as his armoured brigade rolled across the Lebanese border, heading for the line of the El Awali River which the Israelis had decided upon as a useful physical border to their planned demilitarized zone. Another column advanced through Metulla and seized Beaufort Castle which had been built by the Crusaders and which, standing on high ground, had for years served as a PLO fortress from which they could launch rocket attacks on the Israeli villages below. During the evening, Israeli paras landed in assault craft at the mouth of the El Awali River, and, on Monday, a third Israeli armoured column began moving towards the Al-Shouf Mountains.

Palestinian forces fought back viciously, killing large numbers of their own people – innocents held hostage by the terrorist forces who were supposed to be acting on their behalf. But, by the end of the first week of fighting, Israeli troops were in the suburbs of Beirut and had linked with the Christian Phalangists in cutting the road from Beirut to Damascus.

General Sharon, who had commanded the Israeli centre on the Suez front during the Yom Kippur War, was itching to get to grips with the Syrians in Lebanon, who were maintaining a distinctly low profile at this stage. His chance came when the Syrians sent tanks to reinforce a PLO unit. Putting Major-General 'Yanosh' Bengal in charge of the retaliatory force was no accident: Bengal had commanded the 7th Armoured Brigade on the Golan Heights in 1973, and his thirst for revenge against the Syrians was not yet quenched. Let off the leash, Bengal pursued the Syrians with vigour and, within two days of intense fighting, had killed at least 1000 men and had destroyed approximately 300 enemy tanks. By the weekend following that on which the invasion began, the Israelis had destroyed the heart of the PLO resistance, given the Syrians a sound thrashing, and established sound links with the Phalangist forces in Beirut.

Now the war entered a new phase as PLO guerrillas established fresh strongpoints, usually around or in the middle of harmless civilian buildings, not excluding hospitals. Intensive street-fighting was the inevitable result as the campaign waxed and waned over the long, hot days of that summer of 1982. The PLO dug in more firmly, while the Israelis were inhibited in their use of aircraft and artillery by the danger to countless innocent lives. During July, *Zahal* succeeded in capturing Beirut airport and various PLO camps in the vicinity, but Palestinian reinforcements were still flooding through from Syria and, on the 22nd of that month, the Israelis responded with a furious artillery bombardment which destroyed a further 70 Syrian tanks – many of them the new Russian T-72s which were pitched into battle in the Lebanon for the first time against the Israeli-designed and -built Merkava (which proved itself superior).

At the end of July, all Israeli reserves were mobilized and, on 1 August, began tightening a ring of steel around Beirut. The PLO had had enough by this time and wanted nothing more than a cease-fire which would allow them

Israeli paras ('The Guys') shuffle forward in the cramped confines of their transport aircraft prior to a drop.

to escape. This Arik Sharon would not permit, and he called up air strikes which for two days pounded every known or suspected PLO strongpoint, leaving Beirut in rubble. Reprisals inside Israel caused Prime Minister Menachem Begin to resign. Although it had administered a severe blow to both the PLO and Syria, the Israeli offensive failed in its ultimate objective of creating a new and peaceful state in the Lebanon, and the after-effects of the war are still being felt to this day.

The Israeli Army today

Surrounded by potential enemies, Israel is the most security-conscious country in the world outside the Soviet Union, and is constantly altering the composition of its forces, their designations, locations and commanders, with the result that, for example, different accounts of the Six-Day War can put one unit in two different places at the same time, or give the same unit two different designations. Israeli vehicles carry none of the divisional or regimental insignia beloved by other armies, but just individual numbers, and repeated efforts by foreign observers and journalists to crack the 'code' have produced even more discrepancies. Thus, it is impossible to say that unit X comprises Y number of men trained in parachute jumping and amphibious warfare, or whatever, as is possible with the élite forces of most other countries in this book. What *can* be said is that *Zahal* possesses airborne, mountain and armoured brigades which have proved their élite status time and time again, and which are believed to be organized as follows.

A parachute or mountain brigade will consist of three combat battalions, one artillery regiment, one reconnaissance company, and supporting signals and engineering units. Each battalion in turn consists of three rifle companies plus a headquarters company which doubles as the support company. The tripod arrangement continues downwards with three platoons to a company and three sections, each of ten men in two squads, to a platoon. An armoured brigade similarly will consist of three battalions, but, depending on its intended role, there may be three or four tank companies to a battalion, together with reconnaissance and self-propelled mortar platoons. Each tank company consists of three troops, each with three tanks, plus an HQ section with three tanks and two armoured personnel carriers.

Conscription in Israel is universal, with men serving for three years and women for two, after which soldiers revert to the reserve, which currently comprises a quarter of a million men and women on permanent 12-hour standby out of a population of only four million! The regular standing army consists of approximately 18,000 soldiers backed by 120,000 conscripts, in addition to which there is a small battalion of approximately 300 naval commandos trained in amphibious assault operations. Specialist trade training in the Israeli army lasts for the remarkably short period of three months, but is 'hi-tech' and intensive.

In any war, Israel's policy – because of the small size of the country – has to be to carry the fighting to the enemy, and *Zahal*'s objective has always been to achieve a quick result, because a prolonged war would bankrupt the country. Leadership from the front is not only encouraged but expected, and this has led to some of *Zahal*'s most spectacular successes, even though it means that the casualty rate among combat officers is higher than in most other countries. Due to their experience, though, the Israeli defence forces today are among the most highly skilled in the world.

CHAPTER SEVEN

WARSAW PACT & IRREGULAR FORCES

While 'never mind the quality, feel the width', may be an old joke, there are few Western observers who would see this expression as a laughing matter when it is used to describe the military forces of Soviet Russia and their allies. The USSR defeated Nazi Germany in World War 2 strictly through numerical superiority in both men and weapons (and would have won the war even without American, British and Allied assistance), and their whole thinking on future global conflict remains the same. The Soviet and Warsaw Pact forces facing Western Europe could overrun a minimum of 30 km (19 miles) a day on an 800 km (500 mile) front by sheer weight of numbers, regardless of tactics, *if* the NATO countries hesitated to use tactical nuclear weapons; two-thirds of their first-wave assault troops are, with oriental casualness, regarded as expendable. The balance would be sufficient to overrun and occupy the Continent.

If this is genuinely the case – as can be proved – then why, it may well be asked, do the Soviets and their allies bother with special forces at all? The answer is simple: although an accomplishment may be militarily possible, it is not necessarily desirable.

Speed, secrecy and surprise

Speed, secrecy and surprise have for millennia been regarded as the key ingredients in military success, and, as we have already seen, these goals are pursued assiduously by the élite forces of many nations. For the Russians, however, they have a special meaning as their whole military posture is based upon an offensive strategy, as compared with NATO's, which places its emphasis on defence and deterrence.

Despite their two-to-one superiority in men, tanks, guns and aircraft in Europe, Soviet forces would rely heavily on the preparatory work of 'desant' units to weaken the West's defence and to create confusion and disorganization. The word 'desant' itself does not have a precise parallel in Western military terminology, combining elements of both 'landing' and 'assault'. It is best described by example, although here we are handicapped by the fact that Soviet soldiers are not free to give press interviews! However, in an SAS-style 'desant' operation, men of the VDV (*Vozdushno-Desantnyye-Voyska*, or airborne troops, most probably comprised largely of *Vysotniki* or *Raydoviki*, the Russian equivalents of the SAS or Rangers) would be dropped by MI-8 *Hip* battlefield assault helicopters, or by parachute from I-76 *Candid* four-jet transports, in small groups of about twenty men behind enemy lines.

Their targets would be very much the same as those of the SAS under similar circumstances, and were described in a Royal United Services Institute (RUSI) bulletin. The principal objective of each group would be to reconnoitre an area for a later, large-scale, airborne assault, sounding out enemy positions and noting optimum sites for the invaders to occupy. Once this had been accomplished and the information radioed back, each team's task would become one of sabotage.

In one typical exercise, teams were parachuted by night into a 'defended' zone. Dressed in lightweight camouflage smocks, and carrying silenced assault rifles, they would melt into the background if they encountered substantial opposition, since full-scale firefights would have hindered them from reaching their prime objectives. However, reports of such obstructions would be radioed back immediately. (Here, the Russian reliance on quantity rather than quality would prove a hindrance because, compared with the sophisticated, miniaturized and computerized battlefield radios used by the Americans and British, the Soviet radio operators would have to change frequencies manually, and to a pre-arranged schedule, to avoid interception.)

Sabotage

Having reconnoitred their designated area, surviving members of the 'desant' team would begin sabotaging vital Western installations, in particular communications posts; laying landmines to disrupt counter-offensives; and placing markers on suitable landing zones for the far larger back-up force. A typical target – a tactical nuclear weapon site – could be 'taken out' by a mere half-dozen men of the *Vysotniki*, and the fact that Russian exercises emphasize such objectives shows clearly that the Soviet Union knows that NATO would have to resort to nuclear defence within a maximum of five days following a full-scale conventional attack.

One major difference between the Soviet 'desant' teams and their American or British counterparts is that they are only intended to operate in isolation for short periods of time – hours rather than days – and are regarded very much as small cogs in a large machine rather than as units able to act intelligently and damagingly on their own, as the SAS teams did so convincingly in the Falklands. The main assault would follow the *Vysotniki* operations at daybreak, huge AN-12 *Cub* transports dropping whole divisions of airborne troops and support equipment, including armoured personnel carriers and assault guns. Alternatively, especially in difficult terrain such as that to be found on the north of NATO's flank in Norway, heavy-duty helicopters would be deployed.

A measure of the Soviets' dependence on their 'desant' troops to crack open the front line in Europe is demonstrated by the fact that, of nine whole divisions in the VDV, each comprising some 8500 men, no fewer than seven are kept at constant readiness *in peacetime*, even though the number of aircraft available (approximately 1500) means that only two divisions could be deployed at a time.

Russian 'desant' troops have been actively engaged in recent years, the 105th Airborne Division spearheading the invasion of Afghanistan in 1979, while the 103rd – which had captured Prague airport during the Dubcek crisis of 1968 – was on instant alert standby to be flown out to Egypt in 1973, had the Israelis not stopped their advance at the Suez Canal.

'Desant' from the sea

Following, or launched simultaneously with, a Soviet attack via Finland into the northern flank of Norway, would almost certainly come a naval pincer movement out of the Baltic and Black Seas to hit Denmark and West Germany on the one hand, and Greece and Turkey on the other. For this reason the Russians maintain strong Marine Infantry formations as well as

WEAPONS OF THE SOVIET UNION AND RUSSIAN-EQUIPPED REGULAR AND IRREGULAR FORCES

Designation	Type	Calibre	Magazine	Rate of fire	Range	Remarks
AK47M	Assault rifle	7.62 mm	30 rounds	600 rpm cyclic	300–400 m	Most widely used assault rifle in the world
AKS74	Assault rifle	5.45 mm	30 rounds	650 rpm cyclic	400 m	New replacement for the AK47
RPK	Light machine-gun	7.62 mm	30, 40 or 75 rounds	660 rpm cyclic	800 m	Standard support weapon used at section level
PKM	Machine-gun	7.62 mm	100-, 200-, or 250-belt	690–720 rpm	1000 m	
M41	Mortar	50 mm	Single-shot	20 rpm	800 m	
M37	Mortar	82 mm	Single-shot	18 rpm	3000 m	
Sagger	Anti-tank missile	120 mm	Single-shot	Not applicable	3000 m	
RPG7	Anti-aircraft missile	85 mm	Single-shot	Not applicable	300 m	

Desant from the sea: Soviet amphibious vehicles, supported by helicopters, come ashore from a tank landing ship.

specially trained small assault teams akin to the SBS. In most respects, however, their philosophy concerning naval 'desant' operations is the same as it is for their application of airborne troops. Small units would be landed, usually and preferably by night, to assess the opposition, reconnoitre strongpoints, mark safe lines of approach and, if necessary, help to safeguard the bridgehead until the main wave of troops arrived at daylight.

A Russian assault from the sea is impressive in the extreme. Landing craft pour inshore, halting at a safe distance, if necessary, to disgorge their waves of amphibious tanks and armoured personnel carriers, while helicopters from ships such as the *Moskva* and *Leningrad* drop yet more troops right on top of the beach defences. 'Jump jets', Yak-36MPs, copied from the Harrier, provide overhead protection while also being able to give ground support fire and, in particular, take out radar and missile installations.

An ominous statistic to consider is that three out of every four Soviet 'desant' exercises against simulated NATO opposition are successful.

Soviets abroad

Russian special forces, including clandestine members of the GRU – the Army Secret Police – are widely known to have served, and to be serving still, as military advisers and actual fighting troops in many Middle Eastern and 'Third World' countries – particularly Cuba – and Russian-trained Cuban advisers and troops have been active in many of the world's trouble spots, notably Angola, during the 1970s.

The Soviet Army also keeps a very strong presence within the countries of the Warsaw Pact alliance, just as America and Britain do in West Germany. The main concentration is obviously in East Germany where, in addition to six German divisions, the Russians maintain no fewer than 9 armoured and 13 mechanized rifle divisions. Similarly, alongside the ten Czech divisions, the Russians field two tank and three mechanized rifle divisions. Only two of the Warsaw Pact countries other than Russia have special forces: Czechoslovakia, which has a long and illustrious military history as well as a sophisticated indigenous armaments industry, has an airborne brigade, including self-propelled armoured assault and anti-aircraft guns; while Poland has both an airborne division and an amphibious assault division. In all the Warsaw Pact countries, there is far greater standardization of both organization and equipment than exists within NATO, so these forces may safely be assumed to be constructed on the Soviet model, with the exception of some home-built weapons and vehicles such as the Czech OT-64 and OT-65 armoured personnel and reconnaissance vehicles, plus Czech Tatra and Polish Star trucks.

Apart from repressing democratic movements in the Warsaw Pact countries of their supposed allies, such as Hungary in 1956, Czechoslovakia in 1967 and Poland in recent years; and aiding and abetting left-wing nationalist movements in Third World countries and terrorist movements everywhere; and from propping up, usually through economic and military aid, various non-aligned countries; Soviet forces had not seen genuine warfare until they invaded Afghanistan in December 1979. 'Advisers' and 'technicians' have seen plenty of action, of course, from Korea and Vietnam to the Middle East, Africa, the Caribbean and Central and South America, but Afghanistan was the first real encounter for regular Soviet troops.

The Russians were no strangers to the country. After Mohammed Daud Khan was overthrown by Nur Mohammed Taraki and Hafizullah Amin in the *coup d'état* of April 1978, the new rulers welcomed further Soviet aid to boost the country's weak and predominantly feudal economy and to assist in the agrarian and other reforms which they were planning. However, Afghanistan is not only one of the poorest, but it is also one of the most medievally conservative countries in the world, and Taraki's reform programme met with considerable opposition, particularly from the landowning classes. Dissent produced repression in a familiar escalating spiral. In February 1979, the American ambassador was kidnapped by an extremist group and later killed, along with his captors, when Afghan security forces attempted to rescue him. A month later, a garrison of Afghan troops murdered all the Russian advisors in Herat, a town near the Iranian border. Amin's secret police stepped up their activities, the country's regular soldiers were confined to their barracks, and an increasing flood of Russian military equipment, including helicopters, began to arrive in the country. At the same time, the number of Afghan civilians leaving their homeland swelled in proportion and, by the time of the formal Russian invasion of Afghanistan in December, some 400,000 had fled over the mountains into Pakistan. Of more military significance is the fact that, by the same time, more than half of Afghanistan's regular troops had deserted and, literally, headed for the hills, where they continue to form the hard core of the resistance movement.

In desperation, Taraki requested – and received – more and more Soviet military aid in order to put down mutinies among the surviving troops and riots among the civilian population, while Amin gradually emerged as the real strong man of the regime. Taraki visited Moscow and asked Leonid Brezhnev's help in removing this thorn in his flesh, but an agent in his staff reported events to Amin, who had Taraki arrested and later executed. The country was in turmoil and Amin was hated by the vast majority of the population. However, he still had a 20-year treaty with the Soviet Union.

The Russians rewarded Amin by invading Afghanistan on 27 December 1979. Tanks and armoured personnel carriers, supported in the air by MiG ground-attack fighters and helicopter gunships, swiftly surrounded the country's capital, Kabul, and ruthlessly suppressed all attempts at opposition. Amin himself was executed.

The Afghan war

As ignorant and conservative as their forefathers, who denied the Khyber Pass to the British Army in the 19th century, the Afghan hill-farmers, who now constitute the heart of Afghan resistance to the Soviet invaders, still look like the mountain bandits from whom they are descended, with their flowing moustaches, billowing trousers, loose shirts and turbans. Unlike the Palestinians, whom they resemble in so many ways, however, the Afghan freedom fighters lack any unified political goal other than that of expelling the invaders, and are even divided into a variety of religious factions. Their advantage lies in the fact that, whereas the Russians have largely been able to secure the towns and cities, the guerrillas control the countryside – and Napoleon lost his war in Spain for exactly the same reason.

As did the Americans in Vietnam, the Russians invaded Afghanistan full of confidence and with the most modern military equipment, spearheaded by élite airborne troops. Like the Vietcong, the Afghan guerrillas have the support of the majority of the local populace and are able to blend innocently into the background, when they are not trekking across the remote mountains in search of a target to ambush. They have more enthusiasm than skill, although their knowledge of the terrain helps them,

A Russian T-72 tank stands guard in a Kabul street. While the Soviets control the towns, the guerrillas hold the country.

while the Russian armoured vehicles must keep to the main roads, such as they are. Soviet armoured columns roam the country in huge convoys, protected from above by helicopter gunships eager to take off against the first hint of armed resistance, while élite airborne troops parallel SAS and Green Beret operations in Vietnam, being dropped secretly to sabotage guerrilla camps and set up ambushes. In some parts of the country, the Russians have deliberately driven people from their homes in an effort to create an inhospitable wasteland out of which the Afghan resistance cannot operate. In other areas, they have seeded tracts of farmland with small and virtually undetectable anti-personnel mines. The Soviets have also taken advantage of the fierce tribal vendettas existing between many members of the resistance groups, winning some to their side by the promise of vengeance against their enemies.

In return, although untutored in modern warfare, the Afghan guerrillas have resorted to the classic tactics of mining roads along which Soviet patrols are known to pass; of attacking isolated military and government posts; and of bomb attacks and assassinations in the towns and cities. The situation has so many military parallels with that prevailing in Northern Ireland that one final question has to be asked:

Freedom fighter or terrorist?

The bulk of this book has been devoted to what the people of most Western countries regard as the guardians of their freedom: the élite military forces of the democratic nations. To others, however, these same forces are the mailed fist of repression, and it must not be forgotten that many of the terrorist groups are as well armed and, in many cases, as well trained and dedicated to a cause as are the marines, paras and special forces of America, Britain or other countries.

At the heart of the terrorist movement lies the Palestine Liberation Organization which, through Moscow, has for at least two decades led the way in financing and training other groups dedicated to the overthrow of existing Western governments, to providing them with intelligence aid, documentation, weapons and ammunition, and to establishing infiltration and escape routes. Such assistance has been particularly prevalent in Latin America and, at the time of writing this book, seems likely to bring upon the people of Nicaragua the same type of American response as befell Grenada.

The PLO is financed today mainly by Saudi Arabia and Kuwait, but still relies heavily on Soviet assistance, particularly in the matter of arms and ammunition. In turn, the PLO trains guerrillas from other countries in camps in the Middle East. In any one year, more than 2000 terrorists take the four-month training courses in Syria, South Yemen and, until recently, Lebanon. They come from Argentina, Brazil, Chile, Uruguay, Mexico and El Salvador in Latin America; from Turkey, Spain, West Germany, Italy and Ireland in Europe; from Pakistan, Bangladesh, Iran, Armenia, the Philippines, Japan and Sri Lanka in Asia; and from South Africa, Zimbabwe, Niger, Somalia, Ghana, Nigeria, Tunisia, Egypt, Togo and Mali in Africa. Simultaneously, PLO veterans are frequently dispatched as advisers in the field to other terrorist organizations around the world. Their affiliations include the Italian *Operaia Autonomia* and *Brigada Rossa* (Red Brigade), the Spanish *Euzcadi Ta Askatauna* (Basque separatists), the Moro National Liberation Front in the Philippines, the Baader-Meinhof Red Army Faction in Germany, the Irish Republican Army, the Japanese Red Army and the Dutch Red-Aid, among others.

What, the objective reader must ask, differentiates these groups from the Afghans? In all cases the ultimate aim is the abolition of what a particular guerrilla group considers a repressive regime, or the establishment of an independent state for an ethnic or religious faction. In the West, it is popular to think of the Russians as the 'bad guys', and therefore their invasion of Afghanistan – regardless of their mutual aid treaties with the two preceding governments – is seen as unnecessary intervention in the affairs of an autonomous state, and the Afghan guerrillas are therefore regarded as 'freedom fighters'. But the Palestinians or the IRA see themselves as fighting for exactly the same reasons. The whole question, 'freedom fighter or terrorist?' is decided by a value judgement, depending on individual circumstances, education, political inclination, geography and a multitude of other factors.

List of Illustrations

A Russian T-72 tank stands guard in a Kabul street. While the Soviets control the towns, the guerrillas hold the country.

while the Russian armoured vehicles must keep to the main roads, such as they are. Soviet armoured columns roam the country in huge convoys, protected from above by helicopter gunships eager to take off against the first hint of armed resistance, while élite airborne troops parallel SAS and Green Beret operations in Vietnam, being dropped secretly to sabotage guerrilla camps and set up ambushes. In some parts of the country, the Russians have deliberately driven people from their homes in an effort to create an inhospitable wasteland out of which the Afghan resistance cannot operate. In other areas, they have seeded tracts of farmland with small and virtually undetectable anti-personnel mines. The Soviets have also taken advantage of the fierce tribal vendettas existing between many members of the resistance groups, winning some to their side by the promise of vengeance against their enemies.

In return, although untutored in modern warfare, the Afghan guerrillas have resorted to the classic tactics of mining roads along which Soviet patrols are known to pass; of attacking isolated military and government posts; and of bomb attacks and assassinations in the towns and cities. The situation has so many military parallels with that prevailing in Northern Ireland that one final question has to be asked:

Freedom fighter or terrorist?

The bulk of this book has been devoted to what the people of most Western countries regard as the guardians of their freedom: the élite military forces of the democratic nations. To others, however, these same forces are the mailed fist of repression, and it must not be forgotten that many of the terrorist groups are as well armed and, in many cases, as well trained and dedicated to a cause as are the marines, paras and special forces of America, Britain or other countries.

At the heart of the terrorist movement lies the Palestine Liberation Organization which, through Moscow, has for at least two decades led the way in financing and training other groups dedicated to the overthrow of existing Western governments, to providing them with intelligence aid, documentation, weapons and ammunition, and to establishing infiltration and escape routes. Such assistance has been particularly prevalent in Latin America and, at the time of writing this book, seems likely to bring upon the people of Nicaragua the same type of American response as befell Grenada.

The PLO is financed today mainly by Saudi Arabia and Kuwait, but still relies heavily on Soviet assistance, particularly in the matter of arms and ammunition. In turn, the PLO trains guerrillas from other countries in camps in the Middle East. In any one year, more than 2000 terrorists take the four-month training courses in Syria, South Yemen and, until recently, Lebanon. They come from Argentina, Brazil, Chile, Uruguay, Mexico and El Salvador in Latin America; from Turkey, Spain, West Germany, Italy and Ireland in Europe; from Pakistan, Bangladesh, Iran, Armenia, the Philippines, Japan and Sri Lanka in Asia; and from South Africa, Zimbabwe, Niger, Somalia, Ghana, Nigeria, Tunisia, Egypt, Togo and Mali in Africa. Simultaneously, PLO veterans are frequently dispatched as advisers in the field to other terrorist organizations around the world. Their affiliations include the Italian *Operaia Autonomia* and *Brigada Rossa* (Red Brigade), the Spanish *Euzcadi Ta Askatauna* (Basque separatists), the Moro National Liberation Front in the Philippines, the Baader-Meinhof Red Army Faction in Germany, the Irish Republican Army, the Japanese Red Army and the Dutch Red-Aid, among others.

What, the objective reader must ask, differentiates these groups from the Afghans? In all cases the ultimate aim is the abolition of what a particular guerrilla group considers a repressive regime, or the establishment of an independent state for an ethnic or religious faction. In the West, it is popular to think of the Russians as the 'bad guys', and therefore their invasion of Afghanistan – regardless of their mutual aid treaties with the two preceding governments – is seen as unnecessary intervention in the affairs of an autonomous state, and the Afghan guerrillas are therefore regarded as 'freedom fighters'. But the Palestinians or the IRA see themselves as fighting for exactly the same reasons. The whole question, 'freedom fighter or terrorist?' is decided by a value judgement, depending on individual circumstances, education, political inclination, geography and a multitude of other factors.

PENGUIN BOOKS

SOMME

Lyn Macdonald is one of the most highly regarded historians of the First World War. Her books tell the men's stories in their own words and cast a unique light on the experiences of the ordinary 'Tommy'. *The Roses of No Man's Land*, *Somme* and *Passchendaele* have been recently reissued by Penguin. She lives near Cambridge.

LYN MACDONALD

————

SOMME

PENGUIN BOOKS

This book is dedicated to a single soldier
of Kitchener's Army.
His name is Legion.

*And he asked him, What is thy name? And he
answered, saying My name is Legion:
for we are many.*
St Mark v, 9

PENGUIN BOOKS

Published by the Penguin Group
Penguin Books Ltd, 80 Strand, London WC2R ORL, England
Penguin Group (USA) Inc., 375 Hudson Street, New York, New York 10014, USA
Penguin Group (Canada), 90 Eglinton Avenue East, Suite 700, Toronto, Ontario, Canada M4P 2Y3
(a division of Pearson Penguin Canada Inc.)
Penguin Ireland, 25 St Stephen's Green, Dublin 2, Ireland (a division of Penguin Books Ltd)
Penguin Group (Australia), 707 Collins Street, Melbourne, Victoria 3008, Australia
(a division of Pearson Australia Group Pty Ltd)
Penguin Books India Pvt Ltd, 11 Community Centre, Panchsheel Park, New Delhi – 110 017, India
Penguin Group (NZ), 67 Apollo Drive, Rosedale, Auckland 0632, New Zealand
(a division of Pearson New Zealand Ltd)
Penguin Books (South Africa) (Pty) Ltd, Block D, Rosebank Office Park,
181 Jan Smuts Avenue, Parktown North, Gauteng 2193, South Africa

Penguin Books Ltd, Registered Offices: 80 Strand, London WC2R ORL, England

www.penguin.com

First published by Michael Joseph 1983
Published in Penguin Books 1993
Reissued in this edition 2013
001

Printed in Great Britain by Clays Ltd, St Ives plc

ISBN: 978-0-241-95238-2

www.greenpenguin.co.uk

Penguin Books is committed to a sustainable
future for our business, our readers and our planet.
This book is made from Forest Stewardship
Council™ certified paper.

Contents

Maps

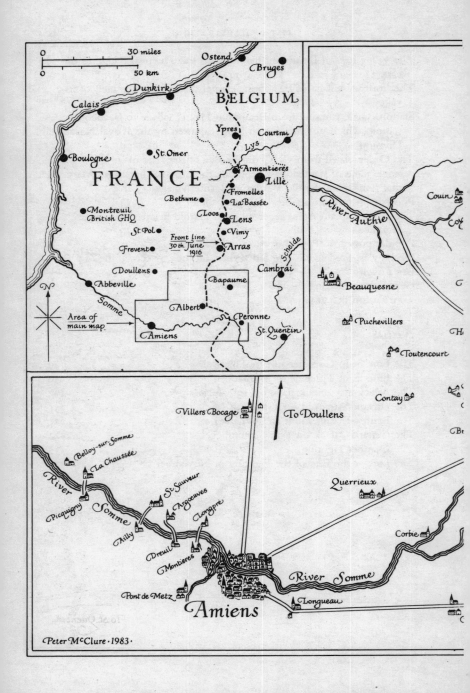

Peter McClure · 1983 ·

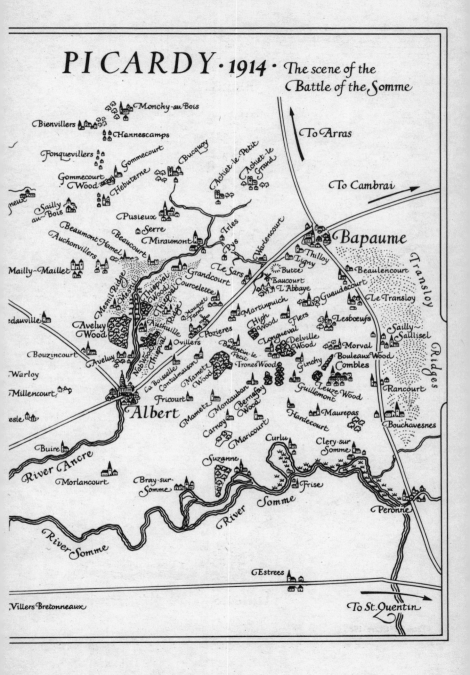

Author's Foreword
and Acknowledgements

If this book had a sub-title it might appropriately be *Whatever happened to Kitchener's Army?* The Somme happened to it. When the Battle of the Somme finished Kitchener's Army was all but finished, too. It seemed at the time that the country would never get over it – and it never has.

In one sense Kitchener's Army was hardly an army at all. Before it was formed in August 1914, the British Army had been a small, tight-knit force of highly-trained professionals (as it is again today) equally skilled in dealing with the impertinent skirmishes in foreign parts which, since the death of Napoleon, had passed as wars, and with the rebellions and insurrections in various parts of the Empire it garrisoned and policed. To the domestic population of Great Britain in those days before instant communication and responsible journalism unrolled international events before the daily judgement of the domestic scene, wars and disturbances alike were remote affairs. Most people were complacent, confident, proud enough of their disciplined and structured society to be content to leave power to the politicians, morality to the churchmen, administration to the Establishment and fighting to the Army.

Nineteen-sixteen was to change all that, although the murmur of the first tentative questioning was drowned by the clamour of the war itself, and the first tremor in the rock-like foundations of British society was masked by the monstrous vibrations of the fighting. A decade was to pass before the murmur grew to a growl and half a century before the tremor was perceived as the first wave of a full-sized earthquake.

From the turbulent present it is seductive to look back on those days before the Great War as on a halcyon age. With the benefit of hindsight and the cultivation of the habit of criticism, it is tempting to condemn those whose duty it was to conduct the war and even to marvel at the attitude of those who saw it as their duty to fight it. The very horror of their experience has given birth to a widely held emotional view of the war in which every Tommy wears a halo and every officer above the rank of captain a pair of horns.

Perhaps it is logical, in the spirit of our times, that some of us should think like that. But it is equally logical that, in every echelon of their society, the Great War generation should have been impelled to act as they did. They were not endowed with the gift of foreseeing the future. It is doubtful, even if they had been, if they would have acted differently, for they were as much the children of their time as we are of ours.

I am constantly amazed by the passion of controversy and argument which discussion of the war can still arouse after the passage of seventy years. It is not my intention to enter the lists. This book does not set out to draw political conclusions and, although it is the story of a battle, it is more concerned with the experience of war than with the war itself. The whole nation experienced that war just as, three generations on, the nation is still experiencing its repercussions.

There was hardly a household in the land, there was no trade, occupation, profession or community, which was not represented in the thousands of innocent enthusiasts who made up the ranks of Kitchener's Army before the Battle of the Somme. By the end of the War there was hardly a family in the land which, in its inner or outer circle, had not suffered bereavement and hardly a young man who was lucky enough to return who would not be affected to the end of his life by his experience of that War to end Wars, and who would not see the world through new eyes because of it.

Most of them survived long enough to see ideals they had nurtured at its outset turn sour in its aftermath. Some survive still, but the voices, like the old soldiers themselves, are rapidly fading away. Soon all that will be left to tell us something of what it was all like in 1914 will be their sepia images in old photographs, grinning in self-conscious khaki, as the mouthless crowds cheer and the silent bands play and the flags fly frozen in the air. When the last of them has gone, a great silence will fall. I hope that these histories of their war will at least continue to transmit the echo.

My first thanks must go to the many old soldiers who with courtesy, patience, kindness and infinite enthusiasm have spent hours talking about the war, who have generously lent me precious souvenirs, books, letters, diaries, photographs, and who (often handicapped by ill-health or disability) have gone to the trouble of writing lengthy accounts of their experiences. Those who have contributed directly to this particular book are listed at the back with my special thanks, but in ten years of research and writing about the Great War I have 'on my books', so to speak, almost 3,000 men and women who served in it. Although it would be impossible to quote them all I owe all of them a debt of gratitude for a plethora of stories, of viewpoints, of first-hand details which have added to my own knowledge and have helped me to learn, to understand and to 'tell it like it was' for them, within a broader context than perhaps these very young people understood themselves at the time. They have done more than that. They have enabled me to build up a considerable collection of oral and written history, documents and ephemera. From a practical point of view a mere fraction can be utilized in the books I write, but, in its natural home in the care of the Imperial War Museum, the collection will, I know, be of value and importance long after we have all 'faded away'.

Ironically, the larger such a mass of material becomes the more difficult it becomes to make use of it unless one is gifted with a computer-like memory. Few working authors (and none whose field is military history!) can rise to the dizzy heights of owning a computer, but my life has been eased and my efficiency increased a hundredfold through the hard work and enthusiasm of members of the (1981) Sixth Form of the Harvey Grammar School, Folkestone, who, with zeal and breath-taking attention to detail, undertook the mammoth task of cataloguing, collating, indexing and cross-indexing some four million words of written and recorded material and then claimed to have enjoyed doing it! I hope they did, and I am very grateful to them, and, in particular, to John Botting and Bill Westall, the two schoolmasters who not only organized the project, guided the boys through it and made themselves responsible for much irreplaceable material, but through their teaching imbued the boys with the enthusiasm and interest which led them to undertake the task in the first place.

I first heard of the Harvey Grammar School one soggy morning on the Somme through a chance meeting with Neill Page, Paul Iverson and Simon Marshall who had just finished A-levels and, inspired by school trips organized by Messrs. Botting and Westall, were making the most of their spare time on a camping holiday exploring the Somme for themselves. Since then Neill and Paul, in particular, have become valuable lieutenants on research trips to the battlefields and in return for sleeping space on the floor, a few beers and a square meal or two, have enthusiastically undertaken all the difficult jobs from patiently teaching me how to read a compass properly to identifying obscure trenches, plotting gun-positions, crawling through tunnels (which they had found in the first place) and digging the car out when it got bogged down on rough tracks where no car should reasonably be expected to go.

I never cease to be amazed at the generosity and willingness of people who volunteer to help. It is obvious that I could never undertake such a mammoth task of research unaided and equally obvious that, so far as the collection of first-hand information is concerned, it is not so much the eleventh hour as two minutes to midnight. Since the publication of *They Called it Passchendaele*, the first of my books on the Great War, I have had amazing luck to acquire a corps of helpers who, between them, have enabled me to enlarge the scope of my work to a degree which would otherwise have been impossible for one person to cover. Some have come through chance meetings in France; many are readers, quite unknown to me, who have volunteered information or introductions to old soldiers; others I have met on the Battlefield Tours I occasionally accompany as guest-lecturer. A good number of them have proved to be first-rate interviewers. Some have made a hobby (valuable to me) of scouring the yellowed files of their local newspapers in search of information about local battalions. Others, like Mollie Jewsbury and Helen McClure, have undertaken the tedious but infinitely worthwhile chore of transforming long and often indecipherable diaries and journals into clean typescript. I am immensely grateful to these ladies, as well as to the people throughout the country who have given much of their time to tracing and talking to old soldiers who would otherwise be out of my reach. Frank Hobson in the North-east, Robert Trafford in the West Country, Alastair McNeilage in East Anglia, Barbara Taylor in Nottingham, Albert Texeira de Mattos and Yves de Kok in Belgium, Elizabeth Ogilvie in New Zealand, Vivien Riches in Australia, and Don Dean, Chris Sheeran, Stan Taylor, Ken Handley, Graham Winton, Hugh Williams, Ken Smallwood and Graham Maddocks.

Of the 'old firm' – the original team who have been helping since the beginning of this project ten years ago – my thanks are yet again due to Guy Francis, to John Woodroff, who checked units, dates and actions against official records with his customary meticulous care, and to my BBC colleague, Ritchie Cogan, for his support and interest both in this country and on forays to the battlefields and particularly for his expert assistance with the illustrations, competently photographed by John Daniel who, like me, will not forget the hair-raising experience of getting the aerial shots from a one-engined aircraft flown by a co-operative but insouciant pilot! It was the way he kept smiling when the engine cut out that made us glad to regain terra firma!

Richard Dunning (who purchased the mine-crater at la Boisselle rather than see it filled in and built on) has given help which I much appreciate, as has Tom Gudmestad in the USA.

The Commonwealth War Graves Commission has, as always, dealt with enquiries in Britain and in France with unfailing courtesy and efficiency and I am particularly grateful to Stuart Campbell at its Headquarters at Maidenhead and to Steve Grady and his staff in Arras.

I must also record my thanks to Eyre Methuen Limited for allowing me to use extracts from *The Private Papers of Douglas Haig*.

Colin Butler deserves a paragraph to himself. I met him in Ypres three years ago and since then he has travelled more miles, conducted more interviews and done more work than anyone else, with the possible exception of myself – although I wouldn't be too sure! His energy is boundless, his enthusiasm inexhaustible and his contribution has been immense. In trying to thank him, words fail me. All I can say is that *he* never does. He even co-opted the services of his long-suffering wife, Wendy, who collated the information on the 13th Service Battalion, The Rifle Brigade, from a multitude of disparate sources and she combined this time-consuming job with having a baby at the same time!

Of my friends 'on location' in France, where most of this book has been researched and written, I must thank Serge and Jeannine Mills, who have not only provided a roof over my head, cosseted, fed, watered and warmed me over two Somme winters and inclement springs, regardless of muddy boots, dripping anoraks and trench maps spread out across half their premises, but have introduced me to many valuable contacts on the Somme and have also indulged me with many hours of relaxing conviviality, hospitality, conversation and friendship. Neither they, nor my other friends in Authuille who have made me feel 'one of the family' (Monsieur Oscar, Mario, Danielle, Roger, Madame Rose, to name but a few) will ever know how much that meant at the end of a long day's slog at the typewriter or out on the ground.

But my unfailing support has been my assistant Alma Woodroff, who has had less than most of us of the interest involved in tramping the Somme or of meeting old soldiers. But, in a sense, she knows them better than any of us, for it is she who transcribes the hundreds of hours of recordings, organizes the research, keeps tabs on everything and keeps everyone in order. Somehow she also managed, uncomplainingly, to fit in the typing of the draft and the manuscript of this book, deciphering the indecipherable, making sense of the unintelligible and, best of all, still came up laughing at the jokes. After three books on the war, if anyone has earned a campaign medal, she has.

My husband, Ian Ross, loathes publicity but I hope he will indulge my feeling that, after ten years of re-fighting the Great War, I owe him my formal thanks for allowing a third of his house to be taken over as archive-cum-office, for putting up with my frequent absences, for his disinterested advice and invaluable judgement, and for only very occasionally complaining of shell-shock.

LYN MACDONALD

Part 1

Lads, You're Wanted!

'Lads, you're wanted! Over there,'
Shiver in the morning dew,
More poor devils like yourselves
Waiting to be killed by you.

E. A. MACKINTOSH

Chapter 1

It was the Romans who first built the long straight road thrusting out from Amiens through Albert to Bapaume, swinging north to Arras and westward to the coast. Now the autoroute speeds down from Calais, swirls into a tangle of highways round Loos and Lens, swoops past the Vimy Ridge and round Arras, vibrating under the wheels of fast cars and Euro-lorries streaming south to Paris and beyond.

In summer, when the stream of traffic swells to a river, the Euro-driver, keeping an ill-humoured eye on his wing-mirror, is moved a dozen times an hour to curse certain motor cars, half-blinded by their right-hand drives, in their wavering attempts to overtake his juggernaut, and shrugs with Gallic resignation as the British registration plates squeeze by.

Past Arras, for the first time since leaving Calais, a driver can relax. The confusion of signboards disappears; the road runs straight; the landscape opens out into a sweep of downs and valleys and, on rising ground to the west, a scattering of copses and villages with the distant spires of country churches, half-hidden by clumps of trees. Curious, map-reading passengers can easily identify them – Gueudecourt, Flers, Lesboeufs, Morval, Combles – and may observe, with idle interest, that the river, soon to be bridged, is the River Somme. But they would have to be quick with the Michelin.

At motorway speed it takes, at most, twelve minutes to cover the twenty-five kilometres from the exit at Bapaume to the exit at Estrées. Between them, the highway, with singular precision, swings across the eastern limits of the battlefield of the Somme. The village of Estrées, at the end of the line attacked by the French Army, was the first and most southerly objective on the first day of the Battle. The British objective was the small town of Bapaume. In five months of almost continuous fighting, they struggled towards it through the summer and autumn of 1916. A hundred and fifty thousand men died. In the end, when the Battle itself died out in the November chill and the slough in front of Gueudecourt, Flers, Lesboeufs, Morval, Combles, they had not quite managed to get there.

★

Later, when it was long over, everyone remembered the bird-song. Doves, cooing beneath the eaves of a shell-racked barn; the faint chirrup of a lark that still, astoundingly, wheeled in the clear sky, far beyond the reach of shot or shrapnel; the song of a nightingale when the guns fell briefly silent and, in the beginning, the endless cawing of rooks in the high trees along the springtime roads of Picardy as the soldiers marched along them in an endless khaki tide.

They were marching towards the Battle of the Somme. But that name, with its tragic connotations destined to ring hollow down the years, had not yet been coined. The soldiers preparing for the fight called it the Big Push. Very few of them were soldiers at all. They were shop assistants, clerks, artisans, aristocrats, butchers, errand boys, farmers, schoolmasters, miners, grocers, sheep-shearers, bankers – but they were united by a simple resolve to put the Germans in their place once and for all. That place, in the universal opinion of the British Tommies, was well below the salt in a world where few would have disputed the right of Great Britain, attended by her Empire, to occupy the head of the table.

Pouring into the Somme, marching to and from the training grounds, moving wholesale from billets in one indistinguishable French village only to tramp in apparently aimless circles to another, the infantry were glad, on the whole, to be on the move. They had been at the front for many months; they had held the trenches, graduating from quiet to 'lively' stretches of the line; they had become hardened to discomfort and cautiously blasé under shellfire. A few of the earlier arrivals had taken part in the Battles of Loos and Festubert, and lively spirits, handy with a knobkerry, had developed a penchant for prowling round No Man's Land and paying rowdy surprise visits to the enemy's trenches, but not one man in five hundred had ever been 'over the top' in a major battle. Until now, by exercising a reasonable degree of caution, the majority of Kitchener's Army had run a slightly greater risk of dying from boredom in the trenches than from the attentions of the enemy. Their philosophy was summed up by the phrase that had become a universal motto, *If you can't take a joke you shouldn't have joined!* They were half a million strong, volunteers to a man and, although there was a leavening of professional soldiers in their ranks, hardly anyone among them had been in khaki for more than twenty-three months. By the early summer of 1916, on the eve of the biggest battle of the war, they were, at best, half trained, and this unpleasant but inescapable truth was at the forefront of the minds of the professional army commanders throughout the long months of planning the battle. It was in their disquiet that the first seeds of the tragedy took root.

The Army had undeniably done its best, but the tide of patriotic enthusiasm which had swept a hundred thousand would-be soldiers into its ranks in the first ten days of the war had completely swamped its resources. At the beginning of August 1914, it had been a small, tight-knit professional force. By the end of the same month it had swelled, willy-nilly, into a vast amorphous mass of men and boys, united only by boundless enthusiasm at the prospect of being turned into soldiers. The problem was how to set about it. The Regular Army was occupied else-where and, by the beginning of September, Commanding Officers of Regimental Depots in Britain were turning grey under the strain of hand-ling a strength that had catapulted from a disciplined body of one or, at most, two reserve battalions, to ten, eleven, twelve, thirteen 'Service' bat-talions of raw recruits, enlisted for the duration of the war, and whose only resemblance to 'battalions' as the Army knew them, was that they consisted of a thousand or so men apiece – all of them devoid of the slightest military skill, but asking nothing more than to be sent to France without delay. In desperation they closed recruiting lists, canvassed the ragged ranks of would-be soldiers for any who had at least seen service in the Boys' Brigade or as Boy Scouts, slapped corporals' stripes on the sleeves of their civilian suits, handed them over to bemused drill-sergeants and turned to the War Office with imperative demands for advice, for ration money, for equipment and, above all, for instructors. The replies, when they came, generally consisted of little more than terse orders to 'Carry On'.

The War Office had problems of its own. It was being besieged from all quarters, not only from the hard-pressed commands of its ballooning Army, wobbling under the weight of its unwieldy expansion, but from a hundred other directions where private enterprise had raised what amounted to a series of private armies.

In the first enthusiastic weeks of war it seemed that every county, town and borough all over the British Isles, each anxious to have at least one battalion of its own, had set itself up as a recruiting agency. As fast as young men poured into Town Halls to enlist, money poured in from the local citizenry to maintain them. Within days, and in numbers that those concerned with the administration of the Army preferred not to contem-plate, they were happily encamped on Wimbledon Common, in Bellevue Park, on the Ayrshire coast and on private estates, village greens and local parks across the length and breadth of the country. There was no hope of Khaki as yet but, tweed-capped and flannel-trousered though they were, the new recruits basked in the glow of local admiration, and drilled as enthusiastically as though their broom handles were rifles in response to the tentative suggestions of young officers whose commissions, at present, emanated from the local Mayor, rather than from the King, and

whose superior knowledge was cribbed shakily from some well-thumbed
army manual dating from the Boer War.

> *Where are our uniforms?*
> *Far far away*
> *When will our rifles come?*
> *P'raps p'raps some day . . .*

It was the first parody of a war whose parodies were to become im-
mortal.

All officers of the Reserve, many of them verging on the antediluvian,
had been called up and, unless actually confined to wheelchairs, had
answered the call. An appeal had gone out for 'old sweats' who had served
in the Boer War or even in the Sudan to come forward to help with
the training. It was necessarily sketchy and not entirely relevant to the
circumstances of modern warfare. In the summer and autumn of 1915,
when certain battalions of the New Army started arriving at the front, it
was not unknown for Divisional Headquarters to receive reports that
were couched in terminology strangely inappropriate to the European
landscape. The old soldiers, who had initiated the New Army into the
military arts, and whose last experience of soldiering had been a dozen
years earlier in South Africa, were accustomed to referring to 'plains' and
'*kopjes*' and their pupils, assuming this to be standard military practice,
had naturally followed suit. A year later, their error having been pointed
out by a score of apoplectic brigadiers, they now knew better.

There was small resemblance between the arid veldt of South Africa
and the dulcet countryside of Picardy. The River Somme ambled towards
Amiens, coiling in long, lazy loops through a marshy valley, joined by a
score of minor tributaries that turned it, here and there, into a waterscape
of straggling streams and islands. Just behind Corbie it met the Ancre,
flowing down through Albert from the north-east, where the British
Army stood astride the river, on the edge of high chalk downs where the
German Army was entrenched.

On 1 July the British had been in position for a bare ten months. But
the enemy had been there for almost two years. The Germans had come
to the Somme early on an autumn morning. It was 27 September 1914,
and, in the tiny hamlet of Authuille, tucked under the high bluff of
the Thiepval Ridge, not a man, woman or child would ever forget the
date.

Swelling out of the valley carved by the River Ancre more than a
hundred feet below, the crest of the Thiepval Ridge was deceptively
gentle. A plateau rather than a summit, with broad shoulders that breasted

the horizon as they ran down to Grandcourt, away on the left and reached towards Aveluy, away on the right. Both villages stood on the banks of the River Ancre and its gentle course, its wooded valleys, the high hills above, had made it a favourite place with holiday-makers who preferred green tranquillity to the elegant bustle of seaside resorts. In the summers before the war they came from as far away as Paris, to swim or fish in the river, to walk and ride in the hills, to climb the winding road to Thiepval village on the summit of the ridge, to admire the view and to take afternoon tea, in the English-style, enjoying the delicious cakes for which the pâtisserie in Thiepval was justly renowned.

Thiepval was a seigniorial village, not much changed from feudal times. It had a few shops, a café or two, a sizeable church and sixty odd houses occupied by the farmworkers who worked the fertile lands around. But what caught the eye from miles away was the Château. Large and imposing, it had stood for three centuries in front of the village, dominating the ridge on the foremost edge of the plateau, a landscape of formal gardens stretching from its elegant stone terrace to the verge of its private wood that ran down the lower slopes to the river valley. It commanded a magnificent view.

Strolling on the terrace of an evening, the old Count, Monsieur de Bréda, could almost have exchanged a nod with his neighbour, who owned a château nearly as grand diagonally across the way on the Mesnil Ridge above the dark mass of Aveluy Wood. Ahead, half concealed by the trees of the Count's own valley, Hamel village straggled up the opposite slope and, away on his right, where the long saddle of the Mesnil Ridge ran into the cleft of a narrow valley, the spire of Beaumont Church could just be seen above it. By strolling no more than a hundred yards from his domain, past the village and up the gradual rise of the hilltop, he could survey miles of lush farmland rolling up towards Pozières; away on the low ground to the right, if he could not actually see the town of Albert, set low in the fold of the valley four miles away, he might easily have caught a glimpse of its famous landmark, when a ray of the setting sun lingered briefly on the gilded Virgin towering above the roof of its cathedral. In structure, in outlook, in situation, the Château of Thiepval occupied a position that was second to none.

The de Brédas owned the Thiepval Ridge, with all its farms and villages, and the only thing that had disturbed the satisfaction of the Count, as he surveyed the rolling hectares of his property, was that there was no heir to succeed to it.

The de Brédas were old and childless. Earlier in the year the Count had died and been laid to rest in the vault of the family sepulchre among his more prolific ancestors whose ancient coffins, it was rumoured by the villagers, contained not merely their earthly remains but all their costly jewels. Now the Comtesse de Bréda had gone too. The local servants had been paid off and Madame de Bréda, with her chauffeur and her maid, had swept through Authuille in the new motor car that had been her husband's pride and joy, making for Amiens and the safety of her sister's house. The Château was empty and its long windows, accustomed to throw back the rays of the evening sun as it drifted down behind the Mesnil Ridge, stood blank and shuttered. The villagers, who had seen the Comtesse depart, deduced that the war was approaching too close for comfort.

It was just thirty-five days since the first shots had been fired and fired far to the north, over the Belgian frontier at Mons. It was almost beyond belief that in one short month the Germans could have swept through France, pushing the French and their British ally in front of them, to the very gates of Paris, that three great battles could have been fought and that, even now, the enemy was pouring apparently limitless forces across the captured plains of the north, as he raced towards the sea. In the past few days, rumour had moved faster than events, in a situation so fluid that the newspapers could hardly keep up with it. The *Voix du Nord* was printing little more than ringing calls to arms and patriotic rhetoric, but word of mouth had it that, three days ago, shooting had been heard at Chaulnes and that, only yesterday, the Germans were in Maricourt, not seven kilometres away from the village of Authuille.

On the morning of the 27th the village and the ridge above were wrapped in a thick September mist. Boromée Vaquette milked his six cows as usual and, as usual by seven o'clock, he was driving them out of his farmyard and up the steep path to their pasture on the ridge above. It was not much of a pasture – less than half a hectare and, each day, Vaquette set the cows to graze in a different corner and put up a moveable fence of chains and pickets to prevent them from wandering. It took him twenty minutes to move the stakes, to hammer them into the ground with a heavy mallet, another five minutes to encourage the cows into the enclosure and ten more to walk back down the road to the farm and his morning bowl of coffee.

That morning he never returned. By seven the children were up and dressed. By half-past seven the younger ones had set off for school, the eldest Vaquette girl was skimming the cream from the milk pans, the coffee pot simmered on the kitchen stove, Madame Vaquette was feeding the hens. By eight o'clock she was mildly concerned; by nine she was anxious; by ten it was all round the village that Boromée Vaquette had disappeared; by lunchtime Madame Vaquette was frantic.

During the morning French soldiers had marched into the village, and a sentry posted on the outskirts, despite all Madame Vaquette's pleading, barred the way to the ridge above. Shots had been heard. Late in the afternoon a French sergeant came into the courtyard and knocked at the farmhouse door. He found it difficult to blurt out his story. They had come out of the wood, he said, early in the morning. They were looking for Germans, expecting to see them any minute; they heard the sound of hammering and, across the field, near the place where the four roads met, they could just distinguish through the mist the figure of a man in grey clothes erecting a barricade. They had taken him for a German, fired a volley and retreated into the wood. The soldier began to cry. It was only now that they understood that they had killed a Frenchman and by now it was too late. The advance guard of the Germans had already moved forward to take up a defensive position on the ridge. A few yards beyond the line they had chosen, the body of Boromée Vaquette lay hidden in the long grass. There was no sign of the cows.

The Germans had occupied Thiepval village and spread purposefully across the hills on either side. That night their senior officers slept in Thiepval Château and their troops were digging trenches on the crest of the Thiepval Ridge.

Madame Rose Glavieux (née Vaquette)

It was a week before they could bring back the body of my father because nobody dared to approach. Then one evening a French officer came to see my mother and he said, 'Madame Vaquette, we must do something for you.' The French soldiers were very upset. The officer said, 'We know the place. We can show it to you, and tonight we can bring him back.' It was a very quiet night and it was dark, with no moon. My mother went with my eldest sister and the soldiers showed them the place. They had to go on stockinged feet, to make no noise, right up almost to the German trench to find my father's body. The soldiers carried him back to the house and next day they carried him to the church and the priest said a mass. There were not many there, just the people from the village and a few of the soldiers. After the mass, we followed the coffin to the cemetery and buried my father in the family grave. It was nine days since he had been killed.[1]

1. Boromée Vaquette, the first man of thousands to die on the Thiepval Ridge, is buried in the family plot (now with a modern headstone) to the right of the gate in the small communal cemetery of Authuille.

During that nine days the fighting had trickled to the north and Germans, French and British had begun to dig themselves in.

When the British had taken over this sector of the line, at the urgent request of the French in the late summer of 1915, it had been easy to sneer at their Ally for 'lacking the offensive spirit'. No one, least of all the French, denied that the Somme had been a 'cushy' front, that *laissez faire* had been the order of the day. It was true that there had been occasional duels between the guns, that the Château of Thiepval was distinctly knocked about, and, with its eyeless windows gazing gauntly westwards from the German front line, it had long ceased to be regarded as a desirable billet for German officers. It was true that there had been intermittent skirmishing, and that German engineers and French alike had developed a predilection for burrowing under the lines of their opposite numbers and springing mines beneath their trenches. But these were mere token gestures compared to the battles which all through 1915 had raged to the north and to the east. On the Somme neither side had had any particular reason to stir things up. There was no particular objective and, short of a major offensive which neither side was in a position to undertake, nothing to be gained by local attacks. In the light of the casualties which both sides had suffered elsewhere, the philosophy of 'live and let live' seemed, on the Somme Front, to be very much to the point.

The French Army was stretched to its limit. Four hundred and seventy-five miles of trenchline stretched from the Belgian coast, sweeping across the face of France to the very doorstep of Switzerland. Until the autumn of 1915, the French were grimly holding on to four hundred miles of its length, while the British Expeditionary Force faced the enemy along a mere seventy miles of the front. Certainly the British had not been idle. They had held the Germans at bay at Ypres, they had fought the enemy at Neuve Chapelle, they had stood alongside the French on the Marne, on the Aisne, at Loos, but it was not enough. It was not nearly enough. The British must shoulder more of the burden – and, for a start, they must take over more of the line. So the British Army came to the Somme, took over the French Front where it faced the arc of the German line from Hébuterne to Thiepval, on the Ancre, from Thiepval to the banks of the River Somme itself.

Unlike the French, fighting on their native soil and pledged to give up their lives rather than to concede a single centimetre to the invader; unlike the British, equally committed to kicking the enemy off the face of France, the Germans had positioned their line with care. Here giving up a stretch of low-lying ground, there withdrawing from a steep river valley, they had backed off to build a line that hugged the high spurs and contours of the chalky downland, so that every slope, every natural ravine, each natural declivity, every wood and hilltop could be turned to maximum advantage for observation, for concealment, for defence. Now a complex of trenches marched from horizon to horizon in two distinct, conspicuous lines, as if a giant chalky finger had zig-zagged across the landscape. As the Germans were well aware, the observers of the Royal Flying Corps, buzzing in inquisitive sorties up and down the front, had charted every twist and turn of the German front line and every undulating stretch of their second line, bristling no less distinctly two miles behind it. But the tell-tale chalk of the subsoil, that blazoned their position to the skies, held deeper secrets. It was easily worked and, with characteristic thoroughness and considerable engineering skill, the Germans had tunnelled beneath their trenches and carved out a network of galleries and shelters, so deep and so secure that nothing short of an earthquake could have dislodged them. By the summer of 1916, every hilltop was a redoubt, every wood an arsenal, every farm a stronghold, every village a fortress.

Chapter 2

If the German Command had been able to choose a single stretch of their five-hundred-mile front on which to beat off an Allied offensive, they would have chosen to meet it on the Somme where their line was virtually impregnable. Intelligence reports left them in no doubt that an offensive was in the offing, and it was perfectly evident that, from the Allied point of view, the British would be bound to attack somewhere along their front, in order to relieve the pressure on the hard-pressed French Army, whose strength was fast ebbing away in a river of blood at Verdun, where they had lost two hundred thousand men since the Germans had launched their own offensive in February. But, had it been suggested that the long-expected attack would take place here on the Somme Front where the two armies met, where, consequently, the Allies' line was at its most confused and vulnerable, had there been a hint that it would be a joint operation and that the undermanned demoralized French would attack alongside the British in a major offensive, there was hardly an officer on the German Staff who would not have vented his disbelief in a hearty belly-laugh at the very idea.

The British Staff did not contemplate the prospect with amusement. The battlefield was not of their choosing; it had been chosen by the French, but, for political reasons and the wish to demonstrate goodwill in practical terms, there had been no choice but to acquiesce. When the idea of a joint offensive had first been agreed on at the Chantilly Conference in January, it had been conceived largely as a French affair. If the French Army attacked on a grand scale south of the River Somme, then the British on their left would support them by mounting a series of local attacks north of the Somme and astride the Ancre. But that was before Verdun. As the French strength diminished, as they threw more and more men and guns and munitions eastwards into the white heat of the melting-pot of Verdun, so the strength of the British Army in France was increasing with every raw battalion of Kitchener's Army that crossed the Channel and with every troopship that sailed into Marseilles bearing the gallant survivors of the sad adventure at Gallipoli. As the balance of manpower gradually shifted, and the plans for the offensive evolved and took shape, it became more and more obvious that the weight of the joint offensive must shift too and that the burden of the attack must now fall on the British Army, with the support of a few French Divisions on its right on a much truncated front.[1] This would unavoidably force the main thrust of the push against the bastion of the German line on the uplands of the Somme.

The plan did not appeal to Sir Douglas Haig. He had already set in motion the preliminaries for an offensive in the north and had not entirely given up hope that he might be in a position to launch it later in the summer. Strategically, there was more to be gained. A purely British attack in the north would be equally effective in taking the heat off Verdun and, he believed, would stand a real chance of breaking through the German line.[2]

But on his appointment as Commander-in-Chief in December 1915, Haig had been categorically informed that 'the closest co-operation between the French and the British as a united Army must be the governing policy'. When the French had pressed their case for a joint campaign at the Chantilly Conference, it was just five weeks since Haig had been entrusted with the Command of the British Army in France, and, with the words of the Supreme War Council still ringing in his ears, he was in no position to disagree. Nevertheless, he had his doubts about what, if any, strategic advantage was to be gained by such a battle. More to the point, he had strong doubts about the ability of his Army to fight it.

Kitchener's Army did not share the pessimism of its Commander-in-Chief. Its members were rather more inclined to have a good opinion of themselves. They were mildly tolerant of the French whose ways they found strange but attractive, and not entirely intolerant of the Germans,

1. The original intention had been for the Allies to attack over a forty-five-mile front, the French with sixty Divisions, across thirty miles. Now the French could spare only eleven Divisions and their frontage was reduced to six miles, mostly south of the Somme.

2. It was a three-stage plan involving firstly blowing up and capturing the Wytschaete Messines Ridge, then breaking out of the Ypres Salient and swinging round to capture the ports of Ostende and Zeebrugge in conjunction with an amphibious attack from the sea. It was eventually put into execution a year later and was to be known as the Third Battle of Ypres. It was doomed to failure, partly because of an unusually wet summer and autumn, but largely because of the magnitude of the German defences, which they had hardly begun building by the summer of 1916. Had 'Third Ypres' been launched that summer, instead of the Battle of the Somme, it would have had an excellent chance of succeeding; thus two disasters of almost equal magnitude might conceivably have been avoided.

referred to familiarly as Fritz, with whom, in the discomfort of their
opposing trenches, they felt a certain fellow-feeling. Officially, fraterniz-
ation had been severely frowned upon since the spontaneous Christmas
Truce of 1914 but, in between bouts of belligerence, there was nothing
to prevent bored Tommies and the equally bored soldiers of the German
infantry across the way from entertaining each other with an exchange
of badinage and, occasionally, with an impromptu concert. On the whole,
the Germans were more musical than the British, although their taste
tended towards the sentimental. In the damp darkness of quiet nights in
the trenches, undisturbed by gunfire or the flash of Very lights, it was
the soulful strains of *Die Wacht am Rhein* or *In der Heimat . . .* which were
most often to be heard drifting across from the German side of No Man's
Land.

Apart from the occasional outburst, the British Tommies were not
much given to singing in the trenches. In their opinion there was not
much to sing about. There was the drudgery of working parties, the long
boredom of sentry duty and, week after week, month upon month, the
tedious routine of living in muddy ditches, enlivened by the excitement
of occasional raids and forays, but more often chastised by punishing
shellfire and inevitable casualties. It all added up to something to be
endured rather than to sing about, and the Tommies reserved their vocal
efforts to while away the tedium of long miles on the march or, when
they happened to be on rest, for jolly evenings in one of the *estaminets*
that were to be found in every village behind the front. After several
months of active service – albeit static warfare – the songs they sang had
altered somewhat in character from the jolly ditties that had lightened the
leaden hours of route-marching around the English countryside a year
before. *Where are our uniforms? Far far away . . .* they had warbled then in
their impatience to get to the front. Now that they had attained that
ambition and the long-awaited uniforms had already turned shabby in
the rigours of trench warfare, the same melody served very well for a
more realistic chorus.[1]

> There is a sausage gun
> Over the way.
> Fired by a bloody Hun
> Three times a day.
> You should see the Tommies run
> When they hear that sausage gun

1. It was a catchy Nonconformist hymn tune sung usually to the words, 'There
is a Happy Land, Far, Far Away . . .'

Fired by a bloody Hun
Three times a day.

The lyrics were a trifle inglorious, but very much to the point, for, if Kitchener's Army had not yet proved itself in a major battle, it had been well and truly 'blooded' in the trenches. There was hardly a man in the ranks who did not consider himself to be a seasoned warrior and as good as the next man. Some battalions of the Regular Army were aghast at the cheek of it. Even the illustrious Guards were not exempt. One scruffy service battalion of the East Surreys, passing a contingent of the Grenadier Guards drawn up in a village square, had the temerity to bellow in unison the traditional army taunt that dated from 1743, 'Where were *You* at Dettingen?' It took all the discipline of the Guards' professional training to prevent them from breaking rank and sorting the East Surreys out.

'Service' battalions of the Worcestershire Regiment as a matter of course threw themselves into a fracas, military or otherwise, with full-throated yells of '*GHELUVELT*'. They themselves had still been mastering the art of shouldering broomsticks in October 1914 when the regular soldiers of their 'parent' battalion were holding off the Germans on the lawns of Gheluvelt Château in the First Battle of Ypres, but this minor circumstance did not abash them. They were 'Worcesters' and that was that. If anything, they considered it something of a distinction to be 'Worcesters' of Kitchener's Army.

This opinion was not infrequently shared by commanding officers of the various Kitchener's Battalions which, by this time, were wearing the insignia of every regiment in the British Army with the exception of those in the exclusive Division of Guards. Until the early part of 1916, many battalion commanders and most brigadiers were 'Dugouts' – Officers of the Reserve who had been winkled out of well-earned retirement to take command of the burgeoning force of assorted civilians who had answered Lord Kitchener's call to arms. In many cases, in the time that had elapsed since those elderly gentlemen had first looked with dismay on the disordered ranks of boyish enthusiasts placed so abruptly under their command, they had developed a strangely paternal attitude towards their men, quite foreign to the general benevolence they had previously entertained towards the troops they had commanded long years ago in peacetime. Indeed, in the necessarily limited Establishment of the small professional Army, very few officers among the Dugouts had ever commanded a battalion before. Senior officers who had earned their colonelcies in peacetime were promptly given brigades; others, who had gone into respectable retirement with the rank of major, were promoted to colonel and put in command of a battalion of the New Army.

For more than a year now, the sole concern of such a colonel had been for 'his' battalion. Day in, day out, and for the best part of every night, he had toiled over every detail of the Herculean task of transforming his force of assorted civilians into troops of the British Army. With assiduous vigilance, he had watched his men progress from their first flat-footed attempts at drill to their final inspection, often by the King himself. He had despaired, or exulted, over their performance on the rifle range, the sports field, the parade ground. He had pondered pleas for compassionate leave, he had promoted the worthy, delivered judgement on defaulters. He had worked out dozens of different training programmes, written scores of reports, preached discipline to the men and the responsibilities of command to young officers and NCOs. He had, almost single-handedly, turned his men into soldiers. Finally, he had brought them to France with a sense of pride which stemmed less from self-congratulation than from recognition of the calibre of the men themselves.

They looked good on the march. They were taller and stronger, on the whole, than the undernourished recruits who had been driven by unemployment or poverty into the ranks of the pre-war Army. The standard of education and intelligence in both officers and men was high. They were enthusiastic, they were cheerful, and they had buckled down admirably to learning the unfamiliar trade of soldiering. They were the pick of the bunch. No matter how much of a martinet their 'Old Man' was held to be in the opinion of a Kitchener's Battalion, there was hardly a colonel who was not secretly convinced that his battalion was second to none.

Trevor Ternan, who had retired as a brigadier-general seven years before the war, went further than that. In his opinion, all four battalions under his command combined to form the finest brigade in the whole of Kitchener's Army and, such was his conviction, that he was determined to bring it to the notice of Lord Kitchener himself.

The 102nd Brigade formed part of the 34th Division. It was better known as the Tyneside Scottish and the paragons who made up its ranks were mainly pitmen and 'Geordies' to a man. The four battalions had been raised by the patriotic efforts of the Tyneside Scottish Committee who, until they had been taken over by the War Office and co-opted into the Army, had contributed every penny for their soldiers' keep, their equipment, their training and their comfort. The men of one battalion had started their military career by bivouacking in the ballroom of Tilley's Assembly Rooms, marching out every day to drill on the Town Moor and returning to hearty meals supplied by a local caterer, and the let-down of their subsequent passage through a succession of leaky tents and draughty huts had been eased by a flow of 'comforts' which had generously redoubled now that they were actually in France and fighting in the trenches.

Best of all the benefits of local munificence were the pipe-bands. Each battalion had its own, and the equipment, the pipes themselves and the pipers' outfits (which alone had cost more than thirty pounds apiece) had been generously paid for by the open-handed Tynesiders at home. The pipers were the real thing, specially recruited on the basis of their musicianship, even though a blind eye had to be turned to certain army regulations which dealt with such niggling inconveniences as the army age limit. It was obvious to all that Pipe-Sergeant Barton must be well over forty, for the family had joined up en masse, and three of Barton's sons were also serving in the bands of the Tyneside Scottish Brigade. Nothing exceeded the delight of the French peasants and their children than when the Tyneside Scottish Brigade swung through a village with a pipe-band blowing lustily at the head of each battalion. Nothing exceeded the pride of their Brigadier as he watched them march past.

The Brigadier was considerably put out when it was announced, at the beginning of February, that Lord Kitchener was to inspect a part of the 34th Division on parade, and that the part selected for this honour was the 101st Brigade. As this Brigade was made up of Royal Scots, Suffolks and Lincolns, it was thought to be a tactful choice which, in view of the well-known rivalry between the two remaining Brigades of the Division – the 102nd Tyneside Scottish and the 103rd Tyneside Irish – would avoid any ructions or accusations of partiality. Brigadier-General Ternan was having none of that! He was acquainted with Field-Marshal Lord Kitchener. He had served under him in two previous wars. They had even shared a billet together, thirty-two years earlier, in the Khedive's Palace at Alexandria. It was true that, as an officer on the Intelligence Staff, Major Kitchener had been lodged in silk and satin splendour in one of the elaborate state apartments, while Ternan, as a junior subaltern, had shared a scullery with the cockroaches, but time and promotion had put their acquaintanceship on a more intimate footing. The Brigadier had no qualms at all about the propriety of waylaying the Field-Marshal's car en route to the inspection, and waving it to a halt. Lord Kitchener was delighted to see him, delighted to see his fine Brigade – which just happened to be lined up on either side of the road ahead – and delighted to accept the Brigadier's invitation to alight and inspect it.

He walked for almost a mile along its ranks and was cheered to the echo by each company as he passed. He complimented the Brigadier in the warmest terms and, when he finally stepped back into his staff car at the end of the line, the pipers skirled him on his way to the strains of

Hielan' Laddie. All in all, the only people who were not entirely delighted with the events of such a satisfactory afternoon were the Corps and Divisional Commanders, who were left kicking their heels for a full hour in front of the drawn-up ranks of the 101st Brigade, at the official inspection point two miles ahead.

Now, just four months later, Lord Kitchener was dead. He had been drowned in HMS *Hampshire* on the way to perform a mission in Russia and his death was to prove to be an irreparable loss to the Army as a whole, particularly with regard to its relations with the French. There was no doubt about the fact that, compared to the Germans, the Allies suffered from their lack of overall command at the highest level. The difficulties involved in working out a joint strategy, of directing independent campaigns in such a way as to contribute effectively to a co-ordinated military effort, and the problems of unanimously deciding who should attack where and when, were never fully resolved. There was too much internecine bickering, both among the French politicians and among the British, and, on both sides, there was too much jockeying for position between the officers of the General Staffs and even between the Commanders of the Armies in the field. In all the joint deliberations there was too much talk, too much time wasted, too much thought given to mutual support in the short-term interest and too little given to the planning of long-term strategy.

By 1916 the situation cried out to be taken in hand by a man who would have the respect of both sides and who, without self-interest or national partiality, would be able to exercise an effective overall command in the common interest of the Allies. Lord Kitchener had been such a man. As Britain's Secretary of State for War, he occupied an eminence which automatically claimed the respect of politicians; as an illustrious soldier of the highest rank, he was unquestioningly honoured by the military. There was no other man who could have taken his place at the hub of the wheeling machinations of a dozen different Franco-British interests, flying off at a dozen different tangents, held them together and sent them bowling smoothly towards a common objective. There was no other man who would have been acceptable to both sides. Now, Kitchener was gone and there was no one to replace him.

In France, and in his dealings with the French, Sir Douglas Haig was left holding the baby. So far as the Somme campaign was concerned, Lord Kitchener's support would have been neither here nor there. Over the preceding months, the sequence of events which had inexorably shifted the main burden of the attack on to the shoulders of the British, had happened so gradually that there had never been a single clear-cut opportunity which might have been seized to re-think the practicalities of the British role in the offensive or to reconsider if, indeed, it should be launched on the Somme Front at all. Even as far back as April, with the plans well under way, and with half the troops already en route to the Somme, it had been far too late to launch into protracted re-negotiations with the French, even if political considerations had not deemed that to be highly inadvisable. The Army was committed to an offensive on the Somme. There was no going back and nothing to be done except to concentrate on training the infantry and to make all possible efforts to rectify their deficiencies before they went into battle.

It was easier said than done.

If midnight oil had been an essential ingredient of victory, the troops would have romped home, for the conferences, the discussion, the debate went on at Army Headquarters and at GHQ itself, long into the night. If the troops could have been swept into Bapaume on a tidal-wave of paper work, they would have been swirling through its streets in no time, for the various Headquarters were pouring out orders, commands, suggestions, memoranda, operational plans and instructions faster than a legion of clerks and printers could keep up with them. If a battle could have been won by planning, then the result would have been a foregone conclusion, for never, in the history of warfare, had a campaign been more meticulously planned down to the last infinitesimal detail. It was self-evident that the New Army – officers and men alike – was rich in morale and the will to win, but it was woefully lacking in knowledge, skill and experience. It was up to the Staff to fill the gaps, to envisage every possible contingency, to anticipate every move, to lay down the plans for every individual unit, and to lay them down within such a rigid framework that they could not fail to be clearly understood. So long as the men of the New Army adhered strictly to the instructions of the professionals, together they would carry the day.

Adhering to instructions was not a characteristic for which the independent spirits of Kitchener's Army were renowned. They had no objection to fighting, which, after all, was what they were here for. Since they had picked up the old soldiers' trick of rubbing candle-grease inside their socks, they had no great objection to marching. They could put up with the trenches and even with the labour involved in fatigues and working parties, for which there seemed to be some reasonable necessity and, on the whole, to a certain philosophic degree, they were willing to acquiesce with the less immediately comprehensible whims of the Army.

Many of the Army's 'whims' sprang from the conviction that, in the final analysis, battles were won by discipline, by the unquestioning, auto-matic response of all ranks to orders. Such traditional discipline, inculcated over long years in the time-serving hierarchy of the peacetime Army, was not so easy to impose on a heterogeneous mass of well-meaning civilians who regarded themselves as very temporary and very private soldiers, with what they considered to be a healthy disrespect for 'bull'. The Army understood this but, in the months of training for the Big Push, it seemed to certain officers, whose brains were whirling in the effort of trying to assimilate the contents of the reams of orders and instructions that were piling up into mountains on their desks, that certain molehills were receiving undue attention.

> *Things which may appear trivial matters to those who have only lately joined the Army are really of great importance, such as saluting, cleanliness, tidiness in dress, manner when speaking to their superiors, strict observance of orders.*
>
> *The strictest attention must continue to be paid to the cultivation of the power of command in young officers, also to discipline, dress, saluting, cleanliness and care of billets.*
>
> *Men must learn to obey by instinct without thinking.*
>
> *Too great stress cannot be laid on developing good morale, a soldierly spirit, and a determination in all ranks to achieve success at all costs.*[1]

In order after order, in tones that varied from the hectoring to the plaintive, the Staff never missed an opportunity of pressing the message home.

The practicalities involved in training some two hundred thousand men to play an effective part in a full-scale battle, was even more of a problem. Brigadiers and Battalion Commanders of long-serving Divisions became sick of complying with insistent demands which reached them almost daily from GHQ, that they should supply immediately: *six men fully qualified to act as instructors in signalling . . . bombing . . . Lewis-guns . . . Stokes mortar . . . bayonet drill . . . musketry . . .* The demands were never ending. They groaned, grumbled, and, in most cases, seized the opportunity of getting rid of the duds.

With more than one hundred and fifty thousand men to be trained for the great attack, the Army could have done with a thousand specialist instructors, and they simply did not exist.

The best that could be done with the few who were available, was to appoint 'specialist' officers and NCOs in each of several hundred battalions and send them, by contingents, on intensive training courses at one of the various Army Schools some distance behind the line. Then to

1. Army Order SS 109. Issued by General Kiggell, 8 May 1915.

depend on them, assisted by voluminous notes and instructions, to pass on their knowledge to junior officers and to train the troops under their command. All the enthusiasm of Kitchener's Army could not prevent the outlines from becoming blurred as they travelled down the chain of command.

Chapter 3

Had it not been for the fact that the Army Schools needed soldiers to 'practise on', the 13th Battalion of The Rifle Brigade would not have received the unexpected bonus of what amounted to a month's holiday. You had to be good to be a demonstration battalion, and Colonel Pretor-Pinney had seen to it that his Battalion *was* good and, as he constantly dinned into them, not so much a Kitchener's Battalion as a Battalion of the Rifle Brigade. He had been an officer of the Regiment for more than thirty years – long enough to have retired twice and twice returned to the Active List to serve in two wars. It was a stroke of luck that he had soldiered in South Africa with Colonel Edward Gordon, for Colonel Gordon was now Assistant Adjutant General of the 37th Division and he regarded the battalion commanded by his old friend with a benevolent eye. He was impressed by its performance and he had chosen it, out of all the battalions in his division, to go to the Army School of Instruction at Auxi-le-Château to show them how things ought to be done. It was a signal honour and a blessed change from a succession of miserable stints in the trenches at le Gastineau.

But Auxi-le-Château, in the spring of 1916, was pure and simple bliss, only slightly mitigated by the fact that it was also hard work. At Auxi perfection was the order of the day, and nothing short of perfection would do. The turn-out of the demonstration squads had to be so immaculate that even the handles of entrenching tools were required to glisten in the early sunshine of morning parades. Their drilling had to be carried out with the precision of a regular battalion on the Regimental Parade Ground at Winchester. Squad by squad, company by company, they were drilled twenty times a day by a succession of self-conscious young subalterns, who squeaked their commands in nervous falsetto under the critical eye of a drill-sergeant to whom mere second-lieutenants were objects of ill-concealed scorn, rather than 'objects of respect'. The appellation 'object of respect' had been a favourite phrase of Corporal Lucas, whose unhappy task it had been to impart to B Company something of the requirements of the Army when they had first joined it nineteen months before, and Corporal Lucas, who was still pursuing the same thankless vocation at

Regimental Headquarters, would have been amazed – if not gratified – had he known how often his words were remembered and quoted. Certain of his expressions had become catch-phrases in the Battalion.

Sergeant Howard Rowlands, B Coy., 13th (S) Btn., The Rifle Brigade

We often remembered old Corporal Lucas during the time we were at Auxi, particularly when it came to company drill and saluting. This was all for the education of the officers in training, and we had to do this saluting over and over and over again, until the lads were weary and sick and tired of it. But it just needed one fellow to say, 'About this serluting . . .' and everybody smiled and saw the joke. Old Lucas used to say, 'About this serluting, what I says is yer don't take it serious enough. Look at me, for example. I always chucks one up every time I meets an object of respect. Don't matter if it's a pretty girl, a Solomon in all his glory – meaning a ruddy general! – or a glass of beer!' We referred to officers as 'Objects of Respect' for a long time. He was a real Cockney. He took us for rifle drill too and, in explaining the aperture of a rifle, he always asked us, 'What is a naperture?' At first he used to give the answer himself. 'Why, a naperture's a nole!' After a while, we decided to convince him that we really understood so, whenever he enquired, 'What is a naperture?' the whole squad would yell back in delight, 'A naperture's a nole.' What agonies we went through trying to hide our amusement, for it was a serious crime to be insolent to a superior officer. But we caught on to these expressions of his and they went right round the Battalion.

The only members of B Company who never saw the point of the joke were the men of No. 5 Platoon who all hailed from Bermondsey.

Drilling on the barrack-square at Winchester, garbed in every form of civilian attire from city suits to boating blazers, shod in civilian shoes, whose thin soles were rapidly giving way under the strain, adorned with headgear that represented every facet of the hatter's trade from bowlers to straw boaters, the infant battalion had looked a motley crew. Behind the uniform khaki front they now presented to the world, they still were. There was The Welsh Mob, of No. 6 Platoon, B Company, actually a group of civil servants from Cardiff who had joined up together. There was the Boys Brigade, who made up all of No. 13 Platoon and half of No. 14. There were the gamekeepers, eight of them, who had left the pheasants on the Wynyard Park Estate to look after themselves for the duration of the war. The Brewery Boys had all worked together at Bass

Rutley. There were twelve pairs of brothers in the battalion. Jack Knotman had been an acrobat on the music halls. Jack Cross, now a sergeant in C Company, had been a footman and valet to Sir Eric Barrington and kept his platoon comfortably supplied with the gloves, socks, scarves and balaclava helmets that must have been knitted non-stop below stairs at 62 Cadogan Place, so regularly did they arrive by every other post. Rifleman Adams, on the other hand, prevailed upon his comrades to carry his rifle on long marches and in return regaled them with the quails in aspic, tinned pineapple, ham galantine and, occasionally, caviare, contained in his parcels from Fortnum and Mason. There was Rifleman Arthur Wright, one of the Bermondsey Boys, who made no bones about having been a professional burglar and who had seen service in one of His Majesty's Prisons before joining His Majesty's Forces. There was Duggie Jones, the baby of the Battalion, burly enough to have got away with enlisting at the age of fifteen and who, in a post-war incarnation, was to become Aubrey Dexter, a successful actor. Rifleman Phipps, known as Old Chelsea, was the oldest member and admitted to having a son in the trenches. Partial to kippers, which his wife despatched to France with faithful regularity, he was still living down the episode when he had caused the entire battalion to 'Stand to' for a gas attack as a result of frying a little supper for himself in the trenches.

The Battalion was proud of its 'characters', but most of all it was proud of its sportsmen. It had The Golfers, seventeen professionals and assistants who had joined up as a body. There were the Stockton Boys, all semi-professional footballers, now, to the fury of the rest of the Brigade, forming a team that made the result of every inter-battalion match a foregone conclusion. There was the youthful Captain Arnold Strode Jackson, a formidable runner, who, as an undergraduate, had won a gold medal at Stockholm in the 1912 Olympic Games. There was Ernie Lowe, the Battalion's boxing champion and, since the South Africans had joined them in October, the 13th Rifle Brigade had been well-nigh invincible on the rugby field.

The 'South African Mob' had banded together and sailed from Port Elizabeth under their own steam and at their own expense, under the aegis of Captain Bill Nothard. It had been his idea. It would have been perfectly possible to join up in South Africa and a South African Brigade was already serving in France. But there were other theatres of war and there was no guarantee that locally recruited troops might not be sent to the Middle East or to fight in German West Africa. The only way to avoid this, to get a sniff at the 'real' war, was to take passage for London and join up on the spot.

Rifleman Percy Eaton, No. 13873, 13th (S) Btn., The Rifle Brigade

We all paid our own passages, and we could afford it because none of us were badly off and sea passages were cheap in those days. There were still passenger ships running and we had a very pleasant voyage. We were quite the heroes on board! There was myself and George Murrell and about twenty others 'recruited' by Nothard. We docked at Southampton, after about three weeks, took the boat train to Waterloo and went straight from the station to the recruiting office in Whitehall. I have a half idea they were expecting us. Nothard had got to know Colonel Gordon when he had been a soldier in South Africa and he must have been in touch with him. Anyway, we were attested, had very sketchy medicals and within half an hour we were given railway warrants for Winchester. So back we went to the station and it really was priceless, because, as we left the recruiting office, there happened to be a Guards' band coming out of Horseguards' Parade and marching down Whitehall, so we joined on behind and we marched behind them all the way to Westminster Bridge. We had no idea of marching and it was very difficult trying to keep time and carrying suitcases and all our gear, but we were as pleased as Punch! We did some very basic training at Winchester and we were soon on our way to France. We joined the 13th at Gommecourt in October 1915 and we were told that this was on the recommendation of Colonel Gordon and that they were the best battalion in the 37th Division. Perhaps because a good few of us had had experience of shooting in South Africa we nearly all became Lewis-Gunners.

Now the South African Mob were appreciating the break at Auxi more than any others in the battalion. The weather was fine, the spring sun shone and, after the unaccustomed rigours of a European winter spent almost entirely in the open in the trenches, or, when out of them, billeted in draughty barns which were not much better, for the first time since arriving in France they felt actually warm. After the intricacies of command on the parade ground had been mastered by the young officers in training, and the perfection of 'serluting' was deemed to have been adequately demonstrated, they had moved on to the real thing – command of troops in battle. That was a lot more fun, at least for the guinea pigs. They mounted mock attack after mock attack. They sniped, they machine-gunned, they mopped up, they consolidated, they signalled, they advanced and they vanquished the Kaiser's imaginary Army a thousand times over.

But the battles and the manoeuvring across the springtime meadows stopped promptly at five o'clock. There was time for a kip and a clean-up, before 'Men's Supper', which in itself was a heartening improvement on the meagre fare that reached the troops at the front, and, afterwards, for those intent on pleasure, an embarrassment of riches to choose from. Auxi-le-Château itself was a real town, with streets where civilians and, in particular, pretty girls, could be seen, just as if there were no war on; there were buildings undamaged by shellfire, cafés and *estaminets*, concerts in the Hôtel de Ville and, best of all, a British Expeditionary Force Canteen which even the most impecunious could afford to patronize. In the 'Officers Only' cafés, earnest young subalterns fought table-top skirmishes and, assisted by Messrs Bryant and May, disposed platoons of matchsticks to illustrate the finer points of the tactical theories they were obliged to master in order to return to their battalions with satisfactory reports. As the spring evenings lengthened, the sportsmen of the battalion preferred to eschew the pleasures of Auxi. Even after the exertions of the day there was pleasure in a scratched up football match. To the golfers, most of whom had found some devious means of bringing a club or two to France, or having them sent on afterwards, the gentle slopes around the green valley of Auxi were natural reminders of Gleneagles, of Turnberry, of Deal or Lytham St Annes. They spent happy competitive evenings, putting and driving, joined occasionally by some officers who shared their passion and were only too happy to pick up a few professional hints.

The rugger players, like the footballers, never tired of training and practising. Since the Rifle Brigade had gone into wartime khaki, they were the only people who were privileged to sport its traditional colours of green and black, admittedly only in the stripes of their team jerseys, but the colours of the Regiment, nevertheless. It was a sore point with some of the non-sporting riflemen who, like Joe Hoyles, had been dazzled by pre-war glamour.

Rifleman Joe Hoyles, MM, No. 3237, 13th (S) Btn., The Rifle Brigade

There were five of us joined up together, Archie Nicholson, Fred Lyons, Frank Bell, Sid Birkett and myself. We all worked at W. H. Smith's in Nottingham. I'd absolutely made up my mind and, when we went up to the barracks to join up, I said, 'We're going into the finest regiment in the British Army.' And they said, 'What's that?' And I said, 'The Rifle Brigade. Left of the Line and pride of the British Army.' I was only seventeen, but it was a unique regiment to me. In my own little town of Oakham, there were two officers of the Rifle Brigade who used to come home on leave and they looked so smartly dressed in the green and black and always with a black sash around their shoulders. It caught my eye. I thought it was wonderful. And there was another fellow in the town who also struck me when I was a boy. He'd been a private, they called him Scotchie Waterfield, and he must have been quite old then. But he'd been in the Rifle Brigade and when you saw him walking down the main street he looked marvellous. It was his quick step. I found out afterwards it was a hundred and forty steps to the minute. From just a young boy I'd thought what a wonderful champion regiment this must be.

The practical wartime khaki which had succeeded green jackets and red coats alike was a poor substitute for the peacock traditions of peacetime, but at least the riflemen sported black buttons on their khaki and they had learned, as generations of riflemen had learned before them, to march at one hundred and forty steps to the minute. It was when the glorious month at Auxi was over and they were marching back to the trenches that this particular aptitude got them into trouble, for, by then, most of the Fourth Army was on the move and fanning out across the face of Picardy.

The sheer logistics of assembling the troops on the Somme in time to familiarize them with their sectors of the trenchline, and to move them back and forwards to rehearse the battle, was a monumental headache that had spread from the apex of GHQ down through the chain of command to furrow the brows of several thousand quartermasters and transport officers at battalion level. A single brigade on the move with its transport occupied at least three miles of road. With the tail of the column an hour's march behind the vanguard and the obligatory ten minutes' rest in every hour, it took two hours and a half, marching easy, to cover that distance. If one such procession met another at a cross-roads proceeding in the opposite direction, the subsequent contretemps could hold up ten thousand men in a chain reaction that stretched for miles and hours behind and could throw out the carefully planned arrangements of a dozen hapless billeting officers, who had earmarked three or four adjacent villages for the accommodation of their brigades that night.

Working out the permutations by which the mass migration could be smoothly achieved, was a task so tortuous that the compilation of *Cook's International Time-table* would have been child's play by comparison. It took long laborious calculations, endless consultations with the scattered commands of a dozen other units and the careful working out of routes over a countryside whose roads could hardly be described as arterial, and where the main access roads must be left clear, so far as possible, for the endless columns of lorries carrying supplies and munitions to the forward areas. Marching along what was little more than a country track, the last thing a battalion of the Royal Warwicks had needed was a quick-stepping battalion of the Rifle Brigade marching up on its heels and creating mayhem in its rear ranks. The ensuing discussion between the two battalions turned the air blue and it was popularly supposed that it was about the time of the move to the Somme that Rifle Regiments earned the epithet 'Black Buttoned Bastards'.

If the 'Black Buttoned Bastards' returning to the trenches in the Third Army area were a touch despondent that their halcyon month was over, the troops of the Fourth Army arriving from the north, although they had no illusions about what was ahead of them, were revelling in the change of scene.

Private Tom Easton, No. 1000, 21st Btn., Northumberland Fusiliers (2nd Tyneside Scottish)

We thought it was lovely country when we got there, because we'd been up in the north before where it was very flat and uninteresting. Here it was all hillier and there were little cottages with gardens and spring flowers coming out. There was a lovely stream nearby and the lads used to bathe in it. It was cold when we first got there but the water gradually got warmer and warmer. What I liked especially was the delight of lying in the grass among the apple trees bursting into blossom and listening to the birds singing, instead of the whistling of the shells. Some lads got fishing rods and gear and were fishing in the stream, and there were plenty of sports and football matches. It was so peaceful you just couldn't believe it. Later on it got more strenuous.

Early in May we marched off again from the lovely peace and quiet and went to la Houssaye, where we joined up with the Third Corps and started training with the 8th and the 21st Divisions for the Battle of the Somme. The ground was supposed to correspond to the ground on the Somme and we were hard at it training; first in platoon and company movement under orders and then even on battalion movement on a wider basis, so that we could practise our art of offensive soldiering. Then we took over our sector of the front but there was always one or two brigades out of the line occupied with training.

They practised moving in the open by platoons, they practised manoeuvring in companies, then moving in waves as a battalion. Then came a whole week when all four battalions trained as a brigade, carrying out the complicated procedures of consolidation, reinforcement, 'leapfrogging' a second line of troops through the first and passing on to the second and third lines of enemy 'trenches' and even beyond. The bombers 'bombed', the snipers 'sniped'. The moppers up went through the motions of bombing 'dugouts', represented by flags inside the shallow 'trenches'. They were mere lines, scratched with spade or plough across the field and they did it all over and over again, until every man from a battalion's colonel downwards knew precisely what to do and when to do it.

It was in the brigade and divisional exercises that signallers like Tom Easton truly came into their own, for the Royal Flying Corps took part, flying up and down the divisional front, swooping down towards the troops and climbing away with a cheerful waggle of wings when the troops signalled back their position in response to a loud klaxon horn sounded by the pilot. They signalled by spreading out white ground-sheets bearing an outsize divisional sign which transmitted the categorical statement, *We are here and so far as we know are the leading infantry and within fifty yards of the firing line*. Some signallers were taught to operate an even more sophisticated piece of equipment.

Private Tom Easton, No. 1000, 21st Btn., Northumberland Fusiliers (2nd Tyneside Scottish)

I was on aircraft communications. All the time we were doing these movements over open countryside, the aeroplanes were going up and down the line all the time and we had to practise communicating with them with flare lamps and ground-sheet signals. We signallers had to carry out a giant shutter, six foot square, lay it on the ground, peg it down, go to one end, grasp the ropes and it pulled open like a venetian blind. The surface was all brown when it was closed but it was a pure white surface when we pulled it open and we had to make coded letters in Morse Code: series of Cs, series of Hs, and so on, which were all part of the code. In my experience as a battalion signaller these were never used. They might have been used by other battalions – though I doubt it – but later on in battle, our reception was so hot that there was no possibility of using it. In fact we never even carried it into the battle.

In the long weeks of conferring and drawing up the battle plans at GHQ, at Army HQ and at Corps Headquarters, the question of signals had an important place in every agenda. Once the troops went over the top, a fool-proof system of communications was the sole means by which the Staff could control the battle. Only on the basis of a constant flow of up-to-the-minute information from the thick of the fight itself, would they be able to send in, or withhold, reinforcements, assist the troops with artillery fire, help them out of difficulties and support them in exploiting success – and do all these things instantly.

The lifeline that would carry vital news of the situation at the front far and fast to command posts in the rear, was the network of telephone wires and cables. For every mile of front, five hundred miles of cable had been buried – and buried six feet deep in the forward areas. Behind Divisional Headquarters, no less than three thousand miles of wire linked the infantry to the artillery, the artillery to the Flying Corps, to balloon sections, to transport lines, to reserves, and to corps and Army HQ in a cat's cradle of circuits and connections that would carry the news from the front, with mercurial despatch, through every stage of liaison and command to the ear of Sir Douglas Haig himself. Thus far the army could make its arrangements, but all would depend, and well they knew it, on the troops sending back information equally fast, once they had gone over the top. Signallers, of course, would go over with them as part of the second wave, reeling out heavy rolls of cable as they went to link up with the communications behind, but, in the hazards of battle, it would be foolish to depend on either all of them or all the cable escaping unscathed. What was needed were fail-safes and in such profusion as to guarantee ten times over that communications could not possibly break down.

There were to be signalling lamps, power buzzers, black and white discs by which Morse messages could be signalled back visually and even the despised semaphore flags were to be carried. There would be helio-graphs, telephones and carrier pigeons, which even now were being taken daily into the trenches and trained to fly back, straight and fast, to the lofts behind the line. There were to be runners – and twice the usual number of them, travelling in pairs – to bring messages back from the forward troops to the old jumping-off line. There were to be marker-pennants, six feet high, carried by the leading man of each company. There were to be coloured flares, five hundred per battalion, to be fired on the instructions of an officer or senior NCO in a complicated series of coded patterns and sequences which they were studiously committing to memory.

Towards the end of the training period, when such instructions as were not marked 'SECRET' reached company level, some officers poring over the long lists of equipment that were to be carried into the attack, came gloomily to the conclusion that the only thing the Army had neglected to consider was the provision of extra pairs of arms for the men to carry them.[1] But, somehow it would have to be managed, for these long and slender lines of communication were the reins by which the Army would direct its fledgling infantry and drive it forward to success.

1. In the first moments of the attack, one German officer, astounded by the sight of the long lines of heavily encumbered Tommies approaching at a slow walk and looking, to his astonished eyes, as if they were setting out on a day's outing, later wrote that, '. . . some were even carrying picnic baskets and others Kodaks as if to take photographs as a souvenir of their outing'. The 'picnic baskets' contained pigeons, the 'Kodaks' were power buzzers.

Chapter 4

Standing on either side of the German Salient at Gommecourt, beyond the northern limit of the planned offensive, the 56th and 46th Divisions did not take much part in extensive rehearsals for the Big Push. For one thing, although they had an important supporting role to play, like the 37th Division they were part of the Third Army; for another they were part of the Territorial Force and they had been part-time soldiers since 1910 when the Territorials were formed as an emergency arm of the Army. But most battalions had long since outgrown the peacetime soubriquet of 'Saturday Afternoon Soldiers'. They had been fighting in France since the early days of the war, and justifiably considered themselves to be as good as the Regulars.

As an officer of the 3rd Londons, Arthur Agius had fought at Neuve Chapelle, at Aubers Ridge, at Festubert and at Loos. In more than a year of heavy fighting, the Battalion had been sadly depleted by casualties and brought up to strength again by drafts of soldiers who were just as inexperienced as any in the ranks of Kitchener's Army, but who had had the foresight to join local Territorial Battalions in August 1914. Even from the start they had considered themselves to be one up on 'Kitchener's Mob'. As Territorials, they were issued with uniforms months before their less fortunate comrades had glimpsed so much as a khaki sock, and they had been equipped with rifles even before they knew how to fire them. They also had the advantage of serving on their own doorsteps. At first, some of the Kensingtons were even allowed to continue living at home and to endow their grateful mothers with the Army billeting allowance of seven and a six a week, travelling daily by tram-car to the White City at Shepherd's Bush, where the Battalion was housed in the garish pavilions left over from the Empire Exhibition of 1913. Fortunately, not all of the temporary buildings had been demolished and the old pavilions made admirable orderly rooms, offices, gymnasiums and dining halls where the troops enjoyed meals supplied by courtesy of Messrs Lyons whose tea rooms adorned almost every corner in the West End of London. Lyons' factory and head offices were conveniently situated nearby at 'Cadby Hall' in High Street, Kensington, where a large staff of girls never failed to rush to the windows to shout and wave to the Kensingtons, marching past on their way to drill in Hyde Park. The Kensingtons, in their turn, never failed to favour this admiring throng with a lusty rendering of their favourite marching song:

> *We are the Kensington Boys*
> *We are the Kensington Boys*
> *We spend our tanners*
> *We mind our manners,*
> *We are respected wherever we go,*
> *When we're marching down the High Street Ken,*
> *Doors and windows open wide.*
> *You can hear the sergeant shout,*
> *Put those blooming Woodbines out,*
> *We are the Kensington Boys.*

The complacency of some of the Kensington Boys was jolted when they were drafted to France and discovered that their seniors in the 56th London Division did not look kindly on such vociferous self-praise. They had adopted as their anthem and marching song a music-hall ditty which had enlivened their peacetime Saturday evenings at Joy's or Wilton's:

> *I'm 'Enery the Eighth I am.*
> *'Enery the Eighth I am, I am,*
> *I got married to the widow next door,*
> *She'd been married seven times before.*
> *AND every one was an 'Enery,*
> *She wouldn't have a Willie or a Sam.*
> *I'm 'er eighth Old Man called 'Enery,*
> *'ENERY THE EIGHTH I AM!*

They marched for miles and miles singing it, and neither its swing nor its charm ever palled. Early in May they had marched to the village of Hébuterne and taken over a trenchline beyond it, facing the Germans to the right of Gommecourt village. Almost their first job had been to dig a trench, which struck some of the troops as being slightly ironic in view of the fact that at Hébuterne there were more trenches than there were troops to fill them. Hébuterne itself consisted of a long village street with a half-ruined church, a few run-down farms whose tenants had long since decamped and which now served, like the tumbledown rows of cottages, as advanced headquarters and billets for signallers, orderlies, and regimental police whose duties kept them near the front line. The front line itself ran parallel to the village street, a few hundred yards ahead of it, and the lanes that ran through orchards to the vestiges of the old fields served as communication trenches to the line – or lines, for the French, during their occupancy, had dug a complete complex of trenches. The British, thinking them too wide, too shallow and 'not much good', had dug a whole new system when they had taken over, a fact which runners of the newly arrived 56th Division frequently cursed whenever their travels between the front and Battalion Headquarters were delayed by involuntary meanderings that terminated infuriatingly in a dead end.

On their left the 46th Division stood in front of the village of Fonquevillers whose tongue-twisting proper name was seldom used by any soldier below the rank of full general. From the Brigadier downwards it was universally known as 'Funky Villas'. Between the two villages and the two Divisions, the woodland of Gommecourt Park stuck its impertinent snout towards the British lines in a salient that formed the westernmost point of the whole of the German trenchline in France. The German trenches followed its angular outline and swept back along both sides of the country road that once led from Puisieux to the village of Gommecourt and on to Fonquevillers. Now the road itself was part of the formidable complex of trenches that stretched southwards and swung over the downs of the Somme facing the Fourth Army. The Gommecourt sector, on the Third Army Front, was immediately adjacent to the left flank of the Fourth.

In front of the 56th Division a shallow valley separated the British trenches from the German line. It was across this valley that the new trench had to be dug, so far out in No Man's Land that it would be within spitting distance of the German front line. It was to be dug by one brigade over only two nights and Arthur Agius, acting under the Brigade-Major, was in charge of the operation.

Captain A. J. Agius, MC, 3rd Btn., Royal Fusiliers, City of London Regiment, 56th Division

Our lines were about eight hundred yards from the Germans. We didn't know we were going to be selected for an attack, but we were told we were to go out and build a complete new trench system, four hundred yards in front and four hundred yards nearer the Germans, which sounded absolute madness. So, I went out with our Brigade-Major one night from a forward sap and we went on for a quarter of a mile, just the two of us, with a soldier carrying a sandbag full of chalk. After taking various measurements and compass directions, we dumped all this chalk and made a cairn of it. (It was chalk country, so it wouldn't be noticed.) We covered the German side with grass so that they shouldn't see the cairn and then we had to work to our left until we came to a road that ran out of our lines. The landmark there was a hawthorn bush that was in full blossom (this was the middle of May) and that made a very convenient point for a marker. It took some doing to lay out a complete front line with traverses and so on. But, in the hours of darkness, we marked all this out with string and pegs and then the next night we set off to do the actual digging.

I went out, almost as soon as it got dark, with a small covering party, a subaltern and about ten men, to lie out in front in case we were rushed by a German patrol. We taped the whole of this thing out and, as soon as we'd finished running the white tape across it, marking all the traverses and every inch of the line, and every angle and turn, the troops filed in and started to dig like billy-o. We had more than five hundred men out there and we dug that whole length of trench in two nights. What a job that was! Of course the Germans knew that something was up. So the second night they pounded us like mad with shellfire and we lost quite a few men. But we got it finished.

It was the Army's intention that the enemy should see that 'something was up'. It was doing its best to convince the Germans that 'something was up' along the whole of the Third Army Front from Gommecourt to Arras. If the Germans could be seduced into the belief that the Big Push was to take place here rather than on the Fourth Army Front on the Somme, then the troops there might be attacking with an element of surprise which could make all the difference. At the very least, the enemy might be misled into believing that the attack would take place on a wider front than was intended and would therefore maintain strong reserves of artillery and infantry opposite the Third Army, rather than sending them south to form part of the unpleasant welcome committee that all too clearly awaited the Fourth Army on the Somme.

The Third Army co-operated enthusiastically in the deception. Its artillery bombarded the enemy lines and cut the barbed wire in front of their trenches as effectively as if they really were about to storm across. Night after night, the infantry raided and patrolled and pushed its line forward as if preparing for a jump-off. They dug complexes of dummy assembly trenches behind the lines. They were only eighteen inches deep, but they looked authentic enough from the air, and some divisions even embellished the illusion by manning them with a phantom army represented by ragged sandbags fluttering on man-sized sticks. After dark, each night, all up and down the sector, convoys of army limbers, piled high with rattling cargoes of empty biscuit tins, clattered about in phantom convoys to simulate intense activity on the roads behind the lines.

At a meeting of corps commanders just two days before the battle, General Snow had the satisfaction of telling the Commander-in-Chief, 'They know we're coming all right!' And Sir Douglas Haig was able to reward him in return with the latest information, gleaned by Intelligence. The Germans had stiffened their Gommecourt front with a whole extra division and its artillery.

The bluff had worked. But, unlike the two Divisions to the north of them, the 46th and 56th ranged in V-shaped formation in front of Gommecourt, were not entirely bluffing. So far as the Germans were concerned, they were indeed 'coming'. At the moment of the attack by the Fourth Army on their right, they too were to attack the Germans on either side of Gommecourt.

It had been Haig's own idea, and he had arrived at it after careful consideration. Any attack which would divert the attention of the Germans away from the Somme was desirable. But an attack at Gommecourt, just two miles north of the limit of the Big Push, would have one insuperable advantage. It would protect the 8th Corps. More particularly, it would protect the 31st Division on the extreme left flank not only of the 8th Corps but of the whole battle line. And, in Haig's opinion, the 31st Division badly needed some protection.

Most of the men in the 31st Division were hardly aware that they were in the Fourth Army, never mind the 8th Corps. It was doubtful if many of them could have reeled off the number of his brigade without hesitation. They seldom even referred to their battalions by their official titles. A man of the 13th or the 14th Battalion of the York and Lancaster Regiment preferred to think of himself as being one of the 1st or the 2nd Barnsley Pals. A man of the 12th Battalion regarded himself as one of the 'Sheffield Pals', while a soldier of any one of the four battalions which made up the 92nd Brigade would claim to belong to 'The Hull Mob'. Even within his own battalion a man's interest seldom extended beyond the limits of his own company. In many cases, it was pretty well confined to his own platoon of twenty or so, because, in the Pals Battalions, the real pals, often from a single village, a single street, a single factory or sports club, stuck together. In all of Kitchener's Army there was hardly a group of more happy-go-lucky amateur soldiers than the Pals and luck, so far, had been on their side. While the majority of the New Army had been enduring the chill and discomfort of winter on the Western Front, the Pals had been wintering in Egypt and had only been brought back to France late in the spring. Most of them had 'souvenirs', including 'lucky scarabs', acquired at swindling expense in some Alexandria bazaar, carried in hopeful optimism that their luck would continue.

The Commander-in-Chief was not quite so optimistic about the prospects of the men as the men were themselves. In the months before the offensive, like grand-masters hunched over an imaginary chessboard that stretched across the fields of France and Belgium, the High Command had moved and rearranged the component parts of divisions, of brigades, and even of battalions, so that almost every Regular division now contained an element of Kitchener's Army, and almost every division of the New Army contained a stiffening quota of experienced troops.

In the case of the 31st Division, a scant three months had not been long enough in which to switch them around. It had hardly been long enough to exchange their pith helmets and khaki drill for tin hats and warm clothing, to school them in the routine of the trenches and to take them through rehearsals of their part in the battle. But, with careful deliberation, the Army deployed its forces so that the Pals should not be overtaxed. Their task was simple. At the northern extremity of the line, all that the Pals were expected to do was to advance a thousand yards, capture Serre, and throw an encircling arm round the northern flank of the front that ran southwards over fifteen straggling miles. They would stand on this position so that, as the Army pursued its inevitable break-through, the whole glorious advance could pivot on this point and swing outwards from it towards the open country. The Pals were to oil the hinge that would open the door to Bapaume, to the French frontier, and, eventually, to Berlin itself.

It should be a piece of cake. On their left they would be protected by a smokescreen, rolling thick across two miles, and, beyond that, by the attack at Gommecourt.[1]

On the right the Regular 4th Division, as tried and tested as any troops could be, would carry the Pals forward by their very momentum. And, beyond them both, the 29th Division, which had proved itself at Gallipoli, could certainly be depended on. It was true that the 4th and 29th Divisions faced the strongpoint of Beaumont Hamel, but the Staff had made provision to trump that particular ace in the Germans' hand.

Beaumont Hamel lay at the foot of a dip in the cleft of a narrow valley, protected at its back by one arm of the deep Y-shaped ravine that ran towards the British line and then swung parallel to it. It was a natural

1. The instructions to the 56th and 46th Divisions were explicitly: *to assist in the operations of the Fourth Army by diverting against itself the fire of artillery and infantry, which might otherwise be directed against the left flank of the main attack near Serre.*

feature, which provided shelter for men and guns alike. Immediately in front, the village was protected by rising ground which ran away to the north towards Serre and it was on this elevation, to the left of Beaumont Hamel and some two hundred yards in front of it, that the Germans had built the massive Hawthorn Redoubt, standing sentinel on the breast of the hill and pushing towards the British lines a mere two hundred yards away on the downward slope. Here, concealed by a sunken track, the British had driven long galleries through the chalky ridge and planted a mine, big enough and powerful enough to blow the Hawthorn Redoubt sky-high and breach the defences of Beaumont Hamel.

But Beaumont Hamel was not the only visible strongpoint on the German line. To the north there was Serre itself and, between it and Beaumont Hamel, another fort on the Redan Ridge. To the south, beyond the River Ancre, the ruins of Thiepval village stood high above the valley and the shoulders of the ridge on either side of it were armoured with defensive works. To the left, the labyrinths of the Schwaben Redoubt and Goat Redoubt were scribbled across the slope of the ridge, facing Beaumont Hamel and Beaucourt across the river. To the right of Thiepval, the complex of trenches they called the Wunderwerk dominated the summit of the ridge and beyond it, the maze of the Leipzig Redoubt thrust like an obstinate jaw towards the British line above Authuille. There it turned to swing over to the twin villages of Ovillers and la Boisselle across the valley beyond. And, around la Boisselle – like Ovillers, a strongpoint in itself – another network of complex defence systems glared, balefully protective, in full view of the British line. Then, to the right, was the great bulging salient where the fortified village of Fricourt was enclosed by the German line as it changed direction and swivelled briefly on an eastward route in front of Mametz and Montauban before turning southwards at the River Somme, where the British Army stood side by side with the French.

Even without positive knowledge of the extent of the German diggings and the concealed fortifications and defences, it was perfectly clear that there were some hard nuts to crack and that, if the advance was to go fast and far in the first vital hours, special attention would have to be given to the problems they presented.

Groaning under the weight of some million pounds of explosive, which had to be carried to the sap-heads over long weary miles by a thousand weary working parties, the infantry did not always bless the solicitous preparations which their Staff were making on their behalf.

Just how to tackle the strongpoints that spiked the German line was a tactical headache, to which the Army had devoted considerable thought and the Fourth Army had issued its own thoughts on the subject in mid-May. But, as they were very well aware and as General Kiggell had stated quite categorically in his memorandum from GHQ, *It must be remembered that officers and troops generally do not now possess that military knowledge arising from a long and high state of training, which enables them to act promptly on sound lines in unexpected situations. They have become accustomed to deliberate action based on precise and detailed orders . . .*

Such 'precise and detailed orders' it was the business of the Army to supply. It was unfortunate that there was not sufficient time to plant mines under all or nearly all the most strongly defended sections of the German Front but there was no help for it. The mine at Beaumont Hamel was well under way and would be ready in good time. A pair of mines on either side of la Boisselle would shake the German garrison to bits along with its defensive outposts. Mines on a smaller scale would give them a nasty surprise at Fricourt and, although the troops would not be attacking the Fricourt Salient directly, would keep them on the *qui vive* while they swept past it on either side and 'pinched it out', while two others, judiciously placed under their line south of Montauban should assist the troops forward in fine style. As for Thiepval, the effect of the explosions on either side of its high fastness, at Beaumont Hamel and at la Boisselle, should be sufficient to rattle the Germans – or, at least, so it was hoped. And, in any event, the whole series of explosions were a mere refinement, extra insurance, the final ounce of thrust that would catapult the troops through and beyond the German line.

The citadels of intricate entrenchments, the battered villages they defended, the deep palisades of barbed wire that lay in front of them, would all long since have been shattered to atoms by the thundering British bombardment, so heavy, so fierce and so continuous that not a man nor a brick could hope to escape destruction.

The barrage opened up on 24 June. It was Midsummer's Day.

Chapter 5

From Frise on the French Front to Arras on the left of the Third Army, the guns opened on the forty-mile front in the full-throated knowledge that ammunition had been dumped in unprecedented quantities behind the batteries. That Sunday morning, 25 June, with a light easterly breeze blowing from the front, they could be heard quite plainly at Montreuil, set high on its fortress hill more than seventy miles away near the coast. At nine o'clock precisely, General Sir Douglas Haig and two ADCs stepped from the front door of the Château of Beaurepaire, mounted their perfectly groomed horses and turned their heads towards Montreuil four kilometres away. It was a pleasant ride along the narrow country road, through the lush greenery of early summer, to the foot of the steep cobbled hill and on up through the encircling ramparts into the town. Centuries earlier, the massive walls had been built to keep the marauding English at bay. From this vantage point, a hundred years before, Napoleon had looked covetously across the English Channel. Now the ramparts were guarding the security of the very people the French had gone to so much trouble to keep out and it was the French themselves who were the interlopers. The whole town had been taken over as the General Headquarters of the British Army and even the three thousand civilians who remained in Montreuil required the authority of the British to pass in or out of it. The civilians were outnumbered, two to one, by the military – almost all of them immaculate staff-officers, whose red hatbands had earned them the troops' nickname of 'geraniums'.

The nerve-centre of GHQ was in the Ecole Militaire in a narrow street a few yards away from the eastern ramparts. So many high-ranking officers passed so often through its exclusive archway, that the presentation of 'military compliments' had to be drastically revised. A mere colonel who, anywhere else, might have expected a full salute, was accorded no more than a token slap on a rifle butt, and generals were so thick on the ground that those who went regularly to and fro only expected to be greeted as befitted their rank once a day. Even the Commander-in-Chief, a stickler for military etiquette, issued orders that he should receive a full salute only on his first appearance – but woe betide the sentry who failed to turn out the guard to receive him. Although the guardroom was only a few yards down the passage leading to the inner courtyard, this was no easy task.

General Haig was in the habit of taking the longer but more pleasant route around the ramparts and, after the briefest of moments when he was just visible through a gap in the buildings, he appeared, only thirty yards away, already turning the head of his charger towards the Ecole Militaire, expecting to be received by an immaculately turned-out guard and full military honours. Under these circumstances, the turning out of the guard was easier to expect than to achieve. After one unfortunate occurrence, when General Haig had caught them unawares, breathless, hastily buckling on belts and fastening buttons, and had insisted that they should do it all over again, the military mind had turned from consideration of weightier problems to contrive a solution which would satisfy both military etiquette and the Commander-in-Chief. It took the form of an electric bell, placed high on the wall at exactly the right height to be pressed by the tip of the sentry's rifle as he caught his first fleeting glimpse of General Haig's approach. There had been no further complaints.

Now, on the eve of the long-planned campaign, the Commander-in-Chief, with his Chiefs of Intelligence, was about to move to Advanced Headquarters for the duration of the battle. A château had been prepared for him at Beauquesne, fifteen miles behind the battle-line. Meanwhile, Sir Douglas Haig was on his way to church.

Some boys were kicking a ball around on the patch of grass in front of the bridge that crossed the moat to the massive citadel, where a pair of immaculate sentries stamped and strutted beneath the Union Jack, fluttering above the postern gate. They stopped to nudge each other and to admire as the small group of horsemen clattered by. Raymond Wable, thirteen years old and home for the weekend from his school at Berck Plage, noticed that they seemed to shine in the sunlight – polished buttons, polished belts, high-polished riding boots, glistening harness and burnished silver spurs against the glossy coats of the horses. ''Aig,' they whispered to each other, their eyes swivelling towards the sentries in delighted anticipation of the full 'Present Arms'.

But the destination of the Commander-in-Chief was not the citadel; it was a modest wooden barrack, twenty yards away on the ramparts, and the flag that fluttered above its modest entrance was the blue and white of the St Andrew's cross, announcing that this was the Church of Scotland Hut. Meticulously punctual, Sir Douglas Haig had arrived with just two minutes to spare before the start of the Sunday morning service. He was in need of a little quiet meditation.

The Reverend Mr Duncan had prepared his sermon with some care. He preached on a text from Chronicles, 'Yea, I will go in the power of the Almighty God,' and he drew from these words a simple theme. God is ever present. His plans rule the Universe. We are merely tools in His hands, used for a special purpose. The Commander-in-Chief listened intently. Duncan's words struck a chord in his mind and, later that day, he carefully noted the details of the sermon. 'He quoted a saying of Abraham Lincoln's when asked if he was sure The Lord was with him. He replied that the important point was that "he should be on the side of The Lord". Mr Duncan also told the story of how, before the attack began, the Scots knelt down in prayer on the battlefields of Bannockburn in 1314. Altogether it was a most inspiring sermon.'

Sir Douglas Haig was a devout man. He was worried about the battle. He was uplifted, even reassured, by the re-statement of one of the tenets of his simple faith. At the door of the hut, shaking hands with the minister after the service, with one ear cocked towards the distant murmur of the bombardment seventy miles away on the Somme, the Commander-in-Chief was struck by a happy thought. Would Mr Duncan care to accompany him when he moved to Advanced Headquarters for the forthcoming battle? Mr Duncan was 'very pleased at the idea'. He would have forty-eight hours to make his arrangements. On Tuesday, the Commander-in-Chief would be moving to Beauquesne.

All across the seventy miles that separated GHQ at Montreuil from the front, in fields and meadows beyond the tumbledown barns and cottages of some hundreds of villages where the troops were encamped, the routine church parades took on a special significance on this last Sunday before the men went into battle. Just as the Church of Scotland Minister at Montreuil had sought to inspire the Commander-in-Chief, padres of all denominations had cast round for themes that would encourage and sustain the men through the ordeal ahead. Most of them automatically struck on the same choice of hymns. *Fight the Good Fight* and *Onward Christian Soldiers* were usually selected as being the most appropriate note to wind up the service before the men marched off. The 6th Battalion of the West Yorkshire Regiment sang them both at their service in the orchard at Puchevillers before marching off to dismiss for dinners and an afternoon of comparative leisure.

There had been no parades for several days. 'Enjoy yourselves,' Colonel Wade had said and, after months of heavy training, the implication of this benevolence was not lost on the troops. There was a wholesale exodus to Beauquesne and, on the philosophical principle that there was no point in going into battle with money in your pocket, champagne corks popped merrily in its cafés all afternoon. The less affluent played cricket or simply indulged in horseplay in the orchard. The favourite pastime which, even after two months' ragging and rough and tumble, still amused a few, was 'testing' the efficiency of the new tin helmets by assaulting hard-headed volunteers with whatever implements were to hand – entrenching tools, knobkerries, or even spades. After 'casualties' amounting to one fractured skull and several cases of concussion the Colonel had forbidden this pastime, but the risk of retribution merely added spice to the proceedings and, if some amateur bookie was willing to give odds, the amusement of a mild flutter. Serious gamblers huddled round the forbidden Crown and Anchor board, set up in a discreetly distant corner of the orchard, and soldiers, at a loose end, strolled through the village, up the country road and gathered in curious groups outside the empty tents of the newly erected casualty clearing station, to indulge in the time-honoured holiday entertainment of watching other people at work. A little distance from the big marquees, the orderlies were hard at it. They were digging graves. The wags of the battalion, with heavy witticism aimed at the new recruits, speculated ghoulishly on who was destined to occupy them.

Forty-eight hours before the march-off there were a thousand details to be seen to and Colonel Wade had called a meeting of his officers to discuss them and to detail those who were to be left behind. Six officers and extra detachments of bombers, Lewis-gunners, signallers and scouts were to march off with the battalion but would stay behind at Bouzincourt ready to move forward to replace casualties. The main body was ordered to Thiepval – not to attack it but, timing their arrival for Zero plus two hours, to pass through the triumphant ranks of the 36th Ulsters of the first wave and to stride on to consolidate the third objective and wait there for the next move.

Now that the maps were actually being distributed, the next move looked interesting. The first was a mere leaflet, a sketchy affair covering three miles at most and showing the area behind and in front of the first three familiar objectives. The officers glanced at it with passing interest and turned their attention to the more beguiling attractions of the maps which only the senior officers would carry into action. They were large maps and, on the scale of one inch to a thousand yards, they illustrated the fifty miles of country between Douai and St Quentin and the thirty miles that lay between it and Bapaume.

There was no Sunday rest for the Gunners. The field guns, ranged in batteries a thousand yards behind the front, and the line of heavy siege guns a mile or so to the rear, were pounding the German defences – sending over 150,000 shells non-stop every twenty-four hours. They went on firing until the recoil buffers of some field guns snapped under the strain. They fired until the breeches were so red hot that they had to be broken open with an axe. And they were firing precisely to programme, for the barrage tables issued to each battery were as finely delineated as the detailed orders to which every battalion of the infantry was expected to adhere.

The 'heavies' in the rear were entrusted with the main task of pulverizing the German trenches and dugouts with shells so numerous and so huge that, if you watched carefully, you could see them in flight on the lowest part of their trajectory as they left the muzzles of the guns. The infantry and the gunners of the field artillery within sight of the Germans, watching the awesome effect of the bombardment, were moved to feel pity for the men caught up in it.

Sheltering in a deep dugout in the Wunderwerk, passing the terrible hours of waiting by scribbling in his diary, young Freiwilliger Eversmann of the 143rd Regiment of Infantry, found that it was not quite deep enough to protect his nerves.[1]

They went at it left and right with heavy calibre guns and hammered us with shrapnel and light calibre pieces. Only with difficulty and distress have we obtained rations today. Two of my comrades got fatal hits while fetching dinner. One of them was Drummer Ollersch, of Gelschenkirchen, a dear chap – three days back from leave and there he's gone . . .

25 June, 7 o'clock: The barrage has now lasted thirty-six hours. How long will it go on?

9 o'clock: A short pause of which we avail ourselves to bring up coffee. Each man got a portion of bread.

10 o'clock: Veritable Trommelfeuer. In twelve hours' shelling they estimate that 60,000 shells have fallen on our battalion sector . . . When will they attack? Tomorrow or the day after? Who knows?

27 June, 4 a.m.: Ran to the cookhouse and fetched coffee, some having been brought up. There was also some bread to be had. By 6 o'clock the fire had increased and soon we had a headache. But, sit tight, it cannot last much longer. They say their munitions will

1. 'Freiwilliger' was a rank equivalent to private (gemeiner) but meaning, literally, 'volunteer'.

soon be done . . . There must be an end sometime to this horrible bombardment . . .

But the British gunners were not having it all their own way. On the other side of the line, a little distance to the south, Sergeant Frank Spencer was also keeping a diary and recording remarkably similar experiences:

Sergeant Frank Spencer, No. 1113, C Bty., 152nd Brigade, Royal Field Artillery

25 June: Lovely morning. Once again still heavy bombardments being carried out on either side. We were shelled for three and a half hours and had to cease our own firing and taking sights to seek refuge in tunnels. One gunner was slightly hit and the adjoining battery on our left was shelled very heavily (several casualties). Myself and four gunners now venture to fetch dinner and we have to dodge the shells which are falling down like rain upon us. We all had to jump into a cable trench. Although the soup is not absolutely spoilt, it is filled with chalk from bursting shells which are again chiefly directed towards C Battery.

26 June, Monday: Bombardments all night.

27 June: Bombardment continues no more than was expected. We still have further trouble due to springs going again, so two more guns are exchanged with ordnance. One was badly damaged as well as having springs broken due to the extraordinary strain from incessant firing. We bombarded all night.

28 June 1916: Bombardment continued. The coming attack is prac-tised on German front lines with heavy curtain fire and 'lifts' at a pre-arranged moment. The infantry raid the enemy lines to report the damage done and bring back with them prisoners from whom we hope to gain some valuable news . . . Our wire was well cut, but the left division had not cut theirs very well.

The field artillery had been schooled and trained in its role with the same scrupulous attention to detail as the infantry had been trained in theirs, for it was the artillery which would orchestrate the battle and the success or failure of the infantry would depend on its playing its part to the full. This had been made very clear to the infantry:

CO-OPERATION OF ARTILLERY WITH INFANTRY

The ideal is for the artillery to keep their fire immediately in front of the infantry as the latter advances, battering down all opposition with a hurricane of projectiles. The difficulties of observation, especially in view of dust and smoke . . . the probable interruption of telephone communications between infantry and artillery . . . renders this idea very difficult to obtain.

Experience has shown that the only safe method of artillery support during an advance, is a fixed timetable of lifts to which both the infantry and artillery must rigidly conform.

This timetable must be regulated by the rate at which it is calculated the infantry can reach their successive objectives:[1]

The calculations had been made with meticulous care. The shallow scratchings on the practice grounds that simulated German trenches had been laid out on the same scale as the known trench system of the enemy.

Stop watches in hand, Staff Officers had watched the Tommies blundering in full battle gear across the carefully measured ground, had timed them and, making allowance for the actual conditions of battle, had made their provisions accordingly.

The guns would operate in a series of carefully planned 'lifts'. For the last hour before the attack, the bombardment would fall with redoubled intensity on the enemy's front line − lifting at Zero to rake forward to his second line and to shell it for precisely as long as it would take the infantry to subdue the first defences and start off for the second. Travelling ahead of the infantry in a series of flea-hops, raining shells on successive lines of German positions, the guns would so prepare the way that all the infantry would have to do would be to take possession of what remained of the trenches and capture such of their defenders as had miraculously survived.

It worked superbly on paper. It would only work on the battlefield if both troops and gunners worked so rigorously hand in hand and adhered so exactly to the timetable that there was no room for error, no room for manoeuvre and no question of failure. The Army thundered instructions accordingly:

No changes must be made in the timetables by subordinate formations without reference to Corps Headquarters or confusion is sure to ensue.

1. *Tactical Notes* issued from Fourth Army HQ, May 1916, for the guidance of divisional commanders.

The warning was reasonable enough. Having completed its part in the massed preliminary bombardment, when the attack started the artillery of each division was to pass back to the 'command' of its Divisional General. But he would not be in a position to know what was happening to his neighbours on either side and, if he adjusted his own fire-power to suit the position of his own men, the 'overs' might fall, with disastrous results, on other troops who were further ahead or less advanced than those in his own battle-line. It was no secret that the guns were getting 'tired' with incessant firing, that they were unreliable and that the gunners were still, for the most part, inexperienced. No matter how carefully they calculated ranges, their firing could not always be described as accurate.

Charlie Burrows, who belonged to the 7th Divisional Artillery and had been firing guns in France and Belgium since October 1914, was firing, for the first time, with sufficient ammunition.

Gunner Charles E. Burrows, 104th Bty., 22nd Brigade, RFA, 7th Division (his diary)

Fritz spots our position and shells us heavily. One gunner blown to pieces, one sergeant and one gunner wounded. One gunpit wrecked by a direct hit and the gun is out of action. They shell us continually for three hours. They get a few hits on our gunpit and smother us with shell-holes. We have a few anxious moments as we have about a thousand rounds of shells in our pits, high explosives. If they had hit us we would all have blown to pieces. They stopped suddenly. We are very relieved and very lucky. We afterwards heard that our heavies had got on to that battery and finished them. There is a quiet time for a short period, and we tidy the position and send the wrecked gun away, and get a new one the same night. Our heavies very busy. I was nearly wounded in the morning from the 25th Battery on our left rear by a premature shell. Something struck me on the left arm but glanced off quickly. Our section fire all night. Heavy artillery fire on both sides the whole night.

26 June: Battery fire all day. All our artillery keep up the bombardment. We have had no sleep for nights. Heard the infantry made another series of raids last night. They were after information.

28 June: Heavy rain last night and tonight towards evening. Bombardment still on. Our section fire all night on the 28th. No sleep for two nights. Still wire cutting.

The week which had started off with a fine Sunday and Monday, gradually deteriorated to chilly, showery weather, unseasonable for late June, hampering the work of the gunners ranging on distant targets and misting the eyes of the Royal Flying Corps as they tried to assess the effects of the bombardment. Because of the weather, the attack was postponed for forty-eight hours.

Whatever the feelings of the infantry, officers of the artillery were glad of this postponement. There was no doubt that they would have to be more sparing with ammunition, that the bombardment would have to be lightened, if they were not to be short of shells in the battle itself; on the other hand there were now two more days to devote to the all important task of wire-cutting.

Major J. Marshall-Cornwall, GSO (Intelligence Officer), GHQ Staff.
(Now General Sir James Marshall-Cornwall, KCB, CBE, DSO, MC)

The infantry had in front of them a triple line of German defences which went back from the front line for six or eight kilometres – three lines of defence, each defended by a chain of concrete pill-boxes, which were machine-gun posts, surrounded by acres of barbed-wire entanglements. The whole thing depended on our artillery being able first of all to locate and then smash up the concrete machine-gun posts and then with the field guns to sweep away the wire entanglements. This was the primary essential. Well, bombardments started with 1,500 British guns – 450 of them were heavies – but, unfortunately, the weather broke. For five days out of the six of the bombardment there was low cloud and drizzle. Air observation was impossible and artillery observation was very hampered. The fact was that neither did they pinpoint the machine-gun posts opposite them, they also failed to cut the wire and the failure of the cutting of the wire was most disastrous.

Our procedure at that time was to use a shrapnel shell which burst about twenty feet above the ground and the hail of bullets going forward when the shell burst in the air swept away the wire entanglements. But it all depended on the accurate setting of the time fuze which ignited the shrapnel shells and our munition factories were only just getting into full swing. There were a lot of manufacturing faults in the fuzes. They didn't all burn the right length and, I'm afraid, a lot of the half-trained gunners of the New Army Divisions didn't set the fuzes exactly accurate. The fact was that many of the shells burst too high and the bullets dropped into

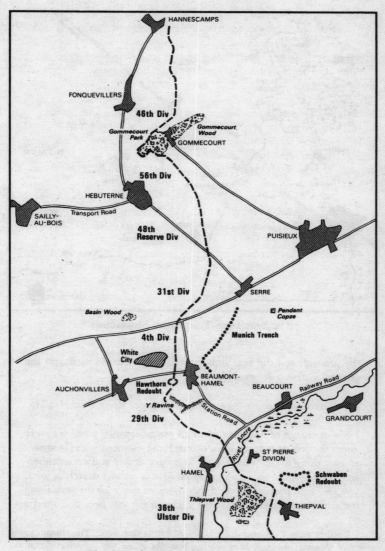

The Line from Gommecourt to Thiepval

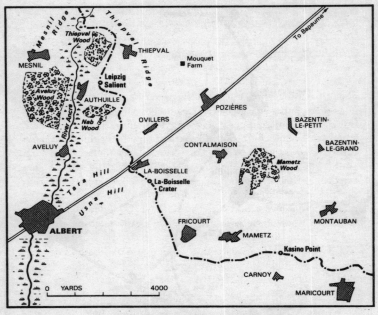

The Line from Thiepval to Montauban

the ground, and the fuze didn't work and it buried itself into the ground so the wire was left.[1]

2nd Lieutenant Kenneth Page, MC, 40 Brigade, Royal Field Artillery

I was in charge of a section of an 18-pounder battery and we were given the job of cutting lanes through the German wire. It wasn't an easy thing to do. You had to do it very slowly and very deliberately. You would go on plugging away at one short stretch of wire, you see, and, bearing in mind that there was wire all the way along the front, the tendency was for a gap to get cut here and then a

1. Further note by General Sir James Marshall-Cornwall: The disappointing effect of shrapnel shells in wire-cutting brought about the introduction in the following year (1917) of a new type of fuze (the 106 fuze). This was a highly sensitive percussion fuze which acted instantaneously as the shell hit the ground and scattered the fragments horizontally, thus effectively destroying the wire entanglements.

gap got cut a little way along there and the infantry had obviously got to get through this wire, so they tended to get in the gaps and, if the Germans knew the gaps were there – after all they'd watched them being cut – they could line their machine-guns up to cover them.

The experts, the 18-pounder battery commanders, were quite good at cutting wire, but it did need very careful laying because guns were rather inaccurate things in those days. They had what was called a 'hundred per cent zone'. That meant that, if you fired a hundred rounds from one gun, at, say, a range of three thousand yards and you then measured up very carefully the area in which all the shells had fallen, you would then call that the hundred per cent zone. But, although most of the hundred rounds – all laid in the same way, remember – would be more or less gathered in the middle, quite a few odd ones would have exploded out towards the extremities of the zone. So, it wasn't easy to go on plugging one gun into the same hole every time, however accurately you laid it. With the inaccuracies of ammunition and fuzes and even the guns themselves, you would get unavoidable errors.

It was quite literally a case of a hit or a miss. In the cloudy moonless nights before the assault, raiding parties, crawling in black-faced cohorts across to the German lines, brought back mixed reports. They had found the German trenches empty and the wire 'well cut'. They had found the wire impassable and the trenches heavily manned. They had found the trenches empty (except for an unfortunate sentry dragged back as a prisoner) but had heard the muffled singing of Germans in their dugouts. But the small bag of prisoners sent back for interrogation were cowed and visibly shaken by the unremitting nervous strain of the bombardment and, like Eversmann, sheltering in a deep dugout from the explosions rocking Thiepval Ridge, willing it to end.

Freiwilliger Eversmann, 143rd German Regiment of Infantry

It is night. Shall I live till morning? Haven't we had enough of this frightful horror? Five days and five nights now this hell concert has lasted. One's head is like a madman's; the tongue sticks to the roof of the mouth. Almost nothing to eat and nothing to drink. No sleep. All contact with the outer world cut off. No sign of life from home nor can we send any news to our loved ones. What anxiety they must feel about us. How long is this going to last?

The answer was, 'not long'. Already the British troops were moving up to the assembly trenches. A few unfortunates, the first to move into position for the attack that should have been launched forty-eight hours before, had already been in them for two chilly and rainy days. There was no question of taking all of them back, for, in the country immediately behind the lines, every tent, every hut, every barn and every house in every village was crammed full of men who had marched up from the rear behind them. Now the weather had cleared. It was a fine night with the promise of a fine day ahead.

Greatcoats had been handed in, tied in bundles of four and, with two hundred thousand packs and three thousand or so officers' valises, were stacked in farm outbuildings all up and down the line. At last-minute parades, brigadiers had bawled through megaphones in cheering tones of encouragement. Commanding officers and adjutants, armed with the printed Summaries of Intelligence sent forward from Headquarters for the purpose, read extracts aloud to their battalions. Based, perhaps selectively, on captured documents, on the interrogation of prisoners, the reports of raiding parties and observations of the result of the bombardment, they pointed without exception to the demoralization of the enemy, to the destruction of his defences, to his lack of fighting spirit, to the casualties he had suffered in the punishing shellfire. Listening to these words, as the shells roared and crashed in the distance, neither the officers nor the men found them difficult to believe.

In the early dusk of the previous evening Major-General Rycroft had gone forward to have a look for himself at the Thiepval Ridge where his 32nd Division was going to attack. Standing at the edge of Aveluy Wood he had no need of binoculars. The ground under his feet quivered with the vibration of the guns and for five days they had been trained on the Thiepval Ridge. Like the tall church and every other building in the village, the château had all but disappeared under a heap of tumbled brick and rubble, half-glimpsed through clouds of yellow smoke that enveloped the ruins with every salvo. Away to the right, the face of the hill was pockmarked with craters. On the skyline above, the clutter of wire and trenches, the forward lines of the great redoubts, seemed to totter behind a curtain of flying chalk. 'My God!' the General had to shout to make himself heard, although the Commanders of his three Brigades were only inches away. 'All we'll find in Thiepval, when we go across, is the care-taker and his dog!'

The Brigadiers, pleased with the aptness of the General's summing-up, had passed it on to the infantry in their reassuring goodbye messages. They all sincerely believed that it was true.

Now the troops were on their way, each man wearing on his shoulder a flash in the identifying colour of his Division. In a spectrum of bright colours they fluttered from two hundred thousand shoulders and on their backs, catching the last rays of the dying sun, were two hundred thousand triangles of tin. Shining in the sun tomorrow morning, they were intended to reveal to distant observers the progress of the infantry's advance. It was the last tiny detail of a million details of the painstaking planning that would direct their destiny.

Even the assembling of such a mass of men had been planned with such care that there was hardly a hold-up or a hitch. Coloured lamps, glowing discreetly at ground level, guided the battalions along their designated tracks to arrive at Divisional Assembly Areas within minutes of the appointed time and with time in hand for a little rest. Although the order had been 'March Easy', it had been hard going; 'Battle Order' meant that every man was weighed down with more than sixty pounds of equipment and, now, at forward divisional dumps, they were dishing out still more spades, pickaxes, and even, to some benighted Tommies in the second wave, rolls of barbed-wire. Cursing at the weight of it all, the infantry could hardly be blamed for failing to appreciate that this burden of extraneous equipment was intended for its protection. After much mulling and weighing of advantage against disadvantage, the Staff had decided that its novice warriors would stand a better chance if they were able to consolidate captured trenches with all speed, rather than run the risk of a counter-attack while they waited for Pioneer Battalions to come up behind them.

Hunched under their assorted burdens, the infantry moved up to the line. Their excitement was mingled with nervousness, but at least the waiting was over. At long last they would have a chance of having 'a proper go' at the Hun. Despite the bellicose array of weapons dangling about their persons, many Tommies had thoughtfully provided themselves with knuckle-dusters, lengths of chain and even vicious knives as their personal contribution to the armoury of battle. Most had never yet seen a German face to face, but, as if anticipating some street corner brawl, they intended to be ready when they did. The fact was that, in spite of the long months of careful rehearsal, of lectures and training, of preparation and of orders, in the untried ranks of Kitchener's Army there was hardly an officer or a man who appreciated the difference between a raid and a general attack.

Part 2

The Big Push

'Old soldiers never die; they simply fide a-why!'
That's what they used to sing along the roads last spring;
That's what they used to say before the push began;
That's where they are today, knocked over to a man.

SIEGFRIED SASSOON

Chapter 6

Morning crept over the Somme spreading a gentle haze that promised a fine day ahead.

The last hour of waiting was the worst.

At 6.35 the guns, which had been firing incessantly all night, roared out in the crescendo of the final bombardment. The shells were too high to be seen but they came screaming so thick and so fast over the front-line trenches that the men packed into them, with only the sky for a view, looked up in spite of themselves, as if expecting to see some thrilling visible sight, like the hail of arrows singing through the air at Agincourt.

In the trenches on either side of Gommecourt, the British troops hardly noticed the stepping up of their own bombardment because the Germans, convinced that the main brunt of the attack would take place here, were returning shot for shot. They were pounding the advanced trench, dug with such bravado well out in No Man's Land, where the first wave of the 56th Division infantry were waiting to go. They were hammering the old front line where the second wave were ready to follow them. Shells were crashing among the support trenches and raining down on Hébuterne where the reserve troops awaited the order to move forward. Captain Agius was there with B Company, ready to go across with bombs and ammunition and to establish contact with the leading companies of the 3rd Londons as soon as they were ensconced in the enemy's front line. In the open street outside the cottage that served as Battalion Headquarters there was no shelter from the bombardment. Brigade Headquarters was even further ahead, for Brigadier-General Loch was a man who liked to see for himself what was going on. The Brigade Orderly Sergeant, Harry Coates, in ordinary circumstances rather admired his fire-eating Brigadier, but now with shells exploding all around the fine observation trench which was Brigade Headquarters for the battle he was not quite so sure. Brigade-Major Philip Neame, originally a Royal Engineer, was a fire-eater of equal calibre to General Loch, and had proved it a year earlier at Neuve Chapelle by winning the Victoria Cross. He had designed the trench, had supervised its construction and, last night, they had moved into it. Luckily, Neame's design had included a good dugout a dozen feet underground and they were sheltering there now. The Brigadier, Neame himself, Coates, and a clutch of runners, orderlies, telephonists and signallers, who were already hunched over their instruments testing the lines as the orderlies dished out the first of the dozen strong cups of tea that each man would drink in the course of the day ahead. The walls were vibrating with every explosion and the Brigadier was looking worried.

Across the two-mile stretch of land that separated the 56th Division from the left flank of the main attack, the two battalions of the 48th Division who were manning the trenches were having an equally bad time. They, at least, were not going 'over the top' although, to make it look as if they were, they had opened conspicuous lanes through the wire in front of their trenches and made the same visible feint 'preparations' as the Third Army on their left. But all they were required to do was to launch a smokescreen to hang like a curtain across the two miles between Gommecourt and Serre and thus to blind and confuse the Germans and their guns. They knew already that they would fail. The wind, which should have carried the smoke forward, had turned and now a gentle breeze blew towards the British from the direction of the German lines.

At Serre the Pals were in position. Waiting in the support trenches with the men of his Vickers machine-gun team, Sergeant Jimmy Myers checked the gun and its components for the umpteenth time and thought for the umpteenth time that, even broken into its component parts and with five men to carry the gun and its thousands of rounds of ammunition, it would be quite a job to hump the gun when they went over with the Bradford Pals. Still, that was more than an hour away. They had practised it all a thousand times – dismantling the gun, slinging the pieces on top of the trench while they clambered out, keeping up with the infantry and, when they reached their advanced position, re-assembling the gun with lightning speed and coming into action. They had got it down to a fine art and, after the final rehearsals, the only observation made by Lieutenant Burrows had been a nod of quiet satisfaction. There was no need to worry about the trek across the width of No Man's Land. As the rehearsals had shown, by nine o'clock when they went over troops of the first wave would already be far ahead and the German outpost line, now staring down at them from the low crest of the hill, would long ago have been rendered harmless.

In the first wave, Willie Parker in the Sheffield Pals was probably the only man who had not rehearsed the battle. He had only been with the Battalion for two weeks. Since he had joined up with his young brother

Reg on the very day the Battalion had started recruiting, his belated arrival was due, in his own view, to unreasoning wilfulness on the part of Authority. First they had trained him as a soldier and then, at the end of six months, had plucked him out of the ranks and sent him back to his proper trade as a skilled engineer. No one from Lord Kitchener downwards could have convinced Willie that the year he had spent making munitions at Armstrong-Whitworth's was more valuable to the war effort than his presence in the khaki ranks of the Sheffield Pals, armed with a rifle that he barely knew how to use. He had badgered the Army, he had petitioned the Lord Mayor, he had made such a nuisance of himself by pestering the factory manager that Armstrong-Whitworth's had given in and released him. The Army had taken Willie back into the fold and he had considered it the greatest piece of luck that a draft of men was on the point of leaving to join the Battalion in France in time for the Big Push. Waiting now in the front-line trench, clad in new khaki, taking pleasure in the unfamiliar weight of rifle and tin hat, Willie would not have changed places with the King himself.

Already they were placing the scaling ladders against the wall of the trench. At twenty-past seven the Sheffields would climb them and crawl out to lie in readiness in front of their own wire. At seven-thirty, when the whistles blew, they would be the first men across.

Over the Redan Ridge, ever since dawn, machine-gun teams to the left of Beaumont Hamel had been looking across at the German line through a tangle of grass and weeds. It was the closest view they had ever had, because they were now well out in No Man's Land on the very edge of the low plateau they called the White City. The British front line ran across it within forty feet of its furthest edge and, in the weeks before the battle, they had driven forward a series of shallow tunnels to within a foot or two of the sunken road in No Man's Land beyond. Just before dawn, they had broken down the last thin barriers of soil in its bank and camouflaged the openings with a thin curtain of tangled vegetation to hide the gun-crews from the prying eyes of any over-zealous observer who might raise his head in the thick of the bombardment. They lay so close – no more than a hundred yards away – that they could almost see the individual barbs of the wire entanglements that stretched across the field, guarding the rising ground where the German trenches furrowed through shattered orchards. The wire looked uncomfortably intact, but there were gaps here and there. Marking them with their eye, the men mentally plotted the rush that would carry them across the ground as they dashed out ahead of the infantry to put paid to any opposition and pave the way ahead. Meanwhile, they were waiting for the word of command to move back along the tunnel, dragging the guns to a safe distance, so that they would not be damaged nor the men concussed when the great mine exploded under the redoubt on the Hawthorn Ridge. That would be the signal to crawl forward again ready for the jump-off ten minutes later.

At twenty minutes past seven, the mine went up in a sheet of flame and a thunderous fountain of debris that leapt a hundred feet into the air. As it fell back to the earth and the last rumblings of the explosion died away, looking across from his observation position behind the White City, Dudley Lissenburg could see quite clearly on the ridge across the valley a small force of two hundred men rush forward and disappear into the cloud of black smoke on their way to capture the crater.

In the stunning aftermath of the explosion, despite the sound of the bombardment on the heights of Thiepval to the right, and a distant mutter of gunfire far, far away to the left, a strange silence seemed to fall. In the moments before the German machine-guns started up, it seemed to Lissenburg uncanny. Across the Redan Ridge the Pals of the 31st Division, crawling out to wait in front of the wire for the signal to go for Serre, remarked on it too. The bombardment which more than two miles away had had to cease to allow two companies of troops to attack four hundred yards of the enemy's defences on the Hawthorn Ridge, had, by some error of judgement or misinterpretation of orders, stopped along the four-mile length of the 8th Corps Front. For the next ten minutes, not a single shot would be fired.

In their jumping-off trench at the edge of Thiepval Wood, waiting to move uphill across the slope to tackle the formidable line that lay in front of the Schwaben Redoubt, the Ulstermen of the 36th Division heard the explosion quite clearly through the roar of their own bombard-ment, and saw the tip of the cone of debris it threw into the sky. They were at a pitch of excitement. It was the 1st July and, according to the old calendar, it was the anniversary of the Battle of the Boyne. To the Ulstermen it was the best of all possible omens and they were raring to go.

A little way behind them, where the 109th Brigade were in readiness to follow up the first-line troops as they left their trenches, Colonel Ricardo stood on the parapet of the assembly trench cheering his men on as they went through the two centre exits on either side. He wanted to wish them luck, but he needed a megaphone to make himself heard. 'They got going without delay; no fuss, no shouting, no running, every-thing solid and thorough – just like the men themselves. Here and there a boy would wave his hand to me as I shouted "Good Luck" to them through my megaphone. And all had a cheery face. Most were carrying loads. Fancy advancing against heavy fire with a big roll of barbed wire on your shoulder!'

Away to the right, at the top of the hill, the ruins of Thiepval village were shuddering under the final tornado of the bombardment. The piles of dusty rubble seemed to hold as little threat as the bleached bones of a long-dead tiger. Not a man among the hundred-strong company waiting to clamber from the trenches across the tumbled terracing of the old château gardens and on to the shattered village beyond, had the slightest doubt that their job would be a piece of cake.

Away to their right, under the crest of the ridge, the vanguard of the 17th Highland Light Infantry was inching forward to lie close up to the belts of wire in front of the Wunderwerk. Somewhere beyond it, in these last moments of the bombardment, Freiwilliger Eversmann, waiting in battle order, was doubtless still wondering, 'When will it end?'

Round the promontory of the Leipzig Redoubt, where the 70th Brigade was also waiting nearly in the shadow of the wire for the bombardment to lift, the line took an almost right-angled turn down into the Nab Valley. Ernest Deighton, of the 8th Battalion King's Own Yorkshire Light Infantry, was the first man out and he had been out since before dawn concealed in a shell-crater halfway across No Man's Land. He had never felt so exposed nor so alone in his life. Deighton was a sniper and a marksman and, ever since it had been light enough to see, he had been training the telescopic sights of his rifle on a gap in the German wire, keeping his eyes peeled for any movement. The Jerries had been keeping their heads well down, and who could blame them, but he was pretty sure that he had bagged at least a couple and that there would be no trouble from that quarter when his comrades dashed across at Zero. The minutes dragged. He had no means of knowing the time – the chance glinting of a watch face might have given away his position – but, like Eversmann, he longed for the bombardment to stop, for the whistles to blow in the trenches behind him, to be on the move, to get going. As soon as the first line of troops reached him, he was to leap up and join them in the charge towards the German trenches.

A mile to the south, Brigadier-General Ternan was furious. Like General Loch at Gommecourt, he had gone to some trouble to make sure of having a good view of the attack and the Royal Engineers had constructed a fine observation post two hundred yards down on the forward slope of the Tara-Usna Ridge overlooking the Ovillers valley and with a fine view to the right over la Boisselle and the 34th Divisional Front. Here, with Brigadier-General Cameron, in command of the Tyneside Irish Brigade, he positioned himself just minutes before Zero, and he had just made the unpleasant discovery that, in spite of the elaborate preparations of the Engineers, it was impossible to see a thing.

The Brigadiers wished in particular to see the effect of the huge mines that were to explode on either side of the village of la Boisselle at Zero Hour. The infantry had already been pulled back to the reserve trenches to protect them from any untoward effects of the explosions and, as Ternan was unhappily aware, this meant that they would have a long way to go, and that they would be exposed to fire even before they started across No Man's Land. Pushing along an assembly trench to their right, the two Brigadiers discovered that, by climbing on the fire step and looking over the parapet, they had a good, if unprotected, view of the valley. Fifty yards down the slope ahead, Ternan could see the first line of the Tyneside Scottish preparing to leave their trenches. At seven twenty-eight the mines went up – one to the left of la Boisselle, a huge one to the right of it and a mile beyond, on the Fricourt Salient, a clutch of smaller explosions. As the noise died away, in a brief spell of comparative silence while the guns lengthened their range, he could hear a strange whining noise from the trenches down the hill. It was the pipers tuning up as they made ready to play the Tyneside Scottish over the top.

The attack of the 18th Division in front of Montauban started with a bang. At the advanced Battalion Headquarters of the 10th Battalion, The Essex Regiment, the waiting officers cheered as the mines went up at Kasino Point. There were casualties from the fall-out and, although it was in the second trench, a few far-flung chunks of debris even flew into their shack, but this was some compensation to Lieutenant Robert Chell who, newly promoted to Adjutant, had been rather disappointed that his place was at Battalion Headquarters rather than in the line with the men. But the men were surging ahead and the first prisoner arrived, incredibly, before the attack was five minutes under way. He was a pitiful specimen, unwashed, unshaven and, as Chell noticed delightedly as he telephoned the details of the prisoner's regiment back to Brigade Headquarters, he was unfed as well by the looks of him and still shaking from his ordeal of seven days in the front line under the bombardment.

This was the first of many reports of good progress that Chell was to send back during the course of the day.

Eight minutes before Zero, where the 30th Division met the French at the end of the British line, Stokes mortar batteries had thundered a hurricane bombardment. Here where the Germans least expected an attack, it was so powerful and so effective that, when it stopped, there was absolute silence from the German lines. As the whistles blew and the troops left the trenches, they presented a sight that would have gladdened the hearts of the Staff who had pored so long and so hard over the battle plans. Extended in lines of companies, a hundred paces apart, they crossed the width of No Man's Land in quick time with rifles slung – British Tommies on the left, French *poilus* on the right. At the point where the two lines met, Colonel Fairfax of the 17th Battalion, The King's Liverpool Regiment, and Commandant Le Petit, in command of the 3rd Battalion of the 153rd Régiment d'Infanterie, found themselves together. Grinning, the French officer crooked his elbow invitingly. Colonel Fairfax took it and, pushing forward, they led the advance arm in arm.

By half-past seven all along the straggling miles of the front the ground mist was beginning to thin. As the first hundred thousand men went over the top, the sun was already shining strongly enough to feel warm on the napes of their necks and it blazed on through the long summer's day.

Ordinarily, on the uplands of the Somme, just a week after midsummer, a balmy evening would have followed such a glorious day and turned imperceptibly into a warm cloudless night. But the night had fallen early, and it fell so thick with the dust and fumes of battle that you could almost touch it. It shook and quivered, blazed lurid yellow in the flash of the guns, swirling into black cloud shot with the flame of exploding shells, swelled into monstrous incandescence, as signal rockets soared through its turbulent mists. A hundred and fifty thousand men, living, or dead, lay out in the inferno.

Peering across at the furnace of Thiepval from the Artillery Observation Post, built four-square in solid concrete high on the Mesnil Ridge, anxious observers were still trying to make sense of the day's events. Their eyes had been glued to the Thiepval Ridge since early morning, but, for all they had seen, for all they had been able to interpret the course of the long day's battle, for all they had been able to make of the conflicting reports that had reached them, for all they we able to understand the significance of the signals and flares that lit the sky above the battle-line, they might have been blind and deaf. In spite of their best endeavours, they did not have the faintest idea of what was happening. But the sight of it awed the mind. The sound of it numbed the senses. And their only sickening certainty was that the position of the line had altered hardly at all since the troops had attacked from it in the morning.

*

But rumours of a breakthrough on the Somme had travelled fast and had been improved in the telling. Barely twenty miles to the north, in a sector of the trenchline between Wailly and Arras where the 6th Battalion, the King's Own Yorkshire Light Infantry was in the line, Lance-Corporal Len Lovell and Private Bill Clegg were suffering from the effects of the exaggerated good tidings. The joke had been conceived on the spur of the moment back at Brigade Headquarters in the euphoria of the first optimistic reports of success in the south and the Brigadier, who was never averse to 'showing Jerry what was what', had sent for a sign-writer from the Pioneer Battalion and set him to work right away. He was to find a trenchboard and embellish it with a suitable inscription. Almost before the paint was dry, it had been sent gleefully to the Headquarters of the 6th Battalion, the King's Own Yorkshire Light Infantry with explicit instructions.

Len Lovell was no stranger to No Man's Land. It had become almost routine to him, and to Clegg as well, to strip off their insignia, to empty their pockets, to blacken their faces, to crawl through the wire and melt into the night.

There was no possibility of dragging the heavy notice-board. First Lovell, then Clegg had to carry it on his shoulders as they crawled, belly down, across No Man's Land, feeling for obstacles in front, freezing in the intermittent glare of flares, inching on when they died down. It took them more than an hour to reach the German wire. Now they had to be doubly cautious, ears cocked for the slightest sound that might warn of an enemy patrol, wary of coming too close to the wire, lest a vibrating 'ping' should give them away, or the inadvertent movement of an arm catch one of them fast in its barbs.

Ten interminable minutes passed before the board was embedded into the earth. It took five more to prime the booby trap, designed to give any Germans who tried to remove it an exceedingly nasty surprise. Then came the slow crawl back to the lines, the ticklish business of finding safe passage through the wire, the hoarsely whispered password. Tonight it was 'WITH' – an everyday word, chosen for its ease of pronunciation by any native-born Britisher, yet containing, in one simple syllable, two complex sounds guaranteed to stump the foreign tongue of all but the most practised linguist.

Experience had shown that a surprisingly large number of Germans had some knowledge of English, so there was little doubt that Jerry would get the message – if not the joke – bright and early in the morning. The sign-writer had gone to some pains to make sure that it would be legible at a distance of thirty yards and, on its black-painted background, the white lettering stood out bold and clear:

10,000 MEN
AND
100'S OF GUNS
CAPTURED ON SOMME!
MORE TO FOLLOW
GOD SAVE THE KING!

A little way to the south, in the confusion of the thundering night, Intelligence Officers, trying to make sense of the day's events on the Somme, would have given a great deal to have been put in possession of such precise information.

At Bouzincourt, where the hundred reinforcements of the 6th Battalion, The West Yorkshire Regiment had been anxiously waiting all day without news, dusk was falling before a message from Brigade Headquarters ordered them forward to join the Battalion. It was not hard to guess that there had been casualties and that the Colonel was among them, for Major Scott, his Second-in-Command, was instructed to go up with the reinforcements and to take charge. Even more disturbing was the fact that they were to rendezvous not, as they might have hoped, at Grand-court, three miles beyond the start line, but at the start line itself in Thiepval Wood. Now they were trying to get there and, although two hours had gone by since they had set off, they had only managed to get as far as Aveluy Wood and here, it seemed, they were stuck. It was almost impossible, even in single file, to make headway through a struggling tide of stretcher-bearers streaming up the narrow tracks against the flow of ration parties and reinforcements pressing down them towards the line. The road to Lancashire Dump was nose-to-tail with limbers, and Lanca-shire Dump itself was a bottleneck, teeming with supply parties and ration parties and endless small bands of reinforcements pouring out from all over the wood on their way up to the line.

Leaving the track they had followed with difficulty through the trees, the West Yorkshires had to wait while a straggle of walking wounded passed, and some from their own regiment, recognizing them as they went through, called out to them, 'It's bloody murder over there, boys.' A signpost at the edge of the wood was confidently marked THIEPVAL-BAPAUME-BERLIN. This time last night it had cheered the troops on their way to the line; now, waiting beside it for the last stragglers to catch up, Lieutenant Hornshaw found it less than reassuring.

A peremptory arrow pointed to the track. It led across the marshy valley to the bottom of the ridge, and to the single route to the trenches below Thiepval which was invisible from the enemy positions above. It

took the West Yorks more than half an hour to shuffle across the mere
half-mile to the opposite bank of the Ancre.

Sheltered by a steep bluff the track turned left, hugging the lower slopes
of the ridge, passing through the ruins of Authuille and, beyond it, rising
gently as it ran towards Thiepval Wood, a mile ahead. Pushing against an
ever-swelling huddle of wounded, of messengers and runners clamouring
urgently to pass, deafened by the din, wearing gas-masks for the last
half-mile, held up in front, pushed forward from behind, the hundred
men of the West Yorkshires struggled on as best they could through the
rank, sour mist, towards the edge of the wood and the rendezvous at
Paisley Dump.

The British Military had taken over Thiepval Wood as surely as they
had taken over Aldershot. For the first year of the war, a tottering signpost,
drunkenly askew, had kept up a pretence that it was '*Proprieté privé.
Entrée Interdite.*' But it had long ago given up the ghost. Now battered
trenchboards nailed to the trees bore directions in uncompromising English: 'To Johnson's Post.' 'To Iniskilling Avenue.' 'To Hamilton Avenue,
Campbell Avenue, Elgin Avenue.' 'To Belfast City.' 'To Paisley Dump.'

Here, at the foot of the ridge on the western edge of the wood,
communication trenches splayed out towards the firing line six hundred
yards above. Here, supplies were unloaded and ammunition dumped.
Here was the meeting-place of every track from Authuille, every causeway
across the marshes. Paisley Dump had regularly been chaotic. Tonight it
was pandemonium.

The reliefs and reinforcements of two divisions were circling in a
sheep-like throng, at a loss to know just where, in the holocaust above,
their presence was so urgently required, and prevented even from getting
up the communication trenches by the rabble of battle-worn soldiers,
relieved from the front line, trying to throng down. Some, at the limit
of their strength, had given up the effort, and the assembly trenches,
where they had waited for the attack, were overflowing with exhausted
troops, lying literally in heaps, so drained by strain and fatigue that they
could sleep in the midst of the inferno. The deafening sound of the battle
above was blotted out by shells screaming closer still, exploding among
the men packed into the clearing and exploding too among the still forms
of the badly wounded as they lay along the edge of the wood waiting to
be evacuated.

As they neared the wood, between the roar of explosions, behind the
sickening gas-soaked mist, in the forefront of the noise that raged at them
from every horizon, the small party of the West Yorkshires became aware
of another sound. It was like nothing they had ever heard before. Later
– and for the rest of his life – Lieutenant Hornshaw was to remember it

as a sound that chilled the blood; a nerve-scraping noise like 'enormous wet fingers screeching across an enormous pane of glass'. It was coming from the wounded, lying out in No Man's Land. Some screaming, some muttering, some weeping with fear, some calling for help, shouting in delirium, groaning with pain, the sounds of their distress had synthesized into one unearthly wail.

As midnight passed and the night of the first day of July turned towards the dawn of the second, as the gunfire died down, it seemed to fill the air. All along the front, from the orchards of Gommecourt to the heights of Beaumont Hamel, from the shoulders of Thiepval to the valley beyond la Boisselle, it rose from the battlefield into the night like the keening of a thousand banshees.

Holding grimly to the remnants of their battered trenches, the battered remnants of the Army shivered as they listened.

Chapter 7

At Gommecourt, Arthur Agius was back where he had started at the beginning of the battle, at Battalion Headquarters at Hébuterne, but this time he was inside it, huddled in a corner with his face to the wall. Technically, Agius was a casualty, but his legs had not been able to support him through a long wait outside the aid post in a crowd of walking wounded, who seemed to him to be in more urgent need of attention than himself.

Captain Arthur Agius, 3rd Btn., Royal Fusiliers, City of London Regiment, 56th Division

I was shell-shocked, I suppose. At any rate, I wasn't much use — inclined to cry, if anything. In fact, I couldn't stop and, being rather young, I was somewhat ashamed of it. But it had been a total shambles. The first two companies had got across and, about an hour after they started, I was told to take B Company across to support them. We had no idea that the whole attack was a diversion. We thought that we were going forward. We had maps and plans of Gommecourt — we knew from information we'd got from the local people exactly where every house was. But the trouble was that Gommecourt stuck out in the middle of the line and we didn't attack it directly. We attacked on one side of the château park and the 46th Division were attacking on the other. We were supposed to encircle it and link up behind. But what we didn't know was that the Germans had so manoeuvred and organized their line that this part which we weren't to attack was really their strongpoint, and they simply had a clear field of fire on either side and nothing to bother about in front. And the shellfire was absolutely appalling. They were simply pouring shells down. We just couldn't get across. We didn't even get as far as the trench we'd dug — well, there was no trench left. It was all hammered to blazes. We got just about as far as our old front line and then it became quite impossible. The company in front of me said, 'It's no use. We can't get over.'

We got orders to turn and try to make our way back to the village. One of my subalterns was newly out. Such a nice chap. He must have had money and we used to tease him a bit because his batman was the family butler! This young officer jumped out of the trench to try to organize the men, pass the word and get them moving to the communication trench, and he was promptly killed. Just disappeared in an explosion. The whole of the valley was being swept with machine-gun fire and hammered with shells. We got the men organized as best we could – those of us who were left. So many gone, and we'd never even got past our own front-line trench! And then we found we couldn't get back. The trenches were indescribable! We were simply treading on the dead. Eventually my Sergeant and I got out on top – we were at the back of the Company. I heard a shell coming. I remember thinking, 'Imagine! Just imagine hearing a single shell in the middle of all this din!' It burst just above my head. The Sergeant was blown one way and I was blown the other. He was killed. I don't know how I got back. I simply don't know how I got back. It was murder.[1]

Trudging along the road away from the battle-line towards Sailly, 'Murder' was a word which Sergeant Henry Coates was finding it difficult to dismiss from his mind and he surmised that the thoughts of the man who was plodding along in silence by his side were probably running along the same lines. He was taking the Brigadier home. From Philip Neame's fine trench they had both had a grandstand view of the battle. The troops had gone over in fine style, behind a smokescreen so thick that they were through the battered German wire and into the front-line trenches almost before the Germans knew what was happening.

And that was the last they had seen of the advance, for the advance had melted away under the relentless German bombardment that had fallen all day on No Man's Land. After the first euphoric hour when markers hoisted above the German trenches triumphantly confirmed that the first wave of troops had reached its first three objectives, they had seen nothing but the perpetual flicker of signal lamps. They had flashed all day long, signalling over and over again the same urgent message: SOS BOMBS. SOS BOMBS. SOS BOMBS.

Looking back on the long day at Brigade Headquarters, Coates could not bring himself to contemplate the number of parties they had ordered out into the maelstrom to try somehow to get bombs and ammunition

1. The casualties of the 3rd Londons on 1 July were four hundred and sixty-eight killed and wounded.

to the troops, cut off in the German lines, battling to hold on to their hard-won gains. Eventually the Brigade Staff had stopped trying. It was very clear, as the day wore on, that no more troops had reached the other side. Even through the tossing sea of explosions, it was plain to see that the fighting was dying down. As dusk gathered in, the lessening flash of rifle fire, the intermittent sparking of a lone Lewis-gun, spoke all too eloquently of one last microscopic stand by a small band of survivors. Without ammunition, without help, without reinforcements, it was a miracle that they had lasted half so long.

As Coates stood in the trench peering at the last few futile streaks of fire, Philip Neame had appeared at his shoulder. 'I think you'd better accompany the Brigadier back.'

Coates had followed Neame down the steps to the dugout. Brigadier Loch sat slumped, staring at the low roof and the hanging lamp that swung and shivered with every crash of the bombardment.

Sergeant Henry Coates, No. 510729, 14th (London Scottish) Btn., London Regiment

He was like a man in a dream. It was terrible to see him like that, because he was quite a chatty old boy, always talking about his little daughter, and friendly, though he could be severe sometimes. The Old Man was a daredevil. A real fighter. He wanted to be in strict control of all that was going on and that's why we had this magnificent dugout with the short trench above it, away in advance of the Battalion HQs. It saved all our lives. If it hadn't been for this deep dugout we'd all have been killed or buried alive. They were simply knocking hell out of us, nearly all day.

I'm sure the Old Man was shell-shocked. I know I was! He was broken. He made no objection to coming with me. He didn't say a word. He just got up, very, very slowly and, in a break in the shelling, we went out. They'd shelled our own trenches so much that the line was absolutely broken, and the trenches were all knocked in and the chaps buried underneath. We were treading over dead bodies and all sorts of things going along. We just struggled back as best we could, past men going forward to try to get the wounded out of the trenches and out of No Man's Land, and past people going up to reinforce the front line – what was left of it! There was hardly anyone there. The Brigadier just followed me and eventually we managed to get through on to the road to Sailly au Bois.

It took them several hours to cover the four miles to Sailly and the old Brigade Headquarters and all the way, neither of them spoke a word.

A sentry snapped to attention as they entered Brigade HQ. The Brigadier hardly returned his salute. The bombardment was still thundering behind them. In silence they went down the steep stair to the cellar and, huddling in opposite corners, still without speaking, they settled down to pass what was left of the night.

Two miles south of Gommecourt, travelling at snail's pace along the congested road that would take them to the reserve trenches in the line in front of Serre, Reg Parker thanked God that he was with the Transport. Things had quietened down early on the Serre Front. By ten in the morning it had all been over. Two out of three of the men who had gone over the top had become casualties and lay dead or wounded on the gentle slope of ground between their trenches and the German lines. The Pals who had joined up in all the euphoria of the early weeks of the war, the lads from Leeds, from Bradford, from York, from Lancaster, from Sheffield, from Hull, had been slaughtered in the first short hour of the great battle. The last echoes of the cheers and the shouting, the last faint remembered notes of the brass bands that had sent them off from the towns and villages of the north, had died out in a whisper that morning in front of Serre.

Private Reg Parker, No. 744, 12th Btn., York & Lancaster Regiment (The Sheffield Pals)

It must have been two or three in the morning before we managed to get the transport and the rations up, though we'd been trying since early in the evening. We could see the fires as we went up. This little country village, this Serre, were a mass of fire that night. We had to take the stuff up to a place called Basin Wood and it was an exposed position, just about 600 yards behind our front line. And it was full of wounded. There were three doctors there, working flat out, and you could hear this groaning in the dark and see them lying round in the flash of the guns. They'd sent a party down to unload the rations but I'd got a water cart and you couldn't just chuck the stuff and get away. You'd got to wait while they emptied it and poured it into petrol tins. You could see it had been a shambles.

I kept trying to find out about my brother. He'd only come to

the Regiment a matter of days before the attack and he couldn't
have come at a worse time. I didn't have time to wangle him on
to the Transport. He was joined up with C Company, in the City
Battalion, and he didn't have time to pal up with any of them. So
nobody knew him. I kept asking, but nobody knew what had
happened to him. While they were unloading the water I saw
our Sergeant-Major and I tried to speak to him but he'd have shot
me! He was brandishing this revolver. Berserk! Didn't know
what he was doing. He was absolutely shell-shocked. They all
were!

You weren't supposed to stop there. You'd got to get out of it
before dawn and I just managed to. I never did find out what
happened to my brother. He must have been blown to smithereens.

Willie Parker was just one of some two thousand men who had fallen
in front of Serre in the first hour of the attack.

Over the Redan Ridge in the Beaumont Hamel valley, blinking mon-
strously under the flashing sky, the white chalk crater of the mine on the
Hawthorn Ridge glowered across at the British lines. It was many hours
since the small force who had captured it and, for a time, held it, had
been killed or pushed back. The Germans still held Beaumont Hamel;
they were still in firm possession of their line. Save for the carpet of dead
that lay in front of it, nothing had changed since morning. The long toil
of the mining operations, the careful preparations, the high optimism,
had all gone for nothing and been cancelled out by the single monstrous
error that had silenced the guns across the whole Corps Front. Even now,
at 8th Corps headquarters, Sir Aylmer Hunter-Weston was fuming over
it, and he was fuming because, in the course of a brief telephone conversation, the Commander-in-Chief had made it plain that he was displeased
with the performance of the 8th Corps. Hours earlier, in a few snatched
moments between conferences, between consultations and the hasty
recasting of plans, Sir Douglas had confided his displeasure to his
journal:

> North of the Ancre, the 8th Corps[1] (Hunter-Weston) said they
> began well, but, as the day progressed, their troops were forced
> back into the German front line, except two battalions which occu-
> pied Serre village, and were, it is said, cut off. I am inclined to

1. The 8th Corps comprised the 29th Division, the 4th Division and the 31st
Division.

believe from further reports, that very few of the 8th Corps left their trenches.[1]

They had 'left their trenches' all right, though not many had got as far as the trenches of the enemy beyond. When the mine had gone up and the bombardment had ceased across the whole length of the 8th Corps Front, it was the last signal of confirmation the Germans had needed to warn them that the assault was under way. That had happened, not at Zero, but ten minutes before the troops were to go 'over the top'. The Germans had ample time to rush up from shelters and dugouts, ample time to garrison their line, ample time to set up machine-guns, to man their hidden posts, to train the guns on the gaps in their own wire and also on the British wire, accurately sighted on the narrow lanes, through which the Tommies would have to pass into No Man's Land. As for the troops already lying beyond the trenches, awaiting the signal to go forward to the assault, it took far less than ten minutes to alert the German artillery and to bring a hurricane of shells crashing down on to the land they would have to cross.

It was incredible that any had succeeded in crossing it at all, and those who did had long ago been cut off, with no hope of reinforcement, of relief, or even of rescue.

Between the remnants of the Pals and the remnants of the divisions flung back at Beaumont Hamel, but far ahead of both at Pendant Copse, Sergeant Harry Butler and a dozen men were still holding on to a tiny stretch of captured trench. They spent the hours of darkness salvaging the rifles of the dead and propping them around the trench in the hope that, when morning came, the glinting bayonets would lead the Germans to believe that fresh troops had come up in the night to reinforce them. For the moment they were safe. There was no shelling to worry about. After the first two hours, after the attack had first dwindled and then withered away, the German guns opposite the 8th Corps Front had been able to swing about and add the full strength of their support to the sectors on either side.

They were still firing now, some northwards to Gommecourt where the last of the survivors were trying to crawl back from the German line under cover of darkness. The rest of the guns, ranged behind Beaumont Hamel, had swung their muzzles towards the Thiepval Ridge and were

1. No troops had 'occupied Serre village', much less two battalions, although later there was evidence that a handful had, incredibly, slipped through the German line and reached it.

firing over open sights at the Schwaben Redoubt where a handful of the Ulsters who had captured it were still holding on.

Later, when the shelling stopped in order to allow the encircling Germans to close in, they managed to struggle back to the shelter of Thiepval Wood through the tiny opening that remained.

Machine-gun fire from Thiepval village was still stuttering into the night.

On the shoulder of the ridge beyond it, the body of Eversmann was lying spreadeagled in front of the Leipzig Redoubt, where the Germans had counter-attacked and been pushed back in the afternoon. Major McFarlane of the 15th Highland Light Infantry had taken A Company out to search for the wounded of the 17th Battalion. That morning, they had punched the Germans hard in the nose of the Leipzig Redoubt and were still, miraculously, holding on to the first two lines of the trenches they had captured. The rescue party stumbled across Eversmann's body. There was no time to spare for the dead; in particular – and in the view of the Jocks, scouring among the carnage of the morning's battle – there was no time to spare for a dead German. But there was always the chance that his pockets contained 'souvenirs'. Later, crouched in a shell-hole in Authuille Wood, two Jocks of the 15th Highland Light Infantry were going over their haul in the first light of morning. The small notebook with its incomprehensible German script might have been tossed aside as useless, but Captain Hunter happened to come along. They handed it over with a jerk of the head. 'We found it up yonder, sir.' It was Eversmann's diary. Hunter tactfully ignored the rest of their booty. The men had had a hard night. Between them they had brought in forty-two of the wounded.

Beyond the wood, across the dip of the Nab Valley, Ernest Deighton had not been quite so lucky for no rescue party had found him nor the four others who lay wounded beside him in the big shell-hole between the first German trench and the second.

Private Ernest Deighton, No. 25884, 8th Btn., King's Own Yorkshire Light Infantry, 8th Division

I thought I was a goner. I didn't think I'd get back. I didn't think I'd *ever* get back.

Lying out there that morning I were within twenty-five or thirty yards of the German front line, looking through this telescopic sight at the gap in their trench. I could have touched it. I had my finger on the trigger all the time, not moving, and I saw a few of them laid to rest. But it didn't do our lads much good. As soon as they started across the machine-guns opened up. It seemed like hours before they got up near to me, but they kept on coming. I still dursn't move. These bullets are flying all over the place. It were Maxims they were firing and they were shooting across each other, with this hissing noise as they went past. I dursn't turn round, but I heard the noise behind me and I knew our fellows were coming. Some of them were getting hit and they were yelling and shouting, but they came on, and when the first wave got up to me I jumped up.

I were in the first row and the first one I saw were my chum, Clem Cunnington. I don't think we'd gone twenty yards when he got hit straight through the breast. Machine-gun bullets. He went down. I went down. We got it in the same burst. I got it through the shoulder. I hardly noticed it, at the time, I were so wild when I saw that Clem were finished. We'd got orders: 'Every man for himself and no prisoners!' It suited me that, after I saw Clem lying there.[1]

I got up and picked up my rifle and got through the wire into their trench and straight in front there was this dugout – full of Jerries, and one big fellow was on the steps facing me. I had this Mills bomb. Couldn't use my arm. I pulled the pin with my teeth and flung it down and I were shouting at them, I were that wild. 'There you are! Bugger yourselves! Share that between you!' Then I were off! It was hand to hand! I went round one traverse and there was one – face to face. I couldn't fire one-handed, but I could use the bayonet. It was him or me – and I went first! Jab! Just like that. It were my job. And from there I went on. Oh, I were wild! Seeing Clem like that!

We were climbing out of the trench, making for the second line, and that's where they got me again just as I were climbing out, through the fingers this time, on the same arm. I still managed to get on. I kept up with the lads nearly to the second line. Then I got another one. It went through my tin hat and down and straight through my foot. Well, that finished it!

After a bit, lying there, I saw two fellows drop into some shell-hole. I crawled after them and, of course, you couldn't see much for the smoke but, next thing we *did* know, the Germans had taken back all their front line again. There were no more of our fellows about. So there we had to stop. When night came I were in a

1. Clem Cunnington is buried in Ovillers Military Cemetery.

deuce of a state. I must have been fainting off and on, what with
the loss of blood. You'd no idea of the passage of time. I didn't
know where I were. I only knew there were Germans in front and
Germans behind and I had no idea which way were the British
lines.

What with having nothing to eat and nothing to drink all day,
my tongue was getting as big as two. I could hardly close my
mouth. My water-bottle was gone. I couldn't realize where I was.
Lights going up all the time. All this noise. Them shelling from
their side and us shelling from ours, and machine-gun in between.
What worried me was getting caught in our own shellfire. I
bothered more about that. Well, they dropped in front of me and
they dropped behind me but they never put one into the shell-hole.

The long night flickered and thundered on. By mid-afternoon on the
previous day, sickened by the terrible sights half-glimpsed through the
smoke that rolled across the valley in the front of Ovillers and la Boisselle,
Brigadier-General Ternan had dodged back through the shelling to his
Brigade Headquarters in the lee of the Tara-Usna Ridge. If any news
was to come back from the line, it would be brought – or telephoned,
if there was a line intact – to Brigade HQ. The fate of the 8th Division,
attacking at Ovillers, was obvious to them all. Few of them had even
managed to cross the wide expanse of No Man's Land to get within
shooting distance of the village. As for his own Brigade, every single
colonel of the Tyneside Scottish had died at the head of his battalion,
and almost every other officer had perished as they went forward to tackle
the line at la Boisselle.[1]

Runner after runner had been sent across and had come back – if they
came back at all – with no news. It was only now, in the deep dark, as
some wounded fragments of the Tyneside Scottish were crawling painfully
back from No Man's Land that they realized, with terrible finality, that
the 1st and the 4th Tyneside Scottish had been virtually annihilated. Later,
when a telephone line was established, Major Acklom reported that he
had gathered the remnants of the other two battalions and was holding
out in a small length of the German line. Both his flanks were in the air.
His men were exhausted. He urgently needed bombs and water. He
recommended 'an early relief by fresh troops'.

It was Tom Easton who had got the line going.

1. Lieutenant-Colonels Lyle and Sillery are buried in Bapaume Post Military
Cemetery. The bodies of Colonel Elphinstone and Major Heniker were never
recovered.

Private Tom Easton, No. 1000, 21st Btn., Northumberland Fusiliers (2nd Tyneside Scottish)

I was in this tunnel with Major Acklom – it was one of the tunnels the Engineers had dug when they laid the big mine. The mine went up all right. We saw it go from the third line. We'd been pulled back because of the explosion and, as a signaller, I was there with all the Battalion Headquarters people.

I could take you to the spot where we set out from. You had a dip coming from Bécourt Château to where the crater is. We were in the deep dip. You couldn't see much when the mine went up, but the noise was terrible. The fallout was tremendous as well, but it fell short of us. Then we got orders to advance. My Colonel had gone sick and Major Heniker was in charge. He got killed by a shell even before we started. Major Neven was Second-in-Command – a big, noble-looking fellow. He got killed too. They all got killed. All the officers. I couldn't do nothing but pray for my mother to protect us. As we went across I kept saying, 'Mother, help me. Mother, help me' – just as if I was praying to her. When we got to the wire, there was my Signal-Officer, Lieutenant McNeil Smith, lying dead. Then Major Acklom came along, and he took command. We didn't have an officer left – and there were few enough of *us*!

We climbed into the German front line. There were any amount of dead and wounded there, ours *and* theirs. We built a barrier in this line for our own defence on the la Boisselle side – the Germans were still in the trench on the other side of it. They'd had a great shock when the mine went up, but they'd found their feet.

We were in this sap and we'd got the telephone lines in and, late in the night, I managed to get through to my Battalion Headquarters at Bécourt Château. The dugout was full of wounded. My Sergeant, Bob Wear, was there, badly wounded. The blood was draining out of him. When it got quieter, after dark, I said to Major Acklom, 'Sir, could I and one or two of the other men try to get this man across to our own front line?' It was only fifty yards away, because we were at the bit where the lines had been closest. Major Acklom studied a bit and then he said, 'Yes, you can go, providing you promise to return.' I said, 'You can have that promise now!' I got these two or three lads and we got a groundsheet. We couldn't carry him. We trailed him on the sheet. One or two shells were coming over. We laid him down to take a bit of a rest and he said, 'I don't know what the hell you're bothering about me for. I'm half bloody dead anyway. You're just risking your own bloody lives.' 'Well,' we said, 'we're going to bother.' We trailed him across to our own front line. We had to watch what we were walking on. We were absolutely trampling on the wounded. You couldn't help it. It's bad enough when you're getting bloody wounded, but it's bloody murder when they're trampling on you as well. Oh, they were crying out! I can hear them now. But there wasn't a thing we could do about it. Just get back to the sap, and hang on. Bob Wear died later.

Gunner Frank Spencer, No. 1113, C. Bty., 152nd Brigade, Royal Field Artillery (his diary)

Still more wounded coming past the guns, day and night. Two of our signallers and an officer who had gone through with the infantry charge return to us. The officer was slightly wounded and the two signallers suffering from severe shock, as they had been buried. Also one of the telephonists was missing and another badly wounded. The duty of this little party had been to run out a telephone wire to keep us in touch with the advancing infantry – but they met with disaster and failed. They say that many of our poor wounded were shot by the enemy while trying to crawl back to the cover of our own trenches. But, on the other hand, a German doctor and his staff was nicely captured whilst tending our own wounded. As nightfall approaches, our infantry are still fighting for la Boisselle, so we are still firing heavily through the night. La Boisselle is now alternately reported in our hands and then in the enemy's. The dogged courage and high fighting qualities of the enemy machine-gunners who had weathered our rain of shells and then breasted and checked the waves of our determined infantry is worthy of admiration. The suggestions one hears that the Germans have not fought well, is no compliment to our own gallant troops.

Beyond the loop of the Fricourt Salient still, as it had been that morning, in German hands, and some four miles to the south-east, the officers of the 10th Battalion, The Essex Regiment, were settling down to enjoy a late dinner in the deep German dugout which some of their Battalion had had the pleasure of helping to capture earlier in the day. It was an extremely convivial occasion and, strictly speaking, there were rather more officers present than there had any right to be. But so many officers had drifted up from the transport lines where the cadre of the Battalion had been left behind when the rest went into action, and they were so anxious to savour the delights of victory, so keen to sightsee in the captured German line, that Colonel Scott did not have the heart to send them packing.

The dugout in 'Mine Alley' near Montauban was the best part of a mile from their jumping-off point of that morning. Their progress had been swift, their casualties had been comparatively few and now their satisfaction was enormous. The 18th Division had well and truly broken the German line on the Somme and, even now, on the other side of Montauban, the troops were probing even further forward. There was no doubt that Jerry was considerably shaken, for only one gun was firing in a desultory fashion from, they guessed, the direction of Delville Wood. It didn't worry them much. They had captured innumerable prisoners, run over a score of gun positions and, once in possession of their new domain, the 10th Essex had even had time to toss out a load of rubbish in the form of the spare uniforms, stores and personal belongings of the previous occupants. They had burned them in a celebratory bonfire. But they had taken care not to dispose of interesting souvenirs or useful commodities. Almost every man in the Battalion, from the Colonel to the cooks, would be able to march out of the line festooned with the coveted German helmets as well as lesser trophies.

Tonight they were having a wonderful time. There was only bully beef to eat, supplemented by cheese and some watery soup, but there was a copious supply of very acceptable German chocolate and, for the officers, excellent German sparkling water to dilute their whisky. General Higginson had enjoyed a generous tot when he had come in person to congratulate them. Now, several hours after his departure, the officers of the 10th Essex, together with those signallers and servants who were lucky enough to be attached to Battalion HQ in its luxurious new abode, were still delightedly smoking good German cigars, celebrating their victory, and looking forward to pressing on tomorrow. It was a whoopee of an evening.

Only the Adjutant, Captain Robert Chell, with his ear clamped to the telephone, doing his best, in the rowdy atmosphere, heavy with cigar-smoke, to comply with the demands of Brigade for precise information, had half an inkling that, elsewhere, things had not gone quite as well as had been expected.

All along the front, of the hundred and fifty thousand men who had gone over the top that morning, more than fifty-seven thousand had been killed or wounded. By a prophetic irony of fate, when the Central War Charities Committee had allocated particular dates in 1916 to particular fund-raising bodies, the first week of July had been designated 'Women's Tribute Week'.

Chapter 8

For the people at home, the parents, the wives, the sweethearts, even the children, of the boys who had mostly gone into battle for the first time, the Big Push would be the story of the year. The Correspondents had watched it from a rise on the Amiens road a mile or so behind Albert.

Spangled with waving poppies and wayward clumps of mustard flowers on its verges, the road ran from Albert through the summer fields of Picardy to the town of Amiens, fifteen miles to the south-west – near enough to the battlefield to hear the constant rumble of gunfire in its streets and to see, from a top floor window, the glowing sky lit by the battle below. But Amiens was another world. With the influx of refugees and of French and British military, the number of residents had almost doubled since the war and they were further augmented by an ever-changing floating population, predominantly masculine and predominantly khaki-clad, drifting in holiday mood through its streets in search of civilian delights. Even after two years of war Amiens still had plenty to offer.

After a spell in the squalor of the trenchline, when a man had perhaps not removed his clothes for a fortnight, when his daily ration of water for washing and shaving had been easily contained in a half-pint mug, and whose head, for most of the time, had been clamped into a steel helmet, the pleasure of a visit to a barber was indescribable. The barber's shop in Rue des Trois Cailloux offered a whole range of sybaritic pleasures – a shampoo, a hair-cut, a shave, hot towels and, greatest luxury of all, a *friction d'eau de quinine* rubbed in until the scalp tingled and glowed. Next door at the parfumier you could buy Eau de Cologne to mask the unpleasant odour that clung to every uniform and person, buy French scent as a lavish present for your girl, or, against the happy day when it would be your turn for a bath, soap that bore no relation at all to the abrasive yellow slabs provided by the Army.

There was the bookshop where Madame Carpentier and her daughter, smiling on purchasers and browsers alike, did a brisk trade in indelible pencils and writing pads and an even brisker trade in copies of the saucy *Vie Parisienne*, whose cut-out pictures enlivened the décor of almost every dugout on the Western Front. They also sold postcards galore and occasionally a book. There were smart cafés, mostly frequented by young officers, and bars in the side streets where drinks were half the price. There was an interesting museum and, although the glorious stonework of the Gothic cathedral had long since disappeared behind a pyramid of sandbags, it was still worth a visit.

Best of all, to palates numbed and wearied by army rations, there were restaurants – la Cathédrale, which specialized in good home cooking, the more expensive Godebert, presided over by the delicious Marguerite and, in a sleazy side street with the curious name of Rue du Corps Nu sans Tête, Josephine's oyster restaurant, cheap, cheerful and none too clean, was run by a virago of a *patronne* who clattered and banged about with the speed of a whirlwind and whom the Tommies had consequently nicknamed 'Hurricane Jane'. A few doors away an establishment which proclaimed itself in white-washed letters across the window to be an 'Officers Dining Room' was much patronized by junior subalterns.

By tacit consent the excellent restaurant of the Hotel du Rhin in the Rue Amiral Courbet was avoided by all but officers of the rank of major and above. There were far too many staff officers about, and staff officers, moreover, whose red-hatted grandeur was further enhanced by the green armbands of the Intelligence Service. They lived and worked across the road in a mansion owned by Madame de la Rochefoucauld but, despite the comfort of their aristocratic billet, despite the pleasant proximity of the Hotel du Rhin and its excellent cellar, despite the civilized surroundings of Amiens, they were not enjoying themselves. They were nursemaids, or so they would have described themselves, to a group of British War Correspondents – or so *they* would have described themselves. To the Army they were 'writer chappies' and the Army, and in particular its Commander-in-Chief, thought them an infernal nuisance.

Always a professional soldier who regarded soldiering as a professional affair, impatient of what he saw as 'interference' by the uninformed (a category in which he included most civilians and all politicians), Haig had accepted the presence of journalists at the front with distaste and reluctance. Since the beginning of the war the military authorities had put every obstacle in the way of those who wished to report it but, by the time Haig had taken over command of the Army six months earlier, the presence of the journalists was already a *fait accompli*. But his attitude towards them was far from helpful.

Official Communiqués were telegraphed from GHQ each evening and, in the opinion of GHQ, they contained all the facts which newspaper readers required to know. Any embellishment by non-military observers might, when published, give useful information to the enemy. More colourful stories were, after all, only 'written for Mary Ann in the kitchen'. Haig had been injudicious enough to say as much to the faces of some of the most distinguished representatives of Fleet Street when they had called on him at GHQ, and had caused deep offence. Faced with the patronizing smile and formidable presence of this 'tall, handsome man who could not see why we wanted more facilities to record the progress of the war', only Philip Gibbs of the *Daily Telegraph* had the courage to speak up. He told the Commander-in-Chief, and in no uncertain terms, that he 'could not conduct his war in secret, as though the people at home, whose sons and husbands were fighting and dying, had no concern in the matter. The spirit of the fighting men, and the driving power behind the armies, depended upon the support of the whole people and their continuing loyalties'.

The Commander-in-Chief was not a man whose opinions were easily swayed, but Gibbs had given him food for thought and, at least on the face of it, his attitude had changed. The Correspondents were given uniforms, the use of the upper storey of the splendid billet in Amiens, and the 'services' of a group of trusted Intelligence Officers as censors-on-the-spot, who were installed on the floor below. Their brief was to escort the Correspondents on their forays to the front, censor their despatches as they wrote them and, so that they might be despatched with all speed, no less a personage than a King's Messenger would carry them daily to London. The Correspondents were also led to believe that there was no part of the front they might not visit, that the Army had been instructed to this effect and that they might write whatever they liked, on the understanding that they might not mention place names other than in the most general of geographical terms, nor the names of individuals or units ever at all. As a final accolade, they too would have the right to wear the green armbands of the Intelligence Service.

It was a brilliant move. From now on, the War Correspondents, attired in the King's uniform, were, to all intents and purposes, Officers of the Army, conscious of their debt to it and conscious too of their duty to keep up morale and to reinforce that 'continuing loyalty' of people at home. It was natural that they should wish to prove themselves worthy of the Army's trust. Their facilities included the right to 'talk to anyone', and they travelled far and wide, doing just that, each accompanied by his Army Watchdog, viewing the battles from convenient vantage points and often taking considerable risks to get closer.

It was human nature that, in the light of their previous difficulties with the Staff, the ease of their new situation should float like a rosy gauze between the Correspondents and their observations. It was also human nature that senior officers who condescended to speak to them confined themselves to sanguine observations on what was apparent to anyone who took the trouble to read Official Communiqués, that field officers confined themselves to platitudes and that other ranks, invited by an officer of senior (if unrecognizable) rank to confide his impressions of the war, inevitably responded with such anodyne observations as would appeal equally to the sentimental heart of 'Mary Ann in the kitchen' and the patriotic fervour of her master at the breakfast table. It was human nature, but it was not journalism. If any breath of criticism ever escaped the lips of the War Correspondents none was detectable in the dutiful columns of print that breathed victory and hope to the 'people at home'.

In Madame de la Rochefoucauld's house in Amiens, the lights had burned into the small hours of the morning of 2 July as half a dozen typewriters clattered out a story which each Correspondent fervently hoped would convey the drama and flavour of his excitement better than any other. Robinson of *The Times*, having exhausted his repertoire of adjectives in eye-witness descriptions of some scores of previous bombardments during his two years in France, was now faced with the difficulty of describing one that outstripped them all. In an attempt to convey the number of shells which burst every minute he resorted, in desperation, to a technique which had all the elements of a parlour game.

> . . . counting was hopeless. Fixing my eyes on one spot I tried to wink them as fast as the lightnings flickered, and the shells beat me badly. I then tried chattering my teeth, and I think that in that way I approximately held my own. Testing it afterwards in the light, where I could see a watch face, I found that I could click my teeth some five or six times in a second. You can try it for yourself and, clicking your own teeth, will get some idea of the rate at which shells were bursting on a single spot . . .

But there was no hint of 'chattering teeth' in the well-oiled lyricism inspired by the sight of the Tommies marching to battle.

> Long before they came close one heard the steady roar of their feet – tramp-*tramp*! Tramp-*tramp*! And always as they passed they whistled softly in unison. Some whistled *Tipperary*, some *Come back my Bonnie, to me*, and some, best of all in the place and surroundings, *La Marseillaise*. As we came back along that road, far behind the front, we saw more companies, more battalions. On the tree-shaded road it was too dark to see them, save only as vague dark masses against the light background of the highway. One felt their presence and heard more than one saw them; always the steady tramp-*tramp*,

tramp-*tramp* as they shouldered by; and they were always whistling. Now and again a laugh broke out at some unheard joke, a completely careless laugh, as of a holidaymaker ...

The Correspondents had only been able to snatch an hour or two of sleep when the morning Communiqué arrived from GHQ. Now, as the censors breakfasted at this unseemly early hour on a Sunday morning, restoring themselves for their duty of scrutinizing the despatches as they were ripped hot from the typewriters, the Correspondents were at it again, stiffening their skeleton impressions with a backbone of positive fact.

... North of the Ancre our principal success was the capture of the hamlet of Serre, which is regarded as an important tactical point; but by the close of the day the Germans had counter-attacked so violently that progress appears to have been partial ... Everything has gone well. Our troops have successfully carried out their missions. All counter-attacks have been repulsed and large numbers of prisoners have been taken ... The enemy apparently still hold Gommecourt, though our troops are on both sides of that village ... On either side of the valley of the Ancre the situation is unchanged ... Our troops were making effective progress near la Boisselle ... The general situation may be regarded as favourable ... Thanks to the very complete and effective artillery preparation, thanks also to the dash of our infantry, our losses have been very slight ... The first impression of the opening of our offensive is that our leaders in the field have amply profited by the experience of the last two years and that they are directing a methodical and well planned advance ... There are already indications that close touch must have been kept throughout, and that the attacking forces were well under control ...

What else could they have written? Could they have told of the painstaking plans that had gone so badly awry? Could they have told of the awful consequences of the blunder which had stopped the guns firing after the explosion at Beaumont Hamel? Could they have criticized the Staff for underestimating the enemy's defences? Could they have dwelt on the supporting barrage of shells, so unalterable in its rigid timing that it went far ahead of the troops, lifting again and again, according to programme, until its shells were tumbling harmlessly miles behind the inviolable German line, leaving its own troops to the mercy of the enemy's machine-guns and shellfire? Could they have been expected to explain that no one had been able to interrupt the programme, to bring the bombardment back, because no one had known what was happening? And were the Correspondents in a position to judge that no reliable news had come back from the fighting line because the painstakingly elaborate system of communications had completely broken down? How could they have arrived at the bitter truth that, despite the plethora of failsafes – of pigeons and wireless and runners and flags, of markers and flashes and lamps and telephones and aeroplanes – in places where no messages had been received it was because no single officer or even sergeant had survived the slaughter to send one?

It was not that GHQ had suppressed this information. The simple fact was that the Army itself did not know. It would be many hours yet before the situation was fully understood. It would take weeks and months of agonized analysis and reappraisal before the truth of what had gone wrong was fully understood and appreciated. And the truth was that the Staff had not trusted Kitchener's Army. Leading it by the hand, it had left it so little room to manoeuvre that, in the end, it had been unable to manoeuvre at all.

Although the reports which were beginning to trickle back gradually from the front were becoming more and more disquieting there were at least some successes to report. It was natural that the GHQ Communiqués should dwell on them. It was in the front line that the troops were dwelling on the failure.

Sergeant Jim Myers, No. 22745, 25th Co., Machine Gun Corps, 31st Division

The biggest mistake that was made on manoeuvres and training was that we were never told what to do in case of failure. All that time we'd gone backwards and forwards, training, doing it over and over again like clockwork and then when we had to advance, when it came to the bit, we didn't know what to do! Nothing seemed to be arranged in case of failure.

Corporal Harry Shaw, No. 12774, 9th Btn., Royal Welsh Fusiliers, 19th Western Division

Whatever was gained, it wasn't worth the price that the men had paid to gain that advantage. It was no advantage to anybody. It was just sheer bloody murder. That's the only words you can use for it.

Rifleman T. Cantlon, No. 33419, 21st Btn., King's Royal Rifle Corps

They said to us, 'You lot are moppers up, that's what you've got to do, follow in after the first wave and mop up.' But, they never told us what mopping up was, and we only had a vague idea. No training, as such, except that we were supposed to chuck bombs at these flags that were supposed to be dugouts. Well, when we got to the real thing and we were supposed to throw them down real dugouts full of Germans when we got into the trench, the first thing was that the bombs weren't nearly powerful enough to do much damage. And the second thing was that they didn't go right down anyway because the Germans built the steps down with a bend to them, so half the time when you chucked your bomb down, it didn't go all the way down and explode at the bottom, it just went off, bang, against this bend in the wall. It maybe brought down a bit of dust, it maybe even blocked the entrance, if you were lucky, except that Jerry always had a back door to go out of, but, when you're rushing along like that, you don't go down to look and see, do you? You just chuck your bomb down, like you've been told. Well, half the time, when you moved on a bit, the Jerries would come rushing up at your back and get you from behind. That's what was happening on the first day and it was happening all over the place in our sector. It must have been, because, when you got into the second trench, and you were bombing away there, you'd get shots coming at you from the way we'd come and you'd turn round and there would be old Jerry at your back potting away, and some of them going for the next lot of troops coming up to this trench that we were supposed to have cleared. We simply didn't know what to do, and that's the truth of it. But we soon learned!

Still in his shell-hole between the Leipzig Redoubt and Ovillers and between the first and second German lines, Ernest Deighton was in no state to analyse what had gone wrong. He only knew, between bouts of unconsciousness, that the sun riding high in the sky marked his second day lying out on the battlefield, that he was in pain and that rescue was a long time coming. He also noticed, without much interest, that one by one his companions had died during the night. For a long time it was mercifully quiet, then, alerted by some movement, a machine-gun started up and the bullets were zipping dangerously close to him. The shell-hole was too shallow for safety but there was no possibility of moving even if he had been able to summon up the strength. A dead comrade was lying just below the edge of the shell-hole. Inch by inch and painfully slowly, using his good shoulder and his uninjured hand, Ernie managed to push the body up above the rim. He was only able to heave up the legs and a part of the trunk; the arms and the head still hung down into the shell-hole. As the gun swung through its traverse, Deighton noticed, almost absently, that the bullets smacking into the body sounded exactly the same as if they were thudding into sandbags. It was all one to the poor chap now and a few more bullets would make no difference but all the same he wished, as he crouched beneath the body and drifted back into unconsciousness, that the dead boy's upside-down contorted face was not suspended quite so near his own.

There were few church parades on the Somme that Sunday morning. Most padres had their hands full succouring the wounded as they were carried out of the line, lending a hand at aid posts or travelling along the still chaotic roads as their battalions were pushed forward, with all haste, to relieve the shattered troops in the line. Such public orisons as were addressed to the Almighty were spoken over the mass graves where, in communal funeral services, they were burying the bodies of severely wounded soldiers who had died at dressing stations. It was a dreary duty that would go on for days, for weeks and even months as the Army inched forward and the dead were gradually recovered from the captured ground. Already some padres, sickened and dispirited, were disinclined to comply with the clearly expressed wishes of the Commander-in-Chief, passed on to them, at his request, by the Deputy Chaplain General, Bishop Gwynne ... *that the Chaplains should preach to the troops about the objects of Great Britain in carrying on this war. We have no selfish motive, but are fighting for the good of humanity.* It was Haig's sincerely held belief that this was true and that the duty of the padres was to underline it constantly, to sustain the troops and bolster their morale just as, in the midst of his own difficulties and responsibilities, he himself was sustained and uplifted by the approval of Higher Authority, obligingly reaffirmed each Sunday in the sermons of Mr Duncan. This good man had no doubts about his mission and his duty and, that Sunday morning, he fulfilled both admirably and to the full satisfaction of the Commander-in-Chief. Early that morning he attended the simple Presbyterian service held in makeshift premises near his headquarters at Beauquesne. With the heavy responsibilities of the Commander-in-Chief at the forefront of his mind, Mr Duncan had chosen as his text: 'Ye are fellow workers with God'.[1]

1. It was a popular sentiment, but it is interesting to note that, on 28 June, in the House of Commons it had been stated, in reply to a question, that: 'The aims of the military machine and those of the New Testament are not compatible.'

The service was necessarily brief because there was much to be done. As early as yesterday afternoon, when Sir Douglas Haig had driven after luncheon to Fourth Army Headquarters at Querrieu to confer with Sir Henry Rawlinson, plans had been hastily recast in the light of the first reports. Even by then, it had been obvious that the attack all along the 8th Corps Front and also at Gommecourt had failed completely, while firmer and more detailed reports had indicated, beyond doubt, that in front of Mametz and Montauban, it had succeeded. It was clear that General Gough's Cavalry, jingling in reserve and ready to dash through to Bapaume, would not be needed in the immediate future – nor would the two held-back divisions (the 12th and the 25th) be required to accompany it forward. Until the situation became clearer, as Sir Douglas Haig tentatively suggested to Sir Henry Rawlinson, courteously leaving him to make the decision, it seemed sensible to concentrate all efforts towards exploiting the gains in the south and, meanwhile, to hold the attack north of the Ancre. By seven o'clock that evening, it had been decided.

Extract from the daily diary of General Sir Douglas Haig

At 7 p.m., as the result of my talk, Sir H. Rawlinson telephones that he is putting the 8th and 10th Corps under Gough at 7 a.m. tomorrow. The 8th Corps seem to want looking after! Gough's command will be the 5th Army.

General Gough's command would therefore stretch from the Thiepval Ridge northwards to Serre. His most important task was to take Thiepval – and to take it at all costs. The Fourth Army, under Sir Henry Rawlinson, would be left free to concentrate on the rest of the line, to exploit the breakthrough on the right and push towards the Thiepval Ridge by its back door at Pozières. But they could not even begin this task, nor even move much further forward on the successful right flank, until they had driven the Germans out of Fricourt and la Boisselle.

Late in the afternoon GHQ received the gratifying tidings that the Germans had retired from the Fricourt Salient. Now, with all the force that they could muster, the troops must consolidate their 'gains' at la Boisselle, capture the village and renew the attack on its twin village of Ovillers across the valley.

At la Boisselle, practically all the force that the troops could muster was represented by some one hundred and fifty men in the small length of the trench they had captured between the big mine crater and the village,

and by Major Acklom, Tom Easton, and a handful of others in the tunnel
behind – so narrow that two men could only squeeze past each other
with difficulty, so low that they could not stand upright and where their
only link with the outside world was the single telephone line that Easton
had managed to connect. It was the only means by which Brigadier-
General Ternan could keep in touch with the sole officer of his entire
Brigade who was still, to his knowledge, in the line. The Brigadier's
cheerful bellow at the other end of the wire, his encouragement to 'hold
on', his reassurances that help was on the way and that fresh troops would
soon relieve them, was some slight comfort in their dilemma.

Ternan was far from feeling as cheerful as he sounded, for the ranks
of the dead and most of the wounded were still lying out where they
had fallen yesterday morning. Behind them the front line was tenuously
held by a company of Pioneers. They were practically all that was left of
the Brigadier's command.

The first priority if la Boisselle was to be taken was to get the survivors
out, to get fresh troops in and to get them in fast. In all but name the
34th Division had ceased to exist.

Chapter 9

The theatre at Bavincourt some miles to the north of the battle was only a barn, but it was a pretty good one. While no one could pretend that it came up to the standard of the London Pavilion, the 37th Division had been in the area for almost nine months and in that time, even with a strenuous programme of normal duties of trench-digging and road-making, the Divisional Pioneer Battalion had had plenty of time to transform the building into a respectable facsimile of a real theatre for the benefit of the 37th Divisional Concert Party. There were curtains, there were footlights, there was a ticket-office and seating for up to three hundred on an assortment of pews and forms rescued from churches rather nearer the line which, having been 'ventilated' by German shells to an unhealthy degree, had been temporarily abandoned by their congregations. If the village of Bavincourt was not precisely the Shaftesbury Avenue of the Western Front, it was conveniently situated within a few kilometres' walk of half a dozen villages occupied as rest-billets by troops out of the line. But, such was the popularity of 'The Barn Owls' that the troops would have walked twice as far to see them.

It was a tidy step from Humbercourt – a good eight kilometres – and among the men of the 13th Battalion, The Rifle Brigade who had marched there the day before, on feet softened by a ten-day tour in the trenches, there were many who were more than content to stroll down to the *estaminet*, make a tour of convenient farmhouses in search of eggs, or simply to 'hang about' – an inexpensive pastime made all the more attractive by the fact that they had not been paid. It had been a miserable day of parades, cleaning up and kit inspections. And it had rained. It was still raining in the evening when a dozen stalwarts set out to tramp the eight kilometres to Bavincourt to enjoy an evening at the theatre and to get together after the show with two members of the Battalion who were in the cast of the concert party. They spotted Bill Tylee and Telly Dillsen as soon as the curtain went up and the full company launched into the opening chorus:

> *We are the Barn Owl Boys,*
> *We make a lot of noise,*
> *We come here nightly,*
> *We just can't get to Blighty,*
> *We are just divisional toys.*
>
> *Don't think that we're just shirkers,*
> *We fight like Leicesters or Gurkhas,*
> *We've got our iron rations,*
> *And all the latest fashions,*
> *We dig like real good workers.*

It was the prelude to a happy evening. For the Riflemen the highlight was a turn by Telly Dillsen who combined a splendid bass voice with a talent for lugubrious comic parody. Tonight he chose to render his own version of *Sentry! What of the Night?*

> *Sentry! What of the night?*
> *The sentry's answer I will not repeat,*
> *Though short in words 'twas with feeling replete.*
> *It covered all he thought and more,*
> *It covered all he'd thought before,*
> *It covered all he might think yet*
> *In years to come,*
> *For he was wet and had no rum.*

There was hardly a member of the audience, other than the Brass Hats in the front row, in whom these sentiments did not strike a sympathetic chord, and they raised the roof. Even Jack Cameron, flirtatiously representing a beautiful blonde, received no greater ovation although 'she' took half a dozen bows, eyelashes a-flutter, before the company joined hands for the closing chorus:

> *We hope you will excuse us,*
> *If you didn't like our show don't abuse us,*
> *For we tell you straight and true,*
> *That like you we're soldiers too,*
> *We don't get any suppers, not any more than you.*
>
> *And why we're not in the trenches just now,*
> *Is because our Gallant Staff,*
> *Have sent us here to try and make you laugh,*
> *But one and all,*

We are ready for the call,
To join our regiments.

There was time for a beer afterwards when Tylee and Dillsen had changed back into uniform, and many handshakes, back-slappings and backward shouts of 'See you soon', as the lads started back on the long tramp through the rain to Humbercourt. They were to see Tylee and Dillsen sooner than any of them expected and it was just as well that they were 'one and all ready for the call to join our regiments', because their orders were already on the way. The following morning they would be saying goodbye to the greasepaint, packing up their kit and making for Humbercourt themselves to rejoin the Battalion on the final stage of its journey to the Somme.

In all their sojourn in France, since they had arrived on the *Mona's Queen* on 30 July almost a year before, and apart from a few jolting rail journeys in unsavoury cattle trucks, it was the first time that the Riflemen had not had to march. The buses arrived at ten o'clock in the evening of 5 July. There were twenty of them to transport the Battalion, and they had seen better days since they had trundled around the peacetime streets of London, shiny red and cheerfully noisy. They were still noisy, and here and there, where the drab khaki of their wartime paint was chipped, a glint of red still hinted of the days when they had plied along Oxford Street, travelling north to Kilburn, or honked through Piccadilly and south to Kensington. The windows were boarded up but, miraculously, on some the conductor's bell was still functioning. And, as the boys clambered aboard, one wag inevitably positioned himself on the platform and rang the bell.

'Do you stop at the Savoy Hotel?' It was the old, old joke that Joe Hoyles couldn't resist asking.

'No, sir!' The 'conductor' was equally familiar with the old chestnut. 'Can't afford it! Did you say a twopenny one, sir? Comes cheaper if you take a return.'

But for one in three of the boys it would be a one-way ticket.

It was not much more than thirty miles to their destination but it took the entire night to get there. Two whole brigades of the 37th Division alone were on the move and there were hold-ups and delays which came as a welcome rest to the war-worn buses if not to their passengers. For the first part of the journey, before the lateness of the hour made it possible to drowse off even in the discomfort of buses whose suspension had never been designed for long distance travel, there was chat and banter and sing-songs – anything to pass the time and to keep at bay disturbing thoughts of the ordeal ahead. Although no one had informed them of the purpose of the journey, the men had a shrewd suspicion that they were 'in for it'. Most of them were excited at the prospect.

Joe Hoyles had a flowery turn of phrase which perhaps sprang from the attachment he had formed for the death-and-glory reputation of the Rifle Brigade as a lad before the war. It was not necessarily to the taste of some of his less flamboyant comrades and it was couched in terms which owed not a little to the prose of the Empire-building adventure stories he had read as a schoolboy, but he had fairly summed up the feelings of many others in the speech he had made to the Company Officers of the Battalion when they had attended the A Company Corporals' Christmas Dinner:

Gentlemen,

On behalf of my fellow corporals and myself, I welcome you here tonight. We are pleased that you have come to see us and regret that convention prevents your partaking of this meal which you have so thoughtfully provided.

We have invited you here tonight, to drink your health. We are fortunate in our officers, and when the time comes we shall show you how we appreciate our good fortune. Yes, gentlemen, when the time comes, when once again we go into the line, you will find us ever ready cheerfully to obey and completely to fulfil our duties. You will find us ready to uphold and, if possible, excel the high traditions of the Rifle Brigade and to emulate the noble example of Britain's sons.

Fellow corporals, I ask you to rise and drink the health of our officers, hoping they will be with us to the end of the war and may that end be speedy and gloriously victorious.

Joe's speech was a *tour de force*. Its eloquence was not unconnected with the generous libations of alcoholic refreshment with which most of the Battalion had been toasting the occasion for most of the day. The 13th Rifle Brigade had had a whale of a Christmas at Hannescamps and, lurching in their unwieldy convoy past the end of the very road that led to that village, which otherwise had little about it to inspire nostalgic memories, they nudged each other and laughed as they remembered it.

B Company had done best of all. Between them they had collected twenty-five pounds towards the Christmas festivities which their officers had generously doubled. Having made their arrangements well in advance, they had actually sent to London to Fortnum and Mason's for special delicacies and, while most of the other companies contented themselves with pork, B Company had enjoyed turkey, pheasant and ham. The dinner started at lunchtime and, when it ended, late in the evening, transport, in the form of wheelbarrows, had to be pressed into service to convey some of the more enthusiastic revellers back to their billets.

Number 13 Platoon had excelled themselves in a way that might have caused some astonishment to those who had known them such a brief time before as earnest members of the Boys' Brigade.

Rifleman Walter Monckton, MM, No. 2765, 13th (S) Btn., The Rifle Brigade

We all gave up our blankets to cover the walls of the barn and we covered the beams with evergreens and paper flowers. We got long tables with forms on either side and at one end of the barn we built a stage and draped it with white blankets and footlights made from biscuit tins and candles for a concert we were going to have later on. In the centre of the barn someone actually managed to construct a 'chandelier' with reflectors made of bits of cut-out biscuit tin and with several dozen candles in it. On the wall opposite the door in the middle of the barn Richardson had built a tablet on a draped blue blanket. At the top was a big Rifle Brigade badge with a Union Jack on one side and a tricolour on the other and immediately below this in huge letters: '13 R.B.' And underneath we had written: 'Its honour we will keep. To its glory we will add.' And we surrounded the whole thing with a shield shaped in cotton wool.

I can't remember where we got the cotton wool from, but we must have had plenty, because, on the wall opposite the stage, we had enough of it to stick up a whole poem of two verses. It took absolutely ages forming the letters of the poem with strips of cotton wool and sticking them on to the wall. It was Sid Daynes who made it up, and it said:

> *There is a good time coming some day!*
> *May that day be very soon.*
> *May we all enjoy that some day,*
> *That's the wish of 13 Platoon.*
>
> *This season is noted for wishes*
> *So here's one from 13 Platoon*
> *May you safely meet your dear ones,*
> *Safely and well and soon.*

It was not great verse and Sid Daynes, the proud composer, did not represent a threat to the status of the official Poet Laureate, but 13 Platoon were delighted with it and guests who visited their festivities were equally impressed, particularly the battalion Pioneer Corporal who insisted on pointing out this and the other insignia, slogans and decorations which beautified the barn, to each individual officer as he did the traditional rounds of 'men's dinners' on Christmas Day. The Corporal had evidently 'done the rounds' himself, but the officers overlooked his occasional stumbles in speech and in gait, took it in good part and dutifully admired it all. They toasted the health of the Platoon in whisky or champagne and presented them with several boxes of good cigars. It was a fitting end to the day. Not only had 13 Platoon dined on roast beef and Christmas Pudding, enjoyed chocolate biscuits and tinned peaches for tea but they had even had supper of cheese sandwiches, nuts, oranges, washed down by yet more champagne and white wine.

The concert was a fiasco but that was only because, by the time it was due to begin, most of the audience and some of the performers had disappeared under the tables.

Like the spring holiday month at Auxi, Christmas at Hannescamps shone like a bright beacon in the Battalion's collective memory as they lurched towards the Somme.

Corporal Joe Hoyles, MM, No. 3237, 13th (S) Btn., The Rifle Brigade

On a night journey most of the boys who could packed into the lower deck, although it got very fuggy in there, what with the crowd, and the smoking, and the windows being boarded up. In one way it was better to be on the top deck, but there wasn't much chance of sleeping. Even in July it was pretty cold and the top was completely open in these old buses. You went up a spiral staircase on the outside to get to it and packed into the wooden seats, completely in the open air. These old buses swayed like anything, especially with the number of troops that were packed on to them, and all our gear and, at times, when we went round a corner we really thought she was going over! Then, another hazard was the wires. There were so many telephone wires slung across the roads, and fairly low too, so we really had to crouch down low in our seats and keep our rifles down too, so as not to get caught up in them. There was a rumour going around, though I don't know how true it was, that one chap had been decapitated travelling on the top of a bus, so we were all scared stiff, but of course we made a joke of it. In spite of the cold, I dozed off a bit, but I remember

waking up because I was sharing a seat with another chap and he
suddenly stood up and shouted, 'Look, boys, the dawn!' And there
was just that little bit of light in the sky in the east. But it was well
after sun-up when we got to Bresle.

The dawn was rising over the Somme and in the first half-light, still
trapped in his shell-hole, half-starved, half-frozen and half-dead, Ernest
Deighton was roused to consciousness by a sound he had been awaiting
for four long days. It was the noise of thundering feet and in another
moment a line of British troops rushed past towards the Germans' second
line. They had already swept over the first, but Deighton had heard not
a hint of the fight. Now he was fully conscious and now he knew from
the direction of the attacking troops where his own trenches lay. He also
knew that it was probably his last chance to get back to them.

*Private E. Deighton, No. 25884, 8th Btn., King's Own Yorkshire Light
Infantry*

I thought, 'Here goes, I'm off.' I knew I were a dead man if I
didn't. I scrambled out and hobbled and crawled back as best I
could and even then I don't know whether I'm going the right
way or the wrong way. When I got to not far off the first trench,
this voice cried out, 'Halt!' and I just tumbled into it. They couldn't
help me back further, they'd just taken that trench and they had
to stop there, so somehow I got out of it and I had to crawl all
the way back across our old No Man's Land to our own front
trench. I managed to get to the barbed wire and I found one bit
of a gap and I went through it. It took me about two hours. It
would have been twelve hundred yards altogether. And when I
tumbled into that trench they said, 'Who are you?' and all I could
say was: 'Orange.' That were our password on the first day.
'Orange.' And I was gone, straight away. Passed out. When I came
round I were lying on the fire step and they said, 'The remnants
of your lot are in Long Valley.' So the stretcher-bearers took me
down to Long Valley.[1] There were none of our lot there. Just the
MO. It was Captain Marshall and he says, 'Good God! This is
87 in now. There'll be no more!' After that they transported me
down to the Canadian Hospital and I was down there six weeks.

Tom Easton was out as well. The 19th Division which had been in reserve

1. Also known as Blighty Valley.

on 1 July had moved up on the left of those who remained and Tom himself had signalled them in.

Private Tom Easton, No. 1000, 21st Btn., Northumberland Fusiliers (Tyneside Scottish)

It was about the middle of the forenoon after the attack. We were still down the dugout. We'd had no rations and nothing to eat except some tea. Major Acklom was a regular officer with the Highland Light Infantry and he knew all the tricks of the old soldiers' trade. He suggested that we should tease out some sandbag rags, put them in a tin with some candlegrease, and set light to them with another tin on the top with some water in it. It took hours to warm up and it was nowhere near boiling, but we put the tea leaves and sugar in and let it all warm up together and eventually we got a fairly hot drink that was better than nothing.

Halfway through the next morning in came this Colonel from the 19th Division. They called them the Butterflies, but he was a hard nut. He said he wanted a signaller and I was instructed to go outside and take a signal flag with me, so out we went in front of what had been the first German line and still not very far away from the enemy. The officer gave me instructions. He said, 'I will give you one letter and you must signal that to our own front line four times.' So he gave me the letter and I made the signal. Suddenly, very slowly and methodically, a whole armed company I'd no idea was there jumped up and came forward in extended order with fixed bayonets and passed us and went forward to the line the Germans were still holding in front of la Boisselle. After a minute or two another letter was given to me and, with exactly the same precision, another company moved forward and passed on their way. By this time, of course, the Germans had seen what was going on and their guns had begun to roar out. But I went on signalling, steady, as he gave me the instructions. The third lot came over and then, after a while, the fourth. When they'd passed by, the Colonel turned to me and said, 'Well done, Signaller!' and then he turned and moved after his troops into the battle. I went back down into the tunnel.

Tom was only too happy to get out of the open for the German guns were now registered on the advancing troops and shells were falling too close for comfort. Roy Bealing was in the thick of it.

Private Roy Bealing, MM, No. 3437, 6th Btn., The Wiltshire Regiment, 19th (Western) Division

We'd been waiting in our old front-line trench. We'd had a rough time even before we got there. There's a ridge getting on towards la Boisselle and then there's a dip and the Germans were all on higher ground and they could see us all coming down in single file, perhaps a thousand of us going to this trench, and they started shelling. One shell pitched right in front of me and knocked out Sergeant Viney and two or three more. We had to keep going and we had to step over one and step over another to carry on. But we had to keep going. We were thankful to get into what was going to be our assault trench, but, what with the shells exploding and what with it being our first time over the top, we felt pretty damned bad as we waited there. It seemed like an age, and then Captain Reid came along the top of the trench – right out in the open! – I suppose it was the only way he could pass the word along the company and he must have had a couple of machine-gun bullets through his water bottle because the water was spouting out of it. He yelled down, 'Fix your bayonets and get ready to go over when you hear the whistle.'

I was beside a young chap called Lucas and he was a bundle of nerves. He was shaking, yes. He was simply shivering and shaking like a leaf. He could hardly hold his rifle, never mind fix his bayonet. So I fixed mine and then I said, 'Here you are, Lucas,' and I fixed his for him. It would have taken him a week to fix his bayonet, the state he was in! He wasn't one of a new draft. He was one of the older ones, and I was right sorry for him.

The worst of waiting in the trench was that the Germans had a machine-gun trained on it going backwards and forwards, backwards and forwards, traversing and coming round every couple of minutes, and the bullets were cutting the sandbags on the parapet just as if they were cutting them with a knife. And, if a bullet didn't get you, this shower of sand and dirt was going straight into your eyes although the sandbags were a couple of feet above our heads. Terrible feeling, knowing you've got to go over the top with your eyes full of sand and watering and not able to see anything. We were to the right of la Boisselle village and the stretch of trench where we had to go across was just in front of this huge mine crater. We didn't know it was there, nobody told us about that, just that we had to go over and on past that line they'd captured, on to the second line of German trenches and take them.

When the whistle went, I threw my rifle on top of the trench and clambered out of it, grabbed the rifle and started going forward. There were shell-holes everywhere. I hadn't gone far before I fell in one. There were so many shell-holes you couldn't get round them. But you had to go on so, every time I stumbled and fell in a shell-hole, I just waited a quarter of a minute, had another breath, then out of it and on again. I must have fallen half a dozen times before I got to the first line, and there were lads falling all over the place. You didn't know whether they were just tripping up, like me, or whether they were going down with bullets in them, because it wasn't just the shells exploding round about, it was the machine guns hammering out like hell from the third German line because it was on slightly higher ground. Lucas went down. He was killed before he even got to the first trench – the one that was partly in our hands.

I got to the parapet – it looked just like a parapet, chalk banked up, and I flung myself over it. Well then, I didn't know where I was! I went straight down sixty feet or more, sliding and slithering. I thought I'd never come to the bottom! Of course it was this big crater where they'd blown the mine. There were half a dozen of us all rattling down, shouting. We picked ourselves up and Captain Lefroy was there and Sergeant Stone and just about fourteen or fifteen of us, at a glance, out of the whole company. Captain Lefroy got us together and we clambered up the opposite side of the crater and lay there, well under cover, halfway up it and looking round to see if any more was coming in. We had two brothers named Moxham and one of them was with us and, looking across, we see his brother coming to the opposite lip of the crater. He stopped and didn't throw himself over it like we had, unexpected like, he just stood there looking down into it. We all shouted, 'Come on, come on! Don't stand there! That bloomin' machine-gun'll come round. He'll catch you!' But he just stood there a moment too long – and it did get him! He was killed there. Of course his brother didn't know what to do with himself. But there was nothing we *could* do – just lay there. We couldn't get forward. There weren't enough of us anyway!

A while after that another chap called Bill Parratt came over and he was getting down the side of the crater, careful like, when a shell dropped almost right beside him. There was a big cloud of smoke and when it cleared we saw that it had dropped him right in the bottom of the crater. He was lying on his back and one of his legs had been blown off and it was two or three yards away from him. He was hurt bad. He must have been in pain and agony, but there was nothing we could do for him. As the day went on, and it got towards evening, he started to cry out. 'Captain Lefroy, come and shoot me.' He kept calling over and over again, 'Captain Lefroy, come and shoot me.' We got fed up with hearing him calling out. Makes you jangly, all this calling, 'Come and shoot me, come and shoot me.' So the Captain crawled down and went over to him and pulled a packet out of his pocket and it was morphia tablets. He knew he couldn't do nothing for him, just give him these morphia tablets, and he got them down Bill and after a bit he went quiet and gradually faded out.

There was nothing to do but to stay there. Huddled into the side of the crater it seemed to the small party of the Wiltshires that they were in the very cone of the volcano the crater so strongly resembled as the night flashed and roared around them. After a brief lull in the early evening, it had all started up again as another brigade of their division had moved up to renew the attack on the village of la Boisselle a few hundred yards away to the left. Although it was dark, with the merest hint of a new moon in the sky, the lines in front of la Boisselle were so close that the German sentries were alerted by a shifting shadowy mass of movement, by the unavoidable clink of equipment, by a hoarse suspiration compounded of a thousand whispers, as a thousand men crept out to lie in front of the British lines, ready to launch an attack. Nervous machine-gunners started firing indiscriminately ahead and, a moment later, the field guns opened up, sending a hailstorm of shrapnel over the waiting troops. The groans and cries of the wounded confirmed the Germans' suspicions, if any confirmation had been needed and, in the glare of the bursting shells, the eerie light of the flares that rocketed from their lines, the British were as visible as if they had been standing up in full view and on parade. In fact, they had their heads well down.

Crouched close to the evil-smelling earth, Fred Darby of the 10th Battalion, The Worcestershire Regiment, found that he was sharing his shell-hole with Tom Turrall, a bomber of C Company. Darby's acquaintance with him was slight, for Turrall was a surly man not given to conviviality and with the reputation of being a rebel. He had spent the previous week in the guardroom – or what passed for a guardroom in the village where the Worcesters had rested behind the line – and although at Lieutenant Jennings' insistence he had been released to go into the battle, he was still, officially, under close arrest. It was far from being the first time that he had been reprimanded and disciplined during his service with the Battalion, and his crime this time had been '*insubordination to an NCO*'. Turrall was a troublesome soldier out of the line. In the line, however, the ugly streak of aggressiveness in his character which made him a thorn in the flesh of the Battalion, also made him a formidable fighter, and Lieutenant Jennings was well aware of it. Now, sheltering from the rain of red-hot shrapnel, noticing that Turrall was carrying a bag of bombs that could easily be set alight, Fred Darby did not regard him as the ideal companion in adversity.

Darby himself had had his own brush with Authority and, although it had been no more than a minor misdemeanour, typical of many a fed up Tommy, it had earned him eight days' field punishment, which had seemed to him a trifle unfair, because it had only been meant as a joke. But the joke had a point. The particular chip on Fred's shoulder was the sparsity of the rations and a shrewd suspicion that a large proportion of the food intended for troops in the line was being filched on the way up. The army biscuits which were all-too-often substituted for bread were nutritious enough once you got your teeth into them, but getting your teeth into them was the problem. They were as hard as cement. Varnished, buffed and polished, with a suitable cavity gouged from the centre, an army biscuit made a handsome and durable frame for a snapshot of wife or sweetheart. Soaked in water, and mixed with jam, or raisins if any were to be had, they made a reasonably palatable slop. Wrapped in a cloth and pounded with a mallet, they could be reduced to a state resembling 'breadcrumbs' which, mixed with mashed-up bully beef, resulted in a hash which was eatable if warmed up or – if there was fat available to fry them in, and a Tommy who had the patience to mould them – made into tasty rissoles. But the purpose for which they were palpably useless was the very purpose for which they were intended – to allay the pangs of hunger when nothing else was available. Fred Darby had sent one home to his wife, Freda. He wrote the message on one side: 'Your King and Country need You, and this is how they feed you.' On the other he wrote his wife's name and address, affixed a stamp and posted it from a civilian Post Office behind the lines.

It was the latter that caused the Army offence. There was no regulation which actually forbade defeatism in correspondence although, for obvious reasons, it was discouraged and could evoke a pointed rebuke from the censoring officer. But posting uncensored 'correspondence' – even an army biscuit – was a serious misdemeanour. Astonishingly, Freda had received the biscuit through the normal channels of the Post Office. Fred had received the backlash and, having taken his punishment, was not encouraged to repeat the experiment. He bore no grudge against the Army and the Army later demonstrated that it bore no grudge against Fred by awarding him the Distinguished Conduct Medal and wiping his 'crime' from its records. But, crouching together in their shell-hole under the bombardment, neither Fred nor Turrall could have guessed that Turrall, the *enfant terrible*, was about to earn even greater distinction.

They went over at three o'clock in the morning. It was less than forty-eight hours since the first general attack had been launched on the Somme Front and it had been much against the will of the British Command that the troops had gone over then in broad daylight. After Saturday's débâcle they were now doubly convinced that they had been right in disagreeing with the French who had pressed for a morning attack. It had been all very well for them to insist that their artillery observers needed daylight but it was glaringly obvious that the daylight had been on the side of the enemy. Now, with no interfering ally to thwart better judgement, the leading battalions rose from their shell-holes and surged forward through the concealing night to the trenches in front of la Boisselle. The 10th Worcesters were in the first wave.

Eight hundred and ten men went in. Four hundred and forty-eight came out.

But they had captured three lines of trenches and, although they had not succeeded in taking the whole village, by mid-day they had succeeded in winning enough ground to establish a line halfway through it and Tom Turrall had earned the Victoria Cross.[1]

It had not been so much a fight as a mêlée. The ruined buildings concealed fortifications, dugouts and hidden strongpoints as apparently invincible as any on the front, but the Worcesters had fought with bayonet and bomb. They had gone on fighting when the Commanding Officer, the Second-in-Command and almost every other officer had been killed or wounded and there was no longer anyone to lead the fight. In the first light of dawn Lieutenant Jennings had gathered some remnants of the men about him and was doubtless thankful to recognize Turrall among the scattered troops who, willy-nilly, had been separated from their platoons. They had pressed on through and beyond the village and into a storm of machine-gun fire. When it ceased, none of the party was left but Turrall and, lying a few feet away from him, his leg shattered and

1. Turrall's citation read: 'For most conspicuous bravery and devotion to duty. During a bombing attack by a small party against the enemy, the officer in charge was badly wounded and the party having penetrated the position to a great depth, was compelled to retire. Eventually, Private Turrall remained with the officer for three hours under continuous and very heavy fire from machine-guns and bombs and notwithstanding that both himself and the officer were at one time completely cut off from our troops. He held his ground with determination and finally carried the officer into our lines after our counter-attack had made this possible.'

Date of Act of Bravery 3 July 1916 *London Gazette* 9 September 1916

useless, Lieutenant Jennings. Turrall had dragged him into a shell-hole. He had bandaged the broken leg, using his entrenching tool as a splint and one of his puttees as a bandage. He had single-handedly repulsed a bombing attack by a party of Germans creeping up at close range. He had survived a counter-attack, by lying as still and apparently lifeless as Lieutenant Jennings himself as the enemy swept past to try to retake the line. One German soldier had even stopped and prodded him with his bayonet, and still, with a monumental effort, Turrall contrived to appear oblivious. Throughout the day he lay with Jennings in the shell-hole at the further end of the village with the enemy in front and behind.

At first light as the fight for la Boisselle was at its height and as Lieutenant Jennings had been gathering up his party and preparing for the dash forward, the small force of the 6th Wiltshires, their number swelled by men who had crept or tumbled into the crater during the night, were facing the German lines on the further rim of the crater, 'standing to' in case the enemy should rush it in a dawn attack. Nothing happened and the fearsome noise of the fighting in the village a quarter of a mile to their left reassured them that, for the moment, the Germans had their hands full. But their first sight of what lay beyond the crater, glimpsed cautiously in the grey half-light, haunted them through the sweltering day. Sweating in the heat, parched with thirst, pressed against the gas-soaked slopes of the crater, dizzied by the fumes of explosions, in the forefront of the clamour of the fight to the left of them they could hear quite distinctly a sound that came closer to home. It was the buzzing of a million flies hovering and settling on the still bodies of the dead, lying in countless numbers beyond the crater. The smell, in the summer heat, was almost overpowering but all Roy Bealing could think of through the endless day of burning heat, was that every dead soldier lying out in front must have a full water-bottle strapped to his body. Their own were long since empty. They could only hope that, when nightfall came, rations would come too. Meanwhile, they could only hold on.

When the darkness deepened, Bealing scrambled over the rim of the crater and crawled in search of water among the ranks of the dead. The shelling had abated. In la Boisselle the fighting had died down. Both sides were glad to draw breath and draw strength for tomorrow. Flares lit the ground from time to time, but there was no fear that Bealing would be spotted. Creeping close to the ground among the huddled dead, he would simply be taken for one of them.

Some few hundred yards away, beyond the captured line that ran through the centre of the village, Tom Turrall was creeping back with infinite caution and also with infinite difficulty. He was carrying his officer on his back and Lieutenant Jennings was in a bad way. He had been wounded twice before Turrall had dragged him into the shell-hole and he had been wounded twice more while he lay there. Now, with his left leg shattered, with wounds in his right thigh and knee and a bullet wound through his left arm, he could do little to help himself. Tom Turrall was not, in general, an admirer of officers, but he admired Lieutenant Jennings. He liked the way he had tackled the first dugout, bombing it himself and capturing it almost single-handed which, in Turrall's opinion, was no mean feat. He had liked the way that he had led the men to the second line and kept on leading even after he was wounded and, when Jennings was beyond carrying on, he had astounded Turrall by his courage as he lay shattered in the shell-hole. Time after time he had fainted with pain and time after time he had roused and chatted in an almost social way and had even smoked a cigarette or two, allowing Turrall to light them but, with his one uninjured arm, waving away his efforts to place the cigarette between his lips. Turrall had liked that too, and he was determined to get Jennings back.

Jennings was a dead weight. He was weak with loss of blood. He was a taller man than Turrall and his one sound arm which Turrall had thrown around his own neck had little grip left in it. All that Turrall could do was to grasp it with one hand of his own, throw his other arm behind him around Jennings' body, and half-carry, half-drag him through the gaps between the German outposts, across the battered ground, to the new British line. There had been little chance to consolidate, and the sentries were edgy, alert to any shadow that staggered from the darkness of the night beyond.

'Halt! Hands Up!' And then, as Turrall raised his hands as far as he could without letting Jennings go, came the heart-stopping snap of the rifle bolt, 'That man behind you too! Quick!' 'For God's sake! He's wounded and I'm bringing him in!' Turrall was just in time to stop the sentry firing and raising the alarm.

Lieutenant Jennings survived long enough to be carried to the field dressing station. He survived the journey by ambulance to the casualty clearing station at Dernancourt. And he lived long enough to tell the story of what had happened and to recommend Tom Turrall for the Victoria Cross. He died of his wounds on the evening of 5 July. Some hours earlier, before Lieutenant Jennings had finally slipped into unconsciousness, they were able to tell him that the Germans had been pushed out of la Boisselle.[1]

*

1. Tom Turrall survived the war and died in 1964.

The 19th Division was still in the line but now it was possible to bring out the Tynesiders of the 34th. The fragments of the battalions came out in pathetically small groups and were collected together in trenches on the Albert side of the Tara-Usna ridge. There was little shelter and, after a fine day, a chilly wind hinted at rain in the morning. They were very near the gun line but neither the roar of the night barrage, nor the absence of greatcoats and blankets disturbed them. Slumped where they had thrown themselves down, the Geordies slept the sleep of the dead.

Next morning, for the first time in five days, they had a hot breakfast to sustain them on the six-mile march through the town of Albert to Millencourt four miles beyond. It was a long slog along the congested roads but there were many welcome rests while they waited at the roadside for a convoy of buses or lorries to pass. All were carrying troops whose clean and cheerful demeanour, in spite of an almost sleepless night of travelling, contrasted vividly with the appearance of the soldiers newly out of the line. Filthy, bedraggled, sunken-eyed with fatigue, they stood by the roadside and grinned and waved back as the cheering convoys passed. Tom Easton, for one, felt that, for the first time, he truly understood the meaning of the word 'relief'.

Chapter 10

With the concentration of troops coming out of the line and whole brigades preparing to go in, the population of Millencourt which had amounted to a few hundreds before the war had expanded to that of a fair-sized town. There was no question that such billets as there were should be reserved for the exhausted ranks of the decimated battalions who, beyond anything else, needed rest. In the barns, stacked high with tiers of short wire-netting bunks, the weary men of the 34th Division lay asleep and replete too, for they had enjoyed a lavish meal. Some of the lads had managed to tuck away as many as four plates of stew and, for once, there had been enough bread to mop it up. With so few to be fed, there was plenty to go round.

Arriving late in the afternoon from his meeting with the Divisional Commander, Brigadier Trevor Ternan was reluctant to rouse the sleeping officers, but it had to be done. A day or so before he had addressed the officers of his Brigade *en masse* in the village school-room. Now there was more than room enough for them all in his office at Brigade Head-quarters. Eighty officers had gone into action with the four Battalions of the Tyneside Scottish Brigade. Ten now remained.

In the Tyneside Irish, it was the same sorry tale. Mere drafts of reinforcements arriving in officerless battalions would be of little use. It had been decided, Ternan announced, that both Brigades should be transferred wholesale to the 37th Division to rest and recuperate, to regroup and retrain with new men in a quiet sector of the line. Meanwhile, two Brigades of the 37th Division would take their places in the 34th to continue the battle. Later, when they were up to strength again, he hoped that they would all return to the Home Division. But his listeners knew, as Ternan knew himself, that, whatever the future held, neither the Tyneside Scots nor the Tyneside Irish would ever be the same again.

The change-over had taken place while the men were sleeping and the 112th Brigade was already resting on the slopes behind the village preparing to move off.

A brisk half-hour's stroll away in the environs of the insalubrious village of Bresle, the boys of the 13th Rifle Brigade had enjoyed a day of comparative rest and, in the course of it, had learned that they were now part of the 34th Division. After their night journey from Humbercourt they had been bivouacking all day in the open and they were not sorry to be stretching their legs and leaving to march nearer the line. Earlier in the afternoon, the Battalion had formed an open square on the hillside, Colonel Pretor-Pinney had addressed them, cautioned them – if caution were needed – to uphold the tradition of the 'Golden Horseshoe' symbol of the 37th Division, even though they had been abruptly transmogrified to the 34th, and wished them luck. A number of the boys felt, super-stitiously, that it was an inauspicious moment in which to be deprived of the lucky horseshoe.[1]

Now they were marching along the road, and they were singing. It was not exactly a marching song, nor one of the rousing airs which the popular mind had been led to believe by the War Correspondents made up the usual repertoire of cheery Tommies singing on the march. It was certainly not the *Marseillaise* – which one fulsome report had attributed to some anonymous battalion the week before. Although they were approaching the first anniversary of their arrival in France, the linguistic abilities of the Battalion did not extend quite so far as mastering the words of the *Marseillaise*, but there was nevertheless a distinctly international flavour about one tuneless dirge which was a favourite of theirs, if only because they had composed it themselves. In its genesis the melody had borne a faint resemblance to *Here We Go Round the Mulberry Bush* but with the passage of time infinite variations had rendered it almost un-recognizable.

> *We don't want a girl from Givenchy-le-Noble,*
> *From Givenchy-le-Noble,*
> *From Givenchy-le-Noble,*
> *If you go for a walk she will get into trouble.*
> *So we don't want a girl from Givenchy-le-Noble.*

> *We don't want a girl from Izel-lez-Hameau,*
> *From Izel-lez-Hameau,*

1. The 111th and 112th Brigades which were exchanged with the 102nd (Tyne-side Scottish) and 103rd (Tyneside Irish) Brigades in the 34th Division comprised:

111th Brigade:	112th Brigade:
10th Royal Fusiliers	11th Royal Warwickshire
13th Royal Fusiliers	6th Bedfordshire
13th King's Royal Rifle Corps	8th East Lancashire
13th Rifle Brigade	10th Loyal North Lancashire

From Izel-lez-Hameau,
She may be all right, but we don't care a damno,
So we don't want a girl from Izel-lez-Hameau.

We don't want a girl who comes from les Comptes,
Who comes from les Comptes,
Who comes from les Comptes,
For they all eat onions, and their breath rather haunts,
So we don't want a girl who comes from les Comptes.

As they marched easy a familiar discussion arose in B Company among the bards of No. 13 Platoon. They felt that they should bring the melodic itinerary up to date by adding a verse in honour of the delightful female inhabitants of Auxi. But inspiration eluded them. No one could come up with a better rhyme than 'poxy' and it seemed singularly inappropriate to the place where they had spent such a pleasant time.

Sergeant Howard Rowlands, B Coy., 13th (S) Btn., The Rifle Brigade

I can see us now – a long column of marching riflemen. We must have recaptured our high spirits of the night before because we're singing again. It was a fair step and the gaps between the platoons got noticeably wider and wider. We marched past a field gun battery, halted for tea. We could have done with a cup ourselves, and we let them know it as we went by! Then we marched past them up a steep bit of road and, as we got to the top of the rise, there were long stretches of canvas fastened to plane trees along the roadside to hide the traffic on the road from enemy observation and, beyond the hill, we could see the town of Albert down in the valley.

It was funny how the singing died away. Shells were bursting away to the north-east and there in front of us was Albert, looking fairly intact, but with the battered cathedral tower standing out above it and the figure of the Virgin holding the Child leaning over the town in this sorrowful attitude. I can still picture that stark outline in my mind's eye and it seemed to me then, as it always did afterwards when I looked back on it, that she seemed to be lamenting the folly of men.

Even before the war, the golden Virgin, triumphantly holding the infant Child in her uplifted arms on the soaring heights of Albert's Cathedral, had been a landmark. Now it was the very symbol of the war itself. Early in 1915, an unlucky shot from a German gun had struck the cathedral tower fair and square and the Virgin had fallen forward to lie precariously horizontal, face downwards above what had once been the market-place and was now the bustling centre-point of troop movements through Albert. It was an awesome sight.

As the shellfire intensified and the cathedral itself became more and more battered and knocked about, the tower with its leaning Virgin remained intact. A superstition grew up among the French troops and it was adopted in their turn by the British when they came to the Somme. When the Virgin fell the war would end – and the Germans would have won! As the Virgin looked likely to fall at any time, an event which would be distinctly bad for morale, French Engineers were ordered to secure the statue with strong steel hawsers. So, there she hung, sorrowing or, according to the various imaginations of the troops, protecting or blessing them as they passed beneath.[1]

It was astonishing that there could still be civilians in Albert a scant two miles behind the British front line. It was the ridge that saved it, for Albert lay cupped in a valley. It was not so much a town as an outsize village and, although some houses were tumbled and ruined and shells had taken a bite out of many others, there was still a remarkable air of normality about Albert although, since the bombardment had started, there were fewer inhabitants to be seen and those who had stayed there were keeping judiciously under cover. There were some villas still intact on the western outskirts and, in the main street by the cathedral, a number of houses which, if a soldier was not too fussy, could provide a reasonably draught-free billet for the night. The individual platoons of the 13th Rifle Brigade were more or less left to fend for themselves, with the proviso that they must be on parade and in battle order in front of the cathedral at 7.30 next morning.

Sergeant Jack Cross, No. 4842, C Coy., 13th (S) Btn., The Rifle Brigade

We had to break into the houses to get the lads under cover, but that was all right as long as the sergeants did it, so all the C Company NCOs got in one place and the company officers were next door. We thought that they were fattening us up for the kill, so to speak, because we actually got issued gammon rashers for supper. We had

1. The hanging Virgin remained in this position until the late spring of 1918 when she was shot down by the British Artillery after the Germans had occupied Albert. They rightly concluded that the Germans would use the tower as an observation post, just as they had used it for this purpose themselves.

to cook them ourselves, of course, but nobody minded that. Well, I'd noticed that the garden next door had a fine crop of potatoes in it, just ready. So Fred Crease and myself, we slipped over the garden wall, took our bayonets and dug up these potatoes. They were lovely. We boiled them, fried the gammon rashers and had gammon and new potatoes that night for hot dinner. We hadn't had such a feed since Christmas.

The fact that the Sergeants of C Company dined so royally was probably because Jack himself had seen to it that the cooks always got a share of the warm garments so lovingly knitted by his fellow servants in Eaton Square. No one enquired too closely where the gammon rashers came from, but the C Company Sergeants did notice that the same appetizing smell drifted from the C Company Officers' billet next door. The officers had not had the good fortune to enjoy the delicious accompaniment of new potatoes, although they had been brazenly filched by the Sergeants from the garden behind their own billet, and had to be content with beans.

The rest of the Battalion supped, that evening, on beans and bully beef. Bob Thompson was mixing it into a tasty mush in his mess tin and warming it over his personal, carefully guarded primus stove, when Major Sir Foster Cunliffe popped his head into the Corporals' billet.

'Lost your saucepan, Thompson?' They exchanged grins.

'Yes, sir. And no custard either!'

It was an old joke, dating back to the previous autumn when the Battalion had been occupying the line that ran through the orchards at Hannescamps. The trees above the communication trenches were heavy with apples, and it had given the signallers of D Company an idea, for they were partial to stewed apples and custard. There was no 'custard', of course; there was no milk to make it with; there was no sugar to sweeten it. There were apples in plenty, actually falling in showers into the trench when a shell happened to explode within fifty yards of them, but there was no saucepan to cook them in. It was Sid Whiting who supplied the deficiency.

Rifleman Sid Whiting, MM, No. S/4229, D Coy., 13th (S) Btn., The Rifle Brigade

We could get Quaker Oats – so I suppose the custard was porridge, really speaking – and bags of apples, but this question of a utensil really bothered us. One day, when we were out of the line, I was sitting in the barn at Bienvillers, when I saw 'Madame' bring out a saucepan of food for the dog. As soon as she turned her back, quick as a flash before the dog could get at it, I nipped over, emptied the food on the ground and 'won' the saucepan.

Next time up the line I was cooking our usual supper of stewed apples and porridge when our Company Commander, who was then *Captain* Sir Foster Cunliffe, came into the dugout and remarked how good it smelt. Well, I naturally asked if he would like some, and he said he would. He asked me how we came by the stuff. So I told him the whole story – including the story of the saucepan. We all thought it was a great joke, and the Captain really enjoyed his supper! But he never let us forget it after that! He said, 'Well, I've attended banquets and eaten off gold plate, but I don't think I've ever before eaten food cooked in a dog's saucepan.' Well, as we used to say, '*C'est la guerre*.'

And '*C'est la guerre*' the boys were saying, as they put their shoulders to the door of a locked-up *estaminet* in the main street of Albert. Major Sir Foster Cunliffe, now Second-in-Command of the Battalion, was fortunately well out of the way, or had turned a judicious blind eye. And any officers in the vicinity later turned a deaf ear to the merrymaking when, pleasantly replete with free beer, Horace Smith and some other stalwarts of B Company dragged the piano from the *estaminet* into the street for a sing-song. Breaking into private property had not over-worried them. If the place had not been locked up when the civilians had hastily evacuated, they would never have dreamed of helping themselves. They had been perfectly willing to buy the beer and, for once, they had money to pay for it. '*C'est la guerre*.'

Sergeant Jack Cross, No. 4842, C Coy., 13th (S) Btn., The Rifle Brigade

Well, what the lads were a bit annoyed about was that we all got paid out that day. They could have done with the money a couple of days before when we were up at Humbercourt. You never knew for sure when you were going to get paid except if you were going into action. They always paid us out then because it was a chance to get rid of this money, so that the Quartermaster-Sergeant wouldn't lose it all in a fight. He'd see you got it first. There was a chap in my platoon called Wright and he used to run a Crown and Anchor board so he said, knowing that the lads had got money, 'I'll get the old board out, Sergeant.' Strictly illegal, of course, and as a Sergeant I shouldn't have had anything to do with it, but I said, 'All right, Arthur, you do what you like. Get the board out and I'll give you a start.' Well, all the lads gathered round and Arthur started on the job and I was putting my bits and pieces down and I was winning! I just kept putting my money down on the right spots. I've never won so much money in my life on a Crown and Anchor board. Four pounds ten shillings I picked up that afternoon – near enough a month's pay for a sergeant. I thought, 'Well, I'll stick it now and hold on to the money.' So, off I went. After a bit, when it got dark and they had to pack up, Arthur came along and found us in this billet and said, 'Sergeant, can you tell me where there's a Field Post Office?' I went out in the street and there was a Military Policeman coming along so I said, 'Say, chum, can you tell us where there's a Military Field Post Office?' He said, 'See that flag fluttering over there? That's it.' 'Right,' said Arthur. 'I'm going over there to get rid of this money. I'm not going up the line for somebody to pick my pockets when I get a bullet.' So he sent the money home in postal orders – and it was a tidy sum too!

It rained that night. It was the last straw for Joe Hoyles and the twenty others of his platoon who had not been fortunate enough to find a billet under cover. Wrapped in waterproof groundsheets they passed an uncomfortable night lying on the broken pavement round the church. They had not required to visit the Field Post Office to send their money home. In a sense, Arthur Wright had done it for them and the few francs that had passed briefly through their hands an hour or so earlier were already on their way to swell Arthur's savings at home. Between them they had lost every bean.

It was just as well that Colonel Pretor-Pinney had not been in the vicinity while the Crown and Anchor game was going on. He was a stickler for discipline.

But Colonel Pretor-Pinney was otherwise engaged, for Major-General Ingouville-Williams, the Commander of the 34th Division, and in spite of his exalted rank disrespectfully known to the troops as 'Inky Bill', had summoned the Brigadiers of his two newly acquired Brigades and the Commanding Officers of their eight Battalions to a meeting. It started at eleven o'clock. The General apologized for the lateness of the hour. As they were already on their way into the line, this was the only opportunity there would be to make mutual acquaintance and to discuss the plans that were to be put into effect tomorrow.

The particular plan for tomorrow was the renewal of the attack on the village of Ovillers, across the valley from la Boisselle, which, in spite of the terrible cost, had resisted all efforts to take it. Strictly speaking, it was not the affair of the 34th Division, because the assault was to be carried out by the right flank of General Gough's newly formed Fifth Army, but it was important that they should know of it because they were to be attached to the 19th Division still holding the adjacent sector and their own fortunes and progress would depend on the result. Unless Ovillers fell, it would be extremely difficult to exploit the gains at la Boisselle and to push on beyond it. Meanwhile, they would move up in support and, when the 19th Division was relieved, take over the front line and push ahead.

The night was heavy with cloud and heavy with noise, for the iron-rimmed wheels of the transport limbers clattered non-stop over the broken pavé, making the most of the hours of darkness to get the supplies up the line, and behind the town the guns were roaring out a bombardment as fierce as any since the first day of the assault. Through the long damp hours between nightfall and dawn the men lay waiting for the morning. They knew that something was up and that, soon enough, they would find out what it was.

What was 'up' was that the Germans were answering back. Behind his line for the last few days the enemy had been engaged in very much the same reorganization as the British behind theirs. After the first onslaught the German Army, which had put up such a rugged resistance to the British efforts to break their line, was exhausted and depleted by heavy casualties, and Royal Flying Corps observers were bringing back reports of long lines of ambulances, of troop movements and trains of supply wagons as units were reshuffled in and out of the line. Both sides had fought almost literally to the death and there was hardly a British or a German soldier coming thankfully out of the front line who did not feel a positive admiration for his opponent. It was impossible for the Germans not to admire 'Tommy' pitting his strength and his will against the steel and concrete of strongholds armoured and designed to be impregnable; it was impossible for the British not to admire 'Fritz', who had fought so valiantly in their defence.

The Germans had been chivalrous. The morning after the Big Push in many places where the attack had utterly failed and there was no fight left in the troops, unofficial truces had lasted for hours and the few troops who were left were allowed to move freely in front of their trenches to rescue as many of the wounded as they could in the time allowed. In front of Beaumont Hamel, a young soldier of the Worcesters who had crawled out concealed by the morning mist to search for a wounded friend and had, miraculously, found him, was seen by the Germans just a few feet from their wire when the mist suddenly cleared. There was a clatter of rifle bolts but, as both soldiers looked up, appalled, a sharp order was given and a German officer sprang on to the parapet of the enemy trench. He shouted across, in astonishingly perfect English, 'You must not stop there with that man. If you want to come in, come along. Otherwise you must go back to your own trenches.' And he added, as the boy hesitated, 'We will look after your comrade.'

'I'll go back to my own trenches, sir.' He didn't dare stand upright, and it seemed a long crawl through the shell-holes and the bodies, down a slope, across dead ground and up again to the British wire. But the Germans had not fired a shot at his retreating back. Nor did they fire at the line of British soldiers in their forward trench who, incautiously poking their heads above the parapet, anxiously watched his approach.

Now, days later, some thousands of dead still lay there and the weak waves and shouts of the wounded had long ago been stilled. Even in sectors where bitter fighting had pushed the line forward, the terrible detritus of the first day's battle lay blackened and decomposing in the open. Awaiting the 13th Battalion, The Rifle Brigade, on their arrival at la Boisselle, was the task of burying them. Someone had to do it.

Now that the Germans, like the British, had replaced their battle-weary front-line forces with fresh troops they had thrown them straight into the battle – not, like their exhausted predecessors, to defend their line but to wrest it back in the places where the British had bitten into it, and to stand fast. They had attacked at dead of night. They threw themselves against the tiny lodgement in their front line north of Thiepval and proceeded to throw the British out of it in short order. They had attacked beyond Thiepval, at the other end of the ridge, battering into the bloody nose of the Leipzig Redoubt and fought and bombed all through the night before their survivors were beaten back. And the Germans had been beaten back even beyond the trench from which they had started. Two companies of the 3rd Worcesters had pulled it off. They had succeeded at last in capturing the whole of the German front line in the Leipzig Salient, and they held it and continued to hold it though the Germans blasted a desperate bombardment back at them.

The Germans had also attacked at Ovillers, streaming out of the village and setting up machine-guns in No Man's Land an hour before the British troops were due to launch an attack themselves. But, by ten o'clock in the morning, by the time the 13th Battalion, The Rifle Brigade, had marched out of Albert up the long straight road to the Tara-Usna Ridge, which overlooked the valleys of Ovillers and la Boisselle, Ovillers had been taken. Or, rather it could have been taken, if there had been survivors enough to hold it. The cost of thwarting the German attack, of pursuing them back to the village, of subduing the nest of strongholds which had repulsed successive waves as a cliff-face repulses the sea, had been too high. Fourteen hundred men of the three Battalions had been killed or wounded. They took the first three lines of trenches but, by the time they had done so, there were not enough of them to hold the enemy. All that could be done, until reinforcements arrived, was to retire from the first line, consolidate the two behind it and hang on. But it was a start. And it was more than a start. It was a victory.

From their position in low-lying Ovillers, had they dared to raise their heads and look to their right, the victors could have seen, two kilometres ahead of them, at the top of the long shallow valley that ran through the gently rising ground, the thick belts of wire that protected the village of Pozières, lying beyond them astride the Albert–Bapaume road. Like Ovillers, Pozières was a fortress.

With the Army now pushing towards it from two separate directions, it seemed to Sir Douglas Haig that Pozières was the next logical objective. He had just discussed the matter with General Rawlinson when the news arrived that the capture of Ovillers was not complete and that the troops had merely gained a foothold in the village. No casualty figures were yet available, but it appeared, from all accounts, that the gain, though small, had been costly. More men must be brought in. Experienced men. Good fighters.

The Commander-in-Chief accordingly issued his orders. He instructed General Gough to complete the capture of Ovillers with such troops as remained at his disposal, and he ordered the Anzac Corps in the Second Army to send two Australian Divisions south to the Somme. For the moment he would hold them in reserve. Later, when the way was open, he would push them in to attack Pozières.

In his conversation with General Rawlinson, the name of the Anzacs and the name 'Pozières' were linked for the first time. As long as battles were remembered, they would never again be separated.

In meadowland near Millencourt, flanked on either side by Major-General Ingouville-Williams and by the Corps Commander, Sir William Pulteney, Brigadier Trevor Ternan surveyed the ranks of his Tyneside Scottish Brigade. After a morning of roll calls the totals returned by each battalion had almost beggared belief, but they were amply confirmed by this afternoon's parade. The whole Brigade, drawn up in open square formation, barely occupied the space of a single battalion. The Generals warmly congratulated the men. Sir William Pulteney dwelt at length on the tactical importance of the part they had played. Their achievement might only be measured in yards, but they had broken the German line. General Ingouville-Williams dwelt on their splendid gallantry. He bade them goodbye and Godspeed. He hoped that they would soon rejoin his command. Trevor Ternan, as sadly conscious of the absence of familiar faces as any man in the ranks, called for three cheers. A voice yelled out with statutory bravado, 'Are we downhearted?' The men obliged with a stentorian 'NO!' No one yelled it louder than Tom Easton. For the last six days he had been sick with worry about his brother Joe. This morning, in the decimated ranks of his battalion, he had found him. By some miracle he was whole – and alive!

At ten o'clock that evening, in pouring rain, the 13th Rifle Brigade left the reserve trenches on the Tara-Usna Ridge for the line at la Boisselle. It was less than a mile ahead, but the shelling was heavy and they lost thirteen men, killed or wounded on the way. Early the next morning, just after stand to, Walter Monckton and Joe Hoyles were brewing tea in the trench when the Colonel came along, accompanied by a Staff Officer. They both rose hastily to their feet as the two officers stopped beside them. The trench ran to the left of the big crater and now, since la Boisselle had fallen, it was a good distance behind the front line. It was exactly a week, almost to the minute, since the 34th Division had gone over the top, and most of them lay there still, with the bodies of the men who had followed them.

Climbing on to the firestep, the Staff Captain cautiously raised his head above the parapet and looked across. 'Good God!' he exclaimed. 'I didn't know we were using Colonial troops!' Pretor-Pinney made no reply. Hoyles and Monckton exchanged grim looks. 'Dear God,' muttered Monckton, when the Colonel and the visitor had moved away to a safe distance, 'has the bastard never seen a dead man before?' It was a rhetorical question. Lying out in the burning sun, soaked by the frequent showers of a week's changeable weather, the bodies of the dead soldiers had been turned black by the elements.

The Battalion spent the rest of the day burying them.

Corporal Joe Hoyles, MM, No. 3237, 13th (S) Btn., The Rifle Brigade

There was a terrific smell. It was so awful it nearly poisoned you. A smell of rotten flesh. The old German front line was covered with bodies – they were seven and eight deep and they had all gone black. The smell! These people had been laying since the First of July. Wicked it was! Colonel Pinney got hold of some stretchers and our job was to put the bodies on them and, with a man at each end, we *threw* them into that crater. There must have been over a thousand bodies there. I don't know how many we buried. I'll never forget that sight. Bodies all over the place. I'll never forget it. I was only eighteen, but I thought, 'There's something wrong here!'

Sergeant Jack Cross, No. 4842, C Coy., 13th (S) Btn., The Rifle Brigade

My job was to take the identity discs off the dead men. Other people were detailed off to collect the rifles and other people collected the equipment and then there was a band of stretcher-bearers who picked up these dead gentlemen and took them to the edge of this crater and tipped them over, rolled them down and they buried themselves in the chalk before they got to the bottom.

Corporal Horace Smith, MM, No. 3697, 13th (S) Btn., The Rifle Brigade

My lot, we had to collect the bodies off the old German wire. Over 200 we counted. And we dumped them in the crater. All the time we were getting shelled, and casualties were happening of course. Some of us was hoping they'd happen. I know I didn't mind it happening! Then I got it! I'd just jumped in a trench between two men, Gomer Evans and Dick Darling, and as I jumped in there was this terrific crash. I didn't know any more until I woke up a few minutes later, and there was old Gomer Evans, he'd got the top of his nut blown off, and Dick Darling, he'd got it in the back. His kidneys blown out. We had to bury them both. But we didn't put them in the crater. We buried them just to the side of it.

Acting-Corporal Rupert Weeber, No. 4477, 13th (S) Btn., The Rifle Brigade

As far as you could see there were all these bodies lying out there – literally thousands of them, just where they'd been caught on the First of July. Some were without legs, some were legs without bodies, arms without bodies. A terrible sight. They'd been churned up by shells even after they were killed. We were just dumping them into the crater – just filling them over. It didn't seem possible. It didn't get inside me or scare me, but it just made me wonder that these could have been men. It made me wonder what it was all about. And far away in the distance we could see nothing but a line of bursting shells. It was continuous. You wouldn't have thought that anybody could have existed in it, it was so terrific.

And yet we knew we were going up into it, with not an earthly chance.

The shells were bursting on the line where the troops were grappling with the enemy at Mametz Wood and, nearer still, struggling to capture the village of Contalmaison. It lay beyond them in the dark, three kilometres ahead of the big crater where the blackened bodies of the dead committed to its depths were sinking, by the weight of their numbers, into the crumbling chalk.

Chapter 11

The road that once flew arrow-straight from Albert to Bapaume bisected the battlefield. Before 1914 the traffic it carried had hardly changed since the Roman Legions had marched along it when France was Gaul. Half a dozen farm carts might trundle down to Albert or up to Bapaume on their respective market days. A bicycle might be seen from time to time, free-wheeling down the hill from Pozières to la Boisselle, but the sight of an occasional motor car, travelling at a dizzy twenty-five miles an hour en route to Albert or Amiens, was enough to interrupt work in the fields on either side for up to five minutes while the peasants goggled and gaped.

The peasants themselves travelled mostly on foot and mostly away from the main road. From the farms and smallholdings in the villages there were easier ways to get to market. The country was criss-crossed with tracks and lanes, linking the villages and running out to the surrounding woods and farmlands, tramped out by ten generations of feet going backwards and forwards to the fields, of woodcutters hauling timber, of women in shapeless country black, work-worn and weather-beaten, plodding to market weighed down by heavy baskets of farm produce. In the morning the oxen lumbered out to the fields; in the evening the cows were driven home for milking and at harvest time carts, heavy with hay or mangel wurzels, gouged ever-deeper the permanent ruts that had finally turned the tracks into roads and put them on the map. There were more roads in the Somme countryside than there were places to go. It was hardly surprising that its inhabitants preferred the by-ways to the hard pavé of the single highway. Living in close-knit communities in their separate villages, few of them ever had much occasion even to cross it.

But the main road was a landmark. A daughter who had married from Contalmaison or Bazentin and gone to live at Ovillers or Courcelette, twenty minutes' walk away, would be described as living '*à l'autre côté*', as if she had gone to the other side of the Atlantic, while the residents of Thiepval and Fricourt, just six kilometres apart on either side of the main road, would refer to each other as '*ces gens là*', as if they inhabited separate planets.

Things had changed only slightly since the coming of the railway but, even in this respect, the country-folk south of the road felt a certain superiority to those who lived to the north of it. Over there the main line thundered through the Ancre valley on its way to Paris. There were stations at Miraumont, at Beaucourt, at Hamel, where a few local trains stopped once or twice a day. There was a single-line track that climbed up behind Aveluy Wood to Mesnil and chuffed behind the ridges past Serre to Puisieux, but it was nothing compared to the network of 'railways' that meandered through the fields and villages of the country south of the main road, in much the same manner as the wayward tracks and lanes. And, although the 'trains' were little more than tram-cars, in this gentler terrain it had been possible to lay a considerable network of track.

North of the Albert–Bapaume road the land swept up to the dramatic bluffs and ridges, the steep slopes and deep valleys on both sides of the River Ancre. South of the road, it dropped away and unrolled a carpet of fields and meadows in a panorama of soft hills and valleys, rising gradually to the horizon where the poplars, marching along the high road to Peronne, stood sentinel on the skyline. In this idyllic landscape, the last idyllic touch was its lush, abundant woodland.

The woods appeared on the British Army maps in a strange conglomeration of names. Mametz Wood, Bernafay and Trones, presented no problem, although anyone who cared to look closely at the pre-war maps might notice that the original 'c' of 'Troncs' had been mis-read or misprinted as an 'e'. 'Thrones' or 'tree trunks' – it made little difference to the troops who were fighting for it now. Getting its name right was the least of their worries.

To the right of Montauban, Bernafay Wood and Trones Wood had been the first big obstacles in the way of the advance when the troops had broken the German line in the south. Even now, when they had swept ahead of Montauban and the bloody stumps of Bernafay Wood were in their hands, although the edge of Trones Wood was only a couple of hundred yards away, they had captured a mere toe-hold, at its southern end. Trones was shaped like a pear-drop and beyond its elongated northern tip lay all the strength of the Germans' second-line position. It was natural that the Germans were going to fight for Trones Wood as savagely as they were fighting to hold on to Mametz Wood away to the other side of Montauban. There too the British troops had only managed to capture the tip of one long spur of woodland projecting from the thick mass of the wood itself, and they had not quite managed to capture all of Contalmaison village lying off to the left.

Now that the Fricourt Salient had been pinched out, it was at Contalmaison that the line swung round and, in a sense, linked up.

The four villages of Ovillers, Pozières, Contalmaison and la Boisselle form a rough rectangle with a village at each corner bisected diagonally by the Albert–Bapaume road, as it runs from la Boisselle (in the bottom left, opposite Ovillers) to Pozières, astride it in the top right 'corner', opposite Contalmaison.

If Pozières could be captured, then Ovillers would automatically fall, and Thiepval, still standing impregnable on its bluff above the Ancre, might be taken in the rear. With Contalmaison in British hands, the way would be open to pour troops into Mametz Wood from the left, to join up with the Welsh who were thrusting into its southern flank and to push on together to crack the Germans' second-line defences at a blow. By the evening of 9 July the line ran through the southern edge of Contalmaison and, swinging northwards a mile to the left of the village, crossed the road that ran between it and la Boisselle. That evening the 13th Battalion, The Rifle Brigade, moved up from la Boisselle and into the new front line. They were facing the open country that lay between the strongpoint that was Contalmaison and the fortress that was Pozières.

It was a slithering, wet shambles of a night. The churning shellfire, the constant traffic, the frequent showers of the ten days' fighting had turned the trenches into ditches running with mud. Next morning, a slight steam rose above them under the hot rays of the sun. It was a beautiful day. It was also a day of hellish noise for the Welshmen of the 38th Division were hammering hard for Mametz Wood and, on the immediate right of the Battalion, the 23rd Division were attacking Contalmaison village. By half-past five in the afternoon the village had been captured.

At eight o'clock two battalions of the 111th Brigade were ordered to prepare to attack. The 13th Battalion in the front-line trench were to lead it. The Germans had last been seen streaming out of Contalmaison north to Pozières, protected by the trenchline on the left which was still in their hands, still strongly held and directly in front of the 13th Rifle Brigade. This was the trenchline the Battalion was ordered to capture. On their left, the 25th Division would attack astride the main road and, at the same time, part of the 23rd Division would attack on their right. There would be a heavy barrage to support them. They lined up, well back, on either side of the country tramway track. It was a beautiful evening.

Corporal Joe Hoyles, MM, No. 3237, A Coy., 13th (S) Btn., The Rifle Brigade

It was a very bright hot day and we'd seen Contalmaison go up in the air. We'd seen the church go up in the air. Marvellous gunnery

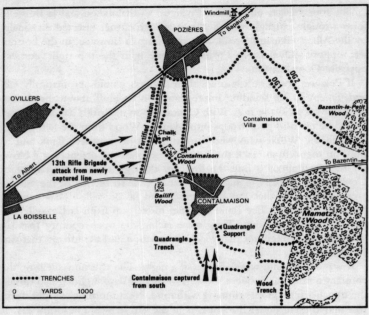

The Attack at Contalmaison on 10th July

it was, our gunnery. *We* had to take to the left of Contalmaison.
I was a section leader and Colonel Pinney came by the Platoon
and he said, 'We're going over at 8.45. Set your watches.' Those
of us in charge of sections had to take our sections over. Where I
got my courage from I don't know. I suppose, being young, one
had an 'Up Guards and at 'em', sort of feeling. Some men funked
it of course. They went over all right, they had to or they'd have
got my bayonet up their arse. But you could tell from their faces
that a lot of people dreaded it. We went over with fixed bayonets
and we all had a Mills bomb in our hands. It was a quarter or a
third of a mile to the first German trench.

Rifleman Ed McGrath, D Coy., 13th (S) Btn., The Rifle Brigade

I can see in my mind's eye, Captain Smith, watch in hand in the
trench, just before we went over. He soon gave the order and over
we went. I remember how I felt like Barnacle Bill, all dressed up like

a Christmas tree. Rifle slung, spade in braces, and two bandoliers of ammo, one Mills bomb in my right hand, pin out, and two in a mess tin cover in my left.

Rifleman George Murrell, B Coy., 13th (S) Btn., The Rifle Brigade

Some of us South African boys were told we were wanted at the other end of the trench. An officer called out, 'Lewis-gunners, over here.' My brother was with me, in the same team. We formed up and I found myself carrying a Lewis-gun pannier and many drums of spare ammunition – at a guess about 800 rounds. Sewrey then took my rifle to carry it and the next thing was – Over the Top! By the time we had got fifty yards or so Sewrey was hit and I was charging the enemy with plenty of bullets but no rifle.

Corporal Bob Thompson, No. 2756, D Coy., 13th (S) Btn., The Rifle Brigade

I had a Lewis-gun team of about six men. We weren't in the front of the first line because, with a Lewis-gun and carrying ammunition, you're not able to do trench attacking really. You let your attacking infantry take the line, then you can go in, you see, because you can't defend yourself with a Lewis-gun. So we were in the second line, or what there was of us. I lost all my lot. I can still hear the bullets zipping up, like a lot of bees and tufts of dirt, thrown up in front of you where the Jerries were shooting. You could see them going zzzp . . . zzzp, like a lot of bees.

Sergeant Jack Cross, No. 4842, C Coy., 13th (S) Btn., The Rifle Brigade

We impressed upon the chaps in the platoon, 'Don't stick together, don't bunch. Keep apart. If you bunch up they'll pick you off like rabbits.' I was on the left of my platoon on one side of the tramway and Sergeant Laney was on *my* left on the other side, because he was the right man of No. 11 Platoon. It was only about a hundred yards, or maybe a hundred and fifty yards in front of us, the first German trench, and we'd got to go straight ahead and capture that position. The whistle went and away they went. As soon as they did you could hear the bullets whistling. I yelled at Laney, 'Look at that lot going through there!' There was a gap in the wire and the platoon in front of us converged on it and into the gap. They went down, just like that! I should think every man was mortally wounded.

Corporal Joe Hoyles, MM, No. 3237, 13th (S) Btn., The Rifle Brigade

I always remember saying to my section, 'Come on Rifle Brigade! The first time Over the Top. Here we go!' And off we went. We were in the first wave, and our platoon officer, Fitzgibbon, was away out in front of us. They just mowed us down! People were falling on your right and your left and of course you had to keep going forward.

Rifleman Ed McGrath, D Coy., 13th (S) Btn., The Rifle Brigade

We hadn't gone very far and our section got less and less until there were only two of us left. I remember calling to the chap I was with, 'I think we're the only ones who are going to get through this lot!' Then I got a jolt in my thigh and my leg came up and hit me in the face. It literally hit me in the face! Down I went!

Rifleman George Murrell, B Coy., 13th (S) Btn., The Rifle Brigade

There was no artillery barrage and so every sniper and machine-gunner had a marvellous target as we advanced in short rushes. I was so laden that I had difficulty in keeping up and I must have made a good single target at times. But all the time I tried to keep up with my brother. Then he went down beside me and I yelled, 'What's the matter? Are you hit?' And he looked up at me, in an absolute fury, and shouted, 'No! I'm picking daisies, you bloody fool!' We had to go on. You couldn't stop for a wounded man – even if it was your own brother! I carried on about thirty yards or so and then suddenly my legs went from under me. I hadn't felt anything. I thought I'd stumbled into a shell-hole. Then I found that my left leg was quite useless. I couldn't move! In the meantime the advance had continued.

Murrell was not alone in noticing that there was no artillery barrage. Pretor-Pinney noticed it too. It had not worried him that there had been no preliminary gunfire, for the attack had been mounted hastily. But the orders which had reached him at eight o'clock had stated clearly that the guns would support the troops as they went across, that the 13th Royal Fusiliers would come up, straight away behind them, that the 23rd and

25th Divisions would be attacking to the left and to the right of them. Now, dodging the bullets, seeing his Battalion falling all around him, even with the hammering of the machine-guns and the cries and the noise of the fight, Pretor-Pinney was not so deafened that he could fail to observe that they had no supporting barrage. Nor was there a barrage to the left or to the right of his Battalion where the other troops should have been attacking. Furthermore, as he glanced anxiously behind him from his position in the last wave, he could see none of the Royal Fusiliers who should have been following on their heels coming up to support them.

There were no troops advancing to support them. There were no troops advancing simultaneously on left and right. In the evening sunlight, the Battalion was advancing alone against the full strength of a triple line of German trenches. This was the long-awaited moment; the climax of the last two years; the first real trial of strength; the first time 'Over the Top'.

In all the rhetoric of the war, like the words dauntless, dogged and gallant, 'at all costs' was an oft-repeated phrase that rang through every report, every Communiqué, every citation, every tale of heroic adventure and misadventure, every celebration of success, every letter of condolence, every justification of failure.

Now, The Rifle Brigade were determined, 'at all costs', to capture the lethal stretch of line. The Germans were equally determined 'at all costs' to hold on to it.

Even without support they made it. Even though men were falling at every step, the survivors kept on. They took the first German line. They bombed and battled their way into the second. With superhuman effort, through a maelstrom of bullets whistling down the hill from the line in front of Pozières, a small force had even got into the strongpoint in the third German line. It appeared on the map as a 'strongpoint' – but, in reality, it was a fort constructed around a small chalk quarry halfway down a sunken track that linked the road from la Boisselle to Contalmaison with the road from Albert to Bapaume. The sunken lane was now a trench, lined with concrete pillboxes. The 'chalk pit' was riddled with dugouts. From its lip machine-guns were firing at pointblank range. They were firing at Tom Jolly and a handful of 13 Platoon as they bombed their way towards it.

It was just about this time that the runner caught up with Colonel Pretor-Pinney as he stopped in a shell-hole to take stock of the situation and to watch as the flurry of fighting intensified around the chalk pit a couple of hundred yards ahead. The runner had only breath enough to gasp, 'Attack cancelled, sir.' And in bleak confirmation he thrust the written message into the Colonel's hand. It had been sent out from Divisional Headquarters, and passed on in good time by Brigade. It had reached the artillery in time to prevent them firing the barrage. It had reached the 23rd Division, which had been preparing to attack on the right. It had reached the 25th Division on the left. It had reached the 13th Royal Fusiliers, in time enough to stop them moving forward in the second wave. Now, belatedly, it had reached the 13th Rifle Brigade.

There was no means of signalling to the men who were already fighting in the German trenches. No flags could be waved without signing the death warrant of the man who waved them. Nobody, in any event, would be looking back for such a signal. No whistle, no bugle, no shout or warning could possibly be heard. Nothing could be done but to send more runners forward, to get word to the boys and to tell those who were still fighting to get out and come back.

Corporal Bob Thompson, Lewis-gunner, No. 2756, D Coy., 13th (S) Btn., The Rifle Brigade

There weren't over-many of us there in the third German trench. I'd lost my Lewis-gunner somewhere or other, and I was on my own for ten minutes or a quarter of an hour and then I picked up another Lewis-gunner. We all knew that, once you occupy a trench, you have to set up a post to consolidate it and defend it in case the Jerry attacks again. Well, we were looking round for a place to plant our gun over the Jerries' side of the trench and, walking round it, I found a Jerry who was wounded sitting on the ground. As we walked up to him very carefully, with a bayonet at the ready to stab him if he started being naughty, he looked up and he said, 'Water, Tommy, water.'

He was badly wounded. What could you do but give him water? So, I slung my rifle and told the other chap to keep watch, and I took my bottle and gave him a drop of water. And then, when he'd drunk it, in a very strange manner – he hadn't got a steel helmet, they had little round hats – he took his little blue hat off and he handed it to me and, in good English, he said, 'Lucky souvenir, you, Tommy.' And he died. Just died, there and then. I was glad I'd given him the water. I stuck the hat in my pocket and forgot all about it. We'd found a place and started setting the Lewis-gun up when Sergeant Holford came running across along the trench beneath us and he shouted, 'The thing's cancelled! We've got to make our way back.'

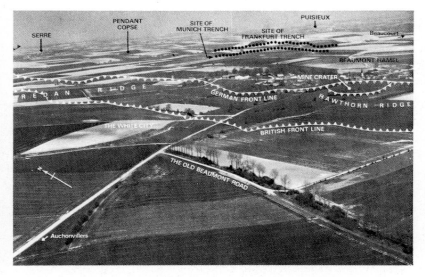

The valley in front of Beaumont Hamel from which British troops attacked on the First of July.

The old trench-lines can still be seen as chalk-marks on the ground. Here on the Thiepval plateau the German line took a sharp turn to run down to the valley of the Ancre and up beyond it to stand guard in front of Beaumont Hamel.

In the fields between Hébuterne village and Gommecourt Territorials of the 56th Division were decimated by shell-fire as they struggled to cross the land to the right of the village to reach the remnants of their first waves, cut off on the high ground beyond. The scars of the intense shelling can still be seen in the foreground. The tip of the wood was the westernmost point of the Germans' trench-line in France. It was known as the Kaiser's Oak.

In front of the British jumping-off line which can still be discerned running across the top corner of the ploughed field on the right and continuing to the edge of the copse on the left, the boys of the Pals Battalions, unprotected by the British barrage for ten minutes before the assault, waited to attack the German line on top of the hill in front of Serre village.

A German's eye view, shot from the lip of the Hawthorn mine crater, of the ground from which the British attacked their line at Beaumont Hamel. Saps were dug right through to the sunken lane to the right of the monument and on the low escarpment of the White City there are many traces of the old tunnels and dugouts. Geoffrey Malins filmed the First of July attack from a position constructed for him by Royal Engineers. Its remains can still be seen where the escarpment runs down to the bend of the track to the left of the memorial to the Scots who eventually captured Beaumont Hamel in November, four and a half months later.

Fortress Thiepval. The complex of German and British front-line trenches in front of Thiepval village, now a small hamlet. The farm buildings to the right of the church are on the site of the old château. The rectangle which encloses them is the line of the original foundations. On the right is the vast Thiepval Memorial to the Missing which records the names of more than 72,000 men who died on the Somme and who have no known graves.

Looking from the German trench-line in front of the old château. The British line followed the edge of Thiepval Wood in the foreground, and ran in front of Hamel village up the slopes on the other side of the valley, facing the German line in front of Beaumont Hamel. On the extreme right of centre is the Ulster Tower, on the site of the 'Pope's Nose', which commemorates the 36th Ulster Division who attacked this sector on the First of July.

The present-day view to the right of old Thiepval village (shot from the Thiepval Memorial). The large mass of woodland on the opposite slope is Aveluy Wood; in the nearer centre is the village of Authuille. The British trenches ran across the slopes of Thiepval Ridge above the village and swung round along the edge of Nab Wood (*left centre*). The isolated clump of trees on the left surrounds the small quarry which was the nub of the German defence in the Leipzig Redoubt.

Rose Vaquette (Madame Glavieux) pointing to the spot where her father, Borro-mée, was shot on 27th September, 1914, coincidentally on the site where the Germans later constructed their Leipzig Redoubt. The swell in the ground, running from the indentation on the nearside verge of the track marks the front-line trench in its 'snout'. In the background the Thiepval Memorial to the Missing stands on the crest of the ridge.

The old well of Thiepval village still looks out across No Man's Land to the old British line round Thiepval Wood.

As this German photograph shows, the walls of Thiepval Château still stood, although ruined and battered, in 1915. It was snapped from the window of the church, which was likewise fairly intact, and the walled village pond in the left foreground still contains water.

A heap of stone in a farmyard – all that remains of the noble Thiepval Château above Thiepval Wood. Beyond it is the Mesnil Ridge and, on the left, the edge of Aveluy Wood.

Above: Thiepval village rebuilt, but a mere hamlet now. The farm in the foreground stands on the site of the old Thiepval Château and the foundations can still be traced. Opposite, in front of the new church the rough uncultivated corner of what is now a field is the site of the village pond. As it was communal property no one, presumably, has the right to use it.

Left: By the summer of 1915 the Germans had built a formidable network of well-constructed trenches like this one which was part of the Ovillers defences.

The Albert-Bapaume road separates the twin village of Ovillers and la Boisselle where the ground still bears witness to the magnitude of the German defences.

The formidable German line still reaches across the fields to the left of la Boisselle to the massive crater of the mine that breached it. Rising from the village the road runs over the Tara and Usna hills on its way to Albert. The village in the distance is Aveluy.

Above left: Boromée Vaquette, the first man to die on the Thiepval Ridge, lies in the family plot, under a modern headstone, in Authuille village cemetery.

Above right: ' . . . the first one I saw were my chum, Clem Cunnington. I don't think we'd gone twenty yards when he got hit straight through the breast. Machine gun bullets.' *Private Ernest Deighton*

Clem Cunnington's grave in Ovillers Military Cemetery.

Below left: Reg Parker (*on left*) with two comrades of the Sheffield Pals. He took the water cart up to the Battalion in the trenches at Serre on the night of the First of July but failed to find his brother Willie who had gone 'over the top' that morning.

Below right: Reg Parker's brother Willie who fought his way out of his 'reserved occupation' job as an engineer to rejoin the ranks of the Sheffield Pals in time to go over the top with them at Serre on the First of July. He was killed in the first wave of the attack.

A view of the still-visible trench-lines to the left of Contalmaison attacked alone by the 13th Rifle Brigade on the evening of 10th July. The chalk-pit in the centre of the photograph was in the 3rd German line. After word reached them that the abortive attack was cancelled more than half the battalion was wiped out by shell-fire as they struggled to get back across the land in the foreground of the photograph.

The road from la Boisselle to Contalmaison, just to the right of where the 13th Rifle Brigade made their unsupported attack on 10th July.

There are still traces in the foreground of the line that formed the Fricourt Salient.
Beyond it the line swung east and from the slopes above Fricourt in the top-right of
the photograph the British attacked almost straight ahead to capture the villages of
Mametz and Montauban.

Contalmaison Château in 1917, a year after its capture.

Right: Entrance to a (possibly British) dugout, one of a line in a sunken road near Contalmaison.

Below: Reserve trenches on the Somme.

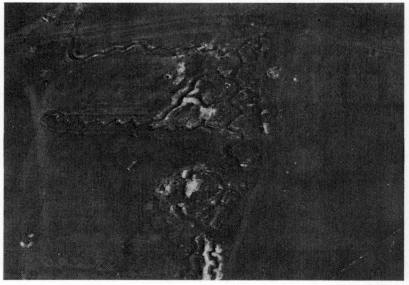

The ground attacked on 14th and 15th July, with the two stumbling blocks of High Wood and Delville Wood.

As Forward Observation Officer Fred Beadle lost his way and turned up this German communication trench to the right of the Crucifix Corner. To his horror he found that it was leading him straight to the enemy line at High Wood.

On the left are the remains of the windmill which concealed a deep dugout. It was from here that astonished British officers were able to look across the waving corn to High Wood and, exploring further, found it empty.

From the windmill above Crucifix Corner, Bazentin, looking across to Longueval and Delville Wood. Although there was still fierce fighting and shelling at Longueval the cavalry galloped across this open country to make their abortive attack on High Wood witnessed by Fred Beadle. The long clump of trees above the remains of the windmill in the foreground is the approximate site of the German communication trench in which Fred Beadle accidentally found himself.

Part of Ethel Bath's letter.

when I tell you he was only out 16 days in all, and he was attached to the Middlesex Regt on the Friday & sent into the trenches the same afternoon and attacked on the Sat at 2-30 in the afternoon, when he was killed, it all seems to quick to give them a chance. Forgive this long letter but it helps one to bear there sorrow to be able to write of it

from

Yours sincerely

Ethel Bath

2nd Lieutenant Reginald Bath, killed in action in Leuze Wood.

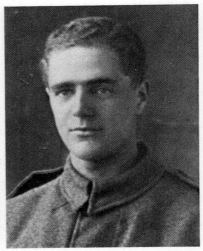

Bill Turner of the 15th Highland Light Infantry with his girl-friend Maggie Gaffney. They were photographed together two days before he was to leave for France – but he was hauled off the train at the last minute when his mother revealed that he was under age.

Above right: Jack Beament of the Church Lads Brigade.

Some of the Church Lads of the 16th Battalion, Kings Royal Rifle Corps. Jack Beament (*second from left, middle row*) and Jack Brown (*fourth from right, back row*) later crawled together out of the debacle at High Wood.

Corporal Joe Hoyles, MM, No. 3237, 13th (S) Btn., The Rifle Brigade

Every officer was wounded or killed. We only had one officer left, Captain Reviere, and he shouted across to me, 'Corporal, gather some men together and capture that machine-gun post that's doing the damage.' We went up this German communication trench and we found this machine-gun. There were only about six of us left in the section and I went ahead and, when I saw the Boche there round the corner, I said, 'Right, lads! Get rid of your bombs!' And over went the bombs! We killed those poor chaps. We captured one prisoner alive. I sent him back, and, just with that, we had the order to retire. It was about ten o'clock by then. Just getting dusk – and after all that massacre, after we'd taken the trenches, we had to retire.

Sergeant Jack Cross, No. 4842, 13th (S) Btn., The Rifle Brigade

How these bullets were whistling! I can still hear them! Now and again a shrapnel shell would burst in the air and these bits of shrapnel showered down, hitting the mud and going flop, flap, flip over the mud. Laney went down. Then he got up and off he went again, and I was going on with him when, suddenly, I got hit and it lifted me up in the air and dropped me flat on my face, just like you see in cowboy films. It knocked me out. I fell down flat on the grass and I stuck my head forward and tipped my steel helmet to the front. I thought, 'I'll hold that on there, and then I won't get one through the napper.' Suddenly, the firing ceased and the machine-guns stopped spluttering just for a moment. I hopped up, doubled back and dived into this shell-hole. I knew I'd just passed one, and as I dived into it my leg came up in the air and I felt a sting in the calf of the leg and I'd got a bullet there as well.

I turned myself round, and faced the enemy and got my head down into the shell-hole and somehow I wiggled my entrenching tool out of the back of my belt and I scratched a hole so I could get deeper down and get the side high between me and the bullets and they still kept singing round the top of this earth around me. After a while, everything went quiet, so I thought, 'This is it, Jack. Now you make your way back to that dressing station – if you can!' And I started crawling back.

Rifleman George Murrell, 13th (S) Btn., The Rifle Brigade

I lay there for a long time. For a while I could hear the Lewis-gun firing in front of me, but the Number One couldn't have had more than one drum of ammunition, because I knew all the rest of the section had been wounded and they'd been carrying the spare drums. When it stopped, I didn't know what had happened. I thought maybe it had only run out of ammunition because the Jerries' guns were still going. But then the remains of the Battalion began to come back past me. One of them stopped to see how I was and he told me it was all over. He couldn't help me. He was a little chap and he was wounded in both arms. After a while it got dark and, although I could hear voices, I didn't know whether they were friends or enemies. So, I just had to stop there.

As the wounded lay waiting for rescue or waiting for dusk to cover the long crawl back and, as the survivors were leaving the captured lines to get back as best they could to their own, the barrage started up. It was fired by the British guns and it was a devastating barrage.

It was not the fault of the artillery. They had been notified in good time about the cancellation of the attack and, as no news had reached them to the contrary, they had no reason to think that it had gone ahead. The guns were firing in response to an SOS signal from troops in Contalmaison. Seeing the affray in the trenches above them to their left, they had assumed that the Germans were about to counter-attack the village from that direction. The guns, trying to balk the counter-attack before it could get going, registered with uncanny accuracy on the trenches the Rifle Brigade had just attacked and also on the ground beyond, where the remnants of the Battalion were struggling to make their way back. Despite the awful losses on the way across, it was under their own bombardment that the 13th Rifle Brigade died, as a battalion, on the way back.

It was dark when the barrage lifted and in the terrible silence that followed those who remained alive and could still move, dragged themselves back to the line.

A little later, the shaken Germans sent a reserve company forward. They trickled down the hill from Pozières to rescue their wounded, to remove their dead and to file back into their empty line to the left of Contalmaison.

The 13th Battalion's own Medical Officer had been killed and, in the nightmare conditions at the Field Dressing Station – a dugout in a deep cutting on the side of the road to la Boisselle – it was impossible to give more than cursory first aid to the wounded. It was not even possible to crowd more than a tenth of them into shelter and so they lay, waiting to be carried back, in the open roadway, sprayed from time to time with bullets from a German machine-gun, firing along the road on fixed sights. It was not a pleasant experience. But they were the lucky ones. They were not so lucky as the men who had escaped uninjured, now gathered in small exhausted groups in the support trenches, but luckier by far than the wounded men who still lay painfully out in front, with little hope of rescue. 'Old Chelsea' was there, and there he would stay for five days and five nights until he was picked up – still alive – when the line advanced.

Ed McGrath lay out for a whole week. Ted Murrell was in, but his brother George was still out. For three days he would be crawling between the lines, dragging his useless left leg, unsure of his direction, until, on the 13th, by a happy chance, he struck the outlying trench of a neighbouring unit.

Company Sergeant-Major Croucher was back, but only because he had been brought in by his sworn enemy, Welch, the most disreputable man in his company whom the Sergeant-Major had personally put on many charges. Inadvertently firing off his rifle on parade while drunk was the most serious of a whole catalogue of Welch's misdemeanours and the very sight of him had been enough to send Croucher into a fury. Now, Welch was at the Field Dressing Station with Croucher on his back, demanding that he should have attention and refusing to take no for an answer. He personally saw to it that the Sergeant-Major was the first casualty to travel down the line. Thompson had followed and, sometime during the night, so had Jack Cross, Weeber and Monckton, among a hundred or so others. Colonel Pretor-Pinney, his left arm mangled by machine-gun bullets, was the last to go.

Most of the officers had been killed, among them all four Company Commanders. Horace Smith kept seeing them in his mind, conferring together in one shell-hole, after the order to retire had reached them. He had also seen the explosion that wiped them out. When the small force of survivors took stock in the morning, there was no sign of the Platoon Commanders. Lieutenant Reviere was the only officer in sight – apart from the Second-in-Command, Major Sir Foster Cunliffe. They would not have seen him had he not tied a handkerchief to his swagger-stick. Now he was waving it above the shell-hole where he lay far out in No Man's Land, close to the German front line. Looking through binoculars, they could easily identify him for the shell-hole, steep on the German side, was shallow where it faced the British.

Fred Lyon and Joe Hoyles stood side by side looking across and Lyon muttered, 'There'll be a VC for whoever brings him in.'

It was broad daylight now. It would be certain death to go back alone. Hoyles was almost too exhausted to shake his head. 'I've had enough, Fred. Enough.' Like Lyon, like Jolly, like Thompson, like Smith, he had got right up to the third line and he had even gone back to it, just before the Germans reoccupied the trench, to rescue his badly wounded officer, Lieutenant Fitzgibbon. Hoyles was not interested in winning the Victoria Cross. He was even a little surprised, when they came out of the trenches, to find that he had been recommended for the Military Medal.

Arthur Wright, burglar, reprobate and King of the Crown and Anchor Board, who had gone out three times to bring in wounded comrades, had earned one too. So had eight others.

Gradually, over the next few days, what was left of the Battalion moved back by stages to the trenches behind the Tara-Usna Ridge. It was just ten days since they had marched into them on their way up the line.

Sergeant Howard Rowlands had gone up with the boys, but almost immediately he had been ordered back again to Albert to join Head-quarters Detail as orderly sergeant. He had spent an anxious ten days. No one at Headquarters knew quite what had happened 'up there' – only that there had been some kind of mess. After a scratch roll-call, all that could be done in the trenches was write the ominous letter 'M' after most of the names. 'M' stood for 'missing'.

Brown . . . *Missing*. Smith . . . *Missing*. Jones . . . *Missing*. Robinson . . . *Missing*. The dreary litany carried on through three hundred names, or more – for no one knew, in the confusion of the aftermath, who was alive, who was dead, who had been wounded and evacuated and who was still lying or dying out in the horrid scrubland that lay between the Battalion and the German line. It would be many weeks before the battlefield could be cleared and bodies – or those that had not been blown out of existence – could be identified and buried. It would be weeks before the names of the wounded, so hastily evacuated, would appear on the returns of clearing stations close to the front, of hospitals at the coastal base and even across the Channel at home.

In the meantime, Howard Rowlands took it upon himself to find out what he could. From morning until night, on foot, near the line and, further afield, on a borrowed bicycle, he scoured every aid post, every dressing station, every casualty clearing station, not once but many times, asking the same questions. 'Any 13th Rifle Brigade here?' 'Any 13th Rifle Brigade been here?' 'Any 13th Rifle Brigade burials here?'

Even the unofficial list that Rowlands was able to compile appalled him. And it appalled Colonel Pretor-Pinney. Rowlands had found the

CO after four days, still in the big dressing station outside Albert, and too ill to be moved. It shook Rowlands, as nothing else had, to see his stiff and disciplined Commanding Officer in tears; to hear him say, over and over again, 'What a mess they've made of my Battalion! What a *mess* they've made of my Battalion.'

On 19 July, the Battalion marched back to Albert, and stopped there for the night. When they marched out again on the road to Bresle, they looked – at least in numbers – something like a battalion, for a large draft of new men had met them in Albert and had been hastily grafted on to the ranks. A new Commanding Officer rode in front of them. Colonel Prideaux-Brune showed his mettle during the march. It was the front ranks who heard him. As they were approaching a village, Keene, who, since his predecessor was 'missing', was now acting-Regimental Sergeant-Major, passed the order: *March to Attention*. Prideaux-Brune put a stop to that with an impatient wave of his hand. 'Cut it out, Sergeant-Major! And the men can smoke if they like.' The Battalion appreciated that.

The road back to Bresle seemed considerably longer than it had seemed eleven days before on the way to the line. But then they had been singing and no one was singing now. Even the men of the new draft were silent and half-embarrassed. But the Battalion stuck it out. They only broke when they got to Bresle. The Colonel had to allow the Sergeant-Major to march the men to attention, for the Divisional Band had paid them the courtesy of turning out to meet them, and it was only good form to 'put on a show'. The band struck up what must have been felt, in all innocence, to be an appropriate tune, and played it in quick time to keep pace with the Riflemen's brisk ceremonial march. The tune was all the rage, and, from a hundred sing-songs, the boys all knew the words.

> *Here we are! Here we are! Here we are again!*
> *There's Pat and Mac and Tommy and Jack and Joe.*
> *When there's trouble brewing –*
> *When there's something doing –*
> *Are we downhearted? NO! Let 'em all come!*
> *Here we are! Here we are! Here we are again!*
> *We're fit and well, and feeling as right as rain.*
> *Never mind the weather.*
> *Now then, all together,*
> *HULLO! HULLO! HERE WE ARE AGAIN!*

Percy Eaton, the only one of the 'South African Mob' who had returned unscathed, found that tears were gushing from his eyes. As they were still marching to attention, they had to gush unchecked. He was not the only one. Not many of the boys had yet reached their twenty-second birthday and it was all a little too much for them.

Part 3

'High Wood to Waterlot Farm, All on a summer's day'

High Wood to Waterlot Farm,
All on a summer's day,
Up you get to the top of the trench
Though you're sniped at all the way.
If you've got a smoke helmet there
You'd best put it on if you could,
For the wood down by Waterlot Farm
Is a bloody high wood.

E. A. MACKINTOSH, August 1916.
(written as a parody of
Chalk Farm to Camberwell Green)

Chapter 12

It was 14 July and neither the Battle of the Somme, neither the struggle still raging at Verdun, nor even the war itself was sufficient reason to deflect the French from celebration of their national day. Before the war, in towns and villages all over France, local bands had turned out, there had been picnics, merrymaking, much toasting of the Republic and, weather permitting, dancing in the streets. Now, in addition to the traditional celebrations, there were military parades, medals were presented, local heroes were fêted and a fever of patriotism added point and poignancy to the occasion. France, always quick to rouse herself to a pitch of nationalistic fervour, had more reason than ever to do so. The French were united in a common hatred of the German invader who had jack-booted across the frontier, just as he had done less than fifty years before, and they were united in their intention of kicking him back where he belonged. So, Bastille Day this year – the second since the war began – had taken on a greater and deeper significance than ever before. In Paris, parades marched down the Champs Elysées, cheered on by crowds who reserved their loudest cheers for the contingents of marching *poilus*, many of them veterans of Verdun, who obliged them, when the parade was over, by peeling off and allowing themselves to be marched into cafés by enthusiastic bystanders, who were only too anxious to buy them drinks and to join them in toasting France and Victory.

More sedate, but no less fervent, toasts were drunk at official ceremonies and receptions at the Hôtel de Ville and also at the Elysée Palace, where the President of the Republic received a large company in which military dignitaries almost outnumbered civilians. There was, after all, something to celebrate. If the Germans had not yet been defeated at Verdun, their defeat, it seemed to its stalwart defenders, was only a matter of time. There was the victory on the Somme, where the French Army had advanced gloriously through the German lines and, so some thought privately, would have advanced a good deal further, had it not been for the less magnificent performance of the British Army beyond their immediate left. But, before the end of the President's reception, Lord Esher was able to give him news which he had just received at first hand by telephone from GHQ. In a series of dawn attacks on a wide front, the British had broken through to the Germans' second line.

But, whatever satisfaction Lord Esher may have felt in conveying such gratifying tidings to President Poincaré in Paris, it was nothing to the satisfaction with which the British on the Somme battlefront itself were able to inform the neighbouring French Army that their attack had succeeded. The French, and in particular General Balfourier, had been bitterly opposed to the whole idea of a night manoeuvre, involving some thousands of troops – and inexperienced troops at that. In their view it was madness to contemplate such a thing and they had forcibly made the point. The sheer assembly of such a force behind the battle-line in darkness, the very idea of sending them stumbling through the night to attack the enemy line, was unutterably foolish. To expect them to make a considerable advance, to capture the bulwark of the Germans' second-line position at a single bound, was insanity. Failure would be inevitable and, in the confusion of the aftermath, the whole front would be left wide open and vulnerable to a German counter-attack. The French feared that the enemy might even be able to seize back most of the ground he had lost and wipe out the gains which the infantry had won, inch by slogging inch, in the first two weeks of July. Furthermore, such a failure would leave the French flank on the right of the British dangerously exposed.

General Balfourier was an advocate of classic warfare. He was a soldier of the old school. He had seen no need to modernize his uniform from the style of the attire in which he had graduated from the military college at St Cyr some forty years earlier. In his high-necked blue coat and wide red trousers, looking much as he might have looked had he been a general in the army of Napoleon III halfway through the reign of Queen Victoria, he had shaken his grizzled head in doubt and consternation and, via his liaison officer, Captain Spears, he had sent repeated messages, begging the British to reconsider.

Captain Spears, weary of fruitless discussions on the same subject, weary of pressing General Balfourier's case with the passion felt by the General himself, weary of bearing back a succession of diplomatic but repetitious replies, returned on the evening of 13 July, having received Fourth Army's last word on the matter from the lips of Major-General Montgomery. 'Tell General Balfourier, with my compliments, that, if we are not on the Longueval Ridge at eight tomorrow morning, I will eat my hat.' Like Captain Spears, Major-General Montgomery had had enough, but, although he had not intended Captain Spears to repeat the message verbatim, the general jubilation at Fourth Army Headquarters was enhanced by much amusement when General Balfourier telephoned through, with Bastille Day bonhomie, to congratulate Major-General Montgomery on having avoided the unfortunate necessity of making such an indigestible breakfast.

General Haig had also telephoned his congratulations early in the morning and they were particularly appreciated by Sir Henry Rawlinson for, as he well knew, Haig had shared the misgivings of General Balfourier and he had made his feelings on the matter very clear. They had come as close to altercation as urbanity and military etiquette would allow and, in the end, Rawlinson had had to insist on going ahead with his plan. Now he had been vindicated, and vindicated triumphantly.

This time there had been no long preliminary bombardment to warn the enemy that the troops were coming. This time there had been no long lines of soldiers advancing in brilliant daylight. The troops had assembled in darkness. Five minutes of brisk and violent bombardment had been sufficient to get the Germans' heads down and send them to their dugouts and, almost before they had time to realize that it had ceased, before the dawn was more than a grey hint in the sky behind their trenchline, the attack was upon them and on a front of more than three miles the German second line was overwhelmed by Kitchener's Army.

Taking off from the northern edge of Mametz Wood, wrested at terrible cost from the enemy's hands, the troops had wheeled east and captured the woods that protected the villages of Bazentin le Grand and Bazentin le Petit in as many hours as it had taken days to capture Mametz Wood. Launching forward into the mangled remains of Trones Wood, they had driven the Germans out of it and carried on to capture most of the village of Longueval in the shadow of Delville Wood and had even penetrated a little way into the wood itself. Now was the moment to press on, and that, as the 7th Division put it to Fourth Army Headquarters, was precisely what they wished to do.

The village of Bazentin le Petit was easily cleared. By nine o'clock, all was quiet. Ominously quiet. In the shelter of the sloping ground – hardly worthy of being called a ridge – which rose beyond a valley on the eastern edge of the village, headquarters had been set up in the village cemetery and in the little quarry which lay conveniently beside it. Quickly, and for once unimpeded by shellfire, cables were run down and communications established. Soldiers filtered down from the village to assemble in the valley while, behind them, Royal Engineers set to work immediately to consolidate the captured line. Officers conferred. Patrols were cautiously sent forward to reconnoitre whatever might lie on the other side of the hill. They brought back astonishing reports. There was not a German to be seen. The commanders decided to look for themselves. General Potter of the 9th Brigade of the 3rd Division, with Lieutenant-Colonel Elliott

and Major-General Watts, Commander of the 7th Division, were not so
foolhardy as to expose themselves by walking along the track at the top
of the slope but, hugging the shelter immediately below, clambered along
to the ruined windmill, a hundred yards or so to the right. Beneath the
jagged outcrop of its rubble, the Germans had constructed a strongpoint
with a dugout running deep down, but it had been hastily vacated and
was as still and empty as the scene that met their eyes as they squinted
across from the shelter of the ruin. They were looking across the gentlest
of valleys, where the ridge on which they stood sloped down to a hollow
and rose almost imperceptibly to the dark mass of High Wood itself, less
than a thousand yards from where they stood, gazing incredulously across
fields of waving corn. Here, behind the Germans' second line, where the
seed corn had dropped from ears heavy with grain in the quiet autumn
of 1915, the unhusbanded crop of 1916 was growing thick and lush and
ripening fast. Some had already been prematurely harvested by the guns
and, only hours before, broad tracks had been trampled through it when
the Germans had beaten their hasty retreat from Bazentin to the shelter
of High Wood. But there were great patches, still untouched, still standing
yellow and rich, and, where the earth had been tumbled by shellfire, red
poppies shone through the standing corn. Off to the right, shells were
screaming on to Longueval village and Delville Wood, the smoke of
battle hung thick in the air, but ahead all was quiet. Nothing stirred in
the cornfields. High Wood was silent.

The officers grew bolder. Tentatively at first, and then, with rising
confidence, they walked down to the little valley, stopped prudently
halfway across in the concealment of a low chalk bank and, peering
through binoculars, surveyed the land ahead. Then they crossed the cornfield almost to the edge of High Wood. Not a shot was fired. High Wood
was empty.

Jubilant, excited, and anxious to push ahead, they almost ran back to
the line. The troops were fresh and ready to go, General Watts had a
brigade of fresh troops in reserve and he could get all four battalions
across within the hour, with more ready to follow.

Fifteenth Corps Headquarters – although congratulatory – was not
impressed with his plan. They had a plan of their own, or rather, GHQ
had a plan, and Thirteen Corps had no choice but to fall in with it. If
they were correct in the belief that the enemy had retired, it would be
pointless to send the infantry forward to take possession of the wood. An
infantryman can move only as fast as his feet will carry him; a cavalryman
can move as fast as his horse, and therefore they must wait for the cavalry
– the fast-moving mobile arm which could exploit the breakthrough and,
who knows, with the infantry behind them, could speed through High

Wood, fan out to Martinpuich, and gallop through le Sars to the very
gates of Bapaume. It was a chance too good to be missed and it was the
chance that both Rawlinson and Haig had been waiting for.

It was unfortunate that the cavalry did not arrive until five o'clock in
the evening. For two weeks now they had been ready, waiting and eager
to go – but the Indian Cavalry, which had been earmarked for the job
of pushing through in this locality, if the opportunity arose, was waiting
at Morlancourt, and Morlancourt, four miles south of Albert, was separated from High Wood by many miles of shell-battered ground. It took
the cavalrymen a long time to negotiate it. They had started to move
forward not long after eight o'clock in the morning, and by midday they
should have been at Carnoy, just behind the old front line of 1 July, a
good seven kilometres from High Wood but with a clear run towards it
from the left of Montauban. By a quarter-past twelve, although the fight
still raged a mile away at Longueval, High Wood and the valley beyond
still lay tranquil under the hot noon sun.

At Fourth Army Headquarters there were anxious conferences. In the
absence of the cavalry, should the 7th Division be sent forward to occupy
the wood? Yes. The order was issued and almost immediately cancelled
in the light of new information that Longueval village had not been
completely captured. Now the cavalry was reported to be arriving in the
Carnoy valley, but would it not be dangerous to send them forward on
a great gallop across open country towards High Wood when they would
have to pass between Longueval and Bazentin le Grand? It was unfortunate
that early reports had been misleading and that it now appeared that part
of the wood north of the village was still holding out. Could they commit
the cavalry, fast moving though it was, to pass between the Scylla and
Charybdis of two embattled points where the enemy was acting in a
manner that was very far from tranquil and where the situation was not,
as yet, fully understood? It was decided to hold the cavalry back and to
wait.

Like the calm epicentre of a whirlpool, the corn in front of High Wood
waved on throughout the long afternoon.

Slowly, cautiously, unable to believe their good fortune, the Germans
filtered back into High Wood and took up defensive positions, and snipers
and machine-gunners crawled out in front to lie low among the thick
corn, on the *qui vive*, for the first hint of attack.

It had been such a day of confusion, of orders and counter-orders, of
brilliant successes and partial reverses, that in the hasty issuing of last-
minute orders it was not entirely surprising that some failed to reach the
units concerned. The 33rd Division arrived in the area at two o'clock in

the afternoon when the situation was at its most muddled and were happily ensconced in the devastated valley at Fricourt, a good seven kilometres away, and they were resting before moving up to the front line early in the evening. The only orders their Divisional General had yet received were that they were to attack through the 21st Division the following day and to consolidate the line beyond High Wood after the cavalry had swept across it and put its German garrison to rout.

For the infantry, there was time enough to rest for a bit, but their guns were already moving forward up the newly constructed plank road to positions less than a thousand yards behind the new front line. Ahead of them went Second Lieutenant Fred Beadle. As Forward Observation Officer in the Divisional Artillery, his job was to survey the ground and to assess the target so that the guns might be ranged and registered for the barrage that would usher the infantry across. Accompanied by a signaller to send back information to the battery, he went up through the battlefield. It was a long trek over unfamiliar ground. Even a map was not much of a help and in a maze of captured trenches it was not surprising that they lost direction. Where two half-obliterated tracks met at Crucifix Corner they took the wrong road, and, instead of leading to the forward observation post in the British line, the old German communication trench led directly to the corner of High Wood. It also led, late in the afternoon, to Fred Beadle's first encounter, face to face, with the enemy, for the Germans were reconnoitring, and one man well out in front of the patrol was creeping down from High Wood as stealthily as Fred Beadle and his signaller were creeping towards it in the opposite direction.

2nd Lieutenant F. W. Beadle, Royal Artillery, 159th Brigade, 33rd Division

I had no idea that we were so near the Germans, but the mass of trenches there were so involved that we had the utmost difficulty and really were simply taking a chance. There was a terrific noise going on with shellfire and it seemed to me extraordinary that this trench was more or less abandoned. We were being very cautious as we went and I had my revolver at the ready – ready for trouble! Then, as we turned the corner of one of the traverses of the trench, there, approaching me, was a German soldier armed with a rifle. The extraordinary thing was that he had his rifle slung on his shoulder and the other odd thing was that he was wearing an overcoat and this was July, although it had been showery.

He saw me at exactly the same time as I saw him and he raised his rifle, but he must have been impeded by this overcoat because he couldn't get it up to his shoulder quick enough. I knew jolly well that if he had I should have caught it. It was either him or me. It was the first time I'd ever fired my revolver in anger, so to speak. The first time I'd ever seen a German soldier, apart from prisoners. I killed him with one shot.

I felt nothing. All I felt was relief. I knew I had no option, but I didn't stop to think of the morality. It was either him or me. Afterwards, I often wondered who he was and where he'd come from and whether he was married and whether he had any family. I've thought about that very often but, at the time, I didn't think of anything except where on earth were we, and where on earth was the infantry we were supposed to contact?

It seemed incredible that the German had been on his own. But his companions, if he had had any, alerted by the shots in front, had beaten a hasty retreat. Five long minutes passed. Resisting the temptation to scuttle back down the trench, Beadle carefully raised himself above the parapet and looked across. He saw with horror that he had brought his signaller more than two-thirds of the way across the valley to within three hundred yards of High Wood, and as he looked he saw the cavalry galloping into action. They were the Deccan Horse, and the 7th Dragoon Guards, and, far across the valley, the infantry were moving towards the northern corner of High Wood to support them.

It was seven in the evening, and the British were attacking more than twelve hours after the Germans had been driven back across the meadows and cornfields to the shelter of High Wood.

2nd Lieutenant F. W. Beadle, Royal Artillery, 159th Brigade, 33rd Division

It was an incredible sight, an unbelievable sight, they galloped up with their lances and with pennants flying, up the slope to High Wood and straight into it. Of course they were falling all the way because the infantry were attacking on the other side of the valley furthest away from us, and the cavalry were attacking very near to where we were. So the German machine-guns were going for the infantry and the shells were falling all over the place. I've never seen anything like it! They simply galloped on through all that and horses and men dropping on the ground, with no hope against the machine-guns, because the Germans up on the ridge were firing down into the valley where the soldiers were. It was an absolute rout. A magnificent sight. Tragic.

The cavalry had advanced in classic historic style with lances glistening in the sun. They entered High Wood. They killed a number of infantry and machine-gunners in the crops in front of it, and killed them with the lance. They captured thirty-two prisoners. When darkness fell they lined the road between Longueval and the corner of High Wood, and held this position through the night. Some must have wondered what had become of their comrades. The fact was that the two remaining cavalry brigades had never left the rendezvous and were now ordered to go 'back to bivouac'. The First and Third Cavalry Divisions waiting all day well south of Albert had received no order at all. The casualties that the cavalry inflicted on the Germans were precisely two less than the casualties they themselves had suffered. The troops were in High Wood – but only just, and now the Germans were answering back with all the fire power they could muster.

By seven o'clock the 33rd Division was in position at Bazentin with the 100th Brigade in front ready, according to the orders they had received, to 'attack through the 21st Division' on the following morning, and they were feeling distinctly uneasy now with the noise hammering from the other side of the slope and shells falling a great deal too close for comfort. At a quarter to eight, while Beadle and his shaken companion were scuttling back, this time in the right direction, Brigadier-General Baird, having seen his troops disposed and having made contact with the 21st Division, now received a nasty surprise. He visited the headquarters of the 91st Brigade in the 7th Divisional sector on his right and he was not greeted with open arms. It came as news to the Brigadier that the 7th Division had been told that his troops would be supporting them, that they had been expected to take part in the attack which was even now in progress and, not to put too fine a point upon it, where the hell had they been and where the hell were they now?

They were bivouacked along the western edge of the wood behind Bazentin le Petit, but they did not stay there for long. Baird had had enough of Army, enough of Corps and even enough of Division. He did not even trouble to refer to HQ for revised orders. There was no time to shilly-shally. On his own responsibility, he ordered two battalions of the 100th Brigade forward to hold the dangerous gap that now existed in the line between High Wood and Bazentin le Petit. So, on the right of the valley, the Glasgow Highlanders moved up into the communication trench so recently and hurriedly vacated by Fred Beadle and, on the left of the valley, the 1st Queen's took up a line along a sunken road. By midnight he had succeeded in moving both battalions into those positions. Only then, as an afterthought, he transmitted a brusque uncompromising message to Divisional Headquarters, informing them that he had done so. Darkness had fallen, the Germans were back in High Wood and all night the shelling and the fighting never abated.

The 16th Battalion of the King's Royal Rifle Corps, although part of the 100th Brigade, had remained behind and were glad of the respite of a night's comparative rest, even in the open air, even on the *qui vive*, even with the din of shelling in front of them at High Wood and away to the right at Longueval and Delville Wood. They were the 'Black Buttoned Bastards' of the 100th Brigade and were as proud as the Rifle Brigade of the traditions of their adopted regiment and of their quick step and rifleman's bearing. Like the 13th Rifle Brigade, the 16th King's Royal Rifle Corps were merely Riflemen 'for the duration' but this did not deter them from patronizing the Rifle Brigade in the well-founded knowledge that they were the senior regiment, nor from perpetuating the traditional rivalry between the regiments which, since 1858, had expressed itself in emotions ranging from friendly sparring to downright animosity. Even the Kitchener's Battalions of the Rifle Brigade had been quick to learn the taunting words that went with their regimental march, composed by some wag years before any of them had been born and they were quick to launch into it whenever they came within jibing distance of a battalion of The King's Royal Rifle Corps.

> The Rifle Brigade is going away
> To leave the girls in the family way.
> The KRRs are left behind,
> They've two and six a week to find.

This sentiment, with all its bawdy implications, and even the strong language of the term 'Black Buttoned Bastards' might reasonably have been expected to bring a blush to the cheeks of the 16th King's Royal Rifle Corps for they had been recruited from the ranks of the Church Lads Brigade. But such piety as they had harboured in the far-off days of peacetime had been well and truly knocked out of them during the two years they had spent in Kitchener's Army and, in particular, by the eight months almost to the day that they had been serving in France and in the trenches. This was a matter to which the Battalion's Padre had become resigned. It was many months now since he had gone looking for a party engaged in digging trenches behind the lines. He had come upon Jack Brown's platoon and announced, as he jumped down among these black sheep of his flock, 'I knew where you all were. I couldn't see you but I knew where you were from the language that was coming up. I knew it was the Church Lads Brigade and I've never heard anything like it in all my life.'

It was fortunate that the Padre had not been within earshot that afternoon at Fricourt. The Church Lads had marched eighteen kilometres to get there and their feet were killing them.

Corporal Jack Beament, MM, A Coy., 16th Btn., King's Royal Rifle Corps (Church Lads Brigade), 33rd Division

It was a terribly hot day and we'd only had ten minutes halt in each hour all the way up. Everywhere was devastated but we spotted a stream and we made for it. There was Jack Brown and old Billy Thompson and his pal Charlie Thompson from West Hartlepool and myself. Billy wasn't a very big chap but how he could swear! I always remember him, after that march taking off his equipment and taking off his boots and socks and swearing like hell. 'Those fucking, bloody bastards! Those bloody fucking bastards!' Between us we said more than a word or two, because it was so hot and we had full equipment and 120 rounds of ammunition to carry. I'll never forget the relief of it, coming to the edge of this stream and bathing my poor bloody feet. We weren't there long, and there was a bit *more* swearing when we were told to pick up our stuff again and march up the line. We regretted having taken our boots off, because it wasn't so easy to get them on again!

I shall never forget that scene as we went up the line. As we marched along there was a corpse of a soldier with no head plonked up against the side of this sunken road, and a bit further on, sticking up above the ground, a hand and obviously a body underneath it, but all you could see was a hand, and, on the lefthand side, just lumps of flesh with the innards and remains of a poor horse all rolled up there together. A shell must have got them. There were bodies all around. You can't describe it! That massacre had happened fourteen days before we got there. It was horrifying. We were all only about twenty years of age and you're a bit callous then. It's a cruel age really. You have no sort of feeling. But it must have made some sort of impression because I can still see it all in my mind's eye, this terrible scene as we went up the line. But we had to take it all in our stride because we couldn't do anything about it. We'd got to go forward. That was our job.

Rifleman Jack Brown, MM, No. 3 Platoon, A Coy., 16th Btn., King's Royal Rifle Corps (Church Lads Brigade), 33rd Division

We was going to High Wood. That's what we was told. It was a hot day and the stench was something awful. The guns were there firing and all the artillery blokes had got their shirts off. There was two banks, one on either side of the road, about chest high – if you could call it a road! And when we actually looked, they weren't banks at all! They were heaps of overturned waggons, dead horses, broken equipment and, not to tell a lie, dead bodies as well. The smell was terrible. We went up to a place and, believe it or not, they called it Happy Valley! On the way up there was a trench at right angles to where we was, and it was full of dead Germans, just standing there where they'd been shot. You could see their heads and shoulders, just stood up there where they'd been firing from. They hadn't fallen down and they'd gone as black as pitch.

You didn't worry when you got in the Army. You didn't – straight! Well I didn't anyhow. I was carrying the rations and I got a bit fed up with them, they was so heavy. So we was told to sit down for a rest and I said, 'What about some of you carrying these rations for a while?' Nobody seemed to want to, so I just said, 'Well, I don't suppose any of us'll want much rations tomorrow.' I dumped them, and that's the last I saw of them. Didn't care really, not among all that. I don't mind saying it, on the way up there, what I did was, I just said a little prayer for myself. I always did it before we went into action, but on the way up there to High Wood, looking around at those terrible things, I just kept saying this little prayer. I suppose it must have been answered, or I wouldn't be here now!

A few little prayers went up from the Church Lads Brigade that night as they waited in the shelter of Bazentin le Petit Wood to go over the top in the morning. From Jack Brown's platoon, at least, they were intermixed with imprecations of a more down-to-earth nature and even Jack himself now rather regretted having dumped the rations. Appetites which had been temporarily sickened on the march to the line had nevertheless been sharpened by the long day's exertions and, with the prospect of going into action in the morning, a little food – even bully beef and army biscuits – would have been a comfort. Jack himself managed to scrounge a bite from his mate Jack Beament in Number One Platoon, but it was as much as his life was worth to let the rest of his own platoon see that he had done so.

It wasn't the first time the two boys had shared a meal. Even before the war, when both had been working for John Dickinson's Paper Company at Croxley Mill, they had shared their lunchtime sandwiches. But munching the dry army biscuit, or sucking it as best he could, that was not what Jack Brown had in mind. He nudged Beament. 'Remember those feeds at Miss Harper's?' 'Yes,' replied Jack Beament, 'And remember the fleas?'

They both well remembered the fleas in the first billet they had shared at Denham. Even the beds had been full of them. It was not that the spinster, Miss Harper, and the two bachelor Harper brothers were anything less than scrupulously clean and they themselves seemed to be impervious to the fleas, doubtless through years of custom, for they were dog breeders to Colonel Wyld and it was on his estate that the Church Lads had been concentrated when the Battalion was first formed, with the Colonel (then Major) as Second-in-Command of the Battalion. The boys had arrived in detachments from all over the country, some from as far away as Scotland and the north. They were a good bunch, but Jack Beament, despite having been a senior sergeant in the Church Lads Brigade, was a youth whose physique it would have been charitable to describe as lanky. When he had first tried to join the Army in August 1914 the Army had described his chest measurements in rather less kindly terms and turned him down flat. Now he was rather glad of it. It had been September before it had been suggested that the Church Lads Brigade should form its own Battalion and there were thirty-two past or present 'Church Lads' working together at the paper mill at Croxley Green. To lose them *en masse* would certainly make a hole in the work-force but the manager, Mr Charles Barton-Smith, was all for it. He was over Army age himself but he had served as a captain in the Church Lads Brigade, so he connived, encouraged them and even supplied a lorry to take them up to London.

Corporal Jack Beament, MM, A Coy., 16th Btn., King's Royal Rifle Corps (Church Lads Brigade), 33rd Division

Every one of us passed the test – including my vital statistics! There was even one lad, Charlie Rogers, who was practically blind in one eye and, when he had his eyes tested by the Colour Sergeant, we were seated on a form at the back. When they covered his good eye and it came to his bad one and he had to read out some numbers off the chart, we were all whispering, 'Twenty-four, forty-eight, nineteen, twenty-eight,' and Charlie repeated them. It's a wonder the Sergeant didn't hear, because he was standing right by Charlie. But if he did, *he* turned a blind eye, so Charlie's blind eye got through. All thirty-two of us got through.

Rifleman Jack Brown, MM, No. 3 Platoon, A Coy., 16th Btn., King's Royal Rifle Corps (Church Lads Brigade), 33rd Division

We got our calling up papers a few days later and we had to go to Sardinia House, Kingsway in London. The mill gave us a lorry and it was waiting outside the Red House, which is the pub at Croxley, and we all bundled in there and it took us to Watford Junction to get the train, not knowing where we was going or anything. We found Kingsway all right but we didn't know where Sardinia House was or anything else but we found it and we got introduced right away to the army regulations. There was a Regimental Sergeant-Major and he took our names and particulars and we got lined up and we marched through the streets. I'd got an old flute and I was playing it. I was playing *The Girl I Left Behind Me* and I played it all the way through London to Paddington Station. We stepped out on that march! Because the Church Lads wasn't just a religious organization. It was a bit like the Boys Brigade, you did drill and all that, and we made a pretty good job of that march to Paddington – or so *we* thought.

Of course we didn't know where we was going and everyone was guessing, would it be Durham, or would it be Bristol or anywhere at all? Anyhow we got in the train and away it went. By this time we'd been all day on the journey because we left Croxley Green quite early in the morning and, blow me, about half an hour later we ended up at Denham – just about seven miles away from Croxley Green where we'd all started out from!

By some miracle, although the Battalion had had its share of trench warfare and casualties, the original thirty-two were still together. They were older, harder, fitter. Even Jack Beament's chest measurements had expanded by a good two inches, but their link with Denham was as strong as ever. 'Lizzie Wyld', as the Battalion had disrespectfully nicknamed their Commanding Officer, was the local squire and, although they had moved on to Clipstone Camp near Nottingham within three months, the residents of Denham still regarded the 16th King's Royal Rifles with proprietary affection as 'their Battalion'. Other troops who had followed them after they had moved north to Nottingham had a kindly reception but the proceeds of every concert, every village fête, every bazaar and jumble sale and the product of hundreds of knitting needles, clicking through miles of khaki wool, were intended for the benefit of the Church Lads and the Church Lads alone. The coffers of the Battalion's Comforts Fund swelled, the Battalion Stores bulged with a plenitude of socks and scarves, gloves and knitted helmets, and there was hardly a man of the original contingent who did not also receive a regular supply of letters and parcels from his old billet at Denham.

Altogether the Battalion was spoilt and Jack Beament was more spoilt than any. He had a share in the collective parcels sent by the Harper household at Denham and parcels from Heanor as well, where he and Harry Chapman had been billeted in Mundy Street with Mr and Mrs Buxton. A parcel had arrived only yesterday. In it was a small tin of patriotic design, adorned by a picture of the King, and Mrs Buxton had filled it with chocolate. Jack had put it in his haversack and now his haversack was on the parapet of the old German trench where they were preparing to pass the night. He considered sharing the chocolate with Jack Brown and Charlie Rogers right away, and then thought better of it. He would keep it for tomorrow.

Machine-gun fire was coming from High Wood across the valley, slowly traversing in the dark in the hope of catching troops assembling for the big attack that would surely come in the morning. It was a random bullet, almost spent, that hit the haversack. It went straight through the tin of chocolate which thus, facetiously, became the first of the Battalion's casualties in the battle for High Wood. Beament was nervously conscious of the fact that, had he not placed the haversack on the parapet, that casualty might have been himself.

Chapter 13

Only two days ago, give or take the occasional spot where a stray shell had created havoc, the trees in High Wood had been in full leaf. But twenty-four hours of fighting and shelling had taken ghastly toll. The leaves were limp and yellowed by cordite. Branches hung splintered from lurching tree trunks. Whole trees had been uprooted and sent crashing into the trampled undergrowth, and the tangle of branches, now seeming to spring out of the ground, gave fine cover for snipers firing from behind them and, looming up fearful and grotesque in the light of the green star shells that rose and fell in the heart of the wood, barred the way to the infantry blundering forward.

It should have been a sylvan scene, the half-full moon riding high on a summer's night over the woods and valleys of the Somme. To observers in the British line, looking across the valley to the wood that swelled and sank in an inferno of flash and fire, the moon, the stars, the warmth seemed strangely incongruous.

Repeated reports had claimed that High Wood had been captured by the 7th Division, and Brigadier-General Baird, in command of a Brigade of the 33rd Division, had sent his men into it with orders to consolidate the line. 'Consolidate' meant 'dig', and on a line running diagonally through the wood, they dug for half the night, cursing the undergrowth, cursing the tentacles of roots that entangled spades and entrenching tools, and cursing the fact that, for all their orders and all the reports and assurances that the wood had been captured, machine-gun bullets were spraying them as they worked. In lulls between the bursts, they could hear voices very close in front of them shouting orders in a language that was unmistakably German. And, occasionally, the alien commands seemed to come from behind their backs.

It was a gruelling and frightful night of fear and crucifying labour. In the first light of the dawn, the weary men were ordered to filter back out of the wood, to abandon the new line, and to prepare the line outside High Wood for a fresh attack. The long night's digging had gone for nothing.

In spite of the insistence of Headquarters that High Wood had been captured – or nearly so – by the 7th Division, it was obvious to Brigadier-General Baird, from the experience of his own troops during the dreadful hours they had spent in it, that this was not the case. Furthermore, the new orders were that the whole division should pivot to face north and, with High Wood on its right, attack the trenchlines that lay between it and Martinpuich. The Glasgow Highlanders were to start out on this affray from the western corner of High Wood and, as no one knew better than the Glasgow Highlanders themselves, the western corner was still clenched in the hands of the Germans. Their orders were therefore inviting them, if not to turn their backs on the enemy, at least to launch into an attack which would bring them, in a matter of yards, within a hail of enfilade fire.

It was suicide to think of attempting it. In remarkably restrained but pungent terms, Brigadier Baird pointed out this fact to Divisional Head-quarters and pointed out furthermore that, no matter how his troops were positioned, the attack could not hope to be successful unless the enemy had been cleared from High Wood. Judging by the experience of his troops in the night, this was palpably not the case. Divisional Headquarters was unperturbed. The troops had perhaps been edgy. It had been categori-cally claimed as long ago as ten o'clock the previous evening that High Wood had been captured, and the casualties which Baird's Brigade had unfortunately sustained, the difficulties they had encountered during the night, must have been due to isolated pockets of resistance – nothing that a little 'mopping up' would not put right. His opinion, they informed him in placatory tones, would be recorded. But the attack would go ahead.

In a lather of impotent fury, all that Brigadier Baird could do was to send a company of the King's Royal Rifle Corps up to the wood itself. When the main attack began they, with the remnants of three platoons of the Glasgow Highlanders, would attack through High Wood. At best they would clear the remaining 'pockets of resistance'. At worst they would divert the Germans' attention from the right flank of the 33rd Division as they pushed towards the north.

The attack was due to start at nine o'clock. The bombardment started at 8.30. It sounded loud and impressive. It had no particular effect.

Rifleman J. Brown, MM, No. 3 Platoon, A Coy., 16th King's Royal Rifle Corps (Church Lads Brigade)

We'd laid there all night in these little shelters what we'd dug and they were just bringing up the breakfast and the order came to march, so we never got no breakfast that morning. Cor' Blimey,

I was frightened. Just thinking, 'Hope I'll get out of it.' But my
legs worked, so I got up and walked out with the rest. We went
across the valley and got up to High Wood and when we got along
the side of the wood we lay down there and had a look down this
valley what we'd come up. There was a Jock regiment marching
up the road in fours and Jerry opened up on them and I remember
two or three shells dropping right in among the column and they
just closed ranks and came on – never faltered! Then our own
bombardment started and, as usual, they was dropping short. They
was falling in the fields behind us. Our own guns! I don't believe
one of them went into High Wood and that's what they were
supposed to be bombarding before *we* went in. They was too far
away to hit us, because we was right up against the wood, and
they certainly didn't hit the wood! I don't know what they was
aiming at or whether they'd just had a good rum ration the night
before! I reckon they were trying to ricochet off on to the target!

*Corporal Jack Beament, MM, No. 1 Platoon, A Coy., 16th King's Royal
Rifle Corps (Church Lads Brigade)*

Just picture a lovely July sunny day. As we were waiting so many
paces apart, I noticed there were hazel trees growing on the edge
of the wood – hazel trees, with nuts on them. I was a stretcher-
bearer in this attack and I was with George Illife who was my
partner, the other stretcher-bearer. Then the Very light went up,
which was the signal, and we had to go into the wood. Illife had
got wounded while we were waiting and he cleared off, so I was
there on my own.

*Rifleman J. Brown, MM, No. 3 Platoon, A Coy., 16th King's Royal
Rifle Corps (Church Lads Brigade)*

The order come. Away we go! I remember Major Cooban – he
was our Company Commander – going into High Wood bent
forward, like, on the trot, with his revolver in his hand, and that's
the last I see of him! We follow on. There was some troops dug in
about twenty yards inside High Wood, in little shell-holes, leaning
forward on their arms, because the machine-gun bullets was whizzing about something awful. We went through past those chaps,
but we didn't get much further. Me and another fellow got into a
shell-hole, because there was no point just going on against these
machine-guns and bullets spitting everywhere, so we had to sit

there for a time and wait to see what was going to happen and if anyone in front was going to knock these machine-guns out so that we could get forward.

Corporal Jack Beament, MM, No. 1 Platoon, A Coy., 16th King's Royal Rifle Corps (Church Lads Brigade)

Major Cooban was a very, very brave man. He ought not to have been in that attack at all. He had lumbago so, technically, he was unfit, but he would insist on leading our Company. I never saw him after we got into the wood. It was an absolutely raging inferno. Shells and rifle fire, machine-gun fire, but, strangely enough, looking back on it, I don't think I felt all that frightened. You couldn't let fear get into your brain. You'd go berserk! All you could do was hope for the best and get on with the job. You hoped you wouldn't get killed though! I came across a chap who came from Cork, he was an Irishman and he was wounded in the head – badly, but I got him into a shell-hole and bandaged him out and he managed to get out of the wood and cleared off. Then I went on a bit further, looking for more wounded but I had to take shelter, which is what all the boys were doing. I don't think that we really got twenty or thirty yards into the wood.

Rifleman J. Brown, MM, No. 3 Platoon, A Coy., 16th King's Royal Rifle Corps (Church Lads Brigade)

All of a sudden something hit me in the back. I thought it was the Jerries up behind me with a mallet! So I puts my hand round on my back and it was covered with blood. I thought to myself, 'I'm going to get out of this!' But when I tried to move my legs, they wouldn't go. I was all on my own in this shell-hole and – this is God's truth! – I lay down, put my arms under my head, laid my head on my arms and laid myself down to die. All I could think of was, 'Fancy training more than fifteen months for this!'

Corporal Jack Beament, MM, No. 1 Platoon, A Coy., 16th King's Royal Rifle Corps (Church Lads Brigade)

I got a bullet in the left shoulder, so I packed up. I started to crawl back where we'd come from and, while I was doing so, I came across a fellow from Redhill called Johnny Redman. He was wounded. He was a very tall, heavy man, but I got hold of him and I half-dragged him and half-carried him out of the wood. I got him somehow on to my shoulder and I remember wondering if the Germans had machine-guns up in the trees because, as we were getting back, I remember the bullets hitting the ground, just like heavy raindrops. They couldn't have been spent bullets from a distance, because they were so near and of course the Germans were shelling as well. There were explosions all over the place. It wasn't very pleasant. But I just had to struggle on as best I could and hope to God we would get back. What a shambles it was. I didn't get more than thirty yards, or forty yards at most. We just couldn't make any advance at all.

Rifleman J. Brown, MM, No. 3 Platoon, A Coy., 16th King's Royal Rifle Corps (Church Lads Brigade)

I was really resigned to dying and I just lay there quiet. After a while I said to myself, 'I'm a long time getting unconscious! I'll have another go.' So I had another go and my legs worked. They told me afterwards that the nerves in my spine must have been numbed with the bang of the bullet in my back, and they'd recovered a bit by then. It wasn't easy, but I chucked my equipment off and my rifle and left it in the shell-hole and when I looked at my haversack as I took it off (I'd got a primus stove in there, one of them little ones) and whatever it was that hit me had smashed that and it was full of petrol. It's a good job it never went up! So I started to crawl back out of the wood and, when I got clear of it, I was able to stand up a bit – but still creeping along like a half-shut knife because of this thing in my back.

Corporal Jack Beament, MM, No. 1 Platoon, A Coy., 16th King's Royal Rifle Corps (Church Lads Brigade)

It was a good struggle back over the open with this chap Redman over my shoulder – the one I *hadn't* got the bullet in! When I got out of the wood I was carrying him over open land. There were no trenches there, and I was going through the remains of this Cavalry. I remember a poor horse with no guts – guts all hanging out – and I had to pass that and get down somehow to the aid post. I passed Colonel Wyld on the way. I couldn't help feeling sorry for him. 'Lizzie Wyld' we called him. He became our CO when we got out to France and he used to ride round and, if he saw something he didn't like, he would bellow, 'I can see you all from my horse and I have the power to send you all home.' It was a joke in the Battalion; we made up a song, or a kind of a song and we used to sing it.

> *I can see you all from my horse*
> *And I have the power*
> *To send you a-a-all home!*

Well! To see him then, I really felt sorry for him. There was a bank halfway across, just a low bank. He wasn't in the wood with us, because he was in charge of the four Companies and the other three were going in the other direction and only 'A' Company had gone into this part of the wood, to fix the Jerries on the right flank, you see. And so he had to stay outside to co-ordinate and give them the orders. He'd had to get messages somehow to each Company as to what action they could take. But things were going so badly against us that I suppose the poor devil didn't know what commands to give! And that look of anguish on his face! Poor old Lizzie! I suppose he must have been a bit shell-shocked. He was sent home after that.

Rifleman J. Brown, MM, No. 3 Platoon, A Coy., 16th King's Royal Rifle Corps (Church Lads Brigade)

There was a little doctor's shelter thing dug into the side of the hill, so I went in there and got bandaged up and that's where I did see Jack Beament. He'd just brought this chap Redman in and he'd got wounded and all. But the doctor said, 'Can you make it further back on your feet?' We both said we could, so we set off back together. What with the loss of blood, we was both feeling pretty queer by the time we got down to Happy Valley and there was a battery of guns firing there, just over the top of a steep bank. You wasn't supposed to go that near the guns but we was just plodding on. Anyhow they stopped firing and let us go by and then they started again when we'd got past. We get down to the dressing station eventually and then we was shipped off to the casualty clearing station in an old general service waggon. The Padre was at the dressing station asking us all when we came in if we'd seen anybody get killed and who they were. See anybody get killed! I should say we did!

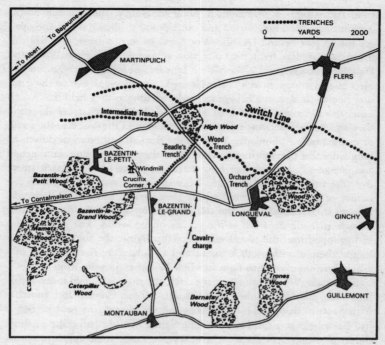

The Ground Attacked on 14th/15th July

Corporal Jack Beament, MM, No. 1 Platoon, A Coy., 16th King's Royal Rifle Corps (Church Lads Brigade)

It was a horrible, terrible massacre. We'd lost all the officers out of our company. We lost all the sergeants, all the full corporals and all the NCOs right down to Herbert King who was the senior Lance-Corporal. He was my pal and he brought 'A' Company out of the wood. He rallied them and brought them out. There were more than two hundred of us went in. And Herbert brought them out. Sixty-seven men. That was all.

It was 15 July. It would be exactly two months to the day, 15 September, before High Wood would be taken.

The trouble was the Switch Line, so long, so deep, so formidable, so heavily manned, so closely interlinked to the trenches that lay in front of it by a network of fortifications, that it was virtually impregnable. It ran from the village of Martinpuich along the valley, through the north-eastern corner of High Wood and out beyond it, slicing across the open ground to pass behind Delville Wood and to form a bastion in front of the village of Flers. Switching direction as it went, with High Wood and Delville Wood beyond it, the Switch Line was an iron gateway, defending Flers and Martinpuich as a portcullis might once have defended the gateway of a castle against a besieging horde. So long as they held the Switch Line, the Germans would hold High Wood. From whatever direction they attacked – frontally or from the boundaries of the wood to the south or to the north – blundering through the thickets and briars or down the long rides that divided it, no matter how they scraped, dug, entrenched and consolidated, no matter how often successive lines of attack swept over the front line that stretched from the north-west to the south-east corner of the wood, no matter how they hacked and battled their way beyond it, again and again the troops came up against the deadly strong triangle that still held out at the corner of the wood. The cavalry who had galloped into the wood with pennants flying, the soldiers who had fought their way through it on 14 and 15 July were the vanguard of a whole host who were to fight in High Wood and to die in it.

At Delville Wood, just along the road, the story was even more appalling. Here they had pushed in the South African Brigade and, together with Scottish troops, they had taken the wood and had held it. But it had been held at a terrible cost. The South Africans had gone in three thousand strong. At roll call, when they eventually came out, seven hundred and sixty-eight men answered their names. The South Africans had suffered more than two thousand casualties – and, in this case, casualties meant dead. It was possibly the greatest sacrifice of the war.

In 'normal' battle conditions the proportion of casualties was reckoned to be, on average, four men wounded or taken prisoner for every man who was killed outright, or died within hours of his wounds. Even on the first black day of July, when the final casualty list had numbered more than fifty-seven thousand, appalling though the total was, roughly one man in every three casualties had been killed. Proportionately, the South Africans' losses had been far greater. Of the three thousand soldiers of the South African Brigade who went into Delville Wood, the handful of wounded were outnumbered, four to one, by the dead. None was taken prisoner.

Sunday, 15 July, dawned a fine morning in Winchester. The cathedral was packed and in the streets outside, the pavements were crowded with bystanders. Accustomed though they were, even in peacetime, to seeing soldiers about the city, the townspeople of Winchester still dearly loved a parade. So they lingered in the warm sun, feathered hats nodding, shoes polished to Sabbath brilliance, to enjoy the sight of the Reserve Battalions of The King's Royal Rifle Corps and The Rifle Brigade as they marched the short distance from the barracks to the cathedral. The soldiers had been roused at dawn and it had taken hours of preparation and spit and polish before their turn-out had achieved the standard of smartness necessary to satisfy the critical eyes of sergeant-majors and inspecting officers. It was no ordinary Church Parade. Even the King, although not actually present in person, would be represented at the head of the city's dignitaries by the venerable Field-Marshal, Lord Grenfell, and as many of its congregation as the cathedral would hold were admitted after the troops and official guests had filed into their places.

In spite of the glorious music and singing, it was a sombre service, dedicated to the memory of the soldiers who had a special bond with Winchester, the home of their Regimental Barracks. They were the officers and the men of The King's Royal Rifle Corps and of The Rifle Brigade who had fallen on the field of battle since the war had begun almost two years before. There were too many of them to enumerate. Besides, precise statistics might have been lowering to morale and might also, perhaps, have taken the edge off the note of ringing patriotism that crowned the solemnity of the service with a full-blooded rendering of the National Anthem.

As the second verse began and the verger swung open the big oak doors, the notes of the anthem spilled out of the cathedral into the streets. Passers-by froze where they stood; men removed their hats and most of them joined in:

> *O Lord our God, arise,*
> *Scatter his enemies,*
> *And make them fall;*
> *Confound their politics;*
> *Frustrate their knavish tricks;*
> *On Thee our hopes we fix,*
> *God save us all!*

There were rather more of the fallen of The King's Royal Rifle Corps to honour than if the service had been held two days earlier. And a hundred and fifty miles away, on the scarred uplands of the Somme where the same morning sunlight shafted through the crippled trees of High Wood, more King's Royal Rifle Corps were dying, even as the patriotic notes swelled through the sunlit streets of Winchester.

The lucky ones, the boys who had been wounded and had dragged themselves or been carried away from the wood, were pressing towards the dressing station. By five in the evening, some one hundred and fifty of them had managed to reach it and had passed through it down the line.

Jack Brown ended up in the mortuary. Such was the chaos and disorganization, such was the flow of casualties pressing towards the second-stage dressing stations in the rear, where ambulances would take them to casualty clearing stations on the other side of Albert, that the walking wounded were literally queuing up for treatment. It was a long wait and, having just received an anti-tetanus injection, Jack was feeling distinctly queer. An orderly ducked out from a tent as the long line of men shuffled slowly past, and, through the flap, Jack glimpsed the still forms of wounded soldiers lying on stretchers inside. It did not occur to him that the soldiers lay very still indeed, only that there was one stretcher unoccupied. 'This'll do me!' he thought, as he slid discreetly from the throng of wounded into the dim half-light of the tent and painfully, gratefully lay down.

It was many hours before he awoke, and, even then, he only had the energy to open one eye, half-blinded by the swinging lantern in the hand of the orderly who bent over him. It was not until he heard the orderly yell as he ran out of the tent that Jack woke up fully and realized that something was wrong. The mistake was soon put right and, early in the morning, Jack was sent off in the first of the day's convoys to the casualty clearing station at Warloy on the first stage of his journey to a long convalescence at home. The unfortunate orderly, whom Jack had scared out of his wits, helped to load him into the ambulance. The parting glance he cast upon him was not a friendly one.

Jack Beament was already on his way to a base hospital at Rouen. His wound was not so serious as Brown's, and, in normal circumstances, his chances of getting home at all would have been slim, but the circumstances were far from normal. For, even two weeks after the disastrous first day of the battle, casualties who had been lying out from the first and later attacks were still being rescued and brought in and the seriously wounded men who had been rescued early from the battlefield, or who had been wounded in the line, were not yet fit to be moved by train, ship, and train again on the long haul back to Blighty. The situation had improved since the first calamitous forty-eight hours of the offensive, when the overflow of wounded arriving at casualty clearing stations was so great that even the vast reserves of spare stretchers were soon used up and, all around the big marquees, men were laid in patient rows on the bare earth, without even the benefit of a blanket to cover them.

It had been a miracle of organization that all had received emergency treatment and had been swiftly sent on to the superior comforts of base hospitals at Rouen or on the coast. But the base hospitals themselves were now packed far beyond their capacity. Beds were moved together, so close that there was barely room for the nurses to pass between them. When the beds ran out, stretchers were pressed into service, laid crossways at the foot and, in the largest marquees, in rows down the middle. And still more wounded were arriving all the time. It was the lightly wounded who came off best – the men who, otherwise, would have been treated for a week or so at the base hospitals, sent to convalescent camps for a few days and then returned to their units in the line. But there was no longer room for them. They, at least, could stand the journey and must be shipped off as quickly as possible to make room for the serious cases. Such fortunate soldiers found little to object to in this arrangement and simply thanked their lucky stars that they were out of it.

In the desperate aftermath of the big attack with every dressing station, casualty clearing station and hospital in France strained ten times beyond its limit, with every orderly, nurse and doctor working hollow-eyed around the clock, some men had not even passed through the base hospitals at all. The transport authorities, at their wits' end, had sent three train-loads of walking wounded straight from the front to the harbour at Boulogne, and, to the delight of their passengers, loaded them directly on to hospital ships bound for home. A few were 'accident cases', suffering from nothing more serious than a sprained ankle, but, now that they had been packaged into the system, they could be sure of at least a few days' rest in a Home hospital, of a period of sick leave and then the blessed respite of a few weeks at their Regimental Base Camp before being drafted back to France and up the line.

Jack Beament, sent to hospital at Rouen, was not quite so fortunate in the short term, but he was nevertheless in for the greatest surprise of his life. It was also the greatest coincidence.

Corporal Jack Beament, MM, No. 1 Platoon, A Coy., 16th King's Royal Rifle Corps (Church Lads Brigade)

It was a hutment hospital on Rouen Racecourse and I was directed to Ward C.3. I could move under my own steam, because my legs were all right. When I got there, the nurse met me at the door and said to me, 'That's your bed over there on the right-hand side.' I thanked her and, as I was making for the bed, I heard a whistle and I looked round. On the other side of the ward, almost immediately opposite my bed, there was my brother Stanley! Just imagine! In all the scores and hundreds of hospitals in France, with all their scores and scores of wards in every hospital, I ended up in the same ward as my brother Stanley. And the even more amazing coincidence was that he had an almost identical wound to mine, only it was in the opposite shoulder. What a reunion that was! And how delighted the nurses were too! They simply couldn't get over it and they made a terrific fuss of us both.

Stanley Beament, in the 20th Battalion of Jack's own regiment, had joined up, on reaching military age, a year after Jack himself, and, as the 20th Battalion of The King's Royal Rifle Corps was a Pioneer Battalion, might have been expected to be immune from wounding by rifle fire. But, twenty-four hours before Jack had been wounded at High Wood, Stanley's company had been attached to the 8th Brigade of the Third Division where they stood in the line ready to launch the dawn attack in the early hours of 14 July. It was while they were consolidating the line between High Wood and Delville Wood, while the Pioneers were digging a new communication trench, that Stanley had been wounded. On his way back to the dressing station, he must have passed within yards of his brother Jack as the Church Lads, in their turn, marched up towards the line. Now, in the hospital at Rouen, the two brothers compared wounds, swapped experiences, gloated over their luck, and, in between painful dressings, thoroughly enjoyed being petted and fussed over and treated as minor celebrities. On 22 July they were bundled aboard a hospital ship and travelled home together.

On the same day, the most illustrious casualty of Bloody July met his death on the Somme. It was Major-General Ingouville-Williams, in command of the 34th Division. He died at Mametz Wood, killed by the explosion of an unlucky shell, as he moved up to reconnoitre the ground for the next stage of the hoped-for advance. It was a severe blow to the Army, for the Somme fighting had taken a heavy toll of colonels and brigadiers who had gone into the line with their troops and had been killed or wounded, and even a colonel or a brigadier was more easily replaced than an experienced major-general in command of a Division. The General's body was brought back and he was buried at Warloy with full military honours. Transport columns and gun batteries were scoured for black horses to draw the gun carriage bearing his coffin and two matching pairs were eventually found in 'C' Battery of the 152nd Brigade.

Sergeant Frank Spencer, No. 1113, 'C' Bty., 152nd Brigade, Royal Field Artillery

23 July: Good progress reported as a result of the strafe and batches of prisoners are continuously marched back to the rear but no definite news is obtainable. We now suffer a great loss by the death

of our Officer Commanding our 34th Division – General Williams
killed by a shell bursting last night. Our No. 2 black team is used
for removal of the body. (Fritz leaves us alone, being evidently too
preoccupied in dealing with infantry as great progress is made during
the day.)

There had been another night attack on High Wood, and this time by
the 51st Division.

*Lance-Corporal David Watson, No. 3721, 9th Btn., Royal Scots, 51st
Division*

We were marched up through Fricourt, which was badly battered.
That was the first real sign of war we had come through and, when
we reached Mametz Wood, we cut through the wood across the
valley and went into a trench behind the Bazentin le Petit wood.
That was the assembly point for the 'do'. And the battle order was
that, if the attack failed, we had to come back to this trench. When
we reached the road at Bazentin village we turned left and moved
up the road. We were in extended order right up that road and,
oh, the German guns were knocking us down wholesale and the
same with these machine-guns. We took up position along the wall
and, at two minutes past twelve, we jumped the wall and ran down
the hill to take, according to orders, a few minutes' rest in a valley.
To me it was like a dried-up water course. A dip. Water would
be there in the winter. And then we were to form up about fifty
yards from High Wood to rush it. The Corporal and three of us,
three privates, we reached the fifty yards spot but no order came
to charge the wood. The Corporal decided to go and see what had
happened but we saw him knocked down about fifty yards away
from us. And he had given us an order, 'Don't move from where
ye are until I get back.' But we couldn't move because we were
pinned down with machine-gun fire. Bullets were flying all roads
and men were dropping on each side. In fact, I saw Sergeant
Thomson who was badly wounded being helped by a Lance-
Corporal who had gone down on one knee and had the Sergeant
sitting up against him, and a big shell splinter came across and
sliced the Sergeant's head off. That poor Corporal, he was nearly
demented. He was inches away from him.

We took up position ready to get into the wood. Nothing happened and our guns didn't seem to hit the wood at all because they
should have been able to knock out these machine-gunners. They

kept firing for a long time and there were only three of us left. One lad lost patience with the strain of waiting, just got up on to his feet and ran away and he went down. He was hit. You saw the flashes coming out of the machine-guns, pointing directly at us. They knew where we were but they hit everything bar the two of us. We could hear the bullets going into the ground in front, behind and at the side. Just never seemed to get us. We decided the best way was just to lie still because it was level ground and the bullets were whizzing over and hitting the earth all round about us. And it took us two hours before we got back to the assembly trench. After, it seemed to quieten down a bit, and it was obvious the thing had failed completely, and we gradually – just one at a time – moved back a little – we took just turn-about moving because, if one movement had been spotted, we would both get it. And we got down into this dip that was at the foot of this steep hill. There was a crucifix at the crossroads – and we got back down to the crucifix, down the road from Mametz Wood and then we climbed the hill behind the Bazentin Wood to get back into the trench. There were only eleven of us left. We were no good to anybody.

Sergeant Bill Hay, No. 1459, 9th Btn., Royal Scots, 51st Division

That was a stupid action, because we had to make a frontal attack on bristling German guns and there was no shelter at all. We were at the back, but C Company really got wiped out. We had a lot of casualties but they lost all their officers, all the NCOs, the lot – cleaned out! We knew it was pointless, even before we went over – crossing open ground like that. But, you had to go. You were between the devil and the deep blue sea. If you go forward, you'll likely be shot. If you go back, you'll be court-martialled and shot. So what the hell do you do? What can you do? You just go forward, because the only bloke you can get your knife into is the bloke you're facing.

There were dead bodies all over the place where previous battalions and regiments had taken part in previous attacks. What a bashing we got. There were heaps of men, everywhere – not one or two men, but heaps of men, all dead. Even before we went over, we knew this was death. We just couldn't take High Wood against machine-guns. It was ridiculous. There was no need for it. It was just absolute slaughter.

When it marched out of the line, the Battalion was a shadow of its former self. They passed through Fricourt in a straggling column, pathetically few in number, and a piper marched at their head. He belonged to the Battalion. He knew the terrible toll that High Wood had taken and, doubtless, his mind was on the bodies of the comrades they had left behind. Since the days of Culloden *The Flowers of the Forest* had been the traditional Highland lament. He chose to play it now. It seemed appropriate to the occasion.

As the Royal Scots marched away from the battle, the Australians were preparing to go into the attack. Their orders were, at all costs, to take Pozières.

Chapter 14

Although the first contingent had arrived only at the end of March, the Australians were already a familiar sight in Northern France – tall men, most of them, broad of physique, hard of muscle, with lean, brown faces tanned to leather by the blistering suns and winds of two seasons on the Gallipoli Peninsula and by their scorching sojourn in Egypt after the evacuation.

True to the British tradition of turning defeat of a kind into victory of a kind, the evacuation of British and Colonial troops from the peninsula had already passed into legend. So carefully had it been planned, so thoroughly had the Turkish enemy been duped, that it had been accomplished without the loss of a single man.

Silence was the essence of the plan. The armada of ships was already moored in the straits and around them bobbed a fleet of lighters ready to creep towards the coast after dark to pick up the men from the narrow beaches at the foot of the cliffs. In places, the tracks that led down to them from the gullies above were steep and so narrow that some thousands of men would have to scramble down them in single file, boots wrapped in sandbags to muffle the sound of their feet, moving slowly, carefully, so that the inadvertent clink or jingle of rifles and accoutrements, multiplied a thousand times, might not give them away.

But it was equally obvious that, if silence fell too suddenly in the trenches above, the Turks would be alerted, might guess what was happening and might open up their guns and bombard the beaches and the rescue fleet beyond. With infinite cunning the Allies planned a great deception. For some hours after the last of the men had filed out of the trenches, it must appear to the Turks that it was still 'business as usual'. Over the last few weeks, they had changed the pattern of activity to accustom the enemy to long periods of silence, alternated with busy periods of fire. At Sari Bair, where the Royal Engineers had been tunnelling for months towards the Turkish lines, preparing a mine beneath the enemy trenches to be blown in conjunction with a big attack which would now not take place, the possibilities of an explosive farewell were not lost on the minds of those who planned the evacuation. The mine could still be fired at the very last minute, as the last man left the trenches. From the deck of a cruiser in the bay, General Birdwood had the satisfaction of seeing 'an eruption that seemed to rival Vesuvius' and to hear, for hours afterwards, a fusillade of fire as the Turks wasted considerable amounts of ammunition firing at the now-empty Allied trenches.

It was a long time before the enemy woke up to the fact that the opposition had melted away, for the troops had exercised considerable ingenuity in order to deceive him. All along the trenches, up and down the length of the peninsula, ready loaded rifles had been left in position with strings of varying lengths attached to the triggers and lighted candles, so positioned that the rifles would fire automatically when the flames burnt through the strings. Similar devices would shoot flares into the sky, carefully timed to reproduce 'normal night-time activity', so carefully established over the past weeks.

As the last troopship bearing the rearguard of the Gallipoli force slid silently down the straits, and the sheer cliffs to starboard began to loom grey in the first light of dawn, the 'Jokes Department' could still plainly be heard drawing enemy fire. With an enormous effort, the troops restrained themselves from spoiling the effect by raising a triumphant cheer. It was a glorious end to an inglorious episode and the story of the *sangfroid* and cool-headedness of the departing warriors had improved in the telling.

Tall stories about the Australians were circulating in France long before they arrived there themselves in the late spring. Most of them could be traced to the Pals Battalions of the 31st Division who had been soldiering alongside them in Egypt. They had every reason to feel slightly resentful of their Anzac comrades. On their arrival in Egypt, the local traders had been quick to notice that the Anzacs, with their six shillings a day, were more affluent than the British troops whose cost of living had immediately rocketed. Oranges, previously obtainable at fifteen for one piastre, soon cost one piastre per orange. The Anzacs, flush with back pay accumulated during service in Gallipoli, rode in taxis while Tommies slogged back to camp on foot or clung precariously to the last tram-car. Prices at the Café Egyptien increased twenty-fold overnight and, within days of the arrival of the Australians, it was rumoured that the sawdust on the floor was swept up by the grasping Egyptians in the small hours of every morning and squeezed between sheets to recover the beer that had soaked into it during the evening's carousal. Souvenir sellers made clear their disdain of customers unadorned by slouch hats and upped their prices accordingly. Touts roamed the streets and cafés to inveigle the well-breeched Australians into dives and dens in sleazy back streets where the charms of women of a dozen different hues and nationalities were available, if not for the asking, at least for the price of one day's Colonial pay.

The Australians were mostly country boys, many of them from the far outback, and it was the first time that they had had the opportunity of indulging in such dubious pleasures. Many had cause to regret it. Within weeks, a huge barbed wire compound was built outside the Mena Camp containing some hundreds of disconsolate Anzacs, mooching about – between doses of unpleasant remedial treatment – as they waited to be shipped home 'in disgrace'. Later the Army took a more realistic view of human frailty and turned its mind towards prophylaxis as well as supplying remedial treatment for venereal disease. But in 1916, 'sin' was supposed not to exist among the upright, adulated troops of Great Britain and her Empire.

The 'sin' which did exist, in the view of the Army, and which must be stamped on hard, was the unforgivable assumption on the part of the Australian soldier that he was the equal of any man whether he wore the desert-stained uniform of a private or the immaculate turn-out of a superior being endowed with the King's Commission. Horrified officers indulging in a civilized aperitif in the palatial bar of Shepheard's Hotel, who had been chummily invited to 'Have one with me, mate' by a slouch-hatted, none-too-clean Australian ranker, had speedily had the hotel put out of bounds to other ranks and, when a whole series of British officers found themselves unable to dine almost anywhere because all the tables had been reserved for convivial parties of noisy Australian troops, other hotels followed suit and were henceforth reserved for 'Officers Only'. There was not much else but 'dives' of dubious reputation where Anzacs and Tommies alike were unmercifully fleeced.

The Australians were nobody's fools and it did not escape their attention that the Egyptians were only too willing to take advantage of their open-handed *bonhomie* and to defraud them at every opportunity. But they seldom got away with it. There were well-authenticated stories of Australians – justifiably enraged by blatant profiteering – overturning market stalls, forcing some unfortunate over-optimistic orange vendor to distribute his entire stock free and administering such corporal punishment to impertinent taxi drivers as their inflated demands deserved.

Real retribution had been reserved for sellers of liquor who had evolved the ingenious ploy of boring a hole in the bottom of a full whisky bottle, draining the contents, filling it with amber-coloured liquid – often urine – and replugging the hole with a ball of molten glass. Few Egyptians tried this ploy more than once if an Aussie caught up with him. He was a lucky man if he escaped with no more punishment than having the bottle broken over his head. The Aussies looked on it as 'safeguarding the interests of future tourists'.

Soon every Egyptian, venturing on a commercial transaction with an

Anzac, was demanding, 'Gibbit money first!' Among the Anzacs this expression became a catch-phrase and a huge joke. Months later in France, the veterans of Gallipoli and Egypt were still bandying it in *estaminets* whenever money changed hands, to the accompaniment of roars of laughter and total incomprehension on the part of the various 'Mamzelles' who served them with the cheap white wine or thin beer which, while it still fell a very long way short of Australian standards, was at least better than the unmentionable liquid which had passed under the name of beer in Egypt.

The Anzacs liked 'Mamzelles'. They prided themselves on their success with the fair sex and fostered the rumour that their turned-up hats were so designed to allow a feminine head to rest comfortably on a broad Australian shoulder and to facilitate kissing, without discommoding the object of admiration by disarranging an elaborate *coiffure* with the broad brim of an Australian hat. The Aussies also prided themselves on their toughness as fighters and now that they had arrived in France they intended to prove it.

It was unfortunate that their first blooding should have been at Fromelles in an attack that turned out to be a catastrophe. Fromelles was not on the Somme at all; it was across the Aubers Ridge in front of Neuve Chapelle and Laventie. The Anzacs were occupying the trenches facing Aubers in what, since the autumn of the previous year, had been a quiet sector and they had been sent here on their arrival from the East to harden them to the harsher climate, and to accustom them to the trenches and trench warfare on the Western Front. Even before the Allies had attacked on the Somme, it had been decided that a subsidiary attack would be useful and that it should be delivered by the 5th Australian Division and by the 61st Division, standing on either side of the Sugar Loaf Salient, both newly arrived in France.

The real tragedy was that it need never have happened at all, for General Monro had been authorized by the Commander-in-Chief to cancel the attack if he saw fit.

From the beginning, Fromelles had been an on-off affair, planned initially to take place on 8 July to pierce the German line towards Lille in one demoralizing blow that would exploit the advances on the Somme. That idea had long gone by the board, but it was the very failure to make a significant advance on the Somme Front which now made a diversionary attack even more desirable. This time it would have quite a different objective. If it were a success, if the preliminary bombardment were strong and powerful enough to induce the Germans to believe that it was the prelude to a major attack, it would have the beneficial effect of preventing the enemy from moving reserves from his line at Aubers Ridge to reinforce his troops facing the hard-pressed British on the Somme Front. But the scale of the attack itself was reduced. There was no possibility of a breakthrough to Lille. Even if the small number of available troops had succeeded in the impossible task of breaking the German line, there were no reserves available to follow up and exploit their success, for every man, every gun, and every available resource to back up the infantry was needed on the Somme where the urgent necessity was to relieve tired divisions and replace them with fresh troops and reinforcements from other parts of the line. The objective must now be limited to the capture of the first three German lines that faced the troops at the foot of the Aubers Ridge.

It was a sad and desolate piece of territory, battered and bruised by the fighting more than a year before, when the troops had tried in vain to capture the low ridge, crowned by the villages of Aubers and Fromelles, and to gain the high ground that guarded the city of Lille. They had failed, but the scars of the fighting, only slightly camouflaged by the sparse green growth of irrepressible summer, still lay like pockmarks on the flat land that separated the British line from the Germans. It was not only flat but muddy. This country had little in common with the dry, chalky landscape of the Somme some thirty miles to the south. It was Flanders, and Flanders meant mud – a deep solid stratum of heavy earth that was the devil to dig in, quick to absorb water, slow to drain. And the weather had broken.

Even on the Somme the deep, dry trenches now had two or three uncomfortable inches of liquid mud at the bottom and the ground above them, churned up by the passage of troops and supply wagons, was now slippery and treacherous. At Fromelles the effect of the rain of the last few days was even more devastating. There were no trenches, dug deep with high head-cover, such as the Aussies had known in Gallipoli. Crouching behind breastworks of mud-filled sandbags, in weather that, even in Flanders, was unseasonable for mid-July, concealed by the mist, the troops took cautious glances across the four hundred yards that lay between their own breastworks and the Germans'. The steady drizzle was seeping into the earth, trickling into every old shell-hole, swelling the brook that meandered across part of the front, and turning every crumbling, ancient trench and ditch into a water course. Remembering the deep, dry entrenchments on the Gallipoli Front this time last year, the damp and dreary Australians felt that they would willingly put up with the clouds of mosquitoes, the legions of bugs that made their lives accursed misery, if they could exchange them for the miserable ditches they now inhabited as they waited to 'have a go at the Fritzes'.

The attack had already been postponed twice while the Command dithered as to whether it should take place at all. Now, with the break in the weather, it was postponed again. The drifting rain and mist hanging over the line had blinded the artillery. Even experienced gunners would have found it impossible in such conditions to register the guns so that the bombardment would fall accurately on the German lines and cut the wire in front of it so that the infantry could get through – and these gunners were far from experienced. Few of them had ever fired a gun in France.

The bombardment was the keystone of the plan. Cunningly applying the bitter lesson that had been learned on the First of July, assuming that the Germans had not failed to notice the rigidly timed 'lifts' when the guns lengthened range with each stage of the attack, the architects of the action hoped to dupe the Germans into thinking that they were using the same technique. But there would be an all-important difference. Giving the Germans five minutes to man the parapets of their front-line trenches against the coming attack, the guns would be brought back to tumble shells among them and, it was hoped, 'to reduce the defenders to a state of collapse before the assault'. As an added refinement, at the moment when the Germans might have expected them to leave their trenches, the troops in the front line were to hoist dummies above the parapet to simulate the vanguard of the attack.

If the Germans had been occupying the line that the gunners were so confidently bombarding, it might have worked. But they were not. They had long abandoned the rain-swept flatlands and, apart from keeping a few fortifications and outposts, had wisely climbed back to the drier ground on the slope of the Aubers Ridge behind. Even if the Australian and the 61st Division succeeded in capturing the line which, according to the trench maps, was still the German Front, they would hardly have improved their position. Their advance would simply bring the line nearer to the foot of the ridge where the Germans, with the advantage of observation, would be able to pick them off as easily as a boy with a catapult. The fact was that the objective of the attack was so limited that the advantage in gaining it would be nil.

General Haig had taken the trouble to make sure that General Monro clearly understood that the operation was no longer urgently needed, and also that he had absolute discretion to cancel or postpone it because of the adverse weather or for any other reason. As the rain continued to fall, as reports brought the disturbing news that not all the Australian gun batteries were yet in position, General Monro began to have serious doubts. Unaccountably, he failed to avail himself of his permission to cancel the attack on his own authority and, on the morning of 17 July, reported to GHQ that he proposed to postpone the attack because of the bad weather and that, unless it cleared up soon, he would have to postpone it again. All things considered, he thought it best to cancel the operation. Was he authorized to do so? He was passing the buck. In an ambiguous message, the Commander-in-Chief promptly passed it back again.

> *The Commander-in-Chief wishes the special operation . . . to be carried out as soon as possible, weather permitting, provided always that Sir Charles Monro is satisfied that the conditions are favourable and that the resources at his disposal, including ammunition, are adequate both for the preparation and the execution of the enterprise.*

It squarely placed on General Monro's shoulders the responsibility of deciding whether or not the attack should go ahead and also hinted that, if he cancelled it, his reasons for doing so would not pass unquestioned. Either way, it must have seemed to General Monro that he could not win. He decided to proceed with the operation.

It was a fatal decision and one that left a legacy of bitterness that the passage of time would never expunge. Bitterness in the mind of General Monro, removed from command of Eleven Corps, as he brooded far away in India over the disaster of Fromelles. Bitterness in the minds of the Australians directed, perhaps fairly, against the Staff and unfairly against the 'Pommy bastards' of the 61st Division, in the unshakeable conviction that they had been let down.

Unlike the Australians who threw themselves over the parapets in a wild enthusiastic rush for the supposed German line, the 61st had been forced to emerge from their wire by sallyports, so few, so narrow, presenting such a target to German machine-gunners, that, in some places, half the men were killed or wounded within yards of their trenches. Unlike the Australians, bronzed, fit and up to strength, the men of the 61st Division could hardly be described as the pick of the bunch. The Division was less than five months old. It had been formed in January 1916 from Reserve Battalions of the second line whose manpower, ever since their formation, had been bled for reinforcements needed by their first-line battalions in France, and their numbers had been made up at frequent intervals by drafts of raw recruits. Their training had been long-delayed by lack of equipment, and was, at best, sketchy. With sixty-plus divisions to supply, against Australia's five, it could hardly have been otherwise.

Half the Australian force had seen service in Gallipoli and were toughened to trench warfare, while hardly a man in the 61st had even seen a trench a month earlier. For the last few days of that month half its strength in men and energy had been expended, in nights of slogging labour, in carrying out from the trenches to a safe distance behind the line fifteen hundred heavy gas cylinders which, days before, they had laboured to carry in. Only two companies of each battalion were fit to go into the attack.

On the extreme flanks of the attack both British and Australians had forged across in fine style. It was in the middle, where they were supposed to meet in the Sugar Loaf Salient, that the real disaster happened. All but a handful of the British failed to get there.

Away on the left flank the Australians were unable to recognize, in any of the tumbled ditches, the German line which had been so clearly marked on the trench maps but, determined to capture something, they had pressed on, in spite of awful casualties, to 'capture' and to hold anything that resembled a trench, a sap, or an outpost. Away on the right, the British had swept across the shattered wire of the line which, according to the maps, had been bombarded by the artillery, but they had ground to a halt against the uncut wire of the actual German line. Before nine o'clock, on that dull evening, dusk had fallen. Long before it did, it had been shatteringly apparent that, apart from ragged fighting by scattered groups of Australians, who were literally choosing to die rather than go back, the attack had fizzled into failure.

There was one ray of hope. The Australians were still fighting in the Sugar Loaf Salient and, if this strongpoint could be captured, some advantage at least might be gained from what was otherwise a débâcle. Late in the evening it was decided to renew the attack on Sugar Loaf, and, in conjunction with one battalion of Australians advancing on their left, to send the depleted Reserves of the 61st Division across to the Sugar Loaf to 'help the Australians'. In a final demonstration of the dithering that had characterized the action since its inception, the attack was cancelled – and cancelled so late that word did not reach the Australians until after their 59th Battalion had advanced, alone and unsupported, to share the fate of their few remaining comrades, still battling at this strongest point of the German line.

It was a terrible repetition of what had happened to the 13th Battalion of the Rifle Brigade at Contalmaison nine days earlier and it created a breach between the Australian fighting troops and their British comrades, which would never be completely closed. It was a sad outcome of the first engagement in which British and Australian troops had fought side by side in France.

For months, for years, for successive decades, the feeling of the Aussies that they had been 'let down' was constantly reinforced by citing the casualty figures as indisputable proof of their own sacrifice and of the British failure.

On the face of it, they looked stark enough. Australian, five thousand three hundred and fifty-five. British, one thousand five hundred and forty-seven. But it was not a comparison of like with like. The 61st Division had gone into the assault at half-strength, and, with fewer than half the number of men engaged, their casualties were proportionately almost as many.

But, for the Australians fighting in France, it was a terrible beginning and no one was more aware of this than the Commander-in-Chief. He kept to himself his thoughts on Fromelles, but, three days later, on 22 July, Haig took the trouble to visit General Gough at his Headquarters 'to make sure that the Australians had only been given a simple task'. He left presumably less than reassured. The following day, the First Australian Division would be attacking on the Somme. Their 'simple task' was to capture Pozières.

Chapter 15

The thronging of troops and supplies into the battlefields reached astounding proportions and the Pioneer troops were slaving night and day to keep the battered roads from disintegrating altogether under the strain of the constant trundling of wheels, the incessant tramping of feet, the pounding of shells that the enemy sent over in unremitting nerve-racking salvoes. Wherever they fell along the roads, they were sure of finding some target.

The road through Fricourt was the single route towards High Wood, Delville Wood, and Guillemont, which, for most of the way, was not overlooked by the enemy. By branching off through Bécourt and going by way of Sausage Valley to the right of la Boisselle, the troops could reach the line in front of Pozières in comparative safety. During the twenty-four hours when the Anzacs were moving into the line, between nine-fifteen on the morning of 21 July to nine o'clock on the morning of the 22nd, the traffic control post at Fricourt Cemetery took a census of the troops and vehicles that passed. The night was dark. The enemy soaked the road with tear-gas and, for a six-hour stretch, the census-takers were forced to wear goggles. This, they explained, accounted for the incompleteness of their returns. But, in spite of this handicap, they had managed to count two thousand four hundred and twenty-three motor vehicles in a steady stream of lorries, motor cars, buses, motor bikes and ambulances, throwing up clouds of white dust that blinded the horses and irritated the eyes and throats of almost four thousand drivers of horse-drawn wagons that rumbled slowly along the road. Five thousand four hundred and four mounted officers and one thousand and forty-three men riding bicycles, stumbled or dodged as best they could through the long column of transport. The Control Post unfortunately did not manage to make a complete count of the infantry moving to and from the line. The nearest approximate figure which could be arrived at was twenty-six thousand five hundred and thirty-six.

These troops, who passed through Fricourt in a single span of twenty-four hours, outnumbered by some hundreds the total force of British troops engaged in the Crimean War. One of them was George Middle.

George Middle was a temporary Anzac. He was also very much a 'temporary gentleman'. Despite his First Class Degree in Mathematics and Physics, obtained in 1914 at the tender age of twenty, he had been a humble lance-corporal until a few months ago, and he had only attained that rank because Army protocol frowned on a humble Sapper lecturing to officers, no matter how much of an expert he might be. George was decidedly an expert, not so much in Maths and Physics, but in the infant science of wireless which he had taken as a subsidiary subject. But his youthful looks had worked against him. Early in the war, the pundits who had interviewed him in the august surroundings of Room 417 at the War Office itself had not been inclined to offer him a commission, but they had been sufficiently impressed by his qualifications to send him as an Instructor to the Wireless Section of the Royal Engineers Training School at Worcester.

Less than a year later, attitudes had changed. In three short months, Middle had risen from lance-corporal (unpaid) first to the dizzy heights of second lieutenant, Royal Engineers and then, with startling rapidity, to the sole command of his own unit of sixty-four men. No one was more surprised than George himself. He had been in France for less than a month and, within days of his arrival, he was ordered to report to Bailleul as Wireless Officer of the First Anzac Wireless Section. It was a daunting task, because the First Anzac Wireless Section did not exist. What did exist was a nucleus of sixty-four burly Australian volunteers without an NCO among them and with precious little in the way of qualifications and experience. Furthermore, the orders of the 'Wireless Section' were that it was to move to the Somme Front on 10 July, which gave Second Lieutenant Middle just forty-eight hours before its departure. He spent most of it interviewing the men, informing himself as to their all-too-scanty experience and, in desperation, winkling out which of them, if any, had done any kind of job in civilian life that would make him useful now. The results were discouraging but among the assorted bunch of sun-toughened warriors, among the one-time jackaroos and salesmen, clerks and sheep shearers, was Harper, who had at least been an electrician at a Melbourne theatre, and whom Middle promptly promoted to temporary acting-sergeant, and there was a handful of army signallers who could act as lance-corporals. It was little enough, but it was a start.

Equipment was another matter. Having disposed his 'command' into sections, having moved them down to the hinterland of the Somme and seen them installed in billets, having instigated some kind of rudimentary training to occupy the waiting time, Middle's real work began. There was plenty to be done, because the 'First Anzac Wireless Section' possessed hardly a single piece of apparatus and Middle himself had to travel mile after weary mile on a far from reliable motor bike, collecting apparatus, conferring with his superiors, checking the equipment and, finally, going into the zone of the battle itself to set up wireless stations in preparation for the coming attack. He had some hair-raising journeys. It was hardly surprising that all was not complete before the Australians went into their first fight on 23 July.

There was an avalanche of paper work to be dealt with, lists of stores to be checked, men to be apportioned to sections, orders to be read, noted, and initialled. In the middle of July, he received a memorandum with disquieting implications.

DIRECTOR OF ARMY SIGNALS
CIRCULAR MEMORANDUM NO. 114

Issued From:
General Head Quarters,
11th July 1916

A memorandum has been issued by the General Staff calling attention to the very serious consequences which have undoubtedly resulted from the enemy overhearing buzzer or telephone messages, and directing severe punishment to be inflicted on anyone communicating in clear by these means information which will be of use to the enemy.

These instructions apply equally to the Signal Service. Signal Service Officers will ensure that all operators including wireless operators are aware of the strict orders against conversation over the wire.

The telephone, or buzzer, or wireless, is not to be used for sending any Service Messages which give in clear the names of Units, their formation, or where they are located. A great deal may depend on the strict observance of these orders and every effort must be taken to detect and punish any disobedience.

(Signed) J. S. Fowler
Brigadier-General
Director of Army Signals
(Noted 17/7/16 by Officer I/C Wireless, 1st Anzacs)

It was not surprising that the Army was edgy about signals. In the last few days it had had several unpleasant revelations and the most unpleasant of all had been at Ovillers where troops who had gained the first foothold in the village had established themselves in a deep dugout, once the German Command Post. In it they had found a complete, verbatim copy of the operation order for the First of July attack at Ovillers, with a German translation appended. A similar unpleasant discovery had been found in similar circumstances at la Boisselle, where the British Corps Commander's 'Good Luck' message to the troops had been read 'in clear' over the telephone to the front line on the eve of the battle. Taken together they explained why the Germans had been ready and waiting, why enemy shells had bombarded the assembly trenches before the attack and why so many of the men, whose bodies were still lying unburied on the battlefield, had met their deaths. It was terrible confirmation of a suspicion which had been growing in the minds of Intelligence Officers for many months. The Germans, with superior equipment, had been listening in on British communications.

It explained too why, for so long, battalions taking over the trenches had been astonished when the Germans had greeted them by name. The latest example was still fresh in everyone's minds. It had happened only days earlier while the Australians waited to attack at Fromelles and, in impotent fury, had shot away the notice-board cheekily hoisted above the German trenches. It read:

ADVANCE AUSTRALIA – IF YOU CAN!

And, although they were to exist in Army mythology for many years, although every man who served on the Western Front would continue to believe them for the rest of his life, they demolished the Spy Stories at a blow. The soldiers had been convinced that certain French civilians were in the pay of the Germans and stories of their perfidy abounded. The hands of a Town Hall clock, not far behind the line, which went mysteriously fast or slow when a relief was under way. The sails of a windmill which appeared to take up a significant position when an attack was imminent. A farmer who unaccountably changed direction in plough-ing a field, who switched one of his pair of brown horses for a grey one or put one white animal in a grazing herd of black cows. Even the French housewife, in some hilltop village, innocently spreading bed-linen to bleach in the sun as a contingent of troops went past, was not above being suspected of signalling to the Germans, and many a volubly protest-ing Madame had been reported and interrogated by Intelligence Officers.

Now, it seemed that there might be a simpler solution. In literally thousands of miles of telephone wires stretching right up to the front line, and even beyond it into forward saps, there was ample opportunity for enemy patrols to creep across No Man's Land after dark and to attach a wire of their own to a junction in the jumble of British cable. In the Somme it was even easier. The chalky sub-soil was ideal for induction and, by using quite simple listening devices, the Germans could pick up signals and conversations with very little difficulty. One unguarded remark, one exchange of friendly badinage between officers of two different units in the line, could give useful, even vital information on plans or dispositions. It was now outrageously evident that the enemy had made good use of his superior technical skill.

Henceforth all this must change. Frivolous use must no longer be made of the telephones and, where possible, wireless must be used and messages transmitted, not simply in Morse Code, but in coded Morse Code. It was not easy to get this message across to the troops and the Army very soon realized that, for every signal circuit set up to serve the troops in the line to send back information during the course of an attack, another must be set up as 'listening circuit', not to listen to the Germans, but to monitor the traffic in their own lines and to trap the unwary and the indiscreet alike.

But George Middle's job was to provide communications for the Australian attack on Pozières. The First Anzac Wireless Company was to serve the 1st and 2nd Australian Divisions as well as the 4th New Zealand Division, but by 23 July when the Australians went over the top, Middle had barely had time to set up the receiving post on Tara Hill and to select the sites for two forward posts. One, code-named U.M., was at the head of Sausage Valley; the other, U.L., was roughly on the line from which the 13th Rifle Brigade had launched their disastrous attack towards Pozières on 10 July. The position of the line had hardly changed since.

Lying astride the Albert–Bapaume Road, the ruined village of Pozières was an island surrounded by deep wire-entangled entrenchments. Strongpoints bristled on the high ground, dominating the land to the south-east, where Sausage Valley ran towards Pozières from the direction of la Boisselle, and to the south-west where Mash Valley crept towards it up the hill from Ovillers. The most formidable was the fortified house – so fortified that it was virtually a concrete tower – which the Germans had christened the 'Panzerturm' and the British troops nicknamed 'Gibralter'.

The Australian attack on Pozières was part of an ambitious exercise. With the 48th Division attacking up Mash Valley on its left, the Australians were to capture Pozières, while, it was hoped, other attacks on their right would have secured the whole of the Bazentin Ridge beyond. The prizes of Delville Wood, High Wood, the Switch Line and even Martinpuich would then be in the hands of the Allies and, if the Australians could capture Pozières and press on a few hundred yards to capture the fortified windmill on the ridge itself, the troops all along the line would be virtually in sight of Bapaume.

Again, it was a night attack, but, on the right, the attack failed. The troops were newly in the line. There had been no chance to reconnoitre. Conflicting orders had changed the timing of Zero Hour and, at the eleventh hour, changed it back again, so that some of the troops were in position barely minutes before the attack was due to begin. Haze and cloud had hindered artillery observation, so the guns had not prepared the way. The fighting troops, many back in the line for the first time since the start of the battle, had been hastily reinforced, but they sorely felt the absence of the experienced officers and NCOs who had led them into the attack on the First of July and who had never come out.

The Australians, on the other hand, were fresh. They were at full strength, they were raring to go and they roared into Pozières. Almost in the first wave they captured the outer trenches of the bastion of Pozières. In an hour they were fighting through the shattered gardens and outbuildings of the houses on the right of the Bapaume road. Here, or just beyond, they should have linked up with the 48th Division attacking from the other side of the Bapaume road. It was just as well that they did not wait for them.

On their own initiative, the Aussies dashed across the road and battered their way through the fortifications on the other side. They conquered 'Gibraltar' even while the 48th Division – or what was left of its men after the Germans had bombarded them in the assembly trenches – was still creeping forward in the face of terrible opposition from the posts beyond. To all intents and purposes, the Australians had captured the village of Pozières. What they had not managed to do, on their right flank, was to subdue the formidable trenches to the north of the village and to strike towards the windmill two hundred yards away.

But the Commander-in-Chief was delighted.

The diary of Sir Douglas Haig

Sunday, 23 July: A general attack was made at 1.30 a.m. The 5th or Reserve Army on our left advanced well to the west of Pozières village with 48th Division, while the First Australian Division captured the village of Pozières itself as far as the Albert–Bapaume Road and reached within two hundred yards of the windmill on the hill north-east of the village . . . The Fourth Army was not so fortunate.

General Haig had received the news early and in time to impart it at breakfast to his illustrious visitor, Lord Northcliffe, who was making one of his frequent visits to the front. Lord Northcliffe was particularly favoured by the Commander-in-Chief, at least by comparison with other journalists. Although he had started in a very small way as a reporter on a provincial newspaper, in the view of General Haig Lord Northcliffe hardly counted as a journalist at all. It was true that he had founded his fortune by means of a magazine of dubious reputation entitled *Answers*, whose content was directly aimed at 'Mary Ann in the kitchen', but, via the *Daily Mail*, he had long ago attained respectability. Now he was proprietor of *The Times* and was a Viscount to boot. Haig was delighted to entertain Lord Northcliffe, and very happy when, after breakfast on the dull, cloudy morning of 23 July, Lord Northcliffe accepted his invitation to accompany him to Mr Duncan's service at the makeshift Church of Scotland. Before leaving, Northcliffe gave the Commander-in-Chief even greater reason to have confidence in him.

The diary of Sir Douglas Haig

Lord N. was, he said, much pleased with his visit, and asked me to ... send him a line should anything appear in *The Times* which was not altogether to my liking. He also said that Repington had now no influence with *The Times*. They employed him to write certain articles but he (Lord N.) knew that he was not reliable.

Tim Repington had incurred the displeasure of the Commander-in-Chief by publishing certain views which emanated more from his own observations and deductions than from the Communiqués and official views of the Army regarding the conduct of the war. He had now been replaced as regular correspondent by Robinson (he of the 'chattering teeth'). Altogether General Haig, if journalists there had to be, found Robinson more to his taste. He was certainly more to his taste than 'John Bull', in the person of the redoubtable Horatio Bottomley, a campaigning journalist who made it his business to find out a good deal more than the Army wished him to know and broadcast it in the vociferous columns of his magazine which the soldiers themselves were beginning to refer to by its unofficial title of 'The Soldiers' Friend'. Already rumours of the débâcle at Fromelles had reached Bottomley's ears and already he was drafting the article which would dub the 61st Division 'The Sacrifice Division'.

Meanwhile the Australians were bracing themselves for a fresh attack on Pozières, to consolidate their gains in the village and to attack beyond it.

Private Fred Russell, No. 524, 22nd Btn., AIF, 6th Victoria Brigade

Our Brigade came in and we had to take over from where the 1st Division were to carry on the fighting and go as far as we could. The place by this time was one shambles of destruction – a wreck. Our headquarters, where I was with the CO of the Battalion, was in a fort called Gibralter. It was a German concrete dugout with a six-foot tower above the ground, right in the centre of the village of Pozières and all the rest of the houses round it were absolutely smashed to pieces.

Orders came along, 'We're to move off at a certain time and we'll advance on the village of Pozières.' Our artillery guns were mounted in a place called Sausage Valley and they were continually firing and, of course, we had to go through them. The main impact of an 18-pounder gun firing is the compression of the shell leaving the muzzle as it goes forward. When you were in front of the guns, you got into that compression. Of course the shell was going up in the air but you got the full blast, where you were, and it was a very hard experience to put up with.

Then we came into the counter-fire of the Germans. The shells were lobbing all over the place. We didn't know where on earth we were. We got into a chalk pit and guides met us there, fellows who were trained for the purpose. They led each party up. There was no front line as such, just a series of shell-holes and timber – no front, no back, no lines of demarcation. It was just an open devastated area. The companies didn't know where they were. You had to put yourself into position and say, 'Well, where are we?' And our CO said, 'Well, you take up fifty yards from here to here – say down to that broken-off tree – and the next company will have to take on from there and co-ordinate it that way.'

That went on all night, with the shelling still going on and they were throwing over big stuff. We got into this Gibraltar HQ – I had to be with HQ, because I was a signaller. We weren't in there ten minutes when a nine-inch shell landed on top of it. There were about twenty or thirty of our fellows down below in there – and down fifteen or twenty feet in a very solid concrete-lined job. But the compression was terrific. All night long they were calling for stretcher-bearers. Every time a salvo came over, after the explosion, you could hear these calls going up outside, 'Stretcher-bearer! Stretcher-bearer!' We took an awful lot of casualties that night, even before the boys went over.

Five days had passed since the first attack. George Middle had got his wireless stations going and they were in position ready for the attack to begin. With the advance of the line, U.L. had moved up and was installed in the chalk pit where the vanguard of the 13th Rifle Brigade had fought so valiantly eighteen days before. The trouble was, that they could not make contact with U.M. a few hundred yards behind, at the head of Sausage Valley.

The signal reached Middle at his station on Tara Hill at 11.25 a.m.: *Am not in contact with U.M. Corporal Love and two men are there but owing to very heavy shelling in that quarter, presume it impossible to erect aerial.*

There was no doubt that the shelling was heavy. It was falling so thick around the island of Pozières that it seemed to the troops advancing that the approaches were encircled by fire. On the right of the road, the Australians were pushing towards the village as best they could and, on the left, the 48th South Midland Division were struggling as best *they* could in a pincer movement up Mash Valley.

Sapper A. E. Comer, No. 474, 48th South Midland Division, Royal Engineers

My lot went up with the troops and we had to go over with rifles. Our own bombardment was terrific. This place, Pozières, was up on top of the ridge and in front of us there was nothing but one sheet of explosives. We went straight up. You grip your rifle and you say, 'Come on, you silly fool, you've got to go.' But all you could do was go a few yards and then drop down as the shells came around, then up again and on, and down again. The only thing you thought of was getting out of it. We engineers had to be there, because the idea was that as soon as we captured a trench we would consolidate it, reverse the parapet so that we'd be able to fire at the Germans from that side. What was even worse than going forward, was trying to keep on working. You drove yourself to it. You made yourself go on but there they were firing at you all the time.

I admit that I was windy. I remember being in a shell-hole and I was clawing at the ground to get my head into it. That's all I was interested in, to get my head right down into the ground. We captured one trench, and then a bit of another. But we didn't get much further. We didn't get to Pozières – and we could see it there, just in front of us. Or, at least, we could have done if you'd dared to look up but all you wanted to do was get on with your job and get out of it.

On the other side of the road, by half-past one, U.L. had succeeded in getting its aerial up and the message went back to Middle, anxiously waiting on Tara Hill: *Everything okay*.

The message should have gone no further. It was unfortunate that a signaller, unnerved by the noise, the barrage, the confusion of his first day in battle, inadvertently sent it on to Divisional Headquarters. It was unfortunate, too, that the message was taken at its face value to mean that the attack was going well, because under the punishing bombardment neither the Australians nor the South Midland Division were able to make much headway.

2nd Lieutenant George Middle, Royal Engineers, Wireless Officer, 1st Anzac Wireless Section

It was really a practice message and it was simply a fluke that it went through to Divisional Headquarters who'd planned the attack. I was still in the dugout at Tara Hill, an hour or so afterwards, and my immediate superior, Major Gordon, came down. I couldn't repeat the language he used. He said to me, 'What the so-and-so and so-and-so is the so-and-so meaning of this so-and-so thing?' And he was flapping this signal. I was a bit taken aback to begin with, but I immediately realized what had happened and said, 'This should never have got to you.' But it didn't do much good. He did belabour me because, as it so happened, everything was far from 'okay' and it had given Headquarters an entirely false impression of what was going on. It was a very bad start because, in a sense, we were demonstrating the use of wireless at that 'do' and supposedly showing how superior it was to telephones and land-lines that were so easily smashed by shell-fire. As a matter of fact, at Pozières, the shelling was so intense that all the lines were shattered and, apart from runners, wireless was really the only communication there was.

By evening, the Australians had borne such casualties and were so exhausted by the ordeal of shelling and fighting that the 2nd Australian Division was ordered into the line to relieve the 1st and, in the early hours, as the relief was taking place, the 17th Royal Warwicks, of the 48th South Midland Division, struggled through and linked up with the Australians to the north-west of Pozières. The village was secured, but the terrible obstacles to the north, trenches O.G.1 and O.G.2, still held out. Until they were captured it would be impossible even for the hard-fighting Aussies to fight their way towards the windmill a few hundred yards beyond. By 29 July, after four days in the line, after repeated efforts, the 2nd Australian Division had lost three thousand five hundred men – and still the windmill held out.

The Commander-in-Chief was sincerely impressed by the performance of Australia's fighting spirit and by the calibre and dash of the Australian soldiers. He was less impressed with the Staff.

The diary of Sir Douglas Haig

Saturday, 29 July: The attack by the 2nd Australian Division upon the enemy's position between Pozières and the windmill, was not successful last night. From several reports I think the cause was due to want of thorough preparation.

After lunch I visited H Q Reserve Army and impressed on Gough and Neill Malcolm that they must supervise more closely the plans of the Anzac Corps. Some of their Divisional Generals are so ignorant and (like many Colonials) so conceited, that they cannot be trusted to work out unaided the plans of attack.

I then went on to H Q Anzac Corps at Contay and saw General Birdwood and his B G S General White. The latter seems a very sound capable fellow, and assured me that they had learnt a lesson, and would be more thorough in future.

General Birdwood, although an Englishman, like George Middle, was an honorary Australian, and popular with his troops. He had gone with them to Egypt and he had brought them to France. In the aftermath of the disaster at Fromelles, he had been following with anguished pride every stage of his Aussies' ordeal at Pozières. Now, in the face of the reproof of the Commander-in-Chief, he kept his own counsel. It was unlikely that he agreed with Haig's opinion that: 'Luckily their losses had been fairly small, considering the operation and the numbers engaged – about a thousand for the whole twenty-four hours.'

Considering the total strength of the Australian force, considering that the A I F had sustained five and a half thousand casualties at Fromelles, considering their losses in the six days since they first launched their strength into Pozières, one thousand men seemed a very large number to have been swallowed up by the maw of the war machine as it ground inexorably towards the end of Bloody July.

On that very day, 29 July, while Haig was in conference with Generals Birdwood and White a letter to the Commander-in-Chief was being written in London. It came from Field-Marshal Sir William Robertson, Chief of the Imperial General Staff, and after the initial euphoria of the

'Big Push' and the heroic stories which had stirred the imagination of the British public, it reflected the unease which was beginning to be felt at home. It was all very well to bandy about the names of villages and ridges as if they were places of metropolitan importance; it was all very well to talk in glowing terms of 'advances', 'leaps forward' and 'captures'; it was right and proper that the troops should be praised for their endeavours, for no praise was high enough, but maps were being published alongside communiqués from the front and the maps were drawn to scale. Assiduous newspaper readers did not have to be geographers or military experts in order to realize that, in terms of distance, if not in terms of strategic importance, the advances were small and that, in some cases, gains of as little as thirty yards were being hailed, in print, with as much enthusiasm as if Berlin itself had fallen to the Allies.

It was equally obvious that the price was high. The whole country had been virtually mobilized to cope with the streams of wounded arriving from the Somme. There had not even been enough ambulances to transport them and even now huge numbers of casualties were being nursed in an extraordinary assortment of temporary premises ranging from village schools and church halls to private houses. They had been pressed into service as temporary hospitals when the civilian and military hospitals had been swamped by the ceaseless convoys of wounded, and every day the Rolls of Honour, those long lists of soldiers reported missing or killed, were growing ever longer.

The letter from Sir William Robertson hinted at the doubts of the powers-that-be and invited the Commander-in-Chief to reply to some pointed questions:

Will a loss of three hundred thousand men really lead to great results? If not should we revise and limit our plans?

Why did it seem that the British were now bearing the brunt of the fighting and the French seemed to be doing little?

Has the primary object of relieving the pressure of Verdun not, at least to some extent, been achieved?

The Commander-in-Chief carefully phrased his reply and sent it immediately to London. Yes, the pressure on Verdun had been relieved. In addition the enemy had been prevented from transferring troops from the Western Front to the Eastern, thereby aiding Russia. He stressed the 'public-relations angle'. The Somme Offensive had proved to the world that the Allies were capable of a vigorous offensive and of 'driving the enemy's best troops from the strongest positions'. This must certainly have shaken the faith of the Germans and those who sided with Germany.

It must also have 'impressed on the world, England's strength and determination, and the fighting power of the British race'. The offensive must be maintained and would eventually result in Germany being overthrown.

The Commander-in-Chief was not persuaded by the casualties. In his view they were not inordinate. Making careful calculations on the expected 'natural wastage' of trench warfare from shelling and skirmishing, he was satisfied that the casualties in the July fighting were only 'about one hundred and twenty thousand more than they would have been had we not attacked'. This, in Haig's opinion, could not be regarded 'as sufficient to justify any anxiety as to our ability to continue the offensive'.

He made it perfectly clear that he intended to continue it and that he expected to be able to maintain the offensive 'well into the autumn'.

General Haig had omitted to take into consideration the fact that the casualties, which the Army was pleased to refer to as 'normal wastage', contained a very much higher proportion of wounded to killed than had been experienced on the Somme since the First of July. By the end of the month the casualties amounted to one hundred and sixty-five thousand. The casualties alone were almost double the entire strength of the British Expeditionary Force which had set off in August 1914 to meet the Germans at Mons. And forty thousand of them were dead.

Chapter 16

At Abbeville, many miles from the front, the lock gates on the River Somme refused to open and divers sent down to investigate found that they were jammed by the bloated bodies of French soldiers carried along by the current of the river as it flowed through to the sea. They had been dead for many weeks.

Although precise casualty figures for each stage of the fighting had not been disclosed, it was common knowledge that they had been heavy. In Britain, parents who had been rather proud of schoolboy sons who had lied their way into the Army, began to bombard the authorities, literally brandishing birth certificates in their anxiety to have under-age soldiers sent back from the front. The Army, while unwilling to remove any of its sadly depleted forces from the line, had no choice, but they had no intention of sending the enthusiastic juveniles home again, still less of discharging them from the Army. Some were, after all, within months of their nineteenth birthday when they would officially come of military age, and, in the meantime, they could be usefully employed at various base camps where every day a thousand or more reinforcements were arriving from Britain in transit to the front. They were flooding into France to replace the early casualties of the Somme and, in the great tract of land that stretched between the Somme battlefield and the coast, the weary battalions which had been struck hard in the first few days' fighting were being rested, revitalized and brought up to strength with new drafts of men. The trouble was that, in the opinion of the Kitchener's Battalions, they were the wrong men.

In the flag waving days of August 1914, when local battalions surged into being on the tide of national enthusiasm, when local boys from Cornwall to John O'Groats had marched arm in arm to join their ranks, almost every battalion had its unique local identity. Now, with a hotch-potch of new arrivals sent to fill the gaps in the ranks of the Kitchener's Battalions with what the troops looked on as arbitrary disregard for their spirit and origins, resentment began to grow. After their ordeal at Gomme-court, the Queen Victoria's Rifles were particularly incensed when the very train that brought a draft of 'strangers' to reinforce them also carried a contingent of men of their own regiment bound for an entirely different unit. The Queen's Westminster Rifles were amused when they were joined by a large batch of the undersized Bantam soldiers and good-humouredly scrounged for empty ammunition boxes to raise the fire-steps of their trenches to a more convenient height, but they were infuriated when their own comrades, coming back to the front on recovering from their wounds, were posted to 'foreign' regiments. Trevor Ternan was equally enraged when precisely the same thing happened to the remnants of the Tyneside Scottish.

The Army allowed it to become known that it was anxious, in the future, to cultivate an 'Army Spirit' rather than the old-fashioned regimental or battalion loyalty. But there were more cogent reasons behind the decision. After the holocaust of the July attacks, local newspapers all over the country were carrying page after page of photographs of local boys who had been killed, casualty lists that were a terrible litany of familiar names, and story after pathetic story of brothers or cousins of one family who had been lost in a single attack. There were rumblings in Parliament where MPs, whose constituencies had been particularly hard hit were beginning to ask awkward questions, and, despite the country's brave acceptance of what amounted to a mass bereavement, the policy of diluting what was left of Kitchener's Battalions, of spreading the risk by splitting up the ranks of boys who all hailed from one town or area, smacked strongly of deliberate political policy.

It was the Scots who took it as a personal insult. It was bad enough when their own Scottish drafts were sent to English regiments, but it was even worse when Scottish battalions were forced to receive 'foreigners' into their ranks and it was particularly resented in the kilted battalions. A large draft of the 51st Division had been relegated to khaki-trousered ignominy in the ranks of the York and Lancaster Regiment, while their Scottish Division was augmented by a contingent of reluctantly kilted warriors who were actually Barnsley men in disguise. Once they had got used to the unaccustomed ventilation of their lower regions, they were not entirely displeased with their metamorphosis. It was a well-known fact, as the Argylls were quick to inform them, that the Germans referred to the 'Kilties' as the Ladies from Hell and that the very sight of the tartan put the fear of God into them.

But, as a Cockney born and bred, Bill Turner found the kilt a distinct embarrassment and, 'Ladies from Hell' or not, was inclined to feel at times that he would just as soon be fighting the Germans in the trenches, than his comrades of the 4th Highland Light Infantry in the only slightly less belligerent territory contained within the walls of Maryhill Barracks in Glasgow. The Scots were of the opinion that the masquerading English-

men were fair game, an opinion which was not shared by Bill Turner
nor by his friend George, who suffered the additional impediment of the
surname 'England'. They became philosophical about being the butt of
rough jokes. In the barrack room they quickly learned to judge just how
far they could go in an argument and to dodge the flying boots and less
savoury missiles that were hurled at their heads if they miscalculated. They
became resigned to the fact that they were the first to be picked on
by the Sergeants, could rely on being on Defaulters' Report as often as
three times a week and that the only way to get off fatigues was to empty
their pockets and bribe the Sergeant with all the money they had.
But the Cockney contingent did not, on the whole, look forward
to Friday evenings when the Highlanders invariably got drunk and,
in their cups, considered it great sport to chase the lads with their 'dirks'.
Being younger, lither and sober, they usually managed to escape with
no more than a volley of imprecations and, once at a safe distance,
hurled back taunts of, 'Who won at Bannockburn?' and, 'What about
Flodden?' But this they would only risk when at a very safe distance
indeed.

It hardly seemed fair. Bill Turner had not asked to be in the Highland
Light Infantry. He had joined the Royal Artillery, and, strictly speaking,
at the age of seventeen, he had no right to be in the Army at all, and
here he was – not only a serving soldier but, what was more, a Regular.

After a dozen attempts to join up, after a dozen recruiting sergeants
had turned him away with a smile as patronizing as a pat on the head, it
had seemed to Bill like the answer to a prayer when, passing Wandsworth
Town Hall, he saw an announcement of a special enlistment scheme for
boys under nineteen to join the Royal Field Artillery.

*Corporal Bugler William Turner, No. B.21097, 15th Highland Light
Infantry (City of Glasgow Corporation Tramways Battalion) 32nd Division*

First thing off, I was sent to Maryhill Barracks in Glasgow. We was
up there three months in the riding school and then we got called
out on the parade ground. It was just after the Battle of Loos and
the Highland Regiments had got badly cut up there, so they wanted
seventeen hundred volunteers to join to refill them. Hardly anybody
volunteered. In the afternoon we was called out on the square again
and the CO says, 'Right. As I call your names and numbers out,
fall in over there.' Blow me, he called out practically everybody's
name and number! I was in a bunch of three hundred and fifty
that was transferred to the Highland Light Infantry. And that was
that! It was real hell for us Cockneys! You was picked out for the

least thing. Up the Orderly Room, three days CB. We were never out of the Orderly Room!

I managed to work myself into the band. It was a pipe-band, of course, but they trained me as a bugler and drummer. It had advantages in the band, and it had disadvantages too! The worst thing was that we weren't a kilted battalion, but the band was all dressed in the kilt. We didn't like it at all. Of course, being young things, we were after the girls, but we were frightened to go out to meet the girls wearing these things. We weren't allowed to wear anything underneath and it *was* cold. We felt half-naked – embarrassed as much as anything – and we knew the girls would see our white knees and that would give away that we were rookies. Even when we could get a pass to go up into the town, we didn't go for weeks. We used to stay in and get hold of some cold stewed tea, or get some permanganate of potash from the chemist and sit there trying to stain our knees to look as if we'd just come down from the Highlands. Then, when we thought we looked respectable, out we went.

I got to like the kilt very much. It was McKenzie tartan and there was eight and a quarter yards of material in it with pleats. They were lovely after a time and really kept you warm when you got used to them. By the time we moved down to Haddington, I felt a real swell and my knees were *really* brown by then. What with playing in the band and swinging around in the kilt, I was a real Cock of the North. I got off with a lovely girl called Maggie Gaffney. She was just about my age and I got very fond of her.

Then came the Battle of the Somme and I was put on a draft to go overseas to replace the casualties of the 15th Highland Light Infantry, which was the Glasgow Tramways Battalion, and they'd got very badly cut up on the First of July. So off I went home to London on four days draft leave. I was all spruced up in my kilt – a real Highland Soldier! There was a well-known tattooist on Waterloo Bridge, name of Birkett, and a lot of the other chaps, the older soldiers especially, they'd got the regimental badge tattooed on their arm. So when I got to Waterloo Station, I went across the bridge and popped in there and took off my tunic, rolled up my shirt sleeve and got this chap to tattoo the Highland Light Infantry badge on my arm. I got home, proud as Punch in my highland uniform, kilt and everything. I took my tunic off and rolled my sleeves up and was flashing my arm about. My mother caught sight of it and she says, 'What's that you've got on your arm?' I says, quite nonchalant, 'That? That's the Highland Light Infantry badge, same as I wear on my hat.'

I didn't half come down to earth then. My mother laid into me. 'How dare you?' she said. 'How dare you get a thing like that put on your arm! Making yourself common!' I said, 'I'm proud of that badge!' 'I'll give you proud!' she said. And she did too! She gave me a good hiding! She really did. Army or not, soldier or not, Highlander or not, she gave me a damn good hiding! And she kept nagging me about my leave. It was well-known that you got four days before you went abroad. She kept saying, 'Is it draft leave?' Of course I kept saying it wasn't – but she went on and on about it.

All in all, Bill's leave had not come completely up to his expectations. He was not sorry to say goodbye and to set off back to Haddington and the charms of Maggie Gaffney. Maggie was on the station platform two days later when the draft left for France. Almost the whole population had turned out to see the lads go. There were many girls like Maggie who claimed a last clinging embrace before the troops piled into the train, slung their kit and rifles on to the racks and struggled in a ten-deep mass behind the open carriage windows in a concerted, futile attempt to shout individual farewells. The shouts were inaudible. A pipe-band, drawn up in front of the train between the soldiers and the tearful tiptoeing civilians, was playing at the pitch of its breath the plaintive strains of *Will Ye No' Come Back Again?* Such of the civilians as were not entirely overcome, were mouthing the words and were disconcerted when the band droned to a halt in the middle of a bar as the train began to move out of the station. It had hardly moved a yard before it came to a jerking halt.

Now the Sergeant-Major was walking up and down the train and calling at the top of his voice, 'LANCE-CORPORAL TURNER!' At the fourth or fifth call, Bill Turner managed to squeeze his way to the window to answer the summons.

Corporal Bugler William Turner, No. B.21097, 15th Highland Light Infantry (City of Glasgow Corporation Tramways Battalion), 32nd Division

He said, 'Fetch your kit and your rifle and come on out here.' I still didn't know what was happening, but I got my stuff and got out and he said, 'Come with me!' He took me up to an officer who had some papers in his hand and the officer said, 'Turner? How old are you?' I said, 'Nineteen.' He said, 'Don't tell lies! I've got a letter here from your mother. You're under age. Get your equipment on, and get back to your billet.'

Maggie Gaffney, interrupted in the full flood of an emotional farewell, was unsure whether to laugh or cry. Plodding back, humiliated and ashamed, with the sound of the cheering and the band and the hoot of the train growing fainter behind him, Bill himself could have wept with disappointment. Six months later, when he had wangled his way on to another draft for France, he made very sure that his mother would not have the least suspicion. This time he had missed his chance, and what galled him most was that he had missed it by just two minutes.

Some under-age boys had joined up with the approval of their mothers. In the case of Jim Dwelly the approval had been strictly conditional on his joining a 'safe' unit, and he had dutifully enlisted in the Army Service Corps. In ribald mockery of its initials the ASC was popularly known in the Army as Ally Sloper's Cavalry. Ally Sloper was a fictional character, of dubious behaviour, the blundering hero of a popular comic strip.

In the opinion of the front-line infantry, the ASC led the life of Riley behind the lines. They firmly believed that they had first pick of the rations, unlimited perks, total protection from the attentions of the enemy and, altogether, led a cushy life. But, without the often gruelling labour of Ally Sloper's Cavalry, the infantry could not have been maintained in the trenches for as much as twenty-four hours. It was the ASC who unloaded the supply ships and loaded the provisions on to divisional trains. Behind the lines it was the ASC who came in for most of the dirty jobs and a great deal of very hard work. At the front, delivering supplies to the line, they were exposed to quite as much dangerous shelling and had rather less protection than the infantry in the trenches. Their tasks were manifold, if humble. They were the underdogs of the Army and their theme song was not only plaintive but pathetic:

> We are the little ASC
> We work all night, we work all day.
> The more we work, the more we may,
> It makes no difference to our pay.

The tune, like a thousand other Army parodies, was a hymn tune, but unlike many of the others it did not have much of a lilt to it. *We are but little children weak*, possibly had a certain charm when warbled by infant Sunday School voices, but rendered in the deeper tones of Ally Sloper's Cavalry, it was distinctly dirge-like. It hardly mattered that it was not a tune that encouraged men to stride out on the march. The ASC did very little marching and many of them hardly knew how. Like Jim Dwelly, the vast majority had been shipped out to France after a mere three weeks in the Army and, with a hundred thousand infantry to be trained, they had been left largely to their own devices. They had mastered the rudiments of saluting, and very little more.

Private J. C. Dwelly, No. 274, Army Service Corps

The most exciting thing that happened to me during the Battle of the Somme was when a sentry-box blew over on the quayside at Boulogne and broke a man's leg. We were down there loading. That was my job at the time, loading up meat – or, rather, supervising the blokes who were loading it, because I couldn't even have lifted one of these huge sides of meat. It was all frozen and it came over by the boat-load, was brought off the ship and dumped on a siding. I had the job of working out the quantities for each division to send it up the line. It would be two thousand pounds of meat for one division and maybe one thousand four hundred and twenty for another, and the quantities were changed every day or two when the divisions were in the line because, of course, they were suffering casualties.

Being there on the Maritime Station we saw a tremendous number of casualties. All that coastline was full of hospitals and there were ambulances driving non-stop past the siding where we were working, taking the wounded to the hospital ships. I felt a bit badly about having a good time in Boulogne. We used to start work at four o'clock in the morning and we were finished by lunchtime and didn't do anything at all for the rest of the day.

I got fed up. I'd only joined the ASC to please my mother and I didn't want to be in it, so I decided to apply for a transfer. So many blokes had been killed that they were asking round all the camps for people who wanted to transfer to a line regiment, so I took my chance.

Jim Dwelly set his sights high. He requested an interview with the Regimental Sergeant-Major at the base camp and announced that he wished to transfer to the Guards. The RSM could hardly conceal his astonishment. He stared at Dwelly in disbelief and said, 'You must be bloody mad!' It was an understandable reaction for the only outward attribute possessed by Dwelly which might remotely qualify him to join the élite of the Army was that he was six feet tall. But quiet persistence had its way. Still marvelling at the very nerve of it, the RSM forwarded Jim's application and it was a moot point which of them was the more astonished when he was accepted by the Grenadier Guards. By the time she found out, his transfer was an accomplished fact, and his mother was slightly mollified by the knowledge that he would spend three months in safety while he trained in England. But, while Jim was waiting for orders to report to the Guards Depot at Caterham, they sent him to the Somme, and to his immense delight they sent him to join up with the Guards.

Private J. C. Dwelly, No. 274, Army Service Corps

I had to report to the Guards Divisional Headquarters at Maricourt. Of course, I wasn't yet in the Guards officially, but they knew I was going to be transferred, so they thought I might as well be with the Division while I waited for my training. The first night I got there, I was put into a room with no roof to it or anything. It was open to the world, all smashed up with bombs and shells. There were a few other blokes in there and I told one of them I was waiting for a transfer into the Grenadier Guards. He said, 'You must be mad! Why didn't you stop where you were?' I said, 'Well, I got a bit fed up with being in the same place and I just thought it would be a change.' He said, 'You're crackers, mate, you really are!' Looking around me, hearing those shells booming away not so far off, I began to think I must be.

They made me clerk to the Veterinary Officer. They had all their horse lines there and the Veterinary Officer was in charge of any that were sick and I had to keep a record of all the things that went wrong with then, stiff legs, wounds, all sorts of things. And I had to keep a record of the horses that were sent away sick and the new horses that were examined when they came in. I was there all the rest of the time the battle was on and even long after. I didn't get to Caterham until April 1917.[1]

The health of horses was of prime importance and every division had its veterinary officer. The Army depended on horses and by 1916 there were more than half a million on military service in France. They came from America, from South America, and the vast numbers that had been requisitioned in 1914 from farmers and stables in Britain were constantly being augmented by fresh 'drafts' from home. They came in a variety of sizes, shapes and breeds from the magnificent charger ridden by the Commander-in-Chief, to the humble mule teams pulling field kitchens along

1. Dwelly successfully passed the rigorous training at the Guards Depot in Caterham, was sent back to France in September 1917 and fought in the Guards until the end of the war.

the cobbled roads in front of the marching battalions. There were huge draught horses, Clydesdales and Shires, to drag the heavy guns and ammunition wagons. There were fast-moving steeds for the Cavalry and Hussars, good mounts for colonels and senior officers and less refined beasts for other officers who needed transport to get around the countryside in a scattered command. There were humbler but powerful teams of hacks and mules to draw the horse-drawn limbers that were part of the transport column of every battalion. They ran into thousands, for the mountain of supplies which was required to keep the Army in the line was gargantuan.

Ammunition, rations and equipment could be taken as far as the nearest railhead; from there they were transported by motor columns to divisional dumps, but it was then up to the humble horse transport of brigades and battalions to make long cross-country journeys to fetch and carry back their own supplies of ammunition and rations for men and for horses. Forage was bulky and it caused the officer in charge of horse transport a good deal more trouble to ensure that his horses were well fed than any battalion quartermaster encountered in supplying rations to the men. A soldier could get by on a tin of bully beef, half a loaf and sufficient tea and sugar for a few brew-ups. Depending on its size and the work expected of it, a horse required between sixteen and thirty pounds of forage a day. The daily requirement of each division was thirty tons.

All over northern France blind horses were being put to the plough, for horses were too badly needed to be shot when they became casualties if there was the slightest chance that they would recover and, even if they were no longer of use for Army purposes, a useful deal could be made with French farmers in return for food or forage. Now that it was harvest time on the Somme, the troops as well as the horses were working in the fields, but on a strictly unofficial basis. There were certain commanding officers who, having marched the remnant of a battalion out of the battle to rest and absorb fresh drafts before going in to the fight again, considered that a day spent in a sunny cornfield engaged in healthy and useful activity in the congenial company of civilians, would do his men as much good as the long periods of drill or route marching laid down by the Army.

The troops and the French civilians got on amazingly well and although neither the French peasantry nor the Tommies, on the whole, were skilled linguists most of the soldiers had picked up enough fractured French to make themselves understood after a fashion, although 'No compree' was probably the most frequently used expression in the pidgin French that served as the *lingua franca*.

The French themselves astutely appreciated the convenience of adopting the Tommies' bowdlerized version of their native tongue and had quickly come to understand that a soldier who might be confused by the polite refusal, '*Il n'y a plus, Monsieur*', would certainly get the message of a blunt '*Napoo!*' and reply with a resigned '*San fairy ann*', whose meaning he plainly understood as '*it doesn't matter*' and which came close enough to '*ça ne fait rien*', to be equally understood by the French. It was more practical, too, when a farm had been cleaned out of produce by some ravenous battalion, to scrawl regretfully on the archway of its courtyard '*Napoo doolay. Napoo oofs,*' which was understood by all to mean 'No more eggs. No more milk,' rather than '*Il n'y a plus d'oeufs. Il n'y a plus de lait,*' which would be understood by few. There were occasional misunderstandings. One soldier, anxious to convey his urgent desire to purchase eggs, squatted and strained in elaborate pantomime of a laying hen, and was astonished and embarrassed to find himself conducted to the outside privy.

On the whole, given their limited vocabulary, the troops managed to communicate exceedingly well with their allies. One farmer's wife, hearing the shout, '*Doolay promenade, Madame!*' had no difficulty in understanding that her errant cow had wandered off. More sophisticated attempts at French construction often resulted in blank incomprehension and the soldier who had taken the trouble to study a booklet entitled *What you want to say and How to say it in French* (kindly supplied free of charge by the manufacturers of Wincarnis who also recommended their tonic wine '. . . *for the relief of nerves in the trenches*'!) occasionally found it more difficult to make himself understood than if he had left well alone and stuck to 'Tommies' French'. One was a soldier of the 51st Division whose uncompromisingly Scottish mind had vaguely registered that the complexities of the French language contained both masculine and feminine nouns. It was the Medical Officer, Major Rory, who overheard him exchanging pleasantries with the lady of the house in the yard of a farm not far behind the lines. She was admiring his kilt and fingering the pleats with a Frenchwoman's appreciation of quality. The Jock, a little unsure of her intentions, was anxious to change the subject and, gazing upwards for inspiration, caught sight of an observation balloon climbing slowly into the sky.

'Voilà, Madame! Voilà le sausage!'

Madame did not follow his meaning. The Jock racked his brains.

'Well, voilà *la* sausage then!'

The Labour Battalions, recruited from all over the world, added an exotic touch to the cosmopolitan population which inhabited the French hinterland behind the lines. At the peak of their strength, in late 1916, they numbered three hundred and eighty-seven thousand and, although

it was chauvinistically reckoned that it took three foreign labourers to do
the work of one European, by undertaking the navvying, road-building
and mending, tree-felling and work on the railways – all essential to keep
the ever-growing Army in the field – they released several thousand
fighting soldiers for service at the front. There were battalions of huge
Fijians and Maoris; there were black labourers from South Africa and,
strictly segregated from them, a Cape Coloured battalion. There was a
battalion of Egyptian labourers and there was the Indian Labour Corps
which had been kept in Europe when the main body of the Indian
contingent had been sent to the Middle East, and were dying like flies in
the harsh northern climate. There were certain Canadian Labour Battalions,
chiefly working in the forests, where the lumberjacks could hardly keep
up with the demand for wood for the trenches, huts and dugouts, for
plank roads that could be quickly laid across the mutilated battlefields and
for sleepers for the ever-lengthening miles of railway track that carried
ever-larger quantities of supplies to the front. There was the Middlesex
Labour Company, British in name only, composed of naturalized British
subjects, many of German origin, who were not eligible to serve in the
fighting ranks of the Army. Most numerous, and most exotic of all, were
the Chinese Labour Battalions. They were also the most troublesome, for
the large majority of the labourers had been recruited from Chinese
prisons, induced by the promise that their sentences would be remitted
and that they would be rewarded by untold riches in return for labour
on the other side of the world. 'Untold riches' amounted to payment of
a franc a day but, by the exercise of oriental wiliness, some of the coolies
amassed considerable sums. Thieving and gambling were the most lucra-
tive pursuits and the ones that caused the Provost-Marshal's biggest
headache.

Like the other Labour Battalions the Chinese were clustered in camps
around Montreuil, and among the camps, the hospitals, the training
grounds and Army camps that filled the narrow strip of coastline that ran
from Calais to le Havre. The Chinese knew nothing of the war and cared
even less. What they did know was that, by the terms of their contract,
they were not to be exposed to shell-fire, a clause they were apt to cite
when occasionally there was an air raid, demanding extra pay as 'danger
money'.

By 1916 there had been so few air raids in the region of Montreuil
that it was generally believed an agreement existed. The Germans, it was
said, would refrain from bombing the British General Staff, if the British
refrained from bombing the German Staff – a deal, cynics remarked, in
which the Germans came off best both ways. The cynics, however, were
mostly to be found in the ranks of the Headquarters troops and Pioneer

Battalions attached to them and among the Tommies who, having been fortunate enough to be transferred to the Chinese Labour Corps, found themselves suddenly elevated from underdogs in the eyes of the Army, to divine personages in the eyes of the Chinese.

Sergeant John Ward, No. 49747, 12th Btn., King's Royal Rifle Corps, and 53rd Company Chinese Labour Corps

After I was wounded I was reclassified C.3., and sent to a base camp at Etaples, doing office work. One day we were paraded and the officer called out, 'Anybody speak Chinese?' I stepped out of the ranks and he said, 'Right, you can come to my office after you dismiss.' When I got there, he said, 'Is it true you can speak Chinese?' Well, of course, I couldn't speak a word of it, but I was fed up with my job and I thought it would be a change so I said, 'No, sir, to be honest, I can't. But I like languages and Chinese is really one I'd like to master.' He said, 'Bloody sauce!' But after a bit of to-ing and fro-ing he said, 'Well, just for your cheek, I'll transfer you.'

They sent me to a big Chinese camp at Crècy, where there were about seven hundred of them. I was in clover! For every twenty labourers there was a Chinese ganger who really did all the work so far as organizing the coolies was concerned, and of course there were interpreters and one or two head-men. And there was quite a number of English NCOs, like myself. We all had batmen! Mine was called Yat-shay-bat-chipa. That wasn't his name. It was his number (14870). None of the Chinese had names, only a brass bracelet with a number on it. The first thing I did was to learn the Chinese for one to ten and it went something like this:

Yat, Ye, Sam, Shay, Ng, Lok, Chat, Bat, Gow, Sap and *Pa*, which was a hundred. After only about a couple of days I was able to call out a dozen men just by using their number. It falls off your tongue when you know it.

This camp was a convalescent camp for Chinese who had been sick or wounded accidentally and they nearly all suffered from Trachoma – weeping red eyes. But that didn't prevent them from working and we used to send them out in gangs on different jobs every morning – light jobs, mostly, until they had fully recovered.

Private Norman Mellor, No. 41728, 4th Bedfordshire Regiment

I had a good time with the Chinese Labour Corps. The only Chinese I ever learned was '*Koydy fidee!*' – and that means 'come on, quick!' They were damned good, hard-working and faithful, if they took to you. But, if they *didn't*, they could slit your throat or do anything. Across from our camp was the 186th Company which was a Prison Company, and all the men in it were under punishment for some crime. They had their own Military Police and they all carried a truncheon.

I was in charge of the Chinese Pay Roll. It was my job to pay them out – a franc a day, but we paid it once a month, so they got thirty francs. That's when there was trouble, when they got all that money. It was a fortune to them! One time we had the office safe broken into and all the money went. No one knew who had done it but of course the Chinese in my own camp had to take the rap for it and I had the unpleasant job of getting all the money back off them. They didn't like it a single bit! Everyone had to pay so much in, because several thousand francs were taken and they all had to contribute to pay it back.

The Chinese were terrible thieves. If I wanted anything at all I just had to mention it to my servant, who spoke a bit of pidgin English, and he'd get it. I never enquired where it came from. But he would never pinch a thing from me. I'd go down in the village the odd time and get tight. Go back to my hut – I'd got a hut of my own – and sling my things off and my money would be lying all over the place and I'd get into bed. Next morning, there he'd be with a cup of tea and the hut all tidied and not a thing touched. And then he'd shave me in bed! He'd do anything for me. It was a life of luxury, and no mistake!

One thing I never ever saw was a drunk Chinaman. Everything else they'd do, but not drink. They liked money, but they didn't like spending it. They'd save it all up, and then someone else would pinch it from them and there'd be trouble over that. Even murder! The only murder we had in our lot was over a girl. One of these coolies had taken a fancy to a French girl who served in some *estaminet*, and he thought one of our Sergeants was just a bit too friendly with her. So one night he went round when everybody was asleep and slit open the NCOs' tents until he found this Sergeant and he bashed his head in. Then he took off! I never heard whether they caught him for it.

The most notorious murder was at Montreuil and it was a murder over gambling debts. After that, an edict from GHQ strictly forbade the Chinese to gamble. GHQ might as well have forbidden them to breathe. Crouched in circles round every corner, the Chinese played Fantan by the hour – and working hours, at that! And they bribed their interpreters to inform the authorities that this was a Chinese religious observance which must be respected. It didn't work for long! The only people who seemed to be able to keep the Chinese in any sort of order were some members of Pioneer Battalions who convinced the Chinese Labourers that their crossed-axe sleeve badges, a symbol of their status as skilled tradesmen, proclaimed them to be official executioners, with the right to summarily chop off the head of any recalcitrant 'coolie'.

The notorious Chinese Secret Societies had come to Europe with the Labour Corps. Every coolie had his own 'Tong' and every coolie was convinced by his Tong leader that a Chinese who died of illness in a European hospital had been foully done to death. So, it followed that, when a coolie fell ill, two men went out of action, for the patient refused to go to hospital unless he was accompanied by a member of his Tong to see that he got a fair deal and that he came out again. This was also the aim of the medical authorities, for a dead Chinaman could be as much of a nuisance as a live one. It was up to the Chinese themselves to conduct the elaborate funeral rites but it was up to the authorities to find a suitable place of burial and 'suitability' was spelt out precisely in an official memorandum on the subject of Chinese graves.

> *The ideal site to secure repose and drive away evil spirits is on sloping ground with a stream below, or gully down which water always or occasionally passes. The grave should not be parallel to the north, south, east or west. This is particularly important to Chinese Mahommedans. It should be about four-feet deep, with the head towards the hill and the feet towards the water. A mound of earth about two feet high is piled over the grave.*

It was not always easy to carry out these instructions to the letter for, at the height of the Somme Battle, the Labour Corps as a whole was suffering almost a thousand casualties a month, and many of them were Chinese. Although they were protected from 'war risk' and were therefore not supposed to be employed within shelling distance of the front line, nothing had been said about salvage operations and during August 1916 salvage was a matter of prime importance to the Army. As the troops fought forward, the Pioneer and Labour Battalions followed behind clearing the ground of unexploded ammunition, recovering lost equipment and rifles lying useless on the ground where there had been heavy casualties during an advance. In packing them and sending them back to the base there were many accidents.

Staff Sergeant James Kain, No. 2282, Army Ordnance Corps

There were fifty-thousand rifles lying out on the battlefield. The Pioneers used to go and fetch them in when the conditions permitted it. They came to us in open trucks and we had to clear them quick. I had a fatigue party of half a dozen men. They were all stood up on the truck passing the rifles down a line and, of course, coming straight off the battlefield, there were live rounds left in them. You grabbed them and threw open the bolt – didn't trouble to look at it – there simply wasn't time – and out flew the rounds, all over the place. The fellows in the truck were just throwing them out one after the other. We had two rifles every three seconds, day after day, and we were working flat out. One day I had thirty-two thousand rifles pass through my hands! I worked it out. Four tons, one load. The only vehicles that could take that load of rifles was the Foden steam engine with a very sturdy truck behind it and even with that we had to have a special steel bar made so that the sides wouldn't bulge.

If the rifles were all right, we just tossed them on to this waiting Foden and they went straight off down the line to the workshops, where they were checked for bent barrels and any faults and then they would be issued to the troops and straight back up the line. But of course we got badly damaged rifles, bits of rifles, all sorts of things and we packed them all together and put them in crates and took them out to sea and sunk them. Some of the others had tight bolts and you would give it a smash with a hammer to make it fly open, or sometimes the catch wouldn't be strong enough to eject the bullets still in it and one would be stuck live in the breech. Once every three weeks or so, one would go off and of course you'd always had to be sure to turn the breech away from you so that the explosion would blow the other way. There was one fellow killed, and one horse was killed and one fellow had his arm shattered, all through the same thing. But that was all the casualties we had, which was remarkable when you think how many rifles we were handling.

Once or twice a day a fellow would have to come round with a broom and sweep all the live rounds up and tip them into the wooden barrel and, further down the road in a field, were four French ladies and they sat there all day long with a special gadget which they stuck into the cartridge and eventually the bullet came out and fell into a box. They emptied the gun powder into a big barrel and their job was to put all the brass and nickel bullets in separate piles to go back home to be remade. Then, every night, they poured the gun-powder out into a heap in the field, ran a fuse to it and it just went up in a puff of smoke.

Kain was one small cog in the vast machine controlled by the Controller of Salvage at GHQ, known unkindly to his fellow officers as 'Old Rags and Bones' or more succinctly as 'Swill'. It was the responsibility of the Royal Engineers to recover their own miles of telephone cable and to return it to the base where it had to be tediously rewound on to cable drums by the signallers themselves. Almost everything else came under the aegis of 'Swill'.

Clothing was cleaned and repaired, or, if beyond redemption, sent back to the United Kingdom as rags. Entrenching tool heads were cleaned and sharpened. Steel helmets were cleaned and relined if they were whole, or, if too battered and holed, were sold as scrap iron after the chin straps had been removed for sale as old leather. Water-bottles were re-covered with a new felt and supplied with new corks. Webbing equipment was dry-cleaned on motor-driven brushes, darned and repaired by local labour or, if beyond repair, had their metal fittings removed and were sent back to the United Kingdom as cotton rags. Leather equipment and saddlery was washed and treated with fish oil, which was also used to restore suppleness to old boots. Even boots whose useful life was at an obvious end had their studs removed for scrap metal before they were abandoned.

There was no item in the detritus of battle which was too insignificant to escape the attention of General 'Swill' Gibbs. He ran the Salvage Corps with an almost missionary zeal, in the firm conviction that every recovered horseshoe nail was another nail in the coffin of the Kaiser and he did his best to transmit his enthusiasm to the troops at the front. Soon, battalions coming out of the line were confronted with notices which demanded in peremptory terms: 'WHAT HAVE *YOU* SALVED TODAY?' The replies of the troops were invariably colourful, if not particularly helpful.

There were cogent reasons for not throwing empty bully beef tins over the parapets of trenches, as careless Tommies were apt to do. It was hardly sanitary. It encouraged flies and rats and, in places where the trenchline had remained static for many months, the clatter of piled up tins in No Man's Land could seriously imperil patrols creeping out under cover of darkness. But a soldier in the fighting line was disinclined to carry his debris with him when he left it, and, even in billets in villages behind the line, it was easier to bury empty tins and bottles than to drag them laboriously to the salvage dump.

The survivors of the July attacks on the Somme, sensing the rapid approach of the day when they would be marching back again, were less inclined than most to concern themselves with the trivia which seemed to them to weigh unduly on the minds of their superiors. In the case of some fortunate battalions, their immediate superiors took the same view and interpreted the periods of drill and fatigues which the Army was pleased to call 'rest' as 'rest' in the civilian sense of the word. Even where a certain amount of route marching and physical training was required to be carried out according to regulations, they organized swimming parades in lieu of PT, and country strolls, thinly disguised as route marches, to pleasant picnic spots or places of interest.

The Colonel of the 1st Queen's Westminster Rifles, whose ordeal by shell-fire at Gommecourt had been followed by a gruelling month of almost uninterrupted fatigues and carrying parties in and out of the trenches, went a little further. The Battalion had had a long slog to get to the back areas. The weather had been intensely hot. Three-quarters of the strength were men newly-arrived to replace the casualties of the First of July and the remainder had done no marching to speak of for a long time. Many of the men had fallen out and Colonel Shoolbred was of the firm and sympathetic opinion that they badly needed a rest. He gave them a whole day off to do nothing but sleep and, if they felt like waking up, to eat. The following day under the guise of the obligatory 'route march' he kindly organized a diversion for his battleworn men. It was a mere stroll, not more than two or three miles, along cool forest pathways to the battlefield of Crécy. On its arrival, by prior arrangement with their Colonel, the Battalion was met by a certain Professor Delve, who spent a long time courteously explaining the various points of interest on the field and expounding on the finer points of the battle, fought by their predecessors in 1346, nearly six hundred years before. The old hands of the Battalion, who had recently had a little too much of battles, listened bemused. They were, nevertheless, grateful to their Colonel. It was a kindly thought.

Colonel Shoolbred's own superiors had to consider the welfare of the 56th Division as a whole and reports had reached Divisional HQ that the performance of the troops on the march out of the line had not come up to the standard to be expected of a Territorial Division – even one which was diluted by a large proportion of raw troops. It was all very well to be sympathetic to men who had had a rough time in the trenches, but their ultimate objective was to go back to them and, for their own good, the time spent at 'rest' must be used constructively – to reimpose discipline, to embark on a programme of vigorous training that would weld new and old troops into a disciplined whole with due regard to the requirements of the war. There must be no slackness, no matter what the excuse. It was not enough to make the men fit, they must be fighting fit. Divisional Headquarters issued its orders accordingly, and commanding officers were obliged to carry them out and pass them on.

After his mild shell-shock on the First of July, Arthur Agius had been kindly treated by his own Commanding Officer, who had arranged for him to spend the last few weeks pleasantly engaged on a not-too-arduous training course at an Army School at Auxi-le-Château. Now, fit and bronzed and fully recovered, he was back with the 3rd Londons. He had rejoined them in time to get to know the new men of his Company, and to take sad stock of the gaps in its old ranks, before the move back to the Somme. It would be a long hike back to the battle and, on 18 August, Agius received the first indication that their 'holiday' was over.

To OC 'B' Company

MARCH DISCIPLINE

The CO wishes all officers to pay particular attention to march discipline. The men should know that it is a disgraceful thing to fall out on the line of march unless absolutely necessary. Straggling is to be considered an offence.

Company Commanders will see that an officer marches in rear of their companies who will check all straggling and take the names of any men who fall out.

On arrival at Destination, companies will render to the Orderly Room a list of names of men who have fallen out.

The battalion has always been known as a good marching battalion and the Commanding Officer feels confident that this good reputation will be maintained.

(Signed). R. D. Sutcliffe,
Captain and Adjutant.
3rd London Regiment.

Two days later, as they were literally packing up for the move, another edict arrived from GHQ:

DISCIPLINE

A practice appears to have arisen of one soldier only saluting where more than one are passing an Officer. This practice must cease.

When several soldiers pass an Officer, unless they are being marched as a party, they will ALL salute, whether there are NCOs among them or not.

When two or more men are sitting or standing about, and an Officer passes them, the senior NCO or oldest soldier will face the Officer, call the rest to attention and alone salute.

Soldiers will salute in the manner laid down in the training manuals.

Officers must return the salutes of their subordinates with a definite motion of the hand and not perfunctorily. Officers will check lack of discipline in saluting and will report to the unit concerned the names of men who fail to salute them. Such men will be severely dealt with.

> (GRO1736, Republished above for compliance
> by all ranks, 20 August 1916)

Agius conscientiously clipped both orders to the squared pages of the notebook he reserved for Battalion Orders, but he was not over-worried. He was rather more concerned about what they were marching back to than about discipline on the march itself, but at least he could set an example. The Colonel and the senior officers would be mounted but Agius chose to travel the long road back on Shanks's Pony – like the men, on his own two feet.

It was good marching weather. Although there had been rain and storms in the middle of the month, it had turned fine. There was a stiff breeze but on the march that was all to the good and better by far than the heat in the early part of the month which had caused so many men to fall out on the way from the line to the rear. Now, marching back again, they were in better fettle and the spirits of the survivors were high enough to inspire them to sing as they went. The new arrivals were shortly introduced to the Battalion's marching song. Being a familiar music-hall ditty it did not take them long to get into the swing of it and, as the Battalion, now back at full-throated strength, passed through the villages of the Somme to the familiar strains of *I'm 'Enery the Eighth I am*, it seemed almost – but not quite – like old times.

Chapter 17

The colonel of any battalion on the march back to the Somme encouraged the men to sing. It whiled away the time between the hourly ten-minute stops — when one hour could feel like two in the dog days of August to men who marched weighed down by pack and rifle, tin helmets slung under rolled-up greatcoats, through clouds of dust that smarted the eyes and settled in a gritty layer at the back of a thousand parched throats. A song was no balm to a battalion of feet, swelling and sweating in woollen socks and heavy boots; it did nothing to lighten the cumbersome weight of equipment on weary backs, but a good song could lighten the spirits and discourage pensive contemplation when boys were going into battle for a second time, still haunted by all-too-vivid memories of the first.

The Tommies had their own ideas of what constituted a good song, and they seldom coincided with those that people at Home fondly imagined them to be singing as they swung along the roads of France on their way to the fields of battle and to victory. Least of all did they coincide with the ideas of a certain Mr Ainger whose patriotic fervour had inspired him to produce a booklet entitled *Marching Songs for Soldiers set to well-known tunes*. The words were appropriately updated and in every syllable they breathed bellicosity and patriotic intent. For the modest price of one shilling — 'all proceeds devoted to the Belgian Relief Fund' — the *Marching Songs* could be purchased in a full-size edition 'with pianoforte accompaniment' and, in the first months of 1915, it sold in such quantities as to suggest that family musical evenings all over the country were being enlivened by the strains of such ditties as:

> *D'ye ken John French, with his khaki suit,*
> *His belt and his gaiters, and stout brown boot,*
> *Along with his guns, and his horse, and his foot,*
> *On the road to Berlin in the morning.*

The pocket-size edition (price twopence) had outsold the original several times over and, lovingly tucked into parcels by mothers, sisters and sweet-hearts, each anxious to lift the spirits of her own particular warrior, the songbooks had arrived in France by the thousand. On the whole, the songs had not caught on. Few battalions of Tommies were to be heard marching to the ringing words:

> To arms! To arms! We bring the Jubilee.
> To arms! To arms! The Flag that calls the Free.
> For the right the foe to smite alike by land and sea,
> While we go marching to Germany!

Marching, if not directly to Germany, at least back to face Germany's soldiers on the battlefield of the Somme, even if the words had not seemed a trifle inappropriate, the strains of *Marching through Georgia* did not exactly fit the Tommies' stolid progress across the miles of 'marching easy' that carried them eastwards. Slower, more lugubrious melodies fitted the pace and were more attuned to their mood. *John Brown's Body* was a favourite, although Mr Ainger, who had matched the melody to his favourite theme ('*Belgium has been harried with fire and with sword . . .*') might have been pained to hear the less elegant version preferred by the troops:

> John Brown's baby's got a pimple on its bum,
> John Brown's baby's got a pimple on its bum,
> John Brown's baby's got a pimple on its bum,
> And the little bugger can't sit down.

He would not have been alone in his disapproval. The Commander-in-Chief himself took a priggish interest in the songs warbled by his now largely youthful army. It was rumoured that General Haig found even the official version of *Mademoiselle from Armentières* offensive to his well-bred ears, even though it had already become popular in the most respectable circles at Home. The Tommies, however, preferred the infinite variations of less respectable versions, and the younger soldiers, in particular, newly drafted to France and into the ranks of the fighting battalions were first aghast, then amazed, then – in most cases – delighted at the bawdy freemasonry of which they had so suddenly and felicitously become a part. Some schoolboy faces, unable to cast off the shibboleths of their rigid and sheltered upbringing, blushed, stayed silent and, as hymn tunes had been so frequently adopted to accompany words that were less than religious in feeling, worried on occasion that the whole blasphemous battalion might be struck down by an avenging thunderclap from Above.

General Haig was more concerned with moral tone than with avenging thunderclaps. No battalion would have ventured to march to a ribald song within miles of his headquarters. No colonel within a considerable radius of any spot where there was a likelihood of meeting a staff officer would have allowed his battalion to march, even in the heat of an August day, with tunics undone and shirt buttons loosened and still less would he have relieved his own sweltering discomfort by replacing his stiff army hat with a khaki handkerchief knotted at each corner in the style of a day-tripper to the beach at Southend. It was unfortunate for one particular Battalion marching towards the Somme that it happened to present precisely this appearance as it passed through a village where a senior Ordnance Officer had his headquarters. It was unfortunate that the Commander-in-Chief, concerned about supplies of ammunition for the coming Push, should have been visiting the Ordnance HQ in person – unfortunate too that the Battalion should have been in full vocal flood and rendering a particular chorus compared to which the bawdiest version of *Mademoiselle from Armentières* might have been considered a suitable serenade for a maiden aunt:

> *Do your balls hang low?*
> *Do they dangle to and fro?*
> *Can you tie them in a knot?*
> *Can you tie them in a bow?*

They had reached the fourth line before the full sense of the words got through to the Commander-in-Chief. It got worse, as he listened:

> *Do they itch when it's hot?*
> *Do you rest them in a pot?*

He crossed to the window and stared in disbelief as the unwitting Battalion shambled past. 'Just as I thought,' he said. 'It's the rear companies! Fetch my horse!'

The Battalion straggled, easy marching, over almost a mile of road. By the time Sir Douglas Haig had mounted and started to trot up the long column, they had started all over again, this time in harmony, for the beauty of their favourite tune was that it could be sung in parts.

> *Do you get them in a tangle?*
> *Do you catch them in the mangle?*
> *Do they swing in stormy weather?*
> *Do they tickle with a feather?*

One by one, as the marching platoons spotted the unmistakable upright

figure of their Commander-in-Chief trotting purposefully past to reach
the head of the Battalion, their voices trailed away into embarrassed
silence. But the men at the head of the column were still lustily singing.

> *Do they rattle when you walk?*
> *Do they jingle when you talk?*

The Colonel had a fine voice. Riding in front of his Battalion, he was
singing louder than any of his men – so loudly that he either failed to
notice the falling-off of the merry chorus behind him or, putting it down
to fatigue, sang louder than ever to encourage his men across the last lap
of the hour's march. Just as General Haig caught up with him, he had
flung back his handkerchiefed head and was bawling in a rousing, oblivious
crescendo:

> *Can you sling them on your shoulder*
> *Like a lousy fucking soldier?*
> *DO YOUR BALLS HANG LOW?*

Haig had to shout to make himself heard. 'I must congratulate you on
your voice, Colonel!'

The unfortunate Colonel could only stare back open-mouthed, fumble
at his unbuttoned tunic, call the Battalion to march to attention and, as
an afterthought, snatch the handkerchief from his head.

'No, no!' Haig raised his hand. 'The men may march easy.' With the
last of his voice the Colonel croaked the command. Haig, on his great
black charger, a full hand higher than the Colonel's horse, trotted beside
him and bent down for a private word in the Colonel's ear, but his
orderly, riding just behind, heard – and later reported – every word.

'I like the *tune*,' he said, 'but you must know that in any circumstances
those words are inexcusable!'

The discomfited Colonel, having now replaced his hat, managed to
salute but before he could stammer an apology Haig was gone, with a
final nod of rebuke, trotting back past the chastened Battalion to resume
his interrupted business. It was a full five minutes before anyone broke
the silence. Then, a wag halfway down the column dared to introduce
another song. It was a song beloved by their virtuous Victorian grand-
mothers and he sang in notes of pure innocence:

> *After the ball was over . . .*

The Battalion exploded. Those of them who were capable of singing took up the refrain. Even the Colonel had to laugh.

In the summer of 1916 soldiers going on leave discovered that London was wriggling, Latin-style, to the strains of *La Cucuracha* and dancing soulfully to *I ain't got Nobody* . . . but the song that struck the mood of the moment was *Roses of Picardy*:

> *Roses are shining in Picardy,*
> *In the hush of the silvery dew,*
> *Roses are flow'ring in Picardy,*
> *But there's never a rose like you . . .*

In Picardy itself the song was not unpopular. In the dusky August evenings it echoed tinnily through a thousand barnyards from the gramophones of a thousand sentimental young officers who never tired of listening to it, hands clasped behind their heads as they lay on some makeshift bed, thinking, remembering, dreaming of some real or imagined 'Rose' waiting in a world far removed from the smelly discomforts of the real Picardy they now inhabited where the noise of battle grumbled and roared round the horizon. But the romantic appeal of the song was irresistible and it was a smash-hit at every concert.

At more makeshift entertainments, where a clutch of soldiers out of the line sat together in a barn or *estaminet*, whiling away an evening with talk and stories and with the occasional song to the quavering accompaniment of a mouth organ, a new mythology of song and doggerel was growing up. There was a verse-smith in most battalions and, although their rough and ready efforts were seldom destined to be included in post-war anthologies, the boys liked them and listened intently as long-ago warriors might well have listened to the 'Odes of Horace', or a Viking Saga, with the feeling that it was their own history, their own experiences that were being immortalized and, to an extent, honoured.

Recovering from their ordeal at High Wood, the remnants of the Church Lads Brigade were particularly struck by the effort of their particular bard. In a sense he was anonymous, because by the time the verses had been passed round the Battalion and almost every man had scribbled out a copy in his own handwriting, no one could remember who had composed them in the first place:

> *There's a Battalion out in France*
> *Its name was spread afar.*
> *And if you want to know its name*

It's the 16th KRR.
They trained for months at Denham
Which made every man quite fit
Then on 16th November
They embarked to do their bit.
The ride it was fairly long
And I'm sure it was no treat.
For the only food that we could get
Was biscuits and bully beef.

Now the first time in the trenches
It was not so very bad,
But on the second of January
A lively time we had.
The shells flew all around us,
Yes, there were many a score!
And the only shelter we could find
Was to lay flat on the floor.

Of course, you know, we lost a few,
Which I am sorry to say,
But we will have our own back
On the Allemands one day.
Since then we've seen the trenches,
Yes many and many a time,
And some of our dear comrades
Got buried by a mine.

And then we went into High Wood.
Of that I cannot speak.
We lost the flower of our flock.
It left us sad and weak.
But still we have to carry on,
Of work we do our share
And unless we have an R.E. fatigue
You seldom hear us swear.

Now when the War is finished
And we return once more,
If they take us back to Denham
There will be a treat in store.
But we shall not forget the lads

> *That we have left behind,*
> *And we all hope they will rest in peace*
> *Where the sun will always shine.*
>
> *Now here's good luck to all of us*
> *No matter where we are,*
> *For we know the name will never fade*
> *Of the 16th KRR.*

To the Church Lads Brigade, High Wood was just part of the saga of the Battalion's collective history. But the 6th Wiltshires, with the memory of their ordeal at la Boisselle still searing their minds, wrote a Battle Song, and Roy Bealing, who had the 'voice' of his platoon, usually led the singing:

> *'Twas on the first day of July,*
> *In the year Nineteen Sixteen*
> *When the Germans held some trenches*
> *And to take them we did mean.*
> *We started with Artillery,*
> *Two thousand guns or more,*
> *And then the lads of the Infantry*
> *Went over with a roar.*
> *And side by side they fought their way*
> *And side by side they fell,*
> *Did those gallant lads of the Infantry*
> *For the Battle of la Boisselle.*

High Wood, la Boisselle, like Thiepval, Beaumont Hamel, Serre and Contalmaison, were in the past. Another name had moved into the forefront of the epic of the Somme where, since the beginning of the month, the troops had been pitting the weight of their effort against the citadel of the Germans' second line at Guillemont.

August. High summer on the Somme, but the sounds of summer were lost behind the warring of the guns. Only one insistent sound vied with the thud of the drumming bombardments – the incessant humming of bluebottles, sated and fat as pigs, preying on the bodies of the dead and hovering above them in black droning swarms, so that in places they seemed to blot out the sky itself.

The bluebottles buzzed everywhere. They infested the trenches. They clung in infuriating clouds around the heads of the men, entered the noses, eyes and ears of soldiers who lay asleep, settled in thousands over sandbags containing rations. Swarms of bluebottles hung permanently above makeshift latrine-saps in a sinister, give-away cloud that was as good as a signpost to any alert sniper who merely had to set his sights beneath them, keep his eyes peeled for the flicker of movement that caused the swarm to disperse momentarily, and squeeze the trigger. An efficient marksman could bag up to a dozen luckless soldiers in the course of one patient day and there was no means of avoiding the danger for, by August, all the troops had diarrhoea. The flies carried the pestilence, alighting on the carrion of the bloated dead, breeding on the decaying flesh and hatching fresh generations to prey in their turn on every crumb of food a soldier ate and to cling and crawl round the rims of tin mugs sticky with the vestiges of a dozen or more brews of strong sweet tea.

In the line a man had precious little chance of washing his face, let alone his mug. In the heat of August, fresh divisions moving up to the line, through the carnage and debris of July, had found the lack of water almost the worst thing to bear. Water-bottles were filled every morning with foul-tasting chlorine-treated water, but they were soon emptied. Later in the month, when sudden thunderstorms turned the shell-holes into stagnant pools, troops in the reserve trenches were tempted to crawl out to augment their meagre water ration. This activity was strictly forbidden and rightly, because gas had permeated the shell-holes and, floating up through the rain-water, it lay in a green, lethal scum on the surface. The troops were well aware of the danger but some, tantalized beyond endurance, were willing to take the risk. The technique was to lower a mess-tin into the water with the upper half clamped tight-shut, to slip it off just far enough to fill the tin with unpolluted water, and replace the lid before lifting it out again. The boys became adept at this trick and there were only a few casualties from stomach upsets and, occasionally, inadvertent gassing.

Signaller W. H. Shaw, No. 12774, 9th Battalion, Royal Welsh Fusiliers, 58th Brigade, 19th Division

I managed to put twelve signallers in hospital when we were out on reserve. Our cook was away for some reason, so I volunteered to do the cooking. I managed to 'find' a bag of flour lying near a certain officers' mess, and some currants and sultanas had come up with the rations, so I decided to give the lads a treat by making a plum duff. We had a bit of sugar and a bit of bacon fat so I mixed it all with the flour and a tin of condensed milk. Then came the question of boiling it. We weren't short of water but the hand of the NCO, who put the chlorine in it, was so heavy that sometimes it just wasn't possible to use it. This was one of the times! So I went out scouting and came across a shell-hole filled with lovely clear water. But, it was a well known fact that all water had to be purified and so I filled my big dixie with water and gave the water a good boil up, then I got hold of a clean sandbag, dumped the pudding into it, tied the top well round with string and boiled it up for hours, hoping for the best but, alas, all my precautions were of no avail. The lads thoroughly enjoyed their unexpected treat but, two hours later, they were all groaning and holding their stomachs and the air was blue with them telling me what they thought of my cooking! I was in just as bad a state myself, because we'd all made pigs of ourselves. The Medical Officer was sent for and he took one look at us and packed us off to the nearest First Aid station. What a scene that was! They had to use stomach pumps on the lot of us – and none too soon either. It was gas! A gas shell had made contact with that particular shell-hole, and after our CO had made contact with *me*, I lost my job as cook!

We were only in hospital for a few days, but, if the lads had carried out what they said they wanted to do to me, I'd have been there for months! But, unpleasant though it was, it was a relief to get out of the line for a bit – even the reserve line. It was only days since I'd been in Mametz Wood when the rations came up and I was standing, holding a loaf of bread in my hands, just about to divide it out, when it was shot to pieces – just crumbled and disappeared! It was a miracle that I wasn't hit myself, and I suppose the loaf saved me, but it gave me a very nasty turn.

In the early days of August it was the 55th Division which was bearing the brunt of the battle. At the beginning of the month they had moved into trenches in front of Guillemont and it was on Guillemont that the attention of the Command was now focussed. The shattered village of Guillemont, its ruins strengthened and fortified as strongly as any front-line positions of a month before, lay a thousand yards beyond the splintered vestiges of Trones Wood on the road that had once led from Mametz to Combles, with Delville Wood away to the left of Guillemont and the tiny village of Ginchy at the apex of a triangle between them.

The line had changed little since the middle of July and from Serre to Thiepval it had changed not at all since Kitchener's Army had broken its back against its granite strength on the first day of the battle. A great bite had been gnawed out of the Leipzig Redoubt. The Australians were in tenuous possession of Pozières village. Contalmaison and the Bazentins had gone. But, beyond them, High Wood held out as obdurately as ever and, despite the valiant efforts of the troops who had gained the greater part of it, a lethal rim still held by the enemy around the edge of Delville Wood stood like a wall of iron between them and the Switch Line. On the road from Delville Wood to Guillemont two unremarkable landmarks of peacetime (a sugar beet factory and, a little further on, the sleepy tramway halt they called Guillemont Station, a lane's length away from the outskirts of the village) were still bristling defiantly behind thickets of barbed wire – links in the menacing chain of defences that lay in formidable strength beyond the British line.

The British line ended just beyond Guillemont and beyond stood the French, cramped into an uncomfortably narrow echelon. Unless Guillemont fell and Ginchy with it, the French could not move. It was no longer a case of breaking the line, but of breaking the impasse, giving the French room to breathe and preparing the way for a concerted push over a wider front. This was the dearest desire of the French General Joffre. General Fayolles, on the other hand, who commanded the force that was jammed into the bottleneck between Guillemont and the River Somme, was rather more concerned that the British should help to relieve the pressure on his immediate area and the British Commander-in-Chief was on his side.

The first priority, as Haig saw it, was 'to help the French forward' by attacking Guillemont and Ginchy in a combined operation, carefully prepared and planned. 'Preparation' meant bombardment and, since the 55th Division had moved into the line, its artillery had been ceaselessly pounding the German trenches and the Germans had been retaliating with indiscriminate bombardments of their own. They were directed against the British gun batteries and also against the unfortunate infantry as they waited eight long days for the attack.

Gunner George Worsley, No. 690452, C Bty., 276th Brigade, R.F.A. (2nd West Lancashire Brigade), 55th Divisional Artillery

The night we took over we had a terrible time going up the line. There was a tremendous bombardment going on and we were getting nearer and nearer to it. We had to move into a gun position to the right of Trones Wood, alongside the road, with Guillemont just in front and the battery we were taking over from was firing right up to the last minute. Then they pulled out and we pulled in and started firing. We only had five guns to fire with, because even before we started one gun was knocked out. I was in the Signallers' dugout, so I didn't see it, but we heard the shell exploding and saw a stretcher being carried past. A little while later, we got a signal through from Dublin Trench. It said *Please send down a burial party at once to 1/3 West Lancashire Field Ambulance Regimental Aid Post* and it was signed by the Medical Officer of the 277 Brigade, a Major Reilly. It was naïve of him really. But it was his first night in there and he probably didn't realize the situation. We had no one to spare to send a burial party for one man! When the daylight came, there were bodies all over the place – bloated bodies, they hadn't been able to clear away. The guns were literally wheel to wheel and we were firing, firing, firing twenty-four hours a day. There were gun lines everywhere – a continuous row of them. There was no end to them – and all of them were firing almost non-stop, right round the clock.

It began to get on your nerves after a while. It wasn't so much that we were being shelled – although we were, because the Germans used to put over these big 5.9 shells and then they'd follow them up with shrapnel shells to catch anyone who was running away. But what really began to get me was the sound of our own guns. The sound waves were going over your head all the time, like a tuning fork being struck on your steel helmet. A terrible sound – ping, ping, ping, ping – this terrible vibration day and night and this noise in your head, just like a tuning fork being rung again and again. It went right through you. You couldn't get away from it. It went right down into your nerves.

On the 8th, the infantry went for Guillemont and the French attacked simultaneously on their right on a front that stretched across the valley to the high spur and beyond that to the River Somme. Just as they had done on the morning of the First of July the two armies went forward shoulder to shoulder. But this time they did not sweep all before them. The French edged forward on their right but, where their line met the British, they were stopped by a hail of enfilade fire. In spite of attacking with two divisions ranged against the short line on either side of Guillemont, in spite of a week's backbreaking work digging advanced trenches for the jump-off, in spite of a carefully planned protective barrage, the German bombardment had stopped the British soldiers in their tracks. A few gallant parties, pitifully small, broke through and were annihilated by storms of machine-gun bullets, streaming from Waterlot Farm, from Guillemont Station, and from the trenches that stretched in front of the village itself. The whole débâcle was horribly reminiscent of the attack at Serre just five weeks earlier and the lessons which had been learned there seemed already to have been forgotten. Once again the 'supporting'

barrage went ahead in a series of predetermined lifts in accordance with
a rigid timetable. Once again no messages came back. Once again the
infantry attacked with all the panoply of visual communications, bearing
on their backs those shining markers, the cut-out diamonds of tin that
would glint in the sun as they made their way forward, carrying the flares
that would signal their position to patrolling aeroplanes.

But there was no sun. There were no aeroplanes. There was mist –
heavy, thick mist that mingled with the smoke and fumes of the crashing
bombardment and swirled and clung round the infantry in a blinding
suffocating curtain as impenetrable as the German line itself.

Later, when darkness fell, when the reliefs came up and the remnants
of the shattered battalions stumbled back to the rear to lick their wounds,
to hold scratch roll calls, to make the first sickening estimates of how
many of their number had been killed or wounded or were missing, the
rumour began to spread that, in the mist and confusion, two British
battalions had attacked each other.

The bombers of the 5th King's Liverpools had somehow managed to
work their way forward, had somehow managed to capture a length of
trench, but they were sharing it with the Germans. They blew in part of
the trench to block the passage and somehow managed to hold on. They
called it Cochrane Alley, and its capture was the only real gain of the
day. Some troops had managed to penetrate the field of heaped-up rubble
that once was Guillemont village, where – as at Thiepval, as at Ovillers, la
Boisselle, Pozières and Beaumont Hamel – every tumbled ruin concealed a
warren of deep dugouts and fortifications. Sure of their own terrain,
German reserves attacked through the mist and the smoke and the British
battalions were overwhelmed. They could ill be spared, for these were
no amateurs, no lambs sent in the innocence of inexperience to the
slaughter. The 8th King's were the Liverpool Irish, like the rest of their
brigade, hard-fighting, experienced Territorials. The 1st King's were
Regulars and they had been in France since the first days of the war.

The 8 August was a black day and an inauspicious day for the King's
arrival in France. Sir Douglas Haig would have liked dearly to show him
a victory.

The King had reached Boulogne by destroyer in the same morning
mist that enveloped the troops attacking at Guillemont and motored to
Montreuil where he lunched at GHQ before driving on to Haig's
advanced headquarters at Beauquesne. The Commander-in-Chief was
waiting to receive him with his mounted escort of the 17th Lancers and
a guard of honour of fifty Artists' Rifles. The two men were old friends.
Ten years earlier while on leave from India Douglas Haig had met and,
after an uncharacteristically whirlwind courtship, had married Miss

Dorothy Vivian who was Maid of Honour to Queen Alexandra and a close connection of the Royal Family. The wedding had been held in the private chapel at Buckingham Palace, graciously offered by the King and Queen who were delighted to see their protégée marry a distinguished soldier whom King Edward held in high regard.

The intimacy had continued into the next reign and now, after inspecting the troops drawn up to await him, after exchanging courtesies when the General presented his Staff, King George V was anxious to broach a subject which he suspected might be troubling the mind of the Commander of his armies. It was 4.30 in the afternoon. The two men repaired to Haig's writing room and tea was brought.

The Commander-in-Chief gave the King a general outline of the situation along the front, touching on Guillemont, where Cochrane Sap was still being held, where some troops were reported to be in the village and more were holding out round Guillemont Station.

If the attack had not been an overwhelming success, the scant information which had reached GHQ gave no reason to suppose that it was a total failure either. It was, after all, only a local engagement designed to assist the French – and the matter was still not concluded. Fresh troops of the Reserve Battalions would be attacking again tomorrow. They might well succeed. Short of omniscience Haig could hardly have given more information.

The King had confidence in his Commander-in-Chief, but, like Haig, he was subject to the Government. Already there had been rumblings in the Cabinet, but it was an outsider, Winston Churchill, who was causing the most trouble, and the King was furious.

Churchill had written a carefully considered paper criticizing the whole conception of the Somme offensive and, weighing the awful cost of losses against gains measured in yards rather than miles, against stalemate rather than advance, and against the grand strategy which had been swept away on a tide of bloodshed, he had concluded that little or nothing had been achieved and questioned the wisdom of continuing what he saw as a vain sacrifice of life and endeavour for what appeared to be no foreseeably fruitful result. Churchill had circulated the paper to every member of the War Cabinet, and the Cabinet had been just sufficiently perturbed to make polite enquiries of the Commander-in-Chief as to his intentions. That very day (although Haig had penned his answer on 1 August) his reply was being read to the War Committee by Sir William Robertson. The occasion was recorded in the Minutes:

The C.I.G.S. read a letter from General Sir Douglas Haig dated August 1st, giving his appreciation of the general military situation, more particularly as affected by the offensive of the Allies on the Somme. It was agreed that the C.I.G.S. should circulate it to the Cabinet.

It was further agreed that the C.I.G.S. should send a message to General Sir D. Haig assuring him that he might count on full support from home.

(August 8th)   WAR OFFICE

The following day Sir Douglas would have the gratification of receiving that message. In the meantime he had the natural gratification of hearing the King express the utmost personal confidence in him and the very human satisfaction of hearing him refer to Churchill and his 'cabal' at length and in terms of robust disapprobation which entirely coincided with the General's own opinion. Thus fortified and encouraged Haig bowed his monarch off the premises to be driven off to a château near St Pol forty kilometres to the north, well away from the battle zone and behind the 'quiet sector' at Arras.

This billeting arrangement had not in the least suited the King who, short of running the unconstitutional risk of going into the actual firing zone, was anxious to get as near the battle as possible. A message from Buckingham Palace, a day or so before his arrival, had made this fact plain and had asked for a change to be made. But Haig had quietly insisted that the present arrangement should stand. He confided his annoyance to his diary:

Extract from the diary of General Sir Douglas Haig

Friday, 4 August: A château in the area of the battle further south is desired. These courtiers at home evidently do not realize the congestion of troops and the dust on the roads when fighting is in progress.

Even miles back from the line, with the constant movement of troops, of long slow cavalcades of transport, of speeding despatch riders and powerful staff cars carrying supplies and ammunition, the roads were a nightmare of flying chalk, grit, dust and eternal sweating hold-ups. And, all along the roadsides, the spectral dust-covered figures of Pioneer troops and sullen patient German prisoners leaned on shovels as they waited for a gap in the traffic which would let them resume the end-less task of repairing surfaces which, as fast as they worked, were ground back in the same old shambles of ruts and potholes with every passing day.

Beyond the old front line where battered tracks ran across land that had been wrested from the enemy, the shambles reached horror proportions. There were miles of abandoned trenches, pounded almost out of recognition. There were old artillery positions surrounded by mountains of empty shell cases that advertised the weight of fire thrown back at the Germans. There were live shells too, the duds that had failed to explode, and they lay in disturbing quantities wherever the plodding battalions looked. There were shattered limbers, dead mules, tumbled mounds that once were villages, splintered sticks that once were woods. And there were the dead.

Corporal O. W. Flowers, No. 133480, Motor Transport Section, Army Service Corps

I was a driver. I'd been a driver before the war, and a fitter as well. I had a licence but, in those days, it didn't matter if you didn't have any legs on, if you didn't have any arms or even any eyes, if you wrote up for a driving licence and sent five shillings you got one.

I joined up in 1915. There was an offer advertised in the papers – six shillings a day for drivers and fitters if they joined the Army. Well, the Tommy was only getting a shilling a day, and if I joined up I knew I'd get my choice of job. But if conscription came in, that would be that! It wasn't just the money. I wanted to go into something where I didn't need to use a gun.

It was all right until the Somme got really bad. We were running from a village just outside Doullens, and we had twenty-four lorries parked in the main street. We used to run the rations up to the line, or as near as we could get. We used to help the Tommies too, because there was a tremendous number of troops going up. And one of the worst jobs I used to have was when a division was going up (they were marching up of course) and we would relieve them of their blankets, so that they wouldn't have to carry them. Well, they was all rolled up and it wasn't a case of, 'This is my blanket, that's your blanket.' You got a blanket and it didn't matter whose it was when you got to the end of your journey. Of course these were all stuffed into my lorry until it was completely full. It wasn't so much a lorry full of blankets as a lorry full of lice! We were all covered. They were all over us! And that happened again and again.

I was attached to the motor transport department of the Army Service Corps and it was mainly supplies we were taking up to the dumps. We used to load up in the afternoon and deliver in the morning and there was every kind of thing we had to carry – including food and stuff for the horses and mules, because the horse transport was further up the field than we were. One day you would load up with coal for the cooks to cook the meals with. The next day, perhaps, you would be on tinned stuff. That was all in boxes. Next day you would be on hay. If you got that you were well away because we had to sleep on our lorries after we'd loaded up – sleep literally on top of the load. One night we had frozen sides of beef!

There were so many casualties that they kept trying to run the ambulances up nearer and nearer the line and these ambulances kept breaking down or they got damaged by shelling or knocked out. But the further the ambulance could get up to the line, the better it was for the wounded men, so they decided that they would have an advanced workshop and, being a fitter, I was sent up to it. It was at Mametz – an old barn that was more hole than wall – and it wasn't a case of the ambulances coming in there, we had to go up to fetch them. I was running to Guillemont, just to the right of Delville Wood.

There was no road at all – neither road nor anything else! It was a track for the ambulances and I don't remember ever seeing another lorry other than my own. They were all a lot further back. Well, there were horses, mules, men, bodies strewed all over the place. If ever hell was let loose, it was let loose then. A few of those nights I went out I used to dread going, not so much because of the danger to myself but because I didn't know what damage I was doing to other people. You couldn't see them. It was too dark. Sometimes a Very light would go up and it would just give you a glimmer of light, for a second or two, and then it was out. But by that time it was too late. You'd gone over somebody. I don't know how many people I may have killed with the lorry, but I'd known I'd gone over them because I'd felt the bump. I didn't hear screams, and I tried to cool myself down with the fact that I'd have heard them if they'd yelled out. I tried to cool myself down with the idea that they must have been dead when I went over them.

Up there at Guillemont it didn't matter where men dropped, they just stayed there with nobody to pick them up. It was days and days before anybody dared to go out to pick them up and bury them. The bodies were piling up all the time, piling up by the roadside.

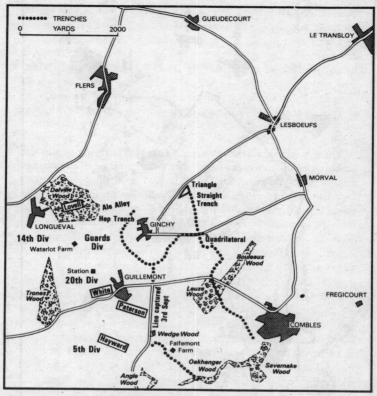

The Battle of Guillemont and Ginchy

One particular night it was a real horror. I was going towards Delville Wood, and what a bombardment there was! There were ever so many ambulances knocked out. They were little ambulances, Tin Lizzies, and they only held two or three wounded, but they were very manoeuvrable. You could just swing your tow rope round the axle and loop it over your hook and away they'd go. Some had tyres blown off and some even had a wheel blown off and I've many a time towed one with three wheels on. (You could do it with a Ford as long as you changed the weight so that there's no one on the side where the wheel's come off.) But that night!

Quite a few ambulances had had a direct hit and we couldn't

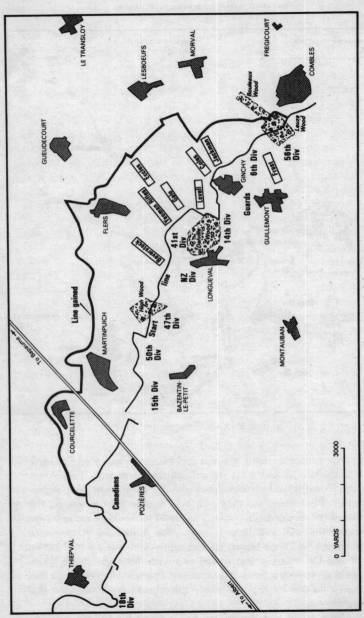

The General Attack on 15th September

do much about those, but some of the others had been pretty well splintered with shrapnel and the wounded men they'd put inside had been wounded again after they'd been put in the ambulance. When you looked inside you got the shock of your life! All we could do was load them into the lorry, try and get them back as quick as you can, because this shelling's going on all the time. When we got back there were five dead in the lorry and the lorry floor was swimming with blood. We made six runs that night towing in ambulances and taking these poor wounded chaps out of the ones we couldn't shift. When I got back from the last run, my mates in the advanced workshop, said, 'What's the matter with you? You look like a ghost!'

I simply couldn't speak. It was a long time before I could speak, I was so terrified. Once we'd handed the wounded over I just crawled into the lorry and lay on the floor and went to sleep. The following morning my uniform was soaked in blood, sodden with it. They had to give me a new one. I looked at it and I can remember thinking, 'If the British people could see what I've seen and experience what I experienced last night, this war would stop. They wouldn't have it!'

I've never been able to stand the sight of blood since. If I prick my finger, I feel sick, even after sixty-five years and more.

The next night, when I had to go up, my heart was in my mouth every foot of the journey – driving in the dark all the time, not knowing where you were going, not knowing what you were hitting. But you just had to do it. You know it's your duty. It has to be done and there's men there that may be in the ambulance and we had to get those ambulances back. It was as simple as that. They were going down by the hundred. It was a blood bath, running up to Guillemont. It was a terror. And the shelling never ceased.

The Germans were shelling indiscriminately behind the immediate front line with far less accuracy of registration on distant targets (as they themselves admitted) than the British. During the Battle of the Somme the Royal Flying Corps exulted in the fact that it 'had the sky to itself' and it was only a slight exaggeration. Far above the duelling guns, the fliers of both sides were duelling in the air in a battle of quite another kind. Few German reconnaissance planes got far behind the British lines without being challenged by a buzz of British fighters swooping in pursuit like a swarm of angry bees and, far above the battle, soundless and graceful as kites, the fighting machines soared and dipped, circled and manoeuvred and were cheered to the echo by watchers below when a burst of flame, a spiralling stream of smoke, signified a kill.

No one greeted a kill with more enthusiasm and relief than the men who were the eyes of the guns, the Observers, swinging lonely in fragile baskets beneath the gas-filled balloons riding cloud-high behind the British lines. They were particularly vulnerable to attack from the air. One burst of machine-gun fire, even a well-aimed rifle shot, could destroy the balloon in a fiery explosion that sent its cable whiplashing to earth and its observer to Kingdom Come.

British reconnaissance planes flying with fighter escorts behind the German lines were not allowed to go about their business entirely unmolested but they managed, to a far greater degree than the enemy, to produce vast quantities of photographs of fine definition which, even taken from high altitude, pinpointed with extraordinary accuracy the enemy's supply and ammunition dumps, his transport depots and gun positions, the roads which carried his soldiers to and from the line. The Army cartographers were consequently able to produce maps so finely delineated that the guns were able to range and fire on such targets with a precision that was distinctly disturbing to the Germans. In a secret report, later captured by British Intelligence, the Germans observed:

> It is worthy of remark that our enemy's guns apparently have a much smaller zone of dispersion than our own. He also appears to have better and more accurate data for shooting from the map than we have. This seems to be proved by the fact that, in weather that excludes all possibility of observation, and under conditions very different from those prevailing during previous shoots, he obtains hits on small targets with great accuracy.

The Germans' answer during the bloody days of August was to keep firing with every gun they had in continuous bombardments – haphazard, but so intense that, raking and ranging methodically back and forth behind the British line, the sheer intensity of the fire-power was bound to wreak destruction somewhere and lower the morale of the British troops as much as it raised the morale of their own men. On one such night of thundering retribution, they scored a hit that sent the morale of C.276 Battery plummeting to the edge of despair.

In the Signallers' dugout a little way behind the guns, George Worsley and Fred Sharples were only twenty yards from the ammunition dump when the shell hit it and if the 2,000 eighteen-pounder shells had gone up in one almighty bang, they would not have lived to tell the tale. It was bad enough that it started a fire.

Gunner George Worsley, No. 690452, C Bty., 276th Brigade, Royal Field Artillery, 55th Division

It was like all hell let loose – an absolute inferno! It was like someone throwing fire crackers into a fire, but multiplied a million times. All the ammunition was exploding in the heat and flying over our heads. There were no officers there and no order was given.

There were three of us stood in a trench and, of course, the top of the trench was crumbling in all the time until our ankles were covered and I screamed at this NCO even though he was a bombardier. I took charge. 'We'll get killed whatever happens!' I screamed. 'We'll be killed whether we stop here or whether we run away. For God's sake, let's be killed trying to get out of it.' And he said, 'Right-o, George.'

It was every man for himself. We ran like hell. The dump was blazing, lighting up the sky, and there was nothing else to do but run because, as soon as the Germans spotted it – and you could see it for miles around – all their guns would be trained on it.

There was a young officer staggering round blinded and screaming and, as we ran, I saw our cook – just his head sticking out of the earth where he'd been buried, and he was screaming too. Not that you could hear anything in the terrible roaring of all these explosives, but you could see by men's faces if they were screaming. And you could see that this man had gone stark staring mad by the frenzy in his face.

You couldn't do anything for him. The idea of digging amidst all that would have been sheer lunacy and everyone was running just to get out of it. I didn't expect to get out of it. I didn't expect to be alive a few seconds afterwards. We ran like hell until we were out of range. Then we dropped down and lay on the ground and watched this thing – a great lurid light, lighting up the whole sky. Blazing!

At dawn, when the fire had burnt itself out, the few survivors, sleepless, shocked and white-faced, began to stumble back towards the guns. But there were no guns to be seen and nothing but a few tangles of twisted metal among the smoking debris to hint that a battery had ever stood there. There was no sign of the cook. No sign of the blinded officer. No sign of a single survivor among the mangled bodies in the wreckage.

A little later a visitor arrived. His appearance was strangely incongruous in the blackened desolation of the burnt-out gun sites and contrasted oddly with the tousled looks of the shocked and filthy gunners. It was a

warm morning and the Staff Officer was jacketless. His shirt sleeves were
neatly rolled up, his breeches immaculately pressed, a cane tucked under
his arm. He was clean, newly shaved and looked as if he had enjoyed an
excellent breakfast before setting off on the difficult journey up to the
gun-line.

*Gunner George Worsley, No. 690452, C Bty., 276th Brigade, Royal
Field Artillery, 55th Division*

He presumed to give us a lecture. Nobody formed up or stood in
a line or anything, we just looked at him and I can remember every
word he said. He said, 'Well, men, I can see you've had a terrible
night. But you haven't seen the worst of war yet.' (We looked at
each other as if to say, 'You should have bloody well been here
last night!') He said, 'It's when you see women and children killed.
That's the worst of war. Now, while you're here, I want you to
forget about your wives and your sweethearts and your friends.
Concentrate on the job in hand, so that, when the time comes for
you to march out, those of you who are fortunate enough to be
left can march out with your heads held high.'

What a lot of rot! We just exchanged looks. So far as we were
concerned, he could have had England for twopence at that
moment! By the time we went out of the line, of the original
forty-two in our battery, there were only six of us left.

In the course of the day a few more survivors drifted back. They included
the Sergeant who, to Worsley's later chagrin, was awarded the Distinguished Conduct Medal for 'putting the fire out'. New guns were
hauled up and dug into fresh positions; new gunners arrived to replace
the casualties and later in the day there was a well-meaning attempt to
provide the men with a hot meal. Worsley's portion was a mess-tin of
what appeared to be warm water with raw mutton fat floating on the
top. His stomach, churning with the stench of the dead, revolted. Captain
Smith happened to be passing and Worsley, shoving the mess-tin under
his nose, snarled, 'Look at that.' The Captain took a step back. Worsley
followed, remorselessly holding the unsavoury dish under the officer's
nostrils. 'Go on! Look at it! It's not fit for swine. If we have to be killed,
for God's sake let us die with something in our bellies.'

It was an extraordinary breach of discipline and protocol, but Smith
and Worsley had served together since the beginning of the war. The
Captain knew his man, though it was difficult to recognize the young
Territorial of two years before in the strained, dishevelled figure who

confronted him now. For more than ten days Worsley, like his comrades, had slept – when sleep was possible – in his clothes. Like his comrades, for the past twelve days he had neither loosened his puttees nor undone the laces of his boots. Like his comrades he was at the point of exhaustion and, as Captain Smith doubtless realized, nearing the end of his tether. The Captain nodded sympathetically, looked at the 'soup' in the mess-tin and murmured, 'I'm sorry.' There was little he could do about it.

Some twenty-five kilometres away, where the King was a guest of honour at a luncheon party at Fourth Army Headquarters at Querrieu, the menu was more elaborate:

MENU

Déjeuner

Oeufs Glacés à la Russe

Poularde Rotie

Viande Froide

Salade

Mousse aux Fraises

Compôte de Framboises

Desserts

The meal had been planned to appeal to the most refined tastes for, besides the King, the party included some senior Commanders of the French Army. In deference to their Gallic appreciation of good food the dishes had been prepared with elaborate care; in deference to the King's wishes, no alcohol was served. At the beginning of the war the King had set an example of sacrifice and abstemiousness to the nation by announcing that neither wine nor spirits would be served at his table until the day of victory. Certain disgruntled courtiers, offered a Hobson's choice of flaccid soft drinks, entertained the ignoble suspicion that the 'ginger ale' served to the King bore a strong resemblance to whisky and soda and that the fizz in Queen Mary's 'fruit cup' owed more to Champagne than to lemonade. Their disgust was as nothing compared to that of General Joffre when Haig's butler, Shaddock, with as much aplomb as if he had been offering Hock or Chablis, invited him to state his preference for ginger beer or orange juice.

Sir Douglas Haig was fond of 'Papa' Joffre; the two men got on well and Haig's excellent French, combined with an instinctive ability to handle Marshal Joffre, had amicably resolved numerous arguments and smoothed many feathers which had been ruffled by disagreements on Allied policy. But he could not resist teasing the old man. His orderly, Secrett (who combined his duties as personal servant to the Commander-in-Chief with

those of mess servant when his master dined or entertained guests) was
consumed by amusement behind a suitably impassive countenance.

Like Secrett, Sir Douglas had observed from the corner of his eye the
meaning look Joffre cast at the waiter, with a half nod towards his empty
wine glass.

Haig beckoned a waiter. 'I think Marshal Joffre wants the bread!' The
waiter dutifully presented the silver bread basket to Joffre who politely
accepted, taking the opportunity of lifting his eyebrows, rolling his eyes
towards the empty glass and then staring the waiter directly in the face
in an endeavour to communicate the telepathic message that man – or
at least a Frenchman – cannot live by bread alone. With the oblivious
exceptions of the King himself and the President of France on his right,
the whole party was now aware of Joffre's predicament. The *entrée* was
brought in and served. Still Marshal Joffre's wine glass remained empty.
Sitting on the King's left, impressed by the proximity of Majesty, he
achieved the difficult feat of appearing to give his full attention to the
royal conversation conducted in the King's schoolboy French and, as soon
as His Majesty turned to talk to the President on his right, pantomiming
to waiter or butler in discreet dumb show, and venturing – as if absent-
mindedly – to toy with the stem of his empty glass.

'I think,' remarked Haig jovially, 'that the Marshal would like some
more bread.'

Again the waiter presented the bread. Again Marshal Joffre snatched a
piece, glaring at Sir Douglas Haig across the table. It was plain to all that
he would have dearly liked to throw it at him.

As soon as the meal was finished and the King was safely closeted in
another room in private conversation with President Poincaré, Haig's
secretary, in response to a nod from the Commander-in-Chief, discreetly
drew Marshal Joffre aside, explained the circumstances and offered him
'a little something'. Joffre refused with disdain. If he could not enjoy a
glass of wine with his meal like any civilized man he would take nothing
at all.

This slightly unfortunate episode did not advance the cause of Anglo-
French understanding. However, it had, on the whole, been a satisfactory
afternoon, particularly for Sir Douglas Haig. He had been able to assure
President Poincaré, who was '. . . most anxious, before the approach of
winter, that we should have made some decisive advance in order to keep
the people of France and England from grumbling . . .', that he expected
at least ten weeks of good weather before winter set in, that he was
unequivocally optimistic that a great deal would be accomplished, and
that he and General Foch were in entire agreement about future plans.
He had also had the honour of playing host to the King at an excellent

lunch which had been sauced by a good joke and, after the French visitors had left, Sir Douglas Haig had the ultimate gratification of being presented by the King with the Grand Cross of the Victorian Order. This honour was in the King's personal gift and, although the immaculate tunic of the Commander-in-Chief already carried several rows of well-earned campaign and service medals, none could approach the value of this mark of his Sovereign's personal esteem and appreciation.

The King, equally pleased with his visit, took his departure to spend a few days with his armies in the north before returning to London. Accompanied by the Prince of Wales, his personal ADC and Major Thompson (an ADC provided by the Commander-in-Chief) the King was driven back to St Pol in a staff car set aside for his personal use. It was a glorious evening. At the King's request they travelled with the hood down. Motor cyclists of the Military Police travelled well ahead to make sure that the road was clear of congestion and the troops, waiting on either side for the royal party to pass, were cheered and delighted with their brief glimpse of the King.

On 14 August, the weather broke.

Chapter 18

It poured with rain on the Somme. On the thinly held front of the Reserve Arm from Serre to Beaumont Hamel, where the line was still stuck precisely where it had been before the First of July, the troops crouched in the trenches, sheltering – if they were lucky – under hastily rigged-up canopies of waterproof sheets that bulged under the weight of the rain and occasionally treated an unfortunate Tommy to an unexpected shower-bath. There was little to do. Apart from the occasional rattle of machine-gun fire from the drier and more comfortably accommodated Germans, and the occasional random salvo of shells designed to keep 'Tommy' from getting too complacent, watch-keeping in daylight hours was more or less confined to keeping a gloomy eye clamped to a trench periscope and watching, through the raindrops that splashed steadily on to its mirror, the same depressingly familiar view of No Man's Land where for six long weeks the bodies of the dead had lain still and silent and beyond recovery. Now, as the rain beat down, a sudden squall would lift some muddied rag of uniform and wave it in grim salutation.

The River Ancre, long liberated by shell-fire from its battered banks, swelled and sent tributaries groping across the valley so that the swamp turned into a lake and water lapped inches above the surface of the wobbling duckboard tracks leading to the line in Thiepval Wood. Below the dripping rubble of Thiepval village, where the Germans were busily pumping out their trenches, gravity carried the water downhill. It ran down the chalky slopes to Thiepval Wood, trickled down through the ragged tree stumps and turned the steep communication trenches into glissades of slime and mud, soon stirred into squelching soup by the constant passage of soldiers slithering to and from the line.

Above the village, on the wide expanse of the Thiepval plateau, there was no shelter from the elements and the wind drove the rain across in curtains from the Leipzig Redoubt, where the British were still trying to increase their hold, to Mouquet Farm, soaking the exhausted Australians still doggedly striving to capture it. But they had won the old windmill to the north of Pozières and, in other parts of their sector, had gained the top of the rain-swept ridge that ran away to Martinpuich, to High

Wood and to Delville Wood beyond. Protected by two great redoubts and by the Switch Line behind them, Martinpuich held out. High Wood held out and the Germans were still clinging on to the edges of Delville. They were clinging on everywhere with exceptional tenacity, fighting back and charging forward in powerful counter-attacks that rocked and sometimes broke the newly captured line.

The Germans were not in an easy situation. Five experienced divisions had been transferred from the Somme to the Eastern Front and, to the fury of General Von Falkenhayn, their replacements had been of such inferior calibre that he had been forced to send them straight back again. At Verdun the French had gained the upper hand. They were now taking the offensive and the Germans, spreading their troops as thinly as they dared, were hard put to it to maintain the illusion that the German Army was as strong as ever. Supplies and transport were a constant headache, and every man going into the line now had to carry on his own person sufficient rations and water for the five days he would remain there. It all added up to the first crack in the mighty armour of the German war machine that had growled into action on the Somme almost two years earlier.

In the British trenches, the Tommies were unaware of the problems that beset the German High Command. They detected no crack in the armour, no lessening of the enemy's fighting spirit. Under the onslaught of his counter-attacks, numbed by the ferocity of his shelling, they were not given to analysing the broader strategy of the battle, still less of the war itself. They no longer lived from day to day, but from hour to hour, minute to minute. Few had a thought to spare for anything but the next man at his shoulder, the next hot brew-up, the next relief. Letters, lovingly penned in ink that ran into blue rivulets under the rain, had an air of unreality. News from home, news of births and bazaars, of deaths and dances, of gossip, of shopping, of all the trivia of everyday events, had little significance. And the pleasure of any brief release from the dank and gloomy trenches was mostly overwhelmed by the knowledge that there would soon be another attack.

The next attack was on 18 August, four squally, stormy days later. Ted Gale's Battalion was attacking to the left of Delville Wood and their objective was Orchard Trench. It was part of a general attack on the line from Guillemont to Thiepval Ridge and, this time, surely, High Wood and Delville Wood would be finally secured and the way ahead would at last be opened. The 18 August would be the fiftieth day of the Battle of the Somme and two years, all but five days, since the first engagement of the war – the Battle of Mons.

Ted Gale had been at Mons. He had been in the Army in the days when, in his opinion, it *was* an Army and he never tired of regaling grumbling comrades who had joined up 'for the duration' with tales of pre-war discipline as a Regular Rifleman: of having been confined to barracks for five days for being two seconds late on ration parade; of the regular duty of polishing the barrack-room floor with brick dust and lead; of having been given pack drill for failing to shine the *soles* of his boots. His companions were not particularly impressed by Ted's early hardships. They thought he had been amply compensated by the enjoyment of a cushy war, for he had twice spent long periods in England. Admittedly he had suffered the loss of all his teeth when a horse kicked him in the mouth early in 1915, but that unlucky episode was followed by several months of safety and comfort at home, while his mouth hardened sufficiently for the Army to fit him with dentures. This fortunate circumstance had resulted in his missing the Battle of Loos. Only a few months later he had gone down with rat poisoning, through eating infected rations, and after the initial discomfort had been blessed with another pleasant period of relaxation and recuperation in Blighty. It was five months now since he had been posted back to France to the 7th (Service) Battalion, The Rifle Brigade, and, after six years of soldiering, he was about to go over the top for the first time.

The 7th Battalion, The Rifle Brigade, were to attack to the left of Delville Wood on the right flank of the 33rd Division, which had been given the ambitious task of capturing the remainder of the ground between Delville Wood and High Wood and securing High Wood itself.

Acting Lance-Corporal E. Gale, No. 3774, 1st (later 7th) Btn., The Rifle Brigade, 41st Brigade, 14th Division

It was the waiting to go over that was the worst, because we didn't go over until almost three o'clock in the afternoon. There was a whole brigade waiting to go over on a battalion front, so we were crowded up like anything. During the morning, the Sergeant came round with the old rum jar and gave us a dessertspoonful of rum, just to put Dutch courage in us. It was strong, that Army rum, and I think he had two or three spoonfuls to our one – or more!

We really needed that rum, waiting to go over the top! Our own guns had put down this terrific barrage but, because we were a bit higher up than the Germans, in order to hit them they'd had to sight the guns so that they would just skim the top of our trenches and there we were, crouching in this terrible noise, and these terrible shells going over us just inches above. You can't describe the feeling! You can't describe the noise! A couple of our own chaps were killed. One fellow had the top of his head took off with one of our own shells. His brains were all over the place. But the artillery couldn't help it. They had a terrible job to get the elevation right and just had to try and skim the top of our trenches and this poor chap Dixon got it. He was only five or six yards away from me. It didn't do much for us to see that sort of thing before we went over!

Five minutes after we went over the top we were finished! The German machine-guns went through our lines just like a mow goes through a field of corn. I don't think we got two hundred yards before we were so mucked up that we just had to lay out in No Man's Land. I was in a shell-hole with the Sergeant – the one who'd been sampling the rum. We were absolutely pinned down but he kept jumping up and shouting, 'Why don't we advance? Why don't we advance?' He was absolutely hollering. How could you advance when there was three of you there and you couldn't see anybody else? I shouted back at him, 'Why don't you keep down? You'll be drawing the guns on us!'

D Company had gone across first and C Company were supposed to be following behind us. From this shell-hole we looked back and we could see C Company there lying on the ground spread out in extended order, just as they'd gone across. We couldn't understand why they weren't coming up to support us. There was just the three of us in the shell-hole – the Platoon Sergeant and Jack Hall, who was the Lance-Corporal, and myself. And the Sergeant said, 'Why the hell don't they come on and give us a hand? We can't go in there on our own!'

This old Sergeant wasn't half going on, nothing would keep him quiet. He was an enlisted man – he wasn't a Regular. There was only two of us Regulars in The 7th Battalion, but the Sergeant had been in the Marines before the war, so he should have known better. Of course he had all this rum in him. Then the third time he jumped up they got him! A bullet went straight in his ear and blew half his face away. Me and Jack had to lay there with him. We lay there for hours and hours and hours with all this clatter going on around us and when it got dusk we started to crawl back.

It was a terrible crawl back and, hunched close to the ground, his ears ringing with the sound of the explosions as the Germans continued to bombard the British line, Ted Gale had not gone far before he realized why C Company had not come up to support them. They were still lying in extended order as he crawled past them – and almost all were dead.

Acting Lance-Corporal E. Gale, No. 3774, 1st (later 7th) Btn., The Rifle Brigade, 41st Brigade, 14th Division

Lieutenant Hall was alive, but only just. He said, 'Can you help me! I've got a bad wound in my hip. I can't move.' I said to Jack, 'Can you hold my rifle and I'll pick him up?'

I picked him up and I carried him back to the trench – it was all of a hundred yards and it took a long, long time, because we had to be careful moving; the whole thing was still like an inferno although it was getting well dark. When we got into the trench, I laid him on the fire step. A few yards beyond him, laying out there, we'd come across a chap we called Corporal Gussie – a machine-gunner. He was badly shot in the stomach and I didn't suppose there was much hope for him, but he was in a bad way. I couldn't do anything, having the Lieutenant with me, but I said to the Corporal, 'I'll come back for you, Gussie.' So, when I'd laid the Lieutenant down and someone else came to see to him, I said, 'Right. I'm going out again.' But the officer wouldn't let me go. I felt very badly about it, because I'd promised Gussie I would go back, but the officer said, 'No you're not. You've had quite enough for one day.' It was nine o'clock at night by then, so I suppose, in a way, he was right. But I tried to insist and, I remember, he said to me, 'Anyone who's left out there isn't worth picking up now!'

He was right. There were twenty-three of us left alive out of my whole company. I don't know how they missed us. It was a miracle! It was a miracle that any of us got back. I don't believe I'd ever cried in my life, but, when I got back and found out what had happened, how many men we'd lost, I cried then. I was a Regular and they were all Volunteers, but we was all mucked in together. I cried then.

Their Battalion was the only one of the Brigade to have failed and they had only failed because the right of the 33rd Division had not succeeded in pushing forward. The Germans still held High Wood. The Tommies had inched forward in Delville, but it would be weeks yet before the wood was finally and permanently in British hands.

Far away on the left flank, across the Albert–Bapaume road, the

Australians had punched their way a little nearer to Mouquet Farm; some lines of trenches beyond the Leipzig Redoubt had been captured and, far away to the right, the troops had crept a little way up the valley to the right of Guillemont and the French had increased their hold on the village of Maurepas on the opposite slopes.

The small gains had been won at the cost of high casualties, but the Staff were satisfied. It was at least something.

Extract from the diary of Sir Douglas Haig

Saturday, 19 August: The operation carried out yesterday was most successful. It was on a front of over eleven miles. We now hold the ridge south-east of and overlooking Thiepval. Nearly five hundred prisoners were taken here while the battalion which carried out the attack only lost forty men! During their advance our men kept close to the artillery barrage.

The artillery, and the Staff who ruled the destiny of infantry and gunners alike, had been thinking on their feet and there had been time, since the catastrophe of the First of July, for shrewd reappraisal of the effectiveness of rigidly timed barrages with 'lifts' so inexorably predetermined. A new technique was now being tried – the 'creeping barrage' which would literally travel like a curtain in front of the infantry as it advanced, so that, when the barrage moved on from the German front line, the infantry would be there, on its heels, ready to engage the enemy, rather than advancing in full view two hundred yards away or more. Perhaps the most satisfactory thing about the limited successes of 18th August was that the technique of the creeping barrage had worked.

But the hard nuts were still holding out. The hardest of all was Guillemont and it was obvious that it would take a full-scale battle and much preparation to capture it. It was equally obvious that, before the Allies could push forward, Guillemont must be captured. There was just the faintest indication that the citadel of the German line was beginning to crumble – but it could be compared to the merest trickle of brick dust on the outer curtain wall. There was a long way to go.

Meantime the survivors of the troops who had been engaging the enemy must be relieved, rested and revived for their next endeavour. So the great chess game of moving troops and transport across the grassless waste of the battlefield, now swept intermittently by rain and winds and thunderstorms, must start all over again. The exhausted troops stumbled thankfully out of the line and, with some trepidation, fresh divisions slogged up through the desolation to take their place.

Alex Paterson was a born soldier, although, unlike Ted Gale, he had not been a Regular before the war. Nevertheless, he had reached the rank of Sergeant in the 11th (Service) Battalion, The Rifle Brigade and furthermore had turned out to be a 'natural'. Officers and men alike depended on Paterson. He had common-sense. He had a steady nerve which inspired confidence. He was a man's man.

Sergeant A. K. Paterson, DCM, MM, No. 52574, A Coy., 11th (S) Btn., The Rifle Brigade

I took to it like a duck to water, which was remarkable because when I joined up I'd never even heard of The Rifle Brigade. I went up to London, to Waterloo Station, and walked across to Scotland Yard and there was a great big Recruiting Sergeant there. I told him I wanted to join the Royal Engineers. He said, 'Well, you can't join the Royal Engineers. They're all full up. But I can give you a jolly good regiment to join.' I said, 'What regiment?' He said, 'The Rifle Brigade.' I told him quite straight that I'd never heard of it. I thought it was the Fire Brigade! It might as well have been the Fire Brigade for all I knew about it.

It was 8 September 1914, and I was still well under military age – I had to lie to get in – but a year later I was Platoon Sergeant and I took my platoon to France.

In the course of his year's service in France, Sergeant Paterson had become adept at trench warfare. He had become a veteran leader of patrols and, for many months in the line in front of Laventie, he had practically lived in No Man's Land. In his view, it was a good deal to be preferred to sitting in a dugout waiting to be shelled. He made it his personal responsibility to cut the zig-zag gaps in the wire in front of the trenches through which the patrols could pass undetected at night. He made it his business to see that every man in his platoon was familiar with the alien land on the other side of the wire. After dark he would take them silently 'over the top' to lie beyond the wire and perhaps to creep a little way ahead, so that they became accustomed to being at large, vulnerable, unprotected by the high sandbagged parapets, with nothing between them and the enemy just two hundred yards away. He taught them to be ready to freeze when a flare went up; ready, when it died down, to scramble back noiselessly through the wire, knowing that such experiences would make his men less apprehensive about leaving the shelter of the trenches when a fatigue party was needed to strengthen the defences or to repair entanglements broken by shellfire.

Daylight patrols called for even greater nerve and skill, but only by daylight could the enemy's positions be properly reconnoitred, his strong-points observed, his dispositions sketched. Day after day, in the hot September month of 1915, Paterson led his patrols out through the long grass towards the German line. The line was newly dug and information was badly needed.

Sergeant A. K. Paterson, DCM, MM, No. 52574, A Coy., 11th (S) Btn., The Rifle Brigade

The grass was just like hay, so anything that was dark or anything that was too light or was coloured would show up. We had to wear as little equipment as possible – no belts or buckles or anything that was likely to glitter in the sunshine. We had to really think about camouflage. We had to brown our hands and faces and, with my black hair, I had to wear a khaki handkerchief over my head with knots at the corners to keep it on and, because the weather was so hot and we knew that our faces would be wet with perspiration – and even *that* could glisten in the sunlight – we covered our faces with grass seed. We crawled on our tummies and we didn't keep to a straight line because, if we'd done that, we might have furrowed the grass as we went through and that would certainly be seen by troops using periscopes on the other side. So we had to move to the left and then to the right on our bellies and, as we got near the line, we had to keep very close so that we could whisper to each other and discuss things that we saw. We even had brown paper instead of white to write our notes on – just a four-inch square which we put in our pockets and then, if there was a bit of a shell-hole, we would get into it and very cautiously make a sketch or two of any sniper posts in the parapet, or any places where it seemed as if they'd got some activity in saps. Sometimes people were captured. We lost an officer and another Sergeant who were a bit too bold. They actually got into one of these German saps. They thought it was empty, but there were Jerries there, or at least they got there pretty soon! Only six officers out of eight got back that day and we didn't know what had happened. There was a certain amount of firing, but firing was going on all the time, all over the place, and you couldn't distinguish one particular lot of fire from the other.

In the best part of a year's foraying in No Man's Land, Alex Paterson had gained a great deal of valuable experience, a Military Medal, and a certain aplomb which was about to be distinctly useful in the trenches in front of Guillemont, for the troops were there to work, to dig, to push the line well out into hostile territory, to push out saps and communication trenches and to so improve the position that when the big attack came they would jump off with every advantage.

Paterson was in his element. Night work suited him. No Man's Land suited him. In spite of harassing fire from the Germans the work went well. Paterson took considerable satisfaction in what had been achieved and was more satisfied than ever when the Brigadier-General came up in person to inspect the results.

Sergeant A. K. Paterson, DCM, MM, No. 52574, A Coy., 11th (S) Btn., The Rifle Brigade

General Shute was the finest offensive officer I've ever come across and he was a man who wanted to be in the line and to know exactly what was going on. The Colonel came with him, and the Adjutant, and they handed him over to me and said, 'Sergeant, will you take the General and do what the General says.' And the General said he wanted to see on the other side of the wire and take a close look at the German line. Well, we had tunnels under our parapets running up through the wire and beyond. So I said, 'Right, you follow me.' He was on his own. I lifted up the sack on one side of the tunnel, I got in and said, 'Now, you come in.' So he came through. Two yards further on was another sack hanging down in the hole in front because, if you left it open all the way through, the Germans would spot the light shining through the other side. I lifted up the curtain at the front end of the tunnel and got through and held it up while he came through. He was a good six feet tall – a big man, taller than me. He went to his right and lay there and had a good look. I said, 'Keep down, sir. You'll have to go right down on your tummy and don't go any distance because there's no cover. I'm going to the right and I'd like you to follow me there, because you can see more.'

I talked to him like my uncle, and he knew perfectly well what I wanted him to do. I crawled along to a safe place and the Brigadier followed me, and I said, 'This is as far as I'm going. You can see all you want to see from here. Now, what do you want to know?' We stayed there for a good five minutes and I pointed things out and he asked me questions. When he'd seen all he wanted to, I said, 'We'll go backwards now. Don't turn round, because you'll be making a target three or four times the length. You go backwards

Left: Death Valley and, running away from it on the right, Caterpillar Wood and valley. It was the only sheltered route to the line as the fighting progressed and the ground still shows the battering it received from the passage of troops and guns.

Below: Looking across to Longueval and Delville Wood from the corner of Trones Wood on the road to Guillemont. The tower-like building in the centre is Waterlot Farm (now a sugar-beet refinery) and the rebuilt Guillemont Station is on the right. Since the railway track has been abandoned it is once again falling into ruins.

After the War the deep dugouts and galleries the Germans had burrowed into the depths of the chalky uplands of the Somme were filled up with the debris and rubble of the ruined villages and the entrances levelled. But this one at Guillemont was overlooked. The kennel-like concrete entries, close to the earth, lead steeply down to a double-chambered German command post, once part of a more extensive underground system.

The remains of a machine-gun post in the Triangle, attacked by the 6th West Yorks. on 3rd September, still looks across the fields to their jumping-off line on the edge of Thiepval Wood.

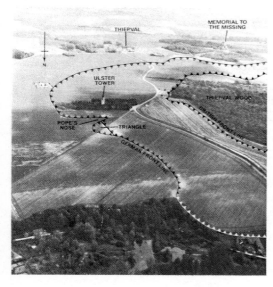

This panorama of the Ancre Valley and the Thiepval Ridge clearly shows the area where the West Yorks. attacked from the edge of Thiepval Wood on 3rd September, and both the Pope's Nose (although the trees surrounding the Ulster Tower mask part of its area) and the infamous Triangle can still be picked out by their outlines on the ground. (*Photograph Richard Dunning*)

The first message to be transmitted by the 1st Anzac Wireless section, under the command of George Middle, during the battle for Pozières.

The statue of Sir Douglas Haig at Montreuil-sur-Mer which was British General Headquarters from 1916 to 1919. The statue was destroyed by the occupying German army in 1940, re-erected after the War and narrowly escaped destruction for a second time when extracts from Sir Douglas Haig's private papers were published in 1952 and what were deemed to be uncomplimentary references to the French Army received wide publicity in the French newspapers, caused a national scandal and violent demonstrations by groups of *anciens combattants* demanding the removal of the statue. The row was smoothed over by the Mayor of Montreuil (the same Raymond Wable who, as a schoolboy, had seen Haig in Montreuil during the War) and the statue still stands today in the market square in front of the old Theatre which was the Army's telephone exchange and main communications centre. As an extra precaution there were duplicated lines in a deep dungeon in the Citadel.

A view of the land between and beyond Ginchy and Guillemont, the scene of the September fighting.

GUILLEMONT   WATERLOT   LONGUEVAL
              FARM
                        QUARRY

The formidable defences of the German Second Line at Ginchy – still clearly visible as chalk-marks on the ground – captured by the Guards Division. The small quarry to the right of the village served as Brigade Headquarters.

Ginchy, Autumn 1982. Almost seventy years on the farmlands of the Somme still yield an annual harvest of steel.

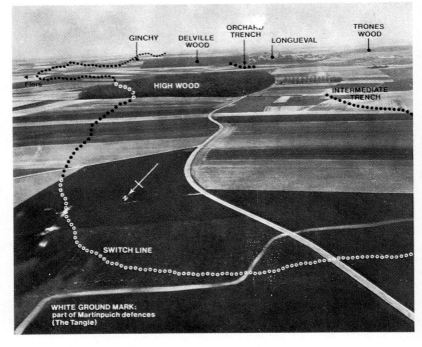

Where the Switch Line ran.

The site of the Triangle and the Quadrilateral from the Guards Memorial on Ginchy Ridge.

Christchurch Boys' High School cricket team in 1908, the year in which they won the Heathcote Williams Shield for the best team in the Dominion of New Zealand. Four of the eleven were killed in the War. Rupert Hickmott is seated left of the shield.

Above: The menacing Quadrilateral which blocked the advance from Guillemont (*in background*). Nearly seventy years later its massive concrete positions still stand – successive attempts to blow them up have merely tilted them.

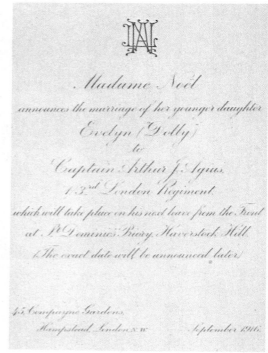

Madame Noël

announces the marriage of her younger daughter

Evelyn (Dolly)

to

Captain Arthur J. Agius.

1. 3rd London Regiment

which will take place on his next leave from the Front

at St Dominic's Priory, Haverstock Hill

(The exact date will be announced later)

45, Compayne Gardens,

Hampstead, London N.W.   September 1916.

Right: The invitation to Arthur Agius's wedding.

The Butte de Warlencourt and the land beyond le Sars where the fighting came to a standstill at the end of the Battle of the Somme in November 1916.

The valley behind Beaumont Hamel and the slopes to the right above it where the boys of the Glasgow Tramways Battalion were cut off in Frankfurt Trench and fought a private battle of their own after the Battle of the Somme officially ended and all attempts to rescue them had to be given up.

The British and German lines on either side of the present-day Newfoundland Park where the trenches (which are chalk-marks beyond it) have been preserved by the Canadian Government as a memorial to the men of the Newfoundland Regiment who died here. Y-Ravine runs just behind the slope on the right and past the foot of the trees in the park.

The valley behind Beaumont Hamel (Station Road) with the Thiepval Ridge to the east, which for obvious reasons had to go before Beaumont Hamel could be captured. The old deep dugouts, so joyfully explored by the boys of the 13th Rifle Brigade after they had helped the Royal Naval Division to capture the valley and many gun positions, can still be seen in the lee of the bush-covered bank in the foreground.

The 'fortress' village of Beaumont Hamel sheltered in the cleft of its valley. The German front line ran across the slopes of the rising ground on either side. The white chalk-marks in front of the copse on the left mark the perimeter of their outpost wired defences, but the ditch-like vestiges of trench running towards the village in the right of middle foreground was dug, after its capture, as a British communication trench. Munich and Frankfurt trenches were on the left of the rising ground behind the village.

Station Road, running from Beaumont Hamel village to Beaucourt station, which was the 'Green Line' captured by the Royal Naval Division supported by the 13th Battalion, The Rifle Brigade, on 13th November. The terrain has been long ago returned to farmland but the rugged vestiges of dugouts, trenches and gun positions show how formidably it was fortified.

Advanced First Army.
Second Army.
Third Army.
Fourth Army.

O.A.104.

3.

June 29

Platoon Comdrs.

Please read to your platoons and initial when you've done so

Capt Lloyd for No 8
Lieut Henri   7
  "   Liddard   6
  "   Thomas   5

The following warning should be communicated verbally to all ranks before taking part in an assault:-

1.   All ranks must be on their guard against the various ruses at which the enemy has shown himself to be an adept, especially the use of British words of command, such as "Retire", etc.

2.   The German machine gun is carried on a sledge, and the Germans sometimes throw a blanket over the gun. This makes the sledge and gun resemble a stretcher.

3.   It is the duty of all ranks to continue to use their weapons against the enemy's fighting troops, unless and until it is beyond all doubt that these have not only ceased all resistance, but that, whether through having voluntarily thrown down their weapons or otherwise, they have definitely and finally abandoned all hope or intention of resisting further. In the case of apparent surrender, it lies with the enemy to prove his intention beyond the possibility of misunderstanding, before the surrender can be accepted as genuine.

G.H.Q.,   Sgd/ L.E. KIGGELL, Lieut-General,

26.6.16.   Chief of the General Staff.

167th Inf. Bde.   - 2 -
168th Inf. Bde.
169th Inf. Bde.

        Herewith 25 copies to provide for a distribution of one per company.

        The importance of the above instructions must be impressed on all ranks.

Hdqrs. 56th Divn.   Lieut. Colonel,

28th June, 1916.   General Staff.

Left: All that remains of old Beaumont Hamel village is a single pane of stained glass depicting the head of the Virgin Mary. In 1916 a German officer picked it out of the rubble of the old church and took it back to Germany as a souvenir. In 1978 he returned it to the village and it was incorporated into a window of the 'new' church (rebuilt in 1922).

Right: This photograph was found by a British soldier in the wallet of a dead German.

Opposite: The Order issued from G.H.Q. on the eve of the First of July which was later denied to be an instruction to 'take no prisoners'.

Left, below and opposite: The letter Captain Agius received from Harold Scarlett's widow Florence.

305 Thorold Rd
Ilford
Oct 3rd 16

Dear Capt. Agius –

I wish to take this opportunity of thanking you for your kind letter of sympathy, and for the few details you were able to give me concerning my dear husband's death. The sad news was a terrible shock to me, and up till now I have felt too ill to write to you, although I have been eager to do so.

If it is not taking too great an advantage of your kindness, will you please let me know whether, at the time my dear one fell, there were any personal possessions on him that could be sent to me. I know there was nothing of real value, but I think you will understand that any little thing, no matter what it is, will became one of my most

cherished possessions.

It was a great relief to know that dear Harold did not suffer any pain although what would I not give to have had just one last message from him. We have been married such a short time (only five months) and I cannot realize that he has gone – never to see him again. The last time we were together he was so happy and well, and eager to do his level best for his country at all cost. This horrible war is dealing some cruel blows, and one is apt to grow hardened to the brutality of it until someone very dear is taken. There is scarcely a home, but what the occupants have some great trouble to bear, and sometimes I think, knowing this, helps us to bear our grief more bravely.

Will you please also tell

me if possible, where my
husband was struck. I feel I
would like to know. After the
War, I hope to be able to visit his
last resting place and in that
case, I suppose I should have
no difficulty in distinguishing
it.

Once again thanking you
for your kindness in writing to
me. With very good wish for
your safe and speedy return to
England

Yours very sincerely,
Florence E. Scarlett

Below: 'Fond Love to my Dear Boy'. Such postcards were more popular with the senders than with the recipients.

Above left: The New Recruits: Joe Hoyles (*standing*), Fred Lyons and Sid Birkett, photographed the day they joined up.

Above right: The Seasoned Warriors. Len Lovell at home on convalescent leave.

Below left: George Roy Bealing, MM 6th Wilts. 19th Div. 1914–18.

Below right: Tom Easton of the Tyneside Scottish in 1914.

on your toes and your knees, into the same curtain and I'll follow you backwards. Don't turn round and put your boots to them!' So we went back, just like that, and, when we'd crawled through the tunnel into the trench, he stood there and he chatted to me and he thanked me and he shook my hand in front of the Colonel and the Adjutant and everybody. They stood there just like stuffed dummies! But the General spoke to me man to man. He was a marvellous chap.

General Shute was no milksop, no remote, godlike figure so detached from his men that he saw them as pawns or statistics. They had done a good job. They had prepared the advanced positions with care. They were tired with long labour and had suffered much from shelling and sniping. Because of the bad weather which had caused the battle to be postponed twice they had been far too long in the line, and General Shute was absolutely determined that they should have a rest before it started. There was very little time, for the assault was now scheduled for 3 September and August was almost at an end. But Shute insisted. On 31 August his Brigade filed out of the trenches and moved back, for two days' holiday, to camp in the Carnoy Valley.

They knew that it would be for a mere breathing space, that in forty-eight hours they would be back – but it was a relief to be out of the line, away from the discomfort of dripping clothing that was soaked again as soon as it began to dry out, away from the gruelling labour of digging trenches that the rainstorms turned into muddy streams even as they dug. Away from the dripping gloom, away from the stench, away from the eternal sound of the guns and the shells that whined through the leaden skies. Yesterday evening, just before dusk, the awful weather had crashed to a climax so furious that it had silenced even the guns. Two observation balloons were struck spectacularly by lightning and exploded. The torrential downpour soaked every man to the skin and turned trenches that had been rivers of water into seas of mud. Duckboards which had provided dry standing of a sort or, at the very least, a foothold, sank a foot or more into the glutinous depths. That night, between sunset and dawn, thirty-seven lorries of supplies and ammunition stuck on the Carnoy–Montauban road alone, and next night, as the boys trudged back towards their unexpected rest, rope-gangs of the ASC were still trying to haul the last of them out.

The night was clear, the rain had gone off, but the Germans chose to send over gas to cheer them on their way. Next morning the sun came out but few of the boys woke up until it was high in the sky. It had not been possible to find them accommodation in a proper camp, even if there had been time to take them so far behind the line. The Brigade found itself lying on the open ground in the vicinity of the Carnoy craters at Casino Point where, exactly two months ago today, in the wake of the exploding mines, the 18th Division had broken the line and forged exultantly ahead with the French at its shoulder.

It was hardly a camp, but, among the debris of abandoned ammunition boxes, the litter of empty shell cases that marked the old gun positions, wigwam-like bivouacs of canvas and canes had been improvised to shelter the men, some captured dugouts served as accommodation for the officers and two big marquees had been put up to serve as dining and recreation halls by day and dormitories by night. There was bacon for breakfast, and plenty to go round, for – discounting the sick – the Brigade had lost six hundred men in its nine-day stint in the trenches in front of Guillemont. There was dinner to look forward to – doubtless only 'His Majesty's stew' but a good deal more palatable than His Majesty's jaw-breaking biscuits, cold beans and bully beef, which was the unvarying diet in the line. Before dinner there was an issue of cigarettes and later the mail came up with letters and parcels from home. The guns still hammering the front two miles away were an unpleasant reminder of what awaited them but, as they lounged on groundsheets on the squelching earth, rapidly drying out under the warm sun, the boys inclined towards the opinion that it all added up to an almost perfect day. The officers, as preoccupied as the men with drying out and catching up on sleep, had kept well out of the way; no sergeants had appeared with lists of obligatory fatigues and, towards evening, Brigadier-General Shute came up himself from Brigade Headquarters to look round with a benevolent eye and see that all was well. By his personal order the boys received a rum ration to which, being out of the line, they had, strictly speaking, no entitlement. When darkness fell, although the sky behind them quivered and pulsated with the glare of battle, almost extinguishing the efforts of the stars to shine through the warm night, although they were allowed no lights, the boys sat on in the open air, reluctant for the day to end.

Fred White and Freddie Stevens (more commonly known in the Army as 'Nobbler and Jerry') sat together replete with sweet biscuits. They did a good Cockney double act – perhaps not quite so good as the original 'Nobbler and Jerry' who had won fame in Fred Karno's Concert Troupe, but good enough to have earned their nicknames. They had been friends since their not-so-long-ago schooldays, near-neighbours at home in Camden Town and members of the same breezy bunch of mates who, on halcyon Sunday evenings before the war, used to walk across Hampstead Heath to Jack Straw's Castle to spend a convivial evening for the price of a glass or two of beer. This outing had been the highlight of the week and, rather more intoxicated on high spirits than on alcohol, they used to swing back across the heath, singing in exaggerated harmony:

> *We were sailing along on Moonlight Bay,*
> *We could hear the voices ringing,*
> *They seemed to say*
> *'You have stolen my heart,*
> *Now don't go 'way!'*
> *As we sang Love's old sweet song,*
> *On Moonlight Bay.*

The weekend the war began they had been singing this favourite as they tramped home in Bank Holiday mood. After that the two Freds had not felt much like singing, nor even like a tramp across the heath. Things had changed after their mates went into the Army. 'Nobbler and Jerry' were equally anxious to join. They had attained the military age of nineteen but what they had not attained was the necessary height. Stevens – with the advantage of one inch over White – was barely five feet four and in the choosy days of August 1914 the Army still stuck to the minimum pre-war requirement of five feet seven. It was a sore subject.

Rifleman F. C. White, No. R.8529, B Coy., Bomber, 10th Btn., King's Royal Rifle Corps, 59th Brigade, 20th Division

Most of our mates were in the London Territorials. Of course they went away immediately the war started and Freddie and I and my brother and one or two others who wasn't in the Territorials always used to march with them wherever they went, so we marched with them to Waterloo Station. That was 4 August, when war was declared. We was all as excited as anything. We all wanted to join up. My brother, who was taller than me, joined up and went in. I went up. They said, 'No, don't want you! You're too small!' Same thing happened to Freddie.

It came to the last day of 1914, and there was only Freddie and me left of the whole bunch. Freddie's brother had just got killed (he was a Regular in the King's Royal Rifle Corps) and me and Freddie was mooching about and we was fed up. We said, 'Come on, let's have another go!' So we goes to a recruiting office in Crowndale Road, St Pancras. Freddie goes in first, up to the Recruiting Sergeant, and I'm standing behind him.

'Yes?' says the Sergeant, 'what do *you* want?'

'Join the Army.'

'What do you want to go in?'

'King's Royal Rifles.'

'You can't go in there. They're full up.'

'Why not? My brother was killed in there!'

The Recruiting Sergeant softened a bit at that, and he says, 'All right. Sign here, take your shilling and away you go.'

Then it comes to me, but I got a flea in my ear! He said, 'You come back when you're a bit taller. We don't want you!' I thought, 'That's good! Freddie's in, I'm out, left on me own – the lone bloke.' When we got outside, Freddie and me talked a bit about what we should do and we decided to have another try. So we walked about three miles from St Pancras to Holloway Road to another recruiting office. I goes in there.

'What do *you* want?'

'Join the army.'

'What do you want to go in?'

'King's Royal Rifles.'

'You can't go in there. Full up!'

'Well, I ain't going in anything at all,' I said. 'My pal's going in there tomorrow.' So, he says, 'Oh, all right. Sign here.' Didn't measure me or anything! Off we went next day, down to the depot at Winchester, and we stuck together all the way along. Never was parted! Of course, later on we had different jobs with the battalion. Freddie went on the Lewis-guns and I stayed in B Company with the bombers. But every time we was out of the line we got together and stuck together.

That evening, sitting under the stars near the Carnoy Craters, was the last time the two Freds would meet until after the war. Tomorrow night they would be on their way back to the line and the battle that loomed ahead. Tonight they were thinking of old times. 'Nobbler' White's mouth organ was worn and battered by long service in the Army and a year or more in the trenches, but he could still squeeze a tune out of it. For most of the evening he had been playing the accompaniment to a selection of the bawdy choruses that had enhanced the Tommies' musical education since their arrival in France. Now he changed the mood.

We were sailing along on Moonlight Bay . . .

Freddie Stevens took up the words but they seemed inappropriate to the circumstances. After a little thought and a few false starts he came up with a better version. The lads liked it, and one by one they joined in.

I was strolling along in Gillymong –
With the Minniewerfers singing
Their old sweet song
And I said to old Fritz,
'We're here to stay!
And we'll kick your arse from here
To Moonlight Bay.'

The best that could be said for it was that it was a good tune.

On the following evening, as they prepared for the long trek back up the line, the boys felt less inclined to sing, and they did not much like the Padre's choice of hymn. Doubtless he meant well, but their thoughts were on the battle ahead and in the circumstances the sentiments expressed in *Nearer, my God, to Thee*, struck a little too close to home. The singing was, to say the least, ragged. The boys stood bare-headed in the low rays of the evening sun waiting for dusk and the order to march off and it was noticeable that the Padre's voice boomed above them all.

Nearer, my God, to Thee,
Nearer to Thee,
E'en though it be a cross
That raiseth me;
Still all my song shall be,
Nearer, my God, to Thee,
Nearer to thee!

In a few minutes' time they would be shouldering rifles and turning their faces towards the sound of the guns. In a few hours they would be going over the top. The 59th Brigade was well under strength, for there had been no time to reinforce them and they were under no illusions as to what lay ahead. Under the circumstances only the most resigned of Christian souls in their ranks could join in the hymn-singing with enthusiasm – and even the voices of that select band trailed off when it came to the third verse.

There let my way appear
Steps unto Heaven.
All that Thou sendest me
In mercy given,
Angels to beckon me,
Nearer, my God, to Thee,
Nearer to thee!

Still, the boys had had a good feed and a good rest and, as the smallest man in the battalion, Fred White was suitably grateful. It was fortunate that he was wiry as well as diminutive for, as a company bomber, he was carrying excess weight in the form of a bomber's jacket with no less than eight Mills bombs tucked into its individual pockets and he was tired already. For most of the day the Bombers had been hard at it priming countless boxes of bombs in preparation for the battle, while their mates had been taking things easy. But one unexpected happening had cheered Fred up. In one of the boxes he had found a note tucked neatly into the top row of bombs. It gave the name and address of the girl munition-worker who had packed them and added the interesting information that she was blonde, blue-eyed and aged nineteen. The message ended encouragingly, *Good Luck, Tommy*. Fred had taken the note as a good omen and was carrying it into battle, tucked like a talisman into his breast pocket, beside a letter from his sweetheart, Ethel.

Chapter 19

Next day the sun shone and the troops splashed across the steaming mud of No Man's Land to capture Guillemont.

It was difficult to see the sun through the fumes, the smoke, the flying debris, the spouting columns of liquid mud that filled the sky and fell back to soak and blind the Tommies as they pressed forward on the heels of the creeping barrage. There was still a 'fixed barrage', a careful timetable of 'lifts', that would move steadily ahead to fall on the second and third German lines as the troops advanced – but this time they were advancing under the umbrella of a second barrage, moving smoothly ahead less than fifty yards beyond them, leading them to the objective and screening them from the enemy as they went.

It was not easy to keep going at a steady pace when every instinct nurtured by training and experience urged every man to throw himself flat. It took one sort of bravado to sing of 'strolling along in Gillymong' but, in the growing mistrust between gunners and infantry, most of whom had tragic experience of the worn-out guns firing short, it took bravado of quite another sort to go forward steadily behind a curtain of explosions in the unswerving belief that they would keep their distance as you progressed.

The mounds of brick dust and rubble which appeared to the naked eye to be all that was left of the village of Guillemont were no longer so innocent-looking to the eye of the Command. With the events at Thiepval, at Ovillers, at la Boisselle, disturbingly fresh in their minds they had no doubt that, beneath the field of ruins, the enemy was waiting in a Pandora's box of tunnels and shelters and dugouts, and that, when the lid was opened, they would be ready to catapult to the surface with the impetus of a tight-coiled spring, suddenly released. The nub of the British plan was to open the lid first – from the outside.

Sergeant A. Paterson, DCM, MM, No. 52574, A Coy., 11th (S) Btn.,
The Rifle Brigade

You went down steps to these places, but the steps didn't go straight
down. They would go down, say, three steps to the left, then three
steps straight followed by four to the right, until they reached the
bottom – the idea being that nobody could throw a bomb directly
down the hole of the entrance. Ordinary bombs, demolition bombs,
would just burst halfway down and the worst they would do would
be block up the passage, and they always had an escape route. So
our job was to demolish the front of them, break down the doors
and entrances, open them up a bit so that the Bombers could get
at them. Well, the Jerries weren't just going to sit there and let us
hammer away demolishing the front of these dugouts, so, first thing,
we had to throw down phosphorus bombs – smoke bombs. You'd
strike the smoke bomb on an ignition brassard you had strapped
round your arm and fling it down the steps. The bombs gave off
a thick suffocating smoke which, being heavy, flowed down the
winding steps and spread out in the large spaces below so that it
would either drive the Germans out or suffocate them.

We had to carry extra haversacks full of these phosphorus bombs
and, as well as that and extra ammunition and all the rest of our
normal equipment, every man had to carry either a pick or a shovel,
one each. It was a wonder we were able to get out of the trench,
because we had to get over a big bank that we'd made ourselves
in front of our trenches for cover, and then beyond that was all
the wire and water.

Zero Hour was supposed to be midday. The idea was that, about
ten minutes before Zero Hour, our bombardment of their lines
increased in volume and, when that noise stopped, which meant
that your covering fire from the field guns was lifting ahead, that
was your signal to go over the top. Well, maybe the firing stopped.
If it did, nobody noticed it, because the Germans were still bombarding our front line and the shells were bursting all over the place
and the shells of our heavy barrage were going over our heads.
The noise was so deafening that, days later, it was still resounding
in our ears – and we were supposed to listen! We went over by
the time on our watches and my platoon was leading, in extended
order, three to four paces between each man. You couldn't say,
'You go straight across that way.' You'd have to go round huge
holes and, with more shells falling all around, it was very difficult
to keep going in a straight line. Very difficult to keep the men

together in any kind of formation. Very difficult to know what was happening.

What was happening was that part of the 59th Brigade, having started off fractionally early, was advancing into the line of its own barrage. It was the 10th Battalion of the King's Royal Rifle Corps, making straight for Guillemont village, who started earliest of all and who took the greatest punishment. But those who survived to reach the German wire and push through gaps to the first objective, just as the barrage lifted, had the advantage of surprise.

Rifleman F. C. White, No. R.8529, B Coy., Bomber, 10th Btn., King's Royal Rifle Corps, 59th Brigade, 20th Division

There was me and this other bloke and our instructions was to make for the church gates at Guillemont. When we got to the church gate there was no church gate! All there was was a pile of bricks! Anyway, we'd been told there was a deep dugout under the church – because there always *was* one in a village church, with the vault and all. We was armed with about half a dozen Mills grenades in a waistcoat in the front of us, and we found the dugout entrance and I stood at one side of it and this other bloke, he stood opposite. There was no door on it – it was open and I got hold of a bomb, pulled the pin out, flung the bomb down. Nothing happened! He pulled the pin out and *he* slung a bomb down. Nothing happened! I got another bomb out, pulled the pin out, flung it down and, as soon as it went down this time, the bloody thing comes straight up again and exploded on the stairs! It didn't half give us a turn! So, I said to this bloke, 'Come on, we'll go somewhere else. It's too hot here!'

Sergeant A. K. Paterson, DCM, MM, No. 52574, A Coy., 11th (S) Btn., The Rifle Brigade

We had to take six German lines and it was all plain to be seen. There was a sunken road, then there was another line of trenches and then there was a pillbox which was the entrance to a line of deep dugouts and a machine-gun was blazing away from it, but the bombers took care of that, and on we went. Every time we got to the next objective there were fewer and fewer men. At about one o'clock, we'd just taken what had been the Germans' support line when I found that our Company Commander had been killed and that the Second-in-Command was severely wounded in the head. Our reserves were just passing through us to take the next objective, which was a sunken road, and that gave us an hour's break, so I spent the time scrounging around in all the smoke and all the deafening noise trying to find out just who was there and who wasn't. There was nobody! No officers to be seen, no other platoon sergeant besides myself, so there was nothing for it but to take charge of the Company because time was going on and we had to line up with the 6th Battalion of the Ox and Bucks Regiment ready to go on to the next objective and over the top again at half-past two. The next objective was supposed to be Wedge Wood Valley. Wedge Wood was the landmark. But there was no Wedge Wood. It had completely disappeared. That was our final objective, on the other side of Guillemont – the line on top of the valley, facing the apex of Leuze Wood.

It was late in the afternoon by the time we got there and I started the riflemen digging a new line near the top of Wedge Wood Valley. By dusk the job was finished after a fashion. In my spare haversack I carried conical-shaped flares, yellow and red, and we had to lay them along the line of our position at three-feet intervals. We lit them when it got dark enough, just as a spotting aeroplane flew over, to show the position of the new front line.

After the flares had died down I took the roll call. Out of our whole company we mustered, besides myself, the Corporal, one Acting Corporal and thirty-seven men, including two stretcher-bearers. I sent one man back to Headquarters with a list of the names and inspected the rifles. Then I posted some sentries and lookouts a short way down No Man's side of Wedge Valley and, after a bit, I called the roll again – just in case anyone had come in or caught up. No one had.[1]

Rifleman F. C. White, No. R.8529, B Coy., Bomber, 10th Btn., King's Royal Rifle Corps, 59th Brigade, 20th Division

It was getting dark and we come across some troops in a slit trench. They were the 16th Irish Division and one of them had found a full bottle of rum. They was all blotto! This was outside Guillemont.

---

1. Sergeant Paterson, who three months before had earned the Military Medal, was awarded the Distinguished Conduct Medal after the Battle of Guillemont. The citation read: 'D.C.M. For conspicuous gallantry in action. When both the officers of his Company had been wounded early in an attack, Sergeant Paterson collected and reformed his Company and pushed on to the final objective. He was twice wounded but displayed the utmost bravery and resource.'

Beyond Guillemont. We was through Guillemont by now, digging
in on the final objective. We felt rough – rough, I'll tell you!
Actually that was our first real experience of warfare. Three or four
times they had a go at Guillemont and they couldn't get it! But
we got it!

In the general attack that had taken place along the length of the line,
they had taken Guillemont – but they had been intended to take more.

For more than two months Thiepval village had scowled from behind
the keep of its defences on the summit of the Thiepval Ridge and it
seemed to the Tommies, creeping slowly towards it from the direction
of the Leipzig Redoubt, and to the Aussies battering out from Pozières
to take it in the rear by way of Mouquet Farm, as dauntingly impregnable
as it had been on 1 July. So long as the Germans held Thiepval, they
would be able to overlook almost the whole British advance and direct
their guns to crush it.

From its heights, Thiepval could look over her shoulder to the high
ridges that climbed up beyond Mametz – to Delville Wood, to High
Wood and to Martinpuich. Just behind her back, the captured village of
Pozières was in full view with the windmill up the hill beyond it and,
beyond even that, the land that swept in a bleak uninterrupted vista to
Courcelette was clearly visible. Nearer still, Mouquet Farm held out and,
as long as it did, Thiepval would hold out too. Looking out from Thiepval
village across the treeless swampland of the Ancre Valley, the Mesnil
Ridge, blasted and pockmarked by continuous bombardment, was bald
of vegetation and, to the vigilant German observers, the chalk-white
furrows of the spiralling communication trenches scarring the face of the
hill pointed unerring fingers to the network of cable communications,
and signposted with awful precision the journeyings of the passageways
that led the British troops towards comparative safety and dubious shelter
on the other side of the ridge.

The longest and most tortuous of the communication trenches, so steep
that in places steps were built into it, was nicknamed Jacob's Ladder. But
it was hardly a stairway to Paradise. By day it was bombarded with high
explosives; by night unfortunate wayfarers were sprayed with shrapnel.
Mingling with the burst of the explosions was the soft dull plopping of
the gas shells that, night after night, soaked the Mesnil Ridge with deadly
fumes. The last straw, in the back-breaking ascent, was having to sweat
it out in the stifling confines of a gas helmet. The trench petered out
into a muddy lane at the village of Mesnil.

The 'muddy lane' was a sunken road that ran from Mesnil past 'Brock's

Benefit' to the trenches facing Beaumont Hamel. Radiating from it, other tracks and even a light railway ran towards the shoulder of the hill where the trenchline faced Y Ravine. One day's fighting and more than two months' incessant bombardment had reduced the battlefield to a waste-land and razed the British trenches almost out of existence. The task of a thousand unfortunate working parties had been to build them up again.

Working under the eyes of the enemy on the ridge beyond it was no easy job.

It was impossible to clear the land between the lines of its gruesome burden of dismembered dead. Even the old front line was so damaged and so choked by bodies, that it could only be held as an outpost and garrisoned by small parties of men. In the few places where the parapet had not been competely shattered, they stood guard, nauseated by the sight and smell of carnage as the working parties laboured to rebuild the line. The few hours of darkness between the long summer evening of one July day and the dawn of the next, were all too brief for the job because there was hardly a foot of trenchline in the sector between the Ancre and Serre which had not been damaged. During the last two weeks of August, in a final spurt of effort, the work on the trenches had been completed and now, on 3 September, the 39th Division filed into them to take part in the general attack from Thiepval to Guillemont which it was hoped would prepare the way for the Big Push that would finally break the line.

Their orders were to attack and capture three lines of trenches on the spur of high land south of Beaumont Hamel Valley; their real task was to cover the 49th Division across the Valley of the Ancre, as they went forward from Thiepval Wood to capture the Schwaben Redoubt and the line that linked it to the village of St Pierre Divion in the valley below. It was almost a blueprint of the attack of the First of July. But a new jumping-off line had been dug precociously near the German line, so close that it seemed inconceivable that, even against this now legendary rampart of steel and fire, the attack could fail. On the night of 2 September, the 6th West Yorks were back in Thiepval Wood – not, this time, in reserve but in the forefront of the attack. Now they were required to bloody the Pope's Nose.

The unflattering sobriquet had been coined, as might have been expected, by the 36th Ulster Division to describe the ugly little salient that thrust out, jagged with defences, to within yards of the British lines. It was armoured to the teeth and it adjoined another fortified strongpoint, dubbed the Triangle, which lay astride the old track that ran through the fields to St Pierre Divion. Concrete machine-gun posts dominated every possible approach but, from the new jumping-off trenches, audaciously far advanced beyond the old ones on the edge of Thiepval Wood, it seemed that one short sharp rush behind the creeping barrage would overwhelm the Pope's Nose and the Triangle at one swift decisive stroke. Meanwhile troops up the hill to the right would rush the German line and swarm across the Schwaben Redoubt. They had done it before. They could do it again. This time they would hold it.

But it was the few remaining old hands who had done it before. The new men, drafted in to fill the gaps in the decimated ranks of the 49th Division, were raw and inexperienced, newly out from home, so innocent that, when the principle of the creeping barrage was explained, there were anxious, mutinous mutterings, exclamations of disbelief. Misunderstanding the concept, the rumour spread that they had been earmarked as a suicide force and were intended to 'draw fire' by walking into the enemy's barrage. The misapprehension was resolved but, in the suspicious minds of the troops, a lingering doubt remained.

Even the officers and experienced NCOs anticipated the attack with misgiving. They knew that their men were exhausted. For the last six days they had spent every waking hour – including many, in the dead of night, which should properly have been devoted to sleep – humping ammunition and reserve rations from Aveluy Wood, across the Ancre and along the slogging miles of Black Horse road to forward dumps in Thiepval Wood. At the end of every exhausting trip, they were put to work again. The advanced trenches and saps had to be dug and there was no one else to do it.

Captain E. V. Tempest, DSO, MC, 1st/6th Btn., West Yorkshire Regiment, 146th Brigade, 49th Division

They returned an hour or two before dawn so exhausted they could hardly walk and would have laid down in hundreds on Speyside or Paisley Dump, anywhere, but for officers and NCOs who were compelled to urge on the men to other fatigues and preparations during the daylight. Moreover, the Battalion was no longer the Territorial Unit of July First, but a mixture of reinforcements from twenty-seven different battalions from all parts of England, who had had no opportunity of shaking down into one efficient unit during the past few weeks of trench warfare. It was said that, if the men reached the assembly trenches on the morning of the battle, it would be a feat worthy of praise! And the most that was hoped for was that, with an extra rum ration, and the excitement of the moment, the attacking waves would reach the enemy support line and remain there from sheer physical inability to go back.

Sergeant J. E. Yates, 1st/6th Btn., West Yorkshire Regiment, 146th Brigade, 49th Division

The experience of my platoon was an average one. When we marched into support on 27 August this platoon was thirty-three strong and in fair condition. After a week of working parties, etc., there remained to go over the top eighteen decrepit old men. The rest were dead, wounded or in hospital. It was my unfortunate duty to wake my men and parade them for the fatigues. They lay like men drunk or dead. For instance, there was one decent average man who, I knew from experience, always pulled his last ounce. One night I could wake him by no ordinary means, and in the end he had to be pulled on to his feet, held there, and kicked into consciousness. He said, 'I can't do it, Sergeant! I'm done!'

I knew he was done, but there were sacks of trench mortar bombs to carry across the marsh up to the line and I had seen men do miracles before. He made an effort to pull himself together, and he moved off with the party. He collapsed after a few steps – but he was one of the eighteen in my platoon who went over the top two days later!

Talking together, the Platoon Sergeants had come to the disquieting conclusion that any remote possibility of success would depend on one of three remote contingencies. First, that the enemy had been completely exterminated by the British barrage. Second, that he was shocked into a state of instant paralysis at the very sight of them. Third, a miracle. Even without a miracle, if the Duke of Wellington's, on their right, had succeeded in capturing the Pope's Nose there might have been some flimsy chance of the West Yorks capturing the infamous Triangle. But they were too weakened by casualties and wearied by labour.

Under cover of the barrage, they had crept up right to the edge of the Pope's Nose, but the barrage of machine-gun fire directed from the Schwaben Redoubt up the hill snuffed out any hopes of holding on to the first few tenuous footholds they managed to gain. When their attack had been easily repulsed, the machine-gun crews in the Pope's Nose were able to swing their guns about to fire at point blank range on the men of the West Yorks who had penetrated the Triangle. And the German barrage, opening up within three minutes of Zero, was pounding the trenches where the troops of the second wave were waiting, with such lethal effect and with such uncanny accuracy that the 'second wave' never materialized at all. Those who were not blown sky-high by the shelling were pinned down and unable to move.

Arthur Wilson, newly commissioned, had joined the battalion in Thiepval Wood only three weeks before.

2nd Lieutenant Arthur Wilson, 1st/5th Btn., West Yorkshire Regiment, 146th Brigade, 49th Division

We had moved forward and we got right up to the German saps, almost under the German wire, but we simply couldn't move. The shelling was so furious and our casualties were so enormous! Most of the Company Commanders were killed – there was no one to lead the men and the number of shells that fell was absolutely fantastic. We were simply blown to blazes and we couldn't do a thing. We were waiting for signals, but of course no word came back. It was a misty morning, so we could see nothing, and no runner could have got through that shelling. It was quite frightful. It was a wonder any of us escaped alive. One shell nearly took my hair off. The blast all went the other way and it killed Company Sergeant-Major Iredale. When we got out, I discovered that my right sock had been unravelled by the force of the explosion. It was completely unknitted for at least six to eight yards by the blast. It was quite extraordinary.

One message got through. It arrived at Battalion Headquarters at ten minutes past six. It had been scribbled by Lieutenant Armistead and it had taken an intrepid and lucky runner more than half an hour to cover the eight hundred yards to Battalion Headquarters. It was the first real information they received and the first they knew of what was happening beyond the thunder of the exploding barrage.

We got part of the front wave into the enemy line. But the rest of the front wave stuck in front of the enemy wire, and then retired, leaving only a few scattered men in front line who have had to come back. I am trying to collect men into front parallel trench, but there are very few.

The few hardened survivors of the original battalion were grimly holding on. The new men, or those of them who had not been knocked out by the vicious whiplash of fire that traversed the Triangle, had indeed retired, fumbling back exhausted to huddle in small terrified groups against the low bank of the sunken road. Later, under repeated questioning, they all told the same story and could not be budged from it. They had been ordered to retire. Some of the men expressed the belief that the order must have been given by a German disguised as a British officer. It was an unlikely tale. Sadly, Captain Temple remarked that the evidence to support this claim was 'not very strong'. But none of the few remaining officers had the heart to blame the few remaining men. They had, quite simply, been asked to do the impossible.

At the pinnacle of the chain of command, opinion, less well-informed, was less sympathetic. General Gough had no hesitation in laying the blame for the failure of the attack squarely on the shoulders of the 49th Division, nor did he hesitate so to inform the Commander-in-Chief.

Extract from the diary of General Sir Douglas Haig

Monday, 4 September: I visited Toutencourt and saw Gen. Gough. The failure to hold the position gained on the Ancre is due, he reported, to the 49th Division. The units of that Division did not really attack and some men did not follow their officers. The total losses of this Division are under a thousand![1] It is a Territorial Division from the West Riding of Yorkshire. I had occasion a fortnight ago to call the attention of the Army and Corps Commanders (Gough and Jacobs) to the lack of smartness, and slackness of one of its Battalions in the matter of saluting when I was motoring through the village where it was billeted. I expressed my opinion that such men were too sleepy to fight well, etc. It was due to the failure of the 49th Division that the 39th (which did well and got all their objectives) had to fall back.

---

1. Even allowing for an understandable delay in the return of casualty figures, it is difficult to deduce on what information General Gough based his confident estimate of the 'total' casualties of the 49th Division. The four under-strength battalions of the 147th Brigade alone suffered more than twelve hundred casualties on the morning of 3 September and, of the 350 men of the 1st/6th West Yorks. who went over the top in the first wave at the Triangle, 244 were killed or wounded. The total casualties of the Division (killed and wounded) including the shellfire casualties of the second wave and Reserve Battalions, were approximately 3,000 – a considerable number for a division which was already under strength. Its total casualties between 1 July and 19 August had been 204 officers and 4,971 other ranks. A division, at full strength, numbered approximately twelve thousand men.

On the crown of the ridge the fortress of Thiepval still stood inviolable and secure. It had been touch and go. If the redoubt at Mouquet Farm had gone, the rear would have been threatened and vulnerable. But Monquet had not fallen, even to the invincible Australians. Exhausted now, waiting for relief, the 1st Australian Division had been urged to make one final effort to take the farm. They had advanced their line, but they had not captured Mouquet. Away to their right, the troops had battered yet again into High Wood and, yet again, they had been hammered out of it. The attack at Delville Wood had resulted in a slight improvement of the line but the Germans were still strongly entrenched on its eastern edge and were fighting on. They were fighting on at Ginchy, waveringly captured, then lost at nightfall in a German counter-attack. But the village was half encircled and, a mile away, in the one real success of that day, the third of September, they had, of course, captured Guillemont.

They had not however captured Falfemont Farm and Harold Hayward believed with youthful egotism that, had he not been prevented by the Colonel from going forward with the rest of his Battalion, it might just have tipped the balance. His Battalion was the 12th Battalion, the Gloucestershire Regiment – the Bristol Battalion, which that city proudly referred to as 'Bristol's Own'.

When the Battalion had been formed in September 1914 a rash of advertisements had invited 'mercantile and professional gentlemen' to join its ranks. The 'mercantile gentlemen' had joined in large numbers. So had their clerks and the commissionaires whose pre-war duties at the entrances of business premises had mainly consisted of opening doors and respectfully saluting the denizens of the commercial world who presided over the offices inside. Now the situation was reversed. Most of the commissionaires were ex-soldiers, bemedalled veterans of previous wars, and they were promptly given the rank of sergeant and entrusted with the task of instructing their erstwhile superiors in the arts of drilling and musketry.

For the first few weeks, before billeting arrangements could be made, most of the mercantile and professional gentlemen continued to live in their own homes and some were even able to continue attending their offices, unless prevented from doing so by the receipt of a polite postcard which expressed the hope that they would find it convenient to attend a drill. The drills themselves did little to lower their dignity. No khaki was available. Attired, as usual, in city suits and bowler hats the new recruits good-humouredly did their best to comply with polite requests from their former employees to 'Right wheel and left turn, if you please, sir.' The first parades were held on the artillery ground in Whiteladies road and, as they seldom lasted for more than an hour, the mercantile gentlemen had ample time in which to continue to look after their commercial interests. Unless, of course, they were courteously requested to perform guard duty.

Ten men each day were required to guard the Cumberland Basin, presumably to thwart the intentions of any German agent with villainous designs on the Bristol Docks. As this duty involved a march in the country, the gentlemen felt it appropriate to turn out in shooting-suits, Norfolk jackets and gaiters. Few of them, however, yet knew how to shoot and they harboured the secret hope that the very sight of the rifles they were privileged to carry (there were only enough of them to go round the guards and sentries) would be sufficient to terrify the enemy – should they be unfortunate enough to meet with Germans in such unlikely surroundings. The rifles were long, heavy, old fashioned and a distinct encumbrance, for the 'guard' did not travel light. They were laden with rugs, umbrellas, and picnic baskets containing wine, pickled herrings, hard-boiled eggs, cold salmon and tongue, and most hip-pockets contained the additional comfort of a brandy-flask. They looked less like a guard than like a party of country gentlemen on their way to a shoot or a picnic and the only enemy they met with in the course of their long day's vigil were groups of children who marched, jeering, behind them and occasionally, from a safe distance, favoured them with a volley of stones and, now and again, a brick.

With the move into permanent camp and later the issue of anonymous khaki uniforms, their dignity and the politeness of their respectful NCOs evaporated overnight.

The Corporals and Sergeants had not considered it necessary to show the same degree of consideration for the younger members of the Battalion. The majority were former pupils of Bristol Grammar School and had only recently left.[1] They all knew each other, hung together, treated the Army as a huge joke and introduced an element of schoolboy ragging that the Battalion could have well done without. There were pillow-fights and water-fights in the barrack-room dormitories where the beds were mere makeshift arrangements of palliasses laid on trestles, and a favourite sport was to ensure a rude awakening for some unfortunate sleeper by pulling the trestle smartly from beneath him so that he landed up on the floor. There was seldom any ill-feeling.

---

1. There was also a sizeable contingent from the Fairfield school and, like Harold Hayward, from Colston's.

2nd Lieutenant H. J. Hayward, MC, No. 14314, 12th (Bristol City) Btn., The Gloucestershire Regiment, 5th Division

We were all firm friends. There were at least a dozen fellows I knew from school, nearly all my senior. My old form-master was our Company Commander. There were some fellows who had left the school before I went there, a few more who were prefects when I was a boy in the first form, and there were two whom had been great chums of mine, although they were both older, because we lived near each other. That was Tom Webber and Harold Howell. We stuck together like glue, even after we went to France. We were in the same section and the same platoon and we shared everything together. Life was more serious when we got to the trenches in France, of course, but we still used to rag and joke. There was one thing we got out there which was *café au lait*. It was coffee-flavoured or cocoa-flavoured condensed milk and it was the most delectable food you could get. I never saw it outside France, and it was a great treat for us. One night Tom and I were going to share a little tin of this and I was on sentry. When I got back I looked at this tin and it was empty! I said to Tom, 'What's happened to the *café au lait?*' He said, 'Well, my half was at the bottom – so I had to eat yours to get at mine.'

We nearly had a rough-house over that! But it was a joke. He'd stowed it away somewhere and there was still half a tin left. It made a wonderful hot drink. It was nectar.

Just before Guillemont the happy trio was broken up when Hayward was ordered out of the line and sent to Battalion Headquarters to act as the Colonel's runner. He was as furious as he might have been two years earlier had he been ordered to remain in the Headmaster's study while the school First Eleven played the most important cricket match of the season. Just as he might have done then, he protested to his form-master. It cut no ice. Major Beckett had been told to nominate one man from each company, he had put forward the name of his old pupil, and that was that. Half-suspecting that Beckett had seized the opportunity of keeping him out of the attack, Hayward protested to the Colonel himself. But the Colonel was adamant. Half his HQ squad had been evacuated with shell-shock. They must be replaced before the Battalion went into action. Hayward could not be spared. It was an appalling disappointment and Hayward did not make a cheerful addition to the personnel of Battalion HQ. He did not even have a sight of the battle when his comrades went over the top at noon on 2 September.

The King's Own Scottish Borderers had gone over several hours earlier, before nine in the morning. Moving forward with the French on their right, under a barrage fired by French guns, they were to capture Falfemont Farm, to knock it out and to hold it until the general attack swept forward at Zero Hour. Falfemont Farm, to the right of Guillemont, lay on the slopes of a valley hidden by the rising land. It was out of observation both from the Gloucesters' HQ and from Guillemont, but the first reports were optimistic. None of the leading lines of men had returned. The assault must have been successful. The black truth was that they had not returned because all had been killed or wounded. The barrage had not materialized. Without informing the British, the French guns had been obliged to swing around to deal with a German counter-attack to the south of them and the French infantry, which should have advanced alongside the Borderers were left, like them, with no artillery support. In the Maurepas Ravine they were mown down by machine-gun fire and there they had stuck. Three hours later the Gloucesters went over the top to renew the attack.

At Battalion HQ it was a long, long day and the long night that followed was full of alarms, reports that the Germans were counter-attacking here in the Guillemont sector, waves of relief when it seemed that they had been beaten off. At dawn Colonel Archer-Shee went forward to see for himself what was happening. He took Hayward with him.

2nd Lieutenant H. J. Hayward, MC, No. 14314, 12th (Bristol City) Btn., The Gloucestershire Regiment, 5th Division

The Colonel had promised me that I could go. He said, 'I'll send you out to see how far the Battalion has gone forward. Just do your job here now and I'll let you go up to the front tomorrow.' I knew he meant when things had quietened down! We went right up to the line. It was fairly safe because we were only going to the line our boys were supposed to have occupied and there were other troops ahead of them. But all the way up, as it got lighter, we could see people lying all over the ground – I was shocked to see people in my own platoon who'd been knocked out. That was terrible!

At first, when we got to the line, we couldn't find the Battalion. There was nothing but a motley array of men in the trenches – not just people from other battalions in our Brigade, but people from other divisions I'd never even heard of. It was an awful mix up! Eventually we did find some of the boys and, by a miracle, I found my pals Tom and Harold. They were in the aid post. A shell had come over and buried Harold when they were going forward and the Company ran over him while he was down with all this earth and stuff on top of him. It was a miracle he got out! Tom Webber was completely shell-shocked. We'd lost a lot of our NCOs and many, many officers.

There was a gap – a big gap – beyond the right of our line, and the ground was hidden, so we couldn't see anybody at all. The Colonel wanted to know who was there and what they intended to do. It was all quiet then, so he told me to run down and find out. We were standing there, quite exposed, and I had just stepped away from the Colonel and turned round when suddenly I was hit by a bullet that came from behind us, from one of the lines of trenches we'd over-run. There must have been a German sniper still holding out there and, of course, the Colonel presented a good target, standing there with his stick and his badges of rank and everything. But the sniper got me instead – right in the backside!

All the Colonel's personal interest and protection did not prevent Harry Hayward from being carried from the battlefield as a casualty. They carried him to the Colonel's own dugout where Lieutenant Fitzgerald extracted the bullet and bandaged the wound. Hayward had to wait until dark before the stretcher-bearers could carry him back to the road where a convoy of horse-drawn ambulances had managed to get up to the line. Alex Paterson was luckier. By the time Hayward was being loaded into the ambulance, Paterson was already settled in the comparative comfort of the casualty clearing station at Corbie. They must have passed within yards of each other that morning for the remnants of Paterson's company had been ordered to the rear to collect the Battalions' rations and Sergeant Paterson had been wounded leading it back to the line.

Sergeant A. K. Paterson, DCM, MM, No. 52574, A Coy., 11th (S) Btn., The Rifle Brigade

I can hardly describe how different the ground was as we went back up through it, compared to what it had been the day before. It had been no picture then, but now there was no sign of any landmark at all, just shell-holes and mud. We had all our equipment and as well as that each one of us was carrying a full sandbag of cheese, bread, jam, whatever they were sending up. We were carry-ing extra ammunition in belts slung over our shoulders and we

were carrying the mail up too, letters and parcels for the boys in
the line. You can imagine that we didn't move very fast.

I spread the men out in single file, with five paces between each
man and put Corporal Bradley with the two stretcher-bearers and
stretcher in the rear, so that they could see to any casualties. When
I got within waving distance of our new Headquarters – about a
hundred yards away – I increased the pace and, just as I gave the
order, I heard a shell coming. I could tell by the sound of it that
it would drop near to my left side, so I dived into a shell-hole on
my right. But I was too late. A lump of shell penetrated my left
thigh and a smaller piece went into my right hand which was
holding the sandbag.

I wouldn't let the men break rank. I signalled to them to double
forward and saw them all arrive safely in the Headquarters' shell-
hole and then I called Corporal Bradley over and handed over my
platoon roll book. During the night I had written out the new roll
of A Company. It didn't take up much room.

The stretcher-bearers carried me out.

Fred White came through unhurt – but fed up.

*Rifleman Fred White, No. R.8529, B Coy., Bomber 10th Btn., King's
Royal Rifle Corps, 59th Brigade, 20th Division*

They relieved us and took us back to the support line and told us
we were going out on divisional rest. We were all formed up ready
to go when who should come in but the sick, lame and lazy –
those blokes who'd gone up to the Medical Officer just before we
went in the line and said they'd got this and they'd got that. They
made a miraculous recovery as soon as we got out! There they
were, about twelve of them, looking all spick and span and smart
and there *we* were, dirty and unwashed and covered with mud and
looking like nothing on earth. Just as we were ready to go, my
Platoon Sergeant came up and he told off five of us – 'You, you,
you, you, you. You've got to stay behind and clean up the battlefield.' Well, you know what cleaning up the battlefield means?
Cleaning up the battlefield means searching all the dead people and
looking for all the information and identities and then burying
them.

I didn't argue with the Sergeant. I just said, 'Excuse me, Sergeant,
take me to Lieutenant Hannay.' That was proper Army procedure,
in the line or out. Sergeant Pearce wasn't very pleased, but he took

me to the officer and he said, 'This man's got a complaint.' 'What is it?' says the Officer. I told him. I said, 'We've been in this action. We've fought this action. These people there have just come out from a tidy place' – meaning the sick, lame and lazy – 'and now we've been told to go back and clean up the battlefield. *They* should go up. They're more fitter than what we are to go up!'

Lieutenant Hannay said, 'I see your point.' So we got off with it and he made them stay behind. I was popular with the platoon for that, but I wasn't so popular with the Sergeant!

Muddy, unshaven, exhausted but with a light tread, the victors of Guillemont went out of the line and the 56th Division went in to pursue the battle beyond the village. The Australians too went thankfully back to billets and the Canadians moved into their place. In every sector of the line divisions were reshuffled. For the next ten days the task of the Army was to pivot on Guillemont, to try to swing forward, to straighten the line to a position of advantage for the Big Push planned for 15 September.

Hopes were high, for the Army would be supported by the new Secret Weapon. The tanks were on their way.

So were the New Zealanders.

Part 4

The Mouth of Hell

Into the mouth of hell,
Sticking it pretty well,
Slouched the six hundred.

E. A. MACKINTOSH,
Autumn, 1916.

Chapter 20

The evening of 5 September was fine and clear but the stiff breeze that had swept away the last of the rain clouds felt distinctly chilly to the soldiers squatting in a muddy field as they enjoyed the unaccustomed treat of an open-air cinema show at Morlancourt, fifteen kilometres from the firing line. Watching the comical misadventures of Charlie Chaplin it was possible to forget the sky beyond, flickering with the bombardment of the 'evening hate'. Even the staccato bark of the guns was masked to some extent by the sound of a tinny piano. With more goodwill than skill, a young officer was doing his best to provide a 'sound track' of appropriate music in the style of professional pianists who performed in the more civilized surroundings of picture palaces at home. Charlie Chaplin was one thing: the second half of the programme baffled the pianist, for in his limited repertoire, there was no music which could add anything to the mood and the drama of the official film of the Battle of the Somme.

It had been filmed by Geoffrey Malins, accredited to the War Office as a cinematograph photographer to capture an official record of troops in action in a major battle. He had ranged far and wide behind the front filming the troops in training, at rest and on the march. He had filmed them kneeling bareheaded on the open ground as surpliced Padres gave a final blessing on the last Sunday in June. He had filmed them moving up the line and assembling for the Big Push. When the battle started on the morning of the First of July he was placed in a hazardously exposed position in a jumping-off trench in front of Beaumont Hamel and, despite the danger, and the unnerving din, turning the handle of his hand-cranked camera at the steady two revolutions per second, he had recorded the scene with coolly professional detachment. Malins had filmed four reels before an explosion knocked the tripod from underneath the camera and very nearly knocked out the cameraman himself. Later, he had turned his lens on the wounded crowding into the aid posts, on disconsolate groups of German prisoners with their triumphant escorts and on troops returning cheerfully from the battle. The film had been shown privately to the King and Queen at Windsor Castle and now it was on show to the general public in halls and cinemas all over the country – half a dozen of them in London alone – and advertised as 'authentic, realistic pictures of Our Boys at the Front'. At the end of every showing rapturous audiences, who had queued for hours to see it, cheered and applauded until their palms ached.

The Boys who actually were at the front viewed the film with mixed feelings. Some senior officers had doubted the wisdom of showing it at all, at least to the troops, like those at Morlancourt, who were about to take their own chance in the Battle of the Somme, but the men watched, rapt and attentive.

The celluloid soldiers marched jerkily at ease, as cheerily – to judge by their grins and inaudible mouthings – as they themselves had marched to Morlancourt. They saw them wink and laugh and salute the camera in a silent bravado of excitement as they waited to go over the top. They saw the awesome soundless swelling of the earth as the mine above Beaumont Hamel tossed half the Hawthorn Ridge into the sky and the men rose like phantoms from the trenches and ran like clockwork toys across the ground beyond. They saw men falling soft to the earth as a rag doll might be tossed down by a child, the gushing fountains of exploding shells, the gauze of cordite fumes that drifted lazily across the erupting earth. To the men who sat watching in the chill and the dark under the open sky it seemed like a spectral battle fought by the long-dead ghosts of soldiers uniformed in phantom grey. In all the images that flickered across the big screen in the corner of the field, there was not an echo of the fight, not a hint of the roar of the guns, the crash of explosions, the crack of rifles, the screams, the shouts, the deadly rattle of machine-guns. It was insubstantial as a dream. But for the rumble of the distant guns they might have been watching from another planet. The reality was that the cinema-goers themselves would soon be on their way to that place where the guns glowed on the thundersome horizon.

The far-off growl of the bombardment had rolled nearer with every step the New Zealanders took on the march from Amiens. By the time they reached Laviéville, just a few kilometres from Morlancourt, they could feel the vibration beneath their feet. It was 8 September. In a bid to rock the line so painfully gained by the British and French, and to thwart the big attack they were clearly preparing, the Germans had mounted a mammoth counter-attack. The line swayed, and held, but the shock-waves of the duelling guns, massed now in thousands on both sides of the line, rippled across the few miles that lay between them and the hutted camp at Laviéville as if to underline the uneasy fact that the N. Zedders were for it. It was not that they had never before heard gun-fire, but they had never before heard it on such a scale.

They had been five days on the march and on the whole it had not been unenjoyable. It was a change to get out of the trenches. It was a change to perambulate in small towns and villages where civilians kept up a semblance of normal life. They had enjoyed ogling the girls, who trailed alongside the long marching columns, fascinated by the strange appearance of the New Zealanders in their lemon-squeezer hats. There had been quaint sights to explore on rest days, wine to be sampled in *estaminets* and, finally, encamped by the River Somme at la Chaussée, a glorious bathing parade to wash away the heat and the dust and soothe swollen and blistered feet. In the 1st Canterbury Battalion Howard Kippenberger, Harry Baverstock and Jack Gee were popularly known as the Three Musketeers and commonly referred to as Kip, Bav and Gee. All three were privates and they were bosom friends.[1]

They were marching together on the last long stretch of road that led from Amiens to Albert – a full eighteen kilometres – and they were finding it hard going. By the time they had covered ten of them the Kiwis were filthy, sweating and bedraggled and there was still a long, long way to go. They were also parched and Platoon Sergeant Geordie Hudson was particular on the subject of water-bottles – so particular that he would scarcely allow his men a drink. 'You never know when your need will be *much* greater than it is now, so keep that bottle intact.' A raging thirst did not add to the delights of the march.

The long straight road between Amiens and Albert had a single bend and at it stood an imposing figure outside an equally imposing gateway. He was only a sentry, only a private like themselves but, from the stiff peak of his hat to the polished toecaps of his boots, his burnished, immaculate turnout was the very antithesis of their own. Despite the splendour of their recently acquired lemon-squeezer hats, the New Zealanders felt like a bunch of grimy hobos. 'Look boys! A soldier!' It was Kip who called out as they passed – and he was only half joking.

The sentry was not only every inch a soldier but every inch a Guardsman. The place was Querrieu and he was on guard outside the château where General Rawlinson presided over 4th Army Headquarters and where, even now, the finishing touches were being put to the plans for the next big effort on 15 September. This time it would not, must not, fail. This time even partial success would not be good enough. This time they would smash the German line and break through, at last, to Bapaume and beyond. Like the New Zealanders, the cavalry was already moving

---

1. 'Kip', however, was at the start of an illustrious military career and eventually became Major-General Sir Howard Kippenberger and Second-in-Command of the New Zealand Forces in the Second World War.

towards the line and the time had surely come, after so many disappoint-
ments, when they would at last come into their own and dash triumphantly
through the German lines to exploit the advance, to finish the job. It
only needed the infantry to punch the first hole and, with the help of
the new Secret Weapon, the infantry could scarcely fail.

There were fewer than sixty tanks, to be sure, and far fewer than the
Commander-in-Chief had desired, but there were enough to scare the
wits out of the Germans. The tank was the ace in the British hand, but there
was one small anxiety. The Germans still held two trump cards on the front
between Delville Wood and Guillemont and, at all costs, they must be
forced to relinquish them before the battle for the breakthrough began.

By some feat of tenacity, which even the British Staff were reluctantly
forced to admire, the Germans still clung on to part of Delville Wood.
They still held Ginchy village to the right of it. Worst of all, they still
held the Quadrilateral. Nothing, it seemed, would push them out of it
and, until they were pushed out, the troops could barely budge beyond
Guillemont.

They wanted to go up the hill. It was such a short distance – a mere
ten minutes' brisk stroll to the woods that lay so tantalizingly close to the
village on either side of the road that led to Combles hidden in the dip
beyond. The maps proclaimed them to be Leuze Wood on the right and
Bouleaux Wood on the left. With natural logic they became, in the
language of the Tommies, 'Lousy' and 'Bollocks' and as they stumbled
and fumbled and fought and died in attempt after attempt to capture the
woods the names seemed more and more to be appropriate.

It was the 56th Division, regrouped, reinforced, rested and refreshed
after their ordeal at Gommecourt who were, for a second time, burning
out their strength in the furnace of Lousy Wood and it was the Quadrilateral that thwarted their every effort. To the right of Guillemont village
the 56th had managed to fight forward in the shelter of the valley to
capture part of the wood, to drive the Germans out of their deep dugouts
and to cling obstinately to one corner, but unless they could advance
from Guillemont itself, straight up the slope of the hill, they could do no
more. The Quadrilateral, away to the left, dominated the road and everything that tried to move along it.

This strongpoint was a complex of entrenchments built round part of
the old railway cutting. It was furnished with fortifications of iron and
concrete, stalwart enough to defy an earthquake and skilfully sited to
command a field of fire which, in every direction, was absolute.[1]

---

1. Until this day they still stand and even explosives have done no more than
tilt them.

Linked by a strongly held trench to another strongpoint (the Triangle) on the Ginchy Ridge which dominated the village of Ginchy beyond, the Quadrilateral was the king-pin and the key to the solid second line of the Germans' defences, built as an impregnable insurance three miles behind the first. Their front line had long been shattered. The Germans were resolved to hold on to the second. The British were equally determined to dislodge them. If, on 15 September, they were still in possession of the Quadrilateral it would imperil the whole attack. Ginchy was taken on 9 September. The Guards moved in to secure the village and, in the scant week that remained before the new offensive, to have one more go at the Quadrilateral.

Two miles away, on the evening of the same day, Arthur Agius found himself in command of his Battalion among the bloody stumps of Lousy Wood. Every other officer had been killed or wounded. He noted rather sadly that, after the day's fighting, there was precious little left of the Battalion to command.

It was as well that Agius had plenty to do. It kept his mind occupied and the responsibility of holding the Battalion together helped him to hold himself together too. His sojourn behind the lines had cured him of his 'nerves' after Gommecourt but now he was shocked to notice the old familiar symptoms of 'shakiness'. He hoped to God that this time he could hang on. Being busy helped. The saddest and most dispiriting of the manifold duties of command were the letters which had to be written – and written as soon as possible – to the relatives of the people who had been killed. Agius sat in the newly captured German dugout and, by the light of a candle that guttered and sank in its evil-smelling, airless depths, penned letter after letter in a hand that showed a disturbing propensity to shake.

Dear Mr and Mrs O'Dell, It is my very sad duty to have to tell you that your son Oliver . . . Dear Mrs Scarlett, I am so very sorry . . . Dear Mr and Mrs Starling, By now you will have received official notification . . .

They were painfully difficult letters to write but there was a formula which eased the process and which Agius, in common with a thousand other officers engaged on the same sad task, fervently hoped would ease the hearts of sorrowing relatives.

. . . always so cheerful. He will be greatly missed . . . much loved by his men who would have followed him anywhere . . . one of our best officers . . . a real loss to the battalion . . . genuinely missed

. . . although he had not been with the battalion for long . . . loyal, reliable and trustworthy . . . the men adored him . . . wise beyond his years . . . hope that it will be at least some comfort to you to know . . . he died bravely, doing his duty . . . was shot through the head and died instantaneously . . . immediately became unconscious . . . killed outright by a bullet through the heart . . . could have felt no pain . . . assure you that he did not suffer . . . Deepest sympathy . . . Deepest sympathy . . . Deepest sympathy.

It was kinder that way. The aim of every man who wrote such a letter was to preserve the illusion of heroic death, of a clean fight, of noble warriors struck down in battle by a bullet which flew straight and true to extinguish a brave life in the execution of some desperate advance or noble act. The ugly truth would be too hard to bear. Few of the bodies that littered the battlefield lay in the classic attitude of the Fallen Warrior. Few bore the single disfiguring mark of a neat bullet wound. Many had not even been killed 'in action' as people at Home could have understood the term. The vast majority had been tossed, mutilated, dismembered, decapitated by monstrous splinters of shells. Some were sliced apart by machine-gun fire. Some, like Harold Scarlett, caught in the epicentre of an explosion, had been scattered to the four winds. It was just two months since Scarlett had joined the Battalion in the wake of the Gommecourt disaster, fresh from England and newly married. How, Agius asked himself, could you tell a young wife of four months that her husband's body had simply been blown out of existence? Agius wrote on . . . *died doing his duty and was buried where he fell* . . . In a sense, it was true. Even as he wrote he could hear, barely a mile away, the awful clamour of the battle bursting in the night. With every breath, with every stroke of his pen, with every ear-splitting explosion, more men were falling wounded and dying in the struggle for the Quadrilateral and already, in preparation for the big breakthrough on 15 September, the troops were moving closer to the line.

The Canterbury Battalion had marched on Sunday morning from Laviéville to bivouac on the hill above Fricourt and 'bivouac' meant bedding down and finding such shelter as they could manufacture by their own efforts. Even the succession of draughty barns and shell-torn attics, which were a good deal too airy by half, seemed, in retrospect, like luxury to the Three Musketeers. There was nothing for it but to dig a man-sized rectangle on the sloping hillside, line it with a waterproof sheet and, with an overcoat masquerading as a blanket, to settle down to uneasy slumber and to try not to dwell on the close resemblance of the 'bivouac' to a grave. To cap it all it rained. Nevertheless, it had been an exciting day.

As the boys marched past Bécordel on the Fricourt road, the New Zealanders, who had moved up ahead of them, were lining the road to cheer them on, and one particular shout directed at Bav came from four pals from his schooldays, Jackson, Ricketts, Biss and Hickmott. Rupert Hickmott had been the idol of Christchurch High School. He was the school's top cricketer – a skilful batsman, a deadly googly bowler and his fielding was an inspiration. It was no surprise to any of his schoolmates that he was chosen to play for New Zealand and, for three years before the war, the school had basked in reflected glory. Now, like the rest of them, Hickmott was in khaki and in France, and a new generation of schoolboys was basking in a glow of patriotism. No less than 786 Old Boys were serving in the forces and, since the entire roll of pupils numbered only 390, the school considered that this was not a bad record. Now that all the New Zealanders were assembled together, Baverstock kept bumping into old friends. Having dug his gloomy bivouac he went visiting and then, with Kip and Gee, indulged in a little sight-seeing.

Private H. Baverstock, No. 11608, 1st Canterbury Btn., New Zealand Division

It was an unforgettable sight. On the other side of the valley was the totally wrecked village of Fricourt. As far as the eye could see there were shattered forests, the mutilated skeletons of the trees. Down below us there were several nine-inch long-barrelled guns and on the opposite slope between Fricourt and Mametz Wood was a long line of six-inch Howitzers about thirty yards apart and, up near the front line, the eighteen-pounders were barking away. The nine-inch monsters just below our bivouacs erupted from time to time in groups of four and the detonation was so terrific that it hurt horribly. Without thinking I stood just a yard away from one of them. There was a sudden rush of hot air and then concussion, so loud that you actually couldn't hear it. That sounds paradoxical, but it is quite true. I caught just a fleeting glimpse of the shell tearing through space.

The same night, we were ordered to go on a road-repairing expedition to just behind the front line. We wandered off with shovels and got as far as the high ground beyond Caterpillar Valley, not far behind where the Aucklands (the Dinks) had gone into the line on the 9th. I hate to say this but, as we had no officers with us, we didn't do a tap of work. The sights we saw were far too tremendous for that.

It was a panorama you could never hope to see again. The sky was deep opalescent blue and it was continuously being stabbed by spurts of flame, just like lightning. The din was diabolic and the devil must have been grinning. All that inferno was right up his street, because it was like hell let loose. Overhead we could just hear the *boom, boom, boom* of huge shells lumbering over to the German back-areas. They were so big and huge that they seemed to take an unconscionable time and occasionally we could see a glare spreading out as they exploded far off in the distance. We had to run the gauntlet of the big guns in Mametz as we went back to our bivouacs.

The Reserve Brigades of some six Divisions were packed in a vast gypsy-like encampment across the slopes of the ridge beyond Fricourt and Mametz and, as they awaited orders to move up to relieve their comrades in the front line, they led a gypsylike existence, sleeping in holes in the ground and, with water strictly rationed, washing infrequently, if at all. Only the Guards managed to conduct themselves as if they were still quartered at Pirbright or Caterham. They were disciplined and immaculate. They kept themselves apart, posted sentries round the limits of their exclusive area and dared any disreputable Tommy to put so much as a toe within it.

Lance-Corporal Len Lovell, No. 18692, A Coy., King's Own Yorkshire Light Infantry

We were lying next to the Guards and you couldn't help admiring them. They were in exactly the same conditions as we were. It had rained on them just the same as it had on us. We were all in the open air, but we were all scruffy and dirty and they were clean and tidy. We didn't know how they did it! Their Quarter Guard was spick and span. Their sentry was on his beat, marching up and down, saluting officers and presenting arms as if they were all still at home in barracks. What discipline! It was marvellous!

Lance-Corporal Charles Frost, MM, No. 17256, 1st Btn., The Leicestershire Regiment

I only joined up two years under age in March 1915 but I was drafted to the 1st Leicesters after they'd had a lot of casualties and, of course, being a Regular Battalion, a bit of their glory rubbed off on us. We thought we were a cut above the rest of Kitchener's mob, but we were nothing to the Guards. We saw a lot of them, because we were in the same Army Corps, and they were often up with us. We used to think they were looked after a damned sight better than we were. Nothing was too good for the Guards! The things they got from home! Well, the officers of the Guards were nearly all moneyed people and their women organized a lot of things for the Guardsmen. They even had a chip van right there, behind Fricourt. They'd got an old caravan frying chips for them! You could smell them all over the place. The smell was all *we* got. That was my biggest worry in the Army – I never got enough to eat and, being only seventeen or eighteen, I was growing all the time.

Private John L. Bouch, No. 1176, 1st Btn., The Coldstream Guards

I enlisted in the Coldstream Guards at the end of August 1914. You'd never believe the training and discipline we went through at the Guards Depot at Caterham. We were subjected to a volume of abuse and scorn which is difficult to imagine. I found out swear words I'd never heard before. I found out a combination of swear words of such degree and magnitude that weren't imaginable! They called us these things in front of officers and nobody said a word.

We were run until we were breathless and then we had to run again simply because we couldn't do a complicated piece of drill as quick as they wanted us to. 'On the left, form SQUAD!' When you found that the man next door had two right feet instead of a left and a right and he went the wrong way, the Drill Sergeant would shout, 'You bloody idiot! Double up the parade ground!' And up we would all have to go, up the parade ground and back again, up again and back again until he shouted, 'Have you had enough, you buggers?' The Drill Sergeant had a voice that carried fifty miles! 'You're in the Guards, remember!' he used to shout. 'This is *not* a regiment of the line. You are supposed to be the people to guard the Sovereign, God help him!'

All our officers were lords, or nearly so. The Honourable Charles Knowles was our Company Commander. Lord Hugh Kennedy was a Lieutenant in charge of Number 12 Platoon. Viscount Holmesdale was another Lieutenant in our Company. I was a Private. We were worlds apart. Even the distinction between Private and non-commissioned officers was very, very marked. In fact a private couldn't speak to an NCO without standing to attention.

At the barracks at Caterham, we even had to stand to attention to speak to an old soldier who was in charge of the barrack rooms – and he was just a private like ourselves!

Private William Jackman, No. 2604675, 3rd and 4th Btn., The Grenadier Guards

I was Captain Morrison's servant. He was a multi-millionaire and he used to pay for a lot of the stuff that came to the Officers' Mess. Before we went to France in 1915 I had to go to Fortnum and Mason's and arrange for what you might call tuck boxes to be sent out to the Battalion regularly. Then I had to go to Berry's, the wine merchants, and place an order with them – a bottle of 1900 port to be sent to us every three days and cases of whisky and brandy. They used to arrive marked with a red cross. Medical comforts!

By the time we went down to the Somme Captain Morrison had left the Battalion, but he never cancelled the order and the stuff kept on coming. It used to arrive in batches and sometimes we'd have as many as a dozen boxes from Fortnum and Mason's arriving at the same time. They were boxes of tinned stuff, mostly, like galantine of chicken, soups, puddings, tins of fruit, tins of grouse and pheasant, ham – everything you could think of for the Officers' Mess. We used to have that much stuff that we couldn't cart it about with us, so we had to make dumps here and there. Often we didn't go back to the same place, so there must have been some farmhouses who did very well out of us!

After Captain Morrison left to go back to England, Lord Henry Seymour, who was our Commmanding Officer, asked me to go into the Officers' Mess, on the catering staff. That suited me! It was a good job with plenty of perks. We were living like lords and I wasn't anxiously looking for promotion, believe me!

When the Battalion went up the line on 9 September I went up with Battalion Headquarters to look after the officers. We had a cook when we were out at rest, but he didn't come with us into the line. I used to take up soup cubes and dried eggs and make scrambled eggs for the Colonel and the officers at Battalion HQ and before we went up I made four sandbags, one for each company to take into the forward line to feed the Company officers. They couldn't do any cooking there, so they were filled with tinned stuff and a bottle of whisky, a bottle of brandy and one of port.

Battalion Headquarters was in a shell-hole – a huge shell-hole. You could have put a bus in it! Of course we were a bit to the rear of the companies and that saved us, although when they started throwing shells and stuff over you had to take what came the same as the rest.

Jackman was better off by far than the Grenadier Guardsmen of the four companies in the front line. It was hardly a line at all. The trenches were so broken and so shattered that in places they had all but disappeared and where they did exist they were littered with the dead of the 47th Brigade whom the Guards were relieving. The relief took a long time. In the grizzly shambles of the ground to the south-east of Ginchy, the Guards had had difficulty in finding the positions so neatly marked on the trench maps. They had been on the move since dusk, but the relief was completed just sixteen minutes before the sun rose beyond the German line to reveal the full havoc and destruction around the Quadrilateral. There was no rest for the Grenadiers after their sleepless night. If the line was to be held, let alone advanced, it would need the efforts of every man to improve it. The Guardsmen slogged at the job all day and they worked on for most of the night. For once, they were cursing the fine weather. For five days it had been warm and summerlike. The night was clear and starry. The moon was not quite full, but it was almost as bright as day and every inadvertent movement brought swift retribution from enemy machine-gunners.

Next night, 11 September, the tanks began their slow grinding journey towards the battle. With no lights of their own they needed the moon to show them the way. They had been parked well back, closely guarded, and shrouded in tarpaulin covers so vast that imagination could barely conceive the nature and the dreadfulness of whatever mechanical mammoth might be skulking underneath. They looked so much like humpback monsters that the troops, agog with rumour and gossip, had begun to call them 'Mastodons'. The Army, hoping that any such rumours as might reach the Germans would be scotched by the supposition that they were portable water tanks for the benefit of the troops in the line, called them 'tanks'. The Admiralty – under whose aegis they had first been developed – called them 'land-ships'. After two years of almost static warfare, of fruitless effort and endeavour, of vulnerable flesh perishing against unyielding iron and concrete, after two months and more of calculating the bitter cost of every painfully captured yard of ground on the Somme, the Staff were calling them a Godsend. Their hopes were high. The trials had been impressive. There was hardly an obstacle the tanks could not run over as easily as a child might propel a wooden toy, step by step, up a flight of stairs. They could uproot trees, over-run trenches, crush barbed-wire entanglements and, given enough of them, surely they could crush the enemy too.

The Army had unfortunately not been given enough of them and the mammoth engines of the fifty prototypes they did receive were already fast degenerating through the wear and tear of the very training exercises, trials and tests which, ironically, were essential to their success. There had been neither enough time nor enough tanks to train the infantry to work with them in new techniques of attack. There had been little enough time to train the embryo tank crews to handle them.

A tank weighed twenty-eight tons. It took one hour and one gallon of petrol to travel half a mile. Ten had been kept in reserve and now, in the light of the full moon, the roads were shaking and vibrating under the weight of forty-two tanks as they went clanking to their assembly positions a mile or two behind the front line between Fricourt and Bray. The soldiers who saw them looming out of the night like immense black whales could hardly believe their eyes.

The tank crews were elated to be on the move at last, but the excitement of some of their Commanders was tinged with unease. They had been training for barely three months. Their instructions for the battle were complicated. Closeted with the Divisional Staff Officers they had spent hours studying maps and aerial photographs of the routes their tanks would take when the battle started. They had studied the Order of Battle and the timetables of each Corps and Division and, finally, each Commander had drawn up his own map, worked out the compass bearings from point to point, the estimated time of his arrival at each place and then readjusted his calculations to fit in with timing of the infantry. They had been bombarded by an avalanche of directions, instructions, advice and dire warnings in such profusion that there had not been enough written copies to go round. It had been almost impossible to memorize them all. They were ordered, furthermore, that their painfully prepared maps must be similarly imprinted on their minds. They were not to be allowed to carry them into action. It was hardly surprising, as the tanks lumbered towards their first engagement, that many brows were furrowed.

Certain Staff Officers at GHQ were worried too. They doubted the advisability of using the tanks at all. If two hundred had been available it might have been a different matter, but could a mere forty-two, spread over the fifteen kilometres of the attack, possibly succeed in breaking the line wide open and ushering the British Army through the gap? It was a moot point. It had been argued, discussed and gone over again and again. There were those who wished to wait until the tanks were available in sufficient numbers to guarantee success. There were those who were tempted to try the few forerunners out as an experiment but were none-theless worried that, by doing so, they would lose the vital element of surprise which in a future massed assault might easily bowl the Germans over. And there were those who, like the Commander-in-Chief, felt that, whatever the risks, the opportunity must be seized to break the deadlock before autumn turned to winter. It would be a gamble but it was their only chance and overall confidence was high. This time there was a good deal more than the hope of success – there was near-certainty.

The guns struck up the overture to the battle on the morning of 12 September and this time they were ranging uncompromisingly on Bapaume. On the 13th, GHQ sent out a ringing call to arms. It was addressed to all ranks of the Fourth and Reserve Armies and appealed to them for 'bold and vigorous action'. It pointed out that the British Infantry outnumbered the Germans by four to one, that the Allies had far more guns and almost total supremacy in the air. It spoke of the cavalry massed to exploit the gains of the infantry. It hinted at the mysterious Secret Weapon which 'may well produce great moral and material effects'. It pointed out the losses and hardships suffered by the enemy, the deterioration of his morale, the 'confusion and disorganization' in his ranks. It assured the troops that there was little depth or strength left in the enemy's defences, that his reserves were weak and 'composed entirely of units which have already suffered defeat'.

It boomed encouragement:

Under such conditions risks may be taken with advantage which would be unwise if the circumstances were less favourable to us.

The assault must be pushed home with the greatest vigour, boldness, and resolution, and success must be followed up without hesitation or delay to the utmost limits of the power of endurance of the troops.

The bombardment redoubled. All day shells thundered on the Quadrilat-eral and on the last uncaptured corner of Delville Wood. The Guards edged forward in front of Ginchy and straightened their line. On their right the 6th Division pushed forward to the Ginchy–Morval road but stopped short in the withering face of the Quadrilateral itself.

That night it poured with rain. Just as he had been a day or two earlier in bivouacs above Fricourt, Len Lovell, in the 6th King's Own Yorkshire Light Infantry, was occupying a position adjacent to the Guards, or at least his Brigade was immediately to the left of theirs. Lovell himself was not aware of being adjacent to anyone, with the exception of Bobby Pearce and a handful of A Company's Bombers. They had been sent forward from the ragged linked-up shell-holes which served the 6th King's Own Yorkshire Light Infantry as a trenchline, to see if, by some miracle, the Germans on the edge of the wood had survived the pounding of the day's bombardment or if, as was fervently hoped, they had had the good sense to retire. In Delville Wood hardly one of the skeleton tree trunks stood more than two feet high. Many were broken off so low that only a few treacherous splinters spiked from their jagged roots in the path of the Bombers crawling belly-down in the pitch-black, feeling ahead for obstacles, striving impossibly for silence, stifling curses when unseen talons of broken timber caught and tore at their hands and clothing, stopping for long moments to listen as they drew near the edge of the wood where the Germans had last been seen. They were experienced raiders. They were used to it and, unlike the Guards, they were handier with bombs than with bullets.

Bobby Pearce had recently proved himself to be just a bit too handy with bombs, or rather, with an unexploded trench-mortar shell he dragged back from one of their patrols in No Man's Land and whose innards – being of a mechanical turn of mind – he was anxious to inspect. It was unfortunate that he accidentally dropped the nose-cap on the floor of the Bombers' billet. Five sleeping men received a rude awakening plus painful, if convenient, Blighty wounds in their feet. In the bedlam that followed the explosion the coke brazier was knocked over and the billet burnt down. As Section NCO Len Lovell received a severe reprimand. Bobby Pearce received a nasty head wound and, following his recovery, a Court-Martial. He had rejoined the Battalion on the march down to the Somme and now, creeping forward through Delville Wood, Lovell was glad of it.

Even before the embellishment of the ugly new scar he now bore on his forehead, Bobby Pearce had a face that only a mother could love. He could neither read nor write. It was Lovell who wrote his letters home and read out, with difficulty, the infrequent, near-illegible replies. Pearce was a rough diamond and an old soldier. He was entitled to wear the campaign medal of the South African War, but he scorned it as a 'bare-arsed medal'. That war had ended before Bobby had got nearer the front than Gibraltar and he did not agree with the opinion of the Army that he qualified for the statutory decoration. Pearce was a hard swearer and a hard drinker. Lovell had covered up for him, had got him out of trouble a dozen times but there was no man he would rather have had at his own shoulder when there was trouble ahead.

Corporal Len Lovell, No. 18692, 6th Btn., King's Own Yorkshire Light Infantry

When we got to within a few yards of what we thought was Jerry's position, we lay there for a long time waiting for a lull in the shelling. All we had to do was see if we could hear them and then creep back and report that they were there. There was no question of making an attack, or anything like that. It seemed like hours before there was a pause in the terrible noise and, when it came, lying there right under the German wire, we could hear them moving about, even talking. That was all we had to know, so I signalled to my nearest man to pass the word to retire. We crept back the way we'd come, keeping low and as quiet as we could. When we were just a few yards from our own position – which was just linked up shell-holes with a few sandbags here and there as a kind of parapet – one of the men jumped up to dash the last few yards to his own shell-hole. At that very moment, there was a break in the clouds and a blink of moon came out. The Jerries must have been suspicious that something was up and looking out for any movement because, instantly, a machine-gun opened fire and the man fell. We got back into the trench, reported to our Bombing Officer and then, as I looked around the party, I realized that we'd lost Bobby Pearce.

Two of us crawled over the parapet, back to where we had seen the body fall and dragged him in. Bobby was completely dead. A bullet had struck him at the back of the head and the whole top of it had gone. He had been my father figure – a much older man than me, who really had looked after me like a father although I was his Section NCO. I felt really terrible.

Before it got light we buried him just a few yards away and stuck a rifle in the ground, bayonet downwards, to mark the spot. The shelling had started up again and, when we went across the following morning to attack Hop and Ale Alley, I noticed that the place where the grave had been was one enormous shell-hole.

Dawn broke shortly after the Bombers had scraped between the tree stumps and buried Bobby in the shallow grave, the rain went off and later in the morning a watery sun did its best to dry out the soldiers bivouacking on the hillsides, waiting for the move. It was 14 September and the wait was almost over. They were issued with bombs and extra ammunition, gathered their kit together, enjoyed a last hot meal and prepared to move up the line. Mail had come up for the New Zealanders and Harry Baverstock was suffering from an embarrassment of riches. He received an accumulated batch of more than twenty letters and no less than four parcels. There were four tins of pipe tobacco, four tins of condensed milk, a mountain of chocolate, a pile of books, a three-month supply of razor blades, sweets, soap, and enough home-knitted woollen goods to start a respectable small business. The best he could do was to put some sweets and chocolate in his pocket, shove a useful looking woollen cap into his light haversack, and stuff the rest of the largesse, as best he could, into his already bulging pack before leaving it, as instructed, at the Battalion dump. He never saw it again.

Shortly after seven o'clock, when the Brigade marched off in the gathering dusk, there was a lull in the shelling. At a quarter to eight, as they were moving past the rubble of Mametz village, the guns opened up behind them in such an intensity of fire that the ears of every man rang. The road to Mametz Wood flashed in the necklace of light that ribboned into the distance from Death Valley just below, where the guns, standing wheel to wheel, were pouring fire towards the German lines. It was the beginning of the great bombardment that was paving the way for tanks, infantry and cavalry. Together, in the morning, they would make the breakthrough.

As the New Zealanders struck across country to their assembly position in the wood, they could see the gunners, working flat out. It was a chilly evening but, sweating with their labour, many had discarded tunics and shirts as well. They looked like demons, bare torsos glowing red as the shells left the muzzles and disappearing into the shadows as the guns recoiled. It seemed to the New Zealanders, half-deafened by the noise, half-suffocated by the fumes, half-mesmerized by the sight, that they were passing through hell itself.

In the evil depths of Mametz Wood Bav, Kip and Gee settled down to pass the night in an old German dugout. The luck of the draw had dictated that their half of the New Zealand Brigade should remain in reserve. The others, who would go across in the morning with the first wave, moved on up the line and into the trenches to the left of Delville Wood. They were facing the Switch Line. It had been the objective of the 7th Rifle Brigade when Ted Gale had gone over the top more than three weeks before and they were back again, for the renewal of the attack. This time they were in Delville Wood itself and Ted Gale was having an unpleasant time for he had mislaid most of his platoon. They were part of the draft of two hundred new men sent to make up the Battalion after the slaughter of Orchard Trench. It was their first time in the line. In the gruesome depths of Delville Wood, with its scattered dead, the remnants of mangled trees clawing grotesquely in the moonlight, the screaming shells, the all-pervading stench, the sickening dread of tomorrow's dawn, it would not have astonished Gale if they had panicked and run. But eventually he rounded them up. They had gone souveniring. Between them they had gathered a fine collection of German revolvers, buttons and badges and a fortunate few, scouring through the ghoulish litter of corpses, had been rewarded with the most prized of trophies – a German helmet.

Unabashed by Gale's fury as he hounded them into the shell-holes where the Battalion was waiting for the jump-off, they were passing them round for less-fortunate scavengers to admire.

Chapter 21

After the early morning mist had cleared it was good flying weather, clear and cold in the upper air where the wind, blowing straight from the north, whistled and twanged through the wires of the aeroplanes, toy-like in the sky, and straight into the goggled faces of the men peering anxiously over the sides of the open cockpits. The goggles were a distinct impediment to observation, for they were flying high above the battle. To venture lower would be to risk a nasty encounter with one of the high-trajectory shells that filled the sky, tearing through it with the speed and sound of an express train. Even the most prudent of pilots could not escape the heart-bumping moments when his eggshell aircraft, swooping down for a closer look, sank, yawing in a rush of turbulence as a 'heavy' passed close beneath its belly, ripping the air apart and leaving a vacuum in its wake. The thrumming of the wind, the howling high-flying shells, the clatter of the aeroplane's own engine shut out the uproar of the battle on the ground below where harmless puffs of smoke flagged the progress of the bombardment.

Between the criss-crossing maze of trenches that divided the grey morass into a jigsaw of crazy pieces, matchstick men bobbed and scurried like ants through the haze of the battle and a million specks of light, a million split-second flashes of fire, flickered in the mist like the shimmering of a host of fireflies. It looked from the air just as such actions had looked a thousand times before. And just as they had done a thousand times before – or so it seemed to them – Corps Commanders sweated with the strain of waiting for the wireless message that would bring the hoped-for news of progress or weary tidings of failure.

The troops went over the top at twenty past six in the morning and two nerve-racking hours later a message was wirelessed from the aircraft observing for 3rd Corps. It was worth waiting for.

TANK SEEN IN MAIN STREET OF FLERS GOING ON WITH
LARGE NUMBERS OF TROOPS FOLLOWING IT.

It was the best news of the whole battle. It was more. It was the best news of the entire war.

In the euphoria of the moment it hardly mattered to General Pulteney at 3rd Corps Headquarters that on his own front of Martinpuich and High Wood things were not going quite so spectacularly well, that it was 15th Corps on their left which had made the breakthrough and that it was to 15th Corps Headquarters that the message should have gone. What *did* matter was that in a single leap the Army was in Flers. Two miles beyond High Wood. Two miles beyond Delville.

General Pulteney passed the signal on to 3rd Corps who flashed it on to 4th Army Headquarters at Querrieu. By ten-fifteen it had reached the delighted ears of Sir Douglas Haig who gave permission for the signal to be passed verbatim to the Press. By early evening it had reached London. The presses in Fleet Street began to roll and before ten o'clock late editions of the evening newspapers were on sale with the glorious news blazoned in banner headlines.

A TANK IS DRIVING DOWN THE MAIN STREET OF FLERS WITH THE BRITISH ARMY CHEERING BEHIND

Someone along the way had taken the trouble to polish the prose a little. It was only a slight and, under the circumstances, a very human exaggeration. For once it was good news. But it was not quite as good as it seemed.

Only twenty-five tanks of the forty-two had succeeded in going forward from the start-lines and, of those twenty-five, the hulks of seventeen were lying destroyed, damaged, broken down or irretrievably ditched on the battlefield. The performance of the tanks had been disappointing but their effect had been enormous. They had terrorized the Germans. More important, they had put heart into the infantry and, by the very fact of their presence, propelled the troops forward with such a thrust of optimism that they had felt themselves to be invincible. It was their morale that had broken the line and it had started to rise on the eve of the battle with their first sight of the tanks.

Some soldiers on their way to the line had even managed to hitch a lift and, as Billy Banks and Roland Otley remarked – or rather roared to each other above the unearthly clatter of the tank – it was not unlike riding on a hay-wain. This time last year, at harvest-time in England, most of the boys who were now in the 21st Battalion of The King's Royal Rifle Corps had been doing exactly that, for they were the Yeoman Rifles. It was the Earl of Feversham who had the idea of raising a battalion of farmers' sons and country lads from the north of England but, by the time he had obtained official approval, arranged his own transfer from the Yorkshire Hussars and enlisted young hopefuls of his acquaintance as fledgling officers – young Anthony Eden fresh from Eton was one of them – it was already September 1915. So many lads of military age were already in the Army that, although the most remote farms and villages were scoured for recruits and although there were accommodating Recruiting Sergeants who needed little persuading to sign up farm-lads whose tender years were belied by a hefty physique, there had not been quite enough 'Yeomen' to make up a full Battalion. They had come in dribs and drabs and it was not until their numbers had been swelled by a draft of recruits of less exclusive origin that they had started training in earnest. And that was months later.

They had come to the front in May, to the quiet, still bucolic surroundings of 'Plugstreet' Wood and one young farmer, standing sentry for the first time in the line, had neatly summed up the Battalion's collective attitude to the war. An officer on his accustomed round stopped by the fire-step.

'Well, Sentry,' he enquired, 'do you see anything?'

'Aye,' replied the Sentry. 'I see a bloody good field of hay going to waste!'

This saying had tickled the Battalion and like its first 'battle' was always good for a laugh. It had happened while they were training on Lord Feversham's estate, Duncombe Park at Helmsley in Yorkshire, under the beneficent eye of Lord Feversham himself, who was struck by the happy idea that the Battalion might practise advancing in open order against a herd of deer which, fortuitously, he wished to move to another part of the estate. The deer were not keen to go. They were not encouraged by the sight of a hundred or so men advancing to the attack! They stood their ground and then turned and charged the Yeomen in a counter-attack, so purposeful that there was no question of dignified 'retirement'. It had been a total rout.

Moving up to Delville Wood under the shrieking bombardment intended to deafen the ears of the enemy to the cacophonous progress of the tanks, the Yeoman Rifles were hoping for better luck in the morning. They were to be supported by the tanks of D Battalion.

At the very head of the long column of machines crawling towards the line, the leading tank – officially known as D1 – was to have the distinction of being the first tank in history to go into battle. It was to cross the front line on a special mission one hour and five minutes before Zero. Len Lovell and the other Bombers of A Company were to go with it, for the 'special mission' was to break the grip of the Germans' last tenuous hold on the edge of Delville Wood and to push them out of Hop Alley and Ale Trench before the start of the main assault.

The noise of a passing tank was deafening. Inside, it was earsplitting.

Even a full-pitched bellow had no chance of being heard above the beat of the mammoth engine, 105 horsepower, the clank and slap of the caterpillar tracks, the crash of the giant gears, the grinding of brakes so powerful that it took all the strength of the brakesman to operate them. At least he benefited from a little light from the narrow slit in the up-front 'cab' where he crouched behind the driver and the officer in charge. The gearsmen were less fortunate. Low down in the middle of the tank it was dark even in daylight. It was hot and it was airless, and on the long haul up, instead of circulating fresh air, the fans were showing a nasty tendency to pick up heavy petrol fumes belching from the exhaust of the vehicle in front and to send them billowing through the tank. Before they had progressed a quarter of the way, the crews were gasping for air, choking and spluttering as they would later choke and splutter in the fumes of the smoke bombs and poison gas.

Of the eight men squeezed into the claustrophobic gloom, the gearsmen were the worst off. They had to have their wits about them, ears pressed close to the sides of the sponsons, alert for orders tapped out by the driver on the cover of the engine, and woe betide them if they failed to pick them up. The gunners' place was in the sponsons themselves. They had a little light, a little air, and just sufficient field of vision to operate the guns that were mounted in the two vast protuberances which stuck out on either side of the tank.[1] They weighed a ton apiece and every man in every tank crew had cause to curse them. With the sponsons fitted, the tanks had been too wide to pass through the tunnels on the French railway system. There had been nothing for it but to take them off and to put them back again at the end of the journey. Their muscles were still aching.

Corporal A. E. Lee, MM, No. 32198, A Btn., Heavy Section, Machine Gun Corps (later Tank Corps)

We joined up with our tanks at Yvrench, a small village near Abbeville, and then came the job of bolting on the sponsons which carried the guns on each side of the tank. They were carried on small trolleys and they had to be manhandled into position, the sponsons lifted off the trolley and manoeuvred into position until the bolt holes in tank and sponson coincided exactly. Then the bolts were inserted and tightened. It sounds easy, and so it was – in theory! But, have you ever tried to lift a ton of metal into a

---

1. The 'male' tank carried two six-pounder cannon, the 'female' tank four Vickers machine-guns.

position where not one but every pair of bolt holes must exactly
coincide? If the fit was not absolutely perfect, even to one-sixteenth
of an inch out, the bolts wouldn't fit. Sometimes the first bolt did
go in but, perhaps because the sponson had warped slightly, none
of the others would! Then it was a case of using drifts, levers and
brute force! But it was done eventually.

Nick Lee, like every other man in A Company, was bitterly disappointed
to be held back in reserve while D and C Company were even now on
their way to the line and the glory of the tanks' first action. The crew
of D1, on the other hand, arriving at the eastern edge of Delville Wood
to lead the infantry in its preliminary action against Hop Alley and Ale
Trench, were disconcerted to discover that they were quite alone. Of the
three tanks which should have been at the rendezvous, only D1 had made
it. At a quarter-past five it left its starting point on the Longueval–Ginchy
Road and with machine-guns firing, with black clouds of smoke snorting
from its exhaust, with a noise that sounded as if all the furies of hell had
been let loose, it lumbered down the edge of Delville Wood lurching,
dipping and rearing its mountainous bulk above the German trenches.
For a full half-minute the Germans were paralysed with shock. Then they
began to run.

The Bombers of the 6th King's Own Yorkshire Light Infantry waited
as near as they dared to the edge of the wood. It was a good ten minutes
before the tank reached a point opposite their position, changed direction,
circled to the right and began to blunder forward up Hop Trench. Smartly
and on schedule, the Bombers jumped up and went forward behind it.

*Lance-Corporal Len Lovell, No. 18692, A Coy., 6th Btn., King's Own
Yorkshire Light Infantry*

It was marvellous. That tank went on, rolling and bobbing and
swaying in and out of shell-holes, climbing over trees as easy as
kiss your hand! We were awed! We were delighted that it was
ours. Up to now Jerry had supplied all the surprises. Now it was
his turn to be surprised!

The tank waddled on with its guns blazing and we could see
Jerry popping up and down, not knowing what to do, whether to
stay or to run. We Bombers were sheltering behind the tank,
peering round and anxious to let Jerry have our bombs. But we
had no need of them. The Jerries waited until our tank was only
a few yards away and then fled – or hoped to! The tank just shot
them down and the machine-gun post, the gun itself, the dead and

wounded who hadn't been able to run, just disappeared. The tank went right over them. We would have danced for joy if it had been possible out there. It seemed so easy! Hop Trench was 'kaput' and in a very few minutes Ale Alley got the same treatment. We were elated.

A Company Bombers were having a thoroughly good time. They were more than a little bit sorry to leave their glorious private victory and to rejoin the Battalion for the main attack. They got back just in time to line up in Delville Wood and just in time to miss the German bombardment which started up in retaliation. The tank was not so fortunate. A shell caught it fair and square and D1, the first tank across, became the Tanks' first battle casualty.

But Hop and Ale which for so long had dominated the eastern edge of Delville Wood were, as Lovell had gloated, 'kaput' and the way had been cleared for the troops. Over at the Quadrilateral, in a similar operation, things had gone badly wrong.

They had planned to send three tanks in to subdue the Quadrilateral twenty minutes before the troops went over at Zero. One tank broke its tail on the way up. Another developed engine trouble. The third appeared but, unlike the solitary tank which so dramatically subdued the Germans' resistance at Delville Wood, it made a tragic error. Lurching along beside what its crew took to be the Germans' front-line trench, they sprayed it with machine-gun fire. The trench was packed with soldiers. The kill was enormous. But it was a British assembly trench and the soldiers were men of the 9th Norfolks waiting to go over the top. It was Captain Crosse who put a stop to that. He leapt out of the trench and rushed up to the tank whose guns were still blazing. It was difficult to make himself heard above its pandemonium, but furious gesticulation was enough. The tank swung away and was last seen turning to the north, moving parallel to Straight Trench. Possibly it did a little damage. Straight Trench *was* the German front line running between the Triangle and the Quadrilateral. But on the Quadrilateral itself not a shot had fallen. The tank moved off leaving it untouched and inviolable in its wake. When the infantry attacked it, the Germans had no difficulty in holding out.

But they were perhaps unnerved. In spite of their losses before the battle even started, the 1st Leicesters and the 9th Norfolks succeeded in rushing Straight Trench and rushed on over the crest beyond. And there they stuck in front of a belt of barbed wire, so formidable, so wide and so deadly that it looked to the astonished troops as if no single shell of the long preliminary bombardment had fallen within a mile of it. They lay all day in front of the wire, waiting for orders, for reinforcements, for the tanks to come up to pave the way for a fresh attack, and as they lay there they were shelled. They could not understand why no British guns were retaliating on their front. But the reason was simple. They were lying in a 'lane' in the barrage. The tanks should have been forging ahead. The artillery had been ordered to leave wide gaps in the supporting barrage rather than run the risk of destroying them or holding up their triumphal progress. But, on the 6th Division Front, no tanks came.

If the Guards Division had waited for their tanks to appear they would never have advanced at all. They had been allotted no less than ten of them, for their task was the hardest of all. They were to make straight for Lesboeufs and Morval – but the Triangle, twin fortress to the Quadrilateral, stood slap in their path. Three of the tanks were to help them subdue it. But, when Zero came, the Guards were on their own. And on their own they advanced.

Private Charles Coles, No. 12245, 4 Platoon, 1st Coy., 1st Btn., Coldstream Guards

We manned the parapets at Zero Hour waiting to go over and waiting for the tank. We heard the chunk, chunk, chunk, chunk, chunk, chunk, chunk. Then silence. The wretched tank never came. There was split-second timing. We couldn't wait for it, so we had to go over the top. We got cut to pieces. Eventually the tank got going and went over past us. The Germans ran for their lives – couldn't make out what was firing at them. The tank did what it was supposed to have done, but too late! We lost hundreds and hundreds of men. Well, what was left of our three battalions of Coldstreams, didn't know what to do. We were all over the place in shell-holes and bits of trenchline, anywhere there was cover. Then Colonel Campbell of the 3rd Battalion Coldstreams got up on the trench and he'd got a hunting horn. He stood right up there in full view and he blew the hunting horn and got us together. He stood on top of the trench. The Germans was firing everything at us! But they say God was in the trenches. If ever God *was* in the trenches He was there then. Colonel Campbell won the Victoria Cross. He was only yards away from me. I saw that V C won. If ever a man deserved it, that man was Colonel Campbell.

The Guards had lost direction. Confused by the creeping barrage (which was actually intended for the adjacent 14th Division) they had strayed to their left and come under enfilade attack from Pint Trench. It was to knock out this danger that Colonel Campbell had rallied the scattered troops.

Private John Bouch, No. 11776, 1st Btn., Coldstream Guards

They were firing and slinging these bombs at us. We had to knock them out and we didn't know where we were really. You're firing at one and firing at another as you run forward and, what with getting on and getting a Lewis-gun Section up to deal with them, you didn't think of anything else. We made a mistake there, because we went off slightly to the left, following this group of Germans. We took prisoners. A lot of them threw up their hands and came forward and the rest of them started to run back and we followed them, rather to the left, when the main attack had gone to the right – and we followed them a long way.

The right flank of the Grenadier Guards attacking the Triangle alone and unsupported were not worried that they were not in touch with the Coldstreams who should have been advancing ahead of them. They assumed that, having captured their objective, the Coldstreams had pressed on and that all the Grenadiers would have to do was to occupy and consolidate the captured position. In fact the Grenadiers were advancing into a gap in the line. The Germans were still in possession of the 'captured' strongpoint.

But, by eleven o'clock, the Triangle had been subdued. The Guards paid a high price for it. Of the officers and men who had gone into action, two-thirds were killed or wounded or missing.

Some of the 'missing' who had wandered to their left were still trespassing in the sector of the 14th Division whose fortunes too had been mixed.

Lance-Corporal Len Lovell, No. 18692, A Coy., 6th Btn., King's Own Yorkshire Light Infantry

We Bombers moved off with the first line and we got to within ten or fifteen yards of Jerry's position. I had a Mills bomb ready in my hand. I pulled the pin out and I was holding down the lever ready to throw it when a Jerry seemed just to pop up out of a hole and let fly. I was struck in the left forearm below the elbow and it spun me round like a top. I fell into a shell-hole with two other fellows. One of them had half his left ear gone and he was drenched in blood, and he was yelling and screaming, hanging on to his ear with blood pouring through his fingers. The other chap had been hit in the right arm. By some miracle I was still clutching my bomb in my right hand – without the pin of course. My big problem was how to get rid of the bomb. My hand and fingers were getting stiff. I couldn't hold on to it for much longer and if I let go of the lever it would explode right away. Besides we knew we must get away quick before Jerry's barrage began to fall behind us to keep our reserves from coming up. I took the risk of standing up to make sure that there was no one else in holes behind us. Then I waved at my two chums to keep low and threw the bomb away into another shell-hole, praying for the best.

We shed our equipment, and took a drink of water out of our bottles. You could hardly make yourself heard above the din but I yelled to the other two that it was time we were off – or else! We hopped in and out of shell-craters as best we could and after a lot of effort we managed to get to the dressing station at Bernafay Wood corner. We thought we should be about the first. But there were hundreds there before us. We joined the queue and there were so many of us that when it came to my turn to reach the doctor there were no splints left. He had to make do with corrugated cardboard and a sling.

It was some hours before Ted Gale reached the same dressing station. His wound was worse than Lovell's and it took a long, long time to walk, to stagger and even, for part of the way, to crawl the best part of two miles to the dressing station at Bernafay Wood. He was losing blood and was half-fainting before he had gone halfway. When he saw the tank parked by the roadside Ted wondered, in his light-headed state, if he might already be delirious. The crew was standing in the roadway and he recognized – or thought he did – an old chum from Chichester. He hadn't seen George Hopkins since their schooldays; he was hardly certain if he was seeing him now, but he took a chance and hailed him with a yell that emerged as a croak. George came running and caught Ted just as he passed out. When he came to he was lying on a stretcher outside the dressing station. There was no sign of the tank. He was still not quite sure that it had not been a dream. But there was nothing dreamlike about the tank he had seen earlier in the morning as his Battalion lay waiting to go over the top in the second wave.

It was one of three that should have led the advance. One had broken down on the way. Another was late. Only D3 arrived – but it was enough.

Corporal E. Gale, No. 3774, D Coy., 7th Btn., The Rifle Brigade, 41st Brigade, 14th Division

The whole Brigade, that's between three and four thousand men, went over on part of the front that would normally have been a one battalion front – so you can imagine how crowded we were. Our job was to take the second line, so we were lying back a bit from the trenches, among the stumps in Delville Wood, ready to go forward. I was keeping a close eye on all this new lot in my platoon, because they were going across for the first time.

Just before Zero Hour we heard this damned racket, and I remember saying, 'What the hell is this?' Then these tanks appeared, one on our front and one a bit away from us. We were all absolutely flabbergasted. We didn't know what to think. We didn't know what they were because we hadn't been told anything about them. It was an amazing sight. It crossed my mind about the old Duke of Wellington's remarks about the Battle of Waterloo. He said, 'I don't know. My troops scare me, I don't know what the hell they're going to do to the French.' They scared Jerry all right! The tanks scared the Jerries more than what we did!

They came up right in front of us and swung round and went straight for the German line. The barbed wire entanglements had been pretty well smashed by our artillery but the tanks just rolled over what remained of them and smashed them all to pieces. They scared the guts out of the Germans. They bolted like rabbits. We saw them! Our tanks went straight over the German first-line trench and straight on and the boys just had to walk across behind it and occupy the front line. It was easy.

It was so easy that the second wave went over just ten minutes after the first, got caught up with the fighting in Pint Trench and, in their enthusiasm, were carried forward to the Switch Line by the momentum of the first wave. The Switch Line, which had loomed so large and so sinister in all the attacks of the last two months, was subdued with comparative ease. And there, according to the battle plan, they should have waited until twenty-past seven before moving on to the second objective at Gap Trench. No orders in the world – no shelling, no machine-gun fire, no casualties, no risk, no battle plan – could compete with the heady thrill of the dash forward. The remnants of the first wave advanced together with the remnants of the second. They lost the tank and they lost Ted Gale almost simultaneously. The tank ground to a half before Gap Trench and almost at the same moment Gale was hit.

Corporal E. Gale, No. 3774, D Coy., 7th Btn., The Rifle Brigade, 41st Brigade, 14th Division

There was another Corporal alongside of me. I grabbed hold of him and I said, 'I've stopped one!' I felt it go through me, into my shoulder, and the feeling was just like somebody jabbing a needle or a pin into your hand. Just a short sharp dig. No pain really. I knew it was a Blighty one – and I was thankful! I can remember what I thought before I passed out. I felt that faintness coming over me and, as I began to fall down, I thought, 'Oh, good! I'm on the way home.'

The rest of the battalion were on the way to Gap Trench in a hurly burly of troops which had become hopelessly mixed up in the excitement and confusion of the advance. For Burton Eccles, one of the new draft, it was the first time over the top.

Rifleman Burton Eccles, No. 203694, 7th Btn., The Rifle Brigade, 41st Brigade, 14th Division

We'd only been with the battalion for a matter of days. I was in a draft of King's Royal Rifle Corps but they called us out in the middle of the night, changed our shoulder badges and put us in the 7th Battalion, The Rifle Brigade. I had my first drink of rum that morning, before we went over. I'd never tasted spirits in my life! I was ready for anything after that.

The bombardment was terrible and, by the time we got over the top, the machine-gun bullets were simply racing at us. You'd wonder how anybody got through it! I had my clothing torn and something hit my tin hat – but the very worst thing was that I had a shovel on my back and a bullet hit the shovel. You never heard such a clang and a row as it made. It scared the life out of me!

I didn't see any Germans at all until the third line of trenches. I must have been looking a lot more fierce than I felt, because out of the trench came about twelve big Germans. I thought, 'Here goes! This is it!' And then they all put their hands up! I thought, 'Thank God for that!' We didn't need to give them any guard to take them back – we just waved them through. As they were running back towards our line one of our chaps turned and he fired at them. I was shocked. I stopped and I yelled at him, 'You dirty dog!' He yelled back, 'We were told not to take prisoners!'

We got into this trench and there wasn't really room for us, there were so many milling about. The trench was really badly knocked about, full of Germans, wounded and dead, and our own chaps as well. You couldn't move. And we stood there while the Germans counter-attacked from further on. We beat them off. Later we went on again.

We had to go through a perfect hail of stuff, branches and bits of tree trunks were flying about in all directions and our chaps were falling all the time. We had to go forward in short bursts from one shell-hole to another. I lost touch with my party in the smoke and, at one point, I found that the fellow in front whom I was following was actually not moving on because he was dead. He had died in a kneeling position.

Of my draft of twenty-five, only ten of us got out and of my own five pals who'd all stuck together, I was the only one to answer the roll call. I never saw anything of them after we started. In an advance over so much ground, in such terrible fire, it is impossible to keep in touch with one's pals.

Perhaps remembering their innocent curiosity of the night before and the jaunt which had so infuriated Ted Gale, Eccles later wrote home, 'I could have got heaps of souvenirs, but I only wanted one. That was myself!' He might also have added that, in any event, he had been rather too busy to collect any.

The 14th Division was advancing across the open country that lay between Lesboeufs and Flers. On their left the 41st Division was advancing on the village of Flers itself.

Afterwards, when the name of the battle had become synonymous with the capture of Flers and Courcelette, when it had been forgotten or only dimly remembered that the tanks had been intended to lead the infantry far beyond, it seemed a signal honour that this youngest and most inexperienced of Divisions had been chosen to attack Flers – and a signal achievement that they had captured it. The 41st had been given ten tanks to help them. Seven had trundled up to the start line, but the troops, lying well out in No Man's Land, were up and away and ahead of them. They went so fast that the tanks had no chance of keeping up. They went so far that they ran into their own barrage and so enthusiastically that the Germans in the first line of trenches were overwhelmed almost before they realized that the attack had begun. And the tanks rumbling up behind bowled them forward to the second line and into the fight for Switch Trench.

The Yeoman Rifles, with the exception of Billy Banks, took off in the first wave. Billy did not see them go. He was oblivious to the tanks, although they must have rumbled past within feet of the shell-hole where he lay. He was oblivious to the victory. He had not even heard the whistle blow at Zero. His last recollection was of waiting in the advanced position to go over and of the whistle of a shell that seemed to be making straight for him.

Rifleman W. Banks, No. 12021, 21st Btn., King's Royal Rifle Corps, 41st Division

It was a long time before I woke up and when I did it was ever so quiet. Oh, I could hear the guns and the sound of fighting in the distance, but there wasn't a sound near me and there wasn't anybody in sight either. I wondered where my pals were. I climbed up out of the shell-hole, looked around and I still couldn't see anybody. I felt myself all over and there wasn't a scratch on me, so I thought I'd better follow on. I went Over the Top by myself!

I kept looking around and, after a bit, I saw a group of men about half a mile away and I thought, 'That'll be the lads.' So I set off to catch up with them and I'd gone no distance when a machine-gun opened up and I got one in the left arm. I looked at it and I thought, 'That's nothing.' So I carried on, and I hadn't gone ten steps when I got hit in the *other* arm. That was it!

Banks never did succeed in catching up with the lads nor in completing his one-man advance on Flers. Fortunately his assistance was not required. D16 was already making its triumphal progress down the main street and D6, D9 and D17 were smashing through a hornet's nest of strongpoints on the eastern edge of the village and putting the Germans to flight. They were the only tanks on the Divisional Front which were still in action. The others lay ditched in the shell-holes along the line of the advance. One wreck, foundered just two hundred yards from the British line, was at least serving some sort of purpose. It had been pressed into service as a makeshift dressing station and the wounded who could hobble or crawl were crouched in the shelter of its battered bulk. Sergeant Norman Carmichael was there with a number of his men, for it was his Number 10 Platoon, in the vanguard of the Yeoman Rifles, which had taken the first shock of the attack and suffered the first casualties.

Sergeant Norman Carmichael, No. 10 Platoon, C Coy., 21st Btn., King's Royal Rifle Corps, 41st Division

Lieutenant Benton and myself took the platoon across. We were the first to go in C Company. I think our Captain gave the order to advance a little bit before the time because we'd been trained that the closer you kept to the creeping barrage the safer you were. But we overdid it. We walked into it and it has to be said that there were a lot of shorts. The artillery was very good but they weren't all that perfect and they couldn't guarantee to put a curtain in a straight line that you could keep behind.

I went down very early and I saw my officer going on just in front of me. He was brandishing his revolver and shouting, 'Come on, Number Ten!' And he just went down. He got a machine-gun bullet right through the head. The Germans had got up by then and my platoon was literally put out of action in a very short time. The last I saw of them there were about half-a-dozen going through the smoke climbing up this ridge to get into the German trenches and I was left lying there. It was a gorgeous summer's day and, after the rest of the Battalion had gone through, I was able to crawl about. I put a bandage round my leg and crept about going to the rest of my lads in the platoon that were wounded. Some of them were shouting. They used to make horrible sounds when they were in pain, when they were wounded and some were wounded pretty badly. I went round to as many as I could, just to try and cheer them up and then I went in and sheltered behind a tank that had broken down trying to get up this ridge. It stopped there all day and we collected as many of the walking wounded as we could. It was doubly safe, behind the ridge and behind the tank.

It was a long time before the Germans got the range and started shelling. When they did, it was a horrible sight. The shells were falling on Delville Wood and it had been fought for over and over again, so it was full of dead bodies and they were being tossed up by the explosions. In a strange sort of way it was fascinating to watch these bodies rising into the air above the tree stumps and circulating almost in slow motion and coming down again. Horrible, but fascinating. It seemed so strange to be lying there on that lovely warm summer's day watching these bodies going up and down.

Beyond Delville Wood, the New Zealanders too had leapt forward ahead of schedule without waiting for the snail-crawling tanks to lead their advance. They too had suffered casualties from their own bombardment but they had kept going, spurred on by the sight of some two hundred Germans running for their lives. They were bellowing and cheering as they went. Disdaining the tanks, lumbering up painfully slowly behind them, they took the Switch Line with the bayonet. They took it so quickly that Harry Baverstock, asleep in his rabbit-warren in Mametz Wood, was roused by '. . . fellows rushing around yelling that the Green Line had been taken by the Dinks'. It was just ten minutes to seven and the attack had been underway for exactly half an hour.

Looking over the parados of the captured trench the New Zealanders could see, on their right, the ruined village of Flers tucked into its shallow valley. They could see the troops and the tanks making steadily towards it. And now that they had a chance to look around, they could see how thin they were in numbers. When they realized the full measure of New Zealand casualties, they sent a message back urging the Reserve Battalion to prepare to take over the line.

At High Wood, on the 47th Divisional Front, the tanks had been a positive hindrance. One of them had even been responsible for a fair number of the New Zealand casualties. It strayed out of the wood, was confused by the lie of the line, unsure of its direction. It opened fire on what it took to be enemy troops. In fact it was firing directly at the New Zealanders as they advanced with the 7th Royal Fusiliers on their left and just behind.

Of course the tanks should never have been ordered into High Wood at all and so the Commander of the 47th Division had told GHQ in the frankest of terms. In the opinion of General Sir Charles Barter, even a child could have seen that the pitted, fought-over ground, the upturned trees, the stockade of jagged stumps, the morass of craters and shell-holes lying lip to lip, were insurmountable obstacles to any vehicle, regardless of its might, regardless of the brilliance of its trials over open country. He had not succeeded in convincing the powers-that-be. They patiently pointed out that the British and German lines lay too close to each other in High Wood for the artillery to bombard and crush the enemy defences. The tanks must do the job. The powers-that-be had not seen for themselves the conditions in High Wood. The General had. Let the tanks go round the perimeter of the wood, he suggested, and the wood itself could then be crushed as easily as a walnut in the jaws of a nutcracker. The General had been overruled, but he had been right. Only one of the tanks had been able to move forward through the wood and, before long, it had stuck. Its crew fought on with the infantry, and the fighting was hand-to-hand.

But, beyond High Wood, the tanks were ranging towards Martinpuich, across the tangle of trenches that had so formidably defended it, followed by the triumphant 50th Division. Soon they were in the outskirts of the village, prisoners were streaming back and the demoralized German line began to crack.

In High Wood the Tommies lay low while trench-mortars poured a short-range barrage into the Switch Line. The bombing parties, creeping forward in its aftermath, found little opposition. By one o'clock, the wood had fallen. It was two months to the day since the three Brigadiers had walked towards it through fields of standing corn and in those two months High Wood had cost the lives of several thousand men.

Just as they had been waiting two months before, the cavalry was massed behind the line, impatient for the order to dash through to Bapaume. Again the order never came. But the German line had been broken. Like the New Zealanders four kilometres away, the Canadians had swept ahead well in advance of their tanks, and swept right into Courcelette. A tank had driven 'up the main street of Flers with the British Army cheering behind'. The British Army had undoubtedly advanced – and further in a few hours than in the previous ten weeks. But they had not advanced quite far enough. The cavalry would not be required to exploit the breakthrough. For the moment the advance had stuck.

It had stuck on the far side of Flers. It had stuck in front of Gueudecourt and in front of Lesboeufs. It had stuck at the Quadrilateral. It had stuck beyond Lousy Wood at the foot of the road that led into Combles. And more than half the tanks which had boosted the infantry on its way had stuck as well, or been wrecked by enemy fire. Most divisions were reduced to half their strength long before the day ended. Most battalions had lost their colonels. Some had lost every single officer.

The 7th Battalion, The Rifle Brigade, were holding five hundred yards of Gap Trench with a modest force of five officers, one warrant officer, four sergeants and no more than one hundred and fifty riflemen. They were uncomfortably aware that, if the Germans decided to counter-attack, they would stand little chance of beating them off. The best they could do was to set up a Lewis-gun in a forward post and reinforce the gun-team with a sergeant and a few riflemen to lend moral support. Burt Eccles was one of the party. The men were exhausted and dazed by the day's fighting. They had had little sleep the night before and another sleepless night lay ahead. They set off up a long narrow trench which, until that morning, had been manned by Germans. The Germans were still there in heaps of contorted bodies that smothered the floor of the trench. Eccles hesitated and stopped. The Sergeant prodded him roughly from behind. 'Get on!' he said. 'What's the matter?' Eccles stood, paralysed. 'I don't like treading on their faces.' The Sergeant had no time for such niceties. 'Never mind their bloody faces! MOVE!' Eccles moved, through the sweet stench of blood, wobbling as the bodies yielded softly under his feet, fighting the impulse to vomit. It was the worst moment of the day.

> Captain Brown had established what passed for Battalion Head-quarters in a 'well-furnished Boche cubby-hole' in Gap Trench. It contained a welcome supply of food. There was rye bread, dried figs, prunes, dates, dried meat, mineral water, lump sugar and cheese. There was not a great deal, but there was plenty to go round what was left of the Battalion.

The Yeoman Rifles were considerably fewer than this time last night when they had been marching to the line with the tanks. Now they were out in the fields beyond Flers and, at the head of a reconnoitring party, Lord Feversham had gone farthest of all. His body still lay in the uncut corn. Billy Banks had been found by stretcher-bearers. Others had got back under their own steam.

When the shelling became too hot, when a battery of guns had moved forward and opened up disconcertingly close to them, when it was only a matter of time before the German guns would register on such a tempting target, Sergeant Carmichael had left the shelter of the tank and made for safety. Nelson Lawson and Geoff Hutchinson went with him. Together they crawled back to the British wire and pulled stakes from the entangle-ments to serve as makeshift crutches. They could never have made it across the moonscape surface of Delville Wood itself, so they worked their way round it and hit on a half-constructed highway of planks and a Pioneer Battalion working flat out to extend it up to the new line. It made the going easier. They must have passed within yards of the New Zealand reinforcements, who were on their way through Carlton Trench to the front.

Now, the ground where their comrades had gone over cheering in the morning was strewn with hideous evidence of the fight. The bodies of four New Zealand soldiers lay staring from one shell-hole. Baverstock's section faltered and the Sergeant urged them on. 'Come on, never mind them. They've only stopped for a rest!' There were a lot of 'resting' bodies about and Baverstock had a black premonition that the bodies of Hickmott, Jackson and Biss were probably among them. He was right. And he was also right in his conviction that they too would be 'for it' in the morning.[1]

1. Harry Jackson survived the war, but the other two had indeed been killed on 15 September.

At dusk it began to rain. Several miles in the rear the disappointed cavalry turned their horses' heads for home. If all had gone according to plan, they should have galloped through the gap many hours ago, past Gueudecourt and Lesboeufs, across the lower ground beyond and by now might have been ranged along the Transloy ridges from Sailly-Saillisel to Bapaume. No trenches there! No barbed wire, few emplacements, nothing to prevent swift-moving patrols from dashing through the night to raid Divisional and even Corps Headquarters to demoralize the enemy's generals much as the tanks had demoralized his infantry that morning.

If all had gone according to plan the victorious tanks would now be sitting behind the new line, waiting for morning and daylight to swing to the north. Then, with the British Army cheering behind, they would have rolled up the German line as they might roll up a carpet laid over their path to Bapaume. But half the tanks were knocked out – and the advance had halted.

The night was kind to the Germans. Rain-clouds gathered low in the sky, glowing red above the guns and concealing the shrinking moon. The Germans were thankful for that. They needed the dark. The Transloy ridges were alive with troops, with guns, with wagons, with supplies, rushing forward to support the sleepless weakened regiments clinging to their beleaguered line. There was no sleep for the German generals nor for their Staff. In their Headquarters' châteaux, which should even now be surrounded, lights burned until dawn and the German Staff who, according to plan, ought to have been quailing under the lances of the cavalry, attempted to make sense of the situation, tried to unravel the riddle of the new 'secret weapon' from incoherent front-line reports, pondered, conferred and planned counter-attacks for tomorrow. At all costs they must force the British to give up ground. At all costs they must capture a tank.

They had, as yet, no clear idea of their losses, except that they must be huge. And they were right. Their dead littered the battlefield and, trotting disconsolately through the drizzle to their billets, the British cavalrymen were overtaking long columns of bemused German prisoners plodding with their escorts to the cages.

Chapter 22

There was no shortage of prisoners after the fighting of 15 September. There had been a disturbing shortage after the First of July. Even where the troops had successfully advanced and where, consequently, large numbers of captives might have been expected, the cages that had been prepared received the merest trickle of Prisoners-of-War. They were full enough now but, even so, in the ten weeks since the start of the campaign, an idea had grown up on both sides of the line that the British infantry would give no quarter and would take no prisoners and that, furthermore, they were acting under direct orders.

This idea was assiduously fostered by the German Staff as a useful means of stiffening the resistance of their front-line infantry. The British Staff, equally anxious to foster the offensive spirit with tales of German atrocities, would have vehemently denied it. The British sense of justice and fair play was renowned throughout the world. It was the Germans who, as all the world was equally aware, brutally hounded innocent civilians, cut off children's hands, bayoneted babies, shot – and even crucified – prisoners. It was the Germans (albeit the descendants of Schubert and Schiller and Göethe) who had first launched upon the unsuspecting Tommies the infamous evils of poison gas and liquid fire. Was it conceivable that the heirs of Nelson, of Wellington, of Clive could descend to such depths of brutality as to shoot enemies who desired to surrender? All the rules of 'honest warfare' forbade it.

But in the minds of many Tommies the conviction that they were directed to take no prisoners had taken a curious hold and it was rooted in an order which had been issued from GHQ on 28 June 1916 – on the eve of the Battle of the Somme.

1. All ranks must be on their guard against the various ruses at which the enemy has shown himself to be an adept, especially *the use of British words of command* such as 'Retire', etc.
2. The German machine-gun is carried on a sledge, and the Germans sometimes throw a blanket over the gun. This makes the sledge and gun resemble a stretcher.

3. It is the duty of all ranks to continue to use their weapons against the enemy's fighting troops, unless and until it is beyond all doubt that those have not only ceased all resistance but that, whether through having voluntarily thrown down their weapons or otherwise, they have definitely and finally abandoned all hope or intention of resisting further. In the case of apparent surrender, it lies with the enemy to prove his intention beyond the possibility of misunderstanding, before the surrender can be accepted as genuine.[1]

It was signed by General Kiggell, Chief of the General Staff. It was sent out to every corps, every division, every brigade, every battalion of British troops on the Western Front and, through colonels and company commanders, to every platoon officer to read and pass on, for it was further instructed that the warning *'should be communicated verbally to all ranks before taking part in an assault'*. The order had never been rescinded and its message, though disguised, was unequivocal. Interpretations inevitably varied in the course of 'verbal communication' by several thousand platoon officers, but there was no doubt that to many soldiers of the infantry the message had come across loud and clear.

Prisoners were a nuisance. Fighting troops had to be spared from the battle to escort them back. Prisoners consumed supplies as well as manpower. 'The more Fritz eats the less there will be for you', was a potent argument. But, an even more powerful argument, as the infantry was rapidly working out for itself, was that brutality to prisoners, failure to give Fritz the benefit of the doubt *in the case of apparent surrender*, if practised on too wide a scale, might result in similar treatment being meted out by the Germans to British soldiers who were forced to surrender. Privately, individually, the Tommies made up their own minds and acted according to circumstance, to character and to conscience. After the advances of 15 September the Prisoner-of-War cages were well populated. They were guarded by Corps Troops of non-combatant units and, in contrast to the slog of trench digging and road building, looking after German prisoners was a sinecure.

Private W. G. Bell, No. 4640, 9th Btn., Army Cyclist Corps

The first thing you did if you got hold of a Jerry was to see what you could get off him – if he'd got a watch or anything like that. Most of our chaps had a load of Mark notes on them that weren't

1. Army Order Number W,19.A.16. O.A.104.

worth the paper they were printed on. All I was after was cap badges. I tried to get some watches but that was no good. None of the scruffy ones that came into our Prisoner-of-War camp had any that were worth having.

There was a lot of talk about Zeppelin raids and the Jerries bombing London and killing a lot of civilians and, just at that time, we had a Jerry airman who'd been brought down. He was handed over to us and one of my mates interrogated him. He tried to find out whether he'd been over, dropping bombs. He said, 'If he's been over *there*, I'll shoot him! He'll never get away!'

He would have done too! Life meant nothing to you. Life was in jeopardy and when you'd got a load of Jerries like that on your hands, all stinking to high heaven, you hadn't much sympathy for them with their *Kamerad* and all this cringing business. It brutalizes you, war does. You don't find that you've got much sympathy. All you're looking after is your own skin all the time. Head down.

Attitudes were hardening at home as well as in France. The casualty lists had burgeoned horribly since July, taking up more and more columns of the daily newspapers, casting a shadow across the summer and a blight over almost every family in the land. Now came the stories of other pathetic events – of homes wrecked by German bombs, of women, children, pet animals and caged birds wounded or killed by 'Hun raiders'.

And then, on 3 September, a raiding Zeppelin was shot down by Lieutenant Leefe Robinson of the Royal Flying Corps. He was acclaimed as a hero and, rightly, in the opinion of Londoners, awarded the Victoria Cross. They had flocked to Potters Bar to gloat over the burnt-out wreck and a brisk market sprang up in souvenirs. Everyone wanted a bit of the Zeppelin and everyone was prepared to pay. At the Polytechnic jumble sale, held on 17 September in aid of comforts for the 'Poly Boys' serving in the forces, the 'Zepp Remnant Corner' was the success of the afternoon. It was presided over by Miss Morel who had spared no effort in collecting, begging, borrowing and even advertising for bits of Zeppelin with which to astound the public who had braved a day of teeming rain to attend. It cost a penny to pass behind a screen to inspect the relics and, as an added bonus, to be regaled by Miss Morel with thrilling stories, graphically related, on the origin of each item. Miss Budgeon and Miss Ross, presiding over the refreshment stall, Mrs Gravelin on Old Clothes, Miss Whitewright in charge of Fancy Goods, Miss Ashby and Miss Bowen well ahead of the season with Christmas cards and calendars, Miss Mitchell and Mrs Bangert persuasively selling rubbish under the title of Penny Odds and Ends and even Miss Cooper, whose Lucky Fish Pond Dip attracted many clients, had lean takings compared to the receipts of the Zepp Remnant Stall. But no one minded. Stall holders and buyers alike had done their bit and raised no less than seventeen pounds. It was estimated with satisfaction that this sum would provide enough khaki wool to enable the knitting committee to provide socks for nearly three hundred 'Poly Boys'.

Like many other organizations and institutions the 'Poly' looked after its own. Since Quintin Hogg had founded the Polytechnic Young Men's Christian Institute, no one was absolutely certain how many boys had passed through its Lower School and gone on to higher education in either the Commercial or the Technical Secondary Department. But they did know that, by September 1916, no less than two thousand six hundred and forty-five Old Boys were serving with the forces. There were probably many more who had not thought of letting them know.

The Polytechnic took a particular interest in boys who had served in the Institute's Cadet Corps and graduated to the Rangers – officially the 12th Londons, but referred to proprietorially as 'The Poly Regiment' – now fighting with the 56th Division in Lousy Wood. Many other 'Poly Boys' in the 47th London Division had helped to make the final thrust that captured High Wood. The September fighting had taken a high toll and, in October, the task of compiling the monthly 'Poly Roll of Honour' was unusually onerous. There were no less than four pages of photographs and obituaries, headed by a verse which was sincerely intended to be of comfort to the bereaved relatives of the boys who had died.

> *Remember what he was, with thankful heart,*
> *The bright, the brave, the tender, and the true.*
> *Remember where he is – from sin apart,*
> *Present with God – yet not estranged from you.*
> *But never doubt that love, and love alone,*
> *Removed thy loved one from this trial scene,*
> *Nor idly dream, since he to God has gone,*
> *Of what, had he been left, he might have been.*

But the currency of such high sentiments had tended somewhat to devalue since the start of the Big Push. There was a growing hint of disillusionment, of doubt, of questioning, not the Cause, but the Execution of the war. It was summed up by Ethel Bath in the letter she wrote in reply to condolences on her shattering news from France.

It is a small comfort to know he gave his life in a successful attack. His Captain wrote that the success was entirely due to the magnificent way the men went forward led by their officers. He also said that of the five officers from the 10th only one was left . . . I am very proud of my boy but at the same time it grieves me dreadfully to think those boys are given such a small chance to show their grit. You will understand what I mean when I tell you he was only out 16 days in all, and he was attached to the Middlesex Regt on Friday 6th, sent into the trenches the same afternoon and attacked on the Saturday at 2.30 in the afternoon, when he was killed. It all seems too quick to give them a chance.

She signed it 'Ethel Bath'. She had hardly had time to get used to the unfamiliar surname. Reg died in Lousy Wood just three weeks to the hour since they were married and, in Lousy Wood itself, where the weary 56th Division was still in the line, letters much like Ethel's were arriving by every mail that came up with the rations from the transport lines. There were several for Arthur Agius. One came from Florence Scarlett and Agius read it in a filthy dugout, not much further advanced than the one in which he had penned his own sad letter to her.

> 305, Thorold Road,
> Ilford.

Dear Captain Agius,

I wish to take this opportunity of thanking you for your kind letter of sympathy, and for the few details you were able to give me concerning my dear husband's death. The sad news was a terrible shock to me, and, up till now, I have felt too ill to write to you, although I have been eager to do so.

If it is not taking too great an advantage of your kindness, will you please let me know whether, at the time my dear one fell, there were any personal possessions on him that could be sent to me. I know there was nothing of real value, but I think you will understand that any little thing no matter what it is will become one of my most cherished possessions.

It was a great relief to know that dear Harold did not suffer any pain, although what would I not give to have had just one last message from him. We have been married such a short time (only five months) and I cannot realize that he has gone – never to see him again. The last time we were together he was so happy and well and eager to do his level best for his Country at all cost. This horrible war is dealing some cruel blows, and one is apt to grow hardened to the Casualty List until someone very dear is taken. There is scarcely a home, but what the occupants have some great trouble to bear, and sometimes I think, knowing this, helps us to bear our grief more bravely.

Will you please also tell me, if possible, where my husband was struck. I feel I would like to know. After the war I hope to be able to visit his last resting-place and, in that case, I suppose I should have no difficulty in distinguishing it.[1]

Once again thanking you for your kindness in writing to me. With every good wish for your safe and speedy return to England.

Yours very sincerely,
Florence E. Scarlett.

Florence Scarlett and Ethel Bath had experienced, between them, just eight days of married life. The letter from Mrs Scarlett worried Agius. The same post had brought a letter from his fiancée, Dolly, full of excited plans for their own wedding and enclosing one of the invitations, hot from the printers. More than a hundred had already gone out to friends and relatives:

Madame Noel
announces the marriage of her younger daughter
Evelyn ('Dolly')
to

Captain Arthur J. Agius
1/3rd London Regiment
Which will take place on his next leave from the Front
at St. Dominic's Priory, Haverstock Hill.
(The exact date will be announced later.)

Agius wondered gloomily if he was being fair to Dolly. He also wondered what the 'exact date' would be. He was 'sweating on leave' but, until another officer came to take over command of the Battalion, there was no hope of getting it.

Leave had been stopped at the beginning of the Somme Offensive. Now it had started again. Filthy, lousy, encrusted with the mud and sometimes with the blood of the trenches, the men poured off the leave trains into seven days of delight. To the families who waited, the long casualty lists, the knowledge of those other families in the land who *have some great*

---

1. Harold Scarlett has no known grave. He is commemorated on the Thiepval Memorial to the missing and his name (one of some 73,000) appears on Pier 9, near the top of Face D.

trouble to bear made it all the more poignant and eagerly awaited. Joe Murray got leave on 18 September. His train arrived at Newcastle at the unearthly hour of twenty-past three in the morning. There were four frustrating hours to pass before the local train left for the mining village of Lintz Green and he put in the first of them by trying to get rid of at least the top layer of the dirt that encrusted his uniform and his body. With the limited facilities available in the station's 'Wash and Brush Up', he made little impression on what seemed to be half the filth of France. At half-past four he set off across the high-level bridge to Gateshead and knocked at his Aunt Maggie's door.

Able Bodied Seaman Joseph Murray, No. TZ.276, Hood Btn., The 63rd (Royal Naval) Division

I said, 'I'm not even going to sit down. I'm as lousy as a cuckoo.' Uncle Bill said, 'Sit down, lad. Bugger the lice. Sit down!' Right off, I got a cup of tea and Aunt Maggie got the frying pan on and I tucked into a good breakfast. First meal in England! My, it was good!

I wanted to send a telegram because I didn't want to give my mother a shock just walking in. So Aunt Maggie and Uncle Bill walked me round to the Post Office as soon as it opened, which was ten minutes before the train went. It took half an hour on the train and then a two-mile walk which took about another half-hour to get home. I didn't mind that, because I didn't want to get home before my telegram. The quickest way was to walk along the track that the colliery trucks used to get down to the main line, and of course in France I'd been walking on railway tracks for months. So I'm walking up the colliery railway and I see somebody waving from the bridge. I thought, 'It's our Mum!'

Apparently the telegram came to our local Post Office and, of course, the Post Mistress knew everybody in the village. She said to the postman, 'Dobson, I've got a telegram here for Mrs Murray.' He said, 'Oh no!' She said, 'No, no. It's good news. Joe's got leave.' So the postman got on his bike and he delivered the telegram before he did his round.

Well! She put the kettle on the fire to boil and then she was off – a pair of slippers on, no shawl, no nothing – straight out of the front door and across the cricket field to meet me. When she got to this bridge, she daren't go any further, in case I was coming by the road. So she waited there and I saw her up on the bridge. I waved and I ran down the embankment and she ran down the bridge and she just collapsed on the wet grass. I had to lean down to give her a hug and a kiss. She didn't faint, but she couldn't walk. All she could do was sit there greetin', sitting on the wet grass. I had to carry her home across the fields, into the cottage and into the kitchen, full of steam from the boiling kettle.

I had a cup of tea but wouldn't sit down. I said, 'Look, Mum, I'm very lousy. I'm going to have a bath.' There was a big rain barrel in the back yard and Mum used to do the washing in there with a big poss stick to agitate the water. So, we got the water boiled again and took it out to the yard, put in some carbolic crystals and I got stripped off and got into the barrel. And she went off to get me some clean clothes. All the neighbours were there, all shouting 'Hello' over our back wall and, 'Welcome home, Joe,' and all that sort of thing. Well, I had my wash and then I had to get out of the rain barrel with all these folk there and I was naked of course. I thought I'd lost all my modesty in France, but I didn't like to stand there drying myself, so I ran in with just a wet towel round my waist and went in front of the fire and Mum dried me – just like she'd done when I used to come home from the pit as a little lad.

A soldier's seven days' leave started officially the moment he arrived at the main-line station nearest his home destination. Before the new ruling, travelling had taken up hours and even days of the precious seven days' leave and it had been commonplace for soldiers, whose homes were in the Hebrides or the far north of Scotland, to arrive home just in time to turn around and set off on the journey back.

For soldiers, like the Colonial troops, who had no homes to go to, London was the Mecca. Many had new-found relatives to visit; many more were at a loose end. From the moment they arrived at Victoria Station, London received them with open arms. There was the YMCA All-Welcome Hut where pretty girl volunteers dished out tea, sandwiches and smiles. There was Paddy's Bar, thick with troops and thick with the smoke of pipes and Woodbines, where from early morning until late at night blasée barmaids pulled endless pints of beer, shrugged off the advances of Tommies who had not seen a girl for months, and prospered on tips from the lavish Aussies. They never bothered to pick up copper coins in their change and were known throughout London as 'the Silver Kings'.

The YMCA was well aware of the temptations of the big city to healthy young men, long deprived of feminine society, and organized leave hostels where a bed could be had for ninepence and a square meal for the same price. They set up canteens, rest and recreation huts where a soldier could enjoy the luxury of a comfortable armchair, a game of draughts or billiards, as many cups of tea as he could consume and the society of pleasant young women of unimpeachable character. At the Shakespeare Hut for New Zealand troops, there were more than two hundred such volunteers, working in shifts, because the ever-vigilant authorities had concluded that a frequent turnover of smiling faces behind the tea urns was the best insurance against the indiscretions and unsuitable attachments that were almost inevitable in the highly charged atmosphere of wartime. They set up Leave Enquiry Bureaux where kindly advisers would arrange accommodation, suggest a sight-seeing programme or per-suade soldiers to join one of their own free tours around London, to Hampton Court or to the Zoo.

The YMCA extended its vigilance to soldiers who disdained such innocent pleasures, and set up night patrols to scour the back streets of Soho and the West End. They were groups of well-meaning volunteers of mature years, 'doing their bit' in work of . . . *a delicate personal nature requiring the utmost tact to separate men from women of known disreputable character.*

Most of the boys were content to goggle at the sights by day and to retire at night to their ninepenny beds, whistling or humming whatever song had been the highlight of their evening at the theatre.

In the theatres and music halls the emphasis was on light entertainment, and every performance was packed out. Few soldiers returned to the front without being able to boast of having seen at least four shows in his seven days' London leave. There was *Ye Gods,* advertised as 'a scream', at the Aldwych. The beautiful Alice Delysia was starring in *Pell Mell* at the Ambassadors. A. E. Matthews toyed sentimentally with Moya Mannering in *Peg O' My Heart* at the Globe. There was *Chu Chin Chow* at His Majesty's, naughty Teddy Gerard in *Bric à Brac* at the Palace and, best of all, among a score of other revues and musicals, George Robey and Violet Loraine at the Alhambra in *The Bing Boys are Here.* Their famous duet was the success of the summer:

> *If you were the only girl in the world*
> *And I were the only boy,*
> *Nothing else would matter in this world today,*
> *If we could go on loving in the same old way.*
> *A Garden of Eden, just made for two,*
> *With nothing to mar our joy,*
> *I would say such wonderful things to you,*
> *There would be such wonderful things to do,*

If you were the only girl in the world,
And I were the only boy.

The Palm Court Orchestra played it at teatime at the Waldorf, errand boys whistled it as they teetered along on bicycles, and they played it every afternoon at Madame Vacani's Dancing School at her famous tea dances. The young lady teachers and the more mature and accomplished of their pupils danced impeccably and mooned just a little in the arms of soulful young officers with nowhere else to go. It was romantic, it was exciting, it was quite respectable and it was well worth the five shillings admission. The charge was fixed high enough to discourage lower ranks from indulging in this genteel entertainment and there was no escaping the eagle eye of Madame Vacani herself. She supervised every dance, played the gracious hostess and introduced the officers to partners who were strictly forbidden, on pain of instant dismissal, to accept any invitation other than to dance. But her eagle eye did not extend beyond the premises of her exclusive school. There was privacy on the dance floor, the music was sentimental, the girls were delightful, the officers were returning soon to France, to an indeterminate and possibly brief future. It was not difficult to persuade the discreet dancing partner of the afternoon to be the charming theatre companion of the evening. They all had a wonderful time.

But there was another side to leave and it was a side that most soldiers dreaded. Since he had been away there was hardly a man who had not lost a comrade, hardly an officer who had not lost a colleague. Relatives at home were avid for visits, for news, for information, for any tiny detail of comfort that would assuage the pain of mourning. It cast a blight over even the most joyous of leaves.

Lance-Corporal Len Lovell, No. 18692, 6th King's Own Yorkshire Light Infantry, 14th Division

When I was safe in hospital, out of that hell of France, I scarcely knew how to adjust to decent society after living like an animal for so long. The only thing that kept worrying me was my promise to go and tell Bobby's people about his end. I dreaded the thought of them asking where he was buried. How could you tell a mother he was blown to pieces? We'd buried him all right, a few yards behind our position in the wood, with a rifle plunged into the earth to mark the grave and his tin hat on top of it. But by the next morning it had entirely disappeared.

Bobby was well in his forties, so his mother was not young. He was separated from his wife – he'd only ever mentioned her to me to rail at her and they had no children. But she was there that day, the day I went to see his mother.

All I could tell them was that he was buried in Delville Wood.

Able Bodied Seaman Joseph Murray, No. TZ276, Hood Btn., The 63rd (Royal Naval) Division

My pal George McCarthy had been killed on 4 June the year before when we were in Gallipoli, and this was my first leave. I had to go to the next village to see his father. He lived in the Aged Miners' Cottages. It was difficult talking to him. I said, 'Look, I didn't see him killed but we *did* bury him.' We didn't of course, because we couldn't! But he was a Catholic and I knew it would be important to his father so I said, 'He had a good Christian burial I can assure you of that!'

Next day I had to go and see another pal's parents. That was even worse. It was another mining family and the father had got his leg broken and he had a permanent limp, so things weren't so good for them. You're paid by the jobs and if you're not fit you don't get any work – and no pay either. Their boy was an old school pal of mine. All the time I sat there talking to the father, his Mum didn't say much and I could sense that she was uneasy. I wasn't in the house ten minutes when the postman knocked at the door with a telegram to say that the other son had been killed in France.

What can a bloke do then? What kind of man from the war, home on leave, goes into a house to make condolences with a fellow's family and a telegram comes to say that the other one's killed?

It spoiled my leave. I felt I could see it on everyone's faces like as if they were saying, 'How come you've come home and *he* hasn't?'

I was sorry I came home on leave. I didn't enjoy it. It's funny, but I wished I hadn't gone. You couldn't get these things out of your mind.

On the whole, Joe Murray was not sorry when his leave came to an end on 25 September. When the night-train from Edinburgh drew into Newcastle it was already filled with troops returning to the front, but Murray squeezed into an overcrowded carriage and sat on his pack on the floor. There was no question of sleep and the talk was all of Zeppelins.

Two had been shot down the night before and newspapers bought to while away the journey were full of dramatic accounts. There was a certain excitement in travelling by night through blacked-out England. With the stepping-up of the air raids a new theory had taken hold in the imaginations of authorities, so sensitive about 'showing a light' that smokers striking matches in the street were being prosecuted and fined. It was now believed that plumes of sparks from the funnels of engines of express trains were guiding the raiders through England.

Whatever guided them, they had arrived in force the night before last and dropped bombs that killed forty civilians and injured a hundred and twenty-six, including four soldiers who were on leave in London. But this time the Zeppelins had not got away with it.

Since the raids had started more than a year earlier, a considerable number of troops had been kept back from the front to stiffen the Home Defences, badly though men were needed in France. Searchlights and gun batteries were set up on the east coast, around the outskirts of important cities and at strategic points in the cities themselves. It had never occurred to Frank Mayhew that his peacetime training as an electrical engineer would lead him to a position in an open field at Cuffley.

Sapper F. L. Mayhew, No. 2259, London Electrical Engineers, Royal Engineers (TF)

Our main job was to keep the searchlights in good order – because Zeppelin raids weren't at all frequent. There was always the possibility, but as a rule weather conditions were so abnormal that the Zeppelins couldn't operate. When the alarm came I was lucky enough to be the operator and to pick up the Zeppelin. It's an extraordinary sight! A Zeppelin in a searchlight beam looks just like a goldfish in a bowl and one could follow it quite easily. The gun was a thirteen-pounder mounted on a three-ton Daimler lorry and it could fire to about sixty degrees. After that, the angle would be so steep that the recoil would have knocked the bottom of the lorry out. On this particular occasion, after holding the Zeppelin for a few minutes, the gun fired four or five rounds and then the angle got too steep for further gunfire so we were out of action and we had to shut down.

To 'shut down' we used to use a copper lid to cover up the beams, but the lamps remained lit under it and a little later the guns thought they should be in action again, so we opened out. Quite by chance I'd sort of mentally followed the Zeppelin and, when we opened out, I was able to pick it up straightaway. But we scored no hits and we had to pass the target on to some other lights.

Trooper Charles Williams, MM, No. 1598, 1st Btn., Royal Buckinghamshire Hussars

It had been a very peaceful day and we were all in bed – except for the people with late passes or the people who'd taken a night off without them. Suddenly there was a whirring noise overhead and we all rushed out and stood looking up and watching. We could see the silhouette up in the sky – a huge cigar-shaped thing caught in a searchlight. Presently we heard the noise of one of our own aeroplanes coming along behind it and the tracer bullets went from the aeroplane to the Zeppelin and the Zeppelin burst into flames and began to fall. It was so huge that it looked as though it was just about half a mile or a mile away.

Some of the fellows rushed in and put on their boots and trousers and started off to see it. There were dozens of them jumping over the fence but most of us stayed behind watching the flare and it was such a blaze that we could even hear the crackling noise from it. While we were watching, the bugles started to sound the alarm and the order to saddle up and get going to where the Zeppelin had come down. We were saddled up and trotting off in no time and, as we went we passed a lot of the boys who were making for the Zepp on foot and we yelled at them that they were wanted and they had to rush off back to the camp to get saddled up and follow us in.

We were to put a guard round the Zeppelin. It had actually fallen some distance away, outside a village just before you get into Billericay. It was much further away than we thought but when we got there it was still burning and it burnt well into the early hours of the morning. What a sight it was! What a sight!

It was a sight that everyone wanted to see. By three o'clock in the morning the road to the farm where the Zeppelin had crashed was jammed with motor-cars, bicycles, pony traps, donkey carts and hundreds of pedestrians who had risen from their beds and walked several miles to gawp, to gaze, to exclaim and to get as near as they could to the wreck. The soldiers, standing guard with bayonets fixed, kept them well back. By dawn there were thousands of people craning their necks from the steep banks of the lane. Some had even climbed trees to get a better look. The wreckage was spread over hundreds of yards and shortly after dawn Bert Williams was one of the party detailed to clear up the area around the smouldering wreckage.

Trooper Charles Williams, No. 1598, 1st Btn., Royal Buckinghamshire Hussars

The worst bit was gathering up the crew. The ground was very soft where they fell and when we picked them up there were indentations in the soft soil of the shape of their bodies, arms, legs, everything – a mould of the bodies really.[1] We carried them to the farmhouse. We picked up wicker chairs, loaves of German bread and bits of burnt silk and pieces of aluminium – all sorts of stuff. It kept us in beer for months! Everybody wanted souvenirs and, when the officers weren't looking, we were selling them to the crowd for half a crown and two bob a time. It was a good morning. Special trains came down with London sightseers and they were all begging us to get souvenirs for them, so those that weren't actually on guard duty were able to get inside the guard-line without the officers noticing and bring out pieces of burnt silk and broken aluminium, to flog it to the Cockneys. You nipped in, got a piece, tucked it up your tunic and then broke it up into small pieces and sold it for about two bob a time. Sergeant Chiltern was in charge of us and he turned a blind eye. Major Francis was in command, but we easily dodged him.

We did two hours guard at a time and the field kitchen even cooked our Sunday dinner for us there. We had beef, roast potatoes and Yorkshire pudding. Some of the sightseers were envious! Some of them said, 'Your dinner smells good, Tommy!' They were starving. They'd been there for hours and hours, some of them, and all day more were arriving. It had been seen for thirty miles around and those that hadn't seen it for themselves had heard about it. It was a fantastic thing – so huge you wouldn't believe it. The wreckage stretched across two fields.

At five o'clock in the afternoon the troopers were relieved and rode back to camp. A fair quantity of Zeppelin wreckage went with them. It turned out to be an excellent investment.

1. The remains of the crew were buried on 27 September in Great Burstead Churchyard. The officiating clergyman felt it appropriate to change the words of the Burial Service from 'our brothers here departed', to 'these men here departed'.

The blacksmiths and the shoeing smiths, like Bert Williams, made the largest profits. As tradesmen they were quick to see the possibilities of exploiting this unexpected windfall and soon they were spending all their time off-duty – and a good deal of on-duty time too – in the Battalion forge, zealously engaged in the manufacture of souvenirs. The light aluminium was easily melted down to make crosses and medallions. As a finishing touch, Trooper Charlie Curtis, whose father worked as a typesetter on the *Daily Mirror*, obligingly got hold of some type. Business flourished. The boys raised their prices and began to take orders for identification discs and bracelets bearing the appropriate name and number and to embellish rings and medallions with the words: *Zeppelin Souvenir. Billericay. 24th September, 1916* stamped into the metal. They hammered it very thin so that it went a long way and they were rich for months.

The 24th had also been an exciting night at West Mersea where the crew of a Zeppelin had, with some difficulty, been captured alive. It was the crew, rather than the captors, who had experienced the difficulty. They hammered on the door of a nearby farmer who was still in such a state of shock at the sight of the monster Zeppelin descending almost in his farmyard that he was too terrified to open up. When the Germans tired of knocking and threw stones at his bedroom window, accidentally breaking it in their anxiety to surrender, it merely reinforced the farmer in his opinion that the beastly Huns were bent on some fresh atrocity. His relief was considerable when he heard them march off towards the village, though he was not reassured by the sound of a salvo of shots as they emptied their pistols towards the sky before tossing them into the undergrowth at the side of the lane. But the prisoners gave no trouble. They allowed themselves to be escorted to the Police Station and accepted cups of tea while awaiting the arrival of a military escort. The Commander, in excellent English, asked politely to be escorted to the Post Office in order to telephone the Dutch Embassy in London who would let his wife know that he was safe. Reporters had quickly arrived on the scene and the next day's newspapers made much of this piece of cheek – typical, they insinuated, of 'Hun arrogance'.

2 MORE ZEPPELINS DOWN, trumpeted the *Daily Mail* in inch-high letters. The *Continental Daily Mail* copied the headlines plus four pages of coverage and carried the news to France.

Three weeks after his experience at Thiepval with the West Yorks on 3 September, Arthur Wilson was at the Base in hospital and he was having a painful time. He had been wounded by a chance shell and wounded in an awkward place. Now the pleasure of being in a real bed, the

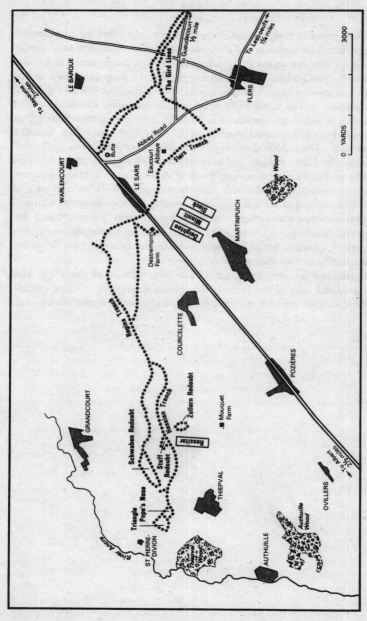

The October Fighting

relief of being in hospital and out of the line, was offset by considerable discomfort. His stomach was distended, his bladder was bursting and he could do nothing about it. It was hell. That morning Sister had come down the ward with a catheter in her hand and a purposeful look in her eye. 'Just another hour!' Wilson begged. Sister relented. 'One hour then, Mr Wilson, and then we really must use the catheter.' Ten minutes had ticked past when the newspapers arrived. Heedless of the dignity that hospital protocol dictated should prevail in an officers' ward, a VAD burst through the door shrieking, 'Two Zeppelins shot down last night!' Wilson's bed was nearest. She brandished the newspaper under his nose and he grabbed it. As he read, he became aware of a warm moist sensation which had nothing to do with excitement, and it went on and on and on. The nurses roared with laughter, produced clean pyjamas, changed the sheets without complaint and teased him without mercy. After a few days the joke began to wear thin. Every nurse who presented him with a bottle or a bedpan felt obliged to remark encouragingly, 'Two Zeppelins brought down, Mr Wilson!'

It was not the only good news. The same edition of the *Daily Mail* reported that Morval and Lesboeufs had been captured. Next day, eighty-eight days after the first attempt, they would at last conquer Thiepval.

Chapter 23

The Germans fought to the death for Thiepval – for every inch of trench dug deep through the pulverized rubble, for every strongpoint hidden in the old vaults and cellars, for every gallery and dugout burrowed into the chalk. One by one they were overwhelmed. When night fell the few who were left were still fighting to retain a last foothold in the north-western corner of Thiepval village. The British infantry paused, drew breath and attacked again in the morning. Before the sun rose through the thick autumn mist, Thiepval was finally captured.

The Germans had been in possession for exactly two years. It was 27 September and, on just such a morning, through just such a mist, two years ago to the day, Boromée Vaquette drove his cows for the last time up the narrow road from Authuille to their pasture on the hump of the ridge above and never came back. It was two years since the villagers of Thiepval had peeped warily through neat cottage windows as German horsemen clattered through the village. Two years since German officers took up their quarters in its spacious château and, dining at a table heavy with the Comtesse de Bréda's china and silver, planned the disposition of their forces who, even as their officers savoured the old Count's best wine, were digging trenches across the meadows of Thiepval Ridge. Now nothing was left. Not a blade of grass. Not a tree. Not a bird. The roads and tracks had all but disappeared. Here and there on the site of the old village a line of brick-dust staining the cratered earth between the trenches hinted at a long-vanished row of cottages. The twisted fragment of a weather-vane, a few chips of brick marked the church; a scattering of jagged grey stones was all that remained of the château and, as far as the eye could see, the churned-up land was covered with the grey humped bodies of British and German dead.

In a terrible travesty of that other harvest-time two years and many lives ago, they looked like haycocks through the morning mist.

In the eighty-nine days since Thiepval had been first attacked, it was Kitchener's Army which had borne the brunt of the fighting on the Somme and it was not surprising that certain people in high places were beginning to question the rate at which the Empire was eating into the capital of its young manhood. In 1914 – in four months' fighting – there had been 90,000 casualties of whom more than 50,000 were killed or missing. That had put paid to the old Regular Army. In 1915, with its dreadful chronology of disaster – Neuve Chapelle, Aubers Ridge, Festubert, Ypres, Loos – the toll of casualties had mounted to 285,000, of whom 92,000 were killed or missing. That had put paid to most of the Reservists and Territorials and it needed no statistician to work out that the Somme Campaign was well on the way to putting paid to Kitchener's Army. Already, between July and September, more than 90,000 men had been killed and the medical records showed that 228,632 others had been sent, badly wounded, to the Base – just 4,000 fewer in three months than in the first sixteen months of the entire war.

For four months now the hotly-debated Military Service Act had been in force. By early next year the first batch of conscripts would be trained and ready for active service. How were they to be used? Among politicians high talk of 'victory' and 'breakthrough' began to give way to mutterings of 'attrition' and to doubts that the High Command of the Army should continue to be given a free hand to prosecute the war on the nation's behalf entirely as they saw fit and to dispose with such profligacy of its young men. It was an over-simplified view but, in some quarters, it was strongly felt – particularly among the cabal within the Cabinet itself which was now actively canvassing peace. Lloyd George was not among them. He had been a champion of conscription but he was not immune to doubt and, now that he was Secretary of State for War, he saw it as a duty to inform himself on matters which were believed by some to lie outside his province.

During the first half of September, Lloyd George had made an extended visit to France on what Haig described as 'a huge joy ride'. Haig looked askance at Lloyd George's untidy dress – the flowing, undisciplined locks, the long shapeless overcoat, the battered trilby hat, the artistic disarray of his floppy ties. He disapproved of Lloyd George's propensity for changing plans at the last minute, sneered at his willingness to be convivial with newspapermen and photographers, and was censorious about his unpunctuality. The Secretary of State spent a mere two days as Haig's guest at GHQ. He had spent five times as long as the guest of the French Army, talking his way along the French Front from Verdun to the Somme – and he had talked a little too much. Lloyd George liked talking to people. Since the start of the Somme Campaign he had gone out of his way to meet officers and men home on leave from the front and to sound out their opinions. But it was one thing to quiz the fighting men; it was quite another to invite General Foch to express his opinion of the performance of British Generals as a whole and of the Commander-in-Chief in particular, and to hint, moreover, that his own confidence in their ability was far from complete. As a high-ranking officer in the French Army, Foch was no stranger to interference by politicians. He was shocked at such a breach of protocol, discreetly replied that he 'had had no means of forming an opinion', and took the first opportunity of repeating this conversation to Sir Douglas Haig. Despite his disapproval of Lloyd George, Haig was genuinely astounded '. . . that a British minister could have been so ungentlemanly as to go to a foreigner and put such questions regarding his own subordinates'.

The Commander-in-Chief was rightly aggrieved, but his own ingrained gentlemanliness and phlegm, and a strong awareness of the importance of 'pulling together', decided him that the whole affair was best ignored. He had more than enough on his plate. Besides, even if they had not achieved the hoped-for breakthrough, the Army's achievements during the latter half of September had been considerable. On the 15th they had crushed the enemy's formidable second line. On the 18th they had captured the Quadrilateral. A week later they had secured Lesboeufs, Morval, Gueudecourt, and one last valley lay between them and the Transloy ridges that snaked round to Bapaume. The Germans had been forced to loosen their grip and retire from Combles. Now the bastion of Thiepval village had crumbled in the face of the British assault, and Mouquet Farm with it.

But although the Germans had been shrugged from the shoulder of the Thiepval Ridge they still held the crest, and the crest was crowned with formidable defences – Schwaben Redoubt, with Stuff Redoubt to the east of it and Zollern Redoubt between that and the Albert–Bapaume Road. The Canadians had pushed well up the road, beyond Courcelette. They were within sight of le Sars and they were almost halfway to Bapaume. It had taken the Army almost three months to get this far and the autumn was well advanced. They must make one last effort to gain the redoubts, to conquer the whole of the Thiepval Ridge with all its advantages of observation, to link up the line that ran along the high ground through Morval and Lesboeufs, through Gueudecourt and Martinpuich to Courcelette on the other side of the Albert–Bapaume road. The September weather had been mixed and could be expected to worsen at any moment. Before it did, there was one last chance – and it was almost a gamble – that they could make the breakthrough. The Commander-in-Chief was convinced that the enemy was almost at his last gasp, that his casualties had been enormous, that his reserves were few, that his morale was quite possibly about to crack.

Along the straggling line of advance between Thiepval Wood and the Albert–Bapaume road the situation was confused and the Signallers were having the worst of it. General Gough, in command of the attack, heard disturbingly conflicting reports and often, by the time a runner had managed to get back through the bombardment with news of an advance made or an objective captured, the fortunes of the troops had been reversed by a German counter-attack. Shells damaged signal lines as soon as they were laid and it was up to the Signallers to mend them and to carry the line forward over the captured ground. Eric Rossiter was not aware that he was performing a personal service for General Gough. He only knew that he was somewhere in the chaos of the thundering battle, that Mouquet Farm was behind him, that Hessian Trench was somewhere out in front and that somehow the cable had to be got up to it. Not far to his left the fighting sounded disconcertingly close, for the 11th Division, also acting under General Gough's instructions, was trying to 'clear up the situation' at Stuff Redoubt. They would finally clear it up on 14 October.

Corporal Eric Rossiter, MM, 7th Canadian Infantry Battalion

Until that moment I'd always considered myself to be a lucky soldier. I'd been at the Signals Headquarters at Ypres the year before, so I'd missed that horrible business when the Germans attacked with gas and the Canadians had to cover up. I'd been in and out of the line on the Somme and never got a scratch. I nearly got it another time at Ypres when the Germans blew a mine right underneath us. We lost seventeen guys, but I wasn't touched. Then we came down to the Somme and this was my second stint in the front line. We'd been out on so-called rest, on fatigues all the time carrying sandbags of rations and supplies up to Pozières and, even then, I'd had a lucky escape just the week before. We were going up in single file in a carrying party and there was a fellow in front of me carrying a sandbag of Mills bombs. A pin in one of the bombs must have worked loose, because suddenly the whole lot went up. It killed and wounded a lot of men. I was only seven or eight yards back, but I never got a scratch.

That night, I suddenly had the feeling that my luck was going to run out. It was the toughest job I'd had. My pal, Jimmy Leaken, and I had to lay a line up from Battalion Headquarters to Hessian Trench. We only had a single Company there, so we didn't have much of a hold on it and it was touch and go if the guys could hang on. We tried to keep in the communication trench as far as we could go but it was so blown in by shellfire that we had to get out in the open. Imagine laying these goddam wires in the daylight, diving from shell-hole to shell-hole and dashing out when the coast seemed to be a bit clear. I was shaking, absolutely.

We made a dash and jumped into one shell-hole and there were five Canadians lying dead there. Jesus! It gave me a fright. Something flashed into my mind that I'd completely forgotten about. I had an uncle who'd dabbled in palmistry and years ago he'd read my hand. He said, 'You're going to get killed before you're twenty years old.' It never hit me till then. There I was, lying there in that shell-hole with those five dead Canadians and I thought, 'Jesus! I've only got four days to go!' It was no comforting thought.

Beyond the Canadians, across the Albert–Bapaume road, Ernest Deighton, now recovered from his wounds and his ordeal at the Leipzig Redoubt on the First of July, was back with the 8th King's Own Yorkshire Light Infantry, but he hardly recognized it as the same Battalion. Most of the new men were not even Yorkshiremen. There were Northumberlands, there were men from the Durham Light Infantry, there were some from the King's Royal Rifle Corps and there was even a bunch of Scots of the Argyll and Sutherland Highlanders. He looked in vain for familiar faces but, like familiar landmarks, there were few to be seen. To crown the confusion the Brigade was no longer apprenticed to the 8th Division but back again with the 23rd and occupying a newly-captured trench on the far side of Martinpuich. An abandoned tank was inextricably ditched half in, half out of the trench, blocking it so effectively that some unfortunates whose positions were on the other side had been obliged to leave the trench and run the gauntlet of the skyline in order to reach them.

Corporal Bernard Minnitt, MC, MM, 11th Btn., The Nottinghamshire and Derbyshire Regiment (The Sherwood Foresters), 70th Brigade, 23rd Division

It was one of the best trenches imaginable – well buttressed, with fine solid fire-steps and beautifully clean deep dugouts. It was pretty evident that the enemy had panicked and left in a hurry and it was probably the tank coming over the hilltop just a few yards away that had put the breeze up them. They could have taken their time if they'd known that the tank's engine was about to give out! There was no sign of any troops in the trench, though it made a sharp turn and appeared to wind away to our right, so we weren't sure if we were alone. To be on the safe side, Lieutenant Lacey strolled up to me and said quite casually, 'Come on, Corporal, let's go for a walk.' I picked up my rifle and we went off down that trench as if we were going for a walk along a promenade. We walked what seemed like half a mile and saw nothing and heard nothing – for which yours truly was really grateful!

Late in the evening I was told to take a fighting patrol of twenty men and go with Lieutenant Benton of B Company on another exploration down the trench. This time we were to go further and try to make contact with another division who someone had a half idea was occupying the same trench about a mile away. I was at the front of the party with my rifle loaded and very cautiously I kept climbing up on the fire-step and looking over the top. I'd taken my bayonet off, because it was very awkward in getting round the trench corners. I pushed the safety catch of my rifle forward and stopped every time we came to the corner of a bay and looked round very carefully before going on to the next. Then a Very light burst just as I was looking round the corner ahead – and there was a face looking back at the other end of the bay!

Lieutenant Benton was just at my back and he whispered, 'Challenge them.' So I said, 'Halt! Who goes there?' There was no reply. I tried again, 'Halt! Who goes there?' Still no reply. Then one of the men behind shouted, 'If you fellows don't reply we'll throw this bloody bomb among you!' Someone shouted back, 'We're the 5th Northants.' What a relief! I walked on round the corner and met this chap halfway along the traverse. It was too dark to tell from the shape of his tin hat if he was English or German but the gleam of his bayonet was at the high port position, above my head and I had my loaded rifle pointed towards him, so it seemed all right. Then a very windy voice behind me shouted, 'Look out, Corporal. They're Boches! The 5th Battalion's a training battalion!'

Then things started happening. The man facing me took a step backwards to bring his bayonet down six inches from my stomach. I knocked it away just as he fired and I heard someone behind me fall with a groan. I fired back, went down on one knee to make a smaller target and reloaded just as a Very light showed up the trench. There was no one in front of me. They had backed round the corner and, when I looked behind me, my 'fighting patrol' had disappeared except for the man who had been hit. He was groaning on the ground and I knew I couldn't move him without help. I dodged back two or three bays, thinking the patrol had moved back for shelter, when someone came jumping over the top of the trench from the direction of the enemy and he shouted, 'Is that you, Corporal?' He was just in time to stop me from shooting him! I said, 'Come and give me a hand. Someone's hurt. Where are the others?' He said, 'They all skedaddled so fast that they knocked the rifle out of my hands and broke my thumb. I can't lift anything.'

We had to leave the wounded man and go back for help. When we got to our sector there was great excitement. The patrol had come rushing in and told the Colonel that we'd run into a crowd of Germans, Lieutenant Benton and Corporal Minnitt were killed and Private Green was missing. They were standing by for an attack when we got there! Dawn was breaking by the time I got back with a stretcher-party to the wounded man. It was Lieutenant Benton and by then he was dead.

It was an awful business – a complete shambles. I was very upset about it and I made it my business to get hold of three men of the patrol we'd clashed with. They were from the 12th Durhams, in our own Brigade, but they hardly knew who they were themselves. They'd joined the Battalion with a new draft a few days before and the man who was out in front as number one bayonet man was on his first patrol and scared stiff. When we'd challenged them everything had gone out of his head but the title of his training battalion in England. He was very down in the mouth over the death of Lieutenant Benton. I told him not to blame himself. It was the fortune of war.

When daylight came, we could see that during the night an assembly trench had been dug at right angles to our old position. It was directly facing the Germans' line where they were dug in in the village of le Sars and our job was to shift them out of it. About half-past twelve we got orders to pack up and move into the assembly trench and keep our heads well down until Zero.

Ernest Deighton was one of the two hundred men who had dug the assembly trench in the night and now he too was crouched in it waiting with the first wave of the 8th King's Own Yorkshire Light Infantry for Zero. Unlike most of the Battalion, Deighton's platoon had lunched after a fashion. A shell exploding in the ragged field behind had fortuitously dug up some potatoes and showered them into the trench along with a fountain of earth. Hardly troubling to clean them, the boys had eaten them like savages. Now, as they waited for the off, the raw potatoes lay heavy on Deighton's stomach. He still had vivid memories of the nightmare of July and the long solitary wait in his sniper's post in No Man's Land. He was now a Lewis-gunner. Charging into a fight with a heavy machine-gun on your shoulder was no joke but at least the course at the

Machine-Gun School had kept him out of the line for a while. For Minnitt waiting fifty yards away, it would be the first time over the top.

Corporal Bernard Minnitt, MC, MM, 11th Btn., The Nottinghamshire and Derbyshire Regiment (The Sherwood Foresters), 70th Brigade, 23rd Division

My position was on the extreme right, next to Lieutenant Coates from Nottingham. As we were on the top of the slope, we could see all the men of the Battalion and they were all looking in our direction for the signal to go. It was a bright sunny day and the whole outlook seemed unreal to me. Suddenly, with one movement, all the bayonets flashed in the sun as the men fixed them on their rifles. Mr Coates' watch showed ten seconds to go, then five, four, three, two, one – then up went his arm and the Battalion went over the top like one man and off at the double into No Man's Land. I was so fascinated at the sight of it all that I suddenly came to my senses and realized that I was still standing there and Lieutenant Coates was thirty yards in front of me. I pulled myself together and jumped over and, just as I did, it seemed as if all hell was suddenly let loose. Every Gunner behind us must have had their fingers itching to fire and thousands of shells started screaming over our heads, firing the creeping barrage and four hundred yards away Jerry's trenches disappeared in smoke and explosions.

I came to a large shell-hole with half a dozen of our fellows in it, scared stiff and sheltering. I ordered them out and rushed on, making sure they came with me, and we came to the one gap in the enemy's barbed wire that seemed to have been broken by our shell-fire. We doubled through it and fanned out again and went on to the German trench. We started taking prisoners right away, and we could see other Germans hopping it, back to their next trench. We'd been given four minutes to get to the first trench, two minutes to clear it and then to move on to number two, but the Germans were obviously so surprised and stunned by our barrage that we jumped the first trench and went straight on to the next and started to clear that and dig ourselves in. We were so far ahead of ourselves that the barrage hadn't lifted past the last trench. Unfortunately we had to put up with being shelled by some of our own missiles before it did lift.

Private Ernest Deighton, No. 25884, 8th Btn., King's Own Yorkshire Light Infantry

My objective was Destremont Farm, just this side of le Sars. We had to pass to the right of it, but I never got any distance! I went over with my whole Lewis-gun section – eight trained gunners and eight reserves, because I was learning them the job. They were carrying extra ammunition and the idea was that if I got hit they would take over the gun. But we all got hit. I lost the lot! The shell hit us all.

We'd just got set up in a shell-hole and I'd started firing the gun when this shell came, and I don't know if it was ours or theirs. That was the last I knew. When I come round I was still in the same position but all I could see was part of the Lewis-gun butt against my face on the side of the shell-hole. Where the rest of the Lewis-gun had gone, I don't know, and there was no sign of any of my section either. I never saw any of them again.

I don't know how long I was knocked out cold. They were still banging away when I came round and my leg was all anyhow and covered with blood. I took my puttee off the other leg and grabbed the shattered one and straightened it and wrapped my puttee round it. Then I pushed in my entrenching tool and turned it round like a tourniquet to stop it bleeding and I reckon that's what saved my life. Then I started to crawl back to the trench the best road I could. It was dark by then, so I couldn't see much and I fell into the trench all anyhow and my legs fell in after me. The stretcher-bearers picked me up straight away and put me on a stretcher and they shoved me for shelter underneath this knocked-out tank that was half over our trench and I stopped there till they were able to carry me down, right the way through to the dressing station under the ruins of the church at Contalmaison. It was a hell of a journey and I was in agony, for the numbness had worn off. My knee was shattered and my whole leg was burning. But I knew I was on my way to Blighty. I'd a fair idea I was on my way out of the war.

But Deighton's Battalion had managed to join hands with the Canadians north of Destremont Farm across the Bapaume road. The Brigade as a whole had taken the first three lines of trenches, but they had not managed to get into le Sars. Later that night the boys were relieved. It had started to rain and the Germans, well aware that troops would be on the move, bombarded the tracks with tear-gas. The new drafts, who now outnumbered the old hands in most battalions, were not familiar with the soft plopping of the gas shells and, by the time the order was passed to don gas helmets, most had received a generous dose. Rain beating on the outside of their goggles and eyes streaming within, did not add joy to the journey.

It rained hard for the next four days. The mud, which had been bad enough after the changeable weather of September, turned to mire. The broken land, raked and cratered by a thousand bombardments, trampled by regiments of feet, scarred and rutted by a million wheels creaking under heavy loads of ammunition and supplies, cut to its chalky bone by the thunderous passage of countless guns, mashed to a porridge by the monstrous weight of the tanks, now sank beneath the lashing rain into a viscous swamp. It engulfed every landmark, every duckboard track, every gun site; it engulfed the bodies of the dead and sucked at the bodies of the living as if to engulf them too. The trenches crumbled and dissolved into runnels of liquid mud that streamed into dugouts and rose in the trenches to the depth of a man's thigh.

Mud. A hundred years earlier, Napoleon's Army, floundering in its glutinous grip, had called it 'the sixth element'. Now, on the Somme, every relief resembled the Retreat from Moscow. Now it took two days to travel from reserve lines to the front through a succession of miserable staging posts, miscalled camps, where the troops could shiver for an hour or two beneath flapping tarpaulins before shouldering mud-encrusted rifles and sloshing on through the waste. Every Battalion on the move left the smell of sodden khaki in its wake. Even the metalled roads – the arteries of the battlefield, the lifelines of supply – were coated with a layer of mud two inches deep, despite the efforts of an army of Pioneers, equipped with heavy brooms and scrapers, to keep them clear. Lorries skidded and gave up the ghost; wagons floundered and sank; for hours at a time traffic ground to a halt and even when it managed to keep going, found no feature or landmark to guide it.

Corporal J. Pincombe, No. 40045, 1st Btn., Queen's Westminster Rifles, 56th Division

A convoy started out on the Somme with the hope of a quiet trip, but each one was an adventure. My job was to take up the Battalion stores – food and, most important, water. By October the conditions had got so bad that we could get nowhere near the line with a limber and so the ration parties from the Battalion had to come down further and further to meet us and carry the stuff back in sandbags. We made the sandbags up at the transport lines – so many to each Company, and the water we poured into old petrol cans. That was an awkward load to carry. The men hated it. It was a terrible job struggling back through the muck with a heavy petrol can of water in each hand and your rifle over your shoulder and the mud two or three feet thick.

On this particular night the battalion rendezvous was at Ginchy. I knew the ration party would be waiting and I knew I was late but I simply couldn't find it in the dusk and the mist. Then, out of the dark, in the flash of the guns I saw a battalion straggling along – a big bunch of soldiers all looking exactly the same in tin hats and capes, and I stopped the limber and shouted, 'Hey! Where's Ginchy, can you tell me?' A Sergeant stopped and came over to me. He said, 'Do you see those two bricks? Well, that's Ginchy!'

Sergeant George Butler, 12th Machine Gun Coy., 4th Division

Sometimes the supplies never came up at all – especially if you weren't attached to a big unit, as we weren't. A guide met us and took us to our positions in a cemetery and, when we got there, there were as many dead on top of the ground as underneath it. We were supposed to be relieving a four-gun platoon and there was just one gun and five men out of a platoon of thirty-odd left. There was no shelter anywhere, only shell-holes. The people we were relieving were glad to be off. They just said, 'There's the front. Fritz attacks with machine-gun fire night and morning.'

It had taken us a long time to get up to the line at Lesboeufs. We walked all the way, through thousands and thousands of shell-holes, rim to rim. Every time you put a foot forward you sank, and you were sinking into a mass of dead as well as mud, because there weren't enough people to collect the bodies in.

We had nothing to eat for three days – no food! Of course, all the time we were under shellfire and that's why they couldn't get the supplies up. We lost three guns and more than a dozen men. Eventually my gun was the only one left. I sent the rest of the fellows off, crawling round the dead looking for food and water and ammunition off dead machine-gun teams. What with this collecting ammunition and running from one shell-hole and one body to another one, we lost a devil of a lot more men, but we collected the best part of seven or eight thousand rounds of ammunition off the dead.

We were in a devil of a state by the time we got to the fifth night. We were starving, nothing to drink or any damned thing and lying there in all the slush in that cemetery. So I thought it out. I decided that we'd fire all the ammunition we had into No Man's Land. We couldn't see the Germans. You could see odd parties when the flares went up, that was all. But we fired off all these guns – I was practically buried in empties when we'd finished. When I'd fired off the last round I said to my men, 'Pick up your kit. We're off out.' I knew I could be shot for it, but I couldn't see the sense in staying. We waded back through the mud and eventually we hit the duckboard track. We'd only gone down it about two hundred yards when we met a party coming up. It was our relief! There was an officer with them, but he said nothing. He probably thought I'd got the order from elsewhere, but I knew myself I was cutting things a bit thin.

Private J. L. Bouch, No. 11776, 1st Btn., Coldstream Guards

We set off. A ghastly night. We followed this line, everybody carrying something and we fell and floundered. There was a fellow who had come to join us and he was a baker and he was a strong man. He could do fifty press ups on his thumbs because he had very strong hands with kneading the dough – a fair, tall chap, very strong. His name was Howarth and we called him Snowball because of his white hair. He went down in the mud. He says, 'It's no good, I can't get up. I can't get up, leave me, leave me here,' and I went to him and I got hold of him. I said, 'I'll kick your bloody guts out if you don't get up,' and he got up and off we went. We came to a sunken road, narrow and fairly steep at the sides. It had been raining and we slithered down to the bottom without any bother. Then we had to get up the other side. Do you think we could get up? No matter how we clawed we just kept slipping back. I threw my can of water up first of all and my rifle and I scrambled and scraped and dug my way up this bank and eventually I managed to get to the top and pulled the others up and we went across to this post that we were relieving.

You couldn't imagine such a shambles. It was a machine-gun post. They would be a machine-gun detachment and possibly twenty men, and it was a round emplacement and it was a shambles of mud and old equipment and rubbish. You couldn't sit down. You sank in the mud. I don't think there would be three rifles that would have fired because you see we'd gone in and out the mud, and down in the mud and some had got it in the barrel and others had all their mechanism covered in mud. Anyhow, the amazing thing was that the following morning in front of us we could see fairly open ground sloping down and no sign of the Germans at all. We'd no rations. I think the only thing we'd got was this can of water, because the rations that we were carrying had gone into the mud. We were a hundred per cent miserable. We had a Sergeant named Dukes and, after a couple of days of this, he said, 'I'm going back to tell them we've got to be relieved,' and he went back and they sent a relief for us and out we went.

When we came out of the line, I didn't appear to be walking on my feet at all. I was walking on my knees. We went into some rest huts and took off our boots and clothing and you were given a ration of tea and rum and you went to sleep like a log and, when I woke up in the morning, my feet were just like huge bladders of lard with the toes sticking out at the top, no feeling at all. Trench feet. No excuse for it. You weren't supposed to have it but, there is was, you got it. All of us had it.

Private Arthur Hales, No. 302, 2nd/2nd London Field Ambulance

On our second night on the Somme the stretcher-bearers were called out and marched off in pitchy darkness, through mud and pouring rain, blindly following an officer. How he found his way is a marvel to me for, even if there had been any landmarks, it would have been impossible to find them on such a night. After about an hour, we struck a surfaced road which made the marching, if anything, more difficult. We were split up and forced through narrow passages between the waggons, up to our eyes in mud. The only objects we could see in the blackness were the roadway filled with traffic and the flashing of the guns nearby. The officer had to ask the way and then we set off again – not on the road, but across a trackless main of mud, down a slope. It was almost impossible to stand upright. Most of us did it on our hands and knees. All over the place were dumps of stretchers, ammunition boxes, shell cases and so on. We stopped at one heap of stretchers and were told that this was our 'station'. They said we could rest for a while before starting our stretcher-bearing stint. We were so dog-tired that we dropped on to the soaking stretchers to try to sleep for a while and forget our misery. Very soon we had to rouse when some stretcher cases arrived from some unknown place in the dark. Our job was to carry them over the sea of mud back to the road and the waggons. It took so long that it was dawn before we completed even the first journey.

Trooper Reg Lloyd, No. 1035, Cheshire Yeomanry (attached to 8th Btn., South Lancashire Regiment, 25th Division)

They were short of troops and no cavalry were wanted by then, so they dismounted us. It was a terrible come-down. To be turned into infantrymen, was like being pole-axed. Of course, we weren't very good at walking at the best of times, never mind in those conditions. We'd just arrived in France and they gave us a couple of weeks' infantry training at the Bull Ring until we were ready for the slaughterhouse. We went up to relieve the Canadians. We'd never seen anything like it. Going up through this area it was just as if an earthquake had been there. It was all mud and I was frightened to death. Eventually we came to a noticeboard. That's all. Just a noticeboard in among a bit of rubble. And the noticeboard said *Pozières*. That was all there was! Just a noticeboard that said *Pozières* to tell us where we were.

Gunner George Worsley, No. 690452, 2nd West Lancashire Brigade, Royal Field Artillery, 55th Division

We'd moved the gun-lines forward and the Headquarters, just behind the gun-line, were set up in some old deep German dugouts and the Germans started firing over gas shells. When a gas shell comes over it makes the same noise as a light shell but, instead of a bang, there's just a plop, although the impact moves the earth. You say, 'Thank goodness, that's a dud!' We got about five of these before we realized that they weren't duds. I said, 'Good Lord, our luck can't be as good as this! All these dud shells!' A couple more came and then we smelled the gas and put our gas masks on. The Germans simply saturated us with gas shells – they reckoned later there must have been more than twenty thousand, trying to knock the gun-lines out and knock out the reserves coming up. We had those gas masks on for twenty-four hours. You can't describe how uncomfortable they are, because they make you feel as if you're choking. There's a grip that holds your nose tightly and you have to breathe through the mouth, through a tube you hold between clenched teeth. Your mouth and throat get unbearably dry.

The telephone lines were down in all the other dugouts so, after twenty-four hours of this, the Colonel came to my telephone to get through to General Headquarters fifteen miles behind. When he asked to speak to the General, some young cub at the other

end, said, 'I'm afraid you can't speak to the General. He's dining.'
Well, the Colonel absolutely howled down the phone. He said,
'Do you realize, young man, that's it's only by the grace of God
I'm speaking to you now? Get me the General at once!' So, after
quite a while, the General came to the phone and the Colonel
said, 'We've had our masks on for twenty-four hours. We can't
live here any longer. What must we do?' Well, the General gave
him orders to abandon the area. The whole Brigade moved out
and that full brigade of guns was left untended for forty-eight hours.

Two of us were ordered to stay to keep the telephone line open
and I was unfortunately one of them. What a night that was! The
dugout was about ten feet under the ground and we took turns
sleeping on the floor. In the early hours of the morning, it was my
turn to keep watch. Shells were coming over steadily and it was
freezing cold in there, with just a tiny dim light. This other chap
was snoring on the floor and I looked at the dugout entrance and
I noticed for the first time that there were five gas cylinders dumped
at it. I knew that, if one of those shells hit one of those cylinders,
we'd absolutely had it.

I'd had a long time in the line with just a few days out and my
nerves weren't too good. I never felt so alone in my life sitting in
that dim dugout and the shells falling all round and the sky flashing
and those five gas cylinders just outside the door. By and by I heard
a voice and it seemed to be coming from a long way away. It was
calling my name – 'George Worsley'. Then a long pause, and then,
'George Worsley. George Worsley.' I was absolutely terrified. I
was too terrified to answer. I thought I was having a hallucination.
So I kept mum. Next day, when the Brigade moved back to the
guns, I discovered that it was one of the chaps who'd been trying
to find me. They'd sent him back up with a message. He didn't
know which dugout I was in so he was going along the lot, dodging
the shells and calling my name all over the place. Down in the
dugout, his voice sounded so faint and ghostly that I thought my
hour had come!

October stormed towards the end of the month. On days when the rain
moved out, winter moved in. Hard night frosts laid a crackle of ice across
the swamps and in the morning the troops pitched forward to the attack
through frozen mud. The fighting went on. The redoubts fell. The Germans were driven from the crest of Thiepval Ridge. Le Sars was captured.

The month ended in a spate of torrential downpours and thunderstorms
so violent that they even out-thundered the guns.

Arthur Agius trudged thankfully out of the line, hitched a lift to Amiens and caught the leave train from the railhead to Boulogne. It was a stormy crossing, but the sun shone on his wedding day, though a blustery wind swept the bride's veil into a tangle that was hard to undo. Agius looked exceedingly smart in a dapper new uniform specially purchased for the occasion. Everyone agreed that it was a wonderful wedding. There was time for a three-day honeymoon in Eastbourne before the bridegroom returned to France to rejoin his Battalion in the trackless swamps in front of Gueudecourt and Lesboeufs, facing the Germans on the Transloy ridges across the valley.

Wallowing in the mud of the front line Fritz was as cold, as miserable, as muddy and despairing as any Tommy. But he suffered less from shortage of ammunition; he was better provisioned; his supplies had a better chance of getting through. Unlike their unfortunate counterparts, German soldiers were not obliged to struggle over six exhausting miles of battered desolation to reach the firing line. There was shelter close behind them. There were usable roads that ran right up to communication trenches, and a network of light-gauge railways to ease the transport of troops and supplies.

But Sir Douglas Haig was right in deducing that the Germans were shaken by the wearing fighting of the past months. He was right in his belief that they were over-stretched and that they were rethinking their position – but they were not thinking of surrender. They were planning to shorten their line.

Three days before the fall of Thiepval, with infinite secrecy, the Germans had put their plans in hand, and miles behind the front, from Arras to the Somme, even as the British Command was planning the next series of attacks that would bring them closer to Bapaume, German engineers were reconnoitring fresh ground and plotting positions of tactical advantage. Early in November they began to draw up blue-prints for a new line of defence – a line so strong, so formidable and so impregnable that, by comparison, their citadel on the Somme had been as fragile as a child's toy fort. In honour of the Wagnerian hero of German victories they code-named it 'The Siegfried Line'. When it was completed they would retire to it. For the winter they would stand where they were, ready to do battle if the British chose to fight the German Army as well as the elements. In the spring, if need be, they could toss them Bapaume, as they might toss a bone to a snarling dog.

Chapter 24

It was 11 November and the boys of the 13th Battalion, The Rifle Brigade, were back on the Somme and none too pleased to exchange the 'cushy' trenches at Calonne for the bleak chill of canvas huts in the muddy environs of Puchevillers. At Calonne the British line ran through the abandoned houses of the village and, although they were something of a shambles, the cellars at least were habitable. Furnished with household goods salvaged from the wreckage of the upper storeys, they made luxurious dugouts. In one section of the line, a soldier could literally step down from the fire-step into a front parlour, complete with sofa, table and chairs, and Joe Hoyles, sent with four others to man an observation post, was delighted to find that some previous occupant had had the foresight to purloin real beds to furnish the cellar beneath it. It was sufficient of an event to warrant a place in his diary: 'I've had the pleasure of laying on something soft for the first time out here!'

By contrast Puchevillers was unanimously voted the most filthy and desolate spot in France, and there they had spent a miserable week, in miserable weather, rehearsing yet again for battle, and that afternoon they had lost the Colonel. Prideaux-Brune had been playing full-back for the Officers against the Other Ranks in a game of rugby organized 'to keep the lads amused' when he was tackled and brought down by Corporal Percy Eaton. It was generally felt that Eaton might have chosen a more convenient time than the eve of a battle to break the Commanding Officer's collar bone.

Joe Hoyles, Tommy Bennett and two other sergeants had pulled rank and had succeeded in getting a canvas hut to themselves. It was freezing cold but, with the help of a little rum purloined from the communal jar, they were managing to pass the evening enjoyably. They fancied themselves as singers and Tommy Bennett of the Welsh contingent undeniably had a fine tenor voice. He sang the harmony for an old favourite.

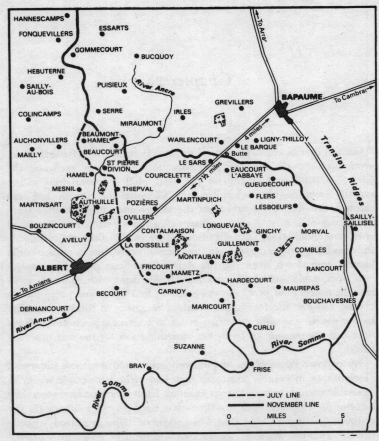

The Line at the end of the fighting in November

> *Just a song at twilight when the lights are low*
> *And the flickering shadows softly come and go.*
> *Though your hearts be weary, sad the day and long,*
> *Still to us at twilight comes love's old song,*
> *Comes love's old, sweet song.*

Under the circumstances, the choice was, to say the least, unusual. But who cared?

The 13th Battalion was temporarily attached to the 63rd Division, now encamped in similarly nasty conditions in the shelter of the Mesnil Ridge as they waited to move up the line. It was more than two years since they had fought at Antwerp in a vain attempt to staunch the flow of the German Army through Belgium; they had spent most of 1915 fighting the Turks in Gallipoli and for eight months now they had been in action in France. In spite of this imposing military record, the men of the 63rd Division did not regard themselves as soldiers. Their Division was the Royal Naval Division and no amount of rifle toting, nor even the indignity of the khaki uniforms and tin hats which the Army now insisted on their wearing, would make them into anything but sailors. Those officers who had gone forward to reconnoitre up the flooded valley of the Ancre saw the irony behind the Army's decision to put the Naval Division in to attack it. It was unfortunate that they had not gone so far as to supply them with boats.

They were a mixed bunch of pre-war naval reservists from seaports round the coast of Britain who had been mildly surprised, when King and Country called them up before even the Army was mobilized, that the mighty British Navy had insufficient ships for them to man and that they had been transmogrified into land-lubber forces of the British Army instead. But God help the British Army if it tried to deprive them of their jealously guarded naval traditions. God help the War Office pundit who suggested changing commanders into colonels, petty officers into sergeants, able seamen into privates, or who suggested, in order to fit in with the Army's arithmetical calculations, that battalions should give up such ringing titles as Howe, Hood, Drake, Nelson, Anson, in exchange for mere numbers. Altogether the Royal Naval Division considered itself to be something special and a cut above mere soldiers with their kow-towing khaki discipline. Their own disciplinary structure, they were happy to say, was as free and easy as their *esprit de corps* was strong. They had recently fallen foul of their new Divisional General who had been sent to replace their own Commander, General Paris, whose leg had been severed by a shell. General Paris was of the well-publicized opinion that 'man for man and officer for officer the Naval Division is incomparably better than nine-tenths of the divisions in France'. His successor, none other than General Shute, did not share this opinion and the antipathy was mutual. The qualities of discipline and leadership, which had so excited Alex Paterson's admiration when he had guided the General into No Man's Land in front of Guillemont, were not appreciated by the Royal Naval Division.

Sub-Lieutenant Jeremy Bentham, Hood Btn., Royal Naval Division

General Shute had no time for the Royal Naval Division and we
had no time for him. The first thing he did was to insist that all
NCOs should wear army rank on one sleeve as well as their naval
rank on the other. They loathed that!

Another bee in his bonnet was Salvage. Actually that's what got
Hall out of trouble. This chap had gone into a dugout and left his
rifle leaning against the wall. Naturally his rifle was absolutely filthy,
because we didn't go in a great deal for spit and polish in our
Division. Along came Shute and spotted this dirty old rifle and
picked it up, bellowing what a disgrace it was and demanding
to know who it belonged to. Of course it was Hall's! But he
had great presence of mind and, knowing how keen Shute was
about salvage, he said, quick as a flash, that it was one he had
picked up in No Man's Land the night before! Shute was pleased
as punch and said, 'Well done!' We enjoyed a good laugh over
that.

*Sub-Lieutenant William Marlow, MC (RNVR), Howe Btn., Royal
Naval Division*

Shute was a proper Army bloke. He never really liked this naval
tradition stuff and when he took over he came and inspected us.
We'd only just gone into the line in the Souchez Sector and we'd
taken it over from the Portuguese. Of course, it was in a bloody
mess, but we hadn't had time to clear it up or anything. Well,
Shute was furious. He went back and wrote an absolute stinker
about the disgusting state of our trenches and really created a most
awful fuss. Alan Herbert was an officer in the Royal Naval Division
– A. P. Herbert, who later became very well known as a writer.
He wrote a poem about this episode, well it was a song really, and
it started off in the wardroom and then it went right down through
all the ranks. It was absolutely filthy!

> *The General inspecting the trenches*
> *exclaimed with a horrified shout,*
> *'I refuse to command a Division*
> *Which leaves its excreta about.'*
>
> *But nobody took any notice*
> *No one was prepared to refute,*

That the presence of shit was congenial
Compared with the presence of Shute.

And certain responsible critics
Made haste to reply to his words
Observing that his Staff advisers
Consisted entirely of turds.

For shit may be shot at odd corners
And paper supplied there to suit,
But a shit would be shot without mourners
If somebody shot that shit Shute.

That song didn't just go through the whole of the Royal Naval Division – it went through the whole of the Army!

But it was the sailors who sang it with particular relish. They sang it to the tune of *Wrap me up in my tarpaulin jacket* and thought it the last word in wit. Small groups of them were singing it now, under their breath, in defiance of the rule of silence as they made their way by various routes across the face of the Mesnil Ridge to assemble behind the line. The assaulting Battalions of the Division had been split up into small parties. Although the Thiepval Ridge, rearing up across the valley, was now in British hands, it was bright moonlight and who knew what unfriendly eyes were marking their passage?

Across the valley, across the heights beyond, across the Albert–Bapaume road where the 50th Division was in the line, Lieutenant Cecil Slack was far from happy about the full moon. Earlier in the day he had received an order which was unequivocal and also, in his opinion, bordered on insanity.

SECRET
TO: O.C. 'C' COMPANY

A series of strongposts is to be formed in advance (75 yards) of our front line tonight. Your Company will have to furnish them and make them. I shall require four posts of an Officer (or good N.C.O.) and 12 men each to go forward at dusk and dig themselves into strongposts by improving shell holes. These posts will work under your supervision and will be provided with a day's rations before dawn.

You had better come and see me at 3 p.m. re above.

W.T.W.

Slack was only too pleased to visit the Commanding Officer in his dugout. He knew that the order had come from Brigade. He also knew that it was suicide, and he challenged the Colonel accordingly.

'Does the General realize that there will be a full moon tonight, sir?'

There was a long pause before the Colonel replied. Then he looked Slack straight in the eye.

'The General is a very able soldier.'

Captain C. S. Slack, MC, 1st/4th Btn., East Yorkshire Regiment, 150th Brigade, 50th Division

A lot of these brainwaves were from people who didn't know what it was like to be in No Man's Land in broad daylight – and broad moonlight is as good as broad daylight. The idea was that, if the Germans made an attack – and they were expecting them to make an attack – there would be a post here, and a post there, to break it up. The Germans were supposed not to know that those four posts were there but you can see 150 yards in broad moonlight and it was a beautifully clear night. You could see everything. You could see your breath going up in front of you in steam. To go out in those conditions was utter suicide, but the General had ordered it, so that was that.

I picked up my first party. As soon as we got out through our own wire the bullets came. A man was killed next to me. We crawled from shell-hole to shell-hole and somehow or other we got to what I thought was a suitable shell-hole to be strengthened. I left my first party there in charge of a corporal and came back to take another party out. I was supposed to take them out seventy yards – and that would be about halfway across No Man's Land – but I didn't. I took them out maybe sixty yards. Then I went back and took the third party out and I had decided by then that I wasn't going to take them out so far. Another man was killed and all the time bullets were crashing round us. The Germans could see us as plain as daylight! Why more of us weren't hit I don't know, because we were being shot at all the time.

Another man was killed at the third post. I crawled back for the fourth party and, this time, I went out twenty yards and stopped.

They were in the line in front of the village of le Sars. It was a month since it had been captured but they had got no further. Just beyond the village the road to Bapaume ran down a gentle slope and, at the foot, where the land flattened out, a long mound of white chalk glistened in the moonlight, dominating the countryside like some cold evil eye. It was not surprising that the soldiers holding the line in front of le Sars were edgy, for the Germans had made a strongpoint of the Butte de Warlencourt. From its rearward slope it looked across to Eaucourt-l'Abbaye – once a farm on the site of an old abbey, now an outpost in the wasteland, captured at the cost of many lives. The Butte also overlooked the country road that once had ambled past on its way to Gueudecourt. It was held now by the Australians, back in the line and fighting for the Maze, the Gird lines, Grassy Lane. Despite their legendary toughness, the Aussies were suffering more acutely than anyone else from the damp and the mud and the chill of the bitter weather.

But the weather had changed with the full moon and, just as the Army Commanders had hoped, it had changed for the better. General Gough's Reserve Army – which, since 30 October, had been redesignated The Fifth Army – stood poised, ready for a battle which, with the season so far advanced, the Germans would scarcely be expecting. On 21 October the cavalry had moved back to winter billets. Shivering in the front line the infantry wished that they could do the same.

The heights of the Thiepval Ridge had been captured but deep in the sharp-cut valley, protected by their tenure of the high land across the river, the Germans still clung fast to St Pierre Divion and Grandcourt on its banks. They still held Beaucourt. They still held Beaumont Hamel and they still held Serre. They had settled down for the winter. One short sharp surprise knock now, when it was least expected, might easily accomplish great things.

Sir Douglas Haig had another reason for wishing to gamble on a late offensive. He had made it clear to General Gough, through his Chief of Staff, General Kiggell, that it should be mounted entirely at the General's own discretion; that, if the weather and conditions weighed unfavourably against the likelihood of success, he need not commit his Army and he was perfectly entitled to cancel the operation. But the weather had cleared up. It had not rained since the 8th. The 12th November dawned unseasonably bright and sunny. It was a perfect autumn day. The air was clear and the cold changed from bone-stiffening chill to a brisk, invigorating freshness that lifted the spirits. It had also, to some extent, dried out the ground. It was a fine day for a ride but the necessity for speedy action forced General Haig to travel by motor car to General Gough's headquarters at Toutencourt. He was anxious to have a private word.

The Commander-in-Chief did not retract the message which his Chief of Staff had passed to General Gough the previous day. General Gough still had a free hand. The final decision was still his. But Haig made it quite clear that the capture of Beaumont Hamel would be useful to him.

Three days hence, on 15 November, he would be conferring at Chantilly with the High Command of the French Army, and at that meeting future strategy would be decided. The French were cock-a-hoop. At long last the tide had turned at Verdun. On 24 October the French Army had recaptured its mighty forts and, if the Germans were not precisely on the run, the initiative had passed decisively to the French. But they could not afford to relax. The enemy must be kept occupied here in the west to prevent him from switching any of his manpower to reinforce his position at Verdun and consequently Marshal Joffre was pressing the British to continue their attacks.

But Haig was worried about his own manpower. The main purpose of the Chantilly Conference was to agree on joint plans for a Spring Offensive. The British Army had informed the Government that it would require 350,000 men as reinforcements. Even if they got them all (which, on past performance, seemed unlikely) Haig was uneasy and doubtful if such a number of new recruits could be trained to full fighting-pitch before he was forced to commit them alongside the French in the spring.

He chatted about these matters to General Gough. It was obvious to both men that Beaumont Hamel, if it could be easily captured, would serve to keep the French quiet and would undoubtedly act in the British interest at the Chantilly Conference. One daring thrust, now that the weather was on their side, might achieve much.

It was a fine night, cloudless and frosty as the troops assembled for the assault. Between Serre and the Ancre they were waiting in precisely the same positions as on the eve of 1 July. Only the season had changed. Two thousand men of the Royal Naval Division were lying on the open ground in the trenches and ruins of the village of Hamel where Joe Murray's billet for the night was a groove of mud between two flooded shell-holes. The water quivered slightly with the vibration of the bombardment and, when it momentarily paused, they could hear steady firing from the German line, like the crackle of twigs in a bonfire, and the fire-cracking explosions of hand-grenades thrown haphazardly into the waterlogged mud in front of their wire. The Germans were uneasy. A major attack at this time of year seemed out of the question but, nevertheless, they had no doubt that something was afoot. The troops, lying out in the dank chill of the November night, dared not reply for fear of bringing the full force of the German artillery down on their tight-packed position.

The Hood Battalion was right down in the valley of the River Ancre – now less of a river than a lake of mud that seeped across the low ground to the foot of Thiepval ridge. Towards midnight haze gathered in the valley and thickened as it spread towards the slopes. The chill deepened. Soon the troops waiting for the assault were enveloped in rolling mist. In Hood Battalion, the Commanding Officer, Lieutenant-Commander Freyberg, taking advantage of its concealing folds, began to move among the lines of his battalion, stopping with a word of encouragement whenever a muffled cough suggested that men were awake. Spirits were not high. The previous evening the officers of B Company had organized a macabre sweepstake. They each wrote a personal cheque for five pounds payable 'to Bearer' and left them, with their kit, in charge of the Quartermaster. Those who survived tomorrow would cash the cheques of those who did not, and share the jackpot.

The 3rd Division was waiting to attack at Serre just as the Pals had waited four months and a half before. The line of attack would be the same, but there were two differences. This time the troops would have twice the number of guns to support them; and this time the ground was a quagmire of oozing mud that stretched back beyond the gun lines one thousand yards behind. The guns had been heaved up on to solid platforms of pit props to keep them from sinking into the swamp and, in the line, the troops crouched and shivered and tried to sleep to the murmur and thud of the pumps that were keeping the trenches comparatively clear of water.

In the White City in front of Beaumont Hamel they had been double-pumping for weeks now to keep the tunnels and trenches reasonably dry. The old tunnels had been refurbished; new ones had been dug; another mine had been laid and they would explode it at Zero under the old crater on the Hawthorn Ridge, for the Germans had re-fortified the redoubt that protected Beaumont Hamel in the cleft of the valley behind. Beaumont Hamel was the main objective – the prize of the battle, and the 51st Highland Division was ordered to take it. They were known to be 'bonny fighters'. They frequently practised by fighting each other. No one recalled the origins of the feud between the 6th and the 8th Battalions of the Argyll and Sutherland Highlanders but, after several *estaminets* had been wrecked in the course of wild rumpuses for which the Army was obliged to foot the bill, it had been generally recognized that, when the Division was out at rest, those in charge of the billeting arrangements of the three Brigades would be well advised to make sure that the 6th and the 8th Argylls were separated by a considerable distance. The 8th Argylls, who came from Argyllshire itself, were largely Gaelic speaking, and sneered at the idea that the 6th, who hailed from Paisley in Renfrewshire, should pass as Highlanders at all. Furthermore, the 8th Argylls considered the 6th to be undeservedly spoilt. Bell's, a local tobacco company, sent out a weekly present of twenty cigarettes per man, and they were vastly superior to the ration of issue cigarettes which came the way of the 8th Argylls. Local football clubs also sent cigarettes and supplied sports kit and equipment. The 6th Argylls never lacked whisky and the Paisley thread manufacturers, J. & P. Coates, who regarded the Battalion as their own, plied the men with comforts. The last straw was when the same firm, in the kindness of its heart, presented every officer with a breast-plate and every man with a heart-shaped mirror of polished steel to place in his breast-pocket as insurance against German bullets. The fact that the 8th Argylls taunted the 6th in Gaelic simply added fuel to the fire. None of the Paisley boys spoke a word of anything but English, but they found no difficulty in understanding the insulting tone of the Highlanders' remarks.

Matters had improved very slightly after the 6th Argylls came out of the Labyrinth in front of Arras with so many casualties that they were reinforced mainly by Englishmen, made into a Pioneer Battalion and transferred to another Division. Although Sergeant 'Wullie' Stevenson was an original member of the 6th Argylls (and of the Auldhouse football team which had joined up en masse), as a machine-gunner he had not suffered the indignity of being reduced with the rest of the Battalion to navvying. Now, in preparation for the battle, he checked and rechecked the four guns of his section and filled his water-bottle with rum against the exigencies of the day ahead. His orders were to make straight for Y Ravine.

The fog thickened. At 5.45 when the bombardment crashed out it was still black night. In order to keep the Germans guessing precisely where the attack would come, the guns opened up from Serre in the north to Lesboeufs in the south and the soldiers holding the muddy draggle of line in front of Lesboeufs and Gueudecourt stood up and cheered as the shells screamed over their heads to crash on the Transloy ridges, in an excess of pleasure that, for once, someone else was going over the top. Astride the Ancre, up the Beaumont Hamel valley, into the slough in front of Serre, the 5th Army went forward through thick swirling fog and were swallowed up.

Sergeant William Stevenson, DCM, MM, No. 3113, 6th Btn., Argyll & Sutherland Hdrs., 51st (Highland) Division

We came straight out of the White City. They put us in the tunnel the night before and in the morning they blew the top off it and the infantry went straight over. The machine-gunners and trench-mortar parties were the last to get out – right near the German lines. The bodies of our boys who'd gone over on 1 July were still lying there between the lines and the stink would have knocked you down. You can believe me or believe me not, but we got right into the German trenches – and there was nobody there! They were all still in their dugouts, because we shelled and knocked hell out of each other every morning and night with shell-fire anyway, and they just thought it was the usual thing and never even bothered to get out of their shelters. They never expected an attack in that weather.

I thought the place was very quiet and I said to Lance-Corporal Hopkins – he was an English boy, a Cockney – I said, 'Come on, Hoppy. You come on with me here. I don't like this!' We went away along the trench, a great wide trench and, as we went along, I heard voices and we listened and Hoppy says, 'They're Germans! I'll tell them to come up.' Well it took a bit of coaxing! They were down in the dugout and there were about twenty to thirty steps, but up they came eventually and all the boys gathered round to see what was going on. We took seventeen prisoners! I sent my batman, wee Hope, an Edinburgh fellow, away back with them to Headquarters. 'March the whole lot back,' I said to him. Lance-Corporal Robertson and myself went in the dugout and, the silliest thing was that there were one or two openings to it. The Germans could easily have got out of them.

We went along and searched and we got all their ammunition and their rifles and revolvers and other souvenirs (later we sold them to the transport boys and the ASC boys at the back!) and then we went up to the top of the hill and Y Ravine was down in front of us. They had this tunnel right along it and there was even electric light in the damned place. There were wire beds for the men to sleep in and everything you could think of. They had machine-gun emplacements and they had concrete emplacements and the tunnel was all linked up to them. No wonder our boys couldn't get into the front-line trenches in July! Beaumont Hamel was really a fortified place and they just couldn't take it.

I believe in other sectors they got it pretty badly but where we were our boys just went sailing through and we followed.

Stevenson was right in thinking that in other sectors things had not gone so well. On the left of Beaumont Hamel another battalion of Argylls lost half their force in their advance towards the same orchards, against the same machine-guns which had mown down the Hampshires on 1 July.

On the right, the Seaforths floundered and groped through the fog searching for gaps in the wire. In front of Serre the infantry waded through
mud, so deep, so heavy, so clinging that more than half of them were
bogged down before they had got halfway to the German trenches. Only
small groups of exhausted men ever succeeded in reaching them and,
when they did, their rifles were so useless, so clogged with mud, that
they were easy prey.

Slogging up the river valley, splaying out over the slopes of the Beaumont Hamel spur, Hood and Hawke Battalions, leading the advance of
the Royal Naval Division, had also run into trouble. To be more precise
they had run past it. Just over the brow, the Germans had well-concealed
strongpoints and unsuspected defensive positions and they were not
marked on the trench maps for the very good reason that no one knew
they were there.

*Able Bodied Seaman Joseph Murray, No. TZ.276, Hood Btn., 63rd
(Royal Naval) Division*

. . . It was very misty, a really wet mist. It wasn't a Scotch mist, it
was a double Scotch mist, nasty, wet and claggy. As soon as the
barrage opened the sky turned red – just like the ironworks at
home across the Derwent valley. When they were drawing their
furnaces you'd get a red glow, and that was the picture I saw
looking back over the lines at our own barrage. The whole sky
was lit up and you could *feel* the shells. You could actually feel the
damned things going over your head like a wind in the fog.

There were twelve or thirteen rows of barbed wire in front of
the first trench and when the bombardment goes into that, it's
supposed to cut it, but it doesn't destroy the wire, it builds it into
a bloody heap with gaps in it here and there and, when the enemy's
alive and awake to the idea that you're coming, they've got their
machine-guns trained on these gaps – therefore you get slaughtered.
But we got through it – some of us anyhow! There didn't seem
to be many of our chaps about as we pressed forward and entered
his second line. The Drakes and the Nelsons got all mixed up and,
on our left, they were all banging and crashing about and there
was terrible fire coming from this redoubt. It was a square of
trenches lined with men manning machine-guns – probably a hundred men in it – and it wasn't even touched by the artillery. How
they missed that, Lord only knows! We had terrible casualties.
When we got to the second line there were hardly any of us about.
We were supposed to rest there for forty minutes and the next lot

were supposed to go through us and take the Green Line – which was the station road. But they'd had such casualties that hardly any of them turned up, so instead of us resting there, we had to go on and *we* had to capture the Green Line. It was Freyberg who got us together and led us on, and there were all too few of us, believe me. But we went on and we captured the Green Line although there was nobody on our left at all by then . . .

Sub-Lieutenant Jeremy Bentham, B Coy., Hood Btn., 63rd (Royal Naval) Division

I had two men with me, two runners to take messages back to Battalion HQ, and my Petty Officer who was to take command of my platoon if I fell. We advanced quite steadily and went on to the Jerry front line and I found myself firing my revolver at anyone I saw emerging from the dugouts. There were plenty of them coming out and running! Unfortunately our 18-pounder guns had got so hot that their shells started falling short and one exploded quite near. The next thing I knew was that I was on the ground with all the chaps who were with me. I had been hit in my left thigh and couldn't walk or even hop. So there we lay while other men jumped over us on their way to catch up with the chaps who were still going forward. I did my best to try and bandage my leg – it was bleeding profusely – and the other men were doing the same, except for one who'd been killed. There was nothing I could do but wait for our surgeon, McCracken. He came along eventually and he bandaged us up as best he could under this terrible shellfire. He was laughing. I'll always remember him laughing as he poured iodine into my wound. 'This will stop you giggling in church!' he said. We settled down to wait for the stretcher-bearers but it was a long time before they came. We were there all day. There were hundreds of us lying there wounded.

Sub-Lieutenant William Marlow, MC, Howe Btn., 63rd (Royal Naval) Division

I hadn't been going half an hour when I was hit in the right wrist. It was my batman who saved me – Molly Milburn. His nickname was Molly. The trouble was that my wound had severed the main artery and I could easily have bled to death. Well, I don't even know how little Molly found me in the fog, but he did and he put a tourniquet on and stopped the flowing of the blood. I was right out for the count. Then he left me and had to go on, naturally. He was a good soldier.

The next thing I knew was that there was a whole load of German prisoners being brought down with two or three blokes guarding them and the Battalion had struck unlucky because we'd struck strongposts that the guns hadn't obliterated. As these prisoners were coming back they were actually being picked off by chaps firing from these strongposts. Germans! They were probably going for the half-a-dozen British who were guarding them, walking on the outside of the lines of prisoners and I remember shouting at them, 'You bloody fools! Get inside of them!' Simple, isn't it? That's what they did – went in the middle of the prisoners and, of course, the Jerries stopped firing. They picked me up on the way past and carried me back the same way – surrounded by German prisoners. When they dumped me at the aid post, there were scores of blokes in there all with terrible wounds, and the quack, old Dr McCracken, said to me, 'Do you think you can make your own way down the line?' I said, 'Too bloody true I can!' So off I went again with the Jerry prisoners and they helped me down to the field dressing station and from there I went to the casualty clearing station.

Bombardier William J. Muir, No. 751367, D 317 Bty., 63rd (Royal Naval) Division Field Artillery

Our gun positions were in Aveluy Wood and I had my signal lines running down this steep communication trench they called Jacob's Ladder. I had to send up a signaller, name of Waugh, not a lot of brains but a big strapping lad, and he had to go up and extend the line as we went forward and he needed two spools of wire of a hundred yards each. I said, 'Look here, two spools are a bit hefty for you to carry up there on your own.' So I got hold of this other chap, Ernest Reevie, a pal of mine from South Shields (we called him Paddy) to go with him. Eighteen-pounder shells come in a case of four with a steel rod going through the middle to keep them in place, so I got hold of two of these rods and put the two reels on them so they could carry them on their shoulders and sent them off up this road on the north side of the Ancre towards where the Division was attacking. Well, of course we didn't know really what was happening up front, and Waugh and Paddy had gone no distance when suddenly they saw hordes and hordes of Germans coming down the road. There were no guards with them, and the lads were quite unarmed, except for these steel rods and two reels of wire. They didn't think they could fight hundreds of Germans with steel rods and they didn't stop to notice that the Germans were unarmed as well! Well, they were just about to dive into a dugout at the side of the road and hope for the best when one of the Germans shouted at them and managed to make himself understood. He wanted to know the way to the prisoners' cage! So Paddy and Waugh just pointed to the rear, and very thankful they were when the Jerries went straight on and didn't bother them.

They must have been about the first lot to be captured, but we saw hundreds that day coming past our positions and we didn't see a single guard with them! I noticed that happening more than once, though. You start a line of prisoners and they all go marching down following each other. The guards can't catch up with them half the time!

By nine o'clock when the fragments of the Royal Naval Division had fought through to the third German line they estimated with amazement, and with a fair degree of accuracy, that the prisoners outnumbered the attackers.

As soon as the line gave way on the Hawthorn Ridge and in front of Beaumont Hamel itself, the geographical accident which had guaranteed its safety now set the seal on its defeat, and the Germans were forced back between the high banks of the valley behind the village. There was nowhere else for them to go. They were waiting there in thousands before the astonished eyes of Lieutenant-Commander Freyberg as he breasted the hill at the head of his tiny force. It was an encouraging sight.

After that it was only a matter of time. By four o'clock the Scots were well established in Beaumont Hamel. They had captured two Battalion Headquarters and, in addition to quantities of maps and papers which British Intelligence would doubtless be glad to receive, they were delighted to find a good supply of canteen stores, a large stock of bottled mineral water and a handsome piano. They also found several sacks of mail from Germany and spared a sympathetic thought for Jerry, trudging towards the Prisoner-of-War cages without the consolation of letters from home.

In the deep-tunnelled dugouts below Y Ravine the stench and the cries were terrible. Tiers of wire bunks were stacked with wounded, terrified by the sight of mud-encrusted Jocks appearing, with bayonets fixed and rifles at the ready, ahead of the stretcher parties. But these Germans were past giving trouble. While the medical teams got on with the job, their escorts began to explore. They were like children in a toyshop. There was Schnapps, there was brandy, there was wine, there was food, there were cigars and, best of all, there was dry clothing.

'Hey, Jimmy,' shouted one Highlander, ecstatic at the discovery of a packing case full of dry socks. 'This is a no' a dugout. It's a shop!'

They could hardly get their boots off quick enough. The dugout was littered with souvenirs and they were theirs for the taking, but, for the moment, dry socks were the most coveted of all the spoils of war.

In the elation of achievement it was easy for the troops, now taking possession of the captured ground, to overlook the fact that they had won a pyrrhic victory. By four o'clock it was dark and new accumulations of fog, thick with the fumes of battle, clammy with damp, rolled up from the river to spread a chill blanket across the bodies of the wounded who still lay on the open ground. There was no hope now that they would be rescued before morning and, for many, little hope that they would survive through the icy November night.

Just as it had done on the sunny evening of the First of July, and just as it had done with haunting regularity in the intervening months, the spectre of partial success laid a dead hand on the decisions of the Command. Partial success, which invariably left the Germans holding certain positions of advantage (from which, with a little more effort, they could surely be evicted) had led to a weary cycle of more 'partial successes'. They were better than total failure, but shabby substitutes for total victory. If General Gough's Army had only partially succeeded in pushing the Germans back, it was axiomatic that the Germans had partially succeeded in stemming the British advance.

There had been stark failure at Serre. A swift advance on the Redan Ridge had soon been forced back when other divisions failed to come forward, and the early advantage was lost. The Germans had been pushed out of St Pierre Divion across the Ancre, but Beaucourt village, further along the river valley, was still unsecured. Thousands of prisoners had been captured, but at a cost of casualties too numerous to calculate. The line had been broken at Beaumont Hamel but the thinned-out ranks of troops who had won through were holding a weak line. If it were not secured, if they did not push on, winter would find them trapped in the valley with the enemy firmly entrenched halfway up the high ground with Munich and Frankfurt trenches guarding the heights.

Sergeant W. J. Hoyles, MM, No. 3237, 13th (S) Btn., The Rifle Brigade, 37th Division

We had to pass across a valley to get to this high hill where the battle was going to go on next morning. We should have dodged across, of course, and gone up in the shelter of the other bank but the Colonel was gone, and we were led by the Second-in-Command. He wasn't one of the original officers – well, we hardly had any of the original officers left – and he was no damned good, this man. He led us in open order right across the valley, across a huge open space, and the Boche were shelling us. We lost no end of men! Freddie Lyon, my great chum, got hit almost right away. I shoved him and some other chaps into a shell-hole on the hillside and I'd hardly turned away when another shell came over and dropped right into it. They were all killed, bar Freddie.

Then I had to find my Battalion and it was pitch dark. Everyone was all mixed up, and the hill itself was nothing but shell-holes and water. Eventually, by a miracle, I stumbled across a bit of a captured trench and this officer chap, this Major who was in command, was in it and he looked up at me and he says, 'Where have you been to?' I said, 'Down there, shifting the wounded – and there are plenty of them! You left us all out in the open. You didn't go far enough!' I didn't care what I said to him, I was so wild. I was shouting at him above the noise, and it was bedlam! He never spoke, so I shouted at him again. I said, 'Where's my Company? Where's A Company?' And he never answered. He was a washout.

I left him and a bit further on I came to a shell-hole and there crouched into it was a Sergeant-Major and two other Sergeants I knew. The extraordinary thing was that I knew these fellows were going to die – and they knew it too. You get that instinct. I said, 'What's the orders? What's happening?' They didn't know. They just looked back at me, absolutely blank. They knew they weren't going to come back.

By the time I got my section up to the top of the hill we were being enfiladed by machine-gun fire. We were crouching in a shell-hole, a very shallow one, waiting to go on and this burst of machine-gun fire took the tops of their heads straight off. I lost the whole of my section – every single man! I got it in the lung, and that was the end for me. The whole thing was an absolute muck-up.

Sergeant C. M. Williams, MM, No. 54556, 13th (S) Btn., The Rifle Brigade

I was in charge of the Battalion Machine-Gunners, and we'd lost a tremendous lot of men in the shelling before we even reached the Green Line where we had to jump off from. But it wasn't until after we'd taken the first German line and a lot of prisoners who gave up without much trouble, that our left flank came under heavy sniper fire and machine-gun fire, because the Battalion to the left of us hadn't got forward. I was in a shell-hole with three of my machine-gunners and I shouted to the men who were round about to drop down and take cover. Rather than dropping where they were, three riflemen made a dash for a shell-hole further away, where there were some other chaps, and, just as they got alongside our position, they were caught in a burst of fire and they literally fell in on top of us. All dead. All killed outright.

Sergeant Johnson collected some bombers and detoured and crawled round the back of the Germans who were firing at us and smashed them out. We went on again and managed to capture another few yards of ground, but again we came into enfilade fire on our left, because the battalion to the left of us was still held up. It was all terrible confusion. We didn't know where anyone was the whole day long, so all we could do was to stop where we were and do the best we could. When dusk fell I collected Corporal Bissell and five other machine-gunners and we crawled out thirty yards or so and dug a position in line with the German sniper position, but beside an old German dugout that gave them a bit of cover and protection. There was terrible firing going on and Very lights started going up. When I'd seen the boys settled, I crawled off again, making for the trench I thought I'd come from, and I hadn't gone a dozen yards before I saw a German in it. It was a German trench I was crawling into! And it wasn't a dozen yards from the machine-gun post we'd just set up. Heaven knows how we'd missed them on the way forward! I crawled backwards, very cautiously indeed, and got back to the boys to warn them.

When I moved off again I didn't know where I was! I knew full well that I'd lost my direction, but I just kept on going, trusting to luck and lying close to the ground when the flares went up and when there were bursts of machine-gun fire. They were spraying the ground practically all the time, but I kept on moving to my right and eventually I struck our line – or rather, the place where most of the boys were! I crawled back again at daybreak and the

Germans had gone out of the post I'd stumbled across. Later we were relieved and by morning we were back where we'd started, on the Green Line.

It was the second time in the space of ninety-five days that the Battalion had lost almost half its fighting strength – three hundred and twelve casualties, of whom ninety-three were dead.

Looking around them at the protective belts of wire, the gun positions sheltered by steep banks, the warren of deep dry dugouts, the survivors marvelled that the Green Line in the valley had ever been captured at all. Even now the dugouts had not been entirely cleared of Germans but those who remained, waiting to be marched back as prisoners, were in no mood to cause any difficulty. Nevertheless, a few of the boys, observing Sergeant-Major 'Rainbow' Oliver sitting on the top step of a dugout occupied by thirty surly Germans, rather admired his nerve. He was unarmed, he was reading a letter from home, and he had every appearance of being completely relaxed. He explained kindly that he had not had time to digest his correspondence before going into action.

Charlie Williams' machine-gunners had 'captured' a Westphalian ham. It was covered with green mould but they had easily scraped that off. Now they were frying thick rashers in a mess-tin lid and pronouncing it a jolly sight better than bully beef. Through the mist the rattle of continued fighting reached towards them from the high ground across the valley.

It was the morning of 15 November and they were conscious of having done well. They had advanced the line halfway up the ridge and D Company on the left had got as far as the edge of Munich Trench. On the right they had taken Beaucourt Trench and linked up with the Royal Naval Division. Lieutenant-Commander Freyberg had rallied a conglomerate force of men and led them, against the odds, to capture Beaucourt village.[1]

The outcome of the gamble had been limited success and less than General Gough had hoped for. But the capture of St Pierre Divion, of Beaucourt and of Beaumont Hamel were three trump cards. The previous evening Gough had had the gratification of placing them in the hand of his Commander-in-Chief and that morning Haig laid them on the table at the opening session of the Chantilly Conference where they had the desired effect of mollifying the French. He played them again next day at the Paris Conference of the British and French Governments and they

1. A feat for which Lieutenant-Commander Freyberg was awarded the Victoria Cross.

even trumped Lloyd George. He had come prepared, with all the powers of his formidable rhetoric, to plead the case for shifting the main arena of the battle away from the atrophy of the Western Front and, even after the Prime Minister had insisted on his deleting the most virulent and inflammatory passages of Lloyd George's prepared speech, it had promised to be a lively meeting. Now all was changed. The Conference, which had set out to curb the powers of the Military, unanimously accepted the conclusions which the Military Commanders had reached at Chantilly and endorsed their plans for the continuance of the war in the spring. A few had doubts. Lord Lansdowne was already mentally composing the memorandum which, on his return to London, he would circulate to the Cabinet. *Are we to continue until we have killed ALL our young men?* But, for the moment, all was accord.

But although, from his own point of view, the outcome of the Conferences had been highly satisfactory, Sir Douglas Haig was not without qualms and he had already sent a message to General Gough clearly stating that he did not wish him to continue with any large-scale attacks during his own absence. Gough was perturbed. His Army had hardly had a fair crack of the whip. The omens were good. He was assured that all ranks were fighting fit and eager to go on. They had captured Beaumont Hamel. They had captured Beaucourt. But the Germans were still dug in on the hump of high ground between them, still holding out in the high redoubts at Munich and Frankfurt trenches. With just a little more effort, one last push, his Army could gain the heights.

Against his better judgement the Commander-in-Chief allowed himself to be persuaded.

General Gough was delighted and put the matter in hand right away.

Part 5

Friends Are Good on the Day of Battle

Translation of the Gaelic inscription on
the 51st Highland Division Memorial which
looks across to Beaumont Hamel.

Chapter 25

The scrag-end of the Glasgow Boys Brigade Battalion – officially the 16th Highland Light Infantry – paraded by companies in a gale-swept field at Mailly Maillet, but the sight was too awful for words and, shortly before General Gough arrived to inspect them, Colonel Kyle ordered the ranks to close up. They were still a sorry sight. Three days earlier, on the heights above Beaumont Hamel, they had advanced through the first snow-storm of the winter to fight the last action of the Battle of the Somme. The Battalion could claim to have been in at the kill. A handful of the originals who had escaped annihilation at Leipzig Redoubt on the first of July could also claim to have been in at the beginning.

General Gough addressed the men with kindly words. He thanked them for their efforts in the battle. It had been a considerable achievement to capture Munich Trench and it was no reflection on their courage and endurance that a counter-attack by a vastly superior force had pushed them out again. They might rest assured that, by their deeds, they had added fresh laurels to the name of the Highland Light Infantry.

The men gave three apathetic cheers. General Gough stood stiffly saluting as they marched off, then he turned to Colonel Kyle.

'What were your casualties?' he asked.

Even after two roll-calls the Colonel was unable to answer with precision. There might yet be stragglers. In the early hours of the 18th they had gone into the attack on Munich and Frankfurt trenches with twenty-one officers and six hundred and fifty other ranks. Eight officers had returned. At the last count 390 men had been killed, wounded, or were missing.

In the afternoon of the same day an urgent signal from Divisional Headquarters brought Colonel Kyle the astonishing news that ninety of his casualties were not 'missing' at all. They had been trapped by the German counter-attack and were lying low, marooned in Frankfurt Trench some distance behind the recaptured German line. At roughly the same time this interesting information also came to the notice of the Germans and, almost as routine, anticipating little trouble, they sent a sergeant and a small armed party down the communication trench to take the Highlanders prisoner. The handful of men who returned reported that half of their number had been killed or captured by the British who had blocked and fortified a stretch of Frankfurt Trench, that they seemed determined to fight and that, to all appearances, they were armed to the teeth.

They were not armed to the teeth. All they had, apart from a length of battered trench and two captured dugouts, were their rifles, four Lewis-guns and a reasonable supply of ammunition, most of it retrieved from the scattered bodies of dead soldiers. They also had the fixed intention of defending their position until the next successful attack brought comrades to the rescue.

But it was 21 November. The Battle of the Somme was over and the long campaign had fizzled out in the failure of Saturday's attempt to seize the heights. Three days had passed. It was Tuesday now and, until winter loosened its grip, there would be no more attacks on Frankfurt Trench. Except, of course, by the Germans, faced with the galling necessity of attacking a part of their own line where a small isolated British force was still, unaccountably, holding out.

They held out until Sunday.

Tuesday evening. In the German front line there is an outbreak of heavy fighting, a frenzy of rapid fire and explosions. Hopes soar in Frankfurt Trench. At midnight the fighting dies down. They listen on for a long time. Eventually there is silence.

By Wednesday, there is no food left. A reconnoitring aeroplane pinpoints the Highlanders' position and flashes an ambiguous message which causes excited speculation. Did it read *Coming tonight* or *Come in tonight*? No one can be sure. They wait, on the *qui vive*. The British do not come – but the Germans do. The Highlanders fight them off. Two men are killed and half a dozen more are wounded. At night they hear another British raid on the front line. The Germans repulse it.

On Thursday, a short-range hurricane bombardment smashes part of the parapet. Explosions in the morass around the trench break up the snow-filled shell-holes. The precious supply of clear water left by the melting snow trickles away and soaks into the mud. A force of German infantry attacks in the wake of the bombardment. The Lewis-gunners guess that they have accounted for at least a dozen. The surviving Germans retire. The Highlanders repair their parapet. There are now more than fifty wounded in the foetid dugout. The last candle has guttered out and they lie there in the dark. Later three men crawl through the freezing slush to search the bodies of the dead Germans. They retrieve their water-bottles. There is another raid on the German line, but no breakthrough.

On Friday, the Germans attack again at close quarters, but without success. Company Sergeant-Major George Lee is hit. He is a foreman in the Glasgow Corporation Roads Department and has taken the lead for the past five days. The bullet strikes him in the head and he slumps across the parapet. As they lift him down he opens his eyes once, and says, 'No surrender, boys.' Then he dies. Some of the wounded have died too, but in the dark of the dugout they cannot tell how many. The night is quiet.[1] Two men crawl to within arm's length of the Germans in Munich Trench in search of water.

On Saturday, a small party of Germans approaches behind a captured British soldier who carries a large white flag and a message from a German Colonel. *Surrender quietly and you will be well-treated. Otherwise you may take what is coming to you.* The Highlanders are given an hour to decide. They ponder, take a vote, and decide to send no reply. After dark they search for water and return with a small quantity which is brackish and polluted. A few are driven to drink it. The night is quiet.

On Sunday, the able-bodied men take stock of their remaining ammunition. There is a single drum of bullets for four Lewis-guns and one Lewis-gunner left alive. They load spare rifles and place them in readiness round the crumbling mud walls of the trench. They spot a continuous line of German helmets moving down the communication trenches and brace themselves for an attack.

The Germans had surrounded the position and they attacked it simultaneously from all sides. The fifteen able-bodied men defending it were easily overwhelmed. Of the original ninety, some thirty badly wounded men were still alive. The rest were dead.

In a mood of understandable pique the Germans ordered the survivors to clear the dugouts of bodies and then, with the dregs of their strength, to carry the wounded back to the transport lines on the other side of the hill. Then they marched them to Brigade Headquarters for interrogation. Starving, filthy, frozen, exhausted and on the verge of collapse, they stumbled to attention in front of a German Major. An interpreter was present. Long years later, Private Dick Manson remained convinced that there was a touch of admiration in his glance as he translated the Major's words.

'Is *this* what has held the Brigade up for a week? Who are you and where have you come from?'

They replied with name, rank and number. They were too weary to

1. After three separate raids which incurred 300 casualties the Army had reluctantly called off the rescue.

say more. But they might have answered that they had come, by a
roundabout route, from Glasgow. That they were a representative cross-
section of their Battalion – shipping clerks, errand-boys, stevedores, railway porters, grocers' assistants, postmen. That they were, in short, fifteen
soldiers of Kitchener's Army.

Bibliography
Author's Note
Index

Bibliography

Military Operations France and Belgium, 1914, Vols. 1–2, compiled by Brigadier-General Sir James E. Edmonds (Macmillan & Co., 1925)

Military Operations France and Belgium, 1915, Vols. 1–2, compiled by Brigadier-General Sir James E. Edmonds (Macmillan & Co. Ltd., 1928)

Military Operations France and Belgium, 1916, Vols. 1–2, compiled by Brigadier-General Sir James E. Edmonds (Macmillan & Co. Ltd., 1932)

Medical Services General History, Vol. 3, Major-General Sir W. G. MacPherson, KCMG, CB, LL D (His Majesty's Stationery Office, 1924)

The Guards Division in the Great War, 1915–1918, Cuthbert Headlam, DSO (John Murray, 1924)

The Story of the 55th (West Lancashire) Division, The Rev. J. O. Coop, DSO, TD, MA (*Liverpool Daily Post* Printers, 1919)

The Eighth Division in War, 1914–1918, Lieutenant-Colonel J. H. Boraston, CB, CBE, and Captain Cyril E. C. Bax (The Medici Society Ltd., 1926)

The History of the Rifle Brigade in the War of 1914–1918, Vol. 1, Reginald Berkeley, MC (The Rifle Brigade Club Ltd., 1927)

The History of the Rifle Brigade in the War of 1914–1918, Vol. 2, William W. Seymour (The Rifle Brigade Club Ltd., 1936)

The 47th (London) Division 1914–1919, edited by Alan H. Maude (Amalgamated Press, 1922)

The West Yorkshire Regiment in the War, 1914–1918, Vol. 1, Everard Wyrall (Bodley Head)

The 56th Division (1st London Territorial Division), Major C. H. Dudley Ward, DSO, MC (John Murray, 1921)

The Worcestershire Regiment, Captain H. FitzM. Stacke, MC (G. T. Cheshire & Sons Ltd., 1928)

The New Zealand Division, 1916–1919, Colonel H. Stewart, CMG, DSO, MC (Whitcombe & Tombs Ltd., Auckland, 1921)

The Cambridgeshires, 1914 to 1919, Brigadier-General E. Riddell, CMG, DSO, and Colonel M. C. Clayton, DSO, DL (Bowes & Bowes, 1934)

The Royal Naval Division, Douglas Jerrold (Hutchinson & Co. Ltd., 1927)

The Story of the Tyneside Scottish, Brigadier-General Trevor Ternan, CB, CMG, DSO (The Northumberland Press, 1918)

The History of the 13th Battalion A.I.F., Thomas A. White (Tyrrells Ltd., Sydney, 1924)

Forward With The 5th, A. W. Keown (The Speciality Press Pty. Ltd., Melbourne, 1921)

The History of the 15th Battalion, The Highland Light Infantry (15th Highland Light Infantry Association, John M'Callum & Co., 1924)

The History of the 16th Battalion, The Highland Light Infantry, edited by Thomas Chalmers (John M'Callum & Co., 1930)

The 17th Highland Light Infantry, John W. Arthur & Ion S. Munro (David J. Clarke, 1920)

History of the 11th Battalion, The Queen's, Captain E. W. J. Neave, MC (The Brixton 'Free Press', 1931)

With the Tenth Essex in France, Lieutenant-Colonel T. M. Banks, DSO, MC, and Captain R. A. Chell, DSO, MC (Burt & Sons, 1921)

The 11th Royal Warwicks in France 1915–1916, Brevet Colonel C. S. Collison, DSO (Cornish Brothers Ltd., 1928)

The 15th Battalion, Royal Warwickshire Regiment in the Great War, Major C. A. Bill (Cornish Brothers Ltd., 1932)

For the Duration, The Story of the 13th Battalion, The Rifle Brigade, D. H. Rowlands (Simpkin Marshall Ltd., 1932)

The 4th Battalion, The King's Own and The Great War, Lieutenant-Colonel W. F. A. Wadham and Captain J. Crossley (privately published, 1920)

History of the 6th Battalion West Yorkshire Regiment, Vol. 1 (1st/6th Battalion), Captain E. V. Tempest, DSO, MC (Percy Lund, Humphries & Co. Ltd., 1921)

The Sherwood Foresters in the Great War 1914–1918 (the 2nd/8th Battalion) Lieutenant-Colonel W. C. Oates, DSO (J. & H. Bell Ltd., 1920)

History and Memoir of The 33rd Battalion Machine-gun Corps, by members of the Battalion (privately published, 1919)

A Record of D.245 Battery 1914–1919, Sergeant A. E. Gee, MM, and Corporal A. E. Shaw (privately published, 1932)

British Regiments 1914–'18, Brigadier E. A. James, OBE, TD (Samson Books)

History of the First World War, B. H. Liddell Hart (Cassell Ltd., 1970)

My War Memories 1914–1918, General Ludendorff, Vol. 1 (Hutchinson & Co. Ltd., 1936)

Sir Douglas Haig's Despatches, edited by Lieutenant-Colonel J. H. Boraston, CB, OBE (J. M. Dent & Sons Ltd., 1919)

The Private Papers of Douglas Haig 1914–1919, edited by Robert Blake (Eyre & Spottiswoode, 1952)

Sir Douglas Haig's Command 1915–1918, G. A. B. Dewar (Constable, 1922)

The Man I Knew, The Countess Haig (The Moray Press, 1936)

Twenty-Five Years with Earl Haig, Sergeant T. Secrett, MM (Jarrolds, 1929)

Haig, Duff Cooper (Faber & Faber Ltd., 1935)

Field-Marshal Earl Haig, Brigadier-General John Charteris, CMG, DSO, MP (Cassell Ltd., 1929)

Le Maréchal Haig à Montreuil-Sur-Mer, Raymond Wable (privately published by the author, 1968)

Goughie, Anthony Farrar-Hockley (Hart-Davis, MacGibbon Ltd., 1975)

The War Memoirs of David Lloyd George (Odham's Press Ltd., 1934)

Tempestuous Journey: Lloyd George, His Life and Times, Frank Owen (Hutchinson & Co. Ltd., 1954)

The Press and the General Staff, Neville Lytton (W. Collins, Sons & Co. Ltd., 1920)

Now It Can Be Told, Philip Gibbs (Harper and Brothers, Publishers, 1920)

The Pageant of the Years, Philip Gibbs (William Heinemann Ltd., 1946)

World War 1914–1918, edited by Sir John Hammerton (The Amalgamated Press Ltd., 1924)

Twenty Years After, Vols. 1–3, edited by Major-General Sir Ernest Swinton, KBE, CB (George Newnes Ltd., 1938)

The Rifle Brigade Chronicle for 1918, compiled and edited by Colonel Willoughby Verner (John Bale, Sons & Danielsson Ltd., 1919)

Unwilling Passenger, Arthur Osburn (Faber & Faber Ltd., 1932)

Twelve Days, Sidney Rogerson (Arthur Barker Ltd.)

Courage Past, Alex Aiken (privately published by the author)

War Letters to a Wife, France and Flanders 1915–1919, Rowland Feilding (The Medici Society Ltd., 1929)

Transport and Sport in the Great War Period, Captain A. O. Temple Clarke (privately published by the author, 1938)

Machine-gunner 1914–1918, compiled and edited by C. E. Crutchley (Bailey Brothers & Swinfen Ltd., 1975)

A Padre in France, George A. Birmingham (Hodder & Stoughton Ltd.)

Frank Maxwell, VC, by his wife (John Murray, 1921)

By-Ways on Service, Notes from an Australian Journal, Hector Dinning (Constable & Co. Ltd., 1918)

Behind the Lines, Colonel W. N. Nicholson, CMG, DSO (Jonathan Cape Ltd., 1939)

Extracts from an Officer's Diary 1914–1918, Lieutenant-Colonel Harrison Jodston, DSO (Geo. Falkner & Sons, 1919)

Happy Odyssey, Sir Adrian Carton de Wiart, VC (Jonathan Cape Ltd., 1950)

A Private in the Guards, Stephen Graham (William Heinemann Ltd., 1928)

Our War, James Milroy McQueen (privately published by the author, 1921)

Treasure Trove of Memories, Hector Macdonald (privately published by the author)

German Spies at Bay, Sidney Theodore Felstead (Hutchinson & Co. Ltd., 1920)

Open House in Flanders, Baroness Ernest de la Grange (John Murray Ltd., 1929)

Quand Montreuil Était sur Mer, Jean Leroy (Quentovic)

GHQ, Montreuil-Sur-Mer, GSO (Philip Allen & Co., 1920)

A Pilgrim in Picardy, B. S. Townrowe (Chapman & Hall Ltd., 1927)

With the British on the Somme, W. Beach Thomas (Methuen & Co. Ltd., 1917)

England in France, Sidney R. Jones (Constable & Co. Ltd., 1919)

Le Temps des Guerres 1914–1939, Gerard Boutet (Editions De Noel, 1981)

L'Hécatombe Sacrée de la Flandre Française 1914–1918, (Imprimerie Desclée, Lille, 1921)

An Der Somme. Erinnerungen der 12 Infanterie-Division an die Stellungskampfe und Schlacht an der Somme Oktober bis November 1916, Verlagsbuchhandlung (Berlin, Ferd. Dümmlers, 1918)

Author's Note

I wish to acknowledge my debt to all of the
following, without whose valuable assistance this book
could never have been written.

Captain A. J. J. P. Agius, MC,
1st/3rd (City of London)
Battalion, London Regiment
(Royal Fusiliers) (TF).

Acting Corporal E. J. Albrow,
7th (S) Battalion, Norfolk
Regiment.

Private J. W. Alderson, 4th
Battalion, Grenadier Guards.

Private F. J. Alhquist, 2nd/20th
(County of London) Battalion,
London Regiment
(Blackheath and Woolwich).

Gunner H. J. Allen, Royal Siege
Artillery.

Lance-Corporal J. F. E. Alpe,
13th (S) Battalion, The Rifle
Brigade.

Corporal F. Arnold, 21st (S)
Battalion (Yeoman Rifles),
King's Royal Rifle Corps.

Private C. D. Ashby, 4th
Battalion, Duke of
Cambridge's Own (Middlesex
Regiment).

Captain A. L. Ashwell, DSO,
8th Battalion (Nottinghamshire
and Derbyshire Regiment)
Sherwood Foresters (TF).

Lieutenant F. Bailey, 3rd
Battalion, Royal Scots.

Lance-Corporal S. F. Bailey, 1st
Life Guards.

Staff Sergeant W. W. Bain, 15th
(S) Battalion, (1st London
Welsh), Royal Welsh
Fusiliers.

Sergeant F. Baker, TD, 1st/5th
Battalion, Lincolnshire
Regiment (TF).

Rifleman J. Baker, 13th (S)
Battalion, The Rifle Brigade.

Private L. M. Baldwin, MM, 8th

(S) Battalion, East Surrey
Regiment.

Signaller H. J. Bale, 308 Brigade,
Royal Field Artillery; 242
Brigade, Royal Field Artillery.

Gunner W. Ballard, D Battery,
290 Brigade, Royal Field
Artillery.

Corporal W. Banks, 21st (S)
Battalion (Yeoman Rifles),
King's Royal Rifle Corps.

Sergeant F. J. Bantock, Royal
Regiment of Artillery.

Private W. J. Barfoot, 11th (S)
Battalion, Queen's (Royal
West Surrey) Regiment.

Rifleman G. W. Barker, 21st (S)
Battalion (Yeoman Rifles),
King's Royal Rifle Corps.

Rifleman G. Barnes, MM, 13th
Battalion, The Rifle Brigade.

Corporal G. Barnes, 8th
Battalion, Oxford &
Buckinghamshire Light
Infantry.

Private W. S. Barnett, 8th
Battalion (City of London),
London Regiment. Post
Office Rifles (TF).

Sergeant A. A. Barron, 16th (S)
Battalion, King's Royal Rifle
Corps.

Trooper G. O. Barson,
Household Battalion, 2nd
Life Guards.

Private P. J. Batchelor, D.
Squadron, Queen's Own
Oxfordshire Hussars.

Sergeant H. Bartlett, 115th
Brigade, Royal Field
Artillery.

Private F. H. Bastable, 7th (S)
Battalion, Queen's Own

(Royal West Kent Regiment).

Private H. S. Baverstock, 12th
Battalion, 1st Canterbury
Regiment, New Zealand
Division.

Lieutenant F. W. Beadle, 156
Brigade, Royal Field Artillery.

Lance-Corporal G. R. Bealing,
MM, Duke of Edinburgh's
2nd Battalion (Wiltshire
Regiment).

Corporal J. Beament, MM, 16th
(S) Battalion, King's Royal
Rifle Corps.

Sergeant S. V. Bearup, 21st (S)
Battalion (Yeoman Rifles),
King's Royal Rifle Corps.

Rifleman S. Bell, 21st (S)
Battalion (Yeoman Rifles),
King's Royal Rifle Corps.

Private W. G. Bell, MM, Army
Cyclist Corps.

Private J. R. Bennett, 22nd
Battalion, Australian Imperial
Forces.

Private J. Bennett, 15th (County
of London) Battalion, London
Regiment (Prince of Wales'
Own, Civil Service Rifles)
(TF).

Lance-Corporal T. A. Bennett,
7th (S) Battalion, The Rifle
Brigade.

Sub-Lieutenant J. H. Bentham,
Hood Battalion, Royal Naval
Division.

Private H. W. Bickerstaff, MM,
19th Battalion, Canadian
Expeditionary Force.

Private W. A. Billingham, 25th
Battalion, Machine Gun
Corps.

Private F. W. Bindley, 2nd

Battalion, Honourable Artillery Company.

Private T. Bingham, 12th (S) Battalion, York and Lancaster Regiment.

Rifleman H. Blackburn, Croix de Guerre, 21st (S) Battalion (Yeoman Rifles), King's Royal Rifle Corps.

Sergeant-Major J. F. Blackemore, MM, 2nd Canterbury Infantry Battalion, New Zealand Division.

Private H. Blankley, 5th Battalion, Northumberland Fusiliers (TF).

Gunner R. Bletcher, 280 Siege Battery, Royal Garrison Artillery.

Rifleman T. S. Bond, 11th (S) Battalion, The Rifle Brigade.

Private G. Boss, 1st/8th (City of London Battalion), London Regiment (Post Office Rifles).

Lance-Sergeant J. L. Bouch, 1st Battalion, Coldstream Guards.

Rifleman W. Bowhill, 13th (S) Battalion, The Rifle Brigade.

Rifleman A. E. Boyland, 13th (S) Battalion, The Rifle Brigade.

Corporal T. Bracey, MM, 9th (S) Battalion, Royal Fusiliers (City of London Regiment).

Major W. J. Brockman, DSO, 15th (S) Battalion, Lancashire Fusiliers (1st Salford).

2nd Lieutenant H. Brooks, 6th Battalion, Tank Corps.

Lance-Bombardier J. H. Bromwich, 138th Heavy Battery, Royal Garrison Artillery.

Private A. B. Brown, 21st (County of London), London Regiment (1st Surrey Rifles) (TF).

Private H. R. Brown, 2nd Battalion, Royal Marine Light Infantry.

Sergeant J. Brown, MM, 16th (S) Battalion, King's Royal Rifle Corps.

Corporal A. T. A. Browne, MM (TD), 20th (S) Battalion, Royal Fusiliers (City of London Regiment).

Sergeant J. Bryant, MM, 8th Battalion, Australian Imperial Forces.

Corporal A. W. Buckingham, 70th Company Motor Transport, Army Service Corps.

Rifleman A. E. Burroughs, 7th (S) Battalion, King's Royal Rifle Corps.

Gunner Charles E. Burrows, 104 Battery, 22nd Brigade, Royal Field Artillery.

Sergeant G. Butler, 12th Machine Gun Company, 4th Division.

Lieutenant S. A. V. Butler, 3rd Battalion, King's Own (Yorkshire Light Infantry).

Private F. Burbeck, 2nd Battalion, Oxfordshire and Buckinghamshire Light Infantry.

Private W. H. Callow, 15th (S) Battalion, Royal Welsh Fusiliers (1st London Welsh).

Rifleman T. E. Cantlon, 18th and 21st Battalions (Yeoman Rifles), King's Royal Rifle Corps.

Corporal C. G. Capel, 1st Battalion, Oxfordshire and Buckinghamshire Light Infantry.

Rifleman N. Carmichael, 21st (S) Battalion (Yeoman Rifles), King's Royal Rifle Corps.

Rifleman C. Carter, 5th (City of London) Battalion, London Regiment, (London Rifle Brigade) (TF).

Private W. F. R. Carter, 7th (S) and 9th (S) Battalions, Leicestershire Regiment.

Private E. S. Cecil, 2nd Battalion, Hampshire Regiment.

Captain Leonard Chamberlen, MC, 13th (S) Battalion, The Rifle Brigade.

Private W. Chambers, 1st Battalion, (Nottinghamshire and Derbyshire Regiment), Sherwood Foresters.

Rifleman A. L. Chapman, 21st (S) Battalion (Yeomans Rifles), King's Royal Rifle Corps.

Rifleman S. F. Charrington, 13th (S) Battalion, The Rifle Brigade.

Private H. M. Chaundy, MC, Motor Transport, Army Service Corps (later Lieutenant).

Pioneer G. T. H. Cheeseman,

7th Signal Troop, 3rd Cavalry Division, Royal Engineers (Signal Service).

Colonel R. A. Chell, DSO, MC, 10th (S) Battalion, Essex Regiment.

Corporal R. T. Chiffey, 33rd Division, Royal Engineers (Signal Service).

Private J. J. Christie, 8th (S) Battalion, Gordon Highlanders.

Private Percy Clark, 5th Battalion, Cheshire Regiment (TF).

Acting Lance-Corporal F. B. J. Cleary, 1st/5th (City of London) Battalion, London Regiment (London Rifle Brigade) (TF).

Private J. Clements, Royal Marine Light Infantry.

Sergeant H. B. Coates, 14th (County of London) Battalion, London Regiment, (London Scottish) (TF).

Sergeant F. H. Cobb, 18th (S) Battalion, King's Royal Rifle Corps.

Company Sergeant-Major W. J. Coggins, DCM, 1st/4th Battalion, Oxfordshire and Buckinghamshire Light Infantry (TF).

Rifleman W. F. Coldrick, 13th (S) Battalion, The Rifle Brigade.

Corporal C. F. Cole, 2nd/21st (County of London) Battalion, London Regiment (1st Surrey Rifles) (TF).

Sapper A. E. Comer, 1st Field Company, Royal Engineers.

Corporal W. E. Cook, Royal Engineers.

Corporal F. H. Corduker, 21st (S) Battalion (Yeoman Rifles), King's Royal Rifle Corps.

Rifleman A. W. C. Corkett, 11th (S) Battalion, The Rifle Brigade.

Trooper J. Cowling, 18th Hussars.

Lieutenant T. C. Cresswell, MC, Hood Battalion, Royal Naval Division.

Gunner A. E. Crook, J. Battery, Royal Horse Artillery.

Sergeant J. T. Cross, 13th (S) Battalion, The Rifle Brigade.

Private R. T. Crowe, 2nd

Battalion, The Highland Light Infantry.

Private Frederick Darby, DCM, 10th (S) Battalion, Worcestershire Regiment.

Sergeant William Darlington, 18th (S) Battalion, Manchester Regiment.

Corporal L. A. Darnell, 11th Battalion, Sussex Regiment.

Sergeant E. J. Davidson, MM, Royal Engineers.

Corporal W. J. Davies, 18th Field Ambulance, Royal Army Medical Corps.

Private J. Dearman, 266th Field Company, Royal Engineers.

Private E. Deighton, 8th (S) Battalion, King's Own Yorkshire Light Infantry.

Private J. W. Dicker, 13th (S) Battalion, The Rifle Brigade.

Sergeant R. Dickson, MM, 3rd Battalion, Grenadier Guards.

Corporal H. Diffey, 15th (S) Battalion (1st London Welsh), Royal Welsh Fusiliers.

Corporal A. W. Dunbar, 236 Brigade, Royal Field Artillery.

Sergeant-Pilot G. F. Duncan, Royal Flying Corps.

Captain F. E. Dunsmuir, MC, 17th (S) Battalion, Highland Light Infantry.

Private J. C. Dwelly, 4th Battalion, Grenadier Guards.

Sergeant H. J. Dykes, Tank Corps.

Private Tom Easton, 21st Battalion, Northumberland Fusiliers (2nd Tyneside Scottish).

Rifleman B. F. Eccles, 7th (S) Battalion, The Rifle Brigade.

Sergeant S. E. Elford, New Zealand Rifle Brigade.

Gunner A. E. Ellingford, MM, 28th Brigade, Royal Field Artillery.

Private C. H. U. Embery, 1st/16th (County of London) Battalion, London Regiment (Queen's Westminster Rifles) (TF).

Lance-Corporal G. England, 3rd Battalion, Grenadier Guards.

Acting Lieutenant-Colonel R. E. England, Croix de Guerre, 13th (S) Battalion (Miners and Pioneers), The King's Own (Yorkshire Light Infantry).

Driver W. Everett, Army Service Corps.

Private V. E. Fagence, 11th (S) Battalion, Queen's (Royal West Surrey Regiment).

Private B. Farrer, Royal Army Medical Corps.

Corporal Signaller H. E. W. Fayerbrother, DCM, 291st Brigade, Royal Field Artillery, 58th Division.

Private B. Felstead, 15th (S) Battalion (1st London Welsh), Royal Welsh Fusiliers.

Private A. W. Fenn, 2nd Battalion, The Suffolk Regiment.

Private W. S. Fisher, 1st Hertfordshire Yeomanry.

Lance-Corporal W. G. Fleet, 7th (S) Battalion, Bedfordshire Regiment.

Corporal O. S. Flowers, Motor Transport Section, Army Service Corps.

Corporal R. A. Ford, 35th Divisional Ammunition Column, 157 Brigade, Royal Field Artillery.

Lance-Corporal H. Forrest, 9th (Dunbartonshire) Battalion, Princess Louise's (Argyll and Sutherland Highlanders) (TF).

Lieutenant-Commander J. C. Forster, Hood Battalion, Royal Naval Division.

Private A. B. Foster, Queen's Own Oxfordshire Hussars.

Private E. Foster, 3rd Battalion, Durham Light Infantry.

Gunner F. Foster, Royal Field Artillery.

Corporal J. Francis, 1st Battalion, Duke of Cambridge's Own (Middlesex) Regiment.

Sapper G. A. Franklin, No. 2 Section, 57th Division, Royal Engineers Signal Company.

Lance-Corporal C. Frost, MM, 1st Battalion, Leicestershire Regiment.

Brigadier R. E. Fryer, OBE, 62 Field Company, Royal Engineers.

Acting-Corporal E. Gale, 1st Battalion and 7th (S) Battalion, The Rifle Brigade.

2nd Lieutenant G. Garnett-Clarke, MC, Royal Field Artillery.

Driver C. Garrard, D. Battery, 87th Brigade, Royal Field Artillery.

Lieutenant P. H. Gates, 2nd Battalion, Lincolnshire Regiment.

Private J. R. Glenn, 12th (S) Battalion, York and Lancaster Regiment (Sheffield Pals).

Captain A. L. Goring, MC, 6th (S) Battalion, Alexandra, Princess of Wales' Own (Yorkshire Regiment).

Private J. Hain, 9th (S) Battalion, Royal Irish Fusiliers.

Private A. Hales, 2/2nd London Field Ambulance, Royal Army Medical Corps (TF).

Private H. Hall, 12th (S) Battalion, York and Lancaster Regiment (Sheffield Pals).

Corporal P. A. Hall, 2nd/4th Battalion, Gloucestershire Regiment (TF).

Corporal W. B. Hand, 1st/7th Battalion (Worcestershire Regiment).

Lieutenant-Colonel P. W. Hargreaves, MC, 3rd Battalion, Worcestershire Regiment.

Corporal H. J. Hart, 9th (S) Battalion, Royal Fusiliers.

Petty Officer H. Hart, Royal Naval Air Service.

Acting Lance-Corporal A. V. Hartland, 2nd/5th Battalion, South Staffordshire Regiment.

Lieutenant R. M. Hawkins, MC, 11th (S) Battalion, Royal Fusiliers.

Private W. Hay, 9th Battalion (Highlanders), Royal Scots (Lothian Regiment).

Private H. J. Haynes, 2nd/6th Battalion, Royal Warwickshire Regiment (TF).

A/B. J. Haynes, Anson Battalion, Royal Naval Division.

Captain E. W. Hayward, DCM, MM, D Battalion (Heavy Branch Machine Gun Corps) (Tanks).

Lieutenant H. J. Hayward, MC, 12th Battalion, Gloucestershire Regiment (Bristol's Own).

Private F. Haywood, 15th (County of London) Battalion (Prince of Wales' Own) Civil Service Rifles (TF).

Brigadier T. E. H. Helby, 59th

Siege Battery, Royal Garrison Artillery.

A/B. E. Henderson, Drake Battalion, Royal Naval Division.

Brigade Trumpeter J. Henderson, 1st Northumberland Brigade, Royal Field Artillery.

2nd Lieutenant G. C. Henry, 2nd Battalion, King's Own Yorkshire Light Infantry.

Lance-Corporal A. C. Hill, Army Service Corps.

Private A. J. Hill, 15th Battalion, Royal Welsh Fusiliers.

Rifleman A. Hill, 2nd/9th Battalion, Queen Victoria's Rifles (London Regiment).

Signaller L. Hill, 16th Battalion, Cheshire Regiment.

Fitter R. Hill, Croix de Guerre, Royal Horse and Royal Field Artillery.

Sergeant T. S. Hogg, 12th (S) Battalion, York and Lancaster Regiment (Sheffield Pals).

Sergeant H. A. Horne, Lincolnshire Regiment.

Corporal J. Hoyles, MM, 13th (S) Battalion, The Rifle Brigade.

Corporal R. Hudson, MC, London Regiment (Queen's Westminster Rifles) (TF); (later Lieutenant).

Lance-Corporal W. R. Hudson, 13th (S) Battalion, The Rifle Brigade.

Private G. H. Huggins, Queen's Own Oxfordshire Hussars.

Colonel N. H. Huttenbach, DSO, OBE, MC, Royal Artillery.

Private F. Ibbotson, 14th Battalion (1st Birmingham City), Royal Warwickshire Regiment.

Private H. H. Innis, 7th Battalion, Northumberland Fusiliers.

Private R. Ison, 9th (S) Battalion, The Rifle Brigade.

Private W. Jackman, 4th Battalion, Grenadier Guards.

Rifleman H. A. Jago, 13th (S) Battalion, The Rifle Brigade.

Private J. H. James, 2nd/7th Battalion, Manchester Regiment (TF).

Private A. J. Jamieson, 11th Battalion, Royal Scots.

Private H. N. Jeary, 1st Battalion, Queen's (Royal West Surrey Regiment).

2nd Lieutenant A. B. Jeffries, 2nd Battalion, Royal Berkshire Regiment.

Corporal F. F. Johnson, A/70 Brigade, 15th (Scottish) Division, Royal Field Artillery.

Lance-Corporal R. G. Johnson, 58th London Signal Company, Royal Engineers.

Private I. A. T. Jones, 2nd Battalion, Royal Welsh Fusiliers.

Lieutenant F. Jones, MC, Tank Corps.

Private S. H. E. Kemp, 14th (County of London) Battalion, London Regiment (London Scottish) (TF).

Private E. C. Kimber, 2nd, 3rd and 4th Battalions, Grenadier Guards.

Sergeant G. W. Kimble, Queen's Own Oxfordshire Hussars.

Lieutenant P. T. King, 2nd/5th Battalion, East Lancashire Regiment.

Lance-Corporal G. Labdon, Machine Gun Corps.

Rifleman H. R. Langley, 16th (S) Battalion, King's Royal Rifle Corps.

Rifleman S. E. Lawrence, 13th (S) Battalion, The Rifle Brigade.

Sub-Lieutenant T. M. Lawrie, CBE, TD, 63rd Royal Naval Division.

Lieutenant-Colonel W. F. Lean, DSO, Croix de Guerre, 3rd Battalion, West Yorkshire Regiment.

Corporal C. A. Lee, 3rd Battalion, The Rifle Brigade.

Corporal A. E. Lee, MM, 'A' Battalion, Heavy Branch, Machine Gun Corps (Tanks).

Lance-Corporal T. C. Levell, MM, 9th (S) Battalion, Norfolk Regiment.

Sergeant W. E. H. Levy, MM, 'D' Battalion, Heavy Branch, Machine Gun Corps (Tanks).

Sergeant E. Lincoln, 13th (County of London) Battalion, London Regiment.

Rifleman H. E. Lister, MM, 12th (S) Battalion, The Rifle Brigade.

Corporal C. W. Lloyd, 13th (S) Battalion, The Rifle Brigade.

Lieutenant R. Lloyd, Royal Horse Artillery.

Corporal L. Longhurst, 16th (County of London), London Regiment (TF).

Private L. Lovell, 6th (S) Battalion, King's Own (Yorkshire Light Infantry).

Corporal J. V. Lowe, 10th (S) Battalion, Cameronians (Scottish Rifles).

Private C. H. Luffman, 7th (S) Battalion, King's (Shropshire Light Infantry).

Gunner W. Lugg, MM, 83rd Brigade, Royal Field Artillery.

Private C. Lunn, 2nd/3rd HCFA, Royal Army Medical Corps.

Warrant Officer W. J. Lush, Royal Garrison Artillery.

Colonel R. Macleod, DSO, MC, Royal Field Artillery (then Captain attached Royal Flying Corps).

Private J. Makin, Medical Unit, Royal Marine Light Infantry.

Gunner Maltby, MM, 29th Brigade, Royal Field Artillery.

Lieutenant F. Mansfield, 8th Siege Battery, Royal Garrison Artillery.

Lance-Corporal H. E. Marden, 13th (S) Battalion, Royal Sussex Regiment.

Sub-Lieutenant W. Marlow, MC, Howe Battalion, 63rd Royal Naval Division.

Private H. Marshall, 9th (S) Battalion, Royal Fusiliers (City of London Regiment).

General Sir James Marshall-Cornwall, KCB, CBE, DSO, MC, Royal Artillery (attached GHQ) (then Captain).

Private M. A. Martino, 149th Brigade, Royal Field Artillery.

Corporal P. Mason, 9th (S) Battalion, Prince of Wales' Own (West Yorkshire Regiment).

Private A. W. Maycock, 13th (S) Battalion (4th Hull), East Yorkshire Regiment.

Corporal F. L. Mayhew, Royal Engineers (London Electrical Engineers).

Private N. Mellor, 4th Battalion, Bedfordshire Regiment.

Gunner D. N. Meneaud-Lissenburg, Royal Horse Artillery.

Lieutenant G. F. Middle, Royal Engineers Wireless Section.

Trooper F. W. Miller, 1st Battalion, Hertfordshire Regiment.

Private H. R. Milson, 2nd Battalion, Royal Welsh Fusiliers.

Corporal B. A. Minnitt, MM, MC, 11th Battalion, Sherwood Foresters (Nottinghamshire and Derbyshire Regiment) (later Lieutenant).

Sergeant J. H. Mitchell, A. Battery, 1st Canadian Motor Machine Gun Brigade.

Rifleman E. G. Morgan, 13th (S) Battalion, The Rifle Brigade.

Lieutenant S. G. Morgan, 2nd Battalion, South Staffordshire Regiment.

Private W. Morgan, 10th/11th (S) Battalion, Highland Light Infantry.

Sergeant L. Morris, Royal Army Medical Corps.

Private W. M. Morriss, 12th Battalion, Canterbury Regiment, New Zealand Expeditionary Force.

Bombardier W. J. Muir, D 317 Battery, Royal Field Artillery, 63rd Royal Naval Division.

Private H. Munday, 5th Battalion, Oxfordshire and Buckinghamshire Light Infantry.

Able Bodied Seaman Joseph Murray, Hood Battalion, Royal Naval Division.

Captain J. Y. Murray, 1st Battalion, Essex Regiment.

Private W. Myatt, 8th Battalion, Tank Corps.

Sergeant J. A. Myers, DCM, 16th (S) Battalion, West Yorkshire Regiment (Bradford Pals).

Gunner J. W. Naylor, Royal Artillery.

Rifleman J. J. Newman, 13th (S) Battalion, The Rifle Brigade.

Private C. J. Nicholls, C Company, Heavy Branch, Machine Gun Corps (Tanks).

Rifleman E. C. Nicholson, MC 21st (S) Battalion (Yeoman

Rifles), King's Royal Rifle Corps (later 2nd Lieutenant).

Private O. Nielsen, 25th Battalion, Australian Imperial Force.

Private W. H. Nixon, DCM, 2nd Battalion, Cheshire Regiment.

Sergeant M. J. O'Connor, MM (and Bar), 13th (S) Battalion, The Rifle Brigade.

Act. RSM L. M. Odell, MM, 1st Canterbury Battalion, New Zealand Expeditionary Force.

Lance-Corporal E. R. Organ, Queen's Own Oxfordshire Hussars.

Corporal R. W. Otley, 21st (S) Battalion (Yeoman Rifles), King's Royal Rifle Corps.

Corporal H. Oxley, 23rd Battalion, Middlesex Regiment.

Brigadier E. K. Page, MC, 130 Battery, Royal Field Artillery (then Lieutenant).

Corporal A. D. Pankhurst, 56th Division, Royal Field Artillery.

Lance-Corporal G. W. Parker, MM, 2nd (City of London) London Regiment (Royal Fusiliers) (TF).

Private R. Parker, 12th (S) Battalion, York and Lancaster Regiment (Sheffield Pals).

Sergeant A. K. Paterson, DCM, MM, 11th (S) Battalion, The Rifle Brigade.

Private A. Paterson, 7th Battalion, Argyll and Sutherland Highlanders (TF).

Lieutenant J. R. Patten, 20th (Light) Division, Royal Field Artillery.

Private W. Pattenden, 2/6th Battalion, Prince of Wales (North Staffordshire Regiment) (TF).

Rifleman F. Pearce, 16th (S) Battalion, King's Royal Rifle Corps (Church Lads Brigade).

The Reverend L. T. Pearson, Chaplain.

Corporal J. Pickard, MM, 78th Winnipeg Grenadiers, Canadian Expeditionary Force.

Rifleman J. A. Pincombe, 16th (County of London) Battalion, London Regiment (Queen's Westminster Rifles) (TF).

Sergeant G. E. Pople, MM and Bar, 8th (S) Battalion, King's (Shropshire Light Infantry).

Rifleman W. T. Poucher, 21st (S) Battalion (Yeoman Rifles) King's Royal Rifle Corps.

Rifleman E. T. Pretty, 9th (S) Battalion, The Rifle Brigade.

Lieutenant B. B. Rackham, MC and Bar, Hawke Battalion, Royal Naval Division.

Corporal A. C. Razzell, 8th (S) Battalion, Royal Fusiliers (City of London Regiment).

Private J. A. Reed, New Zealand Light Railway Engineers.

Private W. G. Reynolds, 4th Battalion, Duke of Cambridge's Own (Middlesex Regiment).

Corporal W. Richards, 1st/8th Battalion, Royal Warwickshire Regiment.

Captain N. Ries, 13th (S) Battalion, The Rifle Brigade.

Acting Corporal J. W. H. Rippin, 7th Battalion, Essex Regiment.

Sergeant F. H. Robbins, 13th (S) Battalion, The Rifle Brigade.

Lance-Corporal F. Robinson, DCM, 8th (S) Battalion, York and Lancaster Regiment.

Rifleman B. Robson, 21st (S) Battalion (Yeoman Rifles), King's Royal Rifle Corps.

Private G. Roden, 22nd (County of London) Battalion, London Regiment (The Queen's) (TF).

Regimental Sergeant-Major A. Roffey, DCM and Bar, 7th (S) Battalion, Queen's Own (Royal West Kent Regiment).

Private F. Rogers, 11th (S) Battalion, Royal Sussex Regiment (1st South Down).

Private R. K. Rolfe, 26th (S) Battalion (Bankers), Royal Fusiliers.

Private H. B. Rose, 1st Battalion, Trench Artillery; 151st Field Artillery, 42nd (Rainbow) Division. U.S. Army.

Rifleman W. T. Rowe, MM, 13th (S) Battalion, The Rifle Brigade.

Rifleman C. P. J. Ruck, 3rd/2nd Battalion, The London Rifle Brigade.

Private E. W. Russell, 5th Canadian Battalion (Western

Cavalry), Canadian Expeditionary Force.

Captain F. C. Russell, 22nd Battalion, Australian Imperial Forces.

Private A. Ryland, 13th (S) Battalion, The Rifle Brigade.

Major R. F. J. Sanders, TD, 16th Heavy Battery, Royal Garrison Artillery.

Rifleman H. F. Saunders, 16th (S) Battalion, King's Royal Rifle Corps.

Rifleman F. Saville, 21st (S) Battalion (Yeoman Rifles), King's Royal Rifle Corps (Church Lads Brigade).

Gunner W. Sayers, 1st/3rd London Regiment, Royal Fusiliers (TF) Tank Corps.

Rifleman A. T. Sears, 11th (S) Battalion, The Rifle Brigade.

Corporal W. H. Shaw, 9th (S) Battalion, Royal Welsh Fusiliers.

Rifleman H. V. Shawyer, 13th (S) Battalion, The Rifle Brigade.

Rifleman C. W. Shepherd, 13th (S) Battalion, The Rifle Brigade.

Rifleman, J. Shrimpton, 13th (S) Battalion, The Rifle Brigade.

Signaller A. V. Simpson, 2nd/6th Battalion, Duke of Wellington's (West Riding Regiment).

Private J. Simpson, 2nd Battalion, Grenadier Guards.

Sergeant J. Skuce, 2nd Battalion, Irish Guards.

Captain C. M. Slack, MC and Bar, 1st/4th Battalion, East Yorkshire Regiment (TF) (then Lieutenant).

Private H. J. Smith, 9th (S) Battalion (Northumberland Hussars Yeomanry), Northumberland Fusiliers.

Corporal H. W. Smith, MM, 13th (S) Battalion, The Rifle Brigade.

Rifleman R. W. Smith, 13th (S) Battalion, The Rifle Brigade.

Corporal R. Smith, 21st (S) Battalion (Yeoman Rifles), King's Royal Rifle Corps.

Warrant Officer S. A. Smith, 11th (S) Battalion, The Rifle Brigade.

Rifleman E. G. Snell, 5th (City of London) Battalion,

London Regiment (London Rifle Brigade) (TF).

Corporal A. E. Somerset, 3rd Battalion, Grenadier Guards.

Corporal R. G. Spearman, 19th Heavy Battery, Royal Field Artillery, Royal Garrison Artillery.

Corporal T. A. Spencer, MM, Royal Scots Fusiliers; 108 Machine Gun Company, Machine Gun Corps.

Rifleman C. Spilsbury, 11th (S) Battalion, The Rifle Brigade.

Private F. G. Staite, MM and Bar, 1st/8th Battalion, Worcestershire Regiment (TF).

Private C. S. Stevens, 1st Battalion, Leicestershire Regiment.

Acting Sergeant-Major W. O. Stevenson, DCM, MM, 6th (Renfrewshire) Battalion, Argyll and Sutherland Highlanders.

Bombardier B. O. Stokes, 3rd Brigade, New Zealand Field Artillery.

Private W. T. Stokes, 2nd/4th Battalion, Royal Berkshire Regiment (TF).

Corporal H. L. Stride, 13th (S) Battalion, The Rifle Brigade.

Private G. C. Stubbs, Royal Army Medical Corps, 12th Field Ambulance, 4th Division.

2nd Lieutenant J. A. Talbot, 10th (S) Battalion, The Rifle Brigade.

Reverend E. Tanner, MC and Bar, Chaplain 4th Class, 2nd Battalion, Worcestershire Regiment.

Corporal J. H. Tansley, 9th (S) Battalion, York and Lancaster Regiment.

Corporal R. Tate, 3rd Battalion, Tank Corps.

Private W. Tate, 4th Battalion (Pioneers), Coldstream Guards.

Private W. R. Thomas, 14th (S) Battalion, Royal Welsh Fusiliers.

Major A. G. C. Thompson, Royal Army Medical Corps.

Corporal R. E. Thompson, 13th (S) Battalion, The Rifle Brigade.

Rifleman A. E. Thorne, MBE, 13th (S) Battalion, The Rifle Brigade.

Lance-Corporal C. Tomlinson, King's Own (Liverpool Regiment).

Corporal F. C. Toogood, 3rd Wellington Battalion, 4th New Zealand Brigade.

Private J. F. Tucker, 1st/13th (County of London) (Princess Louise's Kensington Battalion), London Regiment (TF).

Corporal J. Turnbull, 8th (S) Battalion, King's Own Yorkshire Light Infantry.

Corporal W. B. Turnbull, 12th (S) Battalion, The Rifle Brigade.

Private H. Turner, 50th Divisional Machine Gun Corps.

Lance-Corporal Bugler W. S. Turner, 15th Battalion, Highland Light Infantry (City of Glasgow Corporation Tramways Battalion).

Private J. E. Tyson, 3rd Battalion, King's Own (Royal Lancaster Regiment).

Sergeant F. G. Udall, MM and two Bars, 4th Battalion, London Regiment (Royal Fusiliers) (TF).

Corporal F. G. Vail, MD, Machine Gun Corps.

Private A. Vanpraagh, 253 Tunnelling Company, Royal Engineers.

Corporal E. C. Vickery, 13th (S) Battalion (Forest of Dean) (Pioneers), Gloucestershire Regiment.

Major E. H. Wade, MC and Bar, South Staffordshire Regiment, Machine Gun Corps.

Able-Seaman J. A. Wade, D Company, Hawke Battalion, 63rd Royal Naval Division.

Worker C. H. Wagstaff (now Mrs Brereton), No. 26178, Womens Auxiliary Army Corps.

Company Quartermaster-Sergeant J. Wainwright, 5th Battalion, Machine Gun Corps.

Private A. E. Walker, 4th Battalion, Northumberland Fusiliers.

Sapper F. E. Waldron, 30th

Division, Signals, Royal Engineers.

Sergeant R. Walker, 126 Machine Gun Corps, 42nd Division.

Corporal J. Wallace, Oxfordshire and Buckinghamshire Light Infantry.

Sergeant A. B. Walsh, Royal Engineers.

Trooper H. P. Ward, Queen's Own Oxfordshire Hussars and Machine Gun Corps.

Sergeant W. Ward, MM, 2nd Battalion, Grenadier Guards.

Lance-Corporal D. A. M. Watson, 9th, 12th and 11th Battalions, Royal Scots.

Private F. Watts, 4th Battalion, North Staffordshire Regiment.

Private H. W. H. Watts, 2nd Battalion, Queen's (Royal West Surrey Regiment).

Acting-Corporal R. Weeber, 13th (S) Battalion, The Rifle Brigade.

Private A. E. West, Duke of Cambridge's Own (Middlesex Regiment).

Sergeant F. Wheatcroft, Machine Gun Corps.

Rifleman F. C. White, 10th (S) Battalion, King's Royal Rifle Corps.

Private W. E. White, Oxfordshire and Buckinghamshire Light Infantry.

Lance-Corporal A. J. Whitehouse, MM, Lancashire Fusiliers.

Corporal J. E. H. Whittaker, 21st (S) Battalion (Yeoman Rifles), King's Royal Rifle Corps.

Private E. Wickens, 12th (S) Battalion, Duke of Cambridge's Own (Middlesex Regiment).

Sergeant A. E. Wiffen, 9th Battalion, Essex Regiment.

Corporal H. G. Wild, Royal Flying Corps.

2nd Lieutenant M. C. Wilkinson, 25th Battalion, Royal Welsh Fusiliers.

Trooper C. H. Williams, MM, Royal Buckinghamshire Hussars (TF).

Corporal E. G. Williams, 19th Battalion, King's (Liverpool Regiment).

Gunner G. A. Williams, MM and Bar, 232 Brigade, Royal Field Artillery.

Gunner H. G. R. Williams, 5th Battalion, London Regiment (London Rifle Brigade).

Rifleman CQMS H. Willis, 21st (S) Battalion (Yeoman Rifles), King's Royal Rifle Corps.

Lieutenant A. G. Wilson, MC, 1st/5th Battalion, Prince of Wales' Own (West Yorkshire Regiment) (TF).

Private C. A. Wilson, MM, 1st Battalion, Grenadier Guards.

Lance-Sergeant G. E. Winterbourne, 16th (County of London) Battalion, London Regiment (Queen's Westminster Rifles) (TF).

Lieutenant T. H. Witherow, 8th (S) Battalion (East Belfast), Royal Irish Rifles.

Acting-Corporal L. Wolfe, MM, 6th Battalion, King's Own Scottish Borderers.

Sergeant A. Wolfman, A Company, A Battalion, Heavy

Branch Machine Gun Corps (Tanks).

Private C. T. Wood, Royal Army Medical Corps.

Corporal H. C. Wood, MM, East Surrey Regiment and Royal Flying Corps.

Lance-Corporal J. D. Woodside, 16th (S) Battalion, Highland Light Infantry.

Private F. Woolley, 2nd/4th Battalion, South Lancashire Regiment.

Private J. H. Worker, 1st Battalion, Scots Guards.

Rifleman W. J. Worrell, 12th (S) Battalion, The Rifle Brigade.

Gunner G. Worsley, 276 Brigade, Royal Field Artillery.

Lance-Corporal G. Worth, 6th Battalion, Prince of Wales' Own (North Staffordshire Regiment) (TF).

Gunner E. C. Wright, 62nd Brigade, Royal Field Artillery.

Lance-Corporal F. Wright, Royal Warwickshire Regiment.

Corporal G. Wright, Machine Gun Corps.

Platoon Sergeant G. S. W. Yarnall, 14th Battalion, London Regiment (London Scottish).

Corporal J. H. Yeoman, 21st (S) Battalion (Yeoman Rifles), King's Royal Rifle Corps.

Corporal R. Zealley, 18th (S) Battalion (1st Public Schools) Royal Fusiliers, City of London Regiment.

Index

search with the experts

Win a day with a genealogist

Now that you've read Lyn Macdonald's real life stories of heroism, do you feel inspired to find out about your own family history with the help of an expert?

Enter our competition at **www.findmypast.co.uk/macdonald** for a chance to win a day with a professional genealogist, who will help you learn about your ancestors' lives, and an annual World subscription to leading family history website **findmypast.co.uk**. Three runners-up will each receive a 6 month Britain Full subscription to **findmypast.co.uk**

The competition

Terms and conditions apply, please see www.findmypast.co.uk/macdonald for details and to enter.

Competition runs from 26 September 2013 to 3 January 2014.

Entries must be received by 23:59 GMT on 3 January 2014.

First prize consists of one day's family history consultancy with a qualified professional genealogist, helping you to research your family tree and one annual World subscription to findmypast.co.uk.

Three runner-up prizes each consist of a 6 month Britain Full subscription to findmypast.co.uk.

Prize has no cash alternative, is non-transferable and non-refundable. No purchase necessary.

Promoter: findmypast.co.uk, The Glebe, 6 Chapel Place, Rivington Street, London EC2A 3DQ

Free reader offer

Ever wondered what your ancestors' lives were like? Might they have experienced life at the Front? Here's your chance to uncover their story with **£5 worth of free credits** to **findmypast.co.uk**

Find your ancestors in millions of records dating right back to Tudor times, including local newspapers, birth, marriage and death indexes, census, military, migration, parish and crime records. There are over 1.5 billion family history records at **findmypast.co.uk** covering the UK, Ireland, the United States, Australia and New Zealand. It's free to search these records, and with your free credits you'll be able to view, save and print high-quality scans of original historical documents featuring your own ancestors.

To claim your 40 free credits worth £5 and for advice on getting started, visit **www.findmypast.co.uk/penguin** and enter the promotional voucher code **TRENCH** before **6 November 2013**

Free credit offer

Offer expires at midnight on 6 November 2013. See www.findmypast.co.uk/penguin for terms & conditions.